Cheltenham & Gloucester

Cricket Year

Cheltenham & Gloucester

Cricket Year

Twenty-Third Edition
September 2003 to September 2004

Edited by **Jonathan Agnew**

with additional contributions by
Qamar Ahmed
Charlie Austin
Mark Baldwin
Tony Cozier
Gulu Ezekiel
David Green
Graham Gooch
Jim Maxwell
Telford Vice
Bryan Waddle

BLOOMSBURY

Edited by Jonathan Agnew
Assistant editing by Mark Baldwin
with additional contributions by
Qamar Ahmed
Charlie Austin
Mark Baldwin
Tony Cozier
Gulu Ezekiel
David Green
Graham Gooch
Jim Maxwell
Telford Vice
Bryan Waddle
with special thanks to Nigel Fuller, Kate Laven, Tom Sheldrick,
Jolyon Bond and Neil Manthorp

The publishers would also like to thank the following for their kind permission to
reproduce the following photographs:

Mark Baldwin (p. 52): *The Times*
Glamorgan celebrating (p. 166): Huw John Press Photography, Cardiff

First published in 2004 by
Bloomsbury Publishing Plc
38 Soho Square
London W1D 3HB

www.bloomsbury.com/reference

A copy of the CIP entry for this book is available from the British Library.

ISBN 0 7475 7269 0

10 9 8 7 6 5 4 3 2 1

All papers used by Bloomsbury Publishing are natural, recyclable products made
from wood grown in well-managed forests. The manufacturing processes conform
to the environmental regulations of the country of origin.

Project editor: Chris Hawkes
Design: Kathie Wilson at design, Butler and Tanner
Statistics and County information: Press Association
Pictures researched and supplied by David Munden at
Sportsline Photographic – www.sportsline.org.uk

Printed and bound in Great Britain
by Butler and Tanner, Frome and London

CONTENTS

A MESSAGE FROM
CHELTENHAM & GLOUCESTER

The great successes of Michael Vaughan's England team dominated the headlines and provided most of the talking points during the golden months of March to September. In that time England won ten of their 11 Test matches, beat India in the NatWest Challenge series, and, on 25 September, played in the final of the ICC Champions Trophy, where they lost a thrilling match to the West Indies.

Afterwards, quite rightly, Vaughan said he was immensely proud of his team's achievements in 2004, which had included a morale-boosting Champions Trophy semi-final victory against Australia.

Steve Harmison and Andrew Flintoff were at the heart of England's effort, with Harmison setting the ball rolling with his magnificent and dramatic spell of 7 for 12 in the Jamaica Test in March. England, however, were well served by a clutch of other high-quality performances during the 3–0 series victories against the West Indies and New Zealand, and then in the 4–0 whitewash of the West Indians in July and August.

This winter's campaign in South Africa, and after it the build-up to next summer's mouthwatering Ashes battle against Australia, will ensure that the excitement surrounding English cricket continues apace – but, for now, this 23rd edition of *Cricket Year* enables us to recall the heroic exploits in 2004 of Flintoff, Harmison, Vaughan, Nasser Hussain, Andrew Strauss, Robert Key, Ashley Giles and many others.

Duncan Fletcher, and his England management team, is to be congratulated for the success he has brought to the national team. In partnership with both Hussain and Vaughan, his two captains, Fletcher has helped to build a distinctive team spirit and a very real determination to succeed. Much hard work has also been done behind the scenes by many people within English cricket, and everyone concerned will have been thrilled to see the results achieved on the field by the national team this year.

This book is the perfect companion for England cricket fans looking to relive the great victories of 2004, and Jonathan Agnew provides insightful commentary on each one of those ten Test-match successes. There are also full details of every other international game played around the globe since September 2003, and a comprehensive review of the English domestic summer which featured a Frizzell County Championship title for Warwickshire, yet another one-day triumph for Gloucestershire in the Cheltenham & Gloucester Trophy, and successes for Glamorgan in the totesport League and Leicestershire in the second year of the Twenty20 Cup.

Regular readers will already know that we at Cheltenham & Gloucester were delighted to take over the sponsorship of *Cricket Year* in 2003, and our first edition (the 22nd version of the title) contained several new features. These included the Cheltenham & Gloucester Man of the Year award, won in its inaugural year by Alec Stewart.

Our 2004 award goes to Andrew Flintoff, England's champion, and was voted for by a combination of a special panel and the general public. 'Freddie' is profiled in these pages by Jonathan Agnew, who once again heads up a small army of regular *Cricket Year* contributors from around the world, writes on all matters England and who also provides his usual forthright views in the Introduction.

There are other special features, too, in this year's edition: Graham Gooch, the former Essex and England captain and our greatest Test match run scorer, gives his view of Nasser Hussain, the cricketer and the man; David Green, the former Lancashire and Gloucestershire batsman and now a highly-respected cricket writer for the *Daily Telegraph*, writes on the renaissance of county cricket's Festival Weeks; Tony Cozier relives Brian Lara's world record of 400 not out in Antigua; and Jim Maxwell profiles Steve Waugh, who, like Hussain, announced his retirement from all cricket during these past 12 months.

We would like to express our thanks to every contributor for bringing back the memories of a busy, enjoyable and truly exciting year, as well as to Bloomsbury, who have worked their customary autumn miracle to ensure that *Cricket Year* is published just seven weeks after the end of the English season. So please take some time out, before the events of the next 12 months unfold, to relive all the drama, the achievements and the action from a memorable 2004 cricket year.

Chris Steele
Director of Marketing & Customer Service
Cheltenham & Gloucester

AGGERS' VIEW

Introduction
By Jonathan Agnew

Only twice in the history of cricket have England matched the outstanding success of this year. To win seven consecutive Test matches is a feat that was last achieved in 1928–29, and surely nobody that returned to England from Sri Lanka before Christmas could possibly have predicted that Michael Vaughan's team would win ten out of their next 11 Tests.

It was an emotional scene at the end of the summer at The Oval when, 20 years after the West Indies had so ruthlessly whitewashed England to the cacophony of tin cans, drums, whistles and bugles, the wheel finally turned full circle. How I empathised with the cowed figure of the West Indies' No. 11 batsman, Jermaine Lawson, as he emerged from the dressing room into the sunshine to face inevitable defeat.

Twenty years ago I was in his place, as England's No. 11 at the end of a heavy series beating, and it

Steve Harmison ... the catalyst of England's unforgettable 2004.

was with a sense of real pride that I was now able to commentate on *Test Match Special* as England sealed the match. Beside me, Sir Viv Richards – a member of that West Indies team of 1984 – was not quite so elated, but he was graciously able to accept that this was England's opportunity, and it had been earned the hard way.

On the one hand, England's triumph was unexpected, but on the other it was entirely inevitable. Any team that, overnight, gains a world-class fast bowler who regularly delivers the ball at 92 miles per hour or more, a magnificent all-rounder who has the ability to intimidate any attack, bowls fast and catches brilliantly at second slip, and a busy wicketkeeper who scores a century in only his fourth Test innings, is bound to succeed.

Steve Harmison, Andrew Flintoff and Geraint Jones have all been central to England's glorious sequence of victories. The sudden emergence of Andrew Strauss – all because of a freak injury suffered by Michael Vaughan in the nets – was, meanwhile, a story of *Boy's Own* proportions, and his beautifully paced innings against Australia in the Champions Trophy sealed a summer of tremendous personal achievement. Inevitably, behind the scenes, others have also played a major part.

Troy Cooley is an unfamiliar name to many. He is the quietly spoken man from Tasmania who, after a brief first-class career that was dogged by no-ball problems, turned to coaching. He is now a key member of England's staff and while, from a distance, his array of carefully positioned coloured cones give the impression that he is tutoring his bowlers on a stretch of the M25, he has got through to Harmison, Flintoff and Matthew Hoggard in a spectacular fashion.

Duncan Fletcher's position has grown massively in stature, and there is little doubt that his players would do anything for him. Nasser Hussain also deserves special mention. As I write, he is currently closing what turned out to be his final season as a player with a typically angry, but honest, account of his life. Few have been spared criticism and some are genuinely upset by his comments, but that is Nasser, and it gives an insight into the manner in which he dragged the England team from its knees. He knew when the time was right to resign as captain and hand over to the more popular Vaughan. He also knew when it was right to retire and give way to Strauss.

To a number of people close to Hussain, he has built a reputation for being selfish. That does not sit comfortably with me. Those two decisions – particularly resigning the captaincy – might have

Nasser Hussain (right, talking here to Matthew Hoggard) also deserves a special mention in respect of England's successes.

been inconvenient for some around him for a couple of weeks but, surely, they were utterly selfless, brutally honest and, above all, perfectly timed.

While we spend the winter dreaming about winning the Ashes next year, we must also ask if English cricket will make the most of this big chance. As I write, the England and Wales Cricket Board is considering to whom it should award the television and radio broadcasting rights for the next five years, and we have been hearing threatening noises.

It is one thing to be bullish in an attempt to drive up the price in what is a competitive, albeit devalued market. It is quite another simply to hand the responsibility for the presentation of cricket to the highest bidder, and hang the consequences. Viv Richards knows all about a failure to capitalise on success: it was the cause of the decline of West Indies' cricket.

There is also good reason to be concerned about the ECB's ability to make the right decision. Tim Lamb, their long-serving chief executive, resigned during the summer and so, too, did the head of communications, John Read. Both men appear to have paid the price for the ECB's inability to deal satisfactorily with the vexed question of England's proposed tour of Zimbabwe in November 2004.

The ECB was keen, at the start of the year, to avoid a repeat of the events in Cape Town in 2003 when, in Hussain's own words, England's players were 'hung out to dry' as they attempted to decide whether, or not, to play a World Cup match in Harare.

A document was produced by Des Wilson, a senior member of the Board, in which he set out guidelines for England to decline or defer touring obligations on moral or political grounds. It was well argued and well intentioned, but the timing of its publication and, particularly, the leaking of it to the media before other members of the ECB had read it, was disastrous. Worse still, it tipped off the International Cricket Council, which reacted with unprecedented urgency in New Zealand to pass a resolution that threatened England with enormous financial penalties if they failed to tour Zimbabwe.

The selection process for the tour which, owing to Zimbabwe's suspension from Test cricket, was reduced to five one-day internationals, was also mired in controversy as the ECB tried desperately to avoid exposing itself to accusations of sending a weakened team, and possibly provoke further financial penalty.

The ECB chairman, David Morgan, vetoed a request from Duncan Fletcher and the selectors to rest Michael Vaughan for the futile trip. He was right to do so. For a young player – probably Strauss – to be burdened with leading England on such an unpopular tour would have been both unfair and unkind.

Meanwhile, the ICC's investigation into allegations of racism by the Zimbabwe Cricket Union – a process that could still spare England from making the trip – proceeded slowly in the background.

I admire Wilson for setting out his framework, because his message is correct: sport and politics are inextricably linked, and always have been. It is merely convenient for the ICC to stick blindly to their mantra of considering only issues of safety and security to the players, because it is the less complicated path to take. But it is wrong. The moral argument is not irrelevant and, when it comes to the question of Zimbabwe, the ICC are very wrong indeed.

The ECB has taken its share of flak for its handling of the issue, and that the players should find themselves, once again, in the position of having to make impossible decisions – having been told that the domestic game in England could be destroyed if they do not tour Zimbabwe – is a disgrace.

The fault for that, however, lies squarely with the members of the ICC who produced that proposal in Auckland and, one day, when the whole truth about Zimbabwe comes out, they should hang their heads in shame.

Jonathan Agnew
Leicestershire, September 2004

CHELTENHAM & GLOUCESTER MAN OF THE YEAR AWARD

ANDREW FLINTOFF, the talismanic England all-rounder, has succeeded 2003 winner Alec Stewart as the Cheltenham & Gloucester Man of the Year. Flintoff, who earns the award for his heroic exploits throughout 2004, is profiled here by JONATHAN AGNEW.

It was not so very long ago that Andrew Flintoff was regarded as a bit of a chump. Four years ago, in fact, when Duncan Fletcher despatched him from Lord's after a duck against Zimbabwe with a flea in his ear and a deliberately-placed moan in the media about Flintoff's fitness regime – or, to be precise, his lack of one.

The tabloids had a field day, portraying 'Freddie' as a burger-munching, beer-swilling oaf. One particularly unpleasant kiss-and-tell story by a former girlfriend in a Sunday newspaper suggested that, when it came to the bedroom, she would be lucky to get any more than the equivalent of a quick spell off an old-style Sunday League run-up. It was becoming difficult to take Flintoff, the cricketer, seriously.

It is for that reason that the transformation in Flintoff's stature, from also-ran to world-class player, is all the more remarkable. Ian

Flintoff the batsman ...

Botham, to whom Flintoff is now constantly compared, led a colourful life off the field and attracted a great deal of lurid tabloid attention, but, even in his troubled times, Botham's cricket always spoke for itself and demanded that he was respected, rather than derided. Now Flintoff, the ICC's one-day Cricketer of the Year, the Cheltenham & Gloucester Man of the Year, and first-time father, has come of age in every area of his life.

I am not necessarily turned on by statistics, but in Flintoff's case a study of his career really does need the support of his facts and figures to illustrate fully the remarkable steps he has taken. It is particularly worth remembering that, after his first 12 Test matches, Flintoff averaged 13 with the bat and 44 with the ball.

Since 12 Tests could be considered to be more than enough time to make a judgement about a player's international potential, it is fair to assume that the selectors – and especially Fletcher, I suspect – looked beyond the figures and saw something worth persevering with.

In his next Test – against New Zealand in Christchurch in March 2002 – Flintoff scored his first hundred: a blistering 137 in the second innings of one of the most amazing Tests of modern times. Whether he knew it then, or not, is for him to judge, but that event proved to be the turning point in Flintoff's career, and a triumph for those who had persisted so patiently with him.

Two savage innings in the summer of 2003 gave the touring South Africans notice, and warmed Flintoff up for the period that falls under our spotlight in the *Cheltenham & Gloucester Cricket Year*.

In 14 Tests from October 2003, Flintoff averaged 47 with the bat and 25 with the ball: the figures of a truly outstanding Test all-rounder. Jacques Kallis, in the same period, averaged an astonishing 80 with the bat, but the pressure of scoring those runs clearly told, and 15 wickets at 54 runs each from 11 Tests barely entitle Kallis to a place in the current all-rounder bracket.

Flintoff's contribution to limited-overs matches is even more noteworthy. In 13 innings, he averaged 85 with a strike rate of 105, and his 14 wickets at 21 apiece came at a cost of only three-and-a-half runs per over. Little wonder, then, that when Flintoff was unable to bowl during the NatWest Series this summer, England chose to call him up anyway. By then, his presence in the dressing room alone, and the effect this had on his team-mates, fully justified his selection.

So what is it that turned the chump into a champ, and is our dream of recapturing the Ashes in the summer of 2005 optimistically built on the back of the development of Flintoff and Steve Harmison in particular, the least bit realistic?

The most engaging aspect of watching Flintoff's development this year – and with it, England's wave of success – has been to observe the enormous pleasure he so clearly derives from being in the company of his team-mates. Again, this is a Bothamesque characteristic, but while there seemed to be a touch of 'if you

Flintoff the bowler ...

ain't with me, you're against me' in Botham's case, there is simply no hidden side to Flintoff's camaraderie at all.

He genuinely appears to be as thrilled when someone else claims a wicket as when he does himself, and this can only come through being absolutely comfortable, not only about his place in the team, but also about his value to the team. This rubs off, and Adam Hollioake made the same observation when asked last summer to give a reason for England's dramatic improvement. His answer gave the impression that he was surprised that such a healthy, non-competitive spirit could exist within an environment in which personal success is of such importance.

Flintoff creates this, and also feeds off it, and his growth in confidence has coincided with an uncanny knack of always being in the thick of the action. Is it a coincidence that so many catches fly in his direction at second slip? He certainly does not drop many there, and of all the members of the England team who were on the field at Barbados in April, I can only imagine the relief that must have swamped Matthew Hoggard when he realised that the catch that would give him a Test hat-trick was heading Flintoff's way. Freddie took it nonchalantly, of course, and was the first player to envelope Hoggard in the sort of clinch that Big Daddy used to asphyxiate his victims in the wrestling ring.

There was one brief moment last year when we worried that this rampant confidence might have run away with him. Facing the last over before lunch against the West Indies on the Friday of the Lord's Test, he launched Omari Banks for six into the Nursery End. It was outrageous, bordering on irresponsible, and yet the shouts of caution from the England dressing room were drowned out by the roars of the crowd. With adrenalin surging through his veins, Flintoff went for Banks again and was bowled. Making a fool of yourself in front of 29,000 people is a humbling experience, and I do not think we will see Flintoff treat the business of batting quite so casually again.

There is not quite the same level of anticipation about Flintoff's bowling. There are still dark mutterings about his action in some quarters: at their own instigation, the umpires asked to see video footage during the recent tour of the West Indies. They were happy with what they saw, but some members of the South African media remain convinced that there is occasionally a kink in his right arm.

Flintoff has never been blessed with Botham's astonishing good fortune – you will not find him picking up many 'strangled' wickets in the covers or at deep square leg – but he is becoming increasingly dangerous. He softened up Brian Lara in the first Test at Barbados, and then at Edgbaston and Old Trafford through climbing, bruising deliveries that wore Lara down. If Freddie can do it to him, then what about Matthew Hayden, Justin Langer and Adam Gilchrist?

Surely one crucial factor in determining that is the remarkable fact that, somehow, Flintoff has avoided playing even a single Test against Australia since he made his debut back in 1998.

That amounts to three Ashes series he has missed, largely through injury. So there are no skeletons in his wardrobe, no memories of being humiliated on the field and then ridiculed in the Australian press. Freddie will be fresh when he comes to the fray next summer and yet he will also be established, respected and confident. After a false dawn or two, the Aussies really do have good reason to worry this time.

... and Flintoff, the winner, greets another triumph.

THE YEAR IN PICTURES

October '03: Matthew Hayden (right) celebrates his world record 380 with Steve Waugh. It was to stand for just six months before Brian Lara snatched it back.

January '04: Steve Waugh waves goodbye with a lap of honour at his beloved Sydney Cricket Ground.

May '04: Safe hands – Nasser Hussain, who quit as one of England's best captains in 2003, calls time on his career after winning the first Test against New Zealand at Lord's with an unbeaten hundred.

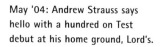

May '04: Andrew Strauss says hello with a hundred on Test debut at his home ground, Lord's.

March '04: Hurricane Harmison announces his arrival as a world-class fast bowler – the West Indies felt the force at Sabina Park.

August '04: The King of Spin, also known as Ashley Giles, returns in triumph to Edgbaston during a summer in which he bewitched the Black Caps, Brian Lara, the West Indians, and his critics ... well done, 'Gilo'.

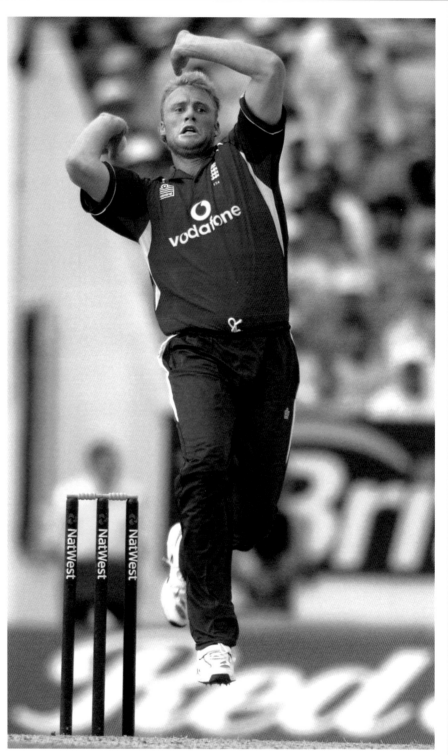

July '04: Andrew Flintoff's return from injury helped England to their only victory of a disappointing NatWest Triangular Series.

June '04: Chris Cairns in familiar pose during his final Test match appearance at Trent Bridge. Cairns' match figures of 9 for 187 were indicative of his wholehearted approach to the game.

July '04: Stephen Fleming's New Zealand lift the NatWest Series trophy at Lord's.

August '04: Brad Hodge and Jeremy Snape run from the field in triumph as Leicestershire snatch the Twenty20 Cup at Edgbaston.

August '04: It's them again ... Mark Alleyne and his Gloucestershire one-day wonders add yet another C&G Trophy to their modern collection.

September '04: Warwickshire are the Frizzell County Championship winners.

September '04: Craig Spearman of Gloucestershire finished the season with a record for the highest individual score in English county cricket – 341– against Middlesex at Gloucester.

September '04: Sting in the tail ... after a year of despair, the West Indies win one of the most important victories in their history with a dramatic ICC Champions Trophy triumph at The Oval.

September '04: A major feature of the West Indies victory was the quick-witted fielding of Dwayne Bravo. Here he runs out Andrew Strauss in the final.

ENGLAND

NEW ZEALAND IN ENGLAND
NATWEST TRIANGULAR ONE-DAY SERIES
WEST INDIES IN ENGLAND
NATWEST CHALLENGE
ICC CHAMPIONS TROPHY

NEW ZEALAND IN ENGLAND
By Jonathan Agnew
and Mark Baldwin

3–5 May 2004 at Fenner's
New Zealand 128 for 3 (35.1 overs) (NJ Astle 64*)
British Universities
Match Drawn

The New Zealanders' opening tour match, against the British Universities at Fenner's, was almost totally washed away by rain. Just 35.1 overs were possible, on the scheduled third and final day, but at least there was time for Nathan Astle, in his first innings since knee surgery, to move smoothly to an unbeaten 64 following the dismissal of the unfortunate Michael Papps for a duck. Mark Richardson, the limpet-like Kiwi Test opener, also took advantage of the opportunity for some crease-occupation.

7–10 May 2004 at Worcester
Worcestershire 270 for 9 dec (77.1 overs)
(BF Smith 92, DR Tuffey 4 for 57) & 318 for 6 dec
(67.4 overs) (GA Hick 204*)
New Zealand 379 for 7 dec (85.3 overs)
(JDP Oram 103*, CD McMillan 86, DL Vettori 51)
& 77 for 1 (23 overs)
Match Drawn

A majestic unbeaten 204 from Graeme Hick, his 15th career score of 200 or more, bruised New Zealand's morale at New Road in a rain-affected draw. Hick's barrage of boundaries came on the final day, after New Zealand had declared overnight with a first-innings lead of 109. It was his 123rd first-class hundred, putting him ahead of Tom Graveney on the all-time list and level with Denis

Compton in equal tenth place. Hick's second hundred took just 73 balls, and it was hardly a comfort to the outclassed Kiwi attack that they would almost certainly not be meeting Hick in an England shirt during their tour. On a more positive note for New Zealand, the match also saw a useful first-innings workout from Daryl Tuffey and powerful innings of 103 not out and 86 respectively by Jacob Oram and Craig McMillan. Both struck 14 fours, with McMillan also hitting two sixes and Oram one in his impressive 120-ball knock.

The run machine: Graeme Hick gives the New Zealand bowlers an early-summer pasting at New Road.

13–16 May 2004 at Canterbury
New Zealand 409 (114.3 overs) (MHW Papps 126, MH Richardson 92, CL Cairns 54, MM Patel 5 for 56) & 211 (52.4 overs) (CL Cairns 73, A Khan 4 for 50)
Kent 432 for 9 dec (91 overs) (RWT Key 114, GO Jones 101, MA Carberry 75, CS Martin 4 for 92) & 189 for 1 (51 overs) (RWT Key 117*, DP Fulton 67)
Kent won by 9 wickets

Robert Key continued to put pressure on the England selectors by taking 114 and 117 not out off the New Zealanders at Canterbury, as Kent won a famous nine-wicket victory. Only Colin Cowdrey and Peter Richardson, against the Australians of 1961 and 1964 respectively, had made two hundreds for Kent in a match against a touring team, and not even they can have batted as fluently as Key did here. His first-innings ton took just 130 balls, and featured 20 fours, and he was pleased with the mental side of adding a 143-ball unbeaten innings which included 18 further boundaries and a straight six off a struggling Daniel Vettori that disappeared into the Kent dressing room. New Zealand, meanwhile, beaten by 25 minutes after lunch on the final day, had reached 244 without loss at the start of the match. Mark Richardson scored 92 and Michael Papps, his diminutive opening partner, completed his seventh first-class hundred before falling for 126. Chris Cairns blasted 54 on the second morning, from just 38 balls, but Min Patel marked a brave comeback from long-term injury – he had not played a senior game since September 2002 – by picking up 5 for 56. Geraint Jones, playing in this match because Kent insisted to England's management that it would do him good ahead of the opening Test, then responded with 101, featuring in stands of 122 with Michael Carberry and 58 with Patel that hauled Kent past New Zealand's first-innings 409. Loose strokeplay from the tourists then cost them dear, with their second innings slipping to 211 all out as Amjad Khan (4 for 50) took advantage. The stage was then clear again for Key, who was joined in a match-clinching opening partnership of 174 by David Fulton (67).

npower FIRST TEST
20–24 May 2004 at Lord's

When Michael Vaughan slipped and twisted his right knee in the nets three days before the start of the first Test at Lord's, most of the ensuing debate was of the negative variety. 'Who would be captain?' 'Marcus Trescothick.' 'Remember his moment of tactical madness last year when he came off for bad

FIRST TEST – ENGLAND v. NEW ZEALAND
20–24 May 2004 at Lord's

NEW ZEALAND

	First Innings		Second Innings	
MH Richardson	lbw b Harmison	93	c Jones GO b Harmison	101
SP Fleming (capt)	c Strauss b Jones SP	34	c Hussain b Harmison	4
NJ Astle	c Jones GO b Flintoff	64	(7) c Jones GO b Harmison	49
SB Styris	c Jones GO b Jones SP	0	c Hussain b Giles	4
CD McMillan	lbw b Hoggard	6	c Hussain b Giles	0
JDP Oram	c Jones GO b Harmison	67	run out	4
DR Tuffey	b Harmison	8	(10) not out	14
CL Cairns	c Harmison b Flintoff	82	c Butcher b Giles	14
*BB McCullum	b Jones SP	5	(3) c Jones GO b Jones SP	96
DL Vettori	b Harmison	2	(9) c Jones GO b Harmison	5
CS Martin	not out	1	b Flintoff	7
Extras	b 9, lb 6, w 2, nb 7	24	b 14, lb 16, nb 8	38
	(102.4 overs)	**386**	(121.1 overs)	**336**

	First Innings				Second Innings			
	O	M	R	W	O	M	R	W
Hoggard	22	7	68	1	14	3	39	0
Harmison	31	7	126	4	29	8	76	4
Flintoff	21.4	7	63	2	16.1	5	40	1
Jones SP	23	8	82	3	23	5	64	1
Giles	5	0	32	0	39	8	87	3

Fall of Wickets
1-58, 2-161, 3-162, 4-174, 5-280, 6-287, 7-324, 8-329, 9-338
1-7, 2-180, 3-187, 4-187, 5-203, 6-287, 7-290, 8-304, 9-310

ENGLAND

	First Innings		Second Innings	
ME Trescothick (capt)	c McCullum b Oram	86	c & b Tuffey	2
AJ Strauss	c Richardson b Vettori	112	run out	83
MA Butcher	c McCullum b Vettori	26	c Fleming b Martin	6
MJ Hoggard	c McCullum b Oram	15		
N Hussain	b Martin	34	(4) not out	103
GP Thorpe	b Cairns	3	(5) not out	51
A Flintoff	c Richardson b Martin	63		
*GO Jones	c Oram b Styris	46		
AF Giles	c Oram b Styris	11		
SP Jones	b Martin	4		
SJ Harmison	not out	0		
Extras	b 4, lb 18, nb 19	41	b 7, lb 12, w 5, nb 13	37
	(124.3 overs)	**441**	(3 wkts 87 overs)	**282**

	First Innings				Second Innings			
	O	M	R	W	O	M	R	W
Tuffey	26	4	98	0	10	3	32	1
Martin	27	6	94	3	18	2	75	1
Oram	30	8	76	2	15	4	39	0
Cairns	16	2	71	1	6	0	27	0
Vettori	21	1	69	2	25	5	53	0
Styris	4.3	0	11	2	13	5	37	0

Fall of Wickets
1-190, 2-239, 3-254, 4-288, 5-297, 6-311, 7-416, 8-428, 9-441
1-18, 2-35, 3-143

Umpires: DB Hair and RE Koertzen
Toss: New Zealand
Test debut: AJ Strauss
Man of the Match: AJ Strauss

England won by 7 wickets

light against South Africa at Headingley?' 'Oh yes. You're right. Who else …?' And on it went, almost to the absolute exclusion of the news that Andrew Strauss, the left-handed Middlesex captain, had been called up as cover. When it dawned on us all that Vaughan would not be fit enough to play and that Strauss would, therefore, take his place, a great argument followed about where Strauss should bat – when, all the time, this most natural of opening batsmen was on the verge of becoming the first Englishman to score a century on debut since Graham Thorpe in 1993, and only the fourth player in history to do so at Lord's. Vaughan might not have thought so at the time of his injury, but even he must have conceded at the end of the game that it had been a blessing in disguise.

Had Nasser Hussain not run Strauss out for 83 in the second innings, he would have become only the third batsman ever to score hundreds in both innings of his first Test. At the time, Hussain was vilified for a dreadful call that left his young partner stranded. Hours later, as Hussain drove exquisitely for boundaries to reach his hundred and then, to win the game, the former England captain was a national hero. Days later, he retired for good.

Trescothick did, indeed, take the reins from Vaughan for what everyone predicted would be a close match. Indeed, England's eventual winning margin of seven wickets seriously over-inflated a domination that only materialised on the last day when they successfully chased 282 – the second highest fourth-innings score ever made at Lord's to win a Test.

The central figure on the opening day was New Zealand's opening batsman, Mark Richardson. Left-handed and obdurate to the verge of being utterly tedious, Richardson is an opening batsman from a bygone age in which 'seeing the shine off the ball and batting until lunch and then until tea' was the accepted way to play. Interestingly, his excellent sense of humour and animated discussions with the media suggest he is merely extremely disciplined at the crease and that he plays strictly to his limitations. Richardson batted for 97 overs for his 93, before a cruel mistake from the usually trustworthy umpire Hair deprived him of a certain hundred. He was the fifth wicket to fall on a first day that was only lit up by a typically breezy 64 from Nathan Astle. England's seam bowling, that had won them the series in the Caribbean, was again a force to be reckoned with and, but for a breathtaking innings from Chris Cairns on the second morning, New Zealand would have fallen well short of a par total.

In his final Test appearance at Lord's, Cairns played an awesome knock in which he hit 82 from only 47 balls. Sixty-four of those runs came in fours and sixes

Andrew Strauss enjoyed a fairy-tale start to his Test career at Lord's.

and, in so doing, he passed Sir Viv Richards' record of 84 sixes in a Test career. The ball was disappearing to all parts of the ground before Harmison clung on to a good running catch at long leg to dismiss New Zealand for 386. In an extraordinary morning's play of 13 overs, New Zealand lost their last five wickets for 102!

By the close of the second day, England were 246 for 2, and Strauss had completed his memorable debut Test innings. What was most obvious throughout his knock was just how thoroughly composed and easy he looked; this was not just a replacement filling in for one game. Strauss needed to be accommodated in the following game, too, and with Vaughan ready to return, the potential selectorial nightmare was already being played out with some relish in the media.

In the true character of this match, New Zealand fought back on the third day to concede a deficit of only 55. Andrew Flintoff and Geraint Jones put on 105 for the seventh wicket, with Flintoff making 63, but England should have capitalised more effectively on the opening stand between Trescothick and Strauss, which was worth 190.

When Hussain took a brilliant catch at short leg to remove Stephen Fleming for four, a collapse of the type we saw several times in the West Indies was a possibility. This time, however, Richardson was not to be denied by Darrell Hair, or anybody else, and he duly reached the hundred he was deprived of in the first innings. Again, it was hardly a pretty innings and, having reached 101 in seven-and-a-quarter hours, he was caught behind off Harmison. Brendon McCullum – batting at No. 3 because of an injury to Astle – scored a very good 96 and, at 180 for 1, New Zealand were in control of the game. But a superb run out by Hussain sparked a collapse in the middle order and, with Giles and Harmison sharing seven wickets in the innings, New Zealand were bowled out for 336, setting England 282 to win and, on the final day, the equation was 274 to win in 90 overs with ten wickets in hand.

Trescothick was caught and bowled in the fifth over by Daryl Tuffey for two and, in the next, Butcher flayed Chris Martin to slip for six. England were 35 for 2 and, apparently, fighting for a draw.

However, Strauss and Hussain combined forces in a partnership that would have played a significant part in Hussain's decision to retire. They took England to 143 for 2, with Strauss having scored the bulk of the runs, before disaster struck. Hussain pushed Martin to point and, calling for a single, set off. Strauss, sensing that the run was not on, hesitated fatally, before dashing for the far end. Hussain stopped and, as Strauss ran helplessly past him, buried his face in his hands as his young partner was run out 17 runs short of his second hundred in the match.

Thankfully for England, Hussain's old friend – and calming influence – Graham Thorpe, joined him at the crease. With Hussain now growing in confidence, the pair saw England to victory with eight overs to spare, with Hussain reaching his hundred and scoring the winning runs from consecutive balls, both of which were driven firmly to the Warner Stand for four.

'I'm going to think about my future for a couple of days,' said an emotional Hussain immediately afterwards, and those who were there as he said it, knew he meant it. Three days later, having spoken with his father and family, Hussain called a press conference and dramatically lowered the curtain on a 96-match career in which he scored 5,764 Test runs at an average of 37, including 14 centuries.

28–31 May 2004 at Leicester
New Zealand 413 (111 overs) (NJ Astle 93, GJ Hopkins 71, BB McCullum 65, SP Fleming 56) & 357 for 5 dec (69.4 overs) (SP Fleming 95, DL Vettori 77, CD McMillan 68*, CL Cairns 62)
Leicestershire 210 (60.4 overs) (JK Maunders 85, CL Cairns 4 for 48, DL Vettori 4 for 60) & 232 (79.3 overs) (DL Maddy 87, JK Maunders 54, DL Vettori 5 for 92)
New Zealand won by 328 runs

The New Zealanders boosted their morale with a comfortable 328-run victory against a lightweight Leicestershire side missing six regulars, but lost Craig

McMillan from their second Test team after the batsman was hit by a ball from Darren Maddy and broke the little finger of his left hand. Skipper Stephen Fleming led the quest for time in the middle, with innings of 56 and 95, but the main plus point of the game for New Zealand came in the bowling of Daniel Vettori, the left-arm spinner. Vettori, who had been struggling for form, and who had not been looking the same bowler following a lengthy lay-off due to a serious back injury, picked up his first five-wicket return for two-and-a-half years as Leicestershire were dismissed for 232 in their second innings. It was the increasingly confident manner in which he bowled, though, as he added 5 for 92 to his first-innings 4 for 60, which delighted the New Zealand

Nasser Hussain jumps for joy after hitting the boundary which brought up his 14th, and last, Test hundred.

NASSER HUSSAIN

GRAHAM GOOCH, the former Essex and England captain, tells NIGEL FULLER about the fiery character and the steely determination to succeed that drove Nasser Hussain to become a fine Test batsman and one of the best captains in England's history.

In charge in the field: Nasser Hussain relished the job of England captaincy, and gave it his all.

It is safe to assume that not many bowlers were shedding tears when Nasser Hussain dramatically announced his retirement after his unbeaten century had carried England to victory in the first Test against New Zealand at Lord's last May.

Not only was he a difficult batsman to get out, he could also prove just as stubborn off the field – a fact readily acknowledged by those who played an influential part in fashioning his career.

No one monitored or helped his development more than Graham Gooch, his captain at both international and county level for a number of years and someone who is the first to admits that his relationship with the former England skipper was not always a bed of roses.

'We've had our run-ins, particularly in the early days,' admits Gooch. 'He was not always the easiest person to get on with and there were several occasions when we didn't see eye to eye and I had to crack the whip.

'But you can't take anything away from him as a cricketer. He was a guy who wore his heart on his sleeve and someone who played with tremendous passion, aggression and with fire in his belly. They were the qualities that made him stand out from the crowd, even if it caused friction down the line on occasions.

'I recall there was a bust-up in the dressing room involving Mark Ilott when Essex were playing Kent. I didn't witness it because I was with England at the time, but I had to sort things out when I returned. After speaking to all the players, I finished up suspending Nasser because it was deemed he was out of order.

'It was the same story 12 months later when Nasser was involved in another altercation at The Oval. It did not affect my admiration for him as a player, though. He was always the type of character you could embark upon a collision course with simply because he was so intense and single-minded. To his credit, however, he was not one to bear a grudge.

'One had to accept he had deep-rooted beliefs and spoke his mind; he had his own way of doing things and that sometimes clashed with what the team ethic might have been. I didn't look upon them as faults, though. As far as I was concerned, they were qualities that strengthened a side. I would much prefer to have a person in my team who is not the easiest to get on with but who is a fighter and a winner. And that's what he was.

'Of course Nasser could explode at times. As his captain, I had to manage situations like that. That's part of the job. Better that than players who are quiet, who do not project themselves and who are not up for the battle ahead.

'He will be the first to admit he could be stubborn and awkward, but, to be fair, he probably mellowed as he matured and became England's captain.'

Hussain was a little leg spinner about eight years of age when Gooch first encountered him, but it was as a promising batsman that he grabbed his attention.

'When he was given his chance in the second XI, I remember Ray East, who was captain and coach at the time, raving about him,' says Gooch. 'And it soon became obvious why Nasser caused so much excitement. His talent was obvious and he also possessed the desire to make full use of it.'

Graham Saville was another figure who played a prominent part in Hussain's career, both as chairman of the Essex cricket committee and when he was coach of the England Under 19 side.

'I remember him scoring 170 against Sri Lanka in Kandy at the beginning of 1987,' said Saville. 'It was a magnificent innings and it convinced me that he was destined to play at the very highest level.

'Following that innings, Doug Insole, then Essex's chairman, contacted me to ask about Hussain. I told him that we should play him in the first XI at every opportunity. Even though he was still short of his 19th birthday, when I offered that opinion there was no doubting that he was a very gifted youngster capable of making his mark at a higher level.'

Saville, like Gooch, found Hussain an intense character that could 'drive you mad' at times. 'According to him he was never out,' he said, a remark that will hardly come as a surprise to those who played both with and against him over the years. 'And when he returned to the pavilion having been dismissed you were advised to steer clear of him for at least an hour to allow him time to simmer down.

'Once he had done so, we would have a chat and he would take things on board. Nasser would also come at you with all guns blazing if things were not right off the field, as I found out to my cost on several occasions at Essex. As the county's cricket chairman, I was the one that was usually approached if players wanted things done.

'He would blow up at the most trivial things, though, like on one occasion when something was wrong with one of the seats in the dressing room.

'I have turned and walked away from his verbal blasts quite a few times and waited for him to calm down, but his outbursts, and the language that went with it, were something you learned to expect. He was not the most diplomatic of people, but whatever faults Nasser had, lacking focus wasn't one of them. He possessed a fierce determination to succeed and had the ability to go with it. Given that combination, it came as no surprise when he went on to have a great career.'

Three years after that innings in Kandy, Hussain was selected for a tour to the West Indies under Gooch and made his debut in the first Test in Kingston. Gooch played a major part in his selection.

'There was a batting place for a young batsman and, basically, the choice was between Nasser, Michael Atherton and John Stephenson, my partner at Essex who had enjoyed a great summer', remembers Gooch.

'I had a bit of influence as captain and I plumped for Nasser. Not only did he have the character and personality I admired, but I knew he could perform in difficult conditions and on bad pitches. I was aware of that from watching him score a century against Kent at Southend a few months earlier and he followed it up with another match-winning innings against Yorkshire in the same Festival Week when batting was far from easy.'

Gooch is not surprised that Hussain went on to make his mark as England's captain.

'From a very early age he was a good tactician and astute at setting fields. When it came to hard work, practice and preparation, he would leave no stone unturned. He was meticulous in everything he did and I would like to think that what he achieved in the game owed much to his early days with Essex when we enjoyed so much success in the 1980s and early 1990s.

'What really impressed me, though, was his man-management as England captain. At the time of his appointment it was a bit of an unknown quantity, but he proved himself a composed and confident leader who won the respect of those who played under him. You can't ask for more than that as captain.'

There are those who saw Hussain's retirement from the game as a selfish act. Certainly many Essex supporters felt that, having turned his back on England, he had a duty to see out the remainder of the season with the county.

Gooch, though, rejects such criticism. 'It is true that he probably played his best cricket for Essex in his last two years, but he retired when he thought the time was right. I will always understand and respect that decision.

Hussain cover drives during his debut Test innings, against the West Indies in Jamaica in 1990.

'It was not one he would have made without a great deal of thought, but, at the age of 36, he quite rightly reasoned that he was nearing the end of his career and what better way to leave the game than with the memory of scoring a century in your last match for both club and country. (His final innings for Essex was 102 against Glamorgan at Cardiff.)

'The biggest compliment I can pay Nasser is that when he walked out onto a cricket field he gave it his all, both as a batsman and also when it came to a battle of words and wills with opponents. He stood up to them and always gave as good as he received. He was a great bloke to have in your side and it's a tribute to him that England became a much better side when he was captain.

'It is stating the obvious that Essex were a better side with him in it, but a playing career can't go on for ever. As I've discovered, as soon as one door closes another opens.

'Nasser is now part of the media, a path followed by many other cricketers when they have called it a day, and I wish him every success. You can rest assured he will still give it his all.'

One can also guarantee that Hussain will continue to express his views without fear or favour, even though it will mean upsetting people. That is the nature of the beast.

Nigel Fuller has reported regularly on Essex cricket for more than 30 years.

management. John Maunders, who scored 85 and 54 in the match, and Maddy, who battled through 207 balls for his second-innings 87, were the only home players to emerge from the four days with any credit.

npower SECOND TEST
3–7 June 2004 at Headingley

Although England arrived at Headingley one up in the series, their exhibition at Lord's still left some locals wondering what all the fuss had been about in the West Indies. Their performance over the next five days, however, will have left no England supporter in any doubt that theirs was now a very fine team indeed.

Typically, a number of side issues dominated the build-up to the match. There was still widespread disbelief that Hussain had retired following the first Test. It was a truly magnanimous gesture, and one which made life much more comfortable for the selectors, but everyone who had great admiration for Hussain's battling and intelligent cricket hoped that he had not acted on the spur of the moment and made a decision that he would regret later in life. As a result of Hussain's departure – and because of the manner in which Strauss had batted at Lord's – Vaughan, quite rightly, made the move down the order to No. 4. Another unusual diversion was the imminent birth of his first child, which was due to arrive anytime between the start of the second and third Tests. Vaughan raised a few eyebrows when he announced that, unless he was actually batting, he would leave Headingley for Sheffield and be present at the birth. Some old timers chuntered, and others wondered if – when the time came – England's captain really would walk off the field. Vaughan had made his choice, however, and at 6.20 pm on the second afternoon, he made a hasty exit which alarmed the ever-alert stewards on the rugby ground who, despite the urgency of the situation, still demanded that Vaughan drive over their precious turf at precisely five miles per hour.

As Vaughan ran from the field, one or two of his team-mates might have been excused a wry smile, because Vaughan had put New Zealand into bat and they were proceeding very comfortably indeed. After just 19 overs were possible on the first day – meaning that Vaughan's decision to field first was entirely justifiable – New Zealand closed day two on 351 for 6. Michael Papps, another patient opener in the Richardson mould, offered three chances on his way to 86, and the most fluent innings came from Fleming, who batted for five hours before falling three short of his hundred when he found a leading edge off Harmison and was caught at mid-off. No one would

SECOND TEST – ENGLAND v. NEW ZEALAND
3–7 June 2004 at Headingley

NEW ZEALAND

	First Innings		Second Innings	
MH Richardson	b Saggers	13	c Jones b Hoggard	40
MHW Papps	lbw b Flintoff	86	(9) c Vaughan b Harmison	0
SP Fleming (capt)	c Vaughan b Harmison	97	(2) c Strauss b Flintoff	11
NJ Astle	c Butcher b Saggers	2	lbw b Hoggard	8
SB Styris	c Jones b Harmison	21	c Jones b Hoggard	19
JDP Oram	c Thorpe b Flintoff	39	(7) not out	36
CL Cairns	c Strauss b Harmison	41	(8) lbw b Hoggard	10
*BB McCullum	b Hoggard	54	(3) c Trescothick b Harmison	20
DL Vettori	b Harmison	35	(11) absent injured	
DR Tuffey	lbw b Hoggard	0	(10) run out	0
CS Martin	not out	0	c Jones b Harmison	7
Extras	b 5, lb 14, w 2	21	b 4, lb 4, nb 2	10
	(143.2 overs)	409	(9 wkts 42 overs)	161

	First Innings				Second Innings			
	O	M	R	W	O	M	R	W
Hoggard	27	6	93	2	15	4	75	4
Harmison	36.2	8	74	4	16	5	57	3
Flintoff	27	7	64	2	6	0	16	1
Saggers	30	6	86	2	5	3	5	0
Trescothick	2	0	3	0	-	-	-	-
Giles	19	1	67	0	-	-	-	-
Vaughan	2	0	3	0	-	-	-	-

Fall of Wickets
1-33, 2-202, 3-215, 4-215, 5-263, 6-293, 7-355, 8-409, 9-409
1-39, 2-75, 3-77, 4-84, 5-91, 6-118, 7-144, 8-149, 9-161

ENGLAND

	First Innings		Second Innings	
ME Trescothick	b Styris	132	not out	30
AJ Strauss	c Tuffey b Vettori	62	c Astle b Tuffey	10
MA Butcher	lbw b Vettori	4	not out	5
MP Vaughan (capt)	c Fleming b Styris	13		
GP Thorpe	b Martin	34		
A Flintoff	c Martin b Styris	94		
*GO Jones	c Fleming b Cairns	100		
AF Giles	c Fleming b Martin	21		
MJ Hoggard	c McCullum b Tuffey	4		
MJ Saggers	c sub b Cairns	0		
SJ Harmison	not out	0		
Extras	b 25, lb 21, w 3, nb 13	62		0
	(133.1 overs)	526	(1 wkt 8 overs)	45

	First Innings				Second Innings			
	O	M	R	W	O	M	R	W
Tuffey	26.1	7	88	1	4	0	28	1
Martin	30	9	127	2	4	1	17	0
Styris	27	5	88	3	-	-	-	-
Cairns	27	6	94	2	-	-	-	-
Vettori	23	2	83	2	-	-	-	-

Fall of Wickets
1-153, 2-174, 3-229, 4-240, 5-339, 6-457, 7-491, 8-526, 9-526
1-18

Umpires: SA Bucknor and SJA Taufel
Toss: England
Man of the Match: GO Jones

England won by 9 wickets

Right: Geraint Jones revealed his high talent as a batsman by scoring a century in only his fourth Test innings.

have denied the amiable New Zealand captain his century, but he is making a habit of failing to convert half-centuries into centuries. Richardson himself had earlier been bowled by Martin Saggers' first delivery of the match – also his first Test delivery in England – and the Kent swing bowler also accounted for Astle for two, albeit through an outstanding catch at point by Butcher.

England's seam bowlers fought back on the third morning, taking 4 for 58, with Cairns forcing Harmison to point for 41 and McCullum impressing for the second time in the series with an innings of 54. Having been put in under cloudy skies, New Zealand would still have been satisfied with their total of 409 all out and an England victory seemed a long way off.

England's new opening pair of Trescothick and Strauss raised the home crowd's hopes with another excellent partnership. This time they put on 153 in only 33 overs before Strauss fell to Vettori's left-arm spin for 62. Butcher and Vaughan – whose mind might have been elsewhere – made just four and 13 respectively, and when Trescothick was bowled by an alarming shooter by Styris for a very good 132, England were still 169 behind with six wickets in hand. The recovery began with a stand of 99 between Flintoff and Thorpe,

who scored 34, and was completed by a thoroughly entertaining partnership between Flintoff and Geraint Jones, who showed once and for all that if England require a wicketkeeper-batsman, then he is their man. With his father listening in over the Internet at his home in Brisbane, Jones helped Flintoff to add 118 priceless runs, and the pair took England into the lead. Flintoff should have been given out lbw for 90, but he made only four more before his 143-ball knock was ended by Styris. Jones found another ally in Giles, who saw Jones to his hundred, that came from 143 balls and contained one six and 15 fours – most of which were hit hard, and square, through the offside.

England's 526 gave them a lead of 117 which, at Leeds, is always a bonus, and before they could pass it, New Zealand had already lost five wickets and were staring defeat in the face. It was the fast bowlers who did the damage again, and it was Matthew Hoggard – whose confidence is never especially high – who led the way. At 75 for 1, New Zealand appeared to be progressing smoothly enough, but Hoggard made one fly at Richardson, and, as England sensed their opportunity, the collapse began. In four overs, New Zealand lost four batsmen for 16 runs, and, at the start of the final day, they were still 15 behind with five wickets left.

Cairns and Oram are dangerous hitters, and they still had the capacity to blast New Zealand out of trouble and set England an awkward target, but after Styris was brilliantly caught by Jones diving to his right in only the second over of the morning, Cairns was quickly lbw to Hoggard and although Oram smashed an entertaining 36 from 31 balls, he had no support and New Zealand were dismissed for 161. England required just 45 runs to take the series.

Strauss experienced his first failure at this level when Astle caught him at third slip for ten, but Trescothick and Butcher completed the task in only eight overs.

npower THIRD TEST
10–13 June 2004 at Trent Bridge

It was a downcast New Zealand team that arrived for the final Test in Nottingham. Even Fleming, their experienced and approachable captain, was unusually downbeat before the game and it was easy to see why. Decimated by injuries, the New Zealanders' plight had now reached farcical proportions to the extent that there were serious grounds for handing England the game as a walkover.

Most crippling of all was the absence of Vettori, who was not only the best spinner in the series, but who is also Fleming's crutch; the man to whom he

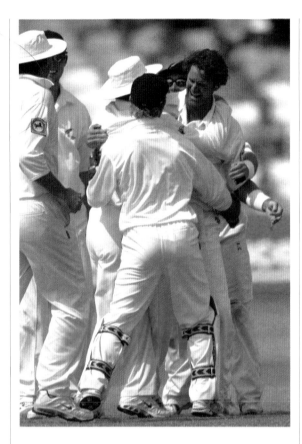

Chris Cairns produced a heroic last Test appearance with the ball ... on his 'home from home' ground of Trent Bridge.

turns to bowl for an entire session to stem the flow of runs. Vettori's hamstring had responded to treatment, but not sufficiently, and he joined Shane Bond and Michael Papps on the sidelines. Others among the walking wounded included Fleming, Oram, Astle and Tuffey. McMillan returned, although with a still-broken finger, and before England's first innings was over, Chris Martin and Kyle Mills had both left the field, never to return.

Despite this crisis, New Zealand showed typical resilience and stomach for a fight they knew they could not win. Chris Cairns' final Test appearance – on his adopted home ground – rewarded him with nine wickets in the match but, sadly, there were to be no heroics from him with the bat. That honour fell to Fleming, Richardson and Styris who, between them, dominated the opening day. Richardson and Fleming put on 163 for the first wicket and although Richardson missed out on his hundred, Fleming made no such mistake this time. He reached his century with a six, but fell for 117 when he edged Flintoff to second slip.

THIRD TEST – ENGLAND v. NEW ZEALAND
10–13 June 2004 at Trent Bridge

NEW ZEALAND

	First Innings		Second Innings	
MH Richardson	c Vaughan b Giles	73	lbw b Giles	49
SP Fleming (capt)	c Thorpe b Flintoff	117	lbw b Flintoff	45
SB Styris	c sub b Giles	108	(4) c Jones b Harmison	39
NJ Astle	b Harmison	15	(5) lbw b Flintoff	0
CD McMillan	lbw b Harmison	0	(6) lbw b Harmison	30
JDP Oram	c Strauss b Saggers	14	(8) c Flintoff b Harmison	0
CL Cairns	c Thorpe b Saggers	12	(9) b Giles	1
*BB McCullum	c Hoggard b Harmison	21	(3) c Flintoff b Giles	4
JEC Franklin	not out	4	(7) c Jones b Flintoff	17
KD Mills	c Jones b Hoggard	0	c Harmison b Giles	8
CS Martin	c Vaughan b Hoggard	2	not out	0
Extras	b 2, lb 14, nb 2	18	b 1, lb 21, nb 3	25
	(121 overs)	384	(81 overs)	218

	First Innings				Second Innings			
	O	M	R	W	O	M	R	W
Hoggard	25	6	85	2	6	2	25	0
Harmison	32	9	80	3	25	7	51	3
Flintoff	14	2	48	1	20	3	60	3
Saggers	22	5	80	2	6	2	14	0
Giles	27	6	70	2	24	6	46	4
Vaughan	1	0	5	0	-	-	-	-

Fall of Wickets
1-163, 2-225, 3-272, 4-272, 5-308, 6-331, 7-366, 8-377, 9-382
1-94, 2-106, 3-126, 4-134, 5-185, 6-198, 7-198, 8-208, 9-210

ENGLAND

	First Innings		Second Innings	
ME Trescothick	c Styris b Franklin	63	c & b Franklin	9
AJ Strauss	c McCullum b Cairns	0	lbw b Cairns	6
MA Butcher	c Styris b Franklin	5	lbw b Cairns	59
MP Vaughan (capt)	lbw b Cairns	61	lbw b Cairns	10
GP Thorpe	c McCullum b Franklin	45	not out	104
A Flintoff	lbw b Cairns	54	c sub b Cairns	5
MJ Hoggard	c Styris b Franklin	5		
*GO Jones	lbw b Styris	22	(7) c Oram b Franklin	27
AF Giles	not out	45	(8) not out	36
MJ Saggers	b Cairns	0		
SJ Harmison	b Cairns	0		
Extras	b 2, lb 5, nb 12	19	b 4, lb 16, nb 8	28
	(85.3 overs)	319	(6 wkts 71.3 overs)	284

	First Innings				Second Innings			
	O	M	R	W	O	M	R	W
Martin	1.5	0	1	0	-	-	-	-
Cairns	23.3	5	79	5	25	2	108	4
Franklin	26.1	4	104	4	17	2	59	2
Mills	6	2	31	0	-	-	-	-
Oram	15	0	47	0	14.3	1	50	0
Styris	11	1	45	1	14	1	43	0
McMillan	2	1	5	0	-	-	-	-
Richardson	-	-	-	-	1	0	4	0

Fall of Wickets
1-1, 2-18, 3-128, 4-140, 5-221, 6-244, 7-255, 8-295, 9-301
1-12, 2-16, 3-46, 4-134, 5-162, 6-214

Umpires: DJ Harper and SJA Taufel
Toss: New Zealand
Man of the Match: GP Thorpe
Men of the Series: SJ Harmison (England) and MH Richardson (New Zealand)

England won by 4 wickets

Right: Graham Thorpe celebrates his match-winning second-innings hundred.

At 225 for 1 on a very good pitch, New Zealand were well placed to score 500-plus, but their last nine wickets fell for 159 runs in 50 overs. Only Styris, on the second day, played as if he was in the throes of a whitewash-saving situation. His 108 apart, the next highest score was McCullum's 21 while, for England, Harmison took 3 for 80.

By the close of the second day, England had plunged recklessly to 225 for 5. It is one thing to bat positively in a Test match, but this approach smacked of over-confidence and, had New Zealand possessed an attack worthy of the name, England might have come unstuck. Strauss experienced his first duck at this level when he edged Cairns to the wicketkeeper in the second over of the innings and after Butcher was caught in the slips off James Franklin – a left-arm swing bowler who was jobbing in the Lancashire League before his emergency call-up – Vaughan and Trescothick took England to 128 for 2, when Vaughan was beautifully undone by Cairns' slower ball for 61.

Trescothick fell for 63, and it was left to Thorpe and Flintoff to steer England out of trouble. Even so, when five wickets were lost for 94 on the third morning, New Zealand had a lead of 65 that, while not

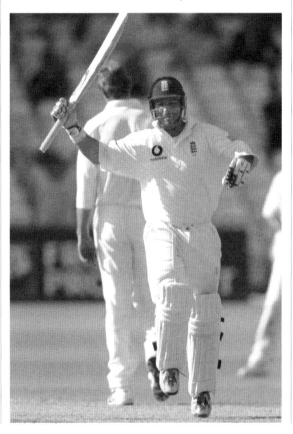

SERIES AVERAGES
England v. New Zealand

ENGLAND

Batting	M	Inns	NO	Runs	HS	Av	100	50	c/st
N Hussain	1	2	1	137	103*	137.00	1	–	3/-
GP Thorpe	3	5	2	237	104*	79.00	1	1	3/-
ME Trescothick	3	6	1	322	132	64.40	1	2	1/-
AF Giles	3	4	2	113	45*	56.50	–	–	-/-
A Flintoff	3	4	0	216	94	54.00	–	3	2/-
GO Jones	3	4	0	195	100	48.75	1	–	14/-
AJ Strauss	3	6	0	273	112	45.50	1	2	4/-
MP Vaughan	2	3	0	84	61	28.00	–	1	4/-
MA Butcher	3	6	0	105	59	21.00	–	1	2/-
MJ Hoggard	3	3	0	24	15	8.00	–	–	1/-
SP Jones	1	1	0	4	4	4.00	–	–	-/-
SJ Harmison	3	3	2	0	0*	0.00	–	–	2/-
MJ Saggers	2	2	0	0	0	0.00	–	–	-/-

Bowling	Overs	Mds	Runs	Wkts	Av	Best	5/inn	10m
SJ Harmison	169.2	44	464	21	22.09	4-74	–	–
A Flintoff	104.5	24	291	10	29.10	3-60	–	–
AF Giles	114	21	302	9	33.55	4-46	–	–
SP Jones	46	13	146	4	36.50	3-82	–	–
MJ Hoggard	109	28	385	9	42.77	4-75	–	–
MJ Saggers	63	16	185	4	46.25	2-80	–	–
ME Trescothick	2	0	3	0	–	–	–	–
MP Vaughan	3	0	8	0	–	–	–	–

NEW ZEALAND

Batting	M	Inns	NO	Runs	HS	Av	100	50	c/st
MH Richardson	3	6	0	369	101	61.50	1	2	2/-
SP Fleming	3	6	0	308	117	51.33	1	1	4/-
MHW Papps	1	2	0	86	86	43.00	–	1	-/-
BB McCullum	3	6	0	200	96	33.33	–	2	6/-
JDP Oram	3	6	1	160	67	32.00	–	1	3/-
SB Styris	3	6	0	191	108	31.83	1	–	3/-
CL Cairns	3	6	0	160	82	26.66	–	1	-/-
NJ Astle	3	6	0	138	64	23.00	–	1	1/-
JEC Franklin	1	2	1	21	17	21.00	–	–	1/-
DL Vettori	2	3	0	42	35	14.00	–	–	-/-
DR Tuffey	2	4	1	29	14*	9.66	–	–	2/-
CD McMillan	2	4	0	36	30	9.00	–	–	-/-
KD Mills	1	2	0	8	8	4.00	–	–	-/-
CS Martin	3	6	3	10	7	3.33	–	–	1/-

Bowling	Overs	Mds	Runs	Wkts	Av	Best	5/inn	10m
JEC Franklin	43.1	6	163	6	27.16	4-104	–	–
CL Cairns	97.3	15	379	12	31.58	5-79	1	–
SB Styris	69.3	12	224	6	37.33	3-88	–	–
DL Vettori	69	8	205	4	51.25	2-69	–	–
CS Martin	80.5	18	314	6	52.33	3-94	–	–
DR Tuffey	66.1	14	246	3	82.00	1-28	–	–
JDP Oram	74.3	13	212	2	106.00	2-76	–	–
MH Richardson	1	0	4	0	–	–	–	–
CD McMillan	2	1	5	0	–	–	–	–
KD Mills	6	2	31	0	–	–	–	–

substantial, gave the visitors an unexpected advantage.

Fleming and Richardson increased that to 159 in the afternoon, giving rise to serious concern in the England camp. This was coupled with the knowledge that Fleming, who had been scouring the field for bowlers, would be hard-pressed to declare but, even so, England were on course for a battle to save the match on the final day.

The lead overnight was 255 with five wickets left, but they were blown away on the fourth morning before many of the crowd had settled into their seats. As usual, it was Harmison who started the collapse when he had McMillan lbw in the fifth over, and Oram, taken low by Flintoff at slip, in his next. The stage was set for Cairns to produce some big hitting in his final innings, but he was bowled by Giles with a beauty out of the rough for only a single, and it was the left-arm spinner who mopped up the innings, taking 4 for 46 and leaving England 284 to win.

In the handful of overs that remained before lunch, England lost both openers and, on 23 for 2 at the break, there was a chance that Fleming's wounded warriors might produce an upset. Vaughan was trapped lbw by Cairns for the second time in the match, so it was 46 for 3 when Thorpe – the ideal man for a perfectly paced run chase – appeared at the crease to join Butcher, his Surrey team-mate.

The left-handers put on 88 before Butcher became Cairns' third lbw victim for 59, and when Flintoff casually drove to extra-cover 28 runs later, England still needed 122 to win with five wickets left.

Jones was dropped in the slips on six, but added 52 before driving Franklin to gully for 27 and, at the scheduled close of play, England needed 25 to win. The extra half-hour was claimed and Thorpe duly reached a terrific hundred. Afterwards, he was the first to pay tribute to Giles' contribution. The pair put on 70 from only 84 balls, with the spinner unbeaten on 36 when the winning runs were struck to complete England's sixth win out of seven Tests, and their first whitewash in a three-or-more match series for 26 years.

16 June 2004 at Derby
New Zealand 258 for 7 (50 overs) (SP Fleming 102, SB Styris 56)
Derbyshire 259 for 6 (48.4 overs) (Hassan Adnan 113*)
Derbyshire won by 4 wickets

Derbyshire, the lowest-ranked county in English one-day domestic cricket, won a famous victory over the side lying fourth in the ICC's limited-overs international rankings. Hassan Adnan, with his first one-day hundred for the club, took Derbyshire past

New Zealand's 50-over total of 258 for 7 with an unbeaten 113 – hitting ten fours and a six and reaching his century from just 101 balls. Adnan, however, who put on 100 for the fourth wicket with his captain Luke Sutton, was dropped before he had got off the mark by Stephen Fleming, off Daryl Tuffey. The Black Caps' skipper had earlier stroked 102 from 119 balls, while Scott Styris and Craig McMillan also batted well in a match designed to give New Zealand limited-overs practice ahead of the NatWest Series. Losing, however, was not supposed to be part of their script.

18 June 2004 at Chelmsford
Essex 243 for 3 (50 overs) (RC Irani 72*, AP Grayson 57)
New Zealand 246 for 5 (38.3 overs) (HJH Marshall 111, CD McMillan 52*)
New Zealand won by 5 wickets

An aggressive 111 by Hamish Marshall, who reached three figures off just 84 balls, swept the New Zealanders to a swashbuckling five-wicket victory over Essex before a 3,000-strong crowd under the Chelmsford lights. The county's total of 243 for 3, featuring half-centuries from Paul Grayson and Ronnie Irani and other good contributions from Aftab Habib and Ravi Bopara, was made to look embarrassingly inadequate as New Zealand rushed home with no fewer than 12 overs in hand. Nathan Astle and Craig McMillan also played some punishing strokes, while Chris Cairns finished off proceedings with a six.

20 June 2004 at Northampton
New Zealand 253 (49.1 overs) (BB McCullum 58, JDP Oram 50, AJ Shantry 5 for 37)
Northamptonshire 241 for 8 (48 overs) (M van Jaarsveld 102, GL Brophy 57*)
New Zealand won by 5 runs

The New Zealanders needed to hold their nerve, both with the bat and then in the field, to see off Northamptonshire by five runs, in a match slightly reduced in playing time by a rain shower. Half-centuries from Jacob Oram and Brendon McCullum, and a hard-hit 46 by acting captain Chris Cairns, were chiefly responsible for New Zealand's recovery from 26 for 3, following a testing new-ball spell by left-arm seamer Adam Shantry, to an eventual 253. Martin van Jaarsfeld's fluent 102 and the big hitting of Gerard Brophy, who finished up on 57 not out, then threatened to take Northants past their adjusted target, but wickets fell regularly after van Jaarsfeld was caught at long on, and, in the end, the 11 runs that Cairns had plundered from the final over proved too much.

NATWEST TRIANGULAR ONE-DAY SERIES
(England, New Zealand and the West Indies)
By Jonathan Agnew

It is no coincidence that one of Britain's wettest summers on record should have played host to a damp squib of a NatWest Series. The darker the cloud cover – and the harder it rained – the more the white ball swung, nipped and bounced. As a result, batting was reduced to a lottery.

That was probably appropriate, however, given that the selection of England's one-day team had more than just a passing resemblance to pulling out winning numbers at a tombola stall.

England's efforts during the series were in complete contrast to their performances in the Test arena which, amazingly, resumed at their formidable best the moment this one-day debacle was consigned to the dustbin.

Without the services of Andrew Flintoff for their first three matches, England appeared to be missing their talisman in every sense. The returning 'Freddie' was given a hero's reception at Headingley where, although he was unable to bowl, he clubbed 21 from 18 balls in what turned out to be England's only victory of the series.

It said everything about the manner in which the conditions affected the standard of cricket that only one game – between England and the West Indies on a fine day at Lord's – was even remotely exciting.

However, although that game went into the last over, the result was never really in doubt because Chris Gayle, who scored an excellent 132, was at the crease and in complete control. This, too, after Andrew Strauss and Andrew Flintoff had both scored centuries as they put on 226. That England could not defend their challenging total of 285 was lamentable.

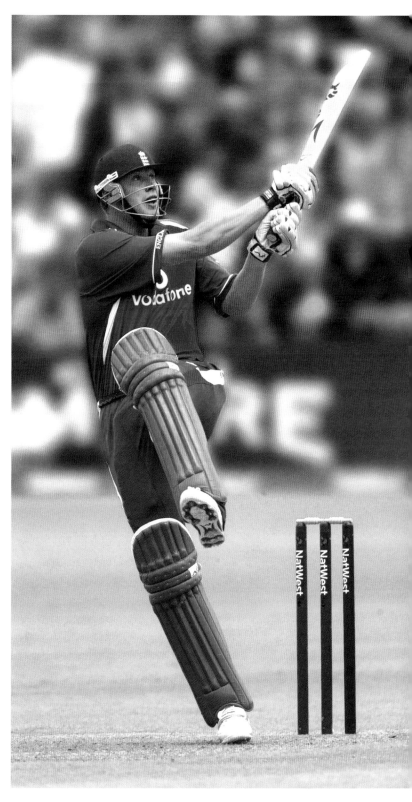

The crowd pleaser: Andrew Flintoff launches another big six into the ranks of his adoring fans.

And yet, this was not the nadir. Not by a long chalk. That came on a damp and drizzly afternoon at Chester-le-Street where England chose an XI that beggared belief. Inexplicably, they selected two left-arm spinners in the seamer-friendly conditions, and were promptly bowled out for 101 in 33 overs. New Zealand knocked them off in the 18th over, thereby rendering the installation of temporary floodlights an expensive waste of time.

The final was contested by New Zealand and the West Indies and, having played the better cricket during the tournament, New Zealand were worthy winners, despite losing seven wickets for 49 runs in ten overs as they set the West Indies 267 to win.

At 106 for 5, the West Indian challenge was over, and thus the final itself joined the swollen ranks of matches that had simply fizzled out. In the end, the West Indies were dismissed for just 159.

Stephen Fleming enjoyed a consistent run of form with the bat, whilst James Franklin and Jacob Oram both enjoyed the conditions and bowled tidily. If the tournament will be remembered for anything, however, it will be for the successive centuries by Flintoff, the hostile bowling of Steve Harmison and further evidence – if any were needed – that floodlit cricket simply does not work in England.

Match One
24 June 2004 at Old Trafford
England v. **New Zealand**
Match abandoned due to rain – 3pts each

Match Two
26 June 2004 at Edgbaston
West Indies 122 for 4 (21 overs)
New Zealand 97 for 2 (13.4 overs)
Match abandoned due to rain – 3pts each

Match Three
27 June 2004 at Trent Bridge
England 147 (38.2 overs)
West Indies 148 for 3 (32.2 overs) (CH Gayle 60*)
West Indies (6pts) won by 7 wickets

Match Four

29 June 2004 at The Riverside
England 101 (32.5 overs) (JEC Franklin 5 for 42)
New Zealand 103 for 3 (17.2 overs)
New Zealand (6pts) won by 7 wickets

Match Five

1 July 2004 at Headingley
West Indies 159 (40.1 overs)
England 160 for 3 (22 overs) (ME Trescothick 55)
England (6pts) won by 7 wickets

Match Six

3 July 2004 at Cardiff
West Indies 216 (46.2 overs) (BC Lara 58,
RR Sarwan 54)
New Zealand 220 for 5 (46 overs) (HJH Marshall 75*)
New Zealand (5pts) beat West Indies (1pt) by 5 wickets

Match Seven

4 July 2004 at Bristol
England 237 for 7 (50 overs) (A Flintoff 106,
AJ Strauss 61)
New Zealand 241 for 4 (47.2 overs) (SP Fleming 99,
HJH Marshall 55, NJ Astle 53)
New Zealand (5pts) beat England (1pt) by 6 wickets

Match Eight

6 July 2004 at Lord's
England 285 for 7 (50 overs) (A Flintoff 123,
AJ Strauss 100)
West Indies 286 for 3 (49.1 overs) (CH Gayle 132*,
RR Sarwan 89)
West Indies (5pts) beat England (1pt) by 7 wickets

Match Nine

8 July 2004 at The Rose Bowl
New Zealand v. **West Indies**
Match abandoned due to rain – 3pts each

	P	W	L	T	NR	Pts	RR
New Zealand	6	3	0	0	3	25	1.40
West Indies	6	2	2	0	2	18	-0.38
England	6	1	4	0	1	11	-0.59

Left: Stephen Fleming lifts the NatWest Series trophy aloft at Lord's, and his New Zealand team were worthy winners of the rain-blighted tournament.

NATWEST SERIES FINAL – NEW ZEALAND v. WEST INDIES
10 July 2004 at Lord's

NEW ZEALAND

SP Fleming (capt)	c Gayle b Bravo	67
NJ Astle	c Gayle b Bravo	57
HJH Marshall	c Sarwan b Gayle	44
SB Styris	c Powell b Smith DR	1
CD McMillan	c Chanderpaul b Best	52
CL Cairns	st Jacobs b Gayle	5
JDP Oram	c Jacobs b Best	15
CZ Harris	c & b Sarwan	1
DL Vettori	c Smith DR b Sarwan	6
*GJ Hopkins	run out	0
IG Butler	not out	0
Extras	lb 8, w 9, nb 1	18
	(49.2 overs)	266

	O	M	R	W
Best	7.2	0	57	2
Bradshaw	6	1	28	0
Smith DR	10	1	27	1
Bravo	10	0	67	2
Gayle	10	0	48	1
Sarwan	6	0	31	3

Fall of Wickets
1-120, 2-143, 3-146, 4-217, 5-233, 6-249, 7-252, 8-265, 9-266

WEST INDIES

CH Gayle	c Styris b Oram	4
DS Smith	run out	44
RR Sarwan	run out	19
BC Lara (capt)	lbw b Vettori	30
DJJ Bravo	c Styris b Vettori	4
S Chanderpaul	c McMillan b Vettori	31
RL Powell	c Marshall b Vettori	18
DR Smith	lbw b Vettori	2
*RD Jacobs	c Cairns b Harris	1
IDR Bradshaw	run out	0
TL Best	not out	1
Extras	lb 2, nb 3	5
	(41.2 overs)	159

	O	M	R	W
Oram	8	2	26	1
Butler	6	0	25	0
Styris	5	0	22	0
Harris	10	0	45	1
Vettori	9.2	1	30	5
McMillan	3	0	9	0

Fall of Wickets
1-5, 2-45, 3-98, 4-105, 5-106, 6-144, 7-149, 8-150, 9-150

Umpires: RE Koertzen and DR Shepherd
Toss: West Indies
Man of the Match: DL Vettori

New Zealand won by 107 runs

WEST INDIES IN ENGLAND
By Jonathan Agnew
and Mark Baldwin

16 June 2004 at Belfast
West Indians 242 (46.2 overs) (BC Lara 106)
Ireland 146 (37.4 overs)
West Indians won by 96 runs

Brian Lara kicked off the West Indies' tour by hitting Ireland's bowlers for 106 and setting up a comfortable victory in the first of two matches in Belfast. Lara had come in, though, at 40 for 3 and was grateful for the support of 20-year-old all-rounder Dwayne Bravo (45) in a fourth-wicket partnership of 139. Ravi Rampaul's three early wickets then ensured that the Irish would not get close to the West Indian total of 242.

17 June 2004 at Belfast
West Indians 292 for 7 (50 overs) (DJJ Bravo 100*)
Ireland 295 for 4 (46.5 overs) (JP Bray 71,
JAM Molins 66, NJ O'Brien 58*)
Ireland won by 6 wickets

Lara did not bat until No. 8 in the tourists' second match at Stormont, scoring just a single when he came in right at the end of the West Indies' 292 for 7. Bravo again caught the eye with a brilliant 100 not out from a mere 65 balls, but both his and the West Indian thunder was stolen by the Ireland top order. Led by openers Jason Molins and Jeremy Bray, who put on 111, Ireland won themselves a victory to fire up memories of their legendary 1969 triumph against a West Indian touring side led by Clive Lloyd. Niall O'Brien, the Kent wicketkeeper, finished on 58 not out and he was kept company by Andrew White, unbeaten on 32, as the Irish reached their target with 3.1 overs to spare. Rampaul's seven overs cost him 74 runs but, overall, perhaps no victory could compare with the drama of Sion Mills' in '69 when Lloyd's team, the morning after a night of traditional Irish hospitality, were bowled out for 25.

19 June 2004 at Hove
Sussex 292 for 6 (50 overs) (MW Goodwin 90,
TR Ambrose 79)
West Indians 184 for 4 (21 overs) (S Chanderpaul 71,
CH Gayle 57)
West Indians won by 6 wickets

Brutal hitting by Chris Gayle and Shivnarine Chanderpaul decimated the Sussex attack at Hove to leave the West Indians clear winners under Duckworth-Lewis regulations. In reply to the county's excellent 50-over total of 292 for 6, in which Murray Goodwin and Tim Ambrose both played fine knocks, the tourists raced to 184 for 4 in just 21 overs following a rain interruption. James Kirtley had reduced the West Indians to 12 for 2, removing Devon Smith and Ramnaresh Sarwan in a new-ball spell of 3–2–4–2, but the rest of the Sussex bowlers took a real hammering, with Luke Wright's four overs costing 61 runs. Earlier in the day, at Cardiff, England had also warmed up for the NatWest Series by beating Wales by six wickets, with Rob Key hitting 83 and Andrew Strauss an unbeaten 92 from 86 balls.

21 June 2004 at Beckenham
West Indians 274 for 8 (48 overs) (RR Sarwan 79,
BC Lara 68, S Chanderpaul 60, MJ Saggers 5 for 51)
Kent 183 (41.1 overs) (ET Smith 54)
West Indians won by 91 runs

A 7,000 capacity crowd at Beckenham were kept waiting when the West Indies' team bus was held up by South London traffic. In a match reduced to 48 overs per side, however, the tourists soon made up for lost time by putting together a total of 274 for 8 that was well out of the reach of a below-strength Kent side. Brian Lara allowed Ramnaresh Sarwan and Shivnarine Chanderpaul to settle in the spotlight after Chris Gayle was defeated by Martin Saggers' second ball of the match, but despite Sarwan's cultured 79 and Chanderpaul's typically industrious 60, the highlight of the day was Lara's effortless 53-ball 68. He drove James Tredwell straight for six and also hit seven fours while dominating a stand of 99 with Sarwan. Ed Smith's 54 was the only innings to compare with the quality of the West Indian strokeplay, as Kent slid to 183 all out in reply.

14–16 July 2004 at Arundel
West Indians 380 (95 overs) (DS Smith 142, BC Lara
113 retired hurt) and 157 (35.5 overs) (CH Gayle 89)
MCC 260 (58 overs) (SG Koenig 79) and 248
(63.3 overs) (AN Cook 89, JP Stephenson 58)
West Indians won by 29 runs

The West Indies suffered a fright before snatching the last five MCC wickets for 35 runs to earn themselves a 29-run win at Arundel. The first day was all about Brian Lara, who hit a magnificent 113 from 105 balls despite 'feeling weak' after a bout of flu and eventually having to leave the field. Devon Smith, the opener, also batted beautifully to score

142 from 211 balls, with 22 fours, and help Lara (two sixes and 18 fours) to put on 196 in 35 overs. The MCC team featured Matthew Hoggard and Simon Jones, playing in search of match fitness ahead of the Test series, and England batsman Graham Thorpe. Hoggard was the pick of a struggling attack on the first day, which ended with the West Indian total on 373 for 6, and he took further wickets on the second morning to end up with highly creditable figures of 4 for 32. MCC's first-innings reply fell away alarmingly from 167 for 1 to 260 all out, despite a quick-fire 32 from Thorpe, but the West Indies collapsed to 50 for 5 late on the second day before a stand of 87 between Chris Gayle and Lara rescued them. Gayle went on to make 89, but Hoggard removed Lara and the tourists lost their last five wickets for just 20 to leave the MCC needing 278 in 78 overs for victory. An eye-catching 89 from 19-year-old opener Alastair Cook, supported by a brave innings from John Stephenson, the former England batsman in the early weeks of his new job as the MCC's head of cricket, took them close.

17–19 July 2004 at Shenley
West Indians 534 for 7 dec (120.1 overs) (DJJ Bravo 118, RD Jacobs 117*, SC Joseph 114, OAC Banks 90) and 283 for 5 dec (59.5 overs) (S Chanderpaul 104*, SC Joseph 68)
Sri Lanka A 346 (70 overs) (GI Daniel 72, J Mubarak 61)
Match drawn

Sri Lanka A had won all seven of their previous one-day tour matches against six counties and the British Universities, but in their first three-day match they found the West Indies batsmen in the mood for some serious practice ahead of the opening Test. On a fine pitch, the West Indians ran up 534 for 7 declared in their first innings and then, after dismissing the Sri Lankans for 346, declined to enforce the follow-on in favour of yet more time at the crease. Shivnarine Chanderpaul was the chief beneficiary, as the match meandered to a draw on the final afternoon, putting some scratchy early-tour form behind him with an unbeaten 104 off 145 balls, an innings that contained 13 fours. Sylvester Joseph also did his Test prospects no harm by adding 68 to his first-day 114, 90 runs of which came in boundaries. Dwayne Bravo's bid for a Test place was reinforced by an aggressive 118 in the first innings, while Ridley Jacobs warmed up for Test action with 117 not out and Omari Banks weighed in with 90.

npower FIRST TEST
22–26 July 2004 at Lord's

Only the most optimistic West Indian supporter could have imagined that Brian Lara's team would have been able to overturn the 3–0 defeat their team had suffered in the Caribbean earlier in the year. In the interim, they had struggled to beat Bangladesh in a two-Test series at home and, of the original tourists, only Lara himself had ever played any first-class cricket in England before.

Lara, whose position as captain was increasingly under threat, had put his job on the line before the second of those matches. He promised to resign if the West Indies did not win the game; his players responded to that, but, in so doing, Lara had undermined his own authority.

Before the opening Test against England at Lord's, I asked him about the Steve Harmison factor, and whether or not his team would be able to stand up to him. Lara's answer would come back to haunt him. 'I'm not sure England have a plan B,' he said, suggesting that England's bowling attack revolved simply around one man. When his old Warwickshire team-mate, Ashley Giles, nabbed his ninth wicket of the game to record the best figures by an English spinner at Lord's for 40 years, Lara must have been forced to review his opinion.

Things could not have gone any worse for Lara on the first day, and if he had been hoping to send a message of positive intent to the passionate cricket-lovers of the Caribbean, his decision to put England into bat backfired horribly. To be fair to Lara, the conditions on the first morning were perfect for seam and swing bowling, and many pundits who gave their opinions at the time believed that he had done the right thing. The trouble was, his enthusiastic, but inexperienced, bowling attack performed so feebly that England closed the first day on 391 for 2, with 158 runs coming in the 33 overs bowled in the final session.

By this time, Robert Key – who had been recalled to play in his ninth Test match because of an injury to Mark Butcher – had scored the small matter of 167 runs and was still unbeaten. He was dropped at slip on 16, but he and Andrew Strauss, who scored his second Test century in three innings at Lord's, added 291 to establish the highest second-wicket partnership for England against the West Indies, the fifth-highest partnership of all time for England, and the biggest partnership for any wicket for ten years. True, they feasted on all manner of garbage that was served up to them as poor Lara searched desperately for someone to restore some measure of control, but

Robert Key acknowledges the applause ringing around Lord's after reaching a magnificent double-hundred on his Test comeback.

as the Queen watched from the pavilion, Key set about cementing his place in the England team after having been absent for more than a year.

Strauss was caught behind off Omari Banks, the off spinner, for 137, but Michael Vaughan settled in and started the second day on 30 not out.

Ten minutes before lunch, England were 527 for 3, and apparently on course for an enormous total. Key had fallen for 221 – scored from 288 balls and including 31 fours – and it had been a morning of total English domination. But Graham Thorpe – who had been sitting and watching as Key and Vaughan had added 165 for the third wicket – edged Dwayne Bravo to Ridley Jacobs for 19 to bring Andrew Flintoff to the crease immediately before the interval. Facing the last over before lunch, Flintoff made his intentions quite clear by lofting Banks for six into the Nursery End. The packed house gasped in amazement at his sheer audacity, but groaned in despair moments later as he

reached for a wide ball outside his off stump and dragged it onto his stumps.

Fifty minutes after the resumption, England were all out for 568. Their last seven wickets had fallen for just 41 runs in 68 balls – the only bright note was that Vaughan had managed to reach his hundred before becoming the eighth wicket to fall. None of the last six batsmen reached double figures and the hard work of the previous day had been squandered – but at least the collapse got the game moving!

Chris Gayle and Devon Smith began the West Indies' reply with a rapid century opening stand, which was finally broken by Giles. 118 for 1 in the 23rd over reads more like a limited-overs score, but, within five overs, two more wickets had fallen – Gayle for a breezy 66 and Sarwan for a single. England's supremacy was total when Lara was given out, caught behind off Giles for 11, when, in fact, replays showed that his bat had not been anywhere near the ball. Any number of English fielders – particularly Geraint Jones, the wicketkeeper – would have known this, and the vehemence of their appeals was especially disappointing. A statement, in which Lara said that he always finds it difficult not to walk when he knows he is out, followed the West Indies captain's understandably reluctant departure from the crease, but there was no need for an apology. It would have been much more relevant if there had been an explanation from England as to why, increasingly, they have no difficulty in appealing when they know that someone is not out.

Shivnarine Chanderpaul stuck it out to make a brave 128 not out, but he was horribly let down by both Tino Best and Fidel Edwards, who both came to the crease, played embarrassingly wild slogs and departed, leaving England with a lead of 152.

England only had to press home their advantage by scoring at a decent rate during the fourth day. Pedro Collins removed Trescothick for 45 and Strauss, 35, but Vaughan batted beautifully to become only the third man, after Graham Gooch and George Headley, to score a century in each innings of a Test at Lord's. When the England captain declared (he had reached 101 not out), the West Indies were set 478 to win – or, perhaps more significantly, were asked to bat for four sessions to save the match.

The visitors were 35 for 2 within 11 overs, and had also lost Gayle for a typically cavalier 81 from only 88 balls before the close of the fourth day. Defiance may be one thing, but Gayle really needs to accept the fact that there are times when blazing strokes on the rise are not in the best interests of the team. The West Indies went into the final day still 363 runs behind, but with their two most experienced batsmen – Lara and Chanderpaul – at the crease.

Lara's was clearly the key wicket for England, and after the pair had added 58 in 18 overs in the morning, Giles made one spit out of the rough as Lara advanced down the pitch, and bowled the West Indian captain for 44 – not a bad scalp for Giles to claim as his 100th Test wicket.

From there, the end came in a rush as the West Indies lost five wickets for 31. Again, it was only Chanderpaul who resisted, and although replays showed he should have been given out caught first ball, there was great disappointment when the last man, Edwards, was dismissed by Flintoff to leave Chanderpaul only three runs away from emulating Vaughan's feat of scoring two centuries in the match.

Michael Vaughan becomes only the third man to score a century in both innings of a Lord's Test.

FIRST TEST – ENGLAND v. WEST INDIES
22–26 July 2004 at Lord's

ENGLAND

	First Innings		Second Innings	
ME Trescothick	c Sarwan b Best	16	b Collins	45
AJ Strauss	c Jacobs b Banks	137	c Sarwan b Collins	35
RWT Key	c Lara b Bravo	221	run out	15
MP Vaughan (capt)	c Smith b Collins	103	not out	101
GP Thorpe	c Jacobs b Bravo	19	c & b Gayle	38
A Flintoff	b Banks	6	c Jacobs b Collins	58
*GO Jones	c Jacobs b Collins	4		
AF Giles	c Smith b Collins	5		
MJ Hoggard	not out	1		
SP Jones	lbw b Collins	4		
SJ Harmison	b Bravo	4		
Extras	b 2, lb 20, w 13, nb 13	48	b 3, lb 14, nb 16	33
	(121.4 overs)	568	(5 wkts dec 76.4 overs)	325

	First Innings				Second Innings			
	O	M	R	W	O	M	R	W
Collins	24	2	113	4	14.4	1	62	3
Best	21	1	104	1	3	1	14	0
Edwards	21	2	96	0	13	0	47	0
Bravo	24.4	5	74	3	7	0	28	0
Banks	22	3	131	2	26	1	92	0
Sarwan	9	0	28	0	4	0	20	0
Gayle	-	-	-	-	9	0	45	1

Fall of Wickets
1-29, 2-320, 3-485, 4-527, 5-534, 6-541, 7-551, 8-557, 9-563
1-86, 2-104, 3-117, 4-233, 5-325

WEST INDIES

	First Innings		Second Innings	
CH Gayle	lbw b Giles	66	b Harmison	81
DS Smith	b Giles	45	lbw b Giles	6
RR Sarwan	lbw b Hoggard	1	lbw b Hoggard	4
BC Lara (capt)	c Jones GO b Giles	11	b Giles	44
S Chanderpaul	not out	128	not out	97
DJJ Bravo	c Jones GO b Jones SP	44	c & b Giles	10
*RD Jacobs	c Jones GO b Hoggard	32	c Thorpe b Hoggard	1
OAC Banks	b Flintoff	45	b Harmison	0
TL Best	b Flintoff	0	st Jones GO b Giles	3
PT Collins	b Flintoff	0	st Jones GO b Giles	2
FH Edwards	b Giles	5	c Jones GO b Flintoff	2
Extras	b 20, lb 11, w 5, nb 3	39	b 5, lb 9, nb 3	17
	(116.4 overs)	416	(79.3 overs)	267

	First Innings				Second Innings			
	O	M	R	W	O	M	R	W
Hoggard	28	7	89	2	14	2	65	2
Harmison	21	6	72	0	21	2	78	2
Jones SP	17	3	70	1	8	3	29	0
Giles	40.4	5	129	4	35	9	81	5
Flintoff	10	4	25	3	1.3	1	0	1

Fall of Wickets
1-118, 2-119, 3-127, 4-139, 5-264, 6-327, 7-399, 8-399, 9-401
1-24, 2-35, 3-102, 4-172, 5-194, 6-195, 7-200, 8-203, 9-247

Umpires: DJ Harper and RE Koertzen
Toss: West Indies
Test debut: DJJ Bravo
Man of the Match: AF Giles

England won by 210 runs

npower SECOND TEST
29 July–2 August 2004 at Edgbaston

The second Test of the four-match series almost mirrored the course of the first, with England racking up a large first-innings total, establishing a lead, and then finishing off the West Indies – this time, though, they did it all with a day to spare.

Neither Strauss nor Key weighed in heavily with the bat in this match. This time it was Trescothick's turn to score two centuries in the game – the first player to do so at Edgbaston – but the real fireworks came lower down the order.

The visitors left out Edwards and were also without the injured Best. A hasty SOS was sent to the Caribbean, and Corey Collymore – who many people thought should have been in the original touring party – arrived in the nick of time to take his place.

The most 'English' of the West Indian seam bowlers, Collymore troubled all of the batsmen, but Trescothick reached his first hundred against the West Indies just before tea. Lara caught him at slip at the second attempt shortly after the break for 105, and, at 210 for 4, there was an opening for the visitors. Thorpe notched up his 26th Test half-century, before falling to Collymore, and the spectators were given a taste of what was to come the following day when Andrew Flintoff and Geraint Jones added 51 to leave England on 313 for 5 at the close.

Lara took the second new ball immediately, but Flintoff and Jones – who already averaged 111 when batting together – simply tore the bowling to shreds. No fewer than 437 runs were scored throughout the day, with an amazing tally of 58 fours and eight sixes, one of those being dropped by Flintoff's father Colin as he tried to cling onto one of his son's enormous hits in the stand. He struck Banks for three sixes in a single over as he and Jones – who played the perfect foil – took their partnership to 170. Jones finally edged Collymore to Jacobs for 74 from only 97 balls, but Flintoff continued the onslaught – 140 runs were scored during the morning – until he was cleverly deceived by a brave slower ball from Bravo, and was lbw for 167. Flintoff had faced just 191 balls, striking 17 fours and seven sixes. Just to rub salt into what were, by then, very open West Indian wounds, even Harmison got in on the act. A reverse sweep for four was the highlight of a remarkable cameo of 31 not out from 18 balls, before Vaughan called a halt to the mayhem with England on 566 for 9. To make matters worse, the West Indies lost both their openers to Hoggard in the five overs before tea.

At least Lara and Sarwan – who had had a poor

Flintoff: 17 fours and seven sixes in his breathtaking 167.

first match – showed that they had the stomach for a fight by batting out the rest of the day. Once again, there was no let up in the scoring rate as they hit 160 runs from 35 overs and, on the third morning, they increased their stand to 209 before Lara – who had appeared to be unsettled by Flintoff – edged him to third slip for 95. It was Flintoff who removed Sarwan, too – bowled off the inside edge for 139 after he and Chanderpaul had taken the score to 297 for 3. The West Indies needed 70 to avoid the follow-on, but there was already some doubt as to whether Vaughan would necessarily enforce it. For the second time in the series, Giles, with 4 for 65, was England's most

A common sight in the summer of 2004: Ashley Giles celebrates after taking yet another wicket. Giles' nine-wicket match haul on his home ground of Edgbaston was particularly pleasing for the likeable left-arm spinner.

successful bowler as the last six wickets fell for just 13 runs in ten overs, and although the West Indies were 230 runs behind, England chose to bat again.

Whilst this was the right decision, it did mean that this wonderfully fast-flowing match lost momentum for a while as England simply went about the business of extending their lead. Trescothick and Thorpe shared a stand of 132 before Trescothick was run out by a direct hit by Sarwan for 107, and England lost seven wickets for 64 runs on the fourth morning to set the West Indies 479 to win – or five sessions in which to survive.

They failed to see out the day, and were bowled out in just 56.3 overs for 222. Hoggard and Giles shared the spoils – another answer to Lara's doubt as to whether there was a plan B – with Giles taking 5 for 57 to take his tally in the series to 18. Gayle made another entertaining 82, but, as the last seven wickets fell for just 50 runs – including five of them for a mere ten – it seemed clear that the West Indies were in freefall. Sir Viv Richards joined the ever-increasing band of former West Indian players to question Lara's leadership skills publicly, but the beleaguered captain vowed to carry on and see out the series.

SECOND TEST – ENGLAND v. WEST INDIES
29 July–1 August 2004 at Edgbaston

ENGLAND

	First Innings			Second Innings	
ME Trescothick	c Lara b Bravo	105		run out	107
AJ Strauss	c Jacobs b Lawson	24		c Jacobs b Lawson	5
RWT Key	c Lara b Collins	29		c Gayle b Lawson	4
MP Vaughan (capt)	c & b Bravo	12		c Gayle b Lawson	3
GP Thorpe	c Jacobs b Collymore	61		st Jacobs b Gayle	54
A Flintoff	lbw b Bravo	167		c Bravo b Gayle	20
*GO Jones	c Jacobs b Collymore	74		b Lawson	4
AF Giles	c Chanderpaul b Bravo	24		b Gayle	15
MJ Hoggard	not out	15		c Smith b Gayle	6
JM Anderson	b Banks	2		(11) not out	8
SJ Harmison	not out	31		(10) lbw b Gayle	1
Extras	lb 6, w 1, nb 15	22		b 8, lb 2, w 5, nb 6	21
	(9 wkts dec 134 overs)	566		(65.1 overs)	248

	First Innings				Second Innings			
	O	M	R	W	O	M	R	W
Collins	18	1	90	1	9	1	29	0
Collymore	30	6	126	2	9	2	33	0
Lawson	23	4	111	1	21	2	94	4
Bravo	24	6	76	4	6	1	28	0
Banks	27	3	108	1	5	1	20	0
Sarwan	12	0	49	0	-	-	-	-
Gayle	-	-	-	-	15.1	4	34	5

Fall of Wickets
1-77, 2-125, 3-150, 4-210, 5-262, 6-432, 7-478, 8-522, 9-525
1-24, 2-37, 3-52, 4-184, 5-195, 6-214, 7-226, 8-234, 9-239

WEST INDIES

	First Innings			Second Innings	
CH Gayle	b Hoggard	7		c Strauss b Giles	82
DS Smith	c Giles b Hoggard	4		c Trescothick b Hoggard	11
RR Sarwan	b Flintoff	139		c Strauss b Giles	14
BC Lara (capt)	c Thorpe b Flintoff	95		c Flintoff b Giles	13
S Chanderpaul	c Key b Giles	45		lbw b Giles	43
DJJ Bravo	b Giles	13		b Giles	0
*RD Jacobs	c Trescothick b Hoggard	0		c Anderson b Hoggard	0
OAC Banks	c Jones b Harmison	4		not out	25
PT Collins	c Flintoff b Giles	6		lbw b Hoggard	0
CD Collymore	lbw b Giles	2		b Anderson	10
JJC Lawson	not out	0		b Anderson	2
Extras	b 9, lb 5, w 1, nb 6	21		b 17, lb 4, nb 1	22
	(91.3 overs)	336		(55.3 overs)	222

	First Innings				Second Innings			
	O	M	R	W	O	M	R	W
Hoggard	18	0	89	3	16	5	64	3
Harmison	14	1	64	1	5	1	29	0
Anderson	11	3	37	0	5.3	1	23	2
Giles	30.3	7	65	4	21	9	57	5
Flintoff	15	1	52	2	5	1	19	0
Vaughan	1	0	8	0	3	0	9	0
Trescothick	2	0	7	0	-	-	-	-

Fall of Wickets
1-5, 2-12, 3-221, 4-297, 5-323, 6-324, 7-324, 8-334, 9-336
1-15, 2-54, 3-101, 4-172, 5-172, 6-177, 7-177, 8-182, 9-210

Umpires: DB Hair and SJA Taufel
Toss: England
Man of the Match: A Flintoff

England won by 256 runs

5–7 August 2004 at Derby
West Indians 223 (40.1 overs) (DR Smith 55,
NRC Dumelow 5 for 51) and 368 for 6 dec (81 overs)
(CS Baugh 150*, SC Joseph 77, RD Jacobs 59*)
Derbyshire 188 (70.2 overs) (SD Stubbings 56,
FH Edwards 5 for 61) and 88 (35.3 overs)
(FH Edwards 5 for 22)
West Indians won by 315 runs

Fidel Edwards blew Derbyshire away with match figures of 10 for 83 at Derby, as the West Indians sought to rebuild morale after two Test defeats. Victory came by the huge margin of 315 runs, but, on the opening day, it did not seem as though the tourists were interested in knuckling down to some serious match practice. Chris Gayle blasted 42 off just 24 balls at the top of the order, but when he played all around a Paul Havell yorker, the innings disintegrated into batting that would have been better suited to an exhibition match. Nathan Dumelow, the off spinner, was the main beneficiary, taking 5 for 51 as the West Indian first innings self-destructed to 223 all out in just 40.1 overs. By the close Derbyshire were 102 for 2 in reply, but Edwards found rhythm and genuine pace on day two to take 5 for 61 as the county were dismissed for 188. Then, boosted initially by Sylvester Joseph's 77, the West Indies now found, in Carlton Baugh, someone else intent on making a bid for Test inclusion. The reserve wicketkeeper went on to score a mightily impressive unbeaten 150, after reaching the end of the second day on 110, and, with Ridley Jacobs, set up a declaration at 368 for 6. Cue Edwards again, with the fast bowler proving far too quick for Derbyshire as they were skittled for just 88.

npower THIRD TEST
12–16 August 2004 at Old Trafford

Of England's four Test victories against the West Indies during the summer, this one was the most remarkable. An entire day was lost to the weather, and England had to come back from a 65-run deficit on first innings to win the match on the final afternoon as the storm clouds miraculously skirted Old Trafford.

A little surprisingly, perhaps, England chose to stick with James Anderson in preference to Simon Jones. Old Trafford has a notoriously harsh square, and one that encourages reverse swing. Anderson bowled less than 17 overs in the match.

As usual, there was a rather chaotic feel to the West Indian preparations. Four changes were made to the

Dwayne Bravo, who came of age as a Test all-rounder in this series, scored 77 at Old Trafford and then followed it up with 6 for 55.

team that had lost at Edgbaston – most notably, Carlton Baugh replaced Ridley Jacobs behind the stumps, and Dave Mohammed, the left-arm wrist spinner, took Banks' place to play in only his second Test. I had witnessed the West Indies' utterly shambolic fielding routine the day before the game, and was saddened by the lack of effort, enthusiasm and purpose to their practice. Inevitably, they then proceeded to play in the same disorganised manner during the Test itself.

Only 70 overs were possible on the first day and England seemed to have gained the upper hand with the West Indies on 275 for 6. Lara had been dismissed for a fifth-ball duck, as Flintoff continued to exert his hold over him. This time, Lara left his leg stump completely exposed – as he tends to do early in his innings – and Flintoff homed in, flicked Lara's boot and the ball deflected off it to hit the stump. That made it 97 for 3, and, four overs later, Sylvester Joseph – playing his first Test innings – was caught by

Thorpe at third slip off Harmison for 45. As usual, the recovery was built around a gutsy effort from Chanderpaul, who put on 157 for the fifth wicket with Bravo, who was rapidly becoming the 'find' of the series. Bravo hit ten fours in his 77 before edging Hoggard to Jones. Hoggard then nipped out Chanderpaul for 76 in his next over – the last of the day – and England were set to demolish the tail the following morning.

Torrential rain saw to that, however, and when England's opportunity came at the start of the third day, they bowled as poorly as they can have done for several months. Rather than pitching the new ball up, and knocking over the lower order, they embarked on a bouncer barrage; an approach that the diminutive Baugh dealt with spectacularly. Swaying to leg and glancing the ball over the slips, he scored an excellent 68 from 84 balls, and received excellent support from both Mohammed and Collins, who was forced to retire hurt with a cut chin.

Graham Thorpe: the Mr Reliable of England's batting line-up sweeps on his way to a 15th Test hundred.

The left-hander finally succumbed to Bravo – who took six wickets in the innings – and when Collins trapped Harmison lbw for eight, the West Indies had a handy lead of 65.

There was even a touch of farce towards the end of the West Indies innings. Collins was apparently due to resume following the lunch break, and informed his captain of this. As Lara visited the gents, the umpires and England's fielders took the field, only for Collins – who was suffering from a headache – to change his mind. On his return, a flustered Lara had no choice but to declare, and the umpires and players trooped off the field again.

England fell to 40 for 3 in no time with Trescothick, Key and Vaughan all dismissed. Vaughan's 12 had taken him an hour to accumulate, but England were rescued by a stand of 177 between Strauss and Thorpe – who was badly missed by Sarwan when on 58. This partnership quickly snuffed out the burst of excitement we saw from the West Indians, and their fielding quickly deteriorated to a level one would not even expect to see on a club ground on a Saturday afternoon. The fundamentals – such as backing up throws – were ignored and, on the fourth morning, they managed to bowl only 22 overs, for which they were heavily fined. Thorpe duly reached his 15th Test century – a brave effort under the circumstances, since his hand had been broken during the course of a refreshingly fiery burst from Edwards. This was Thorpe's final innings of an outstanding summer.

They added only 165 more runs, with Gayle and Sarwan scoring 102 of them. Joseph was the only other batsman to reach double figures as the West Indies folded under pressure.

Flintoff removed Lara once again – this time a brutish lifter that he gloved to slip for seven – and the final wicket of the innings was taken with the 12th delivery of the final morning, leaving England 100 overs in which to score 231.

At 27 for 2, however, and with the threat of rain ever constant, it seemed as though England would be thwarted in their chase for victory. Vaughan survived a stroke of luck on one, when a mistimed pull landed between three fielders, but, with Key, he took the score to 111 before edging Gayle to slip for 33. With Thorpe only capable of holding up one end in the event of staving off defeat, the partnership between Key and Flintoff was critical. Key was put down at slip off Collymore on 57, but as the storms passed by on either side of the ground, the pair carefully added the precious 120 runs that were needed.

Key finished on 93 not out, in every way a better innings than his double hundred in the first Test, while Flintoff – who normally deals in run-a-ball fifties – faced 92 for his 57 not out as England reached their target within 66 overs.

THIRD TEST - ENGLAND v. WEST INDIES
12–16 August 2004 at Old Trafford

WEST INDIES

	First Innings		Second Innings	
CH Gayle	c Strauss b Hoggard	5	c Hoggard b Giles	42
SC Joseph	c Thorpe b Harmison	45	c Vaughan b Flintoff	15
RR Sarwan	b Flintoff	40	c Trescothick b Harmison	60
BC Lara (capt)	b Flintoff	0	c Strauss b Flintoff	7
S Chanderpaul	c Jones b Hoggard	76	c Vaughan b Flintoff	2
DJJ Bravo	c Jones b Hoggard	77	c Flintoff b Giles	6
*CS Baugh	c Vaughan b Anderson	68	c sub b Harmison	3
D Mohammed	c Strauss b Flintoff	23	c Key b Giles	9
PT Collins	retired hurt	19	b Harmison	8
CD Collymore	b Hoggard	5	not out	5
FH Edwards	not out	4	c Flintoff b Harmison	0
Extras	b 9, lb 14, w 6, nb 4	33	b 2, lb 4, w 1, nb 1	8
	(9 wkts 94.3 overs)	395	(59.4 overs)	165

	First Innings				Second Innings			
	O	M	R	W	O	M	R	W
Hoggard	22	3	83	4	7	0	21	0
Harmison	26	5	94	1	13.4	3	44	4
Flintoff	20	5	79	3	12	1	26	3
Anderson	11.3	1	49	1	5	1	22	0
Giles	15	0	67	0	22	6	46	3

Fall of Wickets
1-10, 2-85, 3-97, 4-108, 5-265, 6-267, 7-308, 8-383, 9-395
1-41, 2-88, 3-95, 4-99, 5-110, 6-121, 7-146, 8-152, 9-161

ENGLAND

	First Innings		Second Innings	
ME Trescothick	c Sarwan b Edwards	0	b Collymore	12
AJ Strauss	b Bravo	90	c Chanderpaul b Collins	12
RWT Key	b Collymore	6	not out	93
MP Vaughan (capt)	b Bravo	12	c Lara b Gayle	33
GP Thorpe	c Lara b Bravo	114		
A Flintoff	lbw b Bravo	7	(5) not out	57
MJ Hoggard	c Sarwan b Collymore	23		
*GO Jones	b Bravo	12		
AF Giles	c & b Bravo	10		
SJ Harmison	lbw b Collins	8		
JM Anderson	not out	1		
Extras	b 10, lb 10, w 18, nb 9	47	b 7, lb 3, nb 14	24
	(112.2 overs)	330	(3 wkts 65.3 overs)	231

	First Innings				Second Innings			
	O	M	R	W	O	M	R	W
Edwards	18	2	68	1	11	0	51	0
Collymore	26	6	66	2	16	7	33	1
Bravo	26	6	55	6	12	3	41	0
Joseph	2	0	8	0	-	-	-	-
Gayle	4	1	7	0	8.4	0	32	1
Mohammed	26	2	77	0	6	0	25	0
Collins	10.2	1	29	1	8	2	24	1
Sarwan	-	-	-	-	4	0	15	0

Fall of Wickets
1-0, 2-13, 3-40, 4-217, 5-227, 6-283, 7-310, 8-321, 9-322
1-15, 2-27, 3-111

Umpires: SJA Taufel and Aleem Dar
Toss: West Indies
Test debut: SC Joseph
Man of the Match: GP Thorpe

England won by 7 wickets

npower FOURTH TEST
19–23 August 2004 at The Oval

Twenty years after England were 'blackwashed' at The Oval by the West Indies, the two teams returned with the boot very much on the other foot. It seemed inconceivable that the West Indies would win the Test, but there was always the chance that the weather, or Lara, could prevent England from winning it and so complete the remarkable record of seven wins from the seven Tests played during the summer.

With Thorpe nursing his broken hand, there was scope for the selectors to look to the future, and they called up Ian Bell who had been scoring heavily for Warwickshire all summer. The West Indies recalled Jermaine Lawson, and played Dwayne Smith in order to strengthen the batting. As it was, the current shambolic situation in the West Indies' dressing room was highlighted by Smith's absence from the first innings: he was in hospital having a check-up on a side strain. Unbelievable!

After winning the toss, Vaughan chose to bat immediately. The pitch looked good, there was a chance that it would help the spinners later and the aim was for England to post a huge first-innings total.

Within 27 overs they were 64 for 3, with Trescothick (30), Strauss (15) and Key (10) all falling to rather casual strokes. Bell came in and was immediately softened up by Edwards. He was also instructed to cover up an advertising logo on his shirt, but this did not put the youngster off his stride one bit. Slowly, Bell relaxed and, with Vaughan for company, took to Test cricket with ease. He looks the part at the crease – just as Geoffrey Boycott and Mike Atherton used to do – and brought up his half-century with a perfectly struck off-drive for four. The pair added 146 before Lawson found some extra bounce and Bell edged to Baugh for 70 from 130 balls. Five overs later, England were 236 for 5 after Vaughan aimed to drive Bravo and was taken by Lara at slip for 66.

The second day was set up perfectly. Flintoff and Jones, who have already struck up a formidable reputation when batting together, resumed having added 77 the previous evening. The Oval was full to bursting when the first over was bowled at 10.30 am, so everyone was present when Jones edged the fifth ball of the day to slip for 22 and when Flintoff – who failed to add to his overnight 72 – fell to an outstanding catch by Lawson at mid-on. England were 321 for 7, and the imposing first-innings score they had hoped for looked a long way off. However,

Ian Bell, who took to Test cricket in highly-promising style with a debut innings of 70 at The Oval.

a measure of a successful side is the number of runs the lower order manages to scramble when they are most needed, and the last three wickets put on 149. This included some rather unlikely contributions from the likes of Hoggard (38) and Anderson (12), while Giles reached his third Test half-century. The most remarkable innings came from Harmison, and provided further proof of his

transformation from what had been a quiet and shy individual. He struck three enormous sixes and even played the reverse sweep during his frantic innings of 36 not out from 27 balls. It gave England just the boost they needed, and Harmison then struck with the ball as the West Indies slumped to 26 for 3. Only Lara stood up to the onslaught, playing like a man who had a reputation to protect, but he received precious little support as Bell and Key clung on to outstanding catches. With Smith absent, Lara was the eighth man out for 79 from 93 balls – giving Harmison 6 for 46 – and the West Indies were soon following on, 318 runs behind.

One might have thought that this was the time for the West Indies really to knuckle down. Gayle had other ideas, however, and in the course of a bizarre hundred – the second fastest ever played on English soil – he carted Hoggard for six fours in a single over. At the end of the second day, the West Indies were 84 for 2, still 234 behind, and were destined to lose on the third, so maybe this explains Gayle's odd approach to his innings. He also lost Lara early that third morning when the captain edged Anderson to Trescothick for 15. The manner in which Lara waved farewell as he walked from the ground suggested that we would not see him face England in a Test match again. By his standards, this had been a disappointing series with the bat: he made 264 runs at an average of 33, and failed to score a century. However, it was his record as captain on which he would be judged when he returned home.

Baugh resisted after Bravo (54) had given us a final reminder of his promise, but England were not to be denied, and when Anderson bowled Edwards for two, the scores were level: England needed just one run to win.

Trescothick allowed two balls from Edwards to pass by harmlessly, before thrashing the third through the covers for four, and England's remarkable summer had come to an end in the most emphatic manner imaginable. This was their seventh victory in a row, and their tenth out of 11 Tests. To underscore the chasm that now exists between England and the West Indies, this was their seventh win out of the eight Tests played between the two sides this year.

Right: Michael Vaughan and Steve Harmison are deep in conversation as England strive to complete a series 'whitewash' at The Oval.

FOURTH TEST – ENGLAND v. WEST INDIES
19–21 August 2004 at The Oval

ENGLAND

	First Innings				Second Innings			
ME Trescothick	c Sarwan b Edwards	30			not out			4
AJ Strauss	c Edwards b Lawson	14			not out			0
RWT Key	c Baugh b Bravo	10						
MP Vaughan (capt)	c Lara b Bravo	66						
IR Bell	c Baugh b Lawson	70						
A Flintoff	c Lawson b Edwards	72						
*GO Jones	c Sarwan b Collymore	22						
AF Giles	c Lara b Bravo	52						
MJ Hoggard	c Joseph b Lawson	38						
SJ Harmison	not out	36						
JM Anderson	b Gayle	12						
Extras	b 5, lb 21, w 5, nb 17	48						0
	(123.2 overs)	470			(0 wkts 0.3 overs)			4

	First Innings				Second Innings			
	O	M	R	W	O	M	R	W
Edwards	19	4	64	2	0.3	0	4	0
Collymore	23	8	58	1	-	-	-	-
Lawson	24	4	115	3	-	-	-	-
Bravo	29	4	117	3	-	-	-	-
Smith	14	4	50	0	-	-	-	-
Gayle	7.2	2	18	1	-	-	-	-
Sarwan	7	0	22	0	-	-	-	-

Fall of Wickets
1-51, 2-64, 3-64, 4-210, 5-236, 6-313, 7-321, 8-408, 9-410

WEST INDIES

	First Innings		Second Innings	
CH Gayle	c Jones b Harmison	12	c Flintoff b Anderson	105
SC Joseph	c Giles b Harmison	9	c Jones b Harmison	16
RR Sarwan	c Strauss b Flintoff	2	c Bell b Harmison	7
BC Lara (capt)	c Bell b Harmison	79	c Trescothick b Anderson	15
S Chanderpaul	c Key b Hoggard	14	(6) c Jones b Giles	32
DJJ Bravo	c Jones b Harmison	16	(5) lbw b Hoggard	54
*CS Baugh	c Strauss b Harmison	6	(8) c Jones b Harmison	34
CD Collymore	c Trescothick b Harmison	4	(9) c Jones b Anderson	7
FH Edwards	run out	0	(10) b Anderson	2
JJC Lawson	not out	3	(11) not out	4
DR Smith	absent hurt		(7) c Anderson b Flintoff	28
Extras	lb 7	7	b 1, lb 12, nb 1	14
	(9 wkts 36.5 overs)	152	(84.2 overs)	318

	First Innings				Second Innings			
	O	M	R	W	O	M	R	W
Hoggard	9	2	31	1	12	5	50	1
Harmison	13	1	46	6	18	1	75	3
Flintoff	8	1	32	1	17	3	64	1
Anderson	6.5	0	36	1	15.2	2	52	4
Giles	-	-	-	-	22	5	64	1

Fall of Wickets
1-19, 2-22, 3-26, 4-54, 5-101, 6-118, 7-136, 8-149, 9-152
1-73, 2-81, 3-126, 4-155, 5-237, 6-265, 7-285, 8-312, 9-314

Umpires: DB Hair and RE Koertzen
Toss: England
Man of the Match: SJ Harmison
Men of the Series: A Flintoff (England) and S Chanderpaul (West Indies)

England won by 10 wickets

SERIES AVERAGES
England v. West Indies

ENGLAND

Batting	M	Inns	NO	Runs	HS	Av	100	50	c/st
IR Bell	1	1	0	70	70	70.00	-	1	2/-
A Flintoff	4	7	1	387	167	64.50	1	3	5/-
RWT Key	4	7	1	378	221	63.00	1	1	3/-
GP Thorpe	3	5	0	286	114	57.20	1	2	3/-
MP Vaughan	4	7	1	330	103	55.00	2	1	3/-
ME Trescothick	4	8	1	319	107	45.57	2	-	5/-
AJ Strauss	4	8	1	317	137	45.28	1	1	7/-
MJ Hoggard	4	5	2	83	38	27.66	-	-	1/-
SJ Harmison	4	5	2	80	36*	26.66	-	-	-/-
GO Jones	4	5	0	116	74	23.20	-	1	13/2
AF Giles	4	5	0	106	52	21.20	-	1	3/-
JM Anderson	3	4	2	23	12	11.50	-	-	2/-
SP Jones	1	1	0	4	4	4.00	-	-	-/-

Bowling	Overs	Mds	Runs	Wkts	Av	Best	5/inn	10m
A Flintoff	88.3	17	297	14	21.21	3-25	-	-
AF Giles	186.1	41	509	22	23.13	5-57	2	-
SJ Harmison	131.4	20	502	17	29.52	6-46	1	-
MJ Hoggard	126	24	492	16	30.75	4-83	-	-
JM Anderson	55.1	8	219	7	31.28	4-52	-	-
SP Jones	25	6	99	1	99.00	1-70	-	-

Also bowled: ME Trescothick 2-0-7-0, MP Vaughan 4-0-17-0.

WEST INDIES

Batting	M	Inns	NO	Runs	HS	Av	100	50	c/st
S Chanderpaul	4	8	2	437	128*	72.83	1	2	2/-
CH Gayle	4	8	0	400	105	50.00	1	3	3/-
RR Sarwan	4	8	0	267	139	33.37	1	1	6/-
BC Lara	4	8	0	264	95	33.00	-	2	7/-
DR Smith	1	1	0	28	28	28.00	-	-	-/-
CS Baugh	2	4	0	111	68	27.75	-	1	2/-
DJJ Bravo	4	8	0	220	77	27.50	-	2	3/-
OAC Banks	2	4	1	74	45	24.66	-	-	-/-
SC Joseph	2	4	0	85	45	21.25	-	-	1/-
DS Smith	2	4	0	66	45	16.50	-	-	3/-
D Mohammed	1	2	0	32	23	16.00	-	-	-/-
JJC Lawson	2	4	3	9	4*	9.00	-	-	1/-
RD Jacobs	2	4	0	33	32	8.25	-	-	8/1
PT Collins	3	6	1	35	19*	7.00	-	-	-/-
CD Collymore	3	6	1	33	10	6.60	-	-	-/-
FH Edwards	3	6	1	13	5	2.60	-	-	1/-
TL Best	1	2	0	3	3	1.50	-	-	-/-

Bowling	Overs	Mds	Runs	Wkts	Av	Best	5/inn	10m
CH Gayle	44.1	7	136	8	17.00	5-34	1	-
DJJ Bravo	128.4	25	419	16	26.18	6-55	1	-
PT Collins	84	8	347	10	34.70	4-113	-	-
JJC Lawson	68	10	320	8	40.00	4-94	-	-
CD Collymore	104	29	316	6	52.66	2-66	-	-
FH Edwards	82.3	8	330	3	110.00	2-64	-	-
OAC Banks	80	8	351	3	117.00	2-131	-	-
TL Best	24	2	118	1	118.00	1-104	-	-

Also bowled: SC Joseph 2-0-8-0, DR Smith 14-4-50-0, D Mohammed 32-2-102-0, RR Sarwan 36-0-134-0.

NATWEST CHALLENGE
England v. India
By Jonathan Agnew

With English cricket officials always on the lookout for an opportunity to swell the ECB's coffers, this mini-series of three one-day internationals was billed as the ideal chance for England and India to prepare for the ICC Champions Trophy.

Given that the same opportunity would most likely not have been afforded to Bangladesh or Zimbabwe – let alone the USA – this was clearly a money-making exercise. As expected, the public responded magnificently.

Following such a poor performance in the previous NatWest Series, some crucial changes were made to England's squad. After two excellent one-day centuries for Worcestershire, Vikram Solanki returned to the fold. This involved the inevitable move down the order for Michael Vaughan, who batted at No. 3. There was also a recall for Kabir Ali, but the Worcestershire pace bowler then withdrew through injury, and his replacement, Alex Wharf, performed admirably.

England won the opening match at Trent Bridge comprehensively. India – without the injured Sachin Tendulkar – scored only 170 in 43.5 overs: an innings that was cut short by Steve Harmison's hat-trick. He claimed the wickets of Kaif, for 50, Balaji and Nehra to finish with 3 for 41, while Wharf, on his debut, took three wickets in his first three overs as India slumped to 89 for 5. Solanki rattled up a half-century, and Flintoff biffed 34 from 23 balls as England won with just under 18 overs to spare.

England batted first at The Oval, and scored an impressive 307 for 5 with Flintoff making an outstanding 99 from 93 balls. How this man has come on this year! Flintoff and Collingwood – who made a perfectly paced 79 not out – added 174 and, once again, India's batting was found wanting as they were dismissed for 237.

In the final match, at Lord's, India changed the balance of their team by bringing in Dinesh Karthik, who took over the wicketkeeping duties from Rahul Dravid. The impact was immediate – Dravid scored 52 and put on 93 with Ganguly, who made 90. India set England 205 to win but, at 48 for 5, the hosts were already out of the contest. Vaughan battled away, scoring 74 – his highest one-day score for England in 17 innings – but he was beautifully stumped by young Karthik and, although Giles made 39, England fell 23 runs short.

Above right: Steve Harmison takes a return catch to finish off the India innings with a dramatic hat-trick at Trent Bridge.

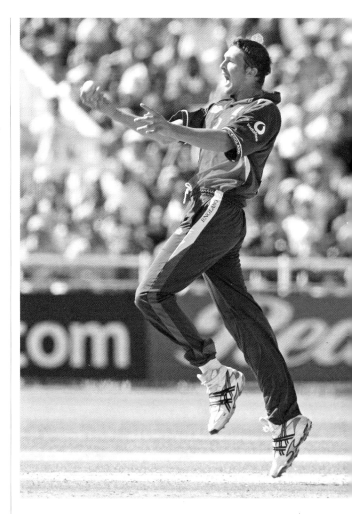

Match One
1 September 2004 at Trent Bridge
India 170 (43.5 overs) (M Kaif 50)
England 171 for 3 (32.2 overs) (VS Solanki 52)
England won by 7 wickets

Match Two
3 September 2004 at The Oval
England 307 for 5 (50 overs) (A Flintoff 99, PD Collingwood 79*)
India 237 (46.3 overs) (M Kaif 51, D Gough 4 for 50)
England won by 70 runs

Match Three
5 September 2004 at Lord's
India 204 (49.3 overs) (SC Ganguly 90, R Dravid 52, SJ Harmison 4 for 22)
England 181 (48.2 overs) (MP Vaughan 74)
India won by 23 runs

ICC CHAMPIONS TROPHY
By Jonathan Agnew

Amid much scepticism, the ICC Champions Trophy got underway in September at the time most professional cricketers are usually heading for the beach for a well-earned holiday.

There were serious concerns both about the 10.15am start to matches and the effect of the white ball in the dewy, autumnal conditions. The last thing a tournament billed as the second World Cup needed was for the toss to influence the outcome of the games.

In fact, because of the four-group structure of the competition, there were no surprise results until the semi-finals. The United States of America – playing in their first major cricket tournament – were dealt with ruthlessly by Australia, who needed less than eight overs to knock off the 66 runs they required to win. When Bangladesh were thrashed by South Africa, the ICC found itself defending the policy of allowing the 'minnows' to play such a prominent part in the Champions Trophy.

Things did hot up, however. England defeated Sri Lanka at the Rose Bowl, where Andrew Flintoff scored his third century in six innings, the West Indies beat South Africa by five wickets and, in a highly charged, but peaceful, encounter at Edgbaston, Pakistan defeated India by three wickets.

And so to the game the whole country was talking about: England against Australia for a place in the final.

Australia had won the previous 14 matches between the two teams, but Michael Vaughan's team was on a high. Australia batted first, and their score of 259 for 9 – with Damien Martyn top scoring with 65 – was more than reasonable under the circumstances.

England lost Solanki for seven, but Trescothick (81) and Vaughan – whose 86 was his highest one-day score for England – added 140, and Strauss completed England's run chase with a brilliantly paced 52 from 42 balls.

At the Rose Bowl, Pakistan surprised everyone by electing to bat first, and their paltry total of 131 was successfully overhauled by the West Indies in only 28 overs.

Marcus Trescothick ... the batting star of England's excellent ICC Champions Trophy campaign.

Therefore it was England and West Indies – the two teams who had been facing each other since March – who squared up at The Oval for the final on a bracing 25 September which, in all probability, would be Brian Lara's last international appearance in England.

Lara won a crucial toss and inserted England without a second thought and, thanks to Ian Bradshaw, the home side never really got going. There was some brilliance in the field by an unusually animated Lara – his catch to dismiss Flintoff for just three was really special – and England were only able to limp to 217 because Trescothick scored 104.

The West Indies quickly fell to 49 for 3, and when Lara was caught behind for 14 off Flintoff, they were struggling on 72 for 4. The West Indians' last hope seemed to be Chanderpaul, who scored 47, but his team were still 70 short of victory with only two wickets left when he drove Collingwood to Vaughan.

With the light closing in, Vaughan turned to Harmison and Flintoff to finish off the game, but Bradshaw and Courtney Browne dug in defiantly. They saw off the fast bowlers and, with 30 runs required, they cannily turned down an invitation to leave the field for bad light.

It was 6.45 pm and in near darkness when Bradshaw drove Wharf to the point boundary to win a game that had seemed well beyond them. In stark contrast to the scenes which had marked their Test-match whitewash on the same ground a month earlier, Lara's team celebrated jubilantly.

Most importantly, and especially at a time when hurricane debris was strewing parts of the Caribbean, they had once again put a smile on the face of West Indian cricket.

Pool A

10 September 2004
at The Oval
New Zealand 347 for 4 (50 overs)
(NJ Astle 145*, SB Styris 75, CD McMillan 64*)
United States of America 137 (42.4 overs)
(JDP Oram 5 for 36)
New Zealand (2pts) won by 210 runs

13 September 2004
at The Rose Bowl
United States of America 65 (24 overs)
(MS Kasprowicz 4 for 14, JN Gillespie 4 for 15)
Australia 66 for 1 (7.5 overs)
Australia (2pts) won by 9 wickets

16 September 2004
at The Oval
New Zealand 198 for 9 (50 overs)
Australia 199 for 3 (37.2 overs) (A Symonds 71*,
DR Martyn 60*)
Australia (2pts) won by 7 wickets

Pool A Table

	P	W	L	T	NR	RR	Pts
Australia	2	2	0	0	0	3.24	4
New Zealand	2	1	1	0	0	1.60	2
USA	2	0	2	0	0	-5.12	0

Pool B

12 September 2004
at Edgbaston
Bangladesh 93 (31.3 overs)

South Africa 94 for 1 (17.4 overs)
South Africa (2pts) won by 9 wickets

15 September 2004
at The Rose Bowl
West Indies 269 for 3 (50 overs) (CH Gayle 99,
WW Hinds 82)
Bangladesh 131 (39.3 overs) (M Dillon 5 for 29)
West Indies (2pts) won by 138 runs

18–19 September 2004
at The Oval
South Africa 246 for 6 (50 overs) (HH Gibbs 101)
West Indies 249 for 5 (48.5 overs) (RR Sarwan 75,
S Chanderpaul 51*)
West Indies (2pts) won by 5 wickets

Pool B Table

	P	W	L	T	NR	RR	Pts
West Indies	2	2	0	0	0	1.47	4
South Africa	2	1	1	0	0	1.55	2
Bangladesh	2	0	2	0	0	-3.11	0

Pool C

11 September 2004
at The Rose Bowl
India 290 for 4 (50 overs) (SC Ganguly 90,
VVS Laxman 79)
Kenya 192 for 7 (50 overs)
India (2pts) won by 98 runs

14–15 September 2004
at Edgbaston
Kenya 94 (32 overs) (Shahid Afridi 5 for 11)
Pakistan 95 for 3 (18.4 overs)
Pakistan (2pts) won by 7 wickets

19 September 2004
at Edgbaston
India 200 (49.5 overs) (R Dravid 67,
Naved-ul-Hasan 4 for 25,
Shoaib Akhtar 4 for 36)
Pakistan 201 for 7 (49.2 overs)
(Yousuf Youhana 81*)
Pakistan (2pts) won by 3 wickets

Pool C Table

	P	W	L	T	NR	RR	Pts
Pakistan	2	2	0	0	0	1.41	4
India	2	1	1	0	0	0.94	2
Kenya	2	0	2	0	0	-2.75	0

Pool D

10–11 September 2004
at Edgbaston
England 299 for 7 (50 overs) (PD Collingwood 80*, VS Solanki 62)
Zimbabwe 147 (39 overs)
England (2pts) won by 152 runs

14 September 2004
at The Oval
Zimbabwe 191 (49.1 overs) (E Chigumbura 57)
Sri Lanka 195 for 6 (43.5 overs)
Sri Lanka (2pts) won by 4 wickets

17–18 September 2004
at The Rose Bowl
England 251 for 7 (50 overs) (A Flintoff 104, ME Trescothick 66)
Sri Lanka 95 for 5 (24 overs)
England (2pts) won by 49 runs – DL Method

Pool D Table

	P	W	L	T	NR	RR	Pts
England	2	2	0	0	0	2.72	4
Sri Lanka	2	1	1	0	0	-0.25	2
Zimbabwe	2	0	2	0	0	-1.88	0

Semi-Finals

21 September 2004
at Edgbaston
Australia 259 for 9 (50 overs) (DR Martyn 65)
England 262 for 4 (46.3 overs) (MP Vaughan 86, ME Trescothick 81, AJ Strauss 52*)
England won by 6 wickets

22 September 2004
at The Rose Bowl
Pakistan 131 (38.2 overs)
West Indies 132 for 3 (28.1 overs) (RR Sarwan 56*)
West Indies won by 7 wickets

FINAL – ENGLAND v. WEST INDIES
25 September 2004 at The Oval

ENGLAND

ME Trescothick	run out	104
VS Solanki	c Browne b Bradshaw	4
MP Vaughan (capt)	b Bradshaw	7
AJ Strauss	run out	18
A Flintoff	c Lara b Hinds WW	3
PD Collingwood	c Chanderpaul b Hinds WW	16
*GO Jones	c Lara b Hinds WW	6
AF Giles	c Lara b Bravo	31
AG Wharf	not out	3
D Gough	st Browne b Gayle	0
SJ Harmison	run out	2
Extras	b 1, lb 7, w 15	23
	(49.4 overs)	**217**

	O	M	R	W
Bradshaw	10	1	54	2
Collymore	10	1	38	0
Gayle	9.4	0	52	1
Bravo	10	0	41	1
Hinds WW	10	3	24	3

Fall of Wickets
1-12, 2-43, 3-84, 4-93, 5-123, 6-148, 7-211, 8-212, 9-214

WEST INDIES

CH Gayle	c & b Harmison	23
WW Hinds	c Solanki b Harmison	3
RR Sarwan	c Strauss b Flintoff	5
BC Lara (capt)	c Jones b Flintoff	14
S Chanderpaul	c Vaughan b Collingwood	47
DJJ Bravo	c Jones b Flintoff	0
RO Hinds	c Jones b Trescothick	8
RL Powell	c Trescothick b Collingwood	14
*CO Browne	not out	35
IDR Bradshaw	not out	34
CD Collymore		
Extras	lb 11, w 19, nb 5	35
	(8 wkts 48.5 overs)	**218**

	O	M	R	W
Gough	10	1	58	0
Harmison	10	1	34	2
Flintoff	10	0	38	3
Wharf	9.5	0	38	0
Trescothick	3	0	17	1
Collingwood	6	0	22	2

Fall of Wickets
1-19, 2-35, 3-49, 4-72, 5-80, 6-114, 7-135, 8-147

Umpires: RE Koertzen & SJA Taufel
Toss: West Indies
Man of the Match: IDR Bradshaw
Man of the Series: RR Sarwan

West Indies won by 2 wickets

Above: Heroes of the hour – Ian Bradshaw (left) and
Courtney Browne celebrate their dramatic
match-winning partnership.

Right: An ecstatic Brian Lara holds aloft the
ICC Champions Trophy.

ENGLAND DOMESTIC SEASON INTRODUCTION
By Mark Baldwin

A revealing little scene was played out at New Road, Worcester, on the final afternoon of the penultimate round of Frizzell County Championship games in mid-September.

Lancashire, in all probability needing a win to have a chance of beating the drop from Division One, were in position to set a target against Worcestershire, who definitely had to achieve victory if they wanted to avoid relegation. If Worcestershire were to win, however, then Lancashire's own demotion would be confirmed.

So what did Lancashire, and their captain Warren Hegg, do? They sat on their hands.

Eventually, with the Worcester crowd seething, Hegg announced his declaration. Worcestershire's target was now 294 in 47 overs and, barring something epic from Graeme Hick, the home side had no chance.

Lancashire's caution was, on the one hand, quite understandable. They had to play the odds, and the four points on offer for the draw mathematically kept them in the hunt for survival. Their next – and final – match was against fellow strugglers Gloucestershire on their own patch at Old Trafford. If they drew here in Worcester and then beat Gloucestershire by a margin of 17 points, or better, they could still stay up.

But was that realistic? Would it not have been better to have taken a bit more of a risk against Worcestershire? What about leaving them, say, 260 in around 55 overs?

At the close, Lancashire indeed could have done with those extra eight overs. Worcestershire, after initially going for broke, but then trying to shut up shop when they lost too many wickets, finished eight down for 199 from the 47 overs they had been given.

Mark Newton, the Worcestershire chief executive, could not conceal his anger as the draw confirmed his own club's relegation. 'I was very unimpressed by the late declaration, and I hope Lancashire come down with us', he said.

Well, Newton got his wish less than a week later, as Gloucestershire fought tigerishly for enough bonus points at Old Trafford to make Lancashire's task a hopeless one. In 2005, Lancashire, the county of Flintoff and Anderson, will be in Division Two alongside Durham, the county of Harmison and Collingwood, Yorkshire, the county of Vaughan and Hoggard, and Somerset, the county of Trescothick. And Worcestershire, of course.

What was particularly interesting about the events at New Road, however, was not the lack of a 'sporting' declaration, or the argument about whether or not Lancashire's caution was excessive, understandable or just downright stupid. It was the reaction of Newton, a marketing man to his finger tips.

What is the point of championship cricket? Is it there to entertain, or to produce the 'tough' cricket and the 'hard' thinking which goes into the approach every nation brings to Test cricket. If championship matches are there to prepare our most promising cricketers for the mental and physical rigours of the Test arena, should they not be played out with the 'give-nothing' and 'expect-nothing' attitute of Test matches themselves?

Newton, and the Worcestershire public that day, clearly felt cheated by Lancashire's reluctance to cut them in on the deal. But English cricket's administrators, acting largely upon the exortations of the marketing men, have, in recent times, imposed upon the championship the current two-division system which – indubitably – has quickly spawned a 'don't-lose-at-all-costs' approach to Division One cricket. In essence, can the marketeers now complain about a lack of entertainment or 'fairness' from opposition captains when it is the system they created which fosters it?

Back in early May at Northampton, meanwhile, I witnessed a degree of caution from the home side that simply defied belief. Struggling to establish themselves in the so-called elite tier, after promotion in 2003, Northants had got Sussex – the champions, no less – on the rack, despite the loss of the equivalent of a day's play to the weather over the previous three days.

They started the final day on six without loss in their second innings, an overall lead of 112, having bowled out Sussex for 294 on the third afternoon with their two off spinners, Jason Brown and Graeme Swann, taking eight wickets between them. This, surely, on a home pitch offering more and more help to their chief attacking assets, was Northants' great chance to start to make an impression on Division One.

Time, said all logic, to risk a little in pursuit of the prize.

So what did they do? On and on they batted, showing little or no urgency until well after lunch. The declaration at 192 for 5 finally arrived at 3.20 pm, leaving Sussex to score a hypothetical 299 for victory in 39 overs! How pitiful it was, then, to see Sussex predictably struggle for survival in worsening conditions – but, ultimately, with Northants rushing through their final overs like dervishes in a bid to get more in before the clock ran down, Sussex held on for the draw at 69 for 7.

As Newton might have said, even though it was in the first week of May, and not September, how Northants deserved to go down. Which, of course, anchored to the bottom for virtually the entire summer, they duly did.

Shane Warne exploded the myth of the two-tier championship when, at the end of a season captaining Hampshire (in Division Two, mind you) he not only praised the overall standard of the cricket around him but also berated Derbyshire for, at one point, 'not wanting to have a game' on the final day. In Division Two, of course, that attitude is unusual, because the whole mindset of the supposedly inferior division is to risk the negative result (often with pitch-preparation, too) in search of the positive.

Warne's support, meanwhile, of the two-division system was because it meant more matches had more riding on them for longer – and he even thought that four-up and four-down would be a good thing because it would create even more yo-yoing between the divisions and therefore more matches in which the result mattered. Learning how to win, or more accurately how to deal with the pressure involved in the pursuit of victory, was the best way for young cricketers to become better, added Warne.

The problem with Division One as it stands, however, and something Warne will no doubt find out in 2005 if he returns to skipper Hampshire in the lead-up to the Ashes series, is that it is the draw which matters the most. Warwickshire won the title itself by drawing 11 of their 16 matches and winning just five.

While Nick Knight's team should be congratulated on playing the system to perfection by clocking up the batting bonus points with a deep and talented batting line-up, and also making themselves incredibly difficult to beat (they lost none), it is to the dishonour of the historic championship that Kent, the runners-up, won two more matches than the champions. In a simple soccer system of three points for a win and one for a draw, Kent would now be the ones celebrating.

Nothing that happened in the championship in 2004, from the issue of Kent's seven wins and Warwickshire's five, to the blatant short-termism of the legions of overseas, EU and Kolpak players now flooding in, to the nonsense of having more than half of England's best Test team for years being associated with 'second-rate' counties, to the comments of Warne and Newton and thousands of others concerned with creating the best product with which both to nurture future stars and entertain the paying public, has dissuaded me from the view that two divisions – in its present format – leaves more questions than it gives answers.

A conference-system in which all 18 counties set off from the same gun, with September play-offs to determine both the title and prize-money share-outs (and in which, with a little imagination, some of the England players could actually take part) would, to my mind, be the proper vehicle for the twin ideals of nurturing and entertaining.

When English cricket comes to re-order the domestic game for 2006, as is planned, I also vehemently hope that the irrelevant and outmoded (and horribly messy) totesport League is scrapped.

We must accentuate the positive and come up with an ordered, easy-to-understand domestic structure which builds on the many good things which are happening in all 18 – yes, all 18 – of the first-class counties. The successes at Test level in the past year of the likes of Andrew Strauss, Robert Key, Geraint Jones, Ian Bell, James Anderson and Martin Saggers shows that it is county cricket as much as National Academies that will produce world-class cricketers. It is a partnership.

Alongside a conference-style championship, which promotes positive cricket and not short-term conservatism, I would like to see an expanded Twenty20 Cup (run initially in two groups of nine, with quarter-finals and a finals day) and an expanded 50-over Cheltenham & Gloucester Trophy that is also structured in mini-league groups leading into a knock-out phase. Just like the World Cup is run, in fact, for those who really need the reason we have domestic cricket at all to be spelled out to them …

Mark Baldwin, a former cricket correspondent of the Press Association, has covered county cricket for The Times *since 1998.*

MCC v. SUSSEX

9–12 April 2004 at Lord's

Champions Sussex warmed up for the defence of their 2003 title by gaining a tenacious draw in the season's curtain-raiser match against the MCC which had been resurrected by the authorities after a gap of 13 years. Beginning on Good Friday, 9 April, the match was somewhat predictably interrupted by bad weather on all but the third day – but, nevertheless, it still developed into an interesting scrap. An MCC line-up consisting almost entirely of young England hopefuls dismissed Sussex for 200 in their first innings on the opening day, with Kent's 22-year-old off spinner, James Tredwell, adding to the favourable impression he had made on winter National Academy duty by picking up three wickets with some skilful bowling. Ian Bell, of Warwickshire, was the next young

Englishman to demonstrate his ability – reaching 70 not out on the eve of his 22nd birthday and going on to 88 the following morning. Andy Flower, the MCC captain, hit 76, but the third day was dominated by the strokeplay of England's forgotten wicketkeeper, James Foster, with his second first-class hundred, and Gloucestershire all-rounder Alex Gidman, who bounced back from an Academy winter cut short by a hand injury to score 91. Mushtaq Ahmed, the leg-spinning hero of Sussex's romantic first championship success, toiled through 40 overs for his 2 for 92 – and was left on 998 first-class career wickets when the MCC declared at 539 for 8. Sternly, however, Sussex then knuckled down to the task of saving the game. In the 32 overs remaining on day three they reached 124 for 1, and although Richard Montgomerie was out early for 50 on the final morning, Murray Goodwin stayed to hit 102, with a six and 18 fours, and Matthew Prior joined the list of young English players producing eye-catching early-season performances with a 112-ball 92. Tim Ambrose, who qualifies at the end of the year as a possible England player himself, made 60 and Michael Yardy remained unbeaten on 37 when bad light disappointingly brought proceedings to an end – 24 overs prematurely. By then, however, Sussex were 60 runs ahead with three wickets still standing at 399 for 7. The champions had only just survived the first challenge of their new status.

James Foster hit the second first-class century of his young career as MCC gave Sussex a stern test of their credentials as county champions in the resurrected season's opener at Lord's.

MCC v. SUSSEX – at Lord's

SUSSEX	First Innings			Second Innings	
IJ Ward	c Key b Harrison	19		c Foster b Saggers	28
RR Montgomerie	c Pietersen b Tredwell	61		c Pietersen b Saggers	50
MW Goodwin (capt)	c Cook b Gidman	17		c Bell b Harrison	102
PA Cottey	c Foster b Napier	20		c Foster b Harrison	19
*TR Ambrose	lbw b Gidman	35		b Gidman	60
RSC Martin-Jenkins	c Napier b Saggers	12		c Foster b Tredwell	0
MJ Prior	c Bell b Tredwell	13		c Foster b Saggers	92
MH Yardy	c Foster b Napier	4		not out	37
Mushtaq Ahmed	st Foster b Tredwell	6		not out	2
JD Lewry	c Bell b Napier	9			
M Akram	not out	1			
Extras	lb 3	3		b 1, lb 6, nb 2	9
	(62.1 overs)	200		(7 wkts 104.4 overs)	399

Bowling
Saggers 16-4-55-1. Harrison 11-3-43-1. Gidman 13-3-41-2. Napier 13.1-1-38-3. Tredwell 9-2-20-3.
Saggers 28-9-67-3. Harrison 14.4-0-65-2. Gidman 16-3-63-1. Napier 24-3-113-0. Tredwell 19-3-68-1. Bell 3-0-16-0.
Fall of Wickets: 1-23, 2-60, 3-87, 4-139, 5-154, 6-177, 7-180, 8-184, 9-190
1-56, 2-135, 3-185, 4-232, 5-235, 6-319, 7-378

MCC	First Innings	
AN Cook	lbw b Akram	12
RWT Key	lbw b Lewry	13
IR Bell	c Yardy b Lewry	88
KP Pietersen	b Martin-Jenkins	17
A Flower (capt)	c Ambrose b Akram	76
APR Gidman	lbw b Mushtaq Ahmed	91
*JS Foster	not out	110
GR Napier	lbw b Mushtaq Ahmed	4
JC Tredwell	c Martin-Jenkins b Akram	40
AJ Harrison	not out	34
MJ Saggers		
Extras	b 14, lb 14, w 6, nb 20	54
	(8 wkts dec 148 overs)	539

Bowling
Lewry 28-2-117-2. Akram 31-7-130-3. Martin-Jenkins 30-10-84-1. Mushtaq Ahmed 40-11-92-2. Yardy 15-1-71-0. Montgomerie 4-0-17-0.
Fall of Wickets: 1-27, 2-31, 3-71, 4-195, 5-254, 6-376, 7-382, 8-459

Match drawn

FRIZZELL COUNTY CHAMPIONSHIP
By Mark Baldwin

Round One: 16–19 April 2004

Division One

On paper, it looked as though Sussex could not have had a tougher start to the defence of their championship title than an immediate visit to The Oval. Surrey, their predecessors as champions and also winners in 1999 and 2000, were understandably up for the fight – but, in the end, it was Sussex who were left agonisingly close to administering the knock-out blow. Early on, both Robin Martin-Jenkins and Jason Lewry impressed with the ball as Surrey slid to 121 for 6. But Azhar Mahmood responded with an aggressive 84, and Martin Bicknell (45), Ian Salisbury (40) and Jimmy Ormond also contributed to the lower-order rally which hauled Surrey up to 304. By the close of the second day, however, it was Sussex who were in total command at 445 for 9. Ian Ward made a highly determined and satisfying 82 against the county he left not altogether amicably the previous winter, while Chris Adams and Tim Ambrose added 104 for the fourth wicket. Adams hit 101, but the Sussex skipper's pleasure was short-lived as rain washed away the entire third day. On the resumption, Lewry thrashed his way on from an unbeaten 44 to a career-best 72 and, with Mohammad Akram scoring

31 not out, Sussex's first-innings total was boosted to 493 by their highly entertaining last-wicket stand of 87. Soon, with the champions closing in hungrily for the kill, Surrey were tottering at 88 for 7 in their second innings, with plenty of time remaining. Opener Scott Newman, however, now batting at No. 7, because he had been off the field during the Sussex innings nursing a hamstring strain, was then joined by Bicknell in a courageous partnership of 100

Round One: 16–19 April 2004 Division One

GLOUCESTERSHIRE v. KENT - at Bristol

GLOS	First Innings		Second Innings forfeited
WPC Weston	b Saggers	0	
CM Spearman	c Stiff b Khan	27	
THC Hancock	c Fulton b Saggers	13	
MGN Windows	lbw b Khan	11	
CG Taylor (capt)	c Carberry b Walker	96	
APR Gidman	c Fulton b Saggers	10	
*RC Russell	b Saggers	2	
AN Bressington	not out	58	
MCJ Ball	not out	28	
JMM Averis			
J Lewis			
Extras	b 10, lb 10, w 4, nb 32	56	
	(7 wkts dec 68.5 overs)	301	

Bowling
Saggers 17.5-7-43-4. Khan 12-0-63-2. Sheriyar 13-2-60-0. Stiff 8-1-24-0. Tredwell 10-1-34-0. Walker 5-0-36-1. Carberry 3-0-21-0.
Fall of Wickets: 1-0, 2-28, 3-60, 4-73, 5-123, 6-141, 7-245

KENT	First Innings forfeited	Second Innings	
DP Fulton (capt)		lbw b Lewis	10
RWT Key		not out	118
ET Smith		b Lewis	36
MJ Walker		c Windows b Gidman	30
MA Carberry		not out	104
JC Tredwell			
*NJ O'Brien			
A Khan			
MJ Saggers			
DA Stiff			
A Sheriyar			
Extras		b 4	4
		(3 wkts 60.4 overs)	302

Bowling
Lewis 16.4-4-62-2. Averis 19-2-97-0. Bressington 6-0-55-0. Gidman 16-1-62-1. Ball 3-0-22-0.
Fall of Wickets: 1-18, 2-66, 3-119

Kent won by 7 wickets – Gloucestershire (3pts), Kent (16pts)

SURREY v. SUSSEX - at The Oval

SURREY	First Innings		Second Innings	
SA Newman	c Ambrose b Akram	14	(7) not out	86
*JN Batty (capt)	lbw b Lewry	10	(1) lbw b Martin-Jenkins	22
MR Ramprakash	c Ward b Martin-Jenkins	25	lbw b Akram	21
JGE Benning	c Mushtaq Ahmed b M-Jenkins	24	c Ambrose b Lewry	1
AD Brown	lbw b Lewry	27	c Ambrose b Martin-Jenkins	13
AJ Hollioake	c Ambrose b Martin-Jenkins	4	c Adams b Martin-Jenkins	0
Azhar Mahmood	c Montgomerie b Lewry	84	(8) b Akram	0
MP Bicknell	c Ambrose b Innes	45	(9) b Mushtaq Ahmed	37
IDK Salisbury	b Mushtaq Ahmed	40	(2) b Akram	18
J Ormond	c Ambrose b Martin-Jenkins	27	c Ambrose b Akram	19
TJ Murtagh	not out	0	not out	9
Extras	b 4	4	b 4, lb 6, nb 14	24
	(81.5 overs)	304	(9 wkts 73.3 overs)	254

Bowling
Akram 19-6-74-1. Lewry 18-4-60-3. Martin-Jenkins 20.5-4-59-4. Innes 11-3-35-1. Mushtaq Ahmed 13-1-72-1.
Akram 19.3-6-85-4. Lewry 16-5-46-1. Martin-Jenkins 20-7-47-3. Mushtaq Ahmed 14-2-54-1. Innes 4-0-12-0.
Fall of Wickets: 1-24, 2-24, 3-65, 4-78, 5-84, 6-121, 7-227, 8-245, 9-304
1-33, 2-51, 3-52, 4-75, 5-79, 6-79, 7-88, 8-188, 9-229

SUSSEX	First Innings	
IJ Ward	lbw b Murtagh	82
RR Montgomerie	c Salisbury b Bicknell	25
MW Goodwin	c Brown b Azhar Mahmood	2
CJ Adams (capt)	lbw b Ormond	101
*TR Ambrose	c Brown b Murtagh	56
MJ Prior	b Murtagh	36
RSC Martin-Jenkins	c Ormond b Bicknell	31
KJ Innes	b Hollioake	22
Mushtaq Ahmed	run out	17
JD Lewry	c Batty b Salisbury	72
M Akram	not out	31
Extras	b 1, lb 12, w 1, nb 4	18
	(135.4 overs)	493

Bowling
Bicknell 24-4-87-2. Ormond 28-6-85-1. Azhar Mahmood 23-2-83-1. Salisbury 23.4-2-86-1. Murtagh 23-8-65-3. Benning 2-0-15-0. Hollioake 6-0-35-1. Brown 6-0-24-0.
Fall of Wickets: 1-85, 2-110, 3-128, 4-232, 5-311, 6-315, 7-364, 8-370, 9-406

Match drawn – Surrey (10pts), Sussex (12pts)

NORTHAMPTONSHIRE v. LANCASHIRE - at Northampton

LANCASHIRE	First Innings	
AJ Swann	lbw b Louw	0
IJ Sutcliffe	c Louw b Swann	104
MJ Chilton	c Brophy b Louw	46
SG Law	c Sales b Louw	108
CL Hooper	c Afzaal b Swann	115
G Chapple	b Phillips	55
KW Hogg	c Sales b Jones	0
DG Cork	b Swann	19
*WK Hegg (capt)	b Louw	45
PJ Martin	not out	2
G Keedy		
Extras	lb 10	10
	(9 wkts dec 149.2 overs)	504

Bowling
Louw 28-7-71-4. Jones 25-2-94-1. Phillips 31-6-112-1. Brown 37-7-110-0. Swann 26.2-4-95-3. Afzaal 2-0-12-0.
Fall of Wickets: 1-0, 2-92, 3-261, 4-270, 5-377, 6-378, 7-412, 8-502, 9-504

NORTHANTS	First Innings		Second Innings	
MJ Powell	lbw b Martin	26	lbw b Hogg	48
TB Huggins	c Swann b Chapple	5	not out	38
TW Roberts	lbw b Martin	89	not out	15
U Afzaal	c Hooper b Hogg	51		
DJG Sales (capt)	run out	84		
*GL Brophy	c Sutcliffe b Hooper	17		
GP Swann	lbw b Keedy	1		
J Louw	c Martin b Keedy	5		
BJ Phillips	c Cork b Hooper	0		
PS Jones	not out	15		
JF Brown	c Law b Keedy	0		
Extras	lb 5	5	b 5, lb 5, nb 2	12
	(112.1 overs)	298	(1 wkt 47 overs)	113

Bowling
Martin 19-10-25-2. Chapple 17-5-50-1. Hogg 13-1-62-1. Cork 15-3-51-0. Keedy 26.1-7-55-3. Hooper 22-10-50-2.
Martin 5-1-12-0. Chapple 7-2-13-0. Hooper 12-2-19-0. Cork 2-0-13-0. Keedy 15-6-29-0. Hogg 5-0-14-1. Swann 1-0-3-0.
Fall of Wickets: 1-6, 2-59, 3-146, 4-200, 5-247, 6-248, 7-260, 8-277, 9-291 1-78

Match drawn – Northamptonshire (8pts), Lancashire (12pts)

WARWICKSHIRE v. MIDDLESEX - at Edgbaston

MIDDLESEX	First Innings		Second Innings	
SG Koenig	c Wagh b Richardson	10	c Frost b Carter	2
BL Hutton	c Frost b Brown	30	c Knight b Trott	20
OA Shah (capt)	c Wagh b Brown	17	not out	20
EC Joyce	c Frost b Carter	39	not out	10
PN Weekes	b Brown	118		
JWM Dalrymple	c Bell b Pretorius	77		
*DC Nash	st Frost b Wagh	55		
SJ Cook	lbw b Hogg	22		
MM Betts	not out	31		
CB Keegan				
M Hayward				
Extras	b 3, lb 10, w 2, nb 18	33	nb 2	2
	(8 wkts dec 124.2 overs)	432	(2 wkts dec 23 overs)	54

Bowling
Pretorius 20-5-95-1. Carter 20-5-59-1. Brown 25-7-65-3. Richardson 24-4-92-1. Bell 2-0-10-0. Hogg 22-5-45-1. Trott 3-0-22-0. Wagh 8.2-0-31-1. Carter 8-3-21-1. Bell 5-2-8-0. Trott 3-1-6-1. Hogg 6-2-15-0. Wagh 1-0-4-0.
Fall of Wickets: 1-17, 2-52, 3-69, 4-119, 5-294, 6-337, 7-373, 8-432 1-12, 2-27

WARWICKSHIRE	First Innings		Second Innings	
NV Knight (capt)	lbw b Keegan	4	not out	5
MA Wagh	c Nash b Weekes	78	not out	19
IR Bell	c Joyce b Hayward	12		
IJL Trott	c Hutton b Weekes	67		
JO Troughton	c Betts b Weekes	4		
DR Brown	b Hayward	42		
GB Hogg	lbw b Weekes	51		
*T Frost	c Nash b Keegan	4		
NM Carter	c Weekes b Keegan	18		
A Richardson	not out	8		
D Pretorius	c Et b Weekes	1		
Extras	b 2, lb 5, w 3, nb 18	28		0
	(70.4 overs)	317	(0 wkts 5 overs)	24

Bowling
Keegan 14-1-63-3. Hayward 3-3-41-2. Betts 8-0-74-0. Cook 14-2-56-0. Weekes 20.4-1-76-5.
Nash 2-0-8-0. Joyce 1-0-4-0. Weekes 1-0-5-0. Shah 1-0-7-0.
Fall of Wickets: 1-8, 2-27, 3-157, 4-167, 5-204, 6-272, 7-283, 8-303, 9-312

Match drawn – Warwickshire (9pts), Middlesex (12pts)

for the eighth wicket. Bicknell, too, was troubled by a sore hamstring, but he hung around gamely for 37 until Mushtaq Ahmed claimed him as his 1,000th first-class victim with Surrey still one run short of making Sussex bat again. Ormond, for the second time in the match, then showed resolve with the bat and, even though he fell before the end, last man Tim Murtagh kept the impressive Newman company until the draw was assured. Adams said afterwards: 'We genuinely believed fate would get us the win, but Newman was brilliant and you have to give credit where it is due. But we must be positive in our reaction to the draw after going so close to forcing victory inside three days. If we play to that level throughout the season we will not only win the title again, but we'll win it by some margin.'

An agreement to open the game up with two forfeitures, early on the final morning, eventually resulted in Gloucestershire losing their gamble at Bristol and Kent romping to a bonus victory. The home side, led for the first time by new skipper Chris Taylor, had only been troubled by the ever-testing Martin Saggers while reaching 202 for 6 on the opening two, rain-affected, days. A complete washout on day three prompted Taylor and opposite number David Fulton to do a deal. Taylor, 58 not out overnight, went on to 96 as Gloucestershire were fed some quick runs en route to a declaration at 301 for 7. Then came the forfeitures, followed by some dashing strokeplay from Rob Key and Michael Carberry. Kent, given 80 overs to score their 302 for victory, rushed over the finishing line in just 60.4, with Key unbeaten on 118 and Carberry celebrating a maiden championship hundred with 104 not out.

Lancashire, whose brave tilt at championship glory in 2003 was undone by the loss of 11 days to bad weather (in one of the best summers in living memory), found the elements ganging up against them once more as they launched their 2004 campaign at Northampton. A solid opening-day total of 306 for 4, based on hundreds by Iain Sutcliffe and Stuart Law, was boosted up to an intimidating 504 for 9 declared by the irresistible power of Carl Hooper's batsmanship the following morning. There were two sixes and 12 fours in Hooper's 115, his 68th first-class century, and Glen Chapple (55) and Warren Hegg (45) also joined in the fun as runs came at a rate of five an over. By the close, Northants were 142 for 2 in reply, with Tim Roberts unbeaten on 85 against his former county, but then the heavens opened to wash away the third day. When Roberts then fell early on day four for 89 and Northants were bowled out for 298 despite new captain David Sales' 84 and a half-

century from Usman Afzaal, there was only enough time left for the home side to reach 113 for 1 in their second innings, following on, before the overs ran out for Lancashire.

A washed-out third day, and other interruptions besides, condemned Warwickshire's meeting with Middlesex to a dull draw at Edgbaston. The evergreen Paul Weekes' 118 illuminated the opening day, and Jamie Dalrymple also impressed with 77 as the visitors reached 432 for 8 declared. Weekes then followed it up by taking 5 for 76 with his off breaks, during a Warwickshire first innings played out mainly on the final day, but Mark Wagh's polished 78, Jonathan Trott's flamboyant 67 and a boisterous 51 from 40 balls from Brad Hogg on his county debut enabled the home team to reply with 317.

Robert Key, who led Kent to victory in a run chase at Bristol in their opening championship fixture.

Division Two

Luke Sutton, who inherited the Derbyshire captaincy when Michael Di Venuto was ruled out for the entire summer with injury, batted through the final three hours of their opening match at Cardiff to earn a draw against Glamorgan. Set 335 in 84 overs, Derbyshire slipped to 114 for 4 before Sutton, with 61 not out, was joined by Graeme Welch (48) in a match-saving partnership. Earlier, Glamorgan's second-innings declaration at 323 for 4 was set up by some excellent strokeplay from Mark Wallace (105), Michael Powell (94) and Matthew Maynard, who remained unbeaten on 59 not out. Both teams had struggled with the bat in their first innings, and Glamorgan needed a spirited unbeaten 37 off 33 balls from No. 11 David Harrison, during a last-wicket stand of 57 with Adrian Dale, to drag themselves up to 185 all out.

A crowd of 3,000 turned up at the Rose Bowl to welcome Shane Warne to the Hampshire captaincy, and the great Australian leg spinner began his reign with a victory against Durham. It could easily have gone against him, however, on a pitch that always made run scoring difficult. Indeed, needing 109 in their second innings, Hampshire plunged to 26 for 5 and then to 52 for 7, against some fine seam bowling from Liam Plunkett and Mark Davies, before cloudy

Shane Warne in the thick of the action as his Hampshire side kicked off the season with a win against Durham.

skies cleared and, in sunshine and aided by three wayward overs from former West Indies Test fast bowler Reon King, they were rushed home by Will Kendall and Dimitri Mascarenhas. Skipper Warne was next man in, but was not required as Kendall and Mascarenhas plundered an unbroken 60 from 12 overs. It was a desperate disappointment for Durham, and especially for Davies, who, in Hampshire's first innings of 221, had returned career-best figures of 6 for 53. Warne took 2 for 27 and 5 for 68, plus three catches on the opening day as Durham were bundled out

Round One: 16–19 April 2004 Division Two

GLAMORGAN v. DERBYSHIRE – at Cardiff

GLAMORGAN	First Innings		Second Innings	
MTG Elliott	c Welch b Mohammad Ali	4	c Bryant b Welch	3
*MA Wallace	run out	20	b Welch	105
DL Hemp	lbw b Mohammad Ali	0	lbw b Dean	20
MJ Powell	b Dean	29	b Botha	94
MP Maynard	lbw b Dean	26	not out	59
A Dale	c Gait b Dean	41	not out	5
RDB Croft (capt)	lbw b Dean	0		
SD Thomas	lbw b Welch	0		
AG Wharf	b Mohammad Ali	17		
MS Kasprowicz	b Mohammad Ali	0		
DS Harrison	not out	37		
Extras	lb 5, nb 6	11	b 2, lb 16, w 3, nb 16	37
	(48.3 overs)	185	(4 wkts dec 75.3 overs)	323

Bowling
Mohammad Ali 16-2-75-4. Sheikh 10-0-40-0. Welch 12-6-24-1. Dean 10.3-2-41-4.
Mohammad Ali 20-2-84-0. Sheikh 3-0-12-0. Welch 21-4-64-2. Dean 14-1-46-1.
Botha 16.3-0-95-1. Hassan Adnan 1-0-4-0.
Fall of Wickets: 1-12, 2-12, 3-38, 4-75, 5-90, 6-90, 7-93, 8-128, 9-128
1-23, 2-99, 3-162, 4-306

DERBYSHIRE	First Innings		Second Innings	
AI Gait	lbw b Thomas	31	lbw b Wharf	4
SA Selwood	b Wharf	2	c Maynard b Kasprowicz	1
CJL Rogers	c Wallace b Kasprowicz	47	lbw b Harrison	43
Hassan Adnan	c Wallace b Wharf	36	c Thomas b Wharf	42
JDC Bryant	b Thomas	6	retired hurt	15
*LD Sutton (capt)	b Harrison	0	not out	61
G Welch	c Wallace b Kasprowicz	1	st Wallace b Croft	48
AG Botha	lbw b Harrison	0	not out	12
MA Sheikh	not out	15		
KJ Dean	run out	0		
Mohammad Ali	lbw b Thomas	0		
Extras	b 1, lb 3, w 1, nb 10	15	b 1, lb 1, nb 10	12
	(55.4 overs)	174	(5 wkts dec 83.4 overs)	238

Bowling
Kasprowicz 17-6-48-2. Wharf 14-2-43-2. Harrison 13-5-31-2. Thomas 11.4-1-48-3.
Kasprowicz 19-6-62-1. Wharf 19-5-54-2. Harrison 13.4-5-27-1. Thomas 15-2-46-0.
Croft 14-3-40-1. Dale 3-1-7-0.
Fall of Wickets: 1-12, 2-75, 3-95, 4-108, 5-126, 6-127, 7-128, 8-139, 9-139
1-7, 2-99, 3-69, 4-114, 5-209

Match drawn – Glamorgan (7pts), Derbyshire (7pts)

HAMPSHIRE v. DURHAM – at The Rose Bowl

DURHAM	First Innings		Second Innings	
JJB Lewis (capt)	c Pothas b Tremlett	3	c Pothas b Tremlett	50
MJ North	c Taylor b Warne	29	lbw b Tremlett	4
GJ Muchall	c Warne b Mullally	0	lbw b Mullally	1
GJ Pratt	c Warne b Mascarenhas	13	c Clarke b Mullally	4
N Peng	lbw b Taylor	49	b Warne	66
GM Hamilton	c Brown b Mascarenhas	6	b Warne	15
*A Pratt	c Et b Mascarenhas	0	c Kendall b Mascarenhas	20
GD Bridge	c Warne b Tremlett	3	b Warne	6
LE Plunkett	not out	15	c Tremlett b Warne	21
M Davies	c Brown b Taylor	0	not out	6
RD King	lbw b Warne	0	b Warne	0
Extras	b 3, lb 5, nb 2	10	b 7, w 1	8
	(54.3 overs)	128	(85 overs)	201

Bowling
Mullally 12-3-26-1. Tremlett 11-6-10-2. Taylor 10-5-23-2. Mascarenhas 12-5-28-3.
Warne 8.3-1-27-2. Clarke 1-0-6-0.
Mullally 10-4-33-2. Tremlett 16-3-42-2. Mascarenhas 17-10-13-1. Warne 29-8-68-5.
Clarke 6-1-24-0. Taylor 7-2-14-0.
Fall of Wickets: 1-3, 2-6, 3-30, 4-75, 5-83, 6-85, 7-88, 8-123, 9-127
1-6, 2-11, 3-19, 4-130, 5-130, 6-164, 7-168, 8-190, 9-199

HAMPSHIRE	First Innings		Second Innings	
DA Kenway	c North b Davies	35	lbw b Davies	9
MJ Brown	c Pratt A b Davies	28	c Hamilton b Plunkett	0
JP Crawley	c Pratt GJ b King	35	(5) lbw b Plunkett	0
MJ Clarke	c Pratt GJ b Davies	75	(6) b Plunkett	0
WS Kendall	c Muchall b King	0	(7) not out	31
*N Pothas	lbw b Davies	10	(8) lbw b Davies	11
AD Mascarenhas	c Muchall b Plunkett	3	(9) not out	33
SK Warne (capt)	c King b Plunkett	3		
CT Tremlett	not out	8	(4) b Davies	10
BV Taylor	c Lewis b Davies	5	(3) c Pratt A b Plunkett	9
AD Mullally	c Lewis b Davies	5		
Extras	lb 6, w 2, nb 6	14	lb 7, nb 2	9
	(56.2 overs)	221	(7 wkts 37.2 overs)	112

Bowling
King 11-1-65-2. Plunkett 17-4-66-2. Davies 17.2-7-53-6. Hamilton 6-1-19-0.
Bridge 5-1-12-0.
Plunkett 18-5-48-4. Davies 15-2-34-3. King 3.2-0-21-0. Hamilton 1-0-2-0.
Fall of Wickets: 1-55, 2-80, 3-165, 4-167, 5-192, 6-199, 7-203, 8-203, 9-208
1-11, 2-13, 3-23, 4-24, 5-26, 6-39, 7-52

Hampshire won by 3 wickets – Hampshire (18pts), Durham (3pts – 1pt deducted for slow over rate)

for 128, and looked thoroughly motivated by his latest cricketing challenge. Warne's fellow Aussie, the highly promising Michael Clarke, reached 50 from just 38 balls on his way to a fine 75 on his county debut, while Nicky Peng – perhaps England's most naturally gifted young batsman – batted beautifully to score 49 and 66. Peng's second-innings dismissal, bowled by Warne in the second over of the leg spinner's second spell after he had put on 111 with Jon Lewis, was possibly the moment the match finally turned against Durham.

Round Two: 21–24 April 2004

Division One

Kent maintained their flying start to the championship season with a remarkable victory over Worcestershire at Canterbury. Set 429 to win in what turned out to be 113 overs, they romped home by five wickets with 3.3 overs to spare. The Kent supporters present on a golden early-summer evening at the St Lawrence Ground witnessed the highest fourth-innings winning total in Kent's long and proud history. Matthew Walker and Michael Carberry were the main architects of the victory, adding 236 for the fifth wicket. Walker was still there at the end with 151 not out, a superlative innings

which included a six and 19 fours, while Carberry's 112 occupied only 157 balls and was just the sort of attacking innings that Kent required on an epic final afternoon. Martin Saggers, the nightwatchman, also played a major part in the drama, however. First surviving the previous evening, which ended with Kent in some trouble at 35 for 2, he then went on to make a career-best 64 and managed to outlast his third-wicket partner Rob Key, with whom he put on 72. Indeed, Saggers did not fall until just after lunch, which Kent had reached on 166 for 3. The game was also something of a personal triumph for David Fulton, the Kent captain, who a year earlier had suffered a pre-season eye injury which threatened his career. Fulton, of course, had managed a courageous comeback midway through the 2003 season, but here he scored his first century since the injury – making it an emotional moment for the 32-year-old opener. However, his first-innings 107, plus half-centuries for Walker and James Tredwell, still left the home side some way short of Worcestershire's 401. Stephen Peters, Vikram Solanki and Andy Bichel had all topped 50 in Worcestershire's first innings, with Peters twice being caught off no-balls as the Kent pace attack struggled with a rash of overstepping, and second time round it was the turn of Stephen Moore, Graeme Hick and Ben Smith to plunder the home bowlers. Moore, a South African batsman in just his

Round Two: 21–24 April 2004 Division One

KENT v. WORCESTERSHIRE - at Canterbury

WORCS	First Innings			Second Innings	
SD Peters	b Sheriyar	76		c Walker b Sheriyar	29
SC Moore	lbw b Khan	5		not out	108
GA Hick	c Tredwell b Saggers	38		c Tredwell b Carberry	89
BF Smith (capt)	c Carberry b Khan	8		not out	78
VS Solanki	lbw b Stiff	84			
DJ Pipe	c Tredwell b Sheriyar	12			
AJ Bichel	c Smith b Tredwell	50			
*SJ Rhodes	not out	42			
MS Mason	c Jones b Sheriyar	16			
SA Khalid	c Fulton b Sheriyar	0			
MN Malik	c Jones b Sheriyar	7			
Extras	b 5, lb 13, w 5, nb 40	63		b 4, lb 4, nb 4	12
	(101.3 overs)	401		(2 wkts dec 60 overs)	316

Bowling
Saggers 26-9-70-1. Khan 20-2-100-2. Sheriyar 22.3-1-94-5. Stiff 17-3-68-1. Tredwell 16-2-51-1.
Saggers 10-3-32-0. Khan 8-1-42-0. Sheriyar 10-1-49-1. Stiff 9-2-46-0. Tredwell 15-1-83-0. Carberry 8-0-56-1.
Fall of Wickets: 1-6, 2-85, 3-130, 4-183, 5-195, 6-317, 7-331, 8-357, 9-357, 1-52, 2-183

KENT	First Innings			Second Innings	
DP Fulton (capt)	c Hick b Mason	107		b Mason	16
RWT Key	c Smith b Malik	13		lbw b Malik	46
ET Smith	c Solanki b Malik	0		lbw b Mason	6
MJ Walker	lbw b Malik	70		(5) not out	151
MA Carberry	c Peters b Mason	10		(6) b Malik	112
*GO Jones	c Rhodes b Mason	0		(7) not out	20
JC Tredwell	not out	51			
A Khan	lbw b Malik	1			
MJ Saggers	lbw b Malik	1		(4) lbw b Mason	64
DA Stiff	b Bichel	4			
A Sheriyar	c Khalid b Mason	5			
Extras	b 6, lb 9, w 2, nb 10	27		b 5, lb 5, nb 4	14
	(84.3 overs)	289		(5 wkts 109.3 overs)	429

Bowling
Bichel 24-5-74-1. Mason 23.3-8-55-4. Malik 20-3-88-5. Khalid 14-4-42-0. Hick 3-0-15-0.
Bichel 21-2-101-0. Mason 24-6-86-3. Malik 19-3-93-2. Khalid 29.3-7-88-0. Solanki 16-1-51-0.
Fall of Wickets: 1-30, 2-30, 3-198, 4-221, 5-225, 6-227, 7-239, 8-249, 9-254, 1-17, 2-33, 3-105, 4-170, 5-406

Kent won by 5 wickets - Kent (19pts), Worcestershire (8pts)

SUSSEX v. LANCASHIRE - at Hove

SUSSEX	First Innings			Second Innings	
IJ Ward	c Cork b Martin	0		c Hegg b Martin	37
RR Montgomerie	not out	60		b Mahmood	27
MW Goodwin	lbw b Cork	33		lbw b Cork	14
CJ Adams (capt)	c Cork b Mahmood	3		c Loye b Mahmood	0
*TR Ambrose	b Cork	0		lbw b Cork	28
RSC Martin-Jenkins	c Loye b Chapple	29		lbw b Cork	5
MJ Prior	b Chapple	11		c Hegg b Chapple	33
KJ Innes	c Cork b Martin	5		c Chilton b Cork	3
Mushtaq Ahmed	c Hegg b Cork	21		run out	2
JD Lewry	c Loye b Mahmood	11		b Cork	0
M Akram	b Mahmood	4		not out	1
Extras	lb 3, w 1, nb 14	18		b 7, lb 1, nb 10	18
	(56 overs)	195		(52.5 overs)	163

Bowling
Martin 14-4-37-2. Chapple 15-4-52-2. Mahmood 13-1-41-3. Cork 13-0-61-3. Keedy 1-0-1-0.
Martin 13-4-25-1. Chapple 15-2-37-1. Cork 13.5-2-58-5. Mahmood 9-1-35-2. Keedy 2-2-0-0.
Fall of Wickets: 1-0, 2-71, 3-76, 4-79, 5-120, 6-132, 7-137, 8-161, 9-184, 1-64, 2-90, 3-90, 4-96, 5-96, 6-153, 7-157, 8-162, 9-162

LANCASHIRE	First Innings			Second Innings	
MJ Chilton	b Akram	5		not out	10
IJ Sutcliffe	b Innes	45		not out	14
MB Loye	b Martin-Jenkins	15			
SG Law	not out	171			
CL Hooper	c Prior b Mushtaq Ahmed	34			
G Chapple	lbw b Mushtaq Ahmed	10			
DG Cork	lbw b Innes	0			
*WK Hegg (capt)	c Prior b Mushtaq Ahmed	0			
PJ Martin	lbw b Mushtaq Ahmed	0			
SI Mahmood	lbw b Akram	9			
G Keedy	lbw b Akram	46			
Extras	b 5, lb 16, w 1, nb 24	46			0
	(98 overs)	335		(0 wkts 8.5 overs)	24

Bowling
Akram 25-3-79-3. Lewry 19-5-60-0. Martin-Jenkins 13-2-37-1. Innes 13-2-50-2. Mushtaq Ahmed 28-3-88-4.
Lewry 4.5-0-12-0. Innes 4-0-12-0.
Fall of Wickets: 1-8, 2-57, 3-120, 4-229, 5-286, 6-287, 7-290, 8-292, 9-331

Lancashire won by 10 wickets -
Sussex (3pts), Lancashire (18pts - 2pts deducted for slow over rate)

MIDDLESEX v. SURREY - at Lord's

SURREY	First Innings			Second Innings	
SA Newman	c Weekes b Hayward	86		c Cook b Hayward	18
*JN Batty (capt)	c Cook b Keegan	35		c Keegan b Hayward	0
MR Ramprakash	b Hutchison	29		c Nash b Keegan	68
JGE Benning	b Hutchison	20		lbw b Keegan	12
AD Brown	b Hutchison	18		c Weekes b Hutchison	4
AJ Hollioake	c Hutton b Keegan	106		run out	4
Azhar Mahmood	c Hutton b Keegan	14		c Hutchison b Weekes	70
IDK Salisbury	c Hayward b Keegan	77		c Nash b Keegan	13
Saqlain Mushtaq	c Hutton b Keegan	2		c Shah b Hayward	1
J Ormond	c Nash b Hayward	1		not out	1
TJ Murtagh	not out	8		b Hayward	0
Extras	b 3, lb 16, w 1, nb 2	22		b 2, lb 9, w 1	12
	(91 overs)	418		(54 overs)	203

Bowling
Keegan 22-0-138-5. Hayward 21-2-100-2. Cook 20-5-57-0. Hutchison 21-4-72-3. Hutton 2-0-5-0. Weekes 5-0-27-0.
Keegan 18-4-47-3. Hayward 11-1-41-4. Hutchison 6-1-11-1. Cook 9-2-44-0. Weekes 10-0-49-1.
Fall of Wickets: 1-119, 2-130, 3-167, 4-189, 5-220, 6-253, 7-378, 8-383, 9-384, 1-4, 2-22, 3-48, 4-59, 5-71, 6-184, 7-191, 8-202, 9-202

MIDDLESEX	First Innings			Second Innings	
SG Koenig	lbw b Azhar Mahmood	1		c Hollioake b Saqlain Mushtaq	62
BL Hutton	b Salisbury	78		c Batty b Saqlain Mushtaq	88
OA Shah (capt)	c Batty b Azhar Mahmood	93		c Brown b Saqlain Mushtaq	65
PM Hutchison	b Azhar Mahmood	2			
EC Joyce	b Salisbury	45		(4) c Et b Saqlain Mushtaq	47
PN Weekes	lbw b Azhar Mahmood	7		not out	9
JWM Dalrymple	lbw b Ormond	0			
*DC Nash	c Newman b Saqlain Mushtaq	26		(5) not out	3
SJ Cook	c Benning b Saqlain Mushtaq	21			
CB Keegan	c Newman b Saqlain Mushtaq	11			
M Hayward	not out	8			
Extras	b 6, lb 8, w 2, nb 18, p 5	39		b 3, lb 9, nb 14	26
	(82.4 overs)	325		(4 wkts 82.4 overs)	300

Bowling
Ormond 18-5-52-1. Azhar Mahmood 19-4-96-4. Murtagh 10-0-55-0. Saqlain Mushtaq 18.4-2-71-3. Salisbury 17-6-32-2.
Ormond 17-3-50-0. Azhar Mahmood 15-2-43-0. Murtagh 5-0-22-0. Saqlain Mushtaq 24-1-107-4. Salisbury 21.4-2-77-0.
Fall of Wickets: 1-1, 2-172, 3-176, 4-209, 5-225, 6-226, 7-273, 8-297, 9-310, 1-114, 2-222, 3-273, 4-291

Middlesex won by 6 wickets - Middlesex (20pts), Surrey (8pts)

third championship match, finished unbeaten on 108 from 162 balls, while Hick thrashed 89 before spearing one to short extra-cover and Smith thumped two sixes and eight fours in his 60-ball 78 not out.

Lancashire underlined their intentions, in terms of the championship, by thrashing champions Sussex by ten wickets at Hove. The opening day of the match saw the launch, in a boundary-side marquee, of *The Longest Journey*, a book commemorating the unique achievement of Sussex's 2003 title success. As the function went on, however, Sussex were collapsing to 195 all out in their first innings. Dominic Cork and Sajid Mahmood both impressed with the ball – with Cork also picking up three sharp catches in the slip and gully area – and Sussex knew they were really up against it once Stuart Law began to tuck in greedily against their attack. Law, who had totalled 1,820 first-class runs at an average of 91 in 2003, merely looked to be carrying on where he had left off as he eased his way to 171 not out. His previous six championship innings against Sussex had been 163

Stuart Law was in peerless early-season form for Lancashire, hitting an unbeaten 171 against champions Sussex at Hove.

not out, 7, 96, 45 not out, 147 and 218. Lancashire's Law-inspired 335 put them firmly in control, and, despite a first-wicket stand of 64, Sussex were soon in Cork's sights once more. The former England fast bowler's 5 for 58 sped Sussex to 163 all out – and the rest was a mere formality. On Mahmood, who picked up five wickets in the match, Cork said: 'He should go on and play for England. He needs time in county cricket to learn his art, but his loping run-up reminds me of Curtly Ambrose.' On the early talk of titles, Lancashire captain Warren Hegg said: 'If it's meant to be, it's meant to be.'

Middlesex had not beaten Surrey in the championship since 1995, but that all changed at Lord's where the tide of recent London derbies finally, and dramatically, turned against the men from south of the Thames. Initially, at least, Surrey seemed to be in control. They reached 418 in their first innings, with the in-form Scott Newman blasting 86 off just 78 balls with 15 boundaries and Adam Hollioake scoring his 17th championship hundred, off 119 balls, and adding 125 for the seventh wicket with Ian Salisbury. Middlesex's response then fell away to 325 all out, after the early promise of Ben Hutton and Owais Shah, and Surrey seemed to be in the process of setting their neighbours a tough fourth-innings target as Mark Ramprakash and Azhar Mahmood put on 113 in 23 overs. However, they then carelessly lost their last five wickets for only 19 runs in the space of just 41 balls and Middlesex suddenly had more than a sniff of a chance. Sven Koenig joined Hutton in an opening stand of 114, after Middlesex had resumed the final day on 32 without loss, and Shah then helped Hutton to add another 108 for the second wicket. Ed Joyce also contributed a quick-fire 47, from only 42 balls, and Saqlain's four wickets were the only obstacles to be laid in Middlesex's way as they cruised to a morale-boosting six-wicket triumph. The famed Surrey strut had, by the time the winning stroke had been made, become no more than a Surrey shuffle.

Division Two

Charlie Shreck, a 6ft 7in Cornish fast bowler, finished with a career-best 6 for 46 as Nottinghamshire blew Durham away by an innings and 80 runs at the Riverside. Shreck's blast on the final morning meant that Durham, 30 for 3 overnight, slid to 93 all out as he and Greg Smith proved too much for the home batsmen. Durham, however, had produced a fighting first-innings effort with the bat, struggling somewhat to reach 175 for 5 on a shortened opening day, but then rallying to 350 with four players getting to 50 and Graeme Bridge also weighing in with 48. Liam Plunkett, Durham's England Under 19 all-rounder, caught the eye with some high-calibre drives and pulls in his 54, but he could not make any impact with the ball. Poor Gavin Hamilton, attempting a

Charlie Shreck was the 6ft 7in spearhead of Nottinghamshire's win at Durham.

Round Two: 21–24 April 2004 Division Two

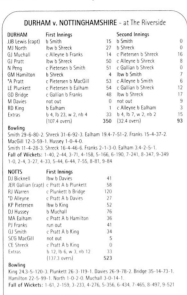

```
        DURHAM v. NOTTINGHAMSHIRE - at The Riverside
DURHAM          First Innings              Second Innings
JJB Lewis (capt) b Smith          15   b Smith              0
MJ North        lbw b Shreck      27   b Shreck             0
GJ Muchall      c Alleyne b Franks 14  c Pietersen b Shreck 16
GJ Pratt        lbw b Shreck      50   b Shreck             8
N Peng          c Pietersen b Smith 51 c Gallian b Shreck   0
GM Hamilton     b Shreck           4   lbw b Smith          7
*A Pratt        c Pietersen b MacGill 53 c Alleyne b Smith  6
LE Plunkett     c Pietersen b Ealham 54 c Gallian b Shreck  12
GD Bridge       c Gallian b Franks 48  not out              17
M Davies        not out            0   not out              9
RD King         b Ealham           1   c Alleyne b Ealham   3
Extras          b 4, lb 23, w 2, nb 4 33  b 4, lb 7, w 2, nb 2 15
                (107.4 overs)      350  (32.4 overs)         93

Bowling
Smith 29-6-80-2. Shreck 31-6-92-3. Ealham 19.4-7-51-2. Franks 15-4-37-2.
MacGill 12-3-59-1. Hussey 1-0-4-0.
Smith 11-4-28-3. Shreck 16-4-46-6. Franks 2-1-3-0. Ealham 3.4-2-5-1.
Fall of Wickets: 1-40, 2-44, 3-71, 4-158, 5-166, 6-190, 7-241, 8-347, 9-349
1-0, 2-4, 3-27, 4-33, 5-44, 6-44, 7-55, 8-81, 9-84

NOTTS           First Innings
DJ Bicknell     lbw b Davies      41
JER Gallian (capt) c Pratt A b Plunkett 58
RJ Warren       c Plunkett b Bridge 120
*D Alleyne      c Pratt A b Davies 27
KP Pietersen    lbw b King        52
DJ Hussey       b Muchall         76
MA Ealham       c Pratt A b Hamilton 36
PJ Franks       run out           41
GJ Smith        c Pratt A b King  34
SCG MacGill     not out            5
CE Shreck       c Pratt A b King   0
Extras          b 12, lb 6, w 3, nb 12 33
                (137.3 overs)     523

Bowling
King 24.3-5-120-3. Plunkett 26-3-119-1. Davies 26-9-78-2. Bridge 35-14-73-1.
Hamilton 22-5-99-1. North 1-0-2-0. Muchall 3-0-14-1.
Fall of Wickets: 1-61, 2-159, 3-233, 4-276, 5-356, 6-434, 7-465, 8-497, 9-521

    Nottinghamshire won by an innings and 80 runs -
       Durham (6pts), Nottinghamshire (22pts)
```

bowling comeback after his trouble with the 'yips' and a move from Yorkshire, was struck for five fours in an over by Russell Warren, who led the way with 120 and an eventual Notts total of 523. Notts' batting strength was also evident with half-centuries also coming from Jason Gallian, Kevin Pietersen and David Hussey and good lower-middle-order contributions from Mark Ealham, Paul Franks and Greg Smith.

Yorkshire's all-round potency was also clear to see at Headingley, where Essex were dismissed for 262 and 273 and beaten by seven wickets. Will Jefferson, Mark Pettini, Alastair Cook and Aftab Habib all batted well for the visitors, but Yorkshire were in charge once accomplished and positive batting from Craig White,

```
        SOMERSET v. DERBYSHIRE - at Taunton
SOMERSET        First Innings              Second Innings
PD Bowler       c Gait b Dean     127  c Rogers b Walker    28
JD Francis      lbw b Dean         17  lbw b Walker         36
NJ Edwards      c Bassano b Hewson 14  c Welch b Dumelow    13
J Cox           c Gait b Walker    68  c Welch b Hewson      6
M Burns (capt)  c Dean b Walker    68  c Rogers b Hewson     5
MJ Wood         c Hassan Adnan b Walker 66 lbw b Hewson     26
AW Laraman      c Hassan Adnan b Walker 20 not out          29
*RJ Turner      lbw b Dean         10  not out              22
RL Johnson      lbw b Dean          1
AR Caddick      c Sutton b Dean     1
NAM McLean      not out             1
Extras          b 1, lb 6, w 1, nb 20 28   lb 5             5
                (110 overs)        388  (6 wkts dec 71 overs) 170

Bowling
Walker 23-0-111-4. Welch 16-5-33-0. Dean 26-6-86-5. Hewson 21-8-48-1.
Dumelow 22-2-92-0. Hassan Adnan 2-0-11-0.
Dean 6-2-10-0. Walker 19-3-49-2. Hewson 18-8-39-3. Dumelow 25-5-60-1.
Hassan Adnan 3-0-7-0.
Fall of Wickets: 1-52, 2-87, 3-182, 4-246, 5-319, 6-367, 7-383, 8-386, 9-387
1-37, 2-59, 3-70, 4-86, 5-117, 6-126

DERBYSHIRE      First Innings              Second Innings
AI Gait         lbw b Laraman      43  not out              36
SA Selwood      c Edwards b McLean 38  c Turner b Caddick   36
CJL Rogers      c Turner b Laraman  8  not out              58
Hassan Adnan    not out           107
CWG Bassano     c Turner b Caddick  8
*LD Sutton (capt) lbw b Laraman     6
DR Hewson       c Turner b Laraman  0
G Welch         lbw b Edwards       9
NRC Dumelow     c Burns b Laraman  18
KJ Dean         not out             0
NGE Walker
Extras          b 8, lb 3, w 1, nb 18 30  lb 6, w 1, nb 8  15
                (8 wkts dec 82 overs) 275  (1 wkt 31 overs) 112

Bowling
Caddick 19-6-61-1. Johnson 20-7-58-0. McLean 21-5-62-1. Laraman 16-4-58-5.
Burns 3-0-9-0. Edwards 3-0-16-1.
Caddick 8-1-27-1. McLean 5-1-15-0. Johnson 4-1-16-0. Laraman 4-0-13-0.
Edwards 6-1-24-0. Francis 4-0-11-0.
Fall of Wickets: 1-84, 2-98, 3-98, 4-118, 5-141, 6-141, 7-170, 8-237
1-3

    Match drawn - Somerset (10pts), Derbyshire (9pts)
```

```
      LEICESTERSHIRE v. GLAMORGAN - at Leicester
GLAMORGAN       First Innings              Second Innings
MTG Elliott     c Nixon b Gibson   37  c Stevens b Henderson 33
*MA Wallace     c Nixon b Gibson   20  c Stevens b Henderson 15
DL Hemp         lbw b Gibson       82  (4) run out           9
MJ Powell       c Cleary b DeFreitas 55 (5) c Robinson b Henderson 3
MP Maynard      c Nixon b Dakin   163  (6) b Dakin          11
A Dale          st Nixon b Hodge   41  (7) c Stevens b Henderson 6
RDB Croft (capt) not out           21  (8) lbw b Gibson      6
SD Thomas       c Stevens b Hodge   5  (9) not out          10
AG Wharf                               (3) c Maddy b Gibson  0
MS Kasprowicz                          c Maunders b Henderson 10
DS Harrison                            not out               0
Extras          b 1, lb 3, w 5, nb 22 31  b 3, lb 5, w 1, nb 2 11
                (7 wkts dec 111.5 overs) 455  (9 wkts dec 38 overs) 125

Bowling
DeFreitas 27-5-109-1. Dakin 21-3-79-1. Cleary 18-3-80-0. Gibson 23-4-97-3.
Henderson 16-3-52-0. Maddy 2-0-7-0. Hodge 4.5-0-27-2.
Gibson 11-2-38-2. Cleary 5-0-31-0. Henderson 15-9-28-5. Dakin 7-2-20-1.
Fall of Wickets: 1-50, 2-77, 3-145, 4-350, 5-415, 6-439, 7-455
1-34, 2-51, 3-73, 4-75, 5-87, 6-91, 7-94, 8-102, 9-121

LEICESTERSHIRE  First Innings              Second Innings
DDJ Robinson    c Guy b Kasprowicz  0  b Thomas             36
JK Maunders     run out             0  lbw b Wharf           5
BJ Hodge        c Harrison b Croft 105 (4) run out          158
DL Maddy        c Hemp b Kasprowicz 26 (3) lbw b Wharf       28
DI Stevens      lbw b Thomas       27  c Wallace b Thomas    0
*PA Nixon       c Powell b Croft   19  c & b Kasprowicz      2
PAJ DeFreitas (capt) c Elliott b Thomas 20 (8) b Harrison    0
JM Dakin        not out            23  (9) b Kasprowicz     15
OD Gibson       lbw b Kasprowicz   22  (10) not out         20
CW Henderson    b Kasprowicz        6  (7) b Harrison       63
MF Cleary       c Maynard b Kasprowicz 4  c Thomas b Croft  23
Extras          lb 8, nb 8         16  b 13, lb 2, nb 8     23
                (64.5 overs)       264  (106.4 overs)       353

Bowling
Kasprowicz 16.5-2-54-5. Wharf 10-0-63-0. Harrison 7-1-24-0. Thomas 15-1-73-2.
Croft 16-4-42-2.
Kasprowicz 27-5-88-2. Wharf 20-4-77-2. Harrison 23-6-61-2. Thomas 20-5-56-2.
Croft 16.4-4-56-1.
Fall of Wickets: 1-0, 2-0, 3-53, 4-102, 5-136, 6-199, 7-221, 8-258, 9-264
1-12, 2-45, 3-100, 4-106, 5-114, 6-244, 7-244, 8-322, 9-343

   Match drawn - Leicestershire (8pts), Glamorgan (12pts)
```

```
        YORKSHIRE v. ESSEX - at Headingley
ESSEX           First Innings              Second Innings
WI Jefferson    c Lumb b Kirby     74  lbw b Blain          20
AN Cook         c Guy b Silverwood  5  c Guy b Blain        52
A Flower (capt) lbw b Blain         7  c White b Lehmann    29
A Habib         c Wood b Harvey    29  c Lumb b Kirby       62
ML Pettini      lbw b Lehmann      67  b Lehmann             0
*JS Foster      c Wood b Kirby      0  c Guy b Silverwood    4
JD Middlebrook  c Guy b Lehmann    25  (8) c Harvey b Kirby  6
GR Napier       c Silverwood b Craven 13 (9) c Wood b Harvey 30
JP Stephenson   not out            10  (10) c Wood b Blain  34
SA Brant        b Silverwood        6  (7) c Wood b Silverwood 2
AGAM McCoubrey  c Guy b Blain       0  not out               0
Extras          b 1, lb 10, nb 14  25  b 5, lb 9, nb 22     36
                (97.2 overs)       262  (91.3 overs)        273

Bowling
Silverwood 23-7-44-2. Kirby 23-5-72-2. Blain 15.2-1-63-2. Harvey 17-8-24-1.
Craven 9-1-28-1. Lehmann 10-3-20-2.
Silverwood 20-5-60-2. Kirby 16-3-50-2. Blain 16.3-3-52-3. Harvey 13-2-32-1.
Lehmann 11-2-25-2. Craven 6-1-20-0. White 9-2-20-0.
Fall of Wickets: 1-17, 2-38, 3-87, 4-159, 5-159, 6-207, 7-236, 8-244, 9-252
1-49, 2-92, 3-135, 4-135, 5-138, 6-142, 7-153, 8-206, 9-267

YORKSHIRE       First Innings              Second Innings
MJ Wood         b Brant            16  lbw b Brant           9
C White (capt)  c Guy b McCoubrey  60  b Napier             39
CR Taylor       b Napier           32  not out              43
DS Lehmann      c Jefferson b Stephenson 53 b Middlebrook    26
MJ Lumb         c & b Middlebrook  76  not out               0
IJ Harvey       lbw b Napier       95
VJ Craven       c Jefferson b Napier 5
*SM Guy         c Flower b Napier   7
CEW Silverwood  c Habib b Brant    37
JAR Blain       lbw b Napier        0
SP Kirby        not out             0
Extras          b 2, lb 1, nb 24   27  nb 12                12
                (102.2 overs)      408  (3 wkts 31.3 overs) 129

Bowling
Brant 25.2-6-86-2. McCoubrey 18.4-3-76-1. Napier 28.2-5-119-4.
Middlebrook 14-1-47-1. Stephenson 15-1-76-2. Habib 1-0-1-0.
Brant 11.3-4-30-1. Napier 10-1-52-1. Stephenson 7-2-29-0. Middlebrook 3-0-18-1.
Fall of Wickets: 1-38, 2-108, 3-149, 4-183, 5-331, 6-338, 7-355, 8-396, 9-404
1-18, 2-66, 3-125

    Yorkshire won by 7 wickets - Yorkshire (22pts), Essex (5pts)
```

Darren Lehmann, Michael Lumb and Ian Harvey had swept them to a first-innings lead approaching 150. White's team were held up a little by stubborn second-innings stands featuring Habib, first with Graham Napier and then with John Stephenson, but victory arrived in the end with few alarms.

The loss of the opening day to rain, and then Somerset's refusal to set any sort of challenging last-day target, condemned the visit of Derbyshire to Taunton to a dull draw. Peter Bowler and Kevin Dean, with a dedicated century and five good wickets respectively, underlined that advancing years were not blunting their effectiveness while, in Derbyshire's first innings, the Lahore-born Hassan Adnan illustrated his ability with an unbeaten 107. The visitors declared more than one hundred runs behind, thus doing their bit to open up the game, but despite seeing Aaron Laraman take 5 for 58 in Derbyshire's first innings, Somerset were unwilling to take a chance on forcing a result. Instead, they plodded through 71 overs before making a token declaration at 170 for 6 – leaving Chris Rogers and Andrew Gait to enjoy some batting practice in the time remaining.

Brad Hodge and Claude Henderson were responsible for turning Leicestershire's game against Glamorgan at Grace Road on its head. Remarkably, too, their efforts almost resulted in a Leicestershire win after they had followed on and begun the final day still 67 runs adrift and with just five second-innings wickets standing. Only 23 overs were possible on the opening day, but after Ottis Gibson celebrated

his return to first-class cricket after more than a three-year absence with two wickets in his first four overs, it was Matthew Maynard who occupied centre stage. The Glamorgan veteran, who had struck five championship hundreds in 2003, hit a six and 24 fours in a wonderful 163 – the 52nd first-class century of his career, and equalling the Glamorgan record jointly held by Hugh Morris and Alan Jones. Mike Kasprowicz then took 5 for 54 and Leicestershire, despite Hodge's 105, looked down and out as they ended the third day on 124 for 5 after being bowled out for 264 in their first innings. Hodge, however, on 42 not out overnight, continued to defy the Glamorgan attack and found a particularly staunch lower-middle-order ally in Henderson. Eventually, the Australian fell for 158 and Henderson for 63, but by then Leicestershire had gained an overall lead of 162. Glamorgan's desperate effort to score the runs in the time left foundered on Henderson's left-arm spin, with the South African and controversial 'Kolpak' signing ending with 5 for 28 from his 15 overs as Glamorgan hung on grimly at 125 for 9.

Round Three: 28 April–1 May 2004

Division One

Bad weather decimated the three matches scheduled in Division One, with just 17 overs being possible on the final day of Worcestershire's match against Sussex at New Road.

Round Three: 28 April–1 May 2004 Division One

WORCESTERSHIRE v. SUSSEX - at Worcester

WORCS	First Innings forfeited	Second Innings	
SD Peters		c Ambrose b Akram	16
SC Moore		b Lewry	12
GA Hick		not out	7
BF Smith (capt)		not out	8
VS Solanki			
DJ Pipe			
AJ Bichel			
*SJ Rhodes			
MS Mason			
MN Malik			
MA Harrity			
Extras		lb 1, nb 2	3
		(2 wkts 17 overs)	46

Bowling
Akram 9-1-37-1. Lewry 8-3-8-1.
Fall of Wickets: 1-28, 2-30

SUSSEX	First Innings forfeited
IJ Ward	
RR Montgomerie	
PA Cottey	
MW Goodwin	
CJ Adams (capt)	
MJ Prior	
*TR Ambrose	
RSC Martin-Jenkins	
Mushtaq Ahmed	
JD Lewry	
M Akram	

Match drawn -
Worcestershire (4pts), Sussex (4pts)

SURREY v. NORTHAMPTONSHIRE - at The Oval

SURREY	First Innings	
SA Newman	c Swann b Jones	131
*JN Batty (capt)	c Sales b Jones	28
MR Ramprakash	c Sales b Jones	34
GP Thorpe	c Sales b Louw	13
AD Brown	b Swann	28
AJ Hollioake	b Brophy b Louw	73
Azhar Mahmood	c Swann b Jones	65
MP Bicknell	not out	9
IDK Salisbury	not out	4
Saqlain Mushtaq		
J Ormond		
Extras	b 4, lb 6, w 6, nb 2	18
	(7 wkts dec 91.3 overs)	403

Bowling
Jones 28-5-114-3. Louw 26.3-3-87-3. Phillips 21-2-100-0. Brown 7-1-48-0. Swann 9-0-44-1.
Fall of Wickets: 1-93, 2-163, 3-218, 4-235, 5-262, 6-383, 7-399

NORTHANTS	First Innings	
MJ Powell	b Ormond	11
TB Huggins	b Bicknell	14
TW Roberts	not out	22
U Afzaal	not out	15
DJG Sales (capt)		
GP Swann		
*GL Brophy		
BJ Phillips		
J Louw		
PS Jones		
JF Brown		
Extras	nb 2	2
	(2 wkts 18.3 overs)	64

Bowling
Bicknell 9.3-3-29-1. Ormond 6-2-28-1. Azhar Mahmood 3-1-7-0.
Fall of Wickets: 1-27, 2-27

Match drawn -
Surrey (9pts), Northamptonshire (6pts)

WARWICKSHIRE v. GLOUCESTERSHIRE - at Edgbaston

GLOS	First Innings	
CM Spearman	c Hogg b Brown	77
WPC Weston	c Richardson b Pretorius	122
THC Hancock	c Frost b Carter	44
MGN Windows	c Knight b Pretorius	48
CG Taylor (capt)	c Frost b Brown	22
APR Gidman	c Frost b Brown	1
MW Alleyne	lbw b Brown	0
*SJ Adshead	not out	56
AN Bressington	not out	19
JMM Averis		
J Lewis		
Extras	lb 2, w 1, nb 8	11
	(7 wkts dec 106.2 overs)	400

Bowling
Pretorius 18-4-69-2. Carter 13-2-57-1. Brown 26-12-75-4. Bell 4-1-34-0. Richardson 14-1-62-0. Hogg 20-5-61-0. Wagh 8.2-0-35-0. Troughton 3-2-5-0.
Fall of Wickets: 1-120, 2-198, 3-296, 4-309, 5-322, 6-322, 7-335

WARWICKSHIRE	First Innings	
NV Knight (capt)	lbw b Lewis	34
MA Wagh	c Adshead b Averis	0
IR Bell	c Adshead b Averis	0
IJL Trott	b Bressington	76
JO Troughton	c Adshead b Lewis	14
DR Brown	c Alleyne b Lewis	0
GB Hogg	not out	8
*T Frost	not out	0
NM Carter		
A Richardson		
D Pretorius		
Extras	lb 3, nb 4	7
	(6 wkts 33 overs)	139

Bowling
Lewis 12-5-21-3. Averis 7-0-40-2. Gidman 5-0-31-0. Bressington 6-0-38-1. Alleyne 3-2-6-0.
Fall of Wickets: 1-4, 2-4, 3-116, 4-120, 5-124, 6-139

Match drawn - Warwickshire (6pts), Gloucestershire (11pts)

Days two and three were also total washouts at The Oval and the first and second days at Edgbaston, where at least Gloucestershire managed to secure seven precious bonus points by totalling 400 for 7 and then reducing Warwickshire to 139 for 6 in reply. Phil Weston twice pulled Alan Richardson for six in his 122, and the tall left-handed opener featured in stands of 120 with Craig Spearman, who went to a half-century off 39 balls with the first of five successive fours off Ian Bell, 78 with Tim Hancock and 98 with Matt Windows. Reserve wicketkeeper Steve Adshead, signed on a one-year deal as Jack Russell's deputy, also made an early impression with an unbeaten 56.

Scott Newman was the in-form batsman at The Oval, reaching an unbeaten 90 from 104 balls in the 38.4 overs possible on the opening day and then going on to hit 131 when play finally resumed three days later. Azhar Mahmood's 65 took him just 60 balls as Surrey achieved maximum batting points.

Division Two

Shane Warne's Hampshire were the only team to beat the weather in Division Two, completing an innings destruction of Leicestershire at the Rose Bowl, despite the loss of both days two and three. Warne and Dimitri Mascarenhas were largely responsible for Leicestershire's slide to 139 all out on the opening day, and Hampshire reached 93 for 1 in reply before the close. After the frustration of watching the rain fall, the home side then built a lead of 129 with 24-year-old opener Michael Brown completing a maiden first-class hundred for the county he had joined following five fruitless years on the Middlesex staff. Warne's declaration, soon after Brown reached three figures, meant that Leicestershire needed to bat through 53 overs to

Round Three: 28 April–1 May 2004 Division Two

HAMPSHIRE v. LEICESTERSHIRE - at The Rose Bowl

LEICESTERSHIRE	First Innings		Second Innings	
DDJ Robinson	b Mascarenhas	11	b Mascarenhas	8
JK Maunders	b Warne	34	c Kendall b Mascarenhas	23
BJ Hodge	c Clarke b Tremlett	1	(5) c Clarke b Warne	29
DL Maddy	lbw b Udal	7	(3) lbw b Mascarenhas	0
DI Stevens	c Pothas b Mascarenhas	11	(4) b Mascarenhas	3
JL Sadler	c Clarke b Warne	1	c Clarke b Tremlett	7
*PA Nixon	c Pothas b Mascarenhas	0	c Brown b Mascarenhas	3
PAJ DeFreitas (capt)	b Tremlett	24	(9) c Clarke b Warne	0
CW Henderson	lbw b Mullally	31	(8) not out	13
DD Masters	b Mullally	5	b Udal	9
MF Cleary	not out	8	lbw b Udal	4
Extras	b 1, lb 5	6	b 4, lb 2, nb 6	12
	(64 overs)	139	(43.4 overs)	111

Bowling
Mullally 11-4-22-2. Tremlett 14-5-33-2. Mascarenhas 15-9-22-3. Udal 12-3-39-1. Warne 12-6-17-2.
Mullally 11-4-18-0. Tremlett 9-1-35-1. Mascarenhas 10-5-22-5. Warne 11-4-26-2. Udal 2.4-2-4-2.
Fall of Wickets: 1-22, 2-29, 3-56, 4-69, 5-69, 6-70, 7-70, 8-104, 9-126
1-24, 2-26, 3-30, 4-37, 5-66, 6-73, 7-80, 8-80, 9-103

HAMPSHIRE	First Innings	
DA Kenway	c Nixon b DeFreitas	23
MJ Brown	not out	102
WS Kendall	c Nixon b Cleary	38
MJ Clarke	b Cleary	0
LR Prittipaul	st Nixon b Henderson	31
*N Pothas	c Hodge b Cleary	21
AD Mascarenhas	run out	2
SK Warne (capt)	not out	29
CT Tremlett		
AD Mullally		
SD Udal		
Extras	b 13, lb 5, nb 4	22
	(6 wkts dec 72 overs)	268

Bowling
Cleary 17-4-57-3. DeFreitas 22-2-62-1. Masters 11-3-24-0. Henderson 12-1-65-1. Maddy 5-1-23-0. Hodge 5-0-19-0.
Fall of Wickets: 1-48, 2-105, 3-105, 4-175, 5-214, 6-222

*Hampshire won by an innings and 18 runs -
Hampshire (19pts), Leicestershire (2pts)*

ESSEX v. SOMERSET - at Chelmsford

SOMERSET	First Innings	
PD Bowler	not out	187
JD Francis	c Pettini b Stephenson	18
MJ Wood	b Kaneria	34
J Cox	c Jefferson b Brant	22
M Burns (capt)	not out	124
AW Laraman		
*RJ Turner		
KP Dutch		
RL Johnson		
AR Caddick		
NAM McLean		
Extras	b 1, lb 11, w 1, nb 2	15
	(3 wkts dec 124.3 overs)	400

Bowling
Brant 32-7-85-1. Napier 31-5-99-0. Stephenson 13-0-43-1. Kaneria 34.3-8-92-1. Middlebrook 11-0-63-0. Habib 3-0-6-0.
Fall of Wickets: 1-32, 2-127, 3-168

ESSEX	First Innings		Second Innings	
WI Jefferson	c Francis b Dutch	85	c Turner b McLean	0
AN Cook	c Turner b McLean	20	not out	20
A Flower (capt)	run out	1	not out	13
A Habib	c Cox b Dutch	25		
ML Pettini	c Burns b Dutch	10		
*JS Foster	not out	75		
JD Middlebrook	c Turner b Caddick	8		
GR Napier	b Caddick	0		
JP Stephenson	c Burns b Dutch	6		
Danish Kaneria	st Turner b Dutch	0		
SA Brant	run out	1		
Extras		0	w 1, nb 2	3
	(73 overs)	231	(1 wkt 10.1 overs)	36

Bowling
Caddick 28-1-114-2. Johnson 6-5-2-0. Dutch 22-3-65-5. McLean 11-3-31-1. Laraman 6-2-19-0.
McLean 5-1-18-1. Laraman 2-0-14-0. Dutch 3-1-4-0. Caddick 0.1-0-0-0.
Fall of Wickets: 1-62, 2-64, 3-124, 4-131, 5-144, 6-173, 7-173, 8-200, 9-204 1-0.

*Match drawn -
Essex (6pts), Somerset (12pts)*

DERBYSHIRE v. DURHAM - at Derby

DERBYSHIRE	First Innings	
AI Gait	c Pattison b Onions	37
SD Stubbings	c North b Onions	9
CJL Rogers	c Pratt b A Plunkett	156
Hassan Adnan	b Breese	72
CWG Bassano	c Davies b Plunkett	22
*LD Sutton (capt)	c Peng b Pattison	27
DR Hewson	c Pratt A b Davies	9
G Welch	not out	37
AG Botha	c Lewis b Davies	2
KJ Dean	not out	17
NGE Walker		
Extras	b 5, lb 7	12
	(8 wkts dec 120.3 overs)	400

Bowling
Plunkett 26.3-4-71-2. Onions 27-7-99-2. Pattison 13-2-42-1. Davies 23-3-67-2. Bridge 14-3-40-0. Breese 17-2-69-1.
Fall of Wickets: 1-14, 2-103, 3-255, 4-294, 5-326, 6-344, 7-350, 8-360 1-1

DURHAM	First Innings	
JJB Lewis (capt)	b Walker	2
MJ North	c sub b Botha	119
GR Breese	lbw b Dean	15
GJ Pratt	c Sutton b Welch	7
N Peng	b Walker	0
I Pattison	lbw b Welch	23
*A Pratt	c Rogers b Welch	44
LE Plunkett	b Botha	7
GD Bridge	c Welch b Botha	0
M Davies	lbw b Botha	0
G Onions	not out	0
Extras	lb 9, nb 6	15
	(57.5 overs)	232

Bowling
Welch 18-2-64-3. Walker 11-3-55-2. Dean 3.3-1-13-1. Hewson 7-2-25-0. Botha 17.5-6-66-4.
Fall of Wickets: 1-5, 2-45, 3-62, 4-85, 5-172, 6-176, 7-226, 8-232, 9-232

*Match drawn - Derbyshire (12pts),
Durham (7pts)*

NOTTINGHAMSHIRE v. YORKSHIRE - at Trent Bridge

YORKSHIRE	First Innings	
MJ Wood	c Hussey b Shreck	15
C White (capt)	c Gallian b Smith	4
CR Taylor	lbw b Smith	0
DS Lehmann	c Sidebottom b Smith	62
MJ Lumb	c Hussey b Ealham	16
IJ Harvey	c Alleyne b Sidebottom	35
*SM Guy	b Franks	0
RKJ Dawson	c Gallian b Shreck	81
TT Bresnan	c Hussey b Sidebottom	0
CEW Silverwood	c Et b Pietersen	14
JAR Blain	not out	28
Extras	lb 4, w 1, nb 4	9
	(72 overs)	264

Bowling
Smith 16-2-75-3. Shreck 16-2-55-2. Sidebottom 17-2-48-2. Franks 7-0-38-1. Ealham 12-3-38-1. Pietersen 4-1-6-1.
Fall of Wickets: 1-5, 2-5, 3-57, 4-88, 5-113, 6-122, 7-151, 8-151, 9-193

NOTTS	First Innings	
DJ Bicknell	c Guy b Silverwood	41
JER Gallian (capt)	c Guy b Lehmann	133
RJ Warren	b Dawson	9
KP Pietersen	b Bresnan	21
DJ Hussey	run out	18
MA Ealham	c Lumb b Dawson	54
PJ Franks	c Lehmann b Harvey	44
*D Alleyne	not out	14
RJ Sidebottom	b Dawson	3
GJ Smith		
CE Shreck		
Extras	b 2, lb 4, nb 10	16
	(8 wkts 89.4 overs)	353

Bowling
Silverwood 17-2-66-1. Blain 14-1-87-0. Bresnan 12-1-55-1. Dawson 30.4-7-102-3. Lehmann 8-2-21-1. White 5-0-12-0. Harvey 3-2-4-1.
Fall of Wickets: 1-110, 2-151, 3-212, 4-212, 5-260, 6-335, 7-336, 8-353

*Match drawn - Nottinghamshire (11pts),
Yorkshire (8pts)*

Dimitri Mascarenhas continued his magnificent early-summer form with the ball as Hampshire beat the weather to dispose of Leicestershire at the Rose Bowl.

escape with a draw. They could not do it, with Warne claiming the vital wicket of fellow Aussie Brad Hodge for 29, but with Mascarenhas emerging as the chief destroyer with 5 for 22 from just ten overs of impressive swing bowling.

Peter Bowler, 40 years old and in his 19th county season, reached the 44th hundred of his first-class career and went on to make an unbeaten 187 as Somerset got the better of a rain-affected draw against Essex at Chelmsford. Bowler, who batted for one minute short of eight hours, added an unbroken 232 in 61 overs with Mike Burns, who finished on 124 not out when he declared Somerset's first innings at 400 for 3. Keith Dutch then took 5 for 65 with his off breaks as Essex were dismissed for 231, despite excellent knocks from both Will Jefferson (85) and James Foster, who remained unbeaten on 75. Jefferson, however, was out for nought to Nixon McLean when Essex were asked to follow on. More bad weather, which had wiped out the entire second day and allowed just 40 overs on the opening day,

arrived to shorten the final day, too.

Both the first and second days were lost to rain at Derby and neighbouring Trent Bridge, consigning both of the matches between Derbyshire and Durham, and Nottinghamshire and Yorkshire, to draws. Chris Rogers, a 26-year-old from Western Australia, hit two sixes and 18 fours in an eye-catching 156 for Derbyshire, while Hassan Adnan also impressed with 72. A new-look Derbyshire at least made sure of maximum bonus points, despite Marcus North's 119, by bowling Durham out for 232 in reply to their own 400 for 8 declared. At Trent Bridge, a fine 133 from Jason Gallian ensured that Notts won the contest for bonus points, after gritty innings from both Darren Lehmann and Richard Dawson had hauled Yorkshire up to 264.

Round Four: 7–10 May 2004

Division One

Inexplicable caution from Northamptonshire cost them the chance of taking the scalp of champions Sussex at Wantage Road. Batting on deep into the final day, Northants only declared their second innings when the Sussex 'win' target had been raised to 299 in a minimum of 39 overs. As it was, by rushing through their last half-dozen overs like mad things, Northants created time to deliver 44 … but finished up three wickets short of victory. Sussex, who survived for a barely deserved draw at 69 for 7, were left to be mightily thankful for Northants' ultra-conservatism. Beginning the final day on six without loss, an overall lead of 112, Northants took a further 57 overs to reach 192 for 5 – the declaration finally arriving at 3.20 pm. Jason Brown, who had shared eight Sussex first-innings wickets with fellow off spinner Graeme Swann, took another three at minimal cost. Swann, though, only had time for nine rather rushed overs as the clock ticked down. Earlier, in a match badly affected by rain on the second day, Usman Afzaal had celebrated his winter move from Nottinghamshire by completing a career-best 167 not out, a skilful effort full of quality strokes and one which suggested that the best was yet to come for a 26-year-old capped three times by England in 2001, but who had then looked to be losing his way. Swann also batted well in both innings, timing his shots enviably, while Ben Phillips helped in a Northants recovery from 186 for 7 by battling to a courageous 73 from No. 9.

Lancashire dug themselves out of a hole against Middlesex at Lord's by topping 400 in a second

Usman Afzaal, pictured during his brief Test career to date, enjoyed a fine start to life with his new county Northants.

innings based upon a gutsy 103 from Mark Chilton and 91 from Stuart Law. Mal Loye also added 60 to his first-innings 101, and Middlesex were unable to press home the advantage gained from a lead of 102 at the mid-point of the match. Constant weather interruptions did not help the home side, after Chad Keegan's opening day 5 for 36 had put them in control. Andrew Strauss, batting down the order after his arrival back from the West Indies the day before, then struck 95 and – despite seven wickets from the ever-competitive Dominic Cork – Middlesex held most of the cards midway through the third day.

Heavy rain in Canterbury, which led to waterlogged run-ups and areas of the outfield even when the weather finally relented, caused the abandonment of Kent's fixture against Gloucestershire after little more than 71 overs of play on the opening day. At least there was no shortage of action in that time, with Kent being tumbled out for 129 by Jon Lewis (5 for 46) and Shabbir Ahmed, who took 3 for 5 in 14 balls at one stage. Gloucestershire had almost moved past Kent's score, with just five wickets down, when bad weather cut short an intriguing contest.

Round Four: 7–10 May 2004 Division One

NORTHAMPTONSHIRE v. SUSSEX - at Northampton

NORTHANTS	First Innings		Second Innings	
MJ Powell	c Ambrose b Lewry	4	b Martin-Jenkins	15
TW Roberts	c Ambrose b Lewry	1	lbw b Akram	10
M van Jaarsveld	lbw b Mushtaq Ahmed	37	lbw b Mushtaq Ahmed	27
U Afzaal	not out	167	c Adams b Davis	25
DJG Sales (capt)	lbw b Mushtaq Ahmed	27	not out	72
GP Swann	c Ward b Davis	54	c Adams b Mushtaq Ahmed	40
*GL Brophy	c and b Davis	4	not out	0
J Louw	b Davis	0		
BJ Phillips	b Lewry	73		
PS Jones	b Mushtaq Ahmed	12		
JF Brown	not out	1		
Extras	b 9, lb 11	20	lb 1, nb 2	3
	(9 wkts dec 128.5 overs)	400	(5 wkts dec 60 overs)	192

Bowling
Akram 33.5-4-105-0. Lewry 25-8-78-3. Mushtaq Ahmed 32-6-119-3. Martin-Jenkins 19-6-44-0. Davis 15-3-34-3.
Akram 9-3-32-1. Lewry 9-4-23-0. Martin-Jenkins 12-6-22-1. Mushtaq Ahmed 17-4-49-2. Davis 12-0-55-1. Adams 1-0-10-0.
Fall of Wickets: 1-2, 2-19, 3-56, 4-90, 5-178, 6-186, 7-186, 8-322, 9-382
1-27, 2-27, 3-68, 4-92, 5-192

SUSSEX	First Innings		Second Innings	
IJ Ward	c Louw b Swann	115	b Louw	0
RR Montgomerie	c van Jaarsveld b Brown	9	c van Jaarsveld b Phillips	13
MW Goodwin	b Brown	3	c van Jaarsveld b Jones	21
CJ Adams (capt)	st Brophy b Brown	11	c Powell b Brown	15
*TR Ambrose	c Sales b Swann	12	c van Jaarsveld b Phillips	1
RSC Martin-Jenkins	c Sales b Brown	51	c van Jaarsveld b Brown	1
MJ Prior	c Brophy b Swann	32	lbw b Brown	6
MJG Davis	lbw b Brown	6	not out	11
Mushtaq Ahmed	lbw b Jones	27	not out	1
M Akram	run out	19		
JD Lewry	not out	1		
Extras	b 4, lb 4	8		0
	(103.2 overs)	294	(7 wkts 43.4 overs)	69

Bowling
Jones 13-1-51-1. Louw 5.2-1-24-0. Phillips 12-6-24-0. Brown 39-6-93-4. Swann 34-6-94-4.
Louw 6-0-19-1. Jones 5-3-11-1. Brown 16.4-6-20-3. Phillips 7-1-9-2. Swann 9-5-10-0.
Fall of Wickets: 1-47, 2-57, 3-74, 4-96, 5-183, 6-231, 7-247, 8-251, 9-290
1-0, 2-29, 3-43, 4-47, 5-50, 6-55, 7-62

Match drawn - Northamptonshire (12pts), Sussex (9pts)

MIDDLESEX v. LANCASHIRE - at Lord's

LANCASHIRE	First Innings		Second Innings	
MJ Chilton	lbw b Keegan	2	c Joyce b Weekes	103
IJ Sutcliffe	c Klusener b Hayward	21	lbw b Hayward	38
MB Loye	c Shah b Keegan	101	lbw b Weekes	60
SG Law	lbw b Hutchison	33	c Nash b Klusener	91
CL Hooper	lbw b Hutchison	0	not out	33
G Chapple	b Keegan	32	c Nash b Klusener	17
KW Hogg	b Hayward	1	b Klusener	12
DG Cork	lbw b Keegan	0	b Klusener	4
*WK Hegg (capt)	c Joyce b Klusener	36	not out	12
SI Mahmood	lbw b Keegan	5		
G Keedy	not out	1		
Extras	lb 4	4	b 8, lb 17, nb 6	31
	(68.5 overs)	236	(7 wkts dec 118.4 overs)	401

Bowling
Keegan 20-3-36-5. Hayward 17-1-75-2. Klusener 13.5-1-60-1. Hutchison 14-2-40-2. Weekes 4-1-21-0.
Keegan 23-6-70-0. Hayward 18-5-36-1. Hutchison 15-2-52-0. Klusener 23.4-1-89-4. Hutton 9-0-26-0. Weekes 21-4-77-2. Joyce 9-2-26-0.
Fall of Wickets: 1-8, 2-26, 3-104, 4-104, 5-193, 6-194, 7-194, 8-194, 9-203
1-75, 2-180, 3-293, 4-331, 5-353, 6-373, 7-377

MIDDLESEX	First Innings		Second Innings	
SG Koenig	lbw b Cork	3	(2) not out	14
BL Hutton	lbw b Cork	4		
OA Shah	b Chapple	34		
EC Joyce	c Hegg b Chapple	44		
AJ Strauss (capt)	c Hegg b Chapple	95	(1) not out	19
PN Weekes	c Hooper b Cork	50		
*DC Nash	lbw b Cork	19		
L Klusener	c Chilton b Cork	19		
CB Keegan	c ⊟ b Cork	26		
PM Hutchison	not out	7		
M Hayward	b Cork	7		
Extras	b 1, lb 11, nb 18	30	lb 2, nb 6	8
	(95.3 overs)	338	(0 wkts 13 overs)	41

Bowling
Chapple 27-7-83-3. Cork 31.3-6-120-7. Mahmood 11-2-48-0. Hogg 7-2-25-0. Keedy 10-3-35-0. Hooper 9-2-15-0.
Hogg 5-2-16-0. Mahmood 5-3-17-0. Hooper 2-0-4-0. Keedy 1-0-2-0.
Fall of Wickets: 1-3, 2-10, 3-78, 4-119, 5-252, 6-266, 7-294, 8-301, 9-326

Match drawn - Middlesex (10pts), Lancashire (8pts)

KENT v. GLOUCESTERSHIRE - at Canterbury

KENT	First Innings	
DP Fulton (capt)	c Gidman b Shabbir	18
RWT Key	c Hancock b Shabbir	11
ET Smith	c Gidman b Shabbir	9
A Symonds	c Adshead b Lewis	33
MJ Walker	b Lewis	21
MA Carberry	b Averis	4
*GO Jones	c Ball b Lewis	1
JC Tredwell	c Adshead b Lewis	14
MJ Saggers	c Adshead b Averis	3
Mohammad Sami	lbw b Lewis	0
A Sheriyar	not out	0
Extras	lb 1, nb 14	15
	(36.3 overs)	129

Bowling
Shabbir 11-2-34-3. Lewis 12.3-1-46-5. Averis 12-1-39-2. Shoaib Malik 1-0-9-0.
Fall of Wickets: 1-26, 2-33, 3-42, 4-77, 5-82, 6-89, 7-124, 8-129, 9-129

GLOS	First Innings	
WPC Weston	c and b Saggers	6
CM Spearman	c Symonds b Saggers	42
THC Hancock	lbw b Sheriyar	0
Shoaib Malik	c Jones b Symonds	18
CG Taylor (capt)	not out	32
APR Gidman	c Walker b Saggers	4
*SJ Adshead	not out	15
Shabbir Ahmed		
MCJ Ball		
J Lewis		
JMM Averis		
Extras	b 4, lb 4, nb 2	10
	(5 wkts 34.5 overs)	127

Bowling
Saggers 10.5-2-30-3. Mohammad Sami 9-1-22-0. Sheriyar 8-0-41-1. Symonds 6-1-24-1. Tredwell 1-0-2-0.
Fall of Wickets: 1-32, 2-39, 3-73, 4-73, 5-77

Match drawn - Kent (5pts), Gloucestershire (7pts)

Division Two

Derbyshire, full of fresh fight under Dave Houghton's guidance as new coach, held on bravely for a draw against Hampshire at the Rose Bowl. It was a close-run thing, though. Dimitri Mascarenhas took 6 for 25 from 17 overs of skilful swing bowling and, in the end, the Derbyshire last pair of Nick Walker and Mohammad Ali survived 14 balls to deny Shane Warne's side victory. Last man Walker, just 19 years old, had included a straight six off Warne in his first-innings 31 not out, from just 22 balls, and he and Ali had batted well first time around to prevent Hampshire from being able to enforce the follow-on. Ali, in fact, took Derbyshire past the follow-on mark by hoisting Alan Mullally for six over square leg. Chris Rogers, with 87, and Chris Bassano (53) led Derbyshire's first-innings reply to a Hampshire total of 419 for 9 declared that was based largely on centuries by Derek Kenway and Nic Pothas. It was an important innings for Kenway, who averaged just 26 in championship cricket in 2003, although he was also dropped three times. The in-form Pothas finished unbeaten on 131. Afterwards, Warne was man enough to admit that victory had eluded his team largely because of his own poor tactics. 'I had in mind setting them a target of 250 in 65 overs, but I lost my rag when

Hampshire could not quite finish off Derbyshire, despite fine batting from Nic Pothas.

they batted on past 300,' said Warne. 'I didn't want to give them a chance of winning, but later I wondered what might have been if I had declared a few overs earlier. But Derbyshire deserve some credit for hanging on through the 53 overs we bowled at them.'

Durham were glad for the contribution of various weather interruptions that did most to consign their fixture against Essex at the Riverside to a draw. By the end of the match they were struggling on 121 for

Round Four: 7–10 May 2004 Division Two

HAMPSHIRE v. DERBYSHIRE - at The Rose Bowl

HAMPSHIRE	First Innings		Second Innings	
DA Kenway	lbw b Botha	101	c & b Welch	33
MJ Brown	lbw b Mohammad Ali	1	c Sutton b Walker	1
WS Kendall	run out	25	c sub b Welch	19
MJ Clarke	c Sutton b Mohammad Ali	21	c Rogers b Moss	45
LR Prittipaul	c Sutton b Walker	40	c Sutton b Mohammad Ali	25
*N Pothas	not out	131	not out	22
AD Mascarenhas	lbw b Moss	46	b Moss	15
SK Warne (capt)	lbw b Mohammad Ali	4	not out	10
SD Udal	c Stubbings b Welch	27		
CT Tremlett	c Sutton b Mohammad Ali	12		
AD Mullally				
Extras	b 5, lb 3, w 1, nb 2	11	b 3, lb 3, nb 2	8
	(9 wkts dec 124.2 overs)	419	(6 wkts dec 32 overs)	178

Bowling
Mohammad Ali 32.2-8-121-4. Welch 33-8-100-1. Moss 26-5-91-1. Walker 10-1-40-1. Botha 23-2-59-1.
Mohammad Ali 14-3-61-1. Walker 5-0-27-1. Welch 8-0-51-2. Moss 5-0-33-2.
Fall of Wickets: 1-9, 2-53, 3-104, 4-185, 5-203, 6-322, 7-334, 8-378, 9-419
1-12, 2-49, 3-66, 4-128, 5-128, 6-152

DERBYSHIRE	First Innings		Second Innings	
SD Stubbings	c Brown b Warne	24	b Mascarenhas	20
AI Gait	b Mascarenhas	9	c Kenway b Warne	20
CJL Rogers	c & b Tremlett	87	c Warne b Mascarenhas	0
Hassan Adnan	lbw b Tremlett	0	c Kenway b Mascarenhas	0
J Moss	c Kenway b Tremlett	9	b Mascarenhas	12
CWG Bassano	c Pothas b Prittipaul	53	lbw b Tremlett	21
*LD Sutton (capt)	c Warne b Udal	8	c Prittipaul b Mascarenhas	5
G Welch	c Pothas b Mullally	40	b Tremlett	12
AG Botha	b Udal	31	lbw b Mascarenhas	0
Mohammad Ali	c Brown b Tremlett	12	not out	3
NGE Walker	not out	31	not out	0
Extras	b 4, lb 10, nb 6	20	lb 5, nb 4	9
	(107 overs)	324	(9 wkts 53 overs)	102

Bowling
Tremlett 16-4-49-3. Mullally 20-4-58-1. Mascarenhas 10-4-25-1. Warne 26-8-75-1. Udal 22-3-78-3. Clarke 7-1-21-0. Prittipaul 5-0-14-1.
Tremlett 11-3-23-2. Mullally 6-2-14-0. Mascarenhas 17-9-25-6. Prittipaul 2-0-11-0. Warne 14-7-18-1. Udal 3-0-6-0.
Fall of Wickets: 1-19, 2-73, 3-90, 4-104, 5-153, 6-183, 7-221, 8-260, 9-279
1-38, 2-38, 3-40, 4-54, 5-56, 6-80, 7-94, 8-99, 9-101

Match drawn - Hampshire (12pts), Derbyshire (10pts)

DURHAM v. ESSEX - at The Riverside

DURHAM	First Innings		Second Innings	
JJB Lewis (capt)	b Napier	8	b McCoubrey	9
MJ North	c Cook b ten Doeschate	15	lbw b McCoubrey	0
GJ Muchall	lbw b Stephenson	94	c Jefferson b Stephenson	40
GJ Pratt	b Napier	43	c Kaneria b McCoubrey	1
N Peng	c Cook b ten Doeschate	6	c Cook b Stephenson	1
GR Breese	c Cook b Stephenson	42	c Cook b Stephenson	4
*A Pratt	st Foster b Kaneria	20	c Habib b Kaneria	19
I Pattison	c & b Kaneria	26	c Cook b Napier	10
Tahir Mughal	lbw b Kaneria	0	not out	17
N Killeen	lbw b McCoubrey	26	not out	9
M Davies	not out	14		
Extras	lb 8, w 1, nb 36	45	b 2, lb 2, w 1, nb 6	11
	(90 overs)	339	(8 wkts 37 overs)	121

Bowling
Napier 23-6-62-2. McCoubrey 18-2-87-1. ten Doeschate 15-2-52-2. Kaneria 23-5-83-3. Stephenson 11-2-47-2.
Napier 11-4-25-1. McCoubrey 11-2-40-3. ten Doeschate 3-0-16-0. Stephenson 9-2-28-3. Kaneria 3-1-8-1.
Fall of Wickets: 1-12, 2-32, 3-111, 4-124, 5-224, 6-244, 7-285, 8-285, 9-300
1-4, 2-21, 3-23, 4-41, 5-62, 6-63, 7-88, 8-95

ESSEX	First Innings	
AN Cook	c Muchall b Davies	20
N Hussain	c Pratt A b Davies	70
WI Jefferson	lbw b Mughal	31
A Flower (capt)	c Pratt A b Davies	15
A Habib	c North b Pattison	8
*JS Foster	c Pattison b Breese	15
GR Napier	c Pratt A b Mughal	25
JP Stephenson	c North b Davies	40
RN ten Doeschate	c Muchall b Davies	7
Danish Kaneria	c Lewis b Killeen	3
AGM McCoubrey	not out	0
Extras	b 12, lb 7, w 4, nb 8	31
	(85.4 overs)	265

Bowling
Mughal 19-4-54-2. Killeen 21.4-7-68-1. Davies 20-11-30-5. Pattison 12-4-30-1. Breese 13-1-64-1.
Fall of Wickets: 1-39, 2-94, 3-149, 4-164, 5-166, 6-205, 7-239, 8-256, 9-265

Match drawn - Durham (10pts), Essex (9pts)

NOTTINGHAMSHIRE v. GLAMORGAN - at Trent Bridge

GLAMORGAN	First Innings		Second Innings	
MTG Elliott	c Alleyne b Franks	41	c Hussey b MacGill	12
*MA Wallace	c Hussey b Sidebottom	13	c Alleyne b MacGill	24
DL Hemp	c Gallian b Smith	82	not out	23
MJ Powell	b Sidebottom	53	not out	0
MP Maynard	c Gallian b Ealham	11		
A Dale	c Alleyne b Ealham	2		
RDB Croft (capt)	c Pietersen b Ealham	2		
SD Thomas	c Pietersen b Sidebottom	13		
AG Wharf	b Sidebottom	0		
DS Harrison	not out	32		
SP Jones	c Bicknell b Sidebottom	11		
Extras	b 1, lb 4, w 3, nb 6	14	lb 2, nb 10	12
	(84.1 overs)	274	(2 wkts 20 overs)	73

Bowling
Smith 18-5-56-1. Sidebottom 25.1-6-86-5. Franks 13-0-45-1. Ealham 20-8-55-3. MacGill 8-3-27-0.
MacGill 10-2-32-2. Pietersen 8-0-33-0. Hussey 2-0-6-0.
Fall of Wickets: 1-30, 2-72, 3-167, 4-180, 5-194, 6-196, 7-221, 8-229, 9-231
1-16, 2-65

NOTTS	First Innings	
DJ Bicknell	c Hemp b Jones	20
JER Gallian (capt)	c Elliott b Wharf	0
RJ Warren	lbw b Harrison	97
KP Pietersen	c Wharf b Thomas	70
DJ Hussey	c Wallace b Jones	55
MA Ealham	c Wharf b Jones	10
PJ Franks	b Croft	45
*D Alleyne	c Wallace b Thomas	28
GJ Smith	c Harrison b Jones	30
RJ Sidebottom	not out	15
SCG MacGill	c Harrison b Croft	0
Extras	b 4, lb 4, w 2, nb 4	14
	(112.1 overs)	384

Bowling
Harrison 17-0-64-1. Wharf 25-7-76-1. Thomas 19-2-82-2. Jones 25-5-98-4. Croft 26.1-9-56-2.
Fall of Wickets: 1-1, 2-40, 3-176, 4-212, 5-257, 6-260, 7-328, 8-351, 9-382

Match drawn - Nottinghamshire (11pts), Glamorgan (9pts)

8 in their second innings, a lead of only 195. Gordon Muchall was the pick of the home batsmen, with scores of 94 and 40, while seamer Mark Davies included the scalp of former England captain Nasser Hussain, for 70, in his bag of 5 for 30 from 20 overs.

Weather problems at Trent Bridge, costing 185 overs of lost play over the four days, made a draw the inevitable result in the match between Nottinghamshire and Glamorgan. Simon Jones, the England fast bowler, picked up Darren Bicknell's wicket with the first ball of his first championship appearance since August 2002, and ended up with four in total as Notts reached a first-innings 384. That earned the home team a lead of 110, but there was only time to reduce Glamorgan to 73 for 2 in their second innings before proceedings were brought to a premature halt.

Round Five: 12–15 May 2004

Division One

James Anderson, bowling with the fire of a man keen to get himself back into England Test reckoning, spearheaded Lancashire's 219-run victory over Worcestershire at Old Trafford. Anderson took ten wickets in the match, including a first-innings haul of 6 for 49, while left-arm spinner Gary Keedy was almost as deadly with an impressive nine-wicket haul. In a low-scoring affair, the batting of Iain Sutcliffe and Carl Hooper also played an important role in Lancashire's win. Hooper scored the 69th first-class hundred of his career in the Lancashire second innings, while opener Sutcliffe grafted his way to 95. Between them, they put the game beyond Worcestershire, who lost Graeme Hick to Anderson for the second time in three days as they slid to 127 all out. Mal Loye's unbeaten 59, from No. 3, was another worthy Lancashire effort in their first innings of 187.

Surrey, initially all at sea against Warwickshire at Edgbaston, looked to have staged one of the best comebacks of recent championship history … before throwing it all away again on the final afternoon and finishing up losing the match by seven wickets. The first four sessions belonged to Warwickshire's batsmen, capped off by a seventh-wicket stand of 191 between Brad Hogg and Ashley Giles. Australian spinner Hogg's career-best 158 included a six and 19 fours, while Giles hit 70. At 133 for 6, in reply to Warwickshire's 546, Surrey seemed doomed. However, under-pressure skipper Jon Batty, with his team disintegrating around him, found support at first from Martin Bicknell in a stand of 50 and then with Ian Salisbury in an eighth-wicket partnership of 84. When Surrey were eventually all out for 302, Batty was still unbeaten

Round Five: 12–15 May 2004 Division One

LANCASHIRE v. WORCESTERSHIRE - at Old Trafford

LANCASHIRE	First Innings		Second Innings	
MJ Chilton	c Hick b Hall	28	lbw b Batty	12
IJ Sutcliffe	c Moore b Bichel	9	c Rhodes b Hall	95
MB Loye	not out	59	(7) c Smith b Batty	20
SG Law	c Kadeer Ali b Mason	8	(3) c Kadeer Ali b Mason	0
CL Hooper	c Peters b Mason	1	(4) c Rhodes b Bichel	100
G Chapple	c Hall b Bichel	21	c Rhodes b Mason	38
DG Cork	b Hall	15	(8) b Bichel	1
*WK Hegg (capt)	c Hick b Malik	15	(9) not out	21
PJ Martin	c Hick b Malik	0	(10) lbw b Malik	2
G Keedy	c Smith b Batty	1	(5) c Rhodes b Batty	1
JM Anderson	c Smith b Batty	0	c Hick b Bichel	3
Extras	b 4, lb 8, nb 12	24	b 2, lb 10	12
	(69 overs)	187	(110.2 overs)	305

Bowling
Bichel 20-3-51-2. Mason 20-7-52-2. Malik 14-5-26-2. Hall 8-0-37-2. Batty 7-4-9-2. Bichel 20.2-6-64-3. Mason 25-8-60-2. Batty 37-8-111-3. Hall 15-5-34-1. Malik 13-3-24-1.
Fall of Wickets: 1-15, 2-44, 3-46, 4-63, 5-87, 6-117, 7-119, 8-119, 9-179 1-31, 2-32, 3-200, 4-209, 5-225, 6-264, 7-265, 8-288, 9-295

WORCS	First Innings		Second Innings	
SD Peters	c Hegg b Keedy	41	c Chilton b Anderson	10
SC Moore	b Anderson	8	st Hegg b Keedy	45
GA Hick	b Anderson	3	c Hooper b Anderson	4
BF Smith (capt)	c Law b Keedy	23	c Keedy b Anderson	10
MN Malik	b Anderson	2	(11) lbw b Anderson	0
Kadeer Ali	c Hegg b Anderson	0	(5) c Cork b Keedy	6
AJ Hall	c Law b Keedy	34	(6) lbw b Chapple	7
GJ Batty	lbw b Anderson	0	(7) not out	31
AJ Bichel	b Anderson	3	(8) c Hegg b Keedy	4
*SJ Rhodes	not out	19	(9) lbw b Keedy	6
MS Mason	st Hegg b Keedy	10	(10) c Law b Keedy	0
Extras	b 1, lb 2	3		0
	(59.2 overs)	127	(42.3 overs)	146

Bowling
Martin 16-4-36-0. Anderson 17-2-49-6. Chapple 14-4-32-0. Cork 4-1-6-0. Keedy 8.2-3-20-4.
Martin 3-1-8-0. Anderson 10.3-1-32-4. Keedy 19-4-62-5. Chapple 8-2-18-1. Hooper 2-1-7-0.
Fall of Wickets: 1-18, 2-36, 3-76, 4-77, 5-77, 6-88, 7-94, 8-102, 9-125 1-22, 2-26, 3-40, 4-61, 5-72, 6-90, 7-112, 8-120, 9-126

Lancashire won by 219 runs - Lancashire (17pts), Worcestershire (3pts)

WARWICKSHIRE v. SURREY - at Edgbaston

WARWICKSHIRE	First Innings		Second Innings	
NV Knight (capt)	c Batty b Saqlain Mushtaq	28	(2) not out	62
MA Wagh	c Azhar Mahmood b Ormond	0	(3) lbw b Saqlain Mushtaq	12
IR Bell	c Ramprakash b Saqlain Mushtaq	34	(4) b Saqlain Mushtaq	31
IJL Trott	lbw b Saqlain Mushtaq	61	(5) not out	35
JO Troughton	st Batty b Salisbury	77		
DR Brown	c Ramprakash b Bicknell	44		
GB Hogg	c Batty b Bicknell	158		
AF Giles	c Azhar Mahmood b Salisbury	70		
*T Frost	c Batty b Bicknell	10		
NM Carter	c Ramprakash b Bicknell	29	(1) run out	24
D Pretorius	not out	2		
Extras	b 11, lb 13, nb 9	33	b 2, lb 3, nb 2	7
	(144.3 overs)	546	(3 wkts dec 32.5 overs)	171

Bowling
Bicknell 27.3-5-130-4. Ormond 29-2-103-1. Saqlain Mushtaq 32-5-77-3. Azhar Mahmood 20-4-94-0. Salisbury 32-8-97-2. Holliaoke 4-0-21-0.
Bicknell 8-0-37-0. Ormond 8-0-48-0. Saqlain Mushtaq 12-1-49-2. Azhar Mahmood 1-0-6-0. Salisbury 7.5-0-44-0.
Fall of Wickets: 1-14, 2-64, 3-71, 4-190, 5-242, 6-306, 7-497, 8-505, 9-544 1-47, 2-64, 3-114

SURREY	First Innings		Second Innings	
SA Newman	c Frost b Pretorius	28	c Knight b Wagh	55
MA Butcher	c Bell b Carter	0	b Pretorius	184
MR Ramprakash	c Wagh b Carter	11	c Pretorius b Giles	35
GP Thorpe	c Frost b Wagh	42	c Frost b Pretorius	89
*JN Batty (capt)	not out	92	b Pretorius	4
AJ Hollioake	c & b Wagh	0	c Frost b Carter	7
Azhar Mahmood	lbw b Hogg	27	c Knight b Carter	7
MP Bicknell	lbw b Giles	37	b Brown	21
IDK Salisbury	lbw b Giles	34	c Wagh b Carter	0
J Ormond	c Carter b Giles	4	not out	3
Saqlain Mushtaq	c Brown b Hogg	14	lbw b Brown	0
Extras	lb 8, w 5	13	lb 5, lb 7	12
	(122 overs)	302	(119.3 overs)	414

Bowling
Pretorius 11-2-47-1. Carter 9-5-22-2. Giles 35-13-55-3. Brown 4-0-14-0. Wagh 26-9-60-2. Hogg 24-0-87-2. Troughton 13-5-9-0.
Pretorius 18-2-88-3. Carter 14-2-39-3. Bell 3-1-10-0. Giles 27-4-73-1. Brown 15.3-3-40-2. Wagh 18-2-65-0. Wagh 18-2-69-1. Troughton 6-0-18-0.
Fall of Wickets: 1-2, 2-32, 3-50, 4-98, 5-98, 6-133, 7-183, 8-267, 9-275 1-124, 2-186, 3-364, 4-382, 5-383, 6-387, 7-395, 8-395, 9-414

Warwickshire won by 7 wickets - Warwickshire (22pts), Surrey (5pts)

GLOUCESTERSHIRE v. NORTHAMPTONSHIRE - at Bristol

NORTHANTS	First Innings		Second Innings	
MJ Powell	c Spearman b Averis	21	c Weston b Shoaib Malik	33
TW Roberts	c Taylor b Gidman	16	b Shoaib Malik	68
M van Jaarsveld	lbw b Gidman	7	c Weston b Lewis	84
U Afzaal	st Adshead b Shoaib Malik	63	run out	64
DJG Sales (capt)	c Spearman b Averis	11	lbw b Gidman	43
GP Swann	b Averis	14	lbw b Shoaib Malik	8
*GL Brophy	b Averis	0	c Spearman b Weston	58
J Louw	not out	26	not out	34
BJ Phillips	c Shoaib Malik b Averis	6	not out	0
PS Jones	c Windows b Shoaib Malik	11		
JF Brown	b Averis	0		
Extras	b 4, lb 8, w 1, nb 30	43	b 5, lb 13, w 1, nb 16	35
	(72 overs)	218	(7 wkts 165 overs)	427

Bowling
Shabbir 16.2-3-78-0. Lewis 17-7-31-1. Averis 19-7-32-6. Gidman 8.4-1-35-1. Shoaib Malik 11-3-30-2.
Lewis 35-13-60-1. Shabbir 5-1-27-0. Averis 28-5-86-0. Gidman 30-10-78-1. Shoaib Malik 45-14-109-3. Hancock 19-5-41-0. Weston 3-1-8-1.
Fall of Wickets: 1-36, 2-52, 3-56, 4-67, 5-90, 6-102, 7-189, 8-200, 9-213 1-111, 2-148, 3-253, 4-294, 5-322, 6-324, 7-420

GLOS	First Innings			
CM Spearman	b Brown	139		
WPC Weston	c Roberts b Phillips	36		
THC Hancock	c Brophy b Brown	65		
MGN Windows	b Swann	31		
CG Taylor (capt)	c Brophy b Phillips	18		
APR Gidman	lbw b Louw	68		
Shoaib Malik	b Louw	63		
*SJ Adshead	lbw b Phillips	14		
JMM Averis	lbw b Phillips	1		
J Lewis	c Sales b Phillips	7		
Shabbir Ahmed	not out	2		
Extras	b 6, lb 14, nb 10	30		
	(154.1 overs)	474		

Bowling
Louw 35-12-81-2. Jones 39-7-115-0. Phillips 34.1-4-106-5. Brown 30-4-83-2. Swann 16-1-69-1.
Fall of Wickets: 1-102, 2-245, 3-260, 4-298, 5-335, 6-439, 7-456, 8-462, 9-471

Match drawn - Gloucestershire (12pts), Northamptonshire (6pts)

on 92 – an innings of huge character, and spread over five-and-a-half hours of bloody-minded defiance. It seemed to have inspired his team-mates, too. Scott Newman helped Mark Butcher to put on 124 for the first wicket, after Surrey were predictably asked to follow on, and by the close of the third day, Butcher was still there on 114. Moreover, an overnight score of 243 for 2 had become 364 for 2 shortly before lunch on the final morning, with Butcher and Graham Thorpe taking their third-wicket stand to 178. Then, however, came the collapse to 414 all out – with Dewald Pretorius and Neil Carter snapping up three wickets apiece. Adam Hollioake, who bagged a pair, gloved a snorter from Carter. That left Warwickshire with 41 overs to score 171, and Nick Knight's unbeaten 62 ensured that they reached it with ease.

A career-best 6 for 32 by James Averis looked as if it would propel Gloucestershire to victory against Northamptonshire at Bristol, with the visitors tumbled out for 218 on the opening day and the home side replying with 474. However, Northants batted solidly all the way down the order in their second innings, with Tim Roberts, Martin van Jaarsfeld and Gerard Brophy all topping 50 and Usman Afzaal continuing his eye-catching early-season form by adding 64 to his first-innings 63. It was an unhappy match for Shabbir Ahmed, one of Gloucestershire's two Pakistani overseas players. On day one, Shabbir refused to continue bowling at the Jessop End because of a fear of slipping in his run-up – this despite Jon Lewis having just completed a lengthy opening spell from the same end without mishap or complaint – and he finished the game with a hamstring strain. Craig Spearman's attractive 139 set up Gloucestershire's first-innings total, with Ben Phillips taking 3 for 8 in 13 balls to snip off the tail and give himself the worthy figures of 5 for 106.

Division Two

A remarkable innings of 165 not out from Gareth Breese, coupled with some equally heroic contributions from the lower order, swept Durham to an astonishing one-wicket win over shell-shocked Somerset at Taunton. Breese, the Jamaican captain who played one Test for the West Indies in 2002 but who holds EU qualifications, led a Durham counter-attack from the depths of 95 for 5 after they had been set a massive 451 to win. Nicky Peng's 88 began the rally, but Breese was the chief architect of an astounding success. Andy Pratt, Shoaib Akhtar with 46, Neil Killeen with 35, and finally Mark Davies also played a part as a Somerset

attack led by Andy Caddick and Richard Johnson was humbled. Caddick had taken four early second-innings wickets, following Johnson's seven-wicket destruction of the Durham first innings, but neither could find a way of denying Breese and company on a memorable final day. Johnson, indeed, finished with figures of 0 for 141, itself an incredible contrast with his 7 for 69 only two days earlier. The match had begun encouragingly for Somerset. James Hildreth, the 19-year-old batsman playing in only his second championship game, included some classy cover driving in his 101, and there were also half-centuries for Jamie Cox, Keith Parsons and Keith Dutch. Having established a first-innings lead of 140, Somerset then set about the Durham bowling for a second time, with Cox hitting two sixes and 14 fours as he moved to a 50th first-class century and with young Hildreth again enjoying himself immensely with 72. How were Somerset to know, when they declared at 310 for 5, that they were going to regret it?

There was perhaps an even better game of cricket

In what turned out to be his final innings for Essex, Nasser Hussain scored 102 against Glamorgan at Cardiff.

at Cardiff. There were no declarations in a contest so closely fought that, by the end of four days uninterrupted by the weather, Essex were just eight runs short of forcing a tie … and with their last-wicket pair at the crease. Glamorgan were docked

Round Five: 12–15 May 2004 Division Two

SOMERSET v. DURHAM - at Taunton

SOMERSET	First Innings		Second Innings	
PD Bowler	lbw b Collingwood	12	lbw b Davies	25
NJ Edwards	lbw b Davies	23	c Lewis b Davies	30
MJ Wood	lbw b Muchall	5	c Collingwood b Killeen	7
J Cox (capt)	c Pratt GJ b Shoaib Akhtar	66	c Killeen b North	124
JC Hildreth	c Pratt A b Shoaib Akhtar	101	c Collingwood b Breese	37
KA Parsons	lbw b Davies	55	not out	36
*RJ Turner	lbw b Shoaib Akhtar	0		
KP Dutch	b Killeen	72		
RL Johnson	lbw b Killeen	1		
AR Caddick	c Breese b Davies	8		
NAM McLean	not out	14		
Extras	b 1, lb 6, w 9, nb 2	18	b 8, lb 7, w 1	16
	(99 overs)	375	(5 wkts dec 87.4 overs)	310

Bowling
Shoaib Akhtar 14-3-63-3. Killeen 20-5-56-2. Collingwood 14-4-50-1.
Davies 22-6-55-3. Muchall 5-0-33-1. Breese 18-3-85-0. North 6-0-26-0.
Shoaib Akhtar 13-3-45-0. Killeen 20-3-59-1. Davies 20-3-69-2.
Collingwood 12-3-37-0. Breese 21-1-79-1. North 1.4-0-6-1.
Fall of Wickets: 1-42, 2-42, 3-52, 4-222, 5-223, 6-223, 7-350, 8-352, 9-354
1-59, 2-62, 3-77, 4-217, 5-310

DURHAM	First Innings		Second Innings	
JJB Lewis (capt)	b Johnson	65	c Turner b Caddick	2
MJ North	lbw b Johnson	20	c Turner b Caddick	33
GJ Muchall	c Turner b Johnson	0	b McLean	19
PD Collingwood	c Hildreth b Johnson	9	lbw b Caddick	4
N Peng	lbw b Caddick	0	lbw b Caddick	88
GJ Pratt	c Turner b McLean	1	c Edwards b Caddick	12
GR Breese	c Turner b Johnson	41	not out	165
*A Pratt	not out	46	c Edwards b Dutch	25
Shoaib Akhtar	b McLean	25	c Wood b Dutch	46
N Killeen	lbw b Johnson	3	b McLean	35
M Davies	c Turner b Johnson	10	not out	4
Extras	b 2, lb 5, nb 8	15	lb 16, nb 4	20
	(72 overs)	235	(9 wkts 113.5 overs)	453

Bowling
Caddick 21-5-53-1. Johnson 23-4-69-7. McLean 9-3-58-2. Parsons 9-2-48-0.
Caddick 42-8-149-5. Johnson 31-5-4-141-0. McLean 31-4-93-2. Parsons 2-0-13-0.
Hildreth 1-0-4-0. Dutch 6-0-37-2.
Fall of Wickets: 1-46, 2-46, 3-60, 4-70, 5-71, 6-136, 7-145, 8-199, 9-209
1-10, 2-57, 3-57, 4-75, 5-95, 6-226, 7-269, 8-357, 9-433

Durham won by 1 wicket - Somerset (7pts), Durham (18pts)

1.5 points for a slow over rate, but this was a great match in which both teams can claim credit. Glamorgan's first-innings 435 was based on a 143-run second-wicket stand between century-maker Matthew Elliott and David Hemp and boosted by a fifth-wicket partnership of 112 by Matthew Maynard and Adrian Dale and then a thumping late-order 78 off 92 balls from Alex Wharf. Essex, initially 115 for 5 in reply, rallied through Aftab Habib's 157 – his best for Essex – and an innings of 80 on his 27th birthday by James Middlebrook. They put on 170 for the sixth wicket, setting the stage for Graham Napier to blast 82 off 104 balls and earn Essex a two-run lead. Maynard and Mike Powell batted well in Glamorgan's second-innings total of 335, but Nasser Hussain, in what was to prove to be his final innings for Essex, almost inspired his county to victory with a determined 102. He and Alistair Cook added 124 for the first wicket, and then Andy Flower's 66 kept them in the hunt for a target of 334 in 69 overs. In the end, Napier and No. 11 Adrian McCoubrey were at the crease as the exciting draw was confirmed.

In an eagerly-awaited clash at Headingley, it was Hampshire who emerged as 119-run winners over Yorkshire to underline their Division Two promotion credentials. Put in by Craig White, Hampshire reached 322 with Nic Pothas scoring 100 and Dimitri Mascarenhas blitzing 11 fours in his 62-ball 49. Yorkshire managed to reach 316 in reply, as irregular bounce and seam movement became more marked

---

GLAMORGAN v. ESSEX - at Cardiff

GLAMORGAN	First Innings		Second Innings	
MTG Elliott	b Middlebrook	114	c Flower b Napier	11
*MA Wallace	c Foster b Napier	0	b Kaneria	14
DL Hemp	b Kaneria	55	c Foster b Napier	14
MJ Powell	st Foster b Kaneria	21	b Kaneria	61
MP Maynard	lbw b Napier	64	c Flower b Middlebrook	6
A Dale	c Foster b Napier	44	(10) not out	28
RDB Croft (capt)	lbw b Kaneria	14	(6) c Cook b Middlebrook	27
DS Harrison	b Gough	0	(7) run out	2
AG Wharf	b Middlebrook	78	(8) b Middlebrook	15
SD Thomas	c Hussain b Napier	23	(9) c Hussain b Gough	39
SP Jones	not out	2	b Middlebrook	35
Extras	b 6, lb 10, nb 6	22	b 10, lb 23, w 1	34
	(94 overs)	435	(98 overs)	335

Bowling
Gough 23-6-77-1. Napier 26-5-91-4. McCoubrey 14-3-59-0. Middlebrook 24.2-4-70-2.
Kaneria 42-9-111-3. Habib 3-1-11-0.
Gough 16-2-61-1. Kaneria 45-13-91-2. Napier 7-1-31-2. McCoubrey 3-0-27-0.
Middlebrook 30-5-92-4.
Fall of Wickets: 1-4, 2-147, 3-195, 4-207, 5-319, 6-324, 7-327, 8-340, 9-404
1-27, 2-46, 3-58, 4-159, 5-217, 6-223, 7-233, 8-291, 9-335

ESSEX	First Innings		Second Innings	
AN Cook	c Croft b Harrison	10	c Wallace b Thomas	51
N Hussain	lbw b Harrison	0	c Maynard b Thomas	102
WI Jefferson	c Wallace b Harrison	4	c Wallace b Jones	5
A Flower (capt)	lbw b Wharf	38	c Jones b Thomas	66
A Habib	b Harrison	157	lbw b Thomas	2
*JS Foster	c Maynard b Croft	17	c Thomas b Jones	6
JD Middlebrook	c Maynard b Thomas	80	b Jones	28
GR Napier	c Maynard b Thomas	82	not out	13
D Gough	c sub b Harrison	16	c sub b Wharf	3
Danish Kaneria	not out	14	lbw b Wharf	0
AGAM McCoubrey	lbw b Thomas	0	not out	20
Extras	lb 6, w 2, nb 12	20	b 5, lb 17, w 1, nb 6	29
	(131.2 overs)	437	(9 wkts 69 overs)	325

Bowling
Harrison 28.1-11-99-5. Thomas 19.3-1-85-3. Croft 21-1-95-1. Jones 22-3-75-0.
Wharf 14-0-77-1.
Harrison 11-1-63-0. Wharf 15-0-71-2. Croft 20-2-78-0. Thomas 11-0-47-4.
Jones 12-0-44-3.
Fall of Wickets: 1-1, 2-10, 3-25, 4-88, 5-115, 6-285, 7-365, 8-401, 9-437
1-124, 2-138, 3-215, 4-228, 5-249, 6-287, 7-311, 8-316, 9-316

Match drawn - Glamorgan (10.5pts - 1.5pts deducted for slow over rate), Essex (12pts)

YORKSHIRE v. HAMPSHIRE - at Headingley

HAMPSHIRE	First Innings		Second Innings	
DA Kenway	c Jaques b Hoggard	4	lbw b Silverwood	20
MJ Brown	lbw b Blain	13	lbw b Blain	20
WS Kendall (capt)	c Wood b Blain	50	c Guy b Silverwood	6
MJ Clarke	b Blain	11	c Jaques b Silverwood	6
LR Prittipaul	c Guy b Harvey	12	lbw b Blain	17
*N Pothas	c Hoggard b Silverwood	100	c Guy b White	77
AD Mascarenhas	c Guy b Dawson	49	c Lumb b Blain	25
SD Udal	c Et b Silverwood	21	c McGrath b White	52
CT Tremlett	b White	13	b Dawson	35
BV Taylor	c Harvey b Silverwood	12	run out	7
AD Mullally	not out	1	not out	22
Extras	b 4, lb 17, w 1, nb 14	36	b 12, lb 8, nb 12	32
	(80.4 overs)	322	(72.4 overs)	313

Bowling
Hoggard 22-5-64-1. Silverwood 17-6-61-3. Blain 19-5-63-3. Harvey 14-4-32-1.
McGrath 8-2-30-0. Dawson 6-1-26-1. White 8-1-11-2.
Hoggard 15-1-60-0. Silverwood 15-3-47-3. Blain 14-1-76-3. White 11-1-46-2.
Harvey 11-3-37-0. Dawson 5.4-1-27-1. McGrath 1-1-0-0.
Fall of Wickets: 1-4, 2-54, 3-80, 4-97, 5-115, 6-195, 7-250, 8-279, 9-317
1-29, 2-29, 3-34, 4-64, 5-73, 6-147, 7-219, 8-284, 9-284

YORKSHIRE	First Innings		Second Innings	
MJ Wood	c Clarke b Mullally	16	c Kenway b Mascarenhas	45
C White (capt)	c Clarke b Tremlett	17	c Pothas b Taylor	36
A McGrath	c Pothas b Mascarenhas	37	lbw b Tremlett	18
PA Jaques	b Taylor	31	c Kenway b Mascarenhas	78
MJ Lumb	c Et b Udal	83	c Clarke b Mascarenhas	0
IJ Harvey	c Udal b Tremlett	22	c Clarke b Mascarenhas	8
*SM Guy	c Kendall b Taylor	7	c Prittipaul b Taylor	8
RKJ Dawson	c Pothas b Tremlett	35	b Taylor	10
CEW Silverwood	lbw b Udal	30	b Tremlett	10
JAR Blain	lbw b Udal	6	b Mascarenhas	4
MJ Hoggard	not out	2	not out	1
Extras	b 9, lb 8, w 5, nb 8	30	lb 3, nb 14	17
	(94 overs)	316	(55.5 overs)	200

Bowling
Mullally 19.4-71-1. Tremlett 21-3-77-3. Mascarenhas 19-3-85-1. Taylor 14-4-46-2.
Clarke 1-0-5-0. Prittipaul 2-0-7-0. Udal 4.4-1-8-3.
Tremlett 15-3-56-2. Mullally 14-3-47-0. Taylor 13-2-50-3. Mascarenhas 13.5-2-44-5.
Fall of Wickets: 1-40, 2-40, 3-110, 4-116, 5-170, 6-193, 7-246, 8-295, 9-305
1-35, 2-79, 3-85, 4-85, 5-89, 6-130, 7-150, 8-172, 9-181

Hampshire won by 119 runs - Yorkshire (6pts), Hampshire (20pts)

LEICESTERSHIRE v. NOTTINGHAMSHIRE - at Leicester

LEICESTERSHIRE	First Innings		Second Innings	
DDJ Robinson	lbw b Sidebottom	4	c Hussey b MacGill	98
JK Maunders	lbw b Shreck	0	lbw b Sidebottom	0
BJ Hodge	b Ealham	30	b Sidebottom	36
DL Maddy	c Gallian b Shreck	3	c Read b Ealham	53
JL Sadler	b Shreck	62	b Shreck	72
JN Snape	lbw b Ealham	0	c Read b Shreck	66
*PA Nixon	c Hussey b Shreck	11	c Read b Shreck	0
PAJ DeFreitas (capt)	c Hussey b Shreck	10	c Read b Franks	10
OD Gibson	not out	57	st Read b Ealham	30
CW Henderson	c Hussey b Shreck	4	(11) not out	8
JM Dakin	lbw b Sidebottom	32	(10) c Pietersen b Sidebottom	34
Extras	lb 8, w 2	10	lb 14, lb 8, w 1	23
	(70 overs)	223	(125.2 overs)	430

Bowling
Shreck 19-5-73-4. Sidebottom 19-7-52-4. Ealham 13-3-30-2. Franks 9-3-19-0.
MacGill 10-1-41-0.
Sidebottom 28.2-4-98-3. Shreck 31-7-87-3. Franks 22-5-92-1. Ealham 15-5-34-2.
Pietersen 6-1-23-0. MacGill 23-3-74-1.
Fall of Wickets: 1-3, 2-9, 3-18, 4-61, 5-63, 6-102, 7-124, 8-128, 9-136
1-3, 2-55, 3-175, 4-221, 5-310, 6-318, 7-337, 8-373, 9-391

NOTTS	First Innings		Second Innings	
DJ Bicknell	b Gibson	17	lbw b Gibson	4
JER Gallian (capt)	b Gibson	1	b DeFreitas	24
RJ Warren	c Robinson b Gibson	72	(4) b Gibson	7
KP Pietersen	c Nixon b Dakin	32	(5) lbw b DeFreitas	2
RJ Sidebottom	lbw b Gibson	0	(3) lbw b Gibson	1
DJ Hussey	c Nixon b DeFreitas	5	c Nixon b DeFreitas	0
*CMW Read	c Henderson b Maddy	31	b Gibson	6
MA Ealham	c Henderson b Maddy	139	c Snape b Gibson	85
PJ Franks	c Maddy b DeFreitas	45	c Sadler b Gibson	51
SCG MacGill	c Sadler b Gibson	1	c Henderson b Maddy	10
CE Shreck	not out	1	not out	0
Extras	b 6, lb 4	10	lb 7, nb 2	5
	(110.4 overs)	366	(70.2 overs)	195

Bowling
Gibson 24-8-98-5. Dakin 24-9-76-1. DeFreitas 26-8-81-2. Maddy 13.4-1-56-2.
Henderson 15-6-33-0. Hodge 6-2-12-0.
Gibson 17-7-43-6. DeFreitas 17-3-53-3. Henderson 16-7-31-0. Dakin 5-1-17-0.
Maddy 11.2-2-35-1. Hodge 4-1-9-0.
Fall of Wickets: 1-3, 2-28, 3-84, 4-90, 5-99, 6-150, 7-172, 8-281, 9-286
1-0, 2-2, 3-12, 4-15, 5-15, 6-22, 7-88, 8-185, 9-195

Leicestershire won by 92 runs - Leicestershire (18pts), Nottinghamshire (7pts)

on the second day. At 114 for 5 by the close, Hampshire were vulnerable, but Pothas again came good with 77 – including two sixes and ten fours – and there were equally valuable lower-order contributions from Shaun Udal, Chris Tremlett and Alan Mullally. Set 320 by Hampshire's gutsy progress to 313, Yorkshire found few answers to the swing and seam of Mascarenhas (5 for 44) and Billy Taylor.

Leicestershire withstood some hurricane hitting by Mark Ealham, and a first-innings deficit of 143, to turn the tables on Nottinghamshire with a 92-run victory at Grace Road. Ealham's first-innings 139 off 168 balls, with eight sixes – four of them off successive balls by Jon Dakin – threatened to take the game away from the home side. It rallied them from 172 for 7, in reply to a Leicestershire first innings boosted by an 87-run last-wicket stand between Ottis Gibson and Dakin – with Ealham dominating stands of 109 and 80 with Paul Franks and Charlie Shreck. But Darren Robinson, who had dropped Ealham on four, then went some way towards atoning for his error by hitting 98 and, with half-centuries from Darren Maddy, John Sadler and Jeremy Snape, Leicestershire managed to haul themselves up to 430. Gibson then sent back both Darren Bicknell and Ryan Sidebottom to leave Notts on 2 for 2 at the close of the third day, and the West Indian went on to take 6 for 43 as he and Phil DeFreitas dismissed the visitors for 195. This time not even Ealham's 85, and a 50 by Franks, could save Notts.

Round Six: 18–22 May 2004

Division One

Kent moved to the top of the championship table with a toughed-out 145-run victory over Northamptonshire at Wantage Road. Pakistan speedster Mohammad Sami was their spearhead, taking ten wickets in the match, but there were also important contributions with the bat from Andy Symonds, Rob Key and David Fulton, plus six more comeback wickets for left-arm spinner Min Patel. Symonds hit one six and 14 fours in a strong-armed 107 on day one to hold Kent's batting together; only reserve wicketkeeper Niall O'Brien otherwise stood out, with an unbeaten 32, as Johann Louw (4 for 33) proved the pick of the home attack. Northants, however, could not get past Kent's first-innings total of 254, despite the fact that three of their top order got themselves established. Sami yorked three batsmen in the space of six balls: the ideal way to negate a sluggish surface. By the close of the second

day, however, Kent's position had been much strengthened by an unbroken partnership of 103 between openers Fulton and Key. The stand grew to 222 the next day, before Fulton was dismissed for 109, but Key went on to reach 173 – with four sixes and 20 fours – while Symonds bludgeoned 61. Kent's declaration at 405 for 6 left Northants with an awkward 13 overs to negotiate on the third evening, and Sami was too quick for both openers as they slipped to 39 for 2. Nightwatchman Louw was not removed until just before lunch on the final morning, however, and Martin van Jaarsfeld looked supremely confident at the other end. The tall South African eventually reached 114 before being unluckily out hitting his own wicket as he attempted to cut Patel. By then, though, van Jaarsfeld had also added 76 for the sixth wicket with Graeme Swann to arrest a mini-slump to 167 for 5. In all, it took Kent 87 overs of toil on the last day to wrap up victory – with Sami finishing with 6 for 99 from 31 overs and Patel wheeling away through 26 to take 3 for 50.

Graeme Hick and Ben Smith built the highest partnership ever seen at New Road – a mammoth 417 – to set up Worcestershire's innings-and-86-run thrashing of Gloucestershire. The scoreboard read 37 for 2 early on the first morning, when Worcestershire captain Smith came in to join Hick. Exactly 24 hours later, to the minute, Smith was out for 187 and the total had moved on to 454 for 3! It was epic stuff from both players, with Hick eventually going on to make 262 before offering an unsurprisingly tired shot against the excellent Jon Lewis, whose figures of 2 for 73 from 32 overs really stood out amidst the carnage going on around him. The third-wicket stand also equalled the tenth highest partnership in championship history and, by the time Vikram Solanki had added 74 runs of his own, Worcestershire were in complete command and their visitors were demoralised. A declaration midway through the second day at 619 for 6 asked Gloucestershire stiff questions about their resolve – at 108 for 6 by the close, they soon showed they were there for the taking. Alex Gidman, who on the first day had seen six overs of his medium pace disappear for 62 as Hick and Smith moved into their stride, tried his best to resist with innings of 54 and 77. Gloucestershire did manage to hold out for just over 100 overs in their second innings, but Matt Mason's 5 for 62 ensured the win for Worcestershire that Hick and Smith – in particular – deserved.

Jamie Dalrymple hit a mammoth, career-best 244 in the London derby at The Oval, putting on 298 in 70 overs of glorious strokemaking with Ed Joyce, but

Middlesex still could not overpower Surrey, and an act of overnight hooliganism before the third day did not help their chances of forcing victory. The visitors also possibly missed the vital trick on the opening day of the match, when they allowed Surrey's last-wicket pair of Tim Murtagh and Jimmy Ormond to add 106 at a jaunty five-and-a-half runs per over. That stand lifted Surrey to 359, with Murtagh's unbeaten 74 his maiden first-class 50. A new-ball spell of 3 for 18 in eight overs by Ormond then reduced Middlesex to 62 for 4, but Joyce and Dalrymple – who was only playing because of Andrew Strauss' late England Test call-up – turned the game on its head with their magnificent partnership. It was also Dalrymple's first championship century, and his progress to 150 was remarkably even-paced … he took 100 balls to reach 50, 150 balls to reach 100 and then 200 balls to complete his 150. The 23-year-old former Oxford blue was not finished there, though, as he racked up 38 boundaries in his 306-ball stay. Middlesex were 363 for 5 at stumps on the second day, poised to build a significant lead over Surrey the following morning, but play could not start on day three until 4.15 pm due to a section of the outfield – near to the square – being dug up by vandals the previous night. In the 34 overs of play possible, Middlesex went on quickly to 487 for 9 declared, before leaving Surrey at 11 for 1 at the close. On the final day, however, Scott Newman hit 87 to pass 1,000 first-class runs for Surrey in only his 20th innings for the club, and there were also half-centuries for Mark Ramprakash (his second of the match) and Alistair Brown.

Ian Bell was the undoubted star of the show at Horsham, but a high-scoring draw between Sussex and Warwickshire had little else of interest – outside

Round Six: 18–22 May 2004 Division One

NORTHAMPTONSHIRE v. KENT - at Northampton

KENT	First Innings		Second Innings	
DP Fulton (capt)	c Brophy b Louw	6	b Afzaal	109
RWT Key	b Louw	16	c Louw b Greenidge	173
ET Smith	run out	35	c Roberts b Swann	1
A Symonds	b Swann	107	c Roberts b Afzaal	61
MJ Walker	c Brophy b Swann	8	b Greenidge	21
MA Carberry	lbw b Louw	22	(7) not out	8
MM Patel	c Sales b Louw	10	(6) c Brown b Afzaal	11
*NJ O'Brien	not out	32		
JC Tredwell	lbw b Swann	11		
MJ Saggers	run out	5		
Mohammad Sami	c Louw b Brown	0		
Extras	lb 2	2	b 2, lb 9, w 2, nb 8	21
	(72.3 overs)	254	(6 wkts dec 105.1 overs)	405

Bowling
Louw 11-4-33-4. Greenidge 7-0-48-0. Phillips 6-2-15-0. Brown 24.3-4-75-1. Swann 24-4-81-3.
Louw 20-3-82-0. Greenidge 12-0-79-2. Phillips 10-1-36-0. Brown 21-2-69-0. Swann 27-6-63-1. Afzaal 15.1-1-65-3.
Fall of Wickets: 1-22, 2-25, 3-120, 4-142, 5-191, 6-197, 7-206, 8-239, 9-246
1-222, 2-223, 3-334, 4-381, 5-393, 6-405

NORTHANTS	First Innings		Second Innings	
MJ Powell	c O'Brien b Saggers	5	c O'Brien b Mohammad Sami	13
TW Roberts	b Mohammad Sami	69	b Mohammad Sami	0
M van Jaarsveld	c Fulton b Mohammad Sami	46	hit wkt b Patel	114
U Afzaal	c Walker b Patel	7	(5) c Walker b Patel	11
DJG Sales (capt)	c Key b Patel	70	(6) lbw b Patel	12
GP Swann	b Mohammad Sami	5	(7) lbw b Mohammad Sami	42
*GL Brophy	b Mohammad Sami	4	(8) c Smith b Mohammad Sami	6
J Louw	c Mohammad Sami b Patel	0	(4) lbw b Mohammad Sami	19
BJ Phillips	c O'Brien b Symonds	4	c O'Brien b Mohammad Sami	5
CG Greenidge	not out	8	b Saggers	5
JF Brown	c Saggers b Symonds	11	not out	4
Extras	b 5, lb 3, w 1, nb 4	13	b 8, lb 14, w 6, nb 8	36
	(92.5 overs)	250	(100 overs)	264

Bowling
Mohammad Sami 22-6-39-4. Saggers 15-4-34-1. Symonds 13.5-3-44-2. Patel 28-6-81-3. Tredwell 14-1-44-0.
Mohammad Sami 31-11-99-6. Saggers 14-6-18-1. Tredwell 20-6-55-0. Patel 28-8-50-3. Symonds 9-3-20-0.
Fall of Wickets: 1-7, 2-123, 3-132, 4-136, 5-143, 6-147, 7-181, 8-219, 9-231
1-1, 2-30, 3-117, 4-134, 5-167, 6-243, 7-250, 8-253, 9-260

Kent won by 145 runs - Northamptonshire (5pts), Kent (19pts)

WORCESTERSHIRE v. GLOUCESTERSHIRE - at Worcester

WORCS	First Innings	
SD Peters	c Weston b Gidman	20
SC Moore	c Weston b Lewis	10
GA Hick	c Spearman b Lewis	262
BF Smith (capt)	lbw b Shoaib Malik	187
VS Solanki	c Windows b Shoaib Malik	74
Kadeer Ali	b Fisher	35
GJ Batty	not out	7
*SJ Rhodes		
MS Mason		
MN Malik		
MA Harrity		
Extras	lb 14, w 2, nb 8	24
	(6 wkts dec 161.3 overs)	619

Bowling
Lewis 32-10-73-2. Averis 33-6-139-0. Gidman 24-3-129-1. Shoaib Malik 39-8-118-2. Fisher 23.3-0-105-1. Hancock 10-1-41-0.
Fall of Wickets: 1-15, 2-37, 3-454, 4-554, 5-600, 6-619

GLOS	First Innings		Second Innings	
CM Spearman	c Smith b Batty	62	(2) c Moore b Harrity	0
WPC Weston	lbw b Malik	26	(1) c Hick b Mason	12
THC Hancock	c Hick b Malik	4	b Mason	68
MGN Windows	c Hick b Batty	1	lbw b Mason	0
CG Taylor (capt)	c Rhodes b Batty	7	c Rhodes b Malik	28
JMM Averis	c Rhodes b Mason	2	(10) b Mason	10
APR Gidman	c Rhodes b Mason	54	(6) b Mason	77
Shoaib Malik	c Mason b Harrity	33	(7) c Rhodes b Harrity	3
*SJ Adshead	c Peters b Malik	10	(8) c Hick b Batty	61
ID Fisher	c Solanki b Harrity	20	(9) st Rhodes b Batty	11
J Lewis	not out	0	not out	24
Extras	b 1, lb 4, nb 8	13	b 2, lb 1, nb 4	7
	(93.2 overs)	232	(100.4 overs)	301

Bowling
Mason 21.2-9-46-2. Harrity 24-6-60-2. Malik 19-4-58-3. Batty 29-10-63-3.
Mason 24-9-62-5. Harrity 28-7-106-2. Malik 15-4-52-1. Batty 24.4-11-48-2. Moore 4-1-10-0. Solanki 5-1-20-0.
Fall of Wickets: 1-55, 2-69, 3-70, 4-105, 5-106, 6-108, 7-149, 8-182, 9-232
1-4, 2-12, 3-12, 4-55, 5-166, 6-181, 7-201, 8-236, 9-264

Worcestershire won by an innings and 86 runs - Worcestershire (22pts), Gloucestershire (2pts)

SURREY v. MIDDLESEX - at The Oval

SURREY	First Innings		Second Innings	
SA Newman	c Keegan b Klusener	56	run out	87
*JN Batty (capt)	lbw b Hayward	3	lbw b Keegan	3
MR Ramprakash	c Dalrymple b Hayward	89	c Hutton b Weekes	66
R Clarke	c Hutchison b Klusener	2	c Dalrymple b Keegan	12
AD Brown	lbw b Hutchison	8	not out	64
AJ Hollioake	c Shah b Hutchison	8	not out	41
JGE Benning	c Nash b Hutchison	4		
MP Bicknell	c Nash b Keegan	19		
IDK Salisbury	c Weekes b Klusener	25		
TJ Murtagh	not out	74		
J Ormond	c Joyce b Dalrymple	40		
Extras	b 5, lb 8, w 11, nb 18	42	b 9, lb 12, nb 6	27
	(86.5 overs)	359	(4 wkts 92.4 overs)	300

Bowling
Keegan 20-2-72-1. Hayward 20-2-72-2. Klusener 17-2-86-3. Hutchison 16-3-50-3. Weekes 13-2-57-0. Dalrymple 0.5-0-9-1.
Keegan 20-6-46-2. Hayward 16-3-53-0. Hutchison 10-2-32-0. Weekes 20-3-53-1. Klusener 14-2-59-0. Dalrymple 8.4-0-33-0. Shah 4-2-3-0.
Fall of Wickets: 1-18, 2-98, 3-104, 4-104, 5-118, 6-126, 7-172, 8-229, 9-253
1-11, 2-166, 3-174, 4-186

MIDDLESEX	First Innings	
BL Hutton	c Hollioake b Ormond	15
SG Koenig	c Batty b Ormond	9
OA Shah (capt)	lbw b Bicknell	0
EC Joyce	c Clarke b Bicknell	123
PN Weekes	c Batty b Ormond	7
JWM Dalrymple	b Murtagh	244
*DC Nash	c Batty b Bicknell	12
L Klusener	lbw b Murtagh	4
CB Keegan	c Bicknell b Murtagh	44
PM Hutchison	not out	1
M Hayward	not out	0
Extras	b 5, lb 8, w 5, nb 10	28
	(9 wkts dec 130 overs)	487

Bowling
Ormond 34-9-117-3. Murtagh 23.5-8-84-3. Bicknell 35-8-109-3. Salisbury 20-0-76-0. Clarke 12-1-65-0. Benning 1-3-0-5-0. Hollioake 4-3-1-18-0.
Fall of Wickets: 1-27, 2-28, 3-28, 4-62, 5-360, 6-396, 7-409, 8-480, 9-487

Match drawn - Surrey (11pts), Middlesex (12pts)

SUSSEX v. WARWICKSHIRE - at Horsham

WARWICKSHIRE	First Innings		Second Innings	
NV Knight (capt)	b Akram	26	c Kirtley b Davis	59
MA Wagh	c Ambrose b Akram	20	lbw b Kirtley	14
IR Bell	not out	262	not out	62
IJL Trott	lbw b Mushtaq Ahmed	26	not out	40
JO Troughton	b Mushtaq Ahmed	10		
DR Brown	c Prior b Mushtaq Ahmed	21		
GB Hogg	c Adams b Mushtaq Ahmed	68		
*T Frost	not out	135		
A Richardson				
NM Carter				
D Pretorius				
Extras	b 1, lb 5, w 1, nb 20, p 5	32	b 7, nb 6	13
	(6 wkts dec 165.4 overs)	600	(2 wkts 54 overs)	188

Bowling
Akram 29-2-94-2. Kirtley 28-3-130-0. Martin-Jenkins 23.4-6-62-0. Mushtaq Ahmed 50-6-194-4. Davis 31-3-96-0. Adams 4-1-13-0.
Akram 6-1-33-0. Kirtley 10-4-23-1. Martin-Jenkins 10-2-36-0. Davis 19-1-68-1. Adams 5-1-12-0. Montgomerie 4-0-9-0.
Fall of Wickets: 1-49, 2-62, 3-108, 4-140, 5-166, 6-311
1-57, 2-91

SUSSEX	First Innings	
IJ Ward	b Pretorius	160
RR Montgomerie	c Richardson b Wagh	61
MW Goodwin	b Wagh	9
CJ Adams (capt)	c Frost b Richardson	144
*TR Ambrose	c Knight b Pretorius	1
RSC Martin-Jenkins	b Pretorius	0
MJ Prior	b Brown	17
MJG Davis	c Frost b Pretorius	39
Mushtaq Ahmed	c Richardson b Pretorius	62
M Akram	b Brown	34
RJ Kirtley	not out	8
Extras	b 9, lb 8, nb 10	27
	(157.3 overs)	562ᵗ

Bowling
Pretorius 33.7-119-4. Carter 29-6-104-0. Hogg 17-4-68-0. Brown 29.3-5-74-2. Richardson 25-7-82-2. Wagh 18-4-81-2. Troughton 6-0-7-0.
Fall of Wickets: 1-143, 2-155, 3-349, 4-383, 5-383, 6-402, 7-418, 8-498, 9-523

Match drawn - Sussex (11pts - five runs deducted for 'illegally' altering the condition of the ball), Warwickshire (11pts)*

of a ball-tampering incident, that is – as only 18 wickets fell in almost four full days. Bell, touted as a future England batsman since making his Warwickshire debut as a 17-year-old in 1999, went to a fifth first-class hundred on the opening day – which the visitors ended on 357 for 6. After Sussex had learned, from umpires Peter Willey and Barrie Leadbeater, that they were to be the first county to be docked five runs for illegally altering the condition of the ball, no wickets at all fell on the second day! Warwickshire moved on to 600 for 6 declared, with Bell becoming the county's youngest double-century maker on his way to an unbeaten 262 and Tony Frost scoring 135 not out in a seventh-wicket stand of 289 which equalled the Warwickshire record. Bell struck five of his six sixes after reaching 200 and also hit 27 fours in an innings which lasted just ten minutes under ten hours. It was the fourth longest innings in Warwickshire history. Sussex, 84 without loss by the close, reached 464 for 7 by the end of day three and

eventually pushed on to 562. It was a spirited effort, after taking such a pounding themselves in the field, with big centuries by both Ian Ward and Chris Adams being especially noteworthy.

Division Two

A crushing victory by 244 runs at Headingley took Nottinghamshire to the top of the Division Two table. Yorkshire, hustled out for just 164 in their first innings in reply to a Kevin Pietersen-led Nottinghamshire total of 393, were not even given an outside chance of fashioning an escape when Notts declined to enforce the follow-on. Instead, David Hussey's run-a-ball 125 – his first hundred for Notts – enabled the visitors to declare their second innings at 269 for 8 early on the third day. Yorkshire could not even take the game into the final day, with leg spinner Stuart MacGill taking his match haul to 7 for 109 as the home team were dismissed for 254 in 62 overs.

Yorkshire's bowling attack, taken apart by Pietersen on the opening day when he struck three sixes and 20 fours in his 167, badly missed the injured pace pair of Chris Silverwood and Steve Kirby. It hardly helped their mood, either, that Yorkshire could see Ryan Sidebottom – who had left them the previous winter – taking three cheap first-innings wickets for Notts.

Mike Powell plundered the fastest first-class hundred of the season so far, off 90 balls, as Glamorgan stepped up their own promotion drive by seeing off Durham by an emphatic 201 runs at the Riverside. Pallav Kumar, a rookie seamer called up as a late replacement from Sunderland University, took three wickets on the opening day for Durham – but the home side still finished it struggling on 4 for 2 in reply to a Glamorgan first innings of 393. David Harrison, who sent back Jon Lewis and nightwatchman Neil Killeen in that initial burst on the first evening, went on to take a career-best 5 for 75 as Durham were dismissed for 220. Matthew Maynard then struck an unbeaten half-century to help set up a Glamorgan second-innings declaration, and only fighting 50s from Lewis and Andy Pratt delayed the Welsh county for long.

More runs for Ian Bell, during his career-best 262 not out at Horsham.

Alex Wharf finished with 5 for 93 and Robert Croft followed up his first-innings 81 by taking 3 for 48.

Injuries to his bowling attack caused Derbyshire captain Luke Sutton to delay his second-innings declaration against Somerset at Derby, a factor which also may have cost them the chance of forcing a win. Derbyshire had the best of the contest, anyway, with 19-year-old Nick Walker providing a real talking point by making the highest score by a No. 11 batsman in the county's history. Walker's 57-ball 80, which lifted their first-innings total from 264 for 9 to 367 all out, was also a highly entertaining affair that featured four sixes and 11 fours. Three of his sixes, moreover, came in one Andy Caddick over – and there was an on-driven, all-run five off Nixon McLean for good measure! Caddick's figures of 6 for 92, though spoilt a touch by Walker's late burst of hitting, were his best for four years and underlined the success of his comeback following the back operation that had kept him out of cricket for a year. Chris Bassano's first-innings 83 was his highest championship score since August 2002, but Ian Blackwell then bludgeoned 111 off 117 balls against his former county to rescue Somerset from the depths of 110 for 5 in reply. Blackwell, who struck three sixes and 12 fours, dominated a stand of 171 in 38 overs with Rob Turner, but Derbyshire ended the first-innings exchanges with a handy 60-run lead thanks once more to the contribution of Walker. The young seamer, discovered by new coach Dave Houghton playing for Sawbridgeworth in the Hertfordshire League in 2003, took a career-best 5 for 68 and then sat back in the dressing room to watch Andrew Gait, Chris Rogers (with 13 fours in his 127-ball 91) and Hassan Adnan build a

Round Six: 18–22 May 2004 Division Two

YORKSHIRE v. NOTTINGHAMSHIRE – at Headingley

NOTTS	First Innings		Second Innings	
DJ Bicknell	run out	48	lbw b Dawson	19
JER Gallian (capt)	c Guy b Blain	0	c Guy b Thornicroft	13
RJ Warren	c Jaques b Blain	8	b White	55
KP Pietersen	b Bresnan	167	(5) c Dawson b White	0
DJ Hussey	b Thornicroft	15	(4) c Dawson b Bresnan	125
*CMW Read	st Guy b Dawson	59	lbw b White	11
MA Ealham	b White	6	c Thornicroft b Bresnan	34
PJ Franks	c Wood b Dawson	17	c Guy b Bresnan	0
RJ Sidebottom	c Guy b Bresnan	4	not out	9
SCG MacGill	b Thornicroft	21		
CE Shreck	not out	1		
Extras	b 13, lb 22, nb 12	47	b 4, lb 2, nb 6	12
	(95.3 overs)	393	(8 wkts dec 64.3 overs)	269

Bowling

Blain 15-3-66-2. Bresnan 19-2-81-2. Harvey 15-6-34-0. Thornicroft 9.3-2-37-2. McGrath 7-1-26-0. Dawson 18-2-74-2. White 12-3-40-1. Blain 0.1-0-5-0. Thornicroft 17.5-3-80-1. Bresnan 14.3-3-57-3. Dawson 13-3-48-1. McGrath 6-1-23-0. White 13-2-50-3.

Fall of Wickets: 1-7, 2-35, 3-91, 4-124, 5-265, 6-288, 7-327, 8-371, 9-372 1-25, 2-39, 3-188, 4-194, 5-215, 6-261, 7-269, 8-269

YORKSHIRE	First Innings		Second Innings	
MJ Wood	b Sidebottom	4	c Read b Sidebottom	9
C White (capt)	c Hussey b Sidebottom	28	lbw b Franks	44
JAR Blain	lbw b MacGill	6	(11) not out	7
A McGrath	b Franks	1	(3) lbw b Sidebottom	25
PA Jaques	c Read b Franks	20	(4) b MacGill	43
MJ Lumb	c Gallian b Sidebottom	4	(5) c Read b Franks	4
IJ Harvey	b MacGill	28	(6) c Read b Franks	18
*SM Guy	c Pietersen b MacGill	9	(7) lbw b MacGill	26
RKJ Dawson	lbw b MacGill	0	(8) c Gallian b Ealham	40
TT Bresnan	not out	21	(9) st Read b MacGill	21
ND Thornicroft	c Franks b Ealham	30	(10) c sub b Ealham	4
Extras	lb 10, w 1, nb 2	13	b 4, lb 7, nb 2	13
	(56.3 overs)	164	(62 overs)	254

Bowling

Shreck 4-0-9-0. Sidebottom 14-7-19-3. Ealham 8.3-3-18-1. MacGill 16-6-54-4. Franks 16-1-54-2. Franks 13-3-62-3. Sidebottom 16-3-52-2. Ealham 19-3-74-2. MacGill 14-1-55-3. **Fall of Wickets:** 1-9, 2-31, 3-40, 4-52, 5-62, 6-75, 7-84, 8-84, 9-125 1-31, 2-76, 3-99, 4-111, 5-141, 6-157, 7-212, 8-222, 9-226

Nottinghamshire won by 244 runs – Yorkshire (3pts), Nottinghamshire (21pts)

DURHAM v. GLAMORGAN – at The Riverside

GLAMORGAN	First Innings		Second Innings	
MTG Elliott	lbw b Davies	37	(2) c Peng b Davies	35
*MA Wallace	c Pratt b A Davies	26	(1) run out	36
DL Hemp	c Pratt A b Kumar	45	(4) c Peng b Collingwood	25
MJ Powell	c Lewis b Killeen	124	(5) c Collingwood b Davies	38
MP Maynard	st Pratt A b Breese	10	(6) not out	54
A Dale	c and b Breese	15	(7) c Muchall b Collingwood	0
RDB Croft (capt)	c Pratt GJ b Davies	81	(8) lbw b Collingwood	6
DS Harrison	c Pratt GJ b Kumar	2	(9) st Pratt A b Breese	32
AG Wharf	lbw b Kumar	2	(10) b Breese	20
SD Thomas	not out	30	(3) c Peng b Killeen	5
DA Cosker	c Pattison b Killeen	1		
Extras	lb 2, w 2, nb 6	20	lb 4, nb 10	14
	(99 overs)	393	(9 wkts dec 67.3 overs)	265

Bowling

Killeen 22-6-62-2. Kumar 15-1-78-3. Davies 21-4-95-3. Pattison 14-1-57-0. Breese 26-6-85-2. Muchall 1-0-4-0. Killeen 22-4-53-1. Davies 17-2-71-2. Kumar 9-1-60-0. Collingwood 11-1-49-3. **Fall of Wickets:** 1-66, 2-73, 3-206, 4-239, 5-261, 6-295, 7-308, 8-326, 9-388 1-60, 2-77, 3-86, 4-153, 5-157, 6-157, 7-165, 8-211, 9-265

DURHAM	First Innings		Second Innings	
JJB Lewis (capt)	b Maynard b Harrison	0	lbw b Wharf	51
MJ North	lbw b Harrison	13	lbw b Harrison	9
N Killeen	c Dale b Harrison	0	(9) b Croft	14
GJ Muchall	c Elliott b Harrison	93	(3) b Thomas	27
GJ Pratt	c Elliott b Wharf	12	(6) lbw b Croft	15
N Peng	c Dale b Wharf	7	(5) c Hemp b Wharf	7
GR Breese	c Thomas b Croft	11	c Elliott b Wharf	4
*A Pratt	c Elliott b Thomas	4	c Thomas b Wharf	59
I Pattison	c Powell b Harrison	33		
M Davies	c Wallace b Cosker	29	not out	0
P Kumar	not out	13	c Dale b Croft	21
P D Collingwood			(4) c Wallace b Wharf	0
Extras	b 4, lb 4, w 1	9	b 1, lb 2, w 1, nb 12	16
	(53.5 overs)	220	(51 overs)	237

Bowling

Harrison 16-2-75-5. Wharf 13-4-31-2. Thomas 8-0-42-1. Croft 15-3-61-1. Cosker 1.5-0-3-1. Harrison 10-0-51-1. Wharf 17-1-93-5. Thomas 9-0-41-1. Croft 13-2-48-3. Cosker 2-1-1-0. **Fall of Wickets:** 1-0, 2-4, 3-23, 4-74, 5-78, 6-105, 7-110, 8-169, 9-176 1-15, 2-58, 3-81, 4-108, 5-115, 6-123, 7-157, 8-191, 9-223

Glamorgan won by 201 runs – Durham (4pts), Glamorgan (21pts)

DERBYSHIRE v. SOMERSET – at Derby

DERBYSHIRE	First Innings		Second Innings	
AI Gait	c Turner b Francis SRG	12	b Johnson	81
SD Stubbings	lbw b Caddick	37	c Turner b Blackwell	17
CJL Rogers	c Turner b Francis SRG	8	c Turner b Caddick	91
Hassan Adnan	lbw b Caddick	45	c Francis SRG b Caddick	60
J Moss	c Edwards b Caddick	9	(6) b Blackwell	9
CWG Bassano	c Francis SRG b Caddick	83	(5) b Caddick	16
*LD Sutton (capt)	c Turner b McLean	17	c Caddick b Francis SRG	41
G Welch	b Caddick	28	not out	45
AG Botha	b Caddick	20	not out	5
MA Sheikh	not out	22		
NGE Walker	b McLean	80		
Extras	b 4, w 1, nb 10	15	lb 9, w 2, nb 4	15
	(113.2 overs)	367	(7 wkts dec 96.5 overs)	387

Bowling

Caddick 30-9-92-6. Johnson 17-2-60-0. Francis SRG 18-3-66-2. McLean 24.2-5-80-2. Blackwell 21-8-58-0. Hildreth 3-0-7-0. Caddick 34-4-119-3. Johnson 13-2-45-1. McLean 10-2-30-0. Francis SRG 6.5-0-53-1. Blackwell 30-4-105-2. Hildreth 3-0-26-0. **Fall of Wickets:** 1-31, 2-41, 3-103, 4-107, 5-112, 6-156, 7-214, 8-256, 9-264 1-73, 2-135, 3-231, 4-270, 5-283, 6-289, 7-360

SOMERSET	First Innings		Second Innings	
NJ Edwards	c Sutton b Walker	54	b Walker	13
JD Francis	c Sutton b Walker	1	st Sutton b Botha	68
J Cox	lbw b Welch	36	b Welch	34
JC Hildreth	c Botha b Sheikh	31	lbw b Sheikh	31
M Burns (capt)	lbw b Walker	4	not out	33
ID Blackwell	c Et b Welch	111	not out	64
*RJ Turner	c Rogers b Botha	45		
RL Johnson	b Walker	9		
AR Caddick	lbw b Welch	9		
SRG Francis	not out	2		
NAM McLean	c Moss b Walker	4		
Extras	b 9, lb 3, w 3, nb 10	25	b 5, lb 5, w 1, nb 16	27
	(93.5 overs)	307	(4 wkts 78 overs)	252

Bowling

Welch 28-12-79-3. Walker 19.5-7-68-5. Sheikh 22-5-68-1. Botha 6-2-76-1. Hassan Adnan 2-0-4-0. Welch 23-4-70-1. Walker 10-1-45-1. Sheikh 15-4-43-1. Botha 25-6-58-1. Hassan Adnan 4-1-26-0. **Fall of Wickets:** 1-2, 2-55, 3-101, 4-101, 5-110, 6-281, 7-287, 8-297, 9-303 1-42, 2-64, 3-114, 4-156

Match drawn – Derbyshire (11pts), Somerset (10pts)

ESSEX v. LEICESTERSHIRE – at Chelmsford

LEICESTERSHIRE	First Innings		Second Innings	
DDJ Robinson	b Gough	56	lbw b Kaneria	53
JK Maunders	lbw b McCoubrey	22	c Foster b Gough	7
BJ Hodge	c Flower b Middlebrook	240	b Brant	5
DL Maddy	c Flower b Kaneria	5	st Foster b Kaneria	23
JL Sadler	c Foster b Gough	46	b Kaneria	43
JN Snape	c Cook b Brant	15	not out	39
*PA Nixon	lbw b Kaneria	41	c Foster b Gough	10
PAJ DeFreitas (capt)	c Jefferson b Middlebrook	47	not out	0
OD Gibson	c Cook b Middlebrook	13		
CW Henderson	not out	10		
MF Cleary	b Kaneria	12		
Extras	b 1, lb 7, w 1, nb 6	15	b 10, lb 3, nb 4	17
	(128.5 overs)	510	(6 wkts 82 overs)	212

Bowling

Gough 18-4-61-2. Brant 20-3-96-1. McCoubrey 14-1-89-1. Kaneria 41.5-7-139-3. Middlebrook 35-3-117-3. Gough 17-3-38-2. Brant 11-3-49-1. Kaneria 31-14-42-3. Middlebrook 12-4-38-0. McCoubrey 10-2-26-0. Grayson 1-0-6-0. **Fall of Wickets:** 1-30, 2-131, 3-162, 4-267, 5-287, 6-367, 7-464, 8-486, 9-502 1-23, 2-34, 3-86, 4-121, 5-147, 6-167

ESSEX	First Innings			
WI Jefferson	b Gough	128		
AN Cook	b Cleary	126		
AP Grayson (capt)	lbw b Gibson	7		
A Flower	b Cleary	22		
A Habib	c Nixon b DeFreitas	97		
*JS Foster	c Nixon b Cleary	212		
JD Middlebrook	b DeFreitas	3		
D Gough	c Cleary b Snape	50		
SA Brant	b Cleary	5		
Danish Kaneria	not out	5		
AGAM McCoubrey				
Extras	b 6, lb 17, w 6, nb 24	53		
	(dec 178.4 overs)	708		

Bowling

Gibson 28-4-97-1. DeFreitas 45-11-145-3. Henderson 29-4-111-0. Cleary 27.4-2-130-4. Hodge 16-2-52-0. Snape 20-2-78-1. Maddy 12-1-67-0. Robinson 1-0-5-0. **Fall of Wickets:** 1-265, 2-291, 3-295, 4-326, 5-510, 6-530, 7-630, 8-666, 9-708

Match drawn – Essex (12pts), Leicestershire (10pts)

Andy Caddick produced his best figures for four years as Somerset drew at Derby.

potentially match-winning position. Derbyshire's ultimate lack of firepower, though, enabled Somerset to depart with a draw following final day half-centuries from John Francis and Blackwell.

Brad Hodge hit a classy 240 for Leicestershire against Essex at Chelmsford, but then almost ended up on the losing side as James Foster replied with a double-century of his own to inspire a determined home response. Hodge's seven-and-a-half hour effort contained a six and 32 fours, but none of the rest of the Leicestershire batting order could support him for long and an eventual total of 510 became almost inadequate as Essex fought back on a pitch which could have been designed to break bowlers' hearts. The young openers, Will Jefferson and Alistair Cook, spearheaded the counter-attack with a partnership of 265 which was the third highest first-wicket stand in the county's history. Cook, a 19-year-old and highly rated product of Bedford School and the England Under 19 team, completed a fine maiden first-class hundred, while

Jefferson was out early on day three for 128. Aftab Habib (97) and Foster then took over, with Darren Gough also contributing a late-order 50. Foster, scoring his maiden championship century and unbeaten on 179 by the close of day three, which Essex reached at 665 for 7, went on to score 212 before a declaration arrived that challenged Leicestershire to bat out 82 overs.

Gough and Danish Kaneria made them wobble, but Jeremy Snape ended up with 39 not out and was joined in the final session by the equally stubborn Leicestershire captain Phil DeFreitas, who repelled 78 balls to finish on 15 not out.

Round Seven: 25–28 May 2004

Division One

Warwickshire won a controversial first West Midlands championship derby in three years by virtue of some whirlwind batting on a dodgy pitch and a more disciplined second-innings bowling effort. Worcestershire felt aggrieved to have lost by nine wickets, not just because of the nature of the Edgbaston pitch, but because – on the opening day – they had reached 223 for 2 at one stage, thanks to Graeme Hick's masterly 125th first-class hundred. Hick went on to score 158 from 263 balls, with a six and 24 fours, and his first-class average for the season stood at 133.50 when he was run out. Worcestershire's eventual total of 379 looked a decent score on a pitch already showing signs of enough inconsistent bounce for the umpires to summon David Hughes, one of the ECB's pitch liaison officers. Warwickshire's top order initially struggled on day two, but, between lunch and tea, an extraordinary 245 runs were plundered from 41 overs as Jim Troughton, Dougie Brown and Neil Carter decided that attack was their best form of defence. Troughton hit 67, Brown's 82 contained ten fours and four sixes and Carter's belligerent 95, from just 81 balls, provided even more fireworks with six sixes and nine boundaries. The calculated assault earned Warwickshire a lead of 26 – and maximum batting points – and by the close of a remarkable day Worcestershire were 70 for 2 in their second innings. Hick had by then fallen for 29 to Naqaash Tahir, a 20-year-old seamer on his county debut who went on to take 4 for 43 (and 8 for 90 in the match), as Worcestershire slumped to 185 all out on day three. Ian Bell's accurate medium pacers brought him 3 for 12 and Warwickshire had suddenly been presented with a smallish target to win the game. Nick Knight and Mark Wagh again approached the task with aggression, with Knight hitting 83 in an opening stand worth 152. After the match, however, Warwickshire had to endure an anxious wait before it was confirmed that a pitch panel of Hughes, Peter Walker and Chris Wood, the ECB's pitch consultants, had chosen not to mete out penalty points. Their verdict was 'below average' and not the 'poor' which would have invoked punishment. Tom Moody, the Worcestershire director of cricket, said: 'County cricket is supposed to prepare people for Test cricket, but all you are going to get on a poor surface like that is a broken thumb or a broken toe'. There were, however, no injuries.

Jon Batty, the Surrey captain, had a rare personal achievement as well as a much-needed seven-wicket win over Kent to celebrate after four hard-fought days at The Oval. Batty's first-innings 129 helped Surrey to an imposing total of 479, and then he took eight catches behind the stumps as Kent's first innings fell away to 239. It was only the second time in first-class cricket history that a wicketkeeper had scored a hundred and taken eight catches in an innings – the other player to do so was Steve Marsh, for Kent against Middlesex at Lord's in 1991. David East, of Essex in 1985, is the only other wicketkeeper to take eight catches in an innings in the championship – while, in all cricket, Batty's feat was only the eighth instance of it. Besides Batty's heroics, it was the batting of

Mark Ramprakash and Rob Key that dominated proceedings – while Surrey's veteran seamer Martin Bicknell also took the 1,000th first-class wicket of his career when he dismissed Matt Dennington on the final day. Ramprakash hit a first-innings 157 to lead a Surrey fightback from the loss of two early wickets on the opening morning, and then an unbeaten 91 to spearhead Surrey's drive towards the 174 from 47 overs that they required for victory on the final afternoon. In between, Key held an almost immovable vigil at the crease as he continued his magnificent early-summer form. His first-innings 86 was followed by an even better and equally fluent career-best 199. In all, Key batted for 12 hours and seven minutes in the match and also fielded for another nine hours. Whoever said county cricket was gentle and soft? Michael Carberry struck a second-innings 61 against his former county, but Azhar Mahmood in the first innings, and Bicknell in the second, chipped away successfully at the visitors and a home victory was the right result – despite the resistance of Key.

Chris Adams became only the third player – after Mark Ramprakash and Carl Hooper – to complete a set of first-class hundreds against all 18 counties, and he did it in some style by going on to make 200 against Northamptonshire at Hove. However, the

Round Seven: 25–28 May 2004 Division One

WARWICKSHIRE v. WORCESTERSHIRE – at Edgbaston

WORCS	First Innings		Second Innings	
SD Peters	c Frost b Tahir	31	b Brown	2
SC Moore	c Trott b Brown	5	c Frost b Tahir	30
GA Hick	run out	158	lbw b Tahir	29
BF Smith (capt)	c Knight b Brown	67	lbw b Carter	41
VS Solanki	lbw b Richardson	12	c Bell b Tahir	21
GJ Batty	c Frost b Bell	21	lbw b Tahir	1
AJ Bichel	c Brown b Bell	35	lbw b Bell	28
*SJ Rhodes	c Frost b Tahir	3	c Knight b Carter	7
MS Mason	not out	14	b Bell	7
MN Tahir	lbw b Tahir	1	not out	0
MA Harrity	lbw b Tahir	0	b Bell	0
Extras	b 8, lb 6, w 10, nb 8	32	b 9, lb 6, nb 4	19
	(106 overs)	379	(45 overs)	185

Bowling
Carter 18-2-70-0. Brown 24-6-83-2. Richardson 17-2-87-1. Bell 26-4-55-2. Tahir 17-1-47-4. Wagh 2-0-13-0. Trott 2-0-13-0.
Brown 7-0-40-1. Carter 12-1-44-2. Tahir 10-0-43-4. Richardson 9-0-31-0. Bell 7-3-12-3.
Fall of Wickets: 1-6, 2-82, 3-223, 4-248, 5-291, 6-357, 7-359, 8-373, 9-373 1-2, 2-61, 3-70, 4-98, 5-111, 6-156, 7-178, 8-182, 9-185

WARWICKSHIRE	First Innings		Second Innings	
NV Knight (capt)	b Bichel	16	b Moore	83
MA Wagh	c Rhodes b Mason	22	not out	63
IR Bell	c Hick b Bichel	8	not out	5
IJL Trott	b Mason	3		
JO Troughton	c Rhodes b Bichel	67		
MJ Powell	lbw b Mason	49		
DR Brown	c Malik b Mason	82		
*T Frost	b Bichel	27		
NM Carter	c Batty b Bichel	95		
N Tahir	c Batty b Malik	16		
A Richardson	not out	0		
Extras	b 9, lb 11	20	lb 2, nb 8	10
	(74.1 overs)	405	(1 wkt 40.3 overs)	161

Bowling
Bichel 20.1-3-126-5. Mason 22-6-80-4. Harrity 8-2-48-0. Malik 11-0-83-1. Batty 13-3-48-0.
Bichel 8-0-51-0. Mason 6-2-10-0. Malik 8-1-21-0. Harrity 5-0-26-0. Batty 7-0-21-0. Moore 6-3-1-30-1.
Fall of Wickets: 1-38, 2-46, 3-46, 4-50, 5-174, 6-174, 7-271, 8-330, 9-370 1-152

Warwickshire won by 9 wickets –
Warwickshire (22pts), Worcestershire (7pts)

SURREY v. KENT – at The Oval

SURREY	First Innings		Second Innings	
SA Newman	lbw b Saggers	0	c Saggers b Carberry	31
N Shahid	c Smith b Mohammad Sami	1	lbw b Saggers	0
MR Ramprakash	b Mohammad Sami	157	not out	91
R Clarke	c Walker b Saggers	44	c Saggers b Walker	15
*JN Batty (capt)	c Ferley b Khan	129	not out	18
AD Brown	st O'Brien b Ferley	79		
AJ Hollioake	lbw b Khan	2		
Azhar Mahmood	b Ferley	27		
MP Bicknell	c Smith b Ferley	6		
J Ormond	c O'Brien b Saggers	6		
Z Khan	not out	2		
Extras	b 10, lb 3, w 1, nb 12	26	b 6, lb 3, nb 10	19
	(127.1 overs)	479	(3 wkts 34.3 overs)	174

Bowling
Mohammad Sami 24-6-75-2. Saggers 31.1-6-111-3. Dennington 21-5-71-0. Khan 27-3-102-2. Ferley 24-2-107-3.
Mohammad Sami 3-0-24-0. Saggers 4-1-9-1. Khan 2.3-0-20-0. Dennington 6-0-21-0. Carberry 12-0-67-1. Walker 7-0-24-1.
Fall of Wickets: 1-1, 2-1, 3-92, 4-323, 5-379, 6-386, 7-440, 8-464, 9-477 1-14, 2-81, 3-116

KENT	First Innings		Second Innings	
DP Fulton (capt)	c sub b Azhar Mahmood	30	c Batty b Azhar Mahmood	13
RWT Key	c Batty b Bicknell	86	c Brown b Bicknell	199
ET Smith	c Batty b Azhar Mahmood	25	b Ormond	23
MJ Walker	c Batty b Azhar Mahmood	20	lbw b Bicknell	0
MA Carberry	c Batty b Azhar Mahmood	17	c Brown b Ormond	61
MJ Saggers	c Batty b Clarke	1	(10) b Bicknell	0
MJ Dennington	b Clarke	11	(6) c Batty b Bicknell	12
*NJ O'Brien	c Brown b Clarke	15	(7) c Batty b Clarke	21
RS Ferley	c Batty b Clarke	0	(8) lbw b Bicknell	4
A Khan	not out	9	(9) not out	22
Mohammad Sami	c Batty b Bicknell	5	c Shahid b Khan	29
Extras	b 1, lb 6, w 1, nb 12	20	b 1, lb 14, nb 14	29
	(73.4 overs)	239	(133.4 overs)	413

Bowling
Khan 11-2-53-0. Bicknell 21.4-6-51-3. Ormond 15-5-25-0.
Azhar Mahmood 15-5-56-4. Clarke 11-2-47-3.
Bicknell 34-8-128-5. Khan 15.4-0-48-1. Azhar Mahmood 22-5-63-1. Ormond 44-14-97-2. Clarke 14-2-49-1. Ramprakash 2-0-7-0. Brown 2-1-6-0.
Fall of Wickets: 1-52, 2-82, 3-142, 4-180, 5-181, 6-199, 7-203, 8-204, 9-220 1-26, 2-109, 3-114, 4-240, 5-272, 6-313, 7-361, 8-364, 9-364

Surrey won by 7 wickets – Surrey (22pts), Kent (4pts)

SUSSEX v. NORTHAMPTONSHIRE – at Hove

NORTHANTS	First Innings	
TW Roberts	c Ambrose b Kirtley	10
TB Huggins	lbw b Martin-Jenkins	7
M van Jaarsveld	b Martin-Jenkins	27
U Afzaal	c Goodwin b Mushtaq Ahmed	69
DJG Sales (capt)	lbw b Mushtaq Ahmed	171
JW Cook	lbw b Davis	7
*GL Brophy	c Ambrose b Martin-Jenkins	181
J Louw	c Montgomerie b Mushtaq Ahmed	9
BJ Phillips	c Prior b Martin-Jenkins	58
PS Jones	c Ambrose b Martin-Jenkins	7
JF Brown	not out	1
Extras	b 6, lb 16, w 2, nb 4	28
	(166.1 overs)	570

Bowling
Kirtley 32-4-106-1. Lewry 32-4-123-0. Mushtaq Ahmed 49-12-143-3. Martin-Jenkins 21.1-5-96-5. Davis 27-8-80-1.
Fall of Wickets: 1-10, 2-44, 3-53, 4-234, 5-250, 6-345, 7-395, 8-527, 9-555

SUSSEX	First Innings		Second Innings	
IJ Ward	c Et b Jones	33	not out	107
RR Montgomerie	lbw b Phillips	82	lbw b Phillips	30
MW Goodwin	c Brophy b Phillips	1	c Brophy b Louw	11
CJ Adams (capt)	c Roberts b Phillips	200	(7) not out	26
*TR Ambrose	c Phillips b Afzaal	28	c Huggins b Brown	0
RSC Martin-Jenkins	b Phillips	25	b Phillips	13
MJ Prior	lbw b Phillips	0	(4) c Afzaal b Brown	70
MJG Davis	c Sales b Jones	0		
Mushtaq Ahmed	not out	8		
RJ Kirtley	b Louw	1		
JD Lewry	b Louw	13		
Extras	b 4, lb 6, w 3, nb 2	15	b 2, lb 2, w 4, nb 6	14
	(133.2 overs)	406	(5 wkts 92 overs)	271

Bowling
Jones 27-4-75-3. Louw 18.2-4-85-2. Phillips 29-8-103-4. Brown 35-12-71-0. Cook 16-3-33-0. Afzaal 8-0-29-1.
Louw 16-0-70-1. Jones 11-4-20-0. Cook 10-2-29-0. Brown 27-9-70-2. Phillips 14-2-34-2. Afzaal 10-3-36-0. van Jaarsveld 4-2-8-0.
Fall of Wickets: 1-58, 2-63, 3-215, 4-330, 5-382, 6-382, 7-383, 8-383, 9-390 1-64, 2-79, 3-192, 4-194, 5-223

Match drawn – Sussex (10pts),
Northamptonshire (12pts)

Jon Batty ... a personal and team triumph in Surrey's win against Kent at The Oval.

Sussex captain's efforts did not prevent his side from having to follow on late on the third day, after a surprising, and sudden, collapse from 382 for 4 to 406 all out. Northants had compiled a massive 570 over the first day and a half, thanks largely to big hundreds from both David Sales and Gerard Brophy, and now they smelt blood. However, Ian Ward ground out a thoroughly professional unbeaten 107 on the last day, with Adams coming in second time around at No. 7 to help the opener to bat out time. When Adams came in, Sussex were just 59 ahead with 27 overs still remaining, but he made sure there was no repeat of the first-innings slide.

Rain washed out all but 5.2 overs of the final day at Old Trafford, although the game between Lancashire and Middlesex looked to be heading for a draw anyway. Sven Koenig, in the side only because Lord's Test hero Andy Strauss was being rested by the England management, responded by grinding his way to 171 – an innings which put a poor spell that had realised just 101 runs from seven previous championship innings behind him. David Nash's unbeaten 81 was also an important factor in allowing Middlesex to reach 382, and then spinners Chris Peploe and Jamie Dalrymple bowled with great discipline and accuracy to peg Lancashire back to 417 after they had powered to 288 for 2 with both Mark Chilton (93) and Mal Loye (98) narrowly missing out on hundreds.

Division Two

Spinners Robert Croft and Dean Cosker bowled Glamorgan to both a 128-run victory and maximum points, against Derbyshire at Derby. They took three wickets each on the final afternoon to thwart Derbyshire's stubborn pursuit of a draw after Glamorgan had batted on for just under 12 overs that morning to allow David Hemp to complete a second-innings hundred. Glamorgan's first-innings total of 474 was full of solid batting, but owed much to an opening partnership of 168 between Matthew Elliott and Mark Wallace. Derbyshire's initial response, however, was a strong one, with Steve Stubbings battling for more than five hours to make 96 and Hassan Adnan including some wonderful strokes in his 95. Glamorgan's eventual success, however, was due to the greater threat provided by their balanced attack, despite a gutsy all-round performance from Graeme Welch.

Nottinghamshire continued their fine progress in championship cricket with a three-wicket win over Durham at Trent Bridge, and thanks to the batting of

LANCASHIRE v. MIDDLESEX - at Old Trafford

MIDDLESEX	First Innings		Second Innings	
BL Hutton	c Anderson b Keedy	27	lbw b Anderson	41
SG Koenig	b Anderson	171	b Anderson	7
OA Shah (capt)	st Hegg b Hooper	35	not out	67
EC Joyce	b Mahmood	0	not out	7
PN Weekes	lbw b Anderson	8		
JWM Dalrymple	lbw b Keedy	17		
*DC Nash	not out	81		
L Klusener	lbw b Anderson	2		
CT Peploe	c Hegg b Chapple	3		
PM Hutchison	lbw b Mahmood	4		
M Hayward	c Hooper b Keedy	1		
Extras	b 6, lb 21, w 2, nb 4	33	b 4, w 3	7
	(133.2 overs)	382	(2 wkts 43 overs)	129

Bowling
Anderson 33-7-95-3. Chapple 34-9-60-1. Mahmood 17-3-58-2. Keedy 34.2-6-99-3. Hooper 15-3-43-1.
Anderson 12-2-45-2. Chapple 9-3-17-0. Keedy 10-1-23-0. Mahmood 3-1-8-0. Hooper 9-1-32-0.
Fall of Wickets: 1-92, 2-180, 3-183, 4-198, 5-237, 6-329, 7-347, 8-362, 9-379 1-8, 2-117

LANCASHIRE	First Innings	
MJ Chilton	b Peploe	93
IJ Sutcliffe	st Nash b Peploe	59
MB Loye	c Joyce b Hayward	98
SG Law	lbw b Dalrymple	49
CL Hooper	b Dalrymple	4
AJ Swann	b Hayward	34
G Chapple	c Nash b Klusener	1
*WK Hegg (capt)	c Weekes b Dalrymple	34
SI Mahmood	lbw b Hayward	0
G Keedy	not out	3
JM Anderson	b Peploe	1
Extras	b 10, lb 13, w 4, nb 14	41
	(147.1 overs)	417

Bowling
Hayward 21-5-39-3. Klusener 25-3-99-1. Peploe 50.1-16-80-3. Hutchison 9-2-35-0. Weekes 4-0-22-0. Dalrymple 37-4-117-3. Hutton 1-0-2-0.
Fall of Wickets: 1-126, 2-189, 3-288, 4-300, 5-370, 6-371, 7-373, 8-373, 9-416

Match drawn - Lancashire (10pts), Middlesex (10pts)

Chris Read on a tense final day. Dropped from the England Test team as a result of Geraint Jones' perceived superior ability with the bat, Read responded here with a timely and courageous 108 not out. It was an innings full of aggression, with a six hit off Gareth Breese and 17 fours besides, but also one in which he assumed full responsibility for the task of seeing Notts past a stiff target of 291 in what had been a closely-fought affair. Indeed, at 152 for 5, it was Durham who seemed to be the favourites, but Read raced to his half-century from just 53 balls to seize back the initiative. Yet the total was still just 221 for 7 when Greg Smith walked out to join Read. One more wicket, and Durham would be clear favourites, but Read kept playing positively and, in the end, the pair had added an unbroken 73 in 19 overs. Earlier in the match, there had been nine wickets for the leg spin of Stuart MacGill, and David Hussey produced the most sparkling strokeplay of the contest with a stunning, unbeaten 166 off just 171 balls. The younger brother of Mike Hussey, who had plundered 469 runs off Durham's bowlers in 2003, he hit seven sixes and 16 fours and was joined by MacGill in a last-wicket stand that raised 120 and was probably the main difference between the two sides in the end. Jon Lewis and Gordon Muchall, in the first innings, and Paul Collingwood and Gary Pratt on day three, also batted attractively for

Durham, but Paul Franks' first five-wicket haul in the championship since July 2002 was another significant contribution to the Notts cause. Mark Davies, of Durham, was the other quicker bowler to emerge with credit from a fine game – his first-innings 6 for 78 underlined his new-found status as the country's leading wicket-taker, and he even commanded the respect of the hard-hitting Hussey.

Essex let Somerset off the hook at Taunton, mainly through their reluctance to declare their second innings, but also because of the batting resistance of the home tail-enders and their evergreen opener Peter Bowler. Approaching his 41st birthday in July, Bowler hit his 45th first-class hundred – and 25th for Somerset – to lead his side to the safety of a draw at 271 for 6 on a final day when 15 overs were also lost to rain. On day two, it had been the flailing bats of the Somerset Nos. 9, 10 and 11 which had prevented Essex from taking full command. At 198 for 8, in reply to Essex's first innings of 400 for 9 declared, Somerset were still 53 runs short of the follow-on target. That they were hauled up to within just 61 runs of the Essex total in the space of just 16 overs, was down to the uncomplicated hitting of Richard Johnson, Andy Caddick and last man Nixon McLean. Johnson's 58 from only 36 balls included four sixes and six fours, while Caddick struck 54 from 51 balls. Even McLean's unbeaten 22 contained

Round Seven: 25–28 May 2004 Division Two

DERBYSHIRE v. GLAMORGAN - at Derby

GLAMORGAN	First Innings		Second Innings	
MTG Elliott	c Sutton b Sheikh	77	(2) c & b Dean	15
*MA Wallace	b Welch	87	(1) c Welch b Botha	46
DL Hemp	b Sheikh	26	not out	102
MJ Powell	lbw b Dean	56	b Welch	6
MP Maynard	st Sutton b Botha	10	c Dean b Welch	17
A Dale	c Gait b Walker	40	c Sutton b Welch	5
RDB Croft (capt)	b Powell	43	c Welch b Sheikh	16
DS Harrison	b Dean	22	c Sutton b Welch	24
AG Wharf	c Powell b Dean	29	c Gait b Welch	10
SD Thomas	c Hassan Adnan b Powell	16	not out	4
DA Cosker	not out	21		
Extras	b 7, lb 9, w 7, nb 24	47	lb 8, w 1, nb 10	19
	(121.1 overs)	474	(8 wkts dec 67.4 overs)	259

Bowling
Powell 20.1-2-85-2. Walker 17-0-83-1. Dean 19-2-77-3. Welch 26-5-96-1. Sheikh 19-6-53-2. Botha 20-5-64-1.
Powell 9-0-47-0. Walker 3-0-14-0. Dean 5-0-21-1. Welch 23-4-123-6. Sheikh 9-3-21-1. Botha 18-4-48-1.
Fall of Wickets: 1-168, 2-184, 3-240, 4-273, 5-297, 6-372, 7-398, 8-436, 9-443
1-36, 2-100, 3-120, 4-144, 5-144, 6-176, 7-218, 8-240

DERBYSHIRE	First Innings		Second Innings	
SD Stubbings	c Wallace b Harrison	96	c Maynard b Croft	9
AI Gait	c Elliott b Harrison	2	c Maynard b Harrison	13
AG Botha	c Wallace b Harrison	0	lbw b Cosker	7
Hassan Adnan	lbw b Cosker	95	c Elliott b Wharf	55
CWG Bassano	c Maynard b Wharf	64	c Maynard b Croft	6
*LD Sutton (capt)	c Cosker b Thomas	24	c Maynard b Cosker	4
G Welch	c Maynard b Croft	22	b Harrison	45
MA Sheikh	st Wallace b Cosker	17	not out	9
KJ Dean	not out	25	c Powell b Croft	8
DB Powell	b Cosker	17	b Cosker	13
NGE Walker	c Thomas b Croft	1	b Wharf	16
Extras	b 2, lb 14, w 5, nb 8	29	b 8, lb 6, nb 14	28
	(129.4 overs)	392	(83.5 overs)	213

Bowling
Harrison 25-9-58-3. Wharf 14-2-57-1. Thomas 23-3-87-1. Croft 39.4-12-79-2. Cosker 27-3-93-3. Dale 1-0-2-0.
Harrison 10-4-23-2. Wharf 15.5-3-68-2. Croft 23-10-35-3. Cosker 26-13-40-3. Thomas 9-1-33-0.
Fall of Wickets: 1-7, 2-13, 3-177, 4-267, 5-281, 6-323, 7-335, 8-367, 9-389
1-21, 2-31, 3-33, 4-53, 5-66, 6-139, 7-161, 8-173, 9-187

Glamorgan won by 128 runs - Derbyshire (7pts), Glamorgan (22pts)

NOTTINGHAMSHIRE v. DURHAM - at Trent Bridge

DURHAM	First Innings		Second Innings	
JJB Lewis (capt)	b Franks	77	c Logan b Franks	16
MJ North	c Bicknell b Sidebottom	17	c Read b Franks	44
GJ Muchall	c Hussey b Franks	60	c Logan b Franks	16
PD Collingwood	c Pietersen b MacGill	31	c Warren b MacGill	68
N Peng	c Pietersen b MacGill	32	b Logan	24
GJ Pratt	lbw b MacGill	14	lbw b MacGill	71
GR Breese	lbw b MacGill	0	c Read b Franks	27
*A Pratt	not out	39	c Sidebottom b Franks	5
N Killeen	c Franks b MacGill	16	not out	2
M Davies	b MacGill	0	b Logan	6
P Kumar	run out	2	lbw b MacGill	21
Extras	b 5, lb 5, nb 2	12	b 3, lb 10, w 4	17
	(93.1 overs)	300	(85.2 overs)	315

Bowling
Smith 19.1-4-44-0. Logan 13-3-72-0. Sidebottom 17-6-40-1. Franks 15-5-53-2. MacGill 24-4-81-6.
Smith 15-2-64-0. Sidebottom 14-3-64-0. Franks 21-9-41-5. Logan 18-1-79-2. MacGill 17.2-3-54-3.
Fall of Wickets: 1-47, 2-157, 3-166, 4-203, 5-235, 6-235, 7-246, 8-288, 9-295
1-40, 2-73, 3-88, 4-120, 5-228, 6-257, 7-279, 8-283, 9-293

NOTTS	First Innings		Second Innings	
DJ Bicknell	lbw b Davies	0	lbw b Collingwood	23
JER Gallian (capt)	c Breese b Davies	36	c Pratt GJ b Killeen	30
RJ Warren	c Pratt GJ b Kumar	31	lbw b Kumar	0
KP Pietersen	c Collingwood b Kumar	20	c North b Davies	19
DJ Hussey	not out	166	c Lewis b Davies	35
*CMW Read	not out	10	not out	108
PJ Franks	c Pratt A b Davies	12	c Pratt A b Breese	14
RJ Logan	c Pratt A b Killeen	7	c Pratt A b Breese	4
GJ Smith	b Davies	2	not out	28
RJ Sidebottom	lbw b Collingwood	13		
SCG MacGill	c Pratt A b Davies	24		
Extras	b 8, lb 9, w 1, nb 6	24	b 1, lb 8, nb 4	13
	(77.5 overs)	325	(7 wkts 75.2 overs)	294

Bowling
Killeen 23-8-81-1. Davies 22.5-2-78-6. Collingwood 14-3-42-1. Kumar 11-1-56-2. Breese 7-0-51-0.
Davies 19-4-78-2. Killeen 18-0-74-1. Collingwood 15-4-57-1. Kumar 7-2-25-1. Breese 16.2-1-51-2.
Fall of Wickets: 1-5, 2-71, 3-71, 4-85, 5-103, 6-135, 7-150, 8-153, 9-205
1-64, 2-65, 3-90, 4-112, 5-152, 6-191, 7-221

Nottinghamshire won by 3 wickets -
Nottinghamshire (20pts), Durham (6pts)

SOMERSET v. ESSEX - at Taunton

ESSEX	First Innings		Second Innings	
WI Jefferson	b McLean	95	b McLean	14
AN Cook	c Turner b Caddick	8	lbw b McLean	10
AP Grayson (capt)	c Edwards b Caddick	4	b Blackwell	30
A Flower	b Caddick	42	c Turner b Caddick	172
A Habib	lbw b Caddick	32	b Blackwell	28
*JS Foster	run out	37	not out	104
JD Middlebrook	c Parsons b Caddick	115	b Caddick	1
GR Napier	c Burns b Caddick	79	c Bowler b Blackwell	9
AJ Clarke	c Edwards b McLean	2	b McLean	28
SA Brant	not out	6	b McLean	2
AGAM McCoubrey	not out	1	b McLean	0
Extras	lb 7, nb 4	11	b 1, lb 8, w 6, nb 2	17
	(9 wkts dec 98.3 overs)	400	(123.1 overs)	413

Bowling
Caddick 24.5-5-80-6. Johnson 21-2-90-0. McLean 20.3-3-75-2. Parsons 17-2-86-0. Blackwell 13-3-44-0. Burns 3-0-18-0.
Caddick 29-5-84-2. Johnson 26-7-79-0. McLean 26.1-4-87-5. Blackwell 39.4-14-146-3. Edwards 3-0-8-0.
Fall of Wickets: 1-17, 2-33, 3-140, 4-140, 5-162, 6-205, 7-380, 8-383, 9-393
1-22, 2-29, 3-100, 4-150, 5-329, 6-335, 7-353, 8-391, 9-405

SOMERSET	First Innings		Second Innings	
PD Bowler	c Flower b Napier	0	not out	138
NJ Edwards	c Foster b Clarke	26	c Foster b Brant	19
J Cox	c Cook b Brant	86	run out	3
JC Hildreth	c Flower b McCoubrey	4	b Middlebrook	41
M Burns (capt)	c Foster b Clarke	32	b Napier	6
ID Blackwell	c and b Napier	3	b Clarke	30
KA Parsons	c Cook b Clarke	12	c Foster b Clarke	11
*RJ Turner	lbw b McCoubrey	25	not out	20
RL Johnson	c Cook b Middlebrook	58		
AR Caddick	c Clarke b Brant	54		
NAM McLean	not out	22		
Extras	b 4, lb 3, w 3, nb 2	12	lb 2, w 1	3
	(78.3 overs)	339	(6 wkts 83 overs)	271

Bowling
Napier 16-7-52-2. Brant 17.3-1-87-2. Clarke 21-2-61-3. McCoubrey 10-1-52-2. Middlebrook 10-1-59-1. Grayson 4-0-21-0.
Napier 22-1-84-1. Clarke 19-5-50-2. Brant 11-4-24-1. Grayson 8-1-24-0. McCoubrey 6-2-35-0. Middlebrook 17-2-52-1.
Fall of Wickets: 1-0, 2-40, 3-51, 4-144, 5-147, 6-162, 7-198, 8-198, 9-291
1-44, 2-56, 3-131, 4-156, 5-192, 6-209

Match drawn - Somerset (10pts), Essex (12pts)

An unbeaten 138 from Somerset veteran Peter Bowler, the 45th century of his first-class career, earned his county a draw with Essex.

Round Eight: 2–5 June 2004

Division One

Warwickshire moved to the top of Division One after trouncing Middlesex at Lord's. Victory, by an innings and eight runs, came on the back of a monumental 303 not out from skipper Nick Knight and an eye-catching all-round contribution from the gifted Ian Bell. It was Knight's first century at Lord's, and he certainly celebrated it in style as he became only the fifth batsman in history to score a triple-century at the game's headquarters. Funnily enough, the fourth player to do so was Knight's current opening partner, Mark Wagh, in 2001 – the last time Warwickshire had played a championship fixture at the ground. Bell's 129 was also his maiden hundred at Lord's, and he also followed it up with something special; in his case, a startling championship-best return of 4–1–4–4 as his medium pacers undermined the Middlesex reply. Dismissed for just 163 in reply to Warwickshire's huge total of 608 for 7 declared, and with only Paul Weekes showing any kind of resistance, Middlesex were seemingly without hope as they followed on. At least they made some sort of fight of it, however, reaching 437 thanks to Ben Hutton's 126 and half-centuries from Sven Koenig, Ed Joyce and Weekes, who added 62 to his first-innings 70.

Kent's seven-wicket win over Lancashire at Tunbridge Wells was their tenth victory in 14 championship games going back to July 2003, and it was a triumph in particular for Andrew Symonds. 'I wouldn't swap him for any other overseas player in the world', said Kent captain David Fulton afterwards, having seen Symonds spearhead a magnificent effort in the field as Lancashire, forced to follow on, were bowled out for 307 and 395. The Australian all-rounder took 8 for 231 in the match, alternating between seam and spin and showing both great stamina and a huge desire to flog the life out of a batsman-friendly surface; he also brought off one of the greatest outfield catches seen in the 174 first-class matches played at the beautiful Nevill Ground. The match also provided a notable achievement for Kent opener Rob Key who, almost a year to the day after the last of his first eight Test caps for England, became the first player to reach 1,000 first-class runs for the season. It was his fifth century in seven innings and the landmark was reached when he late cut a four to go to 94. Key went on to score 180, adding 229 in 58 overs for the second wicket with Ed Smith, whose 116 promised a

two driven sixes, and the West Indian fast bowler then took 5 for 87 in the Essex second innings. The visitors did well to reach 413, thanks in the main to a classy knock of 172 from Andy Flower – a 293-ball effort containing two sixes and 22 fours – and an unbeaten 104 from the in-form James Foster. They clearly batted on too long, however, especially with showers forecast for the final day. That was a disappointment considering the advantage they had worked so hard to claim on the opening day when they withstood Caddick's 6 for 80 to rally from 205 for 6. Will Jefferson's 95 was followed by a seventh-wicket stand of 175 between James Middlebrook – who hit his maiden championship hundred – and Graham Napier.

return to form. Michael Carberry and Matthew Walker also enjoyed themselves as Kent piled up a ground-record score of 615. The Lancashire resistance was led chiefly by Glen Chapple, who scored 102 in the visitor's second innings.

Round Eight: 2–5 June 2004 Division One

MIDDLESEX v. WARWICKSHIRE - at Lord's

WARWICKSHIRE	First Innings	
NV Knight (capt)	not out	303
MA Wagh	c Weekes b Dalrymple	43
IR Bell	b Hayward	129
IJL Trott	c sub b Hayward	3
JO Troughton	lbw b Hayward	0
DR Brown	c Hayward b Klusener	13
GB Hogg	c Hutchison b Dalrymple	71
NM Carter	c Shah b Weekes	13
*T Frost	not out	11
D Pretorius		
N Tahir		
Extras	b 2, lb 11, w 5, nb 4	22
	(7 wkts dec 162.4 overs)	**608**

Bowling
Hayward 26-4-82-3. Klusener 28-3-104-1. Hutchison 32-5-92-0. Hutton 12-1-45-0. Dalrymple 21.4-2-99-2. Peploe 10-2-33-0. Weekes 28-1-120-1. Shah 1-0-3-0. Joyce 4-0-17-0.
Fall of Wickets: 1-118, 2-372, 3-382, 4-382, 5-406, 6-556, 7-579

MIDDLESEX	First Innings		Second Innings	
BL Hutton	c Bell b Pretorius	17	(2) lbw b Wagh	126
SG Koenig	c Frost b Carter	1	(1) c Brown b Wagh	57
OA Shah (capt)	b Carter	0	c Hogg b Wagh	3
EC Joyce	b Carter	5	c sub b Brown	66
PN Weekes	c Trott b Carter	70	c Knight b Brown	62
JWM Dalrymple	st Frost b Brown	19	c Hogg b Tahir	17
*DC Nash	c Brown b Bell	29	c sub b Pretorius	32
L Klusener	lbw b Bell	0	lbw b Bell	12
CT Peploe	c Frost b Bell	3	not out	19
PM Hutchison	b Bell	0	c sub b Pretorius	0
M Hayward	not out	0	c Carter b Pretorius	7
Extras	b 9, lb 9, w 1	19	b 14, lb 21, w 1	36
	(51.3 overs)	**163**	(153.3 overs)	**437**

Bowling
Pretorius 11-2-29-1. Carter 16.3-2-50-4. Brown 11-3-33-1. Tahir 9-1-29-0. Bell 4-1-4-4.
Pretorius 27.3-6-86-3. Carter 29-9-64-0. Tahir 12-3-38-1. Brown 18-4-46-2. Wagh 30-2-85-3. Bell 8-3-14-1. Troughton 6-1-16-0. Hogg 23-8-53-0.
Fall of Wickets: 1-12, 2-12, 3-22, 4-28, 5-72, 6-155, 7-155, 8-163, 9-163
1-167, 2-173, 3-243, 4-339, 5-340, 6-362, 7-393, 8-411, 9-421

Warwickshire won by an innings and 8 runs - Middlesex (1pt), Warwickshire (22pts)

At the foot of the Division One table before this round of games, Gloucestershire hauled themselves off the bottom by beating Surrey by six wickets at Bristol. Player-coach Mark Alleyne, a late replacement for bruised-toe victim Alex Gidman, was the initial star of the Gloucestershire show: he took 5 for 71 – his best bowling figures since 2001 and only his ninth career haul of five or more – as Surrey were dismissed for a first-innings 298. This was an underachievement, despite the indiscipline of Shabbir Ahmed (ten no-balls and two wides) which contributed almost half of a total of 52 extras. Phil Weston soon underlined that fact by hitting a commanding 135 as Gloucestershire replied with 406. Scott Newman fell to Jon Lewis in the eight overs possible on the second evening, and Lewis went on to grab the first seven-wicket analysis of his career as Surrey collapsed limply to 213 all out. Even that total was boosted substantially by a last-wicket stand of 104 between the ever-immaculate Mark Ramprakash (64 not out) and Jimmy Ormond, who hit ten boundaries in a career-best 57. It simply put everything that had gone before into perspective.

Gareth Batty, with a spell of 4 for 2 in eight balls at one stage, undermined Northamptonshire at spin-friendly Wantage Road by taking a career-best 7 for 52 on the opening day. Tom Huggins made a maiden first-class 50, but from 88 for 1 the Northants first innings collapsed to 177 all out against Batty's off

KENT v. LANCASHIRE - at Tunbridge Wells

KENT	First Innings		Second Innings	
DP Fulton (capt)	b Crook	42	c Cork b Chapple	14
RWT Key	lbw b Chapple	180	b Hogg	44
ET Smith	c Keedy b Hogg	116	not out	21
A Symonds	b Crook	33	c Law b Hogg	4
MJ Walker	c Hegg b Swann	72	not out	4
MA Carberry	c Hegg b Chapple	85		
*NJ O'Brien	b Keedy	0		
MM Patel	c Chilton b Chapple	25		
Mohammad Sami	c Hegg b Chapple	0		
DA Stiff	lbw b Chapple	18		
A Sheriyar	not out	5		
Extras	b 9, lb 18, w 4, nb 8	39	nb 4	4
	(150.1 overs)	**615**	(3 wkts 20 overs)	**91**

Bowling
Chapple 36.1-7-136-5. Cork 28-3-116-0. Hogg 17-2-52-1. Crook 25-1-117-2. Keedy 28-2-114-1. Chilton 7-0-23-0. Law 5-1-16-0. Swann 4-2-14-1.
Chapple 4-0-26-1. Cork 5-0-26-0. Keedy 7-2-23-0. Hogg 4-1-16-2.
Fall of Wickets: 1-83, 2-312, 3-398, 4-402, 5-556, 6-561, 7-580, 8-580, 9-602
1-24, 2-79, 3-83

LANCASHIRE	First Innings		Second Innings	
MJ Chilton	run out	37	c Fulton b Patel	25
IJ Sutcliffe	lbw b Symonds	50	lbw b Sheriyar	10
MB Loye	c O'Brien b Symonds	1	lbw b Symonds	34
SG Law	c Walker b Symonds	17	c Fulton b Patel	48
AJ Swann	lbw b Sheriyar	19	b Symonds	6
G Chapple	c Walker b Stiff	28	b Sheriyar	102
SP Crook	lbw b Sheriyar	37	c & b Symonds	68
*WK Hegg (capt)	c Symonds b Mohammad Sami	24	b Symonds	44
KW Hogg	c Walker b Mohammad Sami	4	(10) c sub b Symonds	20
DG Cork	not out	35	(9) c Key b Sheriyar	1
G Keedy	c Walker b Stiff	4	not out	3
Extras	b 4, lb 9, nb 38	51	b 4, lb 9, w 5, nb 16	34
	(67 overs)	**307**	(120.4 overs)	**395**

Bowling
Mohammad Sami 18-3-117-2. Sheriyar 15-4-57-2. Symonds 23-8-51-3. Stiff 9-1-58-2. Walker 2-0-11-0.
Mohammad Sami 8-2-39-0. Sheriyar 20-3-72-3. Symonds 52.4-13-140-5. Patel 32-8-77-2. Stiff 8-0-54-0.
Fall of Wickets: 1-83, 2-96, 3-124, 4-131, 5-183, 6-201, 7-256, 8-267, 9-267
1-30, 2-53, 3-129, 4-129, 5-135, 6-288, 7-360, 8-362, 9-372

Kent won by 7 wickets - Kent (22pts), Lancashire (4pts)

GLOUCESTERSHIRE v. SURREY - at Bristol

SURREY	First Innings		Second Innings	
SA Newman	b Shabbir	18	c Weston b Lewis	10
*JN Batty (capt)	b Lewis	5	c Alleyne b Lewis	11
MR Ramprakash	c Adshead b Alleyne	6	(4) not out	64
R Clarke	c Weston b Alleyne	62	(5) lbw b Lewis	12
AD Brown	c Weston b Averis	5	(6) b Lewis	0
N Shahid	b Alleyne	53	(7) c Adshead b Lewis	0
Azhar Mahmood	lbw b Averis	14	(8) c Alleyne b Lewis	11
MP Bicknell	not out	47	(9) c Hancock b Shoaib Malik	26
TJ Murtagh	b Alleyne	25	(10) c Adshead b Averis	0
J Ormond	c Alleyne b Shabbir	11	(11) c Taylor b Shabbir	57
ND Doshi	c Windows b Alleyne	0	(3) c Adshead b Lewis	11
Extras	b 7, lb 11, w 4, nb 30	52	b 4, lb 5, nb 2	11
	(71.3 overs)	**298**	(58.2 overs)	**213**

Bowling
Lewis 14-6-43-1. Shabbir 18-2-91-2. Alleyne 17.3-4-71-5. Averis 12-2-41-2. Shoaib Malik 10-0-34-0.
Lewis 21-3-72-7. Shabbir 15.2-3-48-1. Alleyne 6-2-24-0. Averis 6-0-24-1. Shoaib Malik 10-0-36-1.
Fall of Wickets: 1-23, 2-31, 3-37, 4-66, 5-155, 6-188, 7-203, 8-264, 9-293
1-16, 2-36, 3-41, 4-53, 5-55, 6-59, 7-75, 8-108, 9-109

GLOS	First Innings		Second Innings	
CM Spearman	lbw b Bicknell	4	(2) c sub b Bicknell	28
WPC Weston	b Murtagh	135	(1) lbw b Bicknell	10
THC Hancock	c Batty b Clarke	43	b Doshi	21
MGN Windows	b Azhar Mahmood	58	not out	23
CG Taylor (capt)	c Brown b Bicknell	24	c Clarke b Doshi	0
Shoaib Malik	c Newman b Bicknell	1	not out	12
MW Alleyne	c Newman b Azhar Mahmood	51		
*SJ Adshead	c Ormond b Bicknell	30		
JMM Averis	lbw b Murtagh	14		
J Lewis	c Ramprakash b Murtagh	8		
Shabbir Ahmed	not out	0		
Extras	b 5, lb 12, w 1, nb 20	38	lb 2, nb 10	12
	(125.2 overs)	**406**	(4 wkts 25.4 overs)	**106**

Bowling
Bicknell 34.2-11-107-4. Ormond 26-5-75-0. Clarke 9-0-58-1. Murtagh 21-5-78-3. Doshi 19-7-26-0. Azhar Mahmood 16-4-45-2.
Bicknell 10-2-46-2. Ormond 4-1-21-0. Azhar Mahmood 5-2-14-0. Murtagh 3.4-0-13-0. Doshi 3-1-10-2.
Fall of Wickets: 1-7, 2-86, 3-196, 4-248, 5-250, 6-338, 7-356, 8-388, 9-404
1-34, 2-51, 3-87, 4-91

Gloucestershire won by 6 wickets - Gloucestershire (22pts), Surrey (5pts)

NORTHAMPTONSHIRE v. WORCESTERSHIRE - at Northampton

NORTHANTS	First Innings		Second Innings	
TB Huggins	st Rhodes b Batty	51	(2) c Smith b Batty	17
TW Roberts	b Batty	30	(1) lbw b Mason	22
M van Jaarsveld	c Smith b Batty	13	c Rhodes b Batty	28
U Afzaal	c Moore b Mason	32	b Solanki	57
DJG Sales (capt)	b Batty	0	c Solanki b Kabir Ali	22
GP Swann	c Solanki b Batty	2	c Moore b Kabir Ali	6
*GL Brophy	b Batty	0	c Smith b Khalid	25
J Louw	c Kabir Ali b Khalid	11	c Solanki b Bichel	28
BJ Phillips	c Hick b Khalid	1	c Solanki b Bichel	4
AJ Shantry	not out	2	not out	0
JF Brown	c Hick b Batty	21	c & b Batty	3
Extras	lb 2, nb 12	14	b 30, lb 3, w 1, nb 18	52
	(67 overs)	**177**	(98.4 overs)	**264**

Bowling
Bichel 13-4-54-0. Kabir Ali 4-0-21-0. Batty 27-10-52-7. Mason 14-5-28-1. Khalid 9-2-20-2.
Bichel 16-4-42-2. Mason 16-4-34-1. Batty 34.4-11-61-3. Kabir Ali 6-0-26-2. Khalid 20-4-53-1. Solanki 6-0-15-1.
Fall of Wickets: 1-56, 2-88, 3-113, 4-113, 5-123, 6-123, 7-141, 8-153, 9-154
1-45, 2-67, 3-99, 4-140, 5-156, 6-208, 7-239, 8-258, 9-261

WORCS	First Innings		Second Innings	
SD Peters	lbw b Swann	63	c Brophy b Phillips	8
SC Moore	c Huggins b Brown	18	not out	66
GA Hick	b Swann	34	not out	63
BF Smith (capt)	c van Jaarsveld b Swann	46		
VS Solanki	run out	32		
GJ Batty	b Brown	36		
AJ Bichel	c and b Swann	21		
Kabir Ali	lbw b Louw	24		
*SJ Rhodes	b Phillips	7		
MS Mason	c Brophy b Shantry	1		
SA Khalid	not out	1		
Extras	b 5, w 2, nb 2	9	b 4, lb 5, w 2, nb 4	15
	(103.3 overs)	**292**	(1 wkt 54.5 overs)	**152**

Bowling
Shantry 12-4-34-1. Louw 8.3-2-18-1. Swann 41-9-111-4. Brown 22-4-83-2. Phillips 20-7-41-1.
Shantry 2-0-9-0. Phillips 5-1-14-1. Swann 22-1-51-0. Brown 19-5-38-0. Afzaal 6.5-1-31-0.
Fall of Wickets: 1-50, 2-123, 3-124, 4-180, 5-229, 6-243, 7-267, 8-283, 9-284
1-20

Worcestershire won by 9 wickets - Northamptonshire (3pts), Worcestershire (19pts)

breaks. Worcestershire did not waste the opportunity to take early control. By the close they were 119 for 1, and, although Stephen Peters did not add to his overnight 63, the visitors still established a useful first-innings lead by reaching 292. There were three more wickets for Batty as Northants ground out 264 second time around, but a potentially tricky win target of 150 was cut down to size by the Worcestershire second-wicket pairing of Stephen Moore and Graeme Hick. Both finished unbeaten,

A brilliant triple-hundred by Nick Knight put Warwickshire on the way to victory against Middlesex at Lord's.

on 66 and 63 respectively, as Worcestershire ran out comfortable winners by nine wickets.

Division Two

It took just two days for Nottinghamshire to complete an innings-and-44-run humbling of Hampshire at their swanky Rose Bowl home. Shane Warne captured the 900th first-class wicket of his great career, but there was little else for Hampshire to celebrate as poor batting let them down. Mark Ealham, meanwhile, thumped the home attack to all parts as he struck two sixes and 17 fours in a fine innings of 96 from 133 balls. Ealham's blitz boosted Notts to 356 all out early on day two, after Darren Bicknell and Kevin Pietersen had taken them to 185 for 5 at the end of a first day that began with Hampshire being dismissed for 199. Six Hampshire batsmen passed 20, but Shaun Udal's 36 was the highest score as the seam and swing of Richard Logan and Paul Franks inflicted significant damage on the home side. Logan took his second four-wicket haul of the game in the Hampshire second-innings slide to 113 all out, while Franks grabbed his second three-wicket return and Greg Smith also got in on the act.

Glamorgan achieved their fourth successive victory at Swansea's seaside St Helens ground, sending Somerset to the bottom of the championship table with a comfortable seven-wicket win. The batting of Matthew Elliott and David Hemp played a big part in the Welsh county's success, while David Harrison also impressed with a five-wicket first-innings haul and Robert Croft, the captain, took the 800th first-class wicket of his career during Somerset's collapse to 229 all out on the opening day. By the close of day one, Glamorgan were already 180 for 1 in reply, with Elliott unbeaten on 129 and scoring exactly 100 of those runs in the final session. The Australian left-hander hit four sixes and 17 fours in his eventual 157, adding 180 for the second wicket with Hemp. Only when they were parted did Richard Johnson and Nixon McLean make inroads into the Glamorgan first innings, and even then a final total of 388 gave the home side a sizeable advantage. That was pressed home further as Somerset subsided to 84 for 3 by the close of the second day, although a pugnacious 131 from Ian Blackwell – an innings that included 22 fours – then took the match into the fourth day. Elliott and Hemp made short work of a target of 212, however, hitting out aggressively for 87 and 57 respectively and adding 109 for the second wicket.

Glamorgan's David Harrison set up a win over Somerset with a first-innings five-wicket haul at St Helens.

Leicestershire, meanwhile, were the club moving off the bottom of the Division Two table as they defeated Derbyshire by six wickets in a thrilling finish at Oakham School. On a pitch that gleamed white in the sunshine, Leicestershire ran up a first-innings total of 534 to take immediate command of the contest. The prolific Brad Hodge led the way with 221 from 290 balls, and although Steve Stubbings made a quick-fire 50 on the second evening, Derbyshire were struggling at 72 for 4 by the close. That they reached 291 was down to 62 from Chris Bassano and a whirlwind 63 not out from No. 11 Nick Walker, who added to his growing reputation as a hitter by reaching his half-century off just 24 balls and striking four sixes and seven fours in all. Even so, Derbyshire were forced to follow on and were 123 for 4 by the end of day three – despite another hard-hit 66 by opener Stubbings, who was out seven balls before stumps. Mark Cleary, the pace bowler, had taken three of those wickets, and had also caused Chris Rogers to retire hurt with a broken thumb. Graeme Welch, though, then took it upon himself to mark his 200th first-class innings with an unbeaten 115 and, with Luke Sutton scoring 58, the gutsy Derbyshire last-day resistance almost embarrassed the home side. Cleary finished with 7 for 80 in a Derbyshire second-innings total of 323, but Leicestershire's target was by now a potentially

Round Eight: 2–5 June 2004 Division Two

HAMPSHIRE v. NOTTINGHAMSHIRE - at The Rose Bowl

HAMPSHIRE	First Innings		Second Innings	
DA Kenway	c Read b Smith	21	c Read b Franks	23
MJ Brown	lbw b Logan	20	b Smith	10
WS Kendall	lbw b Ealham	0	b Logan	21
MJ Clarke	b Logan	28	c Ealham b Franks	7
JP Crawley	c Hussey b Franks	25	c Ealham b Franks	7
*N Pothas	c Hussey b Franks	26	lbw b Logan	3
AD Mascarenhas	c Read b Smith	9	c Read b Smith	18
SK Warne (capt)	c Hussey b Franks	14	c Bicknell b Logan	8
SD Udal	c Read b Logan	36	not out	8
CT Tremlett	c Warren b Logan	11	c Hussey b Logan	3
AD Mullally	not out	5	c Ealham b Smith	0
Extras	lb 2, w 2	4	b 1, lb 4	5
	(54.1 overs)	**199**	(35.4 overs)	**113**

Bowling
Smith 17-6-52-2. Franks 14-5-43-3. Ealham 13-5-46-1. Logan 10.1-2-56-4.
Smith 10.4-0-34-3. Ealham 4-2-5-0. Franks 10-0-35-3. Logan 11-2-34-4.
Fall of Wickets: 1-36, 2-40, 3-73, 4-98, 5-98, 6-124, 7-139, 8-156, 9-194
1-29, 2-33, 3-62, 4-66, 5-76, 6-78, 7-95, 8-109, 9-112

NOTTS	First Innings	
DJ Bicknell	lbw b Mascarenhas	54
JER Gallian (capt)	c Kendall b Tremlett	9
RJ Warren	lbw b Tremlett	0
KP Pietersen	lbw b Udal	49
DJ Hussey	c Pothas b Tremlett	48
*CMW Read	b Udal	5
MA Ealham	c Pothas b Kendall	96
PJ Franks	c Clarke b Warne	32
GJ Smith	c Mascarenhas b Warne	21
RJ Logan	not out	9
SCG MacGill	c sub b Tremlett	4
Extras	b 4, lb 6, nb 19	29
	(95.2 overs)	**356**

Bowling
Tremlett 22.2-3-102-4. Mullally 15-7-29-0. Mascarenhas 20-8-55-1.
Warne 21-3-85-2. Udal 14-3-57-2. Kendall 2-0-12-1. Clarke 1-0-6-0.
Fall of Wickets: 1-19, 2-25, 3-124, 4-130, 5-136, 6-279, 7-291, 8-331, 9-340

Nottinghamshire won by an innings and 44 runs –
Hampshire (3pts), Nottinghamshire (21pts)

GLAMORGAN v. SOMERSET - at Swansea

SOMERSET	First Innings		Second Innings	
PD Bowler	lbw b Kasprowicz	4	lbw b Kasprowicz	2
NJ Edwards	c Powell b Harrison	4	c Wallace b Wharf	15
J Cox	c Wallace b Harrison	2	c Cosker b Wharf	50
JC Hildreth	c Cosker b Harrison	61	c Hughes b Wharf	0
M Burns (capt)	c and b Harrison	11	c Hughes b Cosker	54
ID Blackwell	c Cosker b Croft	64	c Hemp b Croft	131
*RJ Turner	c Cosker b Harrison	2	lbw b Cosker	18
KP Dutch	lbw b Croft	31	c Wallace b Harrison	27
RL Johnson	c Cosker b Croft	17	c Maynard b Croft	27
AR Caddick	not out	1	not out	22
NAM McLean	c Powell b Kasprowicz	1	lbw b Croft	7
Extras	b 1, lb 8, nb 14	23	b 3, lb 11, w 1, nb 2	17
	(54.5 overs)	**229**	(137.4 overs)	**370**

Bowling
Kasprowicz 16.5-1-87-2. Harrison 17-5-48-5. Wharf 10-2-41-0. Croft 11-3-44-3.
Kasprowicz 30-7-101-1. Harrison 20-4-57-1. Croft 38.4-12-78-3. Cosker 33-13-62-2.
Wharf 16-3-58-3.
Fall of Wickets: 1-10, 2-12, 3-16, 4-71, 5-94, 6-112, 7-196, 8-200, 9-227
1-8, 2-28, 3-28, 4-125, 5-152, 6-202, 7-266, 8-324, 9-345

GLAMORGAN	First Innings		Second Innings	
MTG Elliott	c Johnson b Blackwell	157	(2) c Turner b Dutch	87
*MA Wallace	c Turner b McLean	22	(1) c Edwards b McLean	29
DL Hemp	c Turner b Johnson	66	c Burns b Blackwell	57
MJ Powell	b McLean	36	not out	21
MP Maynard	c Hildreth b Dutch	25	not out	31
J Hughes	c Turner b Johnson	35		
RDB Croft (capt)	c Burns b McLean	6		
AG Wharf	c Cox b McLean	0		
DS Harrison	c Turner b Johnson	22		
MS Kasprowicz	b Johnson	0		
DA Cosker	not out	4		
Extras	lb 13, nb 2	15	b 4, lb 1, nb 6	11
	(102.1 overs)	**388**	(3 wkts 48.5 overs)	**212**

Bowling
Caddick 25-1-93-0. Johnson 26.1-8-83-4. McLean 19-5-91-4. Dutch 25-8-85-1.
Blackwell 7-2-23-1.
Caddick 13-4-49-0. Johnson 1-0-10-0. McLean 12-1-62-1. Blackwell 13.5-1-52-1.
Dutch 9-1-34-1.
Fall of Wickets: 1-53, 2-233, 3-253, 4-312, 5-314, 6-324, 7-324, 8-367, 9-367
1-49, 2-158, 3-158

Glamorgan won by 7 wickets – Glamorgan (21pts), Somerset (4pts)

LEICESTERSHIRE v. DERBYSHIRE - at Oakham School

LEICESTERSHIRE	First Innings		Second Innings	
DDJ Robinson	c Welch b Botha	64	c Hassan Adnan b Sheikh	29
JK Maunders	c Sutton b Dean	28	c sub b Sheikh	2
BJ Hodge	b Dean	221	c Walker b Botha	29
DL Maddy	run out	1	(5) not out	12
JL Sadler	c Walker b Botha	41	(6) not out	10
*PA Nixon	c Rogers b Sheikh	40	(4) c sub b Botha	10
PAJ DeFreitas (capt)	b Welch	46		
OD Gibson	b Dean	0		
CW Henderson	c Bassano b Welch	35		
CE Dagnall	c Bassano b Botha	15		
MF Cleary	not out	11		
Extras	lb 7, w 9, nb 16	32	lb 1	1
	(143.4 overs)	**534**	(4 wkts 13 overs)	**83**

Bowling
Welch 35-8-141-2. Walker 18-2-82-0. Dean 29-3-111-3. Sheikh 35-11-97-1.
Botha 24.4-3-92-3. Hassan Adnan 2-0-4-0.
Dean 3-0-24-0. Sheikh 6-0-30-2. Botha 4-0-28-2.
Fall of Wickets: 1-91, 2-111, 3-135, 4-230, 5-422, 6-428, 7-436, 8-503, 9-508
1-4, 2-58, 3-61, 4-75

DERBYSHIRE	First Innings		Second Innings	
AI Gait	c Maddy b Dagnall	6	c Nixon b Cleary	24
SD Stubbings	lbw b DeFreitas	50	c Maddy b Henderson	66
CJL Rogers	lbw b Dagnall	0	retired hurt	0
Hassan Adnan	c Maddy b DeFreitas	5	c Nixon b Cleary	0
CWG Bassano	c Robinson b Dagnall	62	b Cleary	7
*LD Sutton (capt)	lbw b Maddy b Dagnall	14	not out	58
G Welch	c Maddy b DeFreitas	1	not out	115
AG Botha	lbw b Maddy	5	c Nixon b Cleary	2
MA Sheikh	run out	32	c Robinson b DeFreitas	6
KJ Dean	st Nixon b Hodge	35	c Nixon b Cleary	7
NGE Walker	not out	63	b Cleary	10
Extras	lb 4, w 2, nb 12	18	lb 13, nb 14	28
	(86.4 overs)	**291**	(9 wkts 121.3 overs)	**323**

Bowling
Gibson 9.4-1-36-0. DeFreitas 17.2-7-37-3. Dagnall 14-5-37-4. Cleary 15-2-47-0.
Maddy 11.4-1-59-1. Henderson 13-3-41-0. Hodge 6-1-30-1.
DeFreitas 27-6-64-1. Dagnall 20-7-39-0. Henderson 36-16-71-1. Cleary 23.3-5-80-7.
Hodge 6-0-29-0. Maddy 8-3-19-0. Maunders 1-0-7-0.
Fall of Wickets: 1-46, 2-46, 3-68, 4-69, 5-101, 6-112, 7-135, 8-172, 9-215
1-57, 2-57, 3-73, 4-119, 5-249, 6-261, 7-275, 8-297, 9-323

Leicestershire won by 6 wickets –
Leicestershire (22pts), Derbyshire (4pts)

tricky 81 from just 14 overs. With Darren Robinson and Hodge to the fore, the target was achieved with just six balls to spare. This stirring match was also memorable for Phil DeFreitas, the Leicestershire captain and former England all-rounder, who went past Allan Donald to become the highest first-class wicket-taker still playing during the Derbyshire first innings.

Danish Kaneria, the Pakistan leg spinner, achieved match figures of 13 for 186 against Yorkshire at Chelmsford and still ended up on the losing side. Yorkshire's 137-run win came courtesy of a second-innings batting collapse by Essex, who were dismissed for just 116. Until that unexpected disintegration, this had been a closely contested affair. Just four runs separated the two teams at the halfway mark, with Essex replying to Yorkshire's first-day 363 with 359 and Ronnie Irani's 107 all but cancelling out Phil Jaques' 115. The match had started explosively with Darren Gough removing Matthew Wood with just his third ball against his former county, but the strokeplay of Jaques, who struck three sixes and 11 fours, and McGrath (93) threatened to take the game away from Essex until Kaneria picked up four wickets for five runs in the space of 34 balls. Irani, in his first championship appearance of the season, clubbed three sixes and ten fours and lost little time in demonstrating his worth as a specialist batsman following the decision

that a chronic knee injury would curtail his bowling career. Wood and Darren Lehmann were the only Yorkshire batsmen to flourish against Kaneria second time around and, by the close, Lehmann had taken 4 for 35 with his left-arm spin to add to his innings of 86 as Essex crumbled to 108 for 8.

Round Nine: 8–12 June 2004

Division One

A 128-year-old record belonging to WG Grace finally fell to Craig Spearman, the exhilarating strokemaker from Auckland, as Gloucestershire trounced Middlesex by ten wickets at Archdeacon Meadow in Gloucester. The legendary doctor's Gloucestershire first-class record score of 318 not out, made against Yorkshire at nearby Cheltenham in 1876, was passed when 31-year-old Spearman turned a ball from medium pacer Ben Hutton through midwicket for two. Minutes earlier, he had passed both Jack Hobbs' 316 not out for Surrey at Lord's in 1926 (the previous highest score against Middlesex) and Wally Hammond's 317 for Gloucestershire against Nottinghamshire, also at Gloucester, in 1936. Hobbs, Hammond and then Grace: what a trinity to put in the shade! Spearman eventually departed for an epic 341, caught behind off Hutton (another great cricket name!), having batted for almost nine hours and having faced 390 balls, hitting six sixes and 40 fours. 'It hasn't really sunk in yet', said Spearman soon after his great innings, 'but it is something special to beat a WG Grace record. He's the father of cricket. But I wasn't that nervous in the 290s because I was focussing on getting to 319'. Spearman had resumed that historic third day on 208, having dominated an opening partnership worth 227 with Phil Weston, who scored 85. Gloucestershire, who had begun the day on 353 for 2 in reply to Middlesex's 383, finally declared on 695 for 9, with skipper Chris Taylor also batting well for his 100 and Alex Gidman contributing a bright and breezy 51. Middlesex, who must have thought themselves in good shape at 333 for 6 at the end of the opening day, resisted spiritedly second time around through Owais Shah (72) and Ed Joyce (71), but when they both fell early on the final morning, only Paul Weekes and Lance Klusener, with their second half-centuries of the match, held up the Gloucestershire bowlers for long. Spearman, fittingly, then finished unbeaten on 29 (taking his match aggregate and average to 370) as Gloucestershire raced to the 47 runs they

ESSEX v. YORKSHIRE - at Chelmsford

YORKSHIRE	First Innings		Second Innings	
MJ Wood	c Foster b Gough	0	c Foster b Clarke	81
PA Jaques	c Napier b Middlebrook	115	c Foster b Gough	13
A McGrath	c Foster b Danish Kaneria	93	(4) c Danish Kaneria b Gough	5
DS Lehmann	c Foster b Danish Kaneria	27	(5) lbw b Danish Kaneria	86
MJ Lumb	c Napier b Middlebrook	45	(6) c & b Danish Kaneria	36
C White (capt)	lbw b Danish Kaneria	1	(7) lbw b Danish Kaneria	4
*SM Guy	b Danish Kaneria	3	(8) c Flower b Danish Kaneria	6
RKJ Dawson	lbw b Danish Kaneria	49	(9) lbw b Danish Kaneria	5
TT Bresnan	not out	10	(10) lbw b Danish Kaneria	0
CEW Silverwood	b Gough	3	(11) not out	4
SP Kirby	lbw b Danish Kaneria	0	(3) b Danish Kaneria	1
Extras	b 8, lb 7, nb 2	17	lb 7, w 1	8
	(87.5 overs)	363	(75.1 overs)	249

Bowling
Gough 11-1-27-2. Napier 7-0-36-0. Clarke 9-2-42-0. Danish Kaneria 33.5-5-121-6. Middlebrook 27-1-122-2.
Gough 21-7-54-2. Napier 8-0-54-0. Danish Kaneria 23.1-5-65-7. Middlebrook 12-0-40-0. Clarke 11-4-29-1.
Fall of Wickets: 1-0, 2-207, 3-241, 4-254, 5-260, 6-268, 7-310, 8-351, 9-362 1-35, 2-46, 3-53, 4-188, 5-210, 6-226, 7-235, 8-244, 9-244

ESSEX	First Innings		Second Innings	
WI Jefferson	st Guy b Dawson	45	c Wood b Silverwood	8
AN Cook	c White b Kirby	0	lbw b Silverwood	2
A Flower	c Jaques b Dawson	43	c Lumb b Lehmann	37
A Habib	c Guy b Silverwood	80	c Jaques b Lehmann	17
RC Irani (capt)	c Guy b Kirby	107	c Wood b Lehmann	8
*JS Foster	c White b Kirby	20	lbw b Dawson	5
JD Middlebrook	c McGrath b Lehmann	2	(8) c Lumb b Dawson	4
GR Napier	run out	13	(7) c Jaques b Kirby	5
D Gough	b Silverwood	13	(10) c Wood b Silverwood	15
AJ Clarke	c Jaques b Silverwood	12	(9) lbw b Lehmann	0
Danish Kaneria	not out	7	not out	0
Extras	b 5, lb 4, w 4, nb 4	17	b 8, lb 3, nb 4	15
	(104.3 overs)	359	(49.1 overs)	116

Bowling
Silverwood 22.3-1-84-3. Kirby 21-2-86-3. Dawson 32-7-101-2. Lehmann 20-4-61-1. Bresnan 6-2-16-0. White 3-2-2-0.
Silverwood 7-1-18-3. Kirby 6.1-0-20-1. Dawson 19-6-32-2. Lehmann 17-2-35-4.
Fall of Wickets: 1-12, 2-81, 3-118, 4-226, 5-260, 6-265, 7-318, 8-326, 9-348 1-9, 2-18, 3-56, 4-70, 5-77, 6-82, 7-93, 8-95, 9-116

Yorkshire won by 137 runs - Essex (7pts), Yorkshire (21pts)

required to clinch victory in a game that will for ever be remembered as 'Spearman's match'.

Champions Sussex finally recorded their first championship win of the summer as Lancashire, the overwhelming pre-season favourites for the title, slid

Round Nine: 9–12 June 2004 Division One

GLOUCESTERSHIRE v. MIDDLESEX - at Gloucester

MIDDLESEX	First Innings		Second Innings	
BL Hutton	c Adshead b Lewis	14	c Adshead b Lewis	6
SG Koenig	lbw b Smith	45	b Shabbir	3
OA Shah (capt)	c Spearman b Gidman	34	c Shabbir b Lewis	72
EC Joyce	c Weston b Shoaib Malik	28	c Adshead b Shoaib Malik	71
PN Weekes	c Adshead b Shabbir	50	lbw b Fisher	53
JWM Dalrymple	b Lewis	49	lbw b Lewis	0
*DC Nash	run out	12	c Weston b Fisher	16
L Klusener	b Shabbir	63	not out	68
CT Peploe	not out	28	c Shoaib Malik b Fisher	28
PM Hutchison	b Shabbir	8	lbw b Fisher	0
M Hayward	b Shabbir	7	b Shabbir	1
Extras	b 6, lb 6, w 1, nb 28	45	lb 2, w 2, nb 10	40
	(117.1 overs)	383	(94.1 overs)	358

Bowling
Lewis 30-10-88-2. Shabbir 26.1-7-96-4. Smith 16-3-55-1. Gidman 6-0-30-1. Shoaib Malik 20-2-49-1. Fisher 19-4-49-0.
Lewis 12-3-36-3. Shabbir 17.1-4-69-2. Smith 3-0-11-0. Fisher 32-7-110-4. Shoaib Malik 30-3-104-1.
Fall of Wickets: 1-28, 2-102, 3-114, 4-176, 5-212, 6-243, 7-334, 8-334, 9-357 1-17, 2-21, 3-155, 4-195, 5-197, 6-224, 7-263, 8-357, 9-357

GLOS	First Innings		Second Innings	
WPC Weston	c Weekes b Peploe	85	(2) not out	3
CM Spearman	c Nash b Hutton	341	(1) not out	29
MGN Windows	c Nash b Weekes	6		
CG Taylor (capt)	c Nash b Peploe	100		
APR Gidman	c Klusener b Hutton	51		
Shoaib Malik	c Dalrymple b Joyce	0		
*SJ Adshead	not out	35		
ID Fisher	c Hutton b Peploe	6		
J Lewis	c and b Weekes	12		
Shabbir Ahmed	st Nash b Peploe	3		
AM Smith	not out	3		
Extras	b 14, lb 12, w 5, nb 20	51	b 4, w 1, nb 10	15
	(9 wkts dec 149 overs)	695	(0 wkts 11 overs)	47

Bowling
Hayward 9-1-37-0. Hutchison 22-4-91-0. Peploe 43-3-199-4. Klusener 23-1-116-0. Dalrymple 11-2-38-0. Joyce 14-0-62-1. Shah 1-1-0-0.
Hutton 13-1-64-2.
Hutton 4-1-16-0. Peploe 3-0-12-0. Weekes 2-0-10-0. Koenig 2-1-1-0. Shah 0-0-4-0.
Fall of Wickets: 1-227, 2-254, 3-537, 4-610, 5-616, 6-646, 7-659, 8-681, 9-690

Gloucestershire won by 10 wickets - Gloucestershire (22pts), Middlesex (5pts)

disappointingly to an eight-wicket defeat at Old Trafford. Chris Adams, the Sussex captain, finished unbeaten on 150 as his side took command of the match with a sparkling first-innings batting display. Ian Ward and Murray Goodwin put on 148 for the second wicket, and then Adams took over, with Matt Prior also contributing a fine 61, as 458 runs were plundered from 104 overs on the opening day. Lancashire's reply was only boosted to 214 after Sajid Mahmood, emerging at No. 10 to swing the bat with gusto, carved and slashed his way to 94 off a mere 68 balls. His final scoring stroke was a top-edged six over the wicketkeeper's head. Lancashire's game was up, though, the moment that Stuart Law was bowled by a beautiful leg break from Mushtaq Ahmed just before the close of the second day. It was the second time that Mushtaq had dismissed Law that day, and Lancashire were 148 for 4 at stumps as they followed on. Mushtaq, bagging his first five-wicket haul of the season, also removed Carl Hooper for 55 early the next morning and Sussex were only made to bat again because of a 40-run, eighth-wicket stand between Dominic Cork and Mahmood.

Heath Streak, putting his Zimbabwe troubles behind him as Warwickshire's new overseas signing, kept his second county's championship ambitions very much alive by grabbing match figures of 13 for 158 and also scoring 61 on a remarkable debut for the club. The victims of his one-man show of all-round power were Northamptonshire, beaten by eight

LANCASHIRE v. SUSSEX - at Old Trafford

SUSSEX	First Innings		Second Innings	
IJ Ward	c Hooper b Chapple	84	c Cork b Mahmood	26
RR Montgomerie	c Chilton b Cork	5	c Loye b Cork	0
MW Goodwin	c Hooper b Mahmood	83	not out	11
CJ Adams (capt)	not out	150	not out	3
MJ Prior	c Crook b Hooper	61		
*TR Ambrose	b Hegg b Mahmood	8		
RSC Martin-Jenkins	c Cork b Mahmood	9		
RJ Kirtley	c Cork b Chapple	14		
Mushtaq Ahmed	c Law b Cork	6		
M Akram	lbw b Keedy	11		
JD Lewry	b Cork	7		
Extras	b 3, lb 14, w 1, nb 14	32	b 4	4
	(109.3 overs)	470	(2 wkts 12.3 overs)	44

Bowling
Chapple 23.2-2-110-2. Cork 27.3-4-85-3. Mahmood 19-1-102-3. Crook 7-0-50-0. Keedy 19-2-67-1. Hooper 14-2-39-1.
Cork 4-2-11-1. Mahmood 2-0-11-1. Anderson 6.3-1-18-0.
Fall of Wickets: 1-16, 2-164, 3-190, 4-306, 5-317, 6-329, 7-387, 8-430, 9-458 1-2, 2-33

LANCASHIRE	First Innings		Second Innings	
MJ Chilton	c Prior b Akram	9	lbw b Akram	21
AJ Swann	c Ambrose b Akram	6	lbw b Mushtaq Ahmed	27
MB Loye	lbw b Akram	0	c Ambrose b Lewry	24
SG Law	c M'gomerie b Mushtaq Ahmed	25	b Mushtaq Ahmed	42
CL Hooper	lbw b Martin-Jenkins	9	lbw b Mushtaq Ahmed	55
G Chapple	c and b Lewry	21	(8) c M-Jenkins b Mushtaq Ahmed	27
SP Crook	c M'gomerie b Mushtaq Ahmed	4		
*WK Hegg (capt)	b Lewry	7	(7) b Lewry	31
DG Cork	c Montgomerie b Lewry	7	c Akram b Kirtley	31
SI Mahmood	c Adams b Kirtley	94	c Lewry b Mushtaq Ahmed	24
G Keedy	not out	14	(6) c Ambrose b Akram	5
JM Anderson			not out	2
Extras	b 12, lb 4, w 1	17	b 6, lb 14, nb 8	28
	(71.2 overs)	214	(71.2 overs)	297

Bowling
Akram 10-1-49-3. Lewry 16-8-32-3. Martin-Jenkins 7-3-30-1. Kirtley 8-1-23-1. Mushtaq Ahmed 14-0-64-2.
Akram 15.3-2-60-2. Kirtley 16-5-53-1. Martin-Jenkins 4-1-14-0. Lewry 13.3-3-45-2. Mushtaq Ahmed 22.2-2-105-5.
Fall of Wickets: 1-11, 2-11, 3-22, 4-47, 5-73, 6-90, 7-91, 8-100, 9-101 1-46, 2-70, 3-90, 4-142, 5-175, 6-203, 7-207, 8-247, 9-284

Sussex won by 8 wickets - Lancashire (4pts), Sussex (22pts)

WARWICKSHIRE v. NORTHAMPTONSHIRE - at Edgbaston

NORTHANTS	First Innings		Second Innings	
TW Roberts	c Frost b Streak	18	lbw b Streak	0
RA Wine	c Wagh b Brown	18	c Brown b Carter	8
M van Jaarsveld	lbw b Streak	46	c Frost b Streak	48
U Afzaal	c Frost b Streak	21	b Brown	37
DJG Sales (capt)	b Streak	8	c Trott b Carter	76
GP Swann	b Carter	35	b Streak	29
*GL Brophy	b Carter	25	run out	41
J Louw	lbw b Streak	38	c Frost b Streak	10
BJ Phillips	c Carter b Streak	90	lbw b Streak	0
PS Jones	b Streak	18	lbw b Streak	0
JF Brown	not out	0	not out	7
Extras	lb 6, nb 4	12	b 2, lb 11, nb 11	24
	(96.5 overs)	329	(90.1 overs)	280

Bowling
Streak 21.5-4-80-7. Carter 20-8-60-2. Brown 15-4-46-1. Tahir 16-4-39-0. Bell 7-2-24-0. Hogg 6-1-19-0. Wagh 9-2-49-0. Troughton 2-1-4-0.
Streak 21.5-2-78-6. Carter 25.1-5-67-2. Tahir 4-0-17-0. Wagh 3-0-14-0. Bell 11-8-10-0. Brown 23.1-5-73-1. Troughton 2-0-8-0.
Fall of Wickets: 1-24, 2-64, 3-105, 4-110, 5-127, 6-170, 7-185, 8-307, 9-312 1-0, 2-16, 3-83, 4-126, 5-201, 6-234, 7-257, 8-259, 9-261

WARWICKSHIRE	First Innings		Second Innings	
NV Knight (capt)	c Brophy b Phillips	100	not out	56
MA Wagh	b Phillips	92	c Swann b Louw	10
IR Bell	b Phillips	2	b Louw	0
IJL Trott	lbw b Swann	44	not out	22
JO Troughton	c Brown b Louw	54		
DR Brown	c Brophy b Jones	45		
GB Hogg	c Swann b Phillips	20		
HH Streak	b Swann	61		
*T Frost	not out	85		
NM Carter	lbw b White	9		
N Tahir	c Bell b Swann	1		
Extras	b 3, lb 4, nb 4	11		
	(162.3 overs)	524	(2 wkts 17.4 overs)	88

Bowling
Jones 31-5-115-1. Louw 27-6-83-1. Phillips 34-7-110-4. Brown 41-9-128-0. Swann 26.3-5-69-3. White 3-0-12-1.
Louw 7-0-27-2. Jones 4-0-32-0. Phillips 5-1-14-0. Brown 1.4-0-15-0.
Fall of Wickets: 1-189, 2-194, 3-197, 4-249, 5-331, 6-358, 7-368, 8-508, 9-517 1-29, 2-35

Warwickshire won by 8 wickets - Warwickshire (22pts), Northamptonshire (5pts)

WORCESTERSHIRE v. KENT - at Worcester

WORCS	First Innings		Second Innings	
SD Peters	c O'Brien b Sheriyar	123	c O'Brien b Walker	117
SC Moore	b Symonds	15	lbw b Trott	4
GA Hick	c Tredwell b Symonds	2	c Loudon b Trott	27
BF Smith (capt)	c Tredwell b Sheriyar	65	c Key b Trott	127
VS Solanki	c O'Brien b Trott	107	c Walker b Trott	86
AJ Hall	b Cusden	12	not out	9
GJ Batty	b Cusden	36	c Symonds b Tredwell	14
AJ Bichel	c Tredwell b Sheriyar	0		
Kabir Ali	c O'Brien b Symonds	31		
*SJ Rhodes	c O'Brien b Tredwell	8		
MS Mason	not out	35		
Extras	b 2, lb 7, w 2, nb 8	19	lb 5, lb 14, w 2	21
	(127.2 overs)	453	(6 wkts dec 88.5 overs)	405

Bowling
Sheriyar 31-7-106-3. Cusden 26-5-91-2. Symonds 27-8-114-3. Trott 29-4-78-1. Tredwell 13.2-3-54-1. Loudon 1-0-1-0.
Sheriyar 10-2-34-0. Trott 24-1-109-4. Walker 15-5-57-1. Cusden 15-2-63-0. Tredwell 16.5-2-84-1. Loudon 4-0-26-0. Carberry 4-0-13-0.
Fall of Wickets: 1-54, 2-60, 3-179, 4-272, 5-295, 6-355, 7-356, 8-405, 9-414 1-4, 2-80, 3-224, 4-370, 5-384, 6-405

KENT	First Innings		Second Innings	
MA Carberry	c Rhodes b Bichel	8	c Rhodes b Kabir Ali	64
RWT Key	c Rhodes b Hall	29	(7) st Rhodes b Batty	10
ET Smith (capt)	lbw b Mason	1	c Mason b Batty	35
A Symonds	c Smith b Batty	103	c Hick b Batty	9
MJ Walker	c Peters b Hall	62	c Peters b Kabir Ali	14
AGR Loudon	c Moore b Hall	59	c Moore b Hall	12
JC Tredwell	c Hall b Mason	47	(2) b Mason	45
*NJ O'Brien	c Et b Kabir Ali	67	not out	20
BJ Trott	lbw b Kabir Ali	0	(10) c Hick b Bichel	12
A Sheriyar	run out	2	(9) lbw b Hall	0
SMJ Cusden	not out	1		
Extras	lb 8, w 3, nb 26	37	b 6, lb 2, w 1, nb 14	23
	(100.2 overs)	420	(9 wkts 84 overs)	244

Bowling
Bichel 24-6-121-1. Mason 20.2-4-83-2. Kabir Ali 18-2-93-2. Hall 11-2-53-3. Batty 22-6-57-1. Solanki 5-1-5-0.
Mason 14-8-19-1. Kabir Ali 12-1-39-2. Hall 15-5-63-2. Bichel 14-3-55-1. Batty 29-14-60-3.
Fall of Wickets: 1-10, 2-31, 3-116, 4-189, 5-250, 6-281, 7-391, 8-395, 9-403 1-71, 2-107, 3-167, 4-169, 5-194, 6-206, 7-216, 8-221, 9-235

Match drawn - Worcestershire (12pts), Kent (12pts)

Craig Spearman: 'It's something special to beat a WG Grace record. He's the father of cricket.'

wickets at Edgbaston. Streak's 7 for 80 and 6 for 78 gave him the best match analysis by any debutant in the history of the county championship, beating the 12 for 87 claimed by the Reverend Archibald Fargus for Gloucestershire against Middlesex at Lord's in 1900. 'He was outstanding. I don't know any other word to use,' said his grateful captain Nick Knight afterwards. Ben Phillips, coming in at No. 9 at 185 for 7 to thump 90 with two sixes and 17 fours, kept Northants in the hunt on day one, but Knight's 100 and his opening stand of 189 with Mark Wagh (92), provided the base for Warwickshire to go well past the visitors' first-innings 329 and build a match-winning lead. Streak's half-century played an important part in that, with wicketkeeper Tony Frost also batting superbly to hit an unbeaten 85 from 121 balls, an innings that included 12 boundaries. Then came Streak again, and only David Sales, with 76, provided any significant resistance as Warwickshire pressed home their advantage. A modest win target, chased midway through the fourth day, enabled the delighted Knight to add an unbeaten 56 to his earlier century.

Niall O'Brien and last man Alamgir Sheriyar – against his former club – survived the final 31 balls of the match at New Road to deny Worcestershire a win and to earn Kent a valuable draw by ending their second innings on 244 for 9. As a result, Ben Smith, the Worcestershire captain, was left to regret his excessive caution on the last morning, when he batted on for just over half an hour to set Kent a fourth-innings target of 374. He was mindful, no doubt, of Kent's success when they chased 439 on the final day of the two sides' early-season meeting at Canterbury. This time round, though, the in-form Robert Key was unable to bat until No. 7 after being off the field suffering from a migraine during Worcestershire's second-innings romp to 405 for 6 declared. As it was, the still-off-colour Key made only ten and Kent owed much to Michael Carberry, who scored 64 after initially having to retire hurt because of a blow on his helmet, but who then re-entered the fray following the fall of the next wicket. James

Tredwell, promoted to open in Key's enforced absence, also batted well for his 45, but this was a match that Worcestershire should have won after emerging from an attritional first two days to take control, largely through Stephen Peters' second hundred of the game. Peters became only the sixth Worcestershire player to achieve this feat in the championship and Smith, with 127 to add to his first-innings 65, and Vikram Solanki, who added a sublime 86 to his elegant 124-ball 107 on day one – a knock containing two sixes and 14 fours – also enjoyed themselves against a weakened Kent attack. Andrew Symonds, whose continuing Achilles problem prevented him from bowling, hit 103 in Kent's first innings of 420. He reached 93 from just 73 deliveries before Gareth Batty's off breaks at last began to regain some control for Worcestershire captain Smith. O'Brien hit a championship-best 67 to take Kent to within 33 of Worcestershire's imposing first-innings total and there were also attractive half-centuries from Matthew Walker and Alex Loudon.

Division Two

Nottinghamshire continued to assert themselves over their Division Two rivals by beating Somerset at Bath to claim a fourth successive victory. Darren Bicknell's first championship hundred for 21 months – an excellent 150 – and the penetrative seam bowling of Paul Franks and Greg Smith was at the heart of this latest Notts success. Franks, who took 7 for 72 and displayed both pace and bounce in good batting conditions as Somerset were held to 399 in their first innings, underlined the strength of his courageous comeback from a career-threatening knee injury. Ian Blackwell reached his half-century from just 30 balls and went on to score 78, but Bicknell's occupation of the crease – and, in particular, the support he received from Anurag Singh and Chris Read – eventually enabled Notts to earn themselves a handy 61-run first-innings lead. That became even more valuable as Smith provided a telling burst of 5 for 24 in nine overs to undo the Somerset second innings. Left with a final-day target of 160, Notts were swept home by Russell Warren and David Hussey.

An injury to their captain and inspiration, Shane Warne, who suffered a broken bone in his left hand when hit by a ball from Darren Gough, was the only price to pay as Hampshire beat Essex by 114 runs at Chelmsford. The fracture was confirmed by Warne's visit to a local hospital, but his imminent departure for Australia's short Test tour of Sri Lanka meant that Hampshire were not, in effect, going to lose Warne's services for long. In his absence on the third afternoon, after he had sent down four exploratory overs before admitting his hand injury needed examination, Hampshire's victory drive was spearheaded by Billy Taylor's career-

best 5 for 73 and off spinner Shaun Udal's 4 for 55. Chris Tremlett's steep lift had been Essex's undoing the day before, with the fast bowler claiming 4 for 29 as the home side stumbled to 158 in reply to Hampshire's first-innings 353. A third-wicket partnership of 137 between John Crawley and Michael Clarke had initially rallied Hampshire from 38 for 2, and when Crawley finally fell just three short of a hundred, there were useful late-order runs from both Nic Pothas and Udal. Essex, 195 runs adrift on first innings, had their faint hopes kept alive by Danish Kaneria's 5 for 68, but Warne defied the pain from his injured hand to swipe a top score of 34 from No. 10 to boost an ailing Hampshire second innings up to 154. A target of 350 was always going to be beyond Essex in the conditions, even with Warne incapacitated, and only Graham

Matthew Maynard earned himself a Glamorgan county record with his 114 against Leicestershire at Sophia Gardens.

Napier's lively, late, unbeaten 51, containing three sixes and six fours, delayed the end.

Matthew Maynard hit a first-day 114 against Leicestershire at Cardiff to earn himself a record 53rd first-class hundred for his county. Maynard's innings took him above both Alan Jones and Hugh Morris, who both hit 52 centuries, and also laid the foundations for a victory by the massive margin of 409 runs. Leicestershire could make only 255 in reply to Glamorgan's 333, despite a brilliant 145 from Darren Maddy which included three sixes and 20 fours. Robert Croft, the Glamorgan captain, then turned the screw by delaying a second-innings declaration until his side had run up 468 for 9 – a total to which he contributed 138 himself and which contained 14 fours and a six. Jon Hughes was the star of Glamorgan's second innings, however, striking no fewer than three sixes and 16 fours in a maiden first-class hundred. Alex Wharf's hard-hit 51 then piled on the agony for Leicestershire, and the former Yorkshire paceman quickly added three wickets as Glamorgan's weary opponents slid to 137 all out.

Richard Dawson, England's forgotten young off spinner, took his first five-wicket haul for two years and then followed it up with a second-innings 4 for 75 as Yorkshire trounced Durham by 320 runs at the Riverside. Dawson's initial 5 for 40 condemned Durham to a paltry 150 all out in reply to a Yorkshire first-innings total of 331 that had been built on a fine 126 by Anthony McGrath on an untypically baking hot day in the North

East. Matthew Wood then added 71 to his first-innings 55 as Yorkshire, further bolstered by Darren Lehmann's rapid 120, sped to a declaration on 353 for 9. Half-centuries from Marcus North and Paul Collingwood only held Yorkshire, and Dawson, at bay for a while.

Round Nine: 9–12 June 2004 Division Two

SOMERSET v. NOTTINGHAMSHIRE - at Bath

SOMERSET	First Innings		Second Innings	
PD Bowler	c Read b Franks	39	lbw b Ealham	25
NJ Edwards	c Hussey b Franks	87	c Ealham b Franks	15
J Cox	c Read b Franks	1	b Smith	63
JC Hildreth	c Read b Franks	60	b Smith	29
M Burns (capt)	c Hussey b Smith	35	c Hussey b Smith	24
ID Blackwell	b Sidebottom	78	lbw b Smith	9
*CM Gazzard	c Read b Sidebottom	18	(11) absent	
KP Dutch	c Ealham b Franks	5	(7) c MacGill b Sidebottom	22
AR Caddick	c Singh b Smith	27	(8) c Ealham b Smith	3
SRG Francis	not out	1	(9) not out	5
NAM McLean	c Sidebottom b Franks	1	(10) c Hussey b Sidebottom	0
Extras	b 4, lb 15, w 14, nb 8	41	b 8, lb 6, w 9, nb 2	25
	(107.2 overs)	399	(9 wkts dec 54.5 overs)	220

Bowling
Smith 25-4-105-1. Sidebottom 21-6-60-2. Ealham 13-3-56-0. Franks 24.2-5-72-7. MacGill 22-4-85-0. Hussey 2-1-2-0.
Smith 17-4-49-5. Sidebottom 7.5-1-38-2. Franks 8-1-45-1. Ealham 15-3-46-1. MacGill 7-0-28-0.
Fall of Wickets: 1-100, 2-107, 3-211, 4-245, 5-276, 6-352, 7-353, 8-378, 9-396
1-33, 2-88, 3-145, 4-175, 5-184, 6-189, 7-199, 8-220, 9-220

NOTTS	First Innings		Second Innings	
DJ Bicknell	b McLean	150	c Burns b McLean	26
JER Gallian (capt)	lbw b McLean	10	c Hildreth b Caddick	10
A Singh	c Burns b Francis	55	c Burns b Caddick	33
RJ Warren	b Blackwell	32	not out	48
RJ Sidebottom	c and b Caddick	5		
DJ Hussey	c Hildreth b Francis	21	(5) not out	35
*CMW Read	c Hildreth b Caddick	66		
MA Ealham	c Burns b McLean	24		
PJ Franks	b Francis	54		
GJ Smith	c Burns b Francis	5		
SCG MacGill	not out	0		
Extras	b 9, lb 4, w 3, nb 18	34	b 2, lb 1, w 1, nb 4	8
	(113.1 overs)	460	(3 wkts dec 42.3 overs)	160

Bowling
Caddick 36-4-156-2. McLean 24-6-78-3. Francis 25.1-1-106-4. Burns 6-2-28-0. Blackwell 22-5-79-1.
Caddick 19-3-64-2. McLean 8-3-26-1. Francis 8.3-0-41-0. Blackwell 4-1-11-0. Dutch 3-1-15-0.
Fall of Wickets: 1-18, 2-177, 3-257, 4-266, 5-278, 6-304, 7-359, 8-427, 9-441
1-36, 2-40, 3-114

*Nottinghamshire won by 7 wickets -
Somerset (7pts), Nottinghamshire (22pts)*

ESSEX v. HAMPSHIRE - at Chelmsford

HAMPSHIRE	First Innings		Second Innings	
DA Kenway	c Flower b Danish Kaneria	25	lbw b Danish Kaneria	27
MJ Brown	b Napier	0	c Cook b Danish Kaneria	29
JP Crawley	c Cook b Gough	97	c Foster b Danish Kaneria	0
MJ Clarke	c and b Danish Kaneria	69	c Foster b Clarke	8
WS Kendall	c Foster b Gough	19	b Clarke	2
*N Pothas	lbw b Gough	57	b Gough	12
AD Mascarenhas	c & b Danish Kaneria	32	(8) c Jefferson b Danish Kaneria	0
SK Warne (capt)	b Danish Kaneria	6	(10) c Napier b Danish Kaneria	34
SD Udal	not out	43	run out	8
CT Tremlett	b Gough	0	(11) not out	0
BV Taylor	c Foster b Gough	2	(7) c Foster b Gough	22
Extras	b 1, w 4, nb 4	9	b 4, lb 8	12
	(108.5 overs)	353	(49.2 overs)	154

Bowling
Gough 23.5-6-57-5. Napier 19-3-68-1. Clarke 15-3-58-0. Danish Kaneria 35-4-108-4. Middlebrook 15-1-58-0. Bopara 1-0-3-0.
Gough 13-2-36-2. Napier 6-1-26-0. Danish Kaneria 19.2-4-68-5. Clarke 11-6-12-2.
Fall of Wickets: 1-0, 2-38, 3-175, 4-207, 5-224, 6-286, 7-286, 8-325, 9-331
1-55, 2-55, 3-64, 4-64, 5-72, 6-105, 7-108, 8-108, 9-147

ESSEX	First Innings		Second Innings	
WI Jefferson	c Pothas b Taylor	15	lbw b Taylor	26
AN Cook	c Pothas b Tremlett	25	c Kenway b Taylor	22
A Flower (capt)	c Warne b Udal	1	b Brown b Udal	0
A Habib	lbw b Warne	42	c Pothas b Taylor	13
RS Bopara	c Brown b Warne	17	lbw b Mascarenhas	19
*JS Foster	lbw b Tremlett	6	b Taylor	39
JD Middlebrook	not out	30	b Taylor	0
GR Napier	c Kendall b Mascarenhas	7	not out	51
D Gough	c Clarke b Mascarenhas	4	c sub b Udal	20
AJ Clarke	c Clarke b Tremlett	0	c & b Udal	8
Danish Kaneria	b Tremlett	1	c Crawley b Udal	13
Extras	b 5, lb 1, nb 4	10	lb 16, nb 8	24
	(62.5 overs)	158	(55.4 overs)	235

Bowling
Tremlett 16.5-6-29-4. Taylor 16-3-39-1. Mascarenhas 8-3-22-1. Udal 10-2-32-1. Warne 14-6-40-2.
Tremlett 11-1-54-0. Taylor 19-4-73-5. Udal 13.4-1-55-4. Mascarenhas 8-3-17-1. Warne 4-0-20-0.
Fall of Wickets: 1-28, 2-29, 3-73, 4-105, 5-106, 6-118, 7-140, 8-144, 9-150
1-48, 2-51, 3-51, 4-74, 5-108, 6-108, 7-141, 8-184, 9-199

Hampshire won by 114 runs - Essex (3pts), Hampshire (21pts)

GLAMORGAN v. LEICESTERSHIRE - at Cardiff

GLAMORGAN	First Innings		Second Innings	
MTG Elliott	c & b DeFreitas	31	(2) b Dagnall	42
*MA Wallace	c Nixon b Gibson	5	(1) lbw b DeFreitas	19
DL Hemp	c Hodge b Gibson	26	c Nixon b DeFreitas	10
MJ Powell	c Maddy b Gibson	9	st Nixon b Henderson	3
MP Maynard	c Maddy b DeFreitas	114	c Nixon b Cleary	13
J Hughes	c Maddy b Gibson	21	c Nixon b Henderson	110
RDB Croft (capt)	c Maddy b Gibson	20	c Robinson b Henderson	138
AG Wharf	b Gibson	0	b Hodge	51
DS Harrison	c Henderson b Maddy	42	c Sadler b Henderson	21
MS Kasprowicz	c Gibson b DeFreitas	42	not out	14
DA Cosker	not out	1	not out	1
Extras	b 5, lb 7, w 2, nb 8	22	b 15, lb 9, w 6, nb 4	34
	(81 overs)	333	(9 wkts dec 119 overs)	468

Bowling
Gibson 19-3-80-5. Dagnall 18-2-60-0. Cleary 19-1-74-0. DeFreitas 13-4-44-3. Maddy 9-1-41-2. Henderson 3-0-22-0.
Gibson 14-1-66-0. Dagnall 15-0-64-1. DeFreitas 14.1-1-51-2. Hodge 14-2-46-1. Henderson 45-9-146-4. Cleary 11.5-2-53-1. Maddy 5-0-18-0.
Fall of Wickets: 1-14, 2-56, 3-83, 4-90, 5-117, 6-165, 7-169, 8-248, 9-332
1-52, 2-70, 3-79, 4-83, 5-96, 6-314, 7-411, 8-439, 9-445

LEICESTERSHIRE	First Innings		Second Innings	
DDJ Robinson	lbw b Harrison	5	(2) lbw b Kasprowicz	18
JK Maunders	c Elliott b Kasprowicz	3	(1) c Powell b Croft	8
BJ Hodge	b Harrison	5	b Kasprowicz	61
DL Maddy	c Powell b Cosker	145	lbw b Harrison	3
CW Henderson	c Harrison b Cosker	15	(9) c Hughes b Croft	1
JL Sadler	c Hemp b Croft	33	(5) c Wallace b Harrison	1
*PA Nixon	c Wallace b Harrison	4	c & b Wharf	14
PAJ DeFreitas (capt)	c Wallace b Cosker	6	(6) b Harrison	0
OD Gibson	b Croft	15	(8) c Wallace b Wharf	0
CE Dagnall	c Elliott b Croft	1	lbw b Wharf	5
MF Cleary	not out	17	not out	8
Extras	b 5, lb 1	6	b 2, nb 16	18
	(79.1 overs)	255	(50.3 overs)	137

Bowling
Kasprowicz 22-5-60-1. Harrison 18-8-49-3. Cosker 12.1-3-40-3. Croft 20-4-70-3. Wharf 7-0-30-0.
Kasprowicz 16.3-5-43-2. Harrison 11-6-17-3. Wharf 9-1-37-3. Croft 11-5-20-2. Cosker 3-0-18-0.
Fall of Wickets: 1-8, 2-13, 3-13, 4-77, 5-129, 6-146, 7-166, 8-184, 9-194
1-22, 2-51, 3-59, 4-63, 5-63, 6-98, 7-100, 8-105, 9-120

*Glamorgan won by 409 runs -
Glamorgan (20pts), Leicestershire (5pts)*

DURHAM v. YORKSHIRE - at The Riverside

YORKSHIRE	First Innings		Second Innings	
MJ Wood	c Muchall b Shoaib Akhtar	55	lbw b Collingwood	71
PA Jaques	c Shoaib Akhtar b Davies	36	c Shoaib Akhtar b Muchall	53
A McGrath	b Shoaib Akhtar	126	c Pratt b A Davies	8
DS Lehmann	c Pratt A b Killeen	9	c Peng b Davies	120
MJ Lumb	lbw b Collingwood	28	(6) c and b Davies	0
C White (capt)	c Collingwood b Collingwood	27	(7) b Davies	31
*SM Guy	b Breese	0	(8) b Shoaib Akhtar	21
RKJ Dawson	b Shoaib Akhtar	23	(9) b North	21
TT Bresnan	b Shoaib Akhtar	2	(10) not out	4
ND Thornicroft	c Collingwood	6		
SP Kirby	not out	1	(5) lbw b Collingwood	0
Extras	b 5, lb 5, w 6, nb 2	18	b 9, lb 14, w 1, nb 6	30
	(97.2 overs)	331	(9 wkts dec 93 overs)	353

Bowling
Shoaib Akhtar 16.2-3-64-4. Killeen 21-9-69-2. Davies 16-3-66-1. Collingwood 17-8-41-2. Breese 23-3-74-1. North 4-2-7-0.
Shoaib Akhtar 14-3-46-1. Killeen 17-5-40-0. Davies 19-3-51-3. Breese 14-1-78-0. Collingwood 16-3-53-2. Muchall 5-0-17-1. North 8-0-45-2.
Fall of Wickets: 1-79, 2-93, 3-118, 4-171, 5-250, 6-251, 7-297, 8-299, 9-314
1-118, 2-136, 3-156, 4-156, 5-165, 6-306, 7-306, 8-333, 9-353

DURHAM	First Innings		Second Innings	
JJB Lewis (capt)	b Thornicroft	6	c Guy b Kirby	14
MJ North	c McGrath b Kirby	1	b Kirby	59
N Killeen	c Wood b Dawson	3	(10) b Dawson	2
GJ Muchall	c Jaques b Thornicroft	20	(3) c Lehmann b Thornicroft	1
PD Collingwood	c Bresnan b Dawson	26	(4) c Kirby b Dawson	65
N Peng	c Jaques b Dawson	37	(5) c Jaques b Lehmann	0
GJ Pratt	c Guy b White	17	(6) lbw b Dawson	5
GR Breese	b White	6	(7) lbw b White	7
*A Pratt	b Dawson	7	(8) b White	24
Shoaib Akhtar	c & b Dawson	7	(9) not out	16
M Davies	not out	2	c McGrath b Dawson	4
Extras	b 4, lb 6, w 1, nb 8	19	b 7, lb 3, nb 6	16
	(53.5 overs)	150	(65.2 overs)	214

Bowling
Kirby 10-2-25-1. Thornicroft 8-2-27-2. Dawson 16.5-2-40-5. Bresnan 5-2-11-0. White 13-1-38-2. Lehmann 1-0-1-0.
Kirby 13-5-26-2. Thornicroft 9-3-24-1. Dawson 20.2-4-75-4. Bresnan 4-1-17-0. White 10-1-39-2. Lehmann 9-2-23-1.
Fall of Wickets: 1-5, 2-14, 3-27, 4-38, 5-101, 6-110, 7-116, 8-141, 9-141
1-14, 2-23, 3-142, 4-143, 5-158, 6-158, 7-180, 8-197, 9-202

Yorkshire won by 320 runs - Durham (3pts), Yorkshire (20pts)

Round Ten: 18–21 June 2004

Division One

Lancashire, missing seven first-choice players, held Warwickshire to a high-scoring draw in the first county championship match to be staged at Stratford-upon-Avon. Hooper, Cork, Chapple and Sutcliffe were all out injured, while Flintoff, Anderson and Mahmood were away on England duty. The absence of five of their leading seamers hit Lancashire particularly hard as Warwickshire, batting first, amassed 499. Mark Wagh's 167 from 223 balls, containing 30 fours, was the pick – although Brad Hogg's 41-ball 56 provided rich late entertainment. Mal Loye, however, trumped Wagh's effort by anchoring the Lancashire reply with 184, and a draw was made even more certain when, on the third day, a violent hailstorm hit the ground and turned the outfield from green to white just before lunch. *The Times* reported that the Swan's Nest Lane ground – situated just across the river from the Royal Shakespeare Theatre – 'looked more like a scene from *The Tempest*'. Lancashire, however, would have been pleased to have got past Warwickshire's first-innings total and earn themselves 12 points from the draw.

Surrey, on the other hand, were not at all pleased by their failure to beat Gloucestershire at The Oval, despite the loss of 60 overs to bad weather on the

Round Ten: 18–21 June 2004 Division One

WARWICKSHIRE v. LANCASHIRE - at Stratford

WARWICKSHIRE	First Innings		Second Innings	
NV Knight (capt)	lbw b Keedy	53	not out	67
MA Wagh	c Law b Crook	167	c Law b Wood	18
IR Bell	c Law b Crook	49	c Hogg b Keedy	1
IJL Trott	b Martin	54	not out	36
JO Troughton	c Law b Keedy	8		
DR Brown	lbw b Mongia	16		
GB Hogg	b Martin	56		
*T Frost	lbw b Martin	0		
NM Carter	c Swann b Wood	32		
N Tahir	b Martin	26		
D Pretorius	not out	1		
Extras	b 11, lb 5, w 1, nb 20	37	nb 2	2
	(104.5 overs)	499	(2 wkts 35.1 overs)	124

Bowling
Martin 18.5-2-81-4. Wood 20-2-122-1. Chilton 5-1-22-0. Crook 18-2-78-2. Mongia 17-1-82-1. Keedy 26-5-98-2.
Martin 6-1-30-0. Wood 10-1-31-1. Keedy 12-1-31-1. Swann 1-0-1-0. Crook 6.1-0-31-0.
Fall of Wickets: 1-141, 2-295, 3-304, 4-313, 5-356, 6-419, 7-419, 8-446, 9-478 1-46, 2-47

LANCASHIRE	First Innings	
MJ Chilton	c Wagh b Carter	13
AJ Swann	lbw b Bell	20
MB Loye	b Wagh	184
SG Law	c Frost b Tahir	44
D Mongia	lbw b Bell	89
PJ Horton	c Frost b Carter	22
SP Crook	c Knight b Tahir	23
*WK Hegg (capt)	b Hogg	54
J Wood	not out	13
PJ Martin	b Pretorius	2
G Keedy	c Frost b Pretorius	0
Extras	b 5, lb 14, w 3, nb 22	44
	(134.3 overs)	508

Bowling
Pretorius 27.3-6-76-2. Carter 16-1-93-2. Tahir 20-5-47-2. Bell 18-1-66-2. Brown 9-1-34-0. Wagh 19-1-77-1. Hogg 21-2-66-1. Troughton 4-0-30-0.
Fall of Wickets: 1-19, 2-93, 3-162, 4-333, 5-381, 6-409, 7-459, 8-505, 9-508

Match drawn - Warwickshire (11pts),
Lancashire (12pts)

SURREY v. GLOUCESTERSHIRE - at The Oval

GLOS	First Innings		Second Innings	
WPC Weston	c Ormond b Bicknell	19	(2) c Et b Clarke	31
CM Spearman	lbw b Ormond	0	(1) lbw b Bicknell	30
MGN Windows	lbw b Ormond	6	c Hollioake b Clarke	20
CG Taylor (capt)	c Brown b Murtagh	177	c Batty b Ormond	9
APR Gidman	lbw b Bicknell	62	b Murtagh	25
Shoaib Malik	c Hollioake b Murtagh	4	lbw b Ormond	0
*SJ Adshead	c Batty b Murtagh	13	lbw b Hollioake	28
ID Fisher	c Hollioake b Ormond	5	c sub b Hollioake	38
JMM Averis	not out	48	b Ormond	0
J Lewis	c Et b Murtagh	0	not out	34
Shabbir Ahmed	lbw b Murtagh	0	not out	10
Extras	b 6, lb 10, w 2, nb 16	34	b 9, lb 16, w 1, nb 4	30
	(97.5 overs)	368	(9 wkts 94 overs)	255

Bowling
Bicknell 31-10-84-2. Ormond 16.3-2-78-3. Murtagh 16.5-1-74-5. Clarke 7.3-0-47-0. Salisbury 9-0-23-0. Hollioake 6-2-12-0. Doshi 11-1-34-0.
Bicknell 13-4-39-1. Ormond 25-11-53-3. Murtagh 15-3-49-1. Clarke 18-6-38-2. Hollioake 10-1-38-2. Salisbury 11-6-10-0. Doshi 2-0-3-0.
Fall of Wickets: 1-0, 2-6, 3-55, 4-186, 5-191, 6-215, 7-247, 8-368, 9-368 1-49, 2-93, 3-102, 4-110, 5-110, 6-154, 7-171, 8-191, 9-233

SURREY	First Innings	
SA Newman	c Gidman b Fisher	73
AJ Hollioake	run out	0
MR Ramprakash	c Weston b Lewis	5
R Clarke	c Adshead b Shabbir	43
*JN Batty (capt)	c Averis b Fisher	106
AD Brown	c Spearman b Gidman	170
MP Bicknell	c Adshead b Shabbir	36
IDK Salisbury	b Averis	23
J Ormond	c Adshead b Shabbir	39
TJ Murtagh	not out	33
ND Doshi	b Lewis	15
Extras	b 4, lb 12, w 3, nb 36	55
	(132.4 overs)	598

Bowling
Lewis 26.4-3-120-2. Shabbir 30-9-90-3. Gidman 13-0-75-1. Averis 22-1-124-1. Fisher 31-2-132-2. Shoaib Malik 10-0-41-0.
Fall of Wickets: 1-2, 2-64, 3-124, 4-138, 5-381, 6-440, 7-493, 8-525, 9-575

Match drawn - Surrey (12pts),
Gloucestershire (11pts)

MIDDLESEX v. WORCESTERSHIRE - at Lord's

MIDDLESEX	First Innings		Second Innings	
BL Hutton	c Rhodes b Batty	90	not out	3
SG Koenig	not out	104		
OA Shah	lbw b Mason	12	not out	5
EC Joyce (capt)	c Rhodes b Hall	82		
PN Weekes	b Solanki	102		
JWM Dalrymple	c Peters b Solanki	41		
L Klusener	c Mason b Solanki	2		
*BJM Scott	lbw b Solanki	11	(2) lbw b Bichel	0
SJ Cook	c Mason b Solanki	24		
CB Keegan	c Batty b Kabir Ali	0		
TF Bloomfield	b Kabir Ali	8		
Extras	b 4, lb 14, nb 14	32		0
	(175.4 overs)	508	(1 wkt 5 overs)	8

Bowling
Mason 35-8-87-1. Kabir Ali 32-9-84-2. Hall 32-7-92-1. Bichel 27-7-69-0. Batty 33-6-107-1. Moore 3-0-11-0. Solanki 13.4-3-40-5.
Bichel 3-0-6-1. Kabir Ali 2-1-2-0.
Fall of Wickets: 1-167, 2-190, 3-335, 4-439, 5-445, 6-468, 7-475, 8-476, 9-496 1-1

WORCS	First Innings	
SD Peters	c Cook b Keegan	6
SC Moore	c sub b Cook	111
GA Hick	b Klusener	86
BF Smith (capt)	lbw b Klusener	12
VS Solanki	b Klusener	8
AJ Hall	c sub b Cook	28
GJ Batty	run out	52
AJ Bichel	c sub b Bloomfield	53
Kabir Ali	c Dalrymple b Weekes	4
*SJ Rhodes	st Scott b Dalrymple	12
MS Mason	not out	0
Extras	b 9, lb 14, nb 4	27
	(129.2 overs)	399

Bowling
Keegan 24-7-78-1. Cook 25-6-69-2. Bloomfield 20-3-55-1. Klusener 26-5-60-3. Dalrymple 17-5-64-1. Weekes 14.2-3-47-1. Hutton 3-2-3-0.
Fall of Wickets: 1-6, 2-186, 3-200, 4-218, 5-268, 6-271, 7-378, 8-378, 9-399

Match drawn - Middlesex (11pts),
Worcestershire (9pts)

Alistair Brown (left) hit four sixes and 20 fours in his 170 for Surrey against Gloucestershire.

third day. Chris Taylor's 177, his 131-run fourth-wicket stand with Alex Gidman, and a championship-best 48 not out by James Averis, had not been enough to prevent Gloucestershire from being bowled out for 368 – a total which looked inadequate when Jon Batty and Alistair Brown powered Surrey to an eventual 598 with a fifth-wicket partnership worth 243. Brown's hundred was his first in all cricket since September 2002, and, in all, he thumped four sixes and 20 fours in his 234-ball effort. Gloucestershire began the final day on four without loss in their second innings, but held on through a nail-biting three sessions. Surrey chipped away successfully enough to look certain of victory at one point, but the fatal error came when Brown, of all people, dropped Jon Lewis very early in his innings when the Gloucestershire lead was just four runs and there was time for seven more overs to be bowled at them. In the end, Lewis remained on 34 not out and, with last man Shabbir Ahmed, added 22 priceless runs to deny the home side victory.

Middlesex, having lost four of their previous five matches, relieved Owais Shah of the captaincy before meeting Worcestershire at Lord's. Ed Joyce was appointed in his place, and the Irishman followed up an opening stand of 167 between Ben Hutton and Sven Koenig by hitting 82. Koenig eventually retired hurt for a painstaking 104, but Paul Weekes made a more entertaining 102 and even the five-wicket success of Vikram Solanki's off breaks could not prevent Joyce's team from reaching 508. Worcestershire, however, were bolstered in reply by Stephen Moore and Graeme Hick, the former scoring 111 and the latter completing his 1,000 runs for the season in the course of contributing 86 to a second-wicket stand worth 180.

Division Two

Shane Watson, the Australian all-rounder deputising for the injured Shane Warne, marked his first-class debut for Hampshire with an unbeaten 112 which underpinned the 275-run defeat of Somerset at the Rose Bowl. Hampshire's first-innings advantage had been earned by Michael Brown's 81 and half-centuries by both Shaun Udal and Chris Tremlett in a ninth-wicket stand worth 80, but it was Watson and Udal – who shared an eighth-wicket alliance of 158 – which rallied Hampshire from a wobbly 131 for 7 in their second innings. Udal's share was a forthright 74 off 84 balls, and Hampshire's acting captain was even able to declare at 334 for 9 before his bowlers dismissed the visitors for just 146.

Round Ten: 18–21 June 2004 Division Two

HAMPSHIRE v. SOMERSET - at The Rose Bowl

HAMPSHIRE	First Innings		Second Innings	
DA Kenway	c Parsons b Caddick	7	c Dutch b Burns	31
MJ Brown	lbw b Caddick	81	c Hildreth b Burns	23
JP Crawley	c Turner b Francis	3	b Francis	40
WS Kendall	c Edwards b Caddick	13	c Turner b Burns	5
MJ Clarke	c Turner b Caddick	18	c Turner b Caddick	1
SR Watson	st Turner b Dutch	24	not out	112
*N Pothas	c Cox b Dutch	16	(8) b Francis	6
AD Mascarenhas	c Turner b Francis	6	(10) lbw b Francis	9
SD Udal (capt)	c Turner b Francis	50	b Francis	74
CT Tremlett	c Turner b Francis	57	(11) not out	0
BV Taylor	not out	4	(6) lbw b Caddick	0
Extras	lb 9, w 2	11	b 4, lb 12, w 7, nb 10	33
	(91.1 overs)	290	(9 wkts dec.77 overs)	334

Bowling
Caddick 29-9-75-4. Johnson 13-2-38-0. Francis 20.1-5-57-4. Parsons 9-3-36-0. Dutch 20-2-75-2.
Caddick 30-8-119-2. Francis 24-2-113-4. Burns 16-4-46-3. Dutch 4-1-20-0. Edwards 3-0-20-0.
Fall of Wickets: 1-12, 2-31, 3-67, 4-111, 5-146, 6-164, 7-169, 8-175, 9-255
1-48, 2-71, 3-97, 4-103, 5-107, 6-125, 7-131, 8-289, 9-321

SOMERSET	First Innings		Second Innings	
PD Bowler	c Crawley b Tremlett	15	c Crawley b Taylor	6
NJ Edwards	b Taylor	13	lbw b Tremlett	0
J Cox	c Pothas b Mascarenhas	24	lbw b Taylor	23
JC Hildreth	c b b Udal	61	c Pothas b Tremlett	14
M Burns (capt)	c Mascarenhas b Tremlett	36	c Kendall b Udal	30
*RJ Turner	c Pothas b Mascarenhas	4	b Kendall	0
KP Dutch	lbw b Mascarenhas	2	lbw b Tremlett	60
AR Caddick	not out	28	c Pothas b Taylor	5
SRG Francis	c Kendall b Udal	8	not out	0
KA Parsons	absent hurt		absent hurt	
RL Johnson	absent hurt		absent hurt	
Extras	b 3, lb 3, w 2, nb 4	12	b 6, lb 2	8
	(8 wkts 60.2 overs)	203	(8 wkts 40.1 overs)	146

Bowling
Taylor 15.2-3-62-1. Tremlett 18-6-44-2. Watson 8.4-2-28-0. Mascarenhas 10.3-1-45-3. Udal 6.5-1-17-2. Clarke 1-0-1-0.
Tremlett 11.1-1-43-3. Taylor 15-2-38-3. Kendall 8-2-20-1. Udal 6-0-37-1.
Fall of Wickets: 1-21, 2-39, 3-72, 4-153, 5-163, 6-165, 7-169, 8-203
1-1, 2-21, 3-40, 4-49, 5-60, 6-121, 7-130, 8-146

Hampshire won by 275 runs - Hampshire (18pts), Somerset (4pts)

NOTTINGHAMSHIRE v. DERBYSHIRE - at Trent Bridge

NOTTS	First Innings		Second Innings	
DJ Bicknell	lbw b Mohammad Ali	24	not out	25
JER Gallian (capt)	c Mohammad Ali b Botha	190	not out	1
RJ Warren	lbw b Dean	13		
KP Pietersen	c Sutton b Sheikh	107		
DJ Hussey	b Gait b Sheikh	0		
*CMW Read	c Sutton b Dean	130		
MA Ealham	c Gait b Botha	14		
PJ Franks	not out	27		
RJ Logan	not out	25		
CE Shreck				
SCG MacGill				
Extras	b 4, lb 11, w 2, nb 4	21	nb 2	2
	(7 wkts dec.133.2 overs)	551	(0 wkts 3 overs)	28

Bowling
Welch 28-1-101-0. Mohammad Ali 19.2-3-83-1. Sheikh 27-8-78-2. Dean 21-1-138-2. Moss 24-4-65-0. Botha 14-1-71-2.
Welch 2-0-14-0. Mohammad Ali 1-0-14-0.
Fall of Wickets: 1-37, 2-69, 3-286, 4-286, 5-485, 6-489, 7-504

DERBYSHIRE	First Innings		Second Innings	
AI Gait	lbw b Shreck	0	c Pietersen b Shreck	0
SD Stubbings	c Warren b Ealham	0	c Pietersen b Ealham	0
J Moss	c Warren b Shreck	69	c Pietersen b Shreck	20
Hassan Adnan	b Franks	43	not out	129
KJ Dean	run out		(10) b Shreck	8
CWG Bassano	c Read b Ealham	3	(8) c & b Shreck	52
*LD Sutton (capt)	not out	36	(5) lbw b Shreck	8
G Welch	c Read b Franks	29	(6) b Pietersen	9
AG Botha	c Gallian b MacGill	9	(7) lbw b Shreck	40
MA Sheikh	b Franks	1	(9) b Shreck	1
Mohammad Ali	c Gallian b MacGill	14	c Logan b MacGill	50
Extras	b 4, lb 6, w 1, nb 4	15	b 7, lb 13, w 7, nb 6	33
	(59.1 overs)	220	(82.5 overs)	355

Bowling
Shreck 14-4-47-2. Ealham 12-3-35-2. Logan 10-1-69-0. Franks 14-5-43-3. MacGill 8.1-2-16-2. Pietersen 1-1-0-0.
Shreck 25-5-103-6. Ealham 11-1-46-1. Franks 7-0-28-0. MacGill 25.5-5-89-2. Pietersen 6-1-26-1. Logan 8-0-43-0.
Fall of Wickets: 1-0, 2-4, 3-93, 4-107, 5-122, 6-130, 7-177, 8-198, 9-205
1-5, 2-25, 3-26, 4-44, 5-64, 6-158, 7-253, 8-274, 9-291

Nottinghamshire won by 10 wickets - Nottinghamshire (22pts), Derbyshire (3pts)

YORKSHIRE v. LEICESTERSHIRE - at Headingley

LEICESTERSHIRE	First Innings		
DDJ Robinson	c Lumb b Silverwood		22
DL Maddy	c Wood b Bresnan		9
BJ Hodge	lbw b Silverwood		37
JL Sadler	c White b Silverwood		6
DI Stevens	b Kirby		67
*PA Nixon	c Guy b Bresnan		23
PAJ DeFreitas (capt)	c Silverwood b Dawson		78
OD Gibson	c Wood b Bresnan		13
CW Henderson	c Wood b Kirby		1
CE Dagnall	b Dawson		2
MF Cleary	not out		0
Extras	b 8, lb 4, w 1, nb 18		31
	(85.1 overs)		289

Bowling
Silverwood 23-3-78-3. Kirby 26-5-85-2. Bresnan 23-3-88-3. White 4.2-2-12-0. Dawson 5.1-1-12-2. Lehmann 3.4-2-2-0.
Fall of Wickets: 1-36, 2-58, 3-76, 4-91, 5-152, 6-234, 7-276, 8-287, 9-287

YORKSHIRE	First Innings		
MJ Wood	c Hodge b DeFreitas		63
PA Jaques	lbw b Gibson		30
CR Taylor	b DeFreitas		8
DS Lehmann	c Cleary b DeFreitas		17
MJ Lumb	c Gibson b Cleary		77
*SM Guy	c Nixon b Dagnall		24
RKJ Dawson	c Nixon b Maddy		17
TT Bresnan	c Robinson b Dagnall		9
CEW Silverwood	b Dagnall		12
SP Kirby	b Cleary		0
C White (capt)	not out		0
Extras	lb 6, nb 20		26
	(58.4 overs)		283

Bowling
Cleary 12-0-95-2. Gibson 12-2-58-1. DeFreitas 13-3-42-3. Dagnall 12.4-4-46-3. Henderson 3-0-14-0. Maddy 3-0-22-1.
Fall of Wickets: 1-58, 2-79, 3-113, 4-140, 5-210, 6-235, 7-268, 8-274, 9-281

Match drawn - Yorkshire (9pts), Leicestershire (9pts)

A fifth consecutive championship win for Nottinghamshire, who beat Derbyshire by ten wickets in a local derby at Trent Bridge, was based on a massive first-innings total of 551 for 7 declared. Jason Gallian, who turned his 28th first-class ton into a magnificent 190, was joined by Kevin Pietersen (107) and Chris Read (130) in taking the Derbyshire bowling apart. Only Jon Moss provided any first-innings resistance for the visitors, although Hassan Adnan's unbeaten 129 and a violent 32-ball 50 by No. 11 Mohammad Ali, containing ten fours and a six, held Notts up second time around. Indeed, victory for the home side did not arrive until the eighth over of the last 16, with Adnan's determination and Ali's assault causing Gallian and his team some nervous moments in the final hour. Charlie Shreck built further on his fine work earlier in the season by taking 6 for 103.

Rain ruined Yorkshire's fixture against Leicestershire at Headingley, with no play at all on the scheduled first day and just 25 overs possible on the second. In the time remaining, honours were almost exactly even, with Yorkshire failing by a mere six runs to match Leicestershire's first innings of 289.

Round 11: 23–29 June 2004

Division One

Storm clouds had started to gather around Arundel when the champions found that their game against Gloucestershire was the only one to have beaten a band of bad weather that had swept across the country on the first day of this particular round of fixtures. Gale-force winds had the tall trees swaying around one of the country's loveliest settings and, 90 minutes before play began at 11.30, an old oak crashed to earth near to the Castle walls. In such an unsettling atmosphere, it was perhaps no surprise that the Sussex batting should also go crashing, or that Chris Adams' struggling team should eventually bow to a damaging nine-wicket defeat. Jon Lewis, well supported by Mike Smith and Mark Alleyne, was the first-day destroyer for Gloucestershire, and his 5 for 33 was his third haul of five wickets or more for the season. Murray Goodwin's 28 was the top score in the home side's sad first-innings decline to 106 all out, and when bad light drove the players off the field to the sanctuary of the pavilion at 5 pm, the Gloucestershire reply had already reached 63 without loss. On a calmer second day, both weather-wise and on the pitch, the visitors reached 300 – thanks in the end to three straight sixes by Shabbir

Career-best: Stephen Moore hit 146 against Surrey at New Road.

Ahmed off his fellow Pakistani Mushtaq Ahmed, whose 5 for 58 from 30 overs could not prevent a match-winning lead. Lewis and Smith shared six wickets as Sussex collapsed from 113 for 2 to 115 for 7 before Robin Martin-Jenkins and Mushtaq added a defiant 88 in 16 overs for the eighth wicket to force Gloucestershire, at least, to bat again.

More signs of the changing of the old order came at Worcester, where only the elements prevented Surrey – the champions in 1999, 2000 and 2002 – from suffering a heavy defeat against Worcestershire. Surrey were left on 16 for 2 after just seven overs had been possible on the first day, and a fourth-wicket partnership of 52 between Graham Thorpe and Jon Batty could not stop them from sliding to 155 all out early on the second day as Kabir Ali and Matt Mason wreaked havoc. By the close, Worcestershire's openers, Stephen Peters and Stephen Moore, had put on 170 in reply, and their stand reached 240 before Peters fell for 108. Moore, however, went on to record a career-best 146 and although both Graeme Hick and Vikram Solanki both bagged ducks, there was no let-up for Surrey. Ben Smith and Andrew Hall added an unbroken 129 for the fifth wicket to allow a declaration on 400 for 4 and, with one day still to go, Surrey had slumped to 167 for 6 in their second innings. The weather, though, dictated that only 16 overs were bowled on the final day and, with Thorpe making an unbeaten 26, Surrey limped to 187 for 8 – still 58 behind overall – and a fortuitous draw.

Poor weather wrecked Kent's championship return to Beckenham, with the first day a total washout and the final day reduced to just under 30 overs of play. By then, however, Kent were happy to see the rain fall. Bowled out for an inadequate 297, despite Andrew Symonds' barnstorming 156 not out, which contained four sixes and 21 fours, they had been asked to follow on by a Warwickshire team who, in racking up 502 for 6 declared, had achieved maximum batting points for the seventh match in a row. Kent's only previous first-class match at the former Lloyd's Bank Ground in Beckenham had been exactly 50 years earlier, in 1954, but the Warwickshire top three of Michael Powell, Mark Wagh and Jonathan Trott took an immediate liking to a firm, fast pitch. After the match had finally got under way on the second morning, the trio took their team's score to 334 for 1 by the close. Wagh had fallen for 86, following a 171-run opening stand, but Powell then went on to score a determined, if sluggish, hundred in only his second championship appearance of the summer and Trott played some wonderful strokes in reaching 97 not out by stumps. Trott completed his own century the next morning, but the best batting of the game was provided by Symonds, who reached three figures from only 108 balls as the wickets clattered around him.

There was also a rain-hit draw at Liverpool's Aigburth ground, where Lancashire's match against Northamptonshire began on 26 June. Just as had been the case at Beckenham, the first day was washed away, before a diligent unbeaten 133 from Usman Afzaal, from 278 balls, blunted a home attack in which Gary Keedy stood out with his left-arm spin. In reply to a total of 357, Lancashire were in a spot of bother at 169 for 6 before Dominic Cork

found lower-order suport from Steven Crook and went on to reach 74. In the time left, on the final day, there was joy for 19-year-old Oliver Newby, who sent back Martin van Jaarsfeld and Afzaal to claim two distinguished victims in his first-class debut.

Round 11: 23–29 June 2004 Division One

SUSSEX v. GLOUCESTERSHIRE - at Arundel

SUSSEX	First Innings		Second Innings	
IJ Ward	c Alleyne b Lewis	0	lbw b Shabbir	69
RR Montgomerie	b Gidman b Lewis	6	b Alleyne	15
MW Goodwin	c Gidman b Lewis	28	c Adshead b Alleyne	5
CJ Adams (capt)	b Smith	6	c Gidman b Smith	12
MJ Prior	c Adshead b Shabbir	5	lbw b Smith	0
*TR Ambrose	c Adshead b Lewis	14	c Spearman b Shabbir	0
RSC Martin-Jenkins	c Adshead b Alleyne	2	c Smith b Lewis	43
RJ Kirtley	c Adshead b Lewis	17	c Gidman b Smith	0
Mushtaq Ahmed	c Fisher b Alleyne	1	c Adshead b Lewis	54
M Akram	not out	5	c Weston b Lewis	0
JD Lewry	b Smith	7	not out	5
Extras	b 1, lb 8, nb 6	15	b 2, w 1, nb 12	15
	(43.4 overs)	106	(62.5 overs)	218

Bowling
Lewis 13-4-33-5. Shabbir 14-3-33-1. Smith 9.4-3-20-2. Alleyne 7-2-11-2.
Lewis 18.5-3-67-3. Shabbir 16-4-39-2. Smith 16-4-34-3. Alleyne 11-3-45-2.
Gidman 1-0-8-0. Fisher 2-0-23-0.
Fall of Wickets: 1-0, 2-25, 3-42, 4-47, 5-54, 6-73, 7-75, 8-77, 9-99
1-65, 2-81, 3-113, 4-113, 5-113, 6-115, 7-115, 8-203, 9-203

GLOS	First Innings		Second Innings	
WPC Weston	c Ambrose b Akram	81	(2) run out	0
CM Spearman	lbw b Lewry	36	(1) not out	21
MGN Windows	lbw b Mushtaq Ahmed	33	not out	3
CG Taylor (capt)	c Ambrose b Mushtaq Ahmed	47		
APR Gidman	b Akram	26		
MW Alleyne	c Adams b Lewry	10		
*SJ Adshead	lbw b Mushtaq Ahmed	5		
ID Fisher	st Ambrose b Mushtaq Ahmed	21		
J Lewis	lbw b Mushtaq Ahmed	8		
Shabbir Ahmed	not out	34		
AM Smith	b Kirtley	9		
Extras	b 4, lb 19, nb 2	25	lb 1	1
	(94 overs)	300	(1 wkt 3.3 overs)	25

Bowling
Akram 20-3-86-2. Kirtley 15-5-34-1. Martin-Jenkins 18-4-38-0. Lewry 10-0-61-2.
Mushtaq Ahmed 30-10-58-5.
Kirtley 2-0-20-0. Martin-Jenkins 1.3-1-4-0.
Fall of Wickets: 1-83, 2-140, 3-172, 4-177, 5-208, 6-219, 7-221, 8-235, 9-270
1-20

*Gloucestershire won by 9 wickets -
Sussex (3pts), Gloucestershire (20pts)*

WORCESTERSHIRE v. SURREY - at Worcester

SURREY	First Innings		Second Innings	
SA Newman	c Hall b Kabir Ali	23	b Hall	65
MA Butcher	c Rhodes b Kabir Ali	4	c Solanki b Bichel	17
MR Ramprakash	run out	0	c Rhodes b Hall	13
GP Thorpe	lbw b Kabir Ali	41	(7) not out	26
*JN Batty	c Bichel b Mason	53	c Smith b Bichel	10
AD Brown	c Rhodes b Kabir Ali	0	lbw b Mason	31
AJ Hollioake	b Mason	16	(4) b Hall	0
MP Bicknell	lbw b Kabir Ali	9	c Rhodes b Mason	9
IDK Salisbury	c Rhodes b Mason	8	b Kabir Ali	1
J Ormond	c Rhodes b Mason	0	not out	1
TJ Murtagh	not out	2		
Extras	b 1, lb 4	5	b 4, lb 9	13
	(47.1 overs)	155	(8 wkts 60 overs)	187

Bowling
Mason 17.1-5-46-4. Kabir Ali 19-6-60-5. Hall 7-2-16-0. Bichel 4-0-28-0.
Kabir Ali 16-2-65-1. Mason 22-7-47-2. Hall 8-3-10-3. Bichel 10-3-46-1.
Batty 4-3-6-1.
Fall of Wickets: 1-6, 2-14, 3-35, 4-87, 5-87, 6-114, 7-123, 8-142, 9-150
1-45, 2-83, 3-83, 4-106, 5-127, 6-164, 7-178, 8-181

WORCS	First Innings	
SD Peters	c Newman b Hollioake	108
SC Moore	c Batty b Hollioake	146
GA Hick	c Batty b Hollioake	0
BF Smith (capt)	not out	80
VS Solanki	c Batty b Salisbury	0
AJ Hall	not out	53
GJ Batty		
AJ Bichel		
Kabir Ali		
*SJ Rhodes		
MS Mason		
Extras	lb 9, w 2, nb 2	13
	(4 wkts dec 103 overs)	400

Bowling
Bicknell 11-4-27-0. Ormond 31-5-109-0. Murtagh 22-1-107-0. Hollioake 21-3-69-3.
Salisbury 18-0-79-1.
Fall of Wickets: 1-240, 2-245, 3-270, 4-271

*Match drawn -
Worcestershire (12pts), Surrey (4.5pts - 0.5pts deducted
for slow over rate)*

KENT v. WARWICKSHIRE - at Beckenham

WARWICKSHIRE	First Innings	
MJ Powell	c Patel b Trott	134
MA Wagh	c Symonds b Trott	86
IJL Trott	c O'Brien b Saggers	115
IR Bell	c Fulton b Patel	49
JO Troughton	st O'Brien b Patel	21
GB Hogg	c Symonds b Patel	28
DR Brown (capt)	not out	27
NM Carter	not out	1
*T Frost		
N Tahir		
A Richardson		
Extras	b 3, lb 6, nb 32	41
	(6 wkts dec 139 overs)	502

Bowling
Mohammad Sami 25.3-111-0. Saggers 24-5-63-1. Trott 32-7-102-2.
Symonds 8-3-26-0. Loudon 17-1-88-0. Patel 33-8-103-3.
Fall of Wickets: 1-171, 2-354, 3-396, 4-436, 5-463, 6-490

KENT	First Innings		Second Innings	
DP Fulton (capt)	c Powell b Tahir	15	not out	5
MA Carberry	lbw b Carter	13	not out	14
ET Smith	b Tahir	2		
A Symonds	not out	156		
MJ Walker	b Hogg	21		
AGR Loudon	c Trott b Hogg	9		
*NJ O'Brien	lbw b Hogg	13		
MM Patel	b Hogg	24		
MJ Saggers	b Carter	0		
Mohammad Sami	c Frost b Tahir	18		
BJ Trott	run out	0		
Extras	b 5, lb 3, w 6, nb 12	26	nb 4	4
	(75.2 overs)	297	(0 wkts 17 overs)	23

Bowling
Carter 19-7-44-2. Brown 10-2-31-0. Tahir 9-2-50-3. Wagh 2-0-4-0.
Richardson 11-3-55-0. Hogg 22.2-3-90-4. Bell 2-0-15-0.
Tahir 3-0-7-0. Brown 5-3-6-0. Richardson 6-4-4-0. Trott 3-2-6-0.
Fall of Wickets: 1-17, 2-22, 3-50, 4-86, 5-108, 6-146, 7-215, 8-218, 9-296

*Match drawn - Kent (7pts),
Warwickshire (12pts)*

LANCASHIRE v. NORTHAMPTONSHIRE - at Liverpool

NORTHANTS	First Innings		Second Innings	
TW Roberts	c Law b Wood	14	c Cork b Keedy	20
GL Brophy	c Hegg b Crook	36	b Mongia	67
M van Jaarsveld	lbw b Wood	7	c Cork b Newby	0
U Afzaal	not out	133	c Wood b Newby	20
DJG Sales (capt)	c Hegg b Keedy	59		
GP Swann	c Hegg b Crook	2		
BJ Phillips	c Loye b Keedy	5	(5) not out	26
J Louw	lbw b Keedy	2		
*TMB Bailey	lbw b Keedy	5	(6) not out	11
AJ Shantry	c Mongia b Keedy	5		
PS Jones	c Sutcliffe b Mongia	35		
Extras	b 5, lb 7	12	lb 2	2
	(114.4 overs)	357	(4 wkts 53 overs)	146

Bowling
Cork 25-5-69-0. Wood 18-2-70-2. Crook 12-2-33-2. Newby 26-6-75-0.
Keedy 25-3-73-5. Mongia 8.4-0-25-1.
Cork 6-1-19-0. Wood 3-0-20-0. Keedy 23-7-58-1. Newby 9-0-32-2.
Mongia 16-14-1. Loye 1-0-1-0.
Fall of Wickets: 1-21, 2-35, 3-74, 4-158, 5-250, 6-258, 7-260, 8-264, 9-284
1-47, 2-50, 3-96, 4-108

LANCASHIRE	First Innings	
MJ Chilton	b Phillips	35
IJ Sutcliffe	lbw b Swann	48
MB Loye	run out	10
SG Law	c Bailey b Swann	3
D Mongia	c Shantry b Swann	0
*WK Hegg (capt)	c Roberts b Louw	30
DG Cork	c Louw b Shantry	74
SP Crook	c van Jaarsveld b Shantry	20
J Wood	c Sales b Louw	35
G Keedy	lbw b Louw	5
OJ Newby	not out	0
Extras	lb 3, w 3	6
	(97.1 overs)	284

Bowling
Louw 19.1-6-59-3. Shantry 21-6-67-2. Jones 8-1-32-0. Phillips 13-0-52-1.
Swann 32-9-69-3. Afzaal 4-1-4-0.
Fall of Wickets: 1-76, 2-94, 3-97, 4-107, 5-122, 6-169, 7-215, 8-278, 9-284

Match drawn - Lancashire (9pts), Northamptonshire (11pts)

Division Two

This round of matches threw up four rain-affected draws, with no play at all being possible on the first and fourth days at Derby, Cardiff and Taunton. Some play, 10.4 and 14.4 overs respectively, was managed at the Rose Bowl on those days, but to no real avail. Phil Jaques, Yorkshire's Australian

batsman, did, however, find enough time to thrash the Hampshire attack for a scintillating 243 – the highest individual score made at Southampton's new venue. Jaques, who initially arrived at the county to deputise for the injured Ian Harvey, but who then stayed on to act as Darren Lehmann's temporary replacement, also became the first batsman to make a double-hundred both for and against Yorkshire – he had scored 222 for Northants against the White Rose county in 2003. Jaques reached 22 not out on the truncated opening day, and in the 77.2 overs of play that were possible on the second day he accelerated to 193 not out – out of a total of 268 for 3. He hit six sixes to a short boundary on one side of the pitch and, when he was finally dismissed, he had hit 33 fours besides. Vic Craven's 41 was the next highest score and a strange-looking Yorkshire innings then fell away against the swing bowling of Alan Mullally, who added 6 for 68 to the mere seven victims he had picked up in five previous championship appearances. A half-century for John Crawley and some late hitting by Shaun Udal (41) provided the best entertainment for the handful of spectators who then watched the match head towards its watery grave.

Marcus North, yet another of the Australians playing in county cricket, also struck a double-century as Durham had the better of their weather-shortened fixture against Glamorgan. North reached three figures from just 110 balls, and went on to amass a career-best 219. Gareth Breese hit 76 early

Round 11: 23–29 June 2004 Division Two

HAMPSHIRE v. YORKSHIRE - at The Rose Bowl

YORKSHIRE First Innings

MJ Wood (capt)	c Pothas b Tremlett	1
PA Jaques	b Mullally	243
CR Taylor	c Clarke b Udal	22
MJ Lumb	c Pothas b Taylor	18
VJ Craven	c Pothas b Mullally	41
AKD Gray	c Pothas b Mullally	10
*SM Guy	c Taylor b Mullally	13
RKJ Dawson	b Mullally	7
CEW Silverwood	not out	11
MJ Hoggard	c Pothas b Udal	1
SP Kirby	lbw b Mullally	0
Extras	lb 10, nb 18	28
	(126.4 overs)	395

Bowling
Tremlett 23-5-93-1. Taylor 25-8-56-1. Udal 21-2-78-2. Clarke 2-0-7-0. Mullally 31.4-13-68-6. Mascarenhas 22-6-71-0. Kendall 2-0-12-0.
Fall of Wickets: 1-10, 2-125, 3-211, 4-345, 5-354, 6-365, 7-378, 8-385, 9-394

HAMPSHIRE First Innings

DA Kenway	c Guy b Kirby	12
MJ Brown	c Guy b Hoggard	1
JP Crawley	lbw b Craven	53
WS Kendall	c Taylor b Craven	15
MJ Clarke	c Dawson b Kirby	27
*N Pothas	c Dawson b Hoggard	45
AD Mascarenhas	c Craven b Hoggard	22
SD Udal (capt)	b Gray	41
CT Tremlett	not out	0
AD Mullally		
BV Taylor		
Extras	b 6, lb 22, w 3, nb 12	43
	(8 wkts 77.4 overs)	259

Bowling
Hoggard 20.4-6-50-3. Silverwood 13-4-37-0. Kirby 14-4-44-2. Craven 8-2-29-2. Dawson 15-2-51-0. Gray 7-1-20-1.
Fall of Wickets: 1-5, 2-22, 3-55, 4-119, 5-137, 6-182, 7-253, 8-259

Match drawn - Hampshire (9pts),
Yorkshire (10pts)

GLAMORGAN v. DURHAM - at Cardiff

DURHAM First Innings

JJB Lewis (capt)	b Harrison	27
GR Breese	b Cosker	76
GJ Muchall	b Thomas SD	23
MJ North	c Thomas IJ b Croft	219
N Peng	b Thomas SD	28
KJ Coetzer	lbw b Harrison	67
*A Pratt	b Harrison	9
GD Bridge	lbw b Croft	4
N Killeen	b Cosker	4
M Davies	c Hemp b Croft	2
G Onions	not out	0
Extras	lb 7	7
	(129.1 overs)	466

Bowling
Harrison 27-5-116-3. Wharf 18-3-79-0. Thomas S.D. 19-4-62-2. Croft 42-8-128-3. Cosker 23.1-1-74-2.
Fall of Wickets: 1-65, 2-103, 3-143, 4-234, 5-422, 6-438, 7-460, 8-460, 9-466

GLAMORGAN First Innings

IJ Thomas	b Bridge	29
DD Cherry	lbw b Breese	29
DL Hemp	b Killeen	37
MP Maynard	lbw b Davies	17
J Hughes	c and b Onions	7
*MA Wallace	b Onions	0
RDB Croft (capt)	c Peng b Davies	19
AG Wharf	not out	53
SD Thomas	not out	52
DS Harrison		
DA Cosker		
Extras	b 4, lb 9, nb 2	15
	(7 wkts 80 overs)	258

Bowling
Killeen 15-2-50-1. Onions 11-2-34-2. Davies 13-3-31-2. Bridge 23-2-88-1. Breese 18-6-42-1.
Fall of Wickets: 1-42, 2-105, 3-105, 4-121, 5-121, 6-145, 7-150

Match drawn - Glamorgan (9pts),
Durham (11pts)

DERBYSHIRE v. ESSEX - at Derby

DERBYSHIRE First Innings

SD Stubbings	lbw b Clarke	12
AI Gait	b Napier	33
J Moss	lbw b Napier	79
Hassan Adnan	b Napier	1
CWG Bassano	c Foster b Napier	0
*LD Sutton (capt)	c Napier b Danish Kaneria	131
G Welch	b Napier	26
AG Botha	run out	52
MA Sheikh	c Jefferson b Danish Kaneria	10
KJ Dean	not out	8
Mohammad Ali	c Napier b Middlebrook	10
Extras	b 6, lb 11, nb 10	27
	(128.1 overs)	389

Bowling
Brant 18-3-65-0. Clarke 27-2-105-1. Danish Kaneria 40-10-88-2. Napier 23-8-56-5. Middlebrook 20.1-4-58-1.
Fall of Wickets: 1-23, 2-66, 3-68, 4-68, 5-171, 6-231, 7-335, 8-363, 9-371

ESSEX First Innings

WI Jefferson	lbw b Welch	39
AN Cook	c Stubbings b Welch	34
A Flower	not out	88
A Habib	c Stubbings b Welch	3
RC Irani (capt)	not out	51
SA Brant		
*JS Foster		
JD Middlebrook		
GR Napier		
AJ Clarke		
Danish Kaneria		
Extras	b 3, lb 4	7
	(3 wkts 65 overs)	222

Bowling
Mohammad Ali 14-0-48-0. Moss 12-2-39-0. Dean 7-0-30-0. Welch 14-3-40-3. Botha 11-0-31-0. Sheikh 4-2-16-0. Hassan Adnan 3-1-11-0.
Fall of Wickets: 1-67, 2-90, 3-98

Match drawn - Derbyshire (9pts),
Essex (8pts)

SOMERSET v. LEICESTERSHIRE - at Taunton

LEICESTERSHIRE First Innings / Second Innings

DDJ Robinson	b McLean	72	c Laraman b McLean	21
DL Maddy	c Turner b McLean	84	not out	59
BJ Hodge	c Turner b Caddick	2	b Caddick	1
JL Sadler	c Cox b Francis SRG	10		
DI Stevens	c Hildreth b Francis SRG	37	(4) not out	12
*PA Nixon	not out	63		
PAJ DeFreitas (capt)	c Caddick b McLean	13		
OD Gibson	c Turner b McLean	16		
CW Henderson	c Turner b Laraman	52		
MF Cleary	not out	31		
CE Dagnall				
Extras	lb 7, w 3, nb 12	22	nb 2	2
	(8 wkts dec 87.5 overs)	402	(2 wkts 26 overs)	95

Bowling
Caddick 28.5-7-103-1. McLean 22-0-100-4. Francis SRG 19-2-118-2. Laraman 18-2-74-1.
Caddick 10-1-31-1. McLean 6-2-18-1. Francis SRG 7-1-32-0. Francis JD 1-1-14-0.
Fall of Wickets: 1-158, 2-167, 3-167, 4-211, 5-224, 6-255, 7-277, 8-358. 1-27, 2-32

SOMERSET First Innings

PD Bowler	lbw b Cleary	46
JD Francis	c Maddy b Gibson	52
J Cox	c & b Dagnall	2
JC Hildreth	c Stevens b Dagnall	4
M Burns (capt)	b Cleary	27
MJ Wood	not out	33
AW Laraman	c Nixon b Cleary	4
*RJ Turner	c Robinson b Cleary	37
AR Caddick	c Nixon b Maddy	7
SRG Francis	b DeFreitas	6
NAM McLean	c Nixon b Cleary	11
Extras	b 10, lb 9, nb 14	33
	(90 overs)	262

Bowling
DeFreitas 23-8-46-1. Gibson 28-8-83-1. Henderson 2-0-13-0. Dagnall 18-5-49-2. Cleary 16-2-50-5. Maddy 3-2-2-1.
Fall of Wickets: 1-99, 2-113, 3-121, 4-121, 5-170, 6-182, 7-202, 8-236, 9-257

Match drawn - Somerset (8pts),
Leicestershire (12pts - 1.5pts deducted for slow over rate)

Phil Jaques made a remarkable 243 against Hampshire ...
202 more than the next-highest Yorkshire scorer.

on, and then Kyle Coetzer marked his first-class debut by making 67 in a fifth-wicket stand worth 188 with North. Glamorgan slipped to 150 for 7 in reply to Durham's 466 before Alex Wharf and Darren Thomas rallied them with unbeaten half-centuries.

Derbyshire captain Luke Sutton led from the front against Essex with a determined innings of 131 that was chiefly responsible for the home side recovering strongly from a burst of three wickets in five balls by Graham Napier which had reduced them to 68 for 4. Jon Moss and Ant Botha also contributed half-centuries, but it was so cold when the match finally got under way on day two that many of the Essex

fielders sported woolly hats. Andy Flower, with an unbeaten 88, and Ronnie Irani, on 51, were similarly rallying Essex from an uncertain start when the weather intervened for the final time.

Darren Maddy followed up his first-innings 84 with another excellent unbeaten 59 as Leicestershire had the better of what play there was against Somerset. Maddy and Darren Robinson (72) had launched their side's first innings of 402 for 8 declared by adding 158 for the first wicket, and there were also half-centuries, in an eighth-wicket stand of 81, for both Paul Nixon and Claude Henderson. Mark Cleary, the 24-year-old Australia A paceman, then added an impressive 5 for 50 to his merry unbeaten 31 as Somerset slid from 99 without loss in reply to 262 all out.

Round 12: 21–26 July 2004

Division One

Champions Sussex at last showed signs of running into form as they recorded their biggest win over neighbours and rivals Kent for 65 years at Hove. Kent could only make 330 in their first innings, despite 122 from captain and opener David Fulton and a lovely 79 from 104 balls, including 14 boundaries, by Ed Smith. They fell away badly from 173 for 1, as Mark Davis and Mushtaq Ahmed shared six wickets, and, by the end of the second day, Sussex were already in a position to assume command of the match by reaching 396 for 4. Tony Cottey, whose only previous championship appearance had been at the total washout at Worcester, then converted his overnight 114 into a memorable 185 and extended his fifth-wicket partnership with Matthew Prior to 202. The talented Sussex wicketkeeper-batsman made 123 and an eventual first-innings total of 618 was also boosted by 88 extras – just 11 short of the world record! Fulton batted well again second time around, but Kent slipped to 99 for 3 by the close and, on the final day, only Matthew Walker (62) put up any sort of resistance as Davis and Mushtaq got among the wickets once more.

Warwickshire's by-now-familiar formula for success was given a helping hand at Guildford by Surrey captain Jon Batty, who put them in and then saw the championship leaders ease their way to a first-innings total of 537. Ian Bell, who remarkably lay just eighth in the county's batting averages with 58.54 before this game, compiled an elegant 155 and added 214 for the fourth wicket with the resurgent

Michael Powell, who made 110. To cap Surrey's misery, a further 107 was plundered for the seventh wicket by Dougie Brown and Brad Hogg, with the veteran Scottish all-rounder scoring 106 from 145 balls and the Australian thumping 67 off a mere 41

deliveries. In reply, all Surrey had to offer was further technical excellence from Mark Ramprakash, who remained unbeaten on 145 as the home side were asked to follow on after being bowled out for 331. This time Ramprakash could make only a single, as Surrey slid to 24 for 3, but at least some self-respect was achieved as Batty joined Alistair Brown in a fourth-wicket alliance worth 200. Brown then fell for 103, but Batty battled on to reach a courageous 145 until, agonisingly, he was out to the third ball of the third day's final over. Surrey's last three wickets could add only another 49 runs the following morning and although Warwickshire were initially reduced to 37 for 2, they found Bell up to the challenge yet again as the 22-year-old dominated a match-clinching third-wicket stand of 138 with Jonathan Trott. Bell went past his 1,000 first-class runs for the season for the first time during an unbeaten 96, as he guided his side home to a seven-wicket victory.

A brilliant unbeaten 140 from Owais Shah, and a 127-run partnership between a Hutton and a Compton which left older spectators rheumy-eyed, were among the highlights of Middlesex's exciting and hard-fought six-wicket win over Worcestershire at New Road. Ben Hutton's first-innings 108 and Nick Compton's 40 on his championship debut not only had those of a certain age dreaming of their distinguished grandfathers Len Hutton and Denis Compton, but also provided the solid base from

Round 12: 21–26 July 2004 Division One

SUSSEX v. KENT - at Hove

KENT	First Innings		Second Innings	
DP Fulton (capt)	st Prior b Mushtaq Ahmed	122	c & b Davis	47
JC Tredwell	c Kirtley b Akram	17	lbw b Martin-Jenkins	12
ET Smith	b Akram	79	b Mushtaq Ahmed	4
MJ Walker	c Prior b Davis	17	c Montgomerie b Mushtaq Ahmed	62
MA Carberry	c Cottey b Davis	29	c Montgomerie b Akram	3
AGR Loudon	c Prior b Davis	14	b Davis	34
*NJ O'Brien	lbw b Kirtley	6	st Prior b Davis	11
MM Patel	b Mushtaq Ahmed	2	lbw b Mushtaq Ahmed	2
A Khan	b Mushtaq Ahmed	0	c Cottey b Davis	27
IG Butler	not out	16	c Kirtley b Mushtaq Ahmed	17
A Sheriyar	c Adams b Kirtley	12	not out	5
Extras	b 8, lb 6, nb 2	16	b 1, lb 4, nb 14	19
	(115.3 overs)	330	(97.1 overs)	243

Bowling
Akram 19-0-98-2. Kirtley 18.3-4-64-2. Martin-Jenkins 12-4-41-0.
Mushtaq Ahmed 39-13-59-3. Davis 27-10-54-3.
Akram 14-4-38-1. Kirtley 13-1-38-0. Mushtaq Ahmed 42-12-94-4.
Davis 19.1-3-57-4. Martin-Jenkins 9-2-11-1.
Fall of Wickets: 1-51, 2-173, 3-204, 4-264, 5-290, 6-292, 7-294, 8-294, 9-304
1-37, 2-50, 3-94, 4-108, 5-171, 6-181, 7-185, 8-193, 9-228

SUSSEX	First Innings	
IJ Ward	c Fulton b Sheriyar	6
RR Montgomerie	c Tredwell b Khan	20
PA Cottey	b Patel	185
MW Goodwin	b Patel	55
CJ Adams (capt)	b Butler	57
*MJ Prior	c Walker b Patel	123
RSC Martin-Jenkins	run out	25
MJG Davis	not out	17
Mushtaq Ahmed	c Butler b Patel	22
RJ Kirtley	b Loudon	19
M Akram	c O'Brien b Patel	1
Extras	b 9, lb 16, w 11, nb 52	88
	(148.4 overs)	618

Bowling
Butler 24-2-100-1. Sheriyar 27-3-120-1. Khan 20-3-94-1. Patel 39.4-6-138-5.
Tredwell 18-0-88-0. Walker 3-0-5-0. Loudon 17-4-48-1.
Fall of Wickets: 1-21, 2-43, 3-179, 4-283, 5-485, 6-550, 7-553, 8-582, 9-617

Sussex won by an innings and 45 runs -
Sussex (22pts), Kent (5pts)

SURREY v. WARWICKSHIRE - at Guildford

WARWICKSHIRE	First Innings		Second Innings	
NV Knight (capt)	c Azhar Mahmood b Ormond	36	c Clarke b Sampson	21
MA Wagh	c Clarke b Sampson	0	b Ormond	4
IR Bell	c Murtagh b Doshi	155	not out	96
IJL Smith	c Brown b Sampson	25	c Batty b Clarke	61
MJ Powell	lbw b Sampson	110	not out	12
DR Brown	c Clarke b Sampson	106		
N Tahir	c Batty b Ormond	4		
GB Hogg	c Newman b Doshi	67		
*T Frost	lbw b Sampson	0		
A Richardson	c Newman b Doshi	4		
D Pretorius	not out	4		
Extras	b 10, lb 11, w 4, nb 4	29	b 2, lb 3, nb 8	13
	(130.3 overs)	537	(3 wkts 55.3 overs)	207

Bowling
Ormond 31-7-90-2. Sampson 24.3-1-121-5. Murtagh 26-4-105-0.
Azhar Mahmood 20-3-78-0. Doshi 25-0-101-3. Hollioake 4-0-21-0.
Ormond 13-4-37-1. Azhar Mahmood 11-1-40-0. Sampson 8-3-19-1. Murtagh 6-2-22-0.
Doshi 10-1-37-0. Hollioake 2-0-12-0. Clarke 2-0-22-1. Brown 3.3-0-13-0.
Fall of Wickets: 1-6, 2-48, 3-112, 4-326, 5-376, 6-398, 7-505, 8-506, 9-529
1-15, 2-37, 3-175

SURREY	First Innings		Second Innings	
SA Newman	c Frost b Pretorius	9	c Trott b Pretorius	13
R Clarke	b Brown	21	b Brown	6
MR Ramprakash	not out	145	lbw b Pretorius	1
AD Brown	c Frost b Tahir	25	c Frost b Tahir	103
*JN Batty (capt)	c Frost b Richardson	1	lbw b Pretorius	145
AJ Hollioake	c Powell b Hogg	33	[7] lbw b Brown	9
Azhar Mahmood	b Richardson	25	[6] c Frost b Tahir	14
TJ Murtagh	c Wagh b Tahir	0	c & b Brown	57
J Ormond	c Trott b Brown	30	not out	12
PJ Sampson	b Tahir	1	[11] c Wagh b Tahir	1
ND Doshi	c Bell b Tahir	22	[10] st Frost b Hogg	18
Extras	lb 10, w 1, nb 8	19	b 4, lb 15, w 4, nb 10	33
	(78.1 overs)	331	(107.3 overs)	412

Bowling
Pretorius 20-5-66-1. Brown 16-4-57-2. Bell 2-0-11-0. Richardson 19-4-62-2.
Tahir 11.1-2-63-4. Hogg 8-0-46-1. Wagh 3-0-9-0.
Pretorius 18-4-71-3. Brown 25-3-80-3. Tahir 18.3-1-84-3. Richardson 12-3-39-0.
Hogg 13-2-48-1. Wagh 15-1-41-0. Bell 5-0-22-0. Trott 1-0-8-0.
Fall of Wickets: 1-10, 2-38, 3-104, 4-111, 5-183, 6-232, 7-233, 8-283, 9-288
1-14, 2-15, 3-24, 4-224, 5-252, 6-269, 7-363, 8-377, 9-411

Warwickshire won by 7 wickets -
Surrey (6pts), Warwickshire (22pts)

WORCESTERSHIRE v. MIDDLESEX - at Worcester

WORCS	First Innings		Second Innings	
SD Peters	c Hutton b Betts	24	lbw b Betts	13
SC Moore	b Betts	33	b Cook	20
GA Hick	c Betts b Cook	10	lbw b Cook	2
VS Solanki	c Compton b Betts	92	lbw b Cook	9
Kadeer Ali	c Nash b Betts	0	c Shah b Cook	36
AJ Bichel	c Weekes b Agarkar	28	c Weekes b Dalrymple	108
GJ Batty	lbw b Betts	8	c Nash b Cook	0
AJ Hall	c Nash b Agarkar	71	c Compton b Betts	81
Kabir Ali	run out	0	c Nash b Cook	7
*SJ Rhodes (capt)	not out	5	c Hutton b Dalrymple	20
MS Mason	c Nash b Agarkar	6	not out	5
Extras	lb 2, w 3, nb 20	25	b 5, lb 2, w 1, nb 14	22
	(78.3 overs)	305	(106.1 overs)	323

Bowling
Agarkar 20.3-4-72-3. Cook 23-4-61-1. Betts 18-3-89-5. Wright 7-0-31-0.
Hutton 6-1-22-0. Dalrymple 2-0-20-0. Weekes 2-0-8-0.
Cook 32-6-89-6. Agarkar 14-2-62-0. Betts 23.1-5-78-2. Weekes 10-1-25-0.
Wright 13-3-19-0. Dalrymple 14-1-43-2.
Fall of Wickets: 1-59, 2-72, 3-78, 4-78, 5-127, 6-147, 7-280, 8-293, 9-294
1-33, 2-35, 3-37, 4-47, 5-162, 6-162, 7-230, 8-247, 9-307

MIDDLESEX	First Innings		Second Innings	
BL Hutton (capt)	b Batty	108	b Batty	43
SG Koenig	c Rhodes b Mason	37	run out	11
NRD Compton	lbw b Batty	40	c Kadeer Ali b Batty	20
OA Shah	not out	140	b Kabir Ali	11
PN Weekes	b Kabir Ali	42	not out	11
JWM Dalrymple	not out	84	not out	0
*DC Nash	c Hall b Kadeer Ali	12		
SJ Cook	c Peters b Batty	4		
AB Agarkar	c Rhodes b Batty	22		
MM Betts	c Peters b Batty	5		
CJC Wright	lbw b Batty	0		
Extras	b 7, lb 7, w 1, nb 20	35	lb 6, w 2, nb 2	10
	(153.5 overs)	525	(4 wkts 25.4 overs)	105

Bowling
Bichel 21-5-76-0. Mason 30-10-77-1. Kabir Ali 24-1-95-1. Hall 20-3-71-0.
Batty 41.5-5-141-6. Solanki 12-1-36-0. Kadeer Ali 5-1-15-1.
Mason 6-1-21-0. Bichel 6-0-27-0. Kabir Ali 6-0-29-1. Hall 2-0-10-0.
Batty 5.4-2-12-2.
Fall of Wickets: 1-72, 2-199, 3-202, 4-278, 5-432, 6-458, 7-459, 8-519, 9-525
1-15, 2-73, 3-90, 4-94

Middlesex won by 6 wickets -
Worcestershire (4pts), Middlesex (22pts)

GLOUCESTERSHIRE v. LANCASHIRE - at Cheltenham

LANCASHIRE	First Innings		Second Innings	
MJ Chilton	c Adshead b Franklin	69	not out	124
IJ Sutcliffe	run out	10	c & b Ball	61
MB Loye	c Weston b Ball	90	c Hussey b Averis	69
D Mongia	c Franklin b Fisher	111	not out	76
CL Hooper (capt)	c Franklin b Fisher	19		
*JJ Haynes	c Hussey b Franklin	24		
G Chapple	b Franklin	0		
DG Cork	b Franklin	0		
SI Mahmood	b Franklin	0		
PJ Martin	c Weston b Franklin	20		
G Keedy	not out	1		
JM Anderson				
Extras	b 4, lb 8, nb 19	31	b 4, lb 12, nb 8	24
	(111.1 overs)	375	(2 wkts dec 66 overs)	354

Bowling
Lewis 24-4-66-0. Franklin 22.1-7-60-7. Averis 14-1-62-0. Gidman 7-1-27-0.
Ball 25-3-70-1. Fisher 19-1-78-1.
Lewis 14-3-71-0. Franklin 10-4-39-0. Averis 9-3-51-1. Ball 18-1-109-1.
Fisher 15-0-68-0.
Fall of Wickets: 1-20, 2-160, 3-215, 4-263, 5-333, 6-333, 7-333, 8-341, 9-362
1-115, 2-230

GLOS	First Innings		Second Innings	
CM Spearman	c Haynes b Chapple	9	[2] c Loye b Anderson	8
WPC Weston	c & b Anderson	44	[1] lbw b Hooper	65
MEK Hussey	b Martin	5	c Chilton b Hooper	44
CG Taylor (capt)	lbw b Cork	33	b Anderson	74
APR Gidman	b Cork	1	c Sutcliffe b Hooper	21
JEC Franklin	c Haynes b Mahmood	34	[7] lbw b Anderson	0
*SJ Adshead	c Haynes b Cork	40	[6] not out	57
ID Fisher	c Haynes b Cork	1	c Hooper b Keedy	31
MCJ Ball	c Loye b Cork	4	b not out	29
JMM Averis	not out	10		
J Lewis	b Chapple	14		
Extras	b 5, lb 11, w 1, nb 18	35	b 11, lb 12, nb 14	37
	(52.1 overs)	234	(7 wkts 115.4 overs)	366

Bowling
Martin 6-1-24-1. Chapple 11.1-2-23-2. Cork 16-4-54-5. Mahmood 7-0-46-0.
Anderson 19-5-40-1. Keedy 12-3-31-1.
Anderson 28-9-95-3. Chapple 11-3-15-0. Keedy 48.4-14-95-1. Cork 15-4-50-0.
Hooper 29-9-55-3. Mahmood 8-4-24-0. Mongia 4-1-9-0.
Fall of Wickets: 1-19, 2-28, 3-93, 4-99, 5-99, 6-181, 7-188, 8-199, 9-216
1-11, 2-112, 3-160, 4-225, 5-233, 6-233, 7-291

Match drawn - Gloucestershire (8pts), Lancashire (11pts)

which Middlesex struck out to travel a long way past a Worcestershire total of 305 that had owed much to a seventh-wicket stand of 133 between Vikram Solanki and Andrew Hall. Shah's class then told, as he stroked 14 fours and two sixes, while Jamie Dalrymple also impressed with a stylish 84. Gareth Batty's six wickets came at too great a cost, and Middlesex were in control as they reached 525. Simon Cook then took three wickets with the new ball to reduce Worcestershire's second innings to 47 for 4, but Andy Bichel and Kadeer Ali began a recovery which gathered greater momentum as Bichel went on to score a fine 108 and Hall (81) first joined his fellow all-rounder in a seventh-wicket partnership of 68 before adding a further 60 for the ninth wicket with Steve Rhodes. Cook finished with figures of 6 for 89 as the home side were eventually dismissed for 323, but it was all beginning to get a bit tense as Middlesex set out to score 104 in 29 overs for victory. Hutton's 43 was his second vital

contribution of the match, but four wickets were lost before the win was secured with just 20 balls remaining.

A draw at Cheltenham represented a missed opportunity for Lancashire, who, with hindsight, delayed their second-innings declaration by around ten overs too many. Set 496, Gloucestershire managed to bat out 144 overs to claim the four extra points for a draw, finishing on 366 for 7. It was a worthy effort, with Phil Weston and Chris Taylor both hitting top-order half-centuries before Steve Adshead, with 57 not out in 62 overs, was helped by the resistance of the lower order in denying the Lancashire bowlers. Gloucestershire's first-innings 234 was a triumph for Dominic Cork, who took 5 for 54, while Mark Chilton, Mal Loye and Dinesh Mongia were the major run getters in both innings for Lancashire. Mongia's second-innings sprint to 76 not out from just 52 balls – with eight fours and two sixes – was especially entertaining for the good-sized crowds

which again attended the College Ground. There were some mutterings from the home support, however, when, on the second day, James Anderson – hotfoot from being released by England at Lord's – replaced Peter Martin in the Lancashire XI by taking over from him after he had sent down a new-ball spell. In the end, though, even this 'extra-bowler' advantage could not make the difference.

Division Two

Derbyshire gained their first win of the championship season despite a career-best opening-day 6 for 44 from Durham seamer Mark Davies at the Riverside. From 88 for 7, Derbyshire rallied to 195 thanks to a 90-run eighth-wicket stand between Graeme Welch (59) and Ant Botha (42). By the close of a dramatic first day it was Durham who were on the rack, as the home side stumbled to 64 for 7 in reply, and, the following morning, they declined further to 91 all out, despite skipper Jon Lewis stubbornly carrying his bat for 35. Mo Sheikh's 4 for 9 from 11 overs was also a

The class of Owais Shah helped Middlesex to victory at Worcester.

career-best analysis, and as batting conditions improved it was 29-year-old Australian all-rounder Jon Moss, with support from Luke Sutton, who took the game out of Durham's reach. Moss, who went to three figures with a straight six off Graeme Bridge,

Round 12: 21–26 July 2004 Division Two

DURHAM v. DERBYSHIRE - at The Riverside

DERBYSHIRE	First Innings		Second Innings	
AI Gait	b Collingwood	30	c Pratt b Davies	21
SD Stubbings	c Pratt b Davies	8	lbw b Davies	18
J Moss	c Pratt b Davies	0	not out	147
Hassan Adnan	c North b Collingwood	4	c Collingwood b Blignaut	29
JDC Bryant	c Muchall b Davies	3	run out	30
SA Selwood	c Pratt b Davies	8	lbw b Bridge	11
*LD Sutton (capt)	b Davies	45	c Pratt b Davies	45
G Welch	c Pratt b Davies	59	not out	23
AG Botha	c Pratt b Blignaut	42		
MA Sheikh	lbw b Bridge	1		
PMR Havell	not out	1		
Extras	b 8, lb 2, w 1, nb 26	37	b 8, lb 1, w 1, nb 6	16
	(73.5 overs)	340	(6 wkts dec 99 overs)	340

Bowling
Onions 15-4-35-0. Blignaut 11-2-43-1. Davies 18.5-6-44-6. Collingwood 12-3-27-2. Bridge 14-4-32-1. Muchall 3-2-4-0.
Onions 20.4-4-80-1. Blignaut 15-1-48-1. Davies 14.2-2-38-2. Collingwood 12-4-47-0. Bridge 22-1-73-1. Breese 14-2-40-0. Muchall 1-0-5-0.
Fall of Wickets: 1-36, 2-36, 3-45, 4-56, 5-79, 6-83, 7-88, 8-178, 9-181
1-31, 2-46, 3-100, 4-164, 5-204, 6-301

DURHAM	First Innings		Second Innings	
JJB Lewis (capt)	not out	35	b Sheikh	25
GR Breese	c Sutton b Havell	6	b Havell	4
GJ Muchall	c Sutton b Havell	7	c Bryant b Sheikh	49
PD Collingwood	c Sutton b Moss	9	c Sutton b Welch	22
MJ North	c Sutton b Sheikh	3	c Selwood b Welch	68
KJ Coetzer	c Sutton b Sheikh	0	b Welch	5
*A Pratt	c Botha b Moss	1	b Botha	42
AM Blignaut	c Botha b Moss	3	c Botha b Havell	19
GD Bridge	run out	8	lbw b Havell	9
M Davies	c Moss b Sheikh	1	(11)not out	2
G Onions	b Sheikh	0	(10)c Welch b Havell	11
Extras	lb 4, nb 14	18	b 1, lb 5, w 1, nb 16	23
	(46 overs)	91	(76.1 overs)	279

Bowling
Havell 6-0-36-2. Welch 7-4-12-0. Sheikh 11-7-9-4. Moss 17-7-30-3. Havell 16.1-3-75-4. Welch 21-4-56-3. Sheikh 18-2-68-2. Moss 9-1-27-0. Botha 12-2-47-1.
Fall of Wickets: 1-15, 2-23, 3-45, 4-48, 5-48, 6-49, 7-53, 8-77, 9-83
1-19, 2-44, 3-96, 4-128, 5-133, 6-215, 7-243, 8-255, 9-272

Derbyshire won by 165 runs – Durham (3pts), Derbyshire (17pts)

---

remained unbeaten on 147 when the declaration came at 340 for 6. Marcus North made 68, but Paul Havell and Welch ensured that wickets fell regularly and, in the end, the fourth day was not needed as Derbyshire wrapped up a 165-run victory.

Yorkshire, bundled out for just 160 on the third morning in front of 3,000 home fans at Scarborough's North Marine Road, suffered a humiliating ten-wicket defeat at the hands of a Somerset side revitalised by the arrival of an overseas player – Australian captain Ricky Ponting. The West Country side's win was also a triumph for Nixon McLean, the West Indian fast bowler, who took 6 for 79 and 5 for 45, while off spinner Keith Dutch earned considerable plaudits for his second-innings haul of 5 for 26 and eight wickets in the match. The whole Somerset line-up, however, suddenly looked on top of their game as the trials and tribulations of a previously unhappy summer were put behind them. John Francis, the young opener, struck four sixes and 11 fours in his 109 while helping Ponting to add 197 for the second wicket. Ponting, to no great surprise, marked his championship debut by hitting two sixes and 15 fours of his own in a beautiful innings of 112 from 133 balls. Also inspired were Mike Burns, with 74, and Ian Blackwell, who launched no fewer than six sixes and four fours in his violent 73. All this added up to a Somerset reply of 451 to a Yorkshire first innings of 296 that had been sustained by a second-wicket stand of 98 between Matthew Wood

---

YORKSHIRE v. SOMERSET - at Scarborough

YORKSHIRE	First Innings		Second Innings	
MJ Wood (capt)	c Turner b Dutch	59	not out	66
AW Gale	lbw b McLean	0	c Dutch b McLean	9
A McGrath	c Ponting b Dutch	48	(4) c Laraman b Dutch	12
MJ Lumb	c Turner b McLean	10	(3) c Turner b McLean	11
IJ Harvey	lbw b McLean	14	b McLean	10
DS Lehmann	not out	90	c Francis SRG b Dutch	36
*I Dawood	c Ponting b Laraman	8	b Dutch	1
RKJ Dawson	c McLean b Dutch	23	c Burns b Dutch	0
CEW Silverwood	c Blackwell b McLean	26	c Turner b McLean	3
MAK Lawson	lbw b McLean	11	c Turner b McLean	1
SP Kirby	lbw b McLean	0	lbw b Dutch	7
Extras	lb 1, nb 6	7	lb 2, nb 2	4
	(84.5 overs)	296	(42 overs)	160

Bowling
McLean 22.5-6-79-6. Francis SRG 10-2-50-0. Laraman 13-3-43-1. Blackwell 13-2-30-0. Dutch 21-2-87-3. Ponting 5-2-6-0. McLean 15-5-45-5. Francis SRG 10-3-61-0. Laraman 10-1-0-10-0. Dutch 11-2-26-5. Blackwell 5-0-16-0.
Fall of Wickets: 1-3, 2-101, 3-110, 4-129, 5-144, 6-174, 7-227, 8-272, 9-286
1-19, 2-35, 3-54, 4-73, 5-114, 6-116, 7-116, 8-131, 9-135

SOMERSET	First Innings		Second Innings	
PD Bowler	c Dawson b Silverwood	1	not out	1
JD Francis	c Dawood b Silverwood	109	not out	5
RT Ponting	c Gale b Dawson	112		
JC Hildreth	c Wood b Kirby	14		
M Burns (capt)	st Dawood b Dawson	74		
ID Blackwell	c Dawson b Lehmann	73		
AW Laraman	c Lumb b Lehmann	9		
KP Dutch	not out	29		
*RJ Turner	c Harvey b Dawson	1		
SRG Francis	b Lawson	1		
NAM McLean	c Dawson b Lawson	0		
Extras	b 4, lb 6, w 5, nb 8	23		0
	(96.3 overs)	451	(0 wkts 0.4 overs)	6

Bowling
Silverwood 17-1-75-2. Kirby 17-1-92-1. Harvey 17-3-90-0. Dawson 19-4-79-3. Lawson 16.3-1-69-2. Lehmann 10-0-36-2. Lawson 0.4-0-6-0.
Fall of Wickets: 1-31, 2-228, 3-251, 4-292, 5-405, 6-415, 7-430, 8-436, 9-451

Somerset won by 10 wickets – Yorkshire (5pts), Somerset (22pts)

LEICESTERSHIRE v. ESSEX - at Leicester

ESSEX	First Innings		Second Innings	
WI Jefferson	c Maddy b Gibson	29	b Gibson	11
AN Cook	c Nixon b Cleary	0	c Nixon b Gibson	55
A Flower	c Nixon b Dagnall	14	b Gibson	12
A Habib	run out	13	lbw b Dagnall	55
RC Irani (capt)	lbw b Gibson	6	c Maddy b Gibson	49
*JS Foster	b Dagnall	0	lbw b Gibson	0
JD Middlebrook	c Nixon b Dagnall	92	b Gibson	0
GR Napier	c Nixon b Dagnall	7	c Robinson b Henderson	26
AB Adams	b Gibson	124	c Gibson b Dagnall	19
AP Cowan	not out	5	c Henderson b Maddy	6
D Gough	c Robinson b Gibson	11	not out	12
Extras	lb 5, w 1, nb 15	21	lb 6, lb 4, w 3, nb 4	27
	(71.2 overs)	322	(74.1 overs)	272

Bowling
Cleary 14-0-76-1. Gibson 20.2-10-73-4. DeFreitas 4.2-1-11-0. Dagnall 19-1-71-4. Maddy 6.4-1-37-0. Henderson 7-2-49-0.
Gibson 22-5-74-6. Cleary 5-0-20-0. Maddy 10-2-34-1. Dagnall 14-2-65-2. Hodge 1-0-5-0. DeFreitas 15-6-33-0. Henderson 7.1-3-21-1.
Fall of Wickets: 1-11, 2-41, 3-62, 4-71, 5-73, 6-79, 7-108, 8-306, 9-306
1-36, 2-85, 3-86, 4-196, 5-200, 6-200, 7-202, 8-238, 9-250

LEICESTERSHIRE	First Innings		Second Innings	
DDJ Robinson	lbw b Adams	33	c Foster b Cowan	38
DL Maddy	c Foster b Gough	1	c Foster b Gough	25
BJ Hodge (capt)	lbw b Cowan	7	c Cowan b Gough	4
JL Sadler	b Gough	8	lbw b Gough	95
DI Stevens	c Flower b Napier	50	run out	20
*PA Nixon	lbw b Adams	11	(7) lbw b Middlebrook	30
PAJ DeFreitas	c Jefferson b Gough	38	(8) lbw b Napier	39
OD Gibson	c Cowan b Napier	14	(9) run out	39
CW Henderson	lbw b Gough	0	(6) lbw b Adams	0
MF Cleary	not out	14	not out	27
CE Dagnall	c Jefferson b Napier	0	b Gough	0
Extras	b 8, lb 6, w 3, nb 4	21	b 8, lb 12, w 1, nb 11	32
	(59 overs)	197	(116.5 overs)	349

Bowling
Gough 22-7-55-4. Cowan 15-4-54-1. Napier 10-2-33-3. Adams 12-3-41-2. Gough 25.5-6-89-4. Cowan 28-9-75-1. Napier 26-6-85-1. Adams 10-2-30-1. Middlebrook 27-7-50-1.
Fall of Wickets: 1-15, 2-22, 3-39, 4-99, 5-115, 6-153, 7-165, 8-165, 9-197
1-54, 2-60, 3-107, 4-136, 5-140, 6-218, 7-256, 8-305, 9-345

Essex won by 48 runs – Leicestershire (3pts), Essex (20pts)

NOTTINGHAMSHIRE v. HAMPSHIRE - at Trent Bridge

HAMPSHIRE	First Innings		Second Innings	
DA Kenway	c Read b Shreck	0	c Pietersen b Sidebottom	28
MJ Brown	c Read b Sidebottom	74	c Read b MacGill	30
JP Crawley	not out	301		
MJ Clarke	c Hussey b Shreck	140	(3) c Hussey b Pietersen	103
JHK Adams	st Read b MacGill	36	(4) b Bicknell	16
*N Pothas	not out	56		
AD Mascarenhas			(5) not out	41
SK Warne (capt)				
BV Taylor			(6) b Pietersen	27
AD Mullally			(7) c Hussey b Pietersen	27
SD Udal			(8) not out	23
Extras	b 4, lb 9, w 1, nb 20	34	b 8, lb 9, nb 10	27
	(4 wkts dec 152.2 overs)	641	(6 wkts 64 overs)	295

Bowling
Shreck 30-6-106-2. Sidebottom 25-4-108-1. Franks 20-3-102-0. Ealham 24-8-68-0. MacGill 27-0-114-1. Pietersen 7-0-56-0. Hussey 19.2-2-74-0.
Sidebottom 10-3-32-1. Shreck 5-0-53-0. MacGill 14-4-35-1. Franks 4-1-21-0. Hussey 5-0-33-0. Pietersen 13-1-72-3. Bicknell 13-2-32-1.
Fall of Wickets: 1-0, 2-153, 3-391, 4-489
1-61, 2-69, 3-184, 4-200, 5-234, 6-236

NOTTS	First Innings		
DJ Bicknell	c Pothas b Mullally	103	
JER Gallian (capt)	run out	26	
RJ Warren	b Warne	21	
KP Pietersen	c Brown b Warne	0	
DJ Hussey	b Taylor	170	
*CMW Read	c Pothas b Taylor	75	
MA Ealham	not out	113	
PJ Franks	c Pothas b Taylor	30	
RJ Sidebottom	c Udal b Mascarenhas	8	
SCG MacGill	b Mullally	28	
CE Shreck	lbw b Udal	1	
Extras	b 10, lb 5, w 6, nb 16	37	
	(159.2 overs)	612	

Bowling
Mullally 24-3-83-2. Taylor 33-4-159-3. Warne 39-5-133-2. Mascarenhas 28-7-81-1. Udal 22.2-1-93-1. Clarke 9-2-24-0. Crawley 4-1-24-0.
Fall of Wickets: 1-63, 2-93, 3-93, 4-230, 5-408, 6-459, 7-542, 8-573, 9-611

*Match drawn – Nottinghamshire (10pts),
Hampshire (11pts)*

and Anthony McGrath and then by Darren Lehmann's unbeaten 90. Wood, though, was the only Yorkshireman who could hold his head up high after their second-innings capitulation – he carried his bat for 66 as McLean and Dutch blew away his ten different partners.

A fine game of cricket at Grace Road was won in the end by Essex, by 48 runs, but a brave Leicestershire second innings raised the home side's hopes for most of a fascinating final day. It was Darren Gough, with eight wickets in the match, who emerged as the Essex hero – although the whirlwind hitting on the opening day of Andre Adams and James Middlebrook also played a major part in deciding the outcome. Essex had slumped to 108 for 7 in their first innings when New Zealander Adams, signed as an overseas replacement player from the Lancashire League, responded to his sudden elevation by thrashing the fastest hundred of the season so far. It took just 80 balls, it was his maiden first-class century, and he went to three figures with a six over long on off slow left-armer Claude Henderson. With Middlebrook hitting out almost as effectively for 92, the pair put on 198 in just 31 overs for the eighth wicket and, by the end of an action-packed first day, Leicestershire were already 64 for 3 in reply to Essex's unlikely 322. Darren Stevens made 50, but Gough and Graham Napier hastened the home side's decline to 197, and Leicestershire were up against it to an even greater extent when Essex cruised to 196 for 3 in their second innings. However, Ottis Gibson then began to pick up wickets and, as he finished with 6 for 74, a victory target of 398 presented itself. At 145 for 5 at stumps on the third day, it seemed as though Leicestershire's race was almost run, but then John Sadler inspired a late middle-order fightback with a fine innings of 95. Gough, though, adding 4 for 89 to his first-innings 4 for 55, had the last word.

A belting batting pitch at Trent Bridge was the ultimate winner as Nottinghamshire and Hampshire, the two firm favourites for promotion to Division One, slugged out a high-scoring draw. John Crawley's career-best 301 not out, an innings which eclipsed the 286 he made for England A at Port Elizabeth while on tour to South Africa in 1993–94, provided the focal point of Hampshire's march to 641 for 4 declared. Crawley, hitting 35 fours and two sixes in a 442-ball epic, put on 238 with the gifted young Australian Michael Clarke, who scored 140, while Michael Brown and Nic Pothas both passed the half-century mark, but Notts were far from intimidated. Kevin Pietersen may have fallen to

Shane Warne for a duck in an initial struggle to 129 for 3 by the close of day two, but Darren Bicknell anchored the innings with 103 and David Hussey, underlining his growing reputation as a probable Australian Test batsman of the future, struck four sixes and 20 fours in a polished 170. Hussey was presented with his county cap when he left the field for the tea interval on the third afternoon and Warne went wicketless all day as Notts reached 534 for 6 by the close. Chris Read had scored 75 by then and, on the final morning, Mark Ealham took his overnight 79 to 113 not out before the Notts reply finally ran out of juice on 612. Remarkably, both counties had now scored their highest totals against each other, in a fixture dating back to 1843! In the time that remained, Clarke moved to his second hundred of the match.

Round 13: 28 July–1 August 2004

Division One

Northamptonshire gained their first championship victory of the campaign as Surrey let a strong position slip at Wantage Road. The visitors looked to be totally in control of the game after they had reached the end of the opening day on 380 for 6. Mark Ramprakash had led them out of early problems at 57 for 3 with a wonderfully skilful innings of 161 on a pitch that assisted the spinners from the beginning of the match. The former England batsman went past 1,000 runs in the season for the 14th time while hitting 19 fours and a straight six, off Jason Brown, during his 262-ball masterclass. Jon Batty (61) played another important innings for his side and Adam Hollioake's forthright 76 provided lower-middle-order ballast. The next morning saw the innings fall away a little, but 402 still gave Surrey the opportunity to dominate the rest of the game. At 262 for 9, Northants were struggling to stay in contention, but there then followed a last-wicket stand of 70 that, in effect, turned the contest. No. 11 Brown made 34 and home skipper David Sales finished up on 61 not out thanks to the unlikely resistance coming from the other end. Then, with Johann Louw bowling Ramprakash for nought and with Brown and Graeme Swann again revelling in familiar conditions, Surrey's second innings disintegrated to 147 all out. It left Northants suddenly requiring just 218 to win and, when Tim Roberts and Robert White put on 111 for the first wicket, they reached the target at something of a canter.

Kent made Middlesex fight for much of the final day before the home side wrapped up a 119-run win at Southgate to strengthen their chances of staying in Division One. David Fulton, the Kent captain,

Round 13:
28 July–1 August 2004 Division One

NORTHAMPTONSHIRE v. SURREY – at Northampton

SURREY	First Innings		Second Innings	
SA Newman	st Bailey b Brown	28	lbw b Greenidge	4
R Clarke	c Roberts b Greenidge	11	c Love b Greenidge	5
MR Ramprakash	b Greenidge	161	b Louw	0
JGE Benning	b Brown	2	c Love b Brown	33
*JN Batty (capt)	st Bailey b Brown	61	b Brown	4
AJ Hollioake	lbw b Louw	76	b Brown	1
Azhar Mahmood	run out	21	c White b Brown	21
IDK Salisbury	b Brown	17	c White b Swann	24
J Ormond	c White b Louw	15	st Bailey b Swann	19
ND Doshi	lbw b Brown	0	st Bailey b Swann	20
PJ Sampson	not out	1	not out	11
Extras	lb 8, nb 2	10	b 1, lb 4	5
	(120.1 overs)	402	(56.3 overs)	147

Bowling
Louw 17.1-1-68-2. Greenidge 12-1-66-2. Brown 47-10-113-5. Phillips 20-6-46-0. Swann 20-3-76-0. White 4-0-25-0.
Louw 6-1-28-1. Greenidge 5-1-13-2. Brown 23-5-51-4. Swann 22.3-2-50-3.
Fall of Wickets: 1-18, 2-55, 3-57, 4-237, 5-328, 6-356, 7-382, 8-392, 9-402
1-5, 2-10, 3-18, 4-46, 5-51, 6-52, 7-87, 8-109, 9-134

NORTHANTS	First Innings		Second Innings	
TW Roberts	b Doshi	57	c & b Azhar Mahmood	64
RA White	lbw b Ormond	9	b Ramprakash	52
ML Love	c Ormond b Doshi	51	not out	49
U Afzaal	c Batty b Salisbury	29	(6) not out	16
DJG Sales (capt)	not out	61		
GP Swann	c Batty b Ormond	37	(5) c Benning b Doshi	1
J Louw	b Azhar Mahmood	11		
BJ Phillips	b Azhar Mahmood	1		
*TMB Bailey	lbw b Doshi	4	(4) lbw b Ramprakash	20
CG Greenidge	c Hollioake b Doshi	34		
JF Brown	c Clarke b Azhar Mahmood	34		
Extras	b 25, lb 7, nb 6	38	b 11, lb 1, nb 6	18
	(99.4 overs)	332	(4 wkts 74.5 overs)	220

Bowling
Azhar Mahmood 22.4-5-46-3. Ormond 28-8-90-2. Sampson 2-0-14-0.
Clarke 1-0-5-0. Doshi 31-6-103-4. Salisbury 15-2-42-1.
Ormond 13.5-3-56-0. Azhar Mahmood 8-2-27-1. Hollioake 3-0-11-0.
Doshi 27-7-58-1. Salisbury 7-0-21-0. Ramprakash 16-3-35-2.
Fall of Wickets: 1-20, 2-124, 3-147, 4-179, 5-235, 6-252, 7-254, 8-262, 9-262
1-111, 2-125, 3-161, 4-162

Northamptonshire won by 6 wickets –
Northamptonshire (20pts), Surrey (8pts)

scored a determined 121 in six-and-a-half hours at the crease, but Glenn McGrath finally added Fulton's scalp to the 4 for 59 he claimed in a Kent first-innings collapse which, in the end, proved the main difference between the sides. Ed Smith (63) and Matthew Walker (50) were the only players to look comfortable against McGrath and Simon Cook, who shared seven wickets, and Kent were back to square one after Alex Loudon's career-best 5 for 53 had brought them back into the game on day one following Ben Hutton's 100 and a fluent 60 from Owais Shah. Hutton and Sven Koenig then slammed the door shut in Kent's face, with Hutton reaching his second hundred of the match and Koenig finally being run out for 86 after the pair had put on 163 for the first wicket. A declaration at 370 for 8 left Kent to chase an unrealistic target of 530, but they still fought hard to avoid defeat as first Fulton and Michael Bevan, and then Loudon and Niall O'Brien, made the Middlesex bowlers work very hard in sweltering conditions for their ultimate reward.

Worcestershire succeeded where Kent had failed by coming from behind to shock Gloucestershire at Cheltenham. Victory was achieved by five wickets on the last afternoon as Graeme Hick hit a majestic 178, his 126th first-class century, putting him level with WG Grace on the all-time list, and Andy Bichel weighed in with an unbeaten 103 containing four sixes and 11 fours. Hick smote three sixes and 24 boundaries, and Gloucestershire's bowlers were quite unable to resist

MIDDLESEX v. KENT – at Southgate

MIDDLESEX	First Innings		Second Innings	
BL Hutton (capt)	c O'Brien b Patel	100	c Carberry b Patel	107
SG Koenig	b Joseph	31	run out	86
NRD Compton	c Walker b Butler	2	c O'Brien b Joseph	16
OA Shah	b Trott	60	c O'Brien b Joseph	3
PN Weekes	c Walker b Patel	45	lbw b Patel	54
JWM Dalrymple	c Bevan b Loudon	31	c Fulton b Butler	27
*DC Nash	not out	26	c Loudon b Patel	23
SJ Cook	c Walker b Loudon	0	b Patel	29
AB Agarkar	b Loudon	7	not out	1
MM Betts	c & b Loudon	0		
GD McGrath	c Fulton b Loudon	24		
Extras	b 3, lb 5, w 1, nb 16	25	b 12, lb 8, nb 4	24
	(99.3 overs)	351	(8 wkts dec 95.2 overs)	370

Bowling
Butler 15-1-62-1. Trott 15-2-67-1. Joseph 20-3-55-1. Patel 32-8-106-2.
Loudon 17.3-3-53-5.
Butler 14-1-68-1. Trott 10-1-34-0. Patel 33.2-3-94-4. Joseph 11-1-50-2.
Loudon 24-4-88-0. Bevan 3-0-16-0.
Fall of Wickets: 1-68, 2-109, 3-186, 4-228, 5-285, 6-297, 7-305, 8-305, 9-317
1-163, 2-207, 3-213, 4-237, 5-302, 6-316, 7-353, 8-370

KENT	First Innings		Second Innings	
DP Fulton (capt)	c Nash b Cook	8	c Hutton b McGrath	121
MA Carberry	c Shah b Cook	0	c Nash b Cook	14
ET Smith	c Weekes b McGrath	63	c Koenig b Cook	9
MG Bevan	lbw b Dalrymple	14	c Hutton b Weekes	66
MJ Walker	not out	50	lbw b Weekes	14
AGR Loudon	b McGrath	4	lbw b Shah	44
*NJ O'Brien	c Agarkar b Dalrymple	4	not out	67
MM Patel	c Agarkar b Cook	28	b Dalrymple	14
IG Butler	lbw b McGrath	1	c sub b Dalrymple	14
RH Joseph	b McGrath	0	lbw b Dalrymple	10
BJ Trott	c Nash b Betts	8	lbw b Weekes	0
Extras	lb 1, nb 8	9	b 13, lb 8, nb 15	36
	(61.3 overs)	192	(137.3 overs)	410

Bowling
McGrath 22-7-59-4. Dalrymple 15-2-52-2. Cook 14-3-33-3. Agarkar 4-0-27-0.
Betts 4.3-0-14-1. Weekes 2-0-6-0.
McGrath 30-10-71-1. Cook 11-3-46-2. Agarkar 17-6-53-0. Dalrymple 24-5-51-3.
Weekes 44.3-7-128-3. Betts 8-1-31-0. Shah 3-0-9-1.
Fall of Wickets: 1-4, 2-17, 3-74, 4-96, 5-106, 6-121, 7-167, 8-168, 9-168
1-2, 2-20, 3-182, 4-236, 5-268, 6-340, 7-366, 8-386, 9-405

Middlesex won by 119 runs – Middlesex (21pts), Kent (3pts)

GLOUCESTERSHIRE v. WORCESTERSHIRE – at Cheltenham

GLOS	First Innings		Second Innings	
CM Spearman	c Batty b Mason	8	(2) lbw b Kabir Ali	5
WPC Weston	b Kabir Ali	14	(1) c Rhodes b Hall	30
MEK Hussey	c Hall b Mason	0	lbw b Kabir Ali	68
CG Taylor (capt)	c & b Hall	103	c Hick b Hall	7
APR Gidman	c Bichel b Kabir Ali	70	c Hall b Batty	25
*SJ Adshead	lbw b Batty	48	c Smith b Kabir Ali	11
JEC Franklin	lbw b Batty	9	not out	8
MW Alleyne	c Hick b Batty	77	(10) run out	11
ID Fisher	run out	45	(8) c Hall b Kabir Ali	5
MCJ Ball	c Hick b Batty	38	(9) lbw b Batty	5
J Lewis	lbw b Batty	1	c Rhodes b Bichel	0
Extras	b 8, lb 13, w 1, nb 10	32	b 6, lb 7, nb 6	19
	(122.2 overs)	445	(79.1 overs)	189

Bowling
Mason 29-8-82-2. Kabir Ali 22-4-86-2. Bichel 19-2-73-0. Hall 22-0-101-1.
Batty 30.2-8-82-4.
Batty 34-10-68-2. Kabir Ali 13-5-33-4. Mason 31-3-18-0. Bichel 11.1-4-26-1.
Hall 10-3-31-2.
Fall of Wickets: 1-14, 2-14, 3-36, 4-132, 5-229, 6-251, 7-299, 8-387, 9-443
1-14, 2-63, 3-81, 4-142, 5-160, 6-161, 7-161, 8-172, 9-187

WORCS	First Innings		Second Innings	
SD Peters	lbw b Lewis	19	c Ball b Franklin	5
SC Moore	lbw b Franklin	35	lbw b Ball	53
GA Hick	c Fisher b Gidman	26	c Spearman b Fisher	178
BF Smith (capt)	c Gidman b Ball	56	c Taylor b Ball	4
VS Solanki	c Spearman b Gidman	3	st Adshead b Fisher	3
AJ Bichel	c Adshead b Lewis	36	not out	103
GJ Batty	c Weston b Lewis	30	not out	3
AJ Hall	lbw b Lewis	0		
Kabir Ali	not out	11		
*SJ Rhodes	c Spearman b Lewis	4		
MS Mason	c Spearman b Lewis	4		
Extras	b 6, lb 5, w 1, nb 22	34	lb 5, w 1, nb 8	14
	(79.5 overs)	274	(5 wkts 92.1 overs)	363

Bowling
Lewis 18.5-6-38-5. Franklin 17-5-58-1. Gidman 8-1-50-2. Ball 19-3-62-2.
Alleyne 8-3-23-0. Fisher 9-0-32-0.
Lewis 19-3-72-0. Franklin 16-4-53-1. Alleyne 4-0-26-0. Ball 32-2-93-2.
Fisher 19.1-1-100-2. Gidman 2-0-14-0.
Fall of Wickets: 1-59, 2-63, 3-118, 4-126, 5-179, 6-223, 7-229, 8-236, 9-259
1-9, 2-128, 3-138, 4-153, 5-342

Worcestershire won by 5 wickets –
Gloucestershire (8pts), Worcestershire (19pts)

LANCASHIRE v. WARWICKSHIRE – at Old Trafford

WARWICKSHIRE	First Innings		Second Innings	
NV Knight (capt)	c Haynes b Chilton	25	c Keedy b Cork	3
MA Wagh	c & b Keedy	41	c Haynes b Keedy	24
IR Bell	c Hooper b Cork	112	run out	181
UL Trott	c Hooper b Keedy	9	c Cork b Keedy	41
MJ Powell	lbw b Keedy	0	c Keedy b Keedy	0
DR Brown	c Chapple b Hogg	162	(7) c Wagh b Chapple	0
GB Hogg	lbw b Cork	9	(8) not out	72
*T Frost	c Haynes b Keedy	6		
NM Carter	not out	7	not out	7
N Tahir	not out	17	(6) lbw b Keedy	7
A Richardson	c Hooper b Schofield	17		
Extras	b 1, lb 7, w 1, nb 10	19	b 12, lb 2, nb 8	22
	(143.3 overs)	410	(7 wkts dec 95 overs)	353

Bowling
Chapple 26.5-5-73-0. Cork 27-6-53-2. Mahmood 25-4-100-1. Chilton 12-2-39-1.
Keedy 40-7-109-5. Schofield 6.3-1-13-1. Hooper 7-1-15-0.
Chapple 17-1-68-1. Cork 9-2-44-1. Keedy 38-7-109-4. Mahmood 12-0-76-0.
Schofield 11-0-43-0. Mongia 8-1-19-0.
Fall of Wickets: 1-72, 2-78, 3-92, 4-92, 5-346, 6-346, 7-361, 8-368, 9-380
1-3, 2-66, 3-184, 4-190, 5-214, 6-215, 7-332

LANCASHIRE	First Innings		Second Innings	
MJ Chilton	b Carter	20	b Brown	20
IJ Sutcliffe	lbw b Hogg	72	c Frost b Brown	5
MB Loye	retired hurt	44		
D Mongia	c & b Hogg	15	(3) not out	108
MJ Walker	lbw b Hogg	9	c Trott b Carter	11
CL Hooper (capt)	c Brown b Hogg	16	(4) c Trott b Carter	11
CP Schofield	c Wagh b Carter	99	(5) b Wagh	40
G Chapple	c Wagh b Hogg	112	(6) b Wagh	5
DG Cork	b Wagh	23		
*JJ Haynes	lbw b Wagh	0		
SI Mahmood	not out	3		
G Keedy	lbw b Wagh	0		
Extras	b 1, lb 7, w 1	9	b 4, lb 1	5
	(9 wkts 110 overs)	412	(4 wkts 52 overs)	194

Bowling
Carter 20-2-71-2. Brown 18-3-81-0. Wagh 30-7-86-3. Tahir 8-1-29-0.
Hogg 25-2-107-4. Richardson 7-0-18-0. Bell 2-0-12-0.
Brown 7-2-26-2. Carter 16-4-40-1. Wagh 15-4-56-1. Hogg 11-2-53-0.
Tahir 3-1-14-0.
Fall of Wickets: 1-32, 2-130, 3-148, 4-190, 5-358, 6-409, 7-409, 8-412, 9-412
1-21, 2-34, 3-61, 4-178

Match drawn – Lancashire (12pts), Warwickshire (11pts)

Dougie Brown of Warwickshire ... the most influential all-rounder of the championship season.

an onslaught which produced a match-winning fifth-wicket stand of 189. Perhaps justice was done in the end, as Worcestershire won for the 12th time in 14 championship meetings between the two counties, because, on day two, Hick had fallen for 26 to a stupendous diving catch in the outfield by Ian Fisher as he flat-batted an Alex Gidman long hop to deep midwicket. Jon Lewis' 5 for 38 had put Gloucestershire in control after the home side had recovered brilliantly from 36 for 3 to reach a first-innings total of 445, but then Kabir Ali spearheaded a fightback that resulted in Gloucestershire being bowled out a second time for just 189 and leaving Worcestershire 361 to score in the fourth innings. With Hick and Bichel inspired, it was a breeze.

The burgeoning batting talent of Ian Bell was on full display at Old Trafford as Warwickshire and Lancashire played out a well-matched draw. Bell scored 112 and 181 to blunt the Lancashire attack, while Dougie Brown, Glen Chapple and Dinesh Mongia also made hundreds. Chris Schofield was unlucky not to join them, being dismissed an agonising one run short of a maiden first-class ton. Brown's 162 helped Warwickshire to recover from a wobbly 92 for 4 on the first morning, and he and Bell added 254 for the fifth wicket. There was not a lot in the pitch for bowlers throughout the four days, but Gary Keedy's slow left-arm – with nine wickets in the match – still showed up well for Lancashire.

Division Two

There was controversy at Cardiff when Glamorgan refused a request by the England management to play fast bowler Simon Jones, who had been left out of the England team for the second Test, in their important match against fellow promotion rivals Hampshire. 'We have no room for Simon', said John Derrick, the Glamorgan coach. 'Mike Kasprowicz, David Harrison and Alex Wharf all deserve to keep their places, and we also want to play two spinners in this game.' Ironically, neither Wharf nor Dean Cosker, the left-arm spinner, could finish the match because of injuries sustained during Hampshire's first innings. Indeed, everything began to go wrong for Glamorgan on the second day, which had begun with the visitors in trouble on 16 for 3 in reply to the Welsh county's first-innings 301. Harrison, with two wickets, and Wharf had both made new-ball breakthroughs to go some way to vindicating the decision to omit Jones, but then Michael Clarke and Jimmy Adams (75) set about resetting the balance. Hampshire made it to 298 in the end, with Clarke scoring a fine hundred, and by the close of that second day it was Glamorgan who were under pressure on 44 for 2. The next day belonged to Shane Warne, who took 6 for 65 to skittle Glamorgan for 169 and leave his side with the relatively simple task of completing a nine-wicket win – especially against the weakened home attack. The only man to defy Warne was his fellow Victorian, Matthew Elliott, who batted brilliantly to carry his bat to remain on 77 not out.

Another Australian leg spinner, Stuart MacGill, was the player who made the difference at Southend as Nottinghamshire emerged with an eight-wicket win over Essex. Initially, it was the home side who seemed to be on top, with Paul Grayson making his first championship hundred for three years and adding 188 for the first wicket with Will Jefferson, and then Ronnie Irani making an unbeaten 122 and inspiring last man Scott Brant to stay with him while another 105 runs were gathered for the tenth wicket. It was the first three-figure last-wicket stand in the 130-match history of first-class cricket at Southchurch Park, and it saw Essex to a first-innings total of 431. By the end of day two, though, Notts had fought back strongly to reach 370 for 3, with Jason Gallian's 74 providing the firm foundations and hundreds from 104 and 110 balls

Round 13:
28 July–1 August 2004 Division Two

GLAMORGAN v. HAMPSHIRE - at Cardiff

GLAMORGAN	First Innings		Second Innings	
MTG Elliott	c Warne b Mascarenhas	54	(2) not out	77
*MA Wallace	c Clarke b Mullally	23	(1) b Bruce	2
DL Hemp	c Pothas b Mascarenhas	77	b Warne	7
MJ Powell	c Crawley b Udal	72	c Clarke b Warne	10
MP Maynard	c Clarke b Bruce	7	st Pothas b Warne	9
J Hughes	c Pothas b Bruce	23	b Warne	7
RDB Croft (capt)	b Warne	16	c Clarke b Mascarenhas	1
AG Wharf	lbw b Warne	0	lbw b Warne	0
DS Harrison	lbw b Udal	7	c & b Mascarenhas	15
MS Kasprowicz	lbw b Warne	0	c Clarke b Warne	8
DA Cosker	not out	3	c Pothas b Warne	13
Extras	b 1, lb 1, w 1, nb 16	19	b 2, lb 1, w 5, nb 7, p 5	20
	(88.5 overs)	301	(69.5 overs)	169

Bowling
Bruce 15-2-62-2. Mullally 13-3-45-1. Mascarenhas 18-5-69-2. Udal 13.5-2-46-2. Warne 27-5-77-3. Clarke 2-2-0-0.
Bruce 9-1-27-1. Mullally 6-2-9-0. Mascarenhas 25-8-53-3. Warne 27.5-6-65-6. Udal 2-0-7-0.
Fall of Wickets: 1-56, 2-145, 3-182, 4-200, 5-256, 6-287, 7-289, 8-291, 9-291
1-2, 2-37, 3-75, 4-89, 5-97, 6-100, 7-100, 8-120, 9-130

HAMPSHIRE	First Innings		Second Innings	
DA Kenway	lbw b Wharf	5		
MJ Brown	lbw b Harrison	6	c Elliott b Kasprowicz	57
SD Udal	c Powell b Harrison	3		
JP Crawley	lbw b Croft	18	(3) not out	45
MJ Clarke	c Cosker b Croft	109		
*N Pothas	c Powell b Kasprowicz	18		
JHK Adams	c Hemp b Kasprowicz	75	(1) not out	65
AD Mascarenhas	c Powell b Croft	2		
SK Warne (capt)	b Cosker	29		
JTA Bruce	run out	0		
AD Mullally	not out	9		
Extras	b 2, lb 8, w 2, nb 12	24	b 2, lb 2, nb 2	6
	(95 overs)	298	(1 wkt 45.1 overs)	173

Bowling
Kasprowicz 24.5-5-71-2. Harrison 20-8-52-2. Wharf 13-1-56-1. Croft 28-5-68-3. Cosker 10-3-41-1.
Kasprowicz 13-2-49-1. Harrison 10-3-37-0. Croft 18.1-5-59-0. Elliott 1-0-16-0. Maynard 3-0-8-0.
Fall of Wickets: 1-11, 2-16, 3-16, 4-76, 5-147, 6-193, 7-195, 8-251, 9-296
1-99

Hampshire won by 9 wickets - Glamorgan (6pts),
Hampshire (19pts)

ESSEX v. NOTTINGHAMSHIRE - at Southend

ESSEX	First Innings		Second Innings	
WI Jefferson	run out	75	c Smith b MacGill	12
AP Grayson	c and b Pietersen	119	lbw b MacGill	35
A Flower	c Gallian b Pietersen	18	lbw b Shreck	1
A Habib	b Smith	7	c Read b Smith	48
RC Irani (capt)	not out	122	c Ealham b MacGill	60
*JS Foster	c Ealham b Smith	22	not out	44
JD Middlebrook	lbw b Ealham	30	c Ealham b MacGill	8
GR Napier	lbw b MacGill	8	c Hussey b MacGill	13
AR Adams	c Ealham b MacGill	1	c Ealham b MacGill	14
AP Cowan	b MacGill	6	c Read b MacGill	1
SA Brant	b Ealham	19	run out	0
Extras	b 3, lb 8, w 1, nb 12	24	b 2, lb 3, nb 8	13
	(119.1 overs)	431	(65.5 overs)	248

Bowling
Smith 24-6-80-2. Shreck 16-1-84-0. Ealham 17.1-5-57-2. Franks 16-3-52-0. MacGill 35-9-124-3. Pietersen 11-1-23-2.
Smith 9-2-24-1. Franks 7-1-26-0. Shreck 9-2-38-1. MacGill 28-5-109-7. Ealham 5-0-18-0. Pietersen 7.5-1-28-0.
Fall of Wickets: 1-188, 2-219, 3-228, 4-230, 5-234, 6-291, 7-310, 8-312, 9-326
1-55, 2-56, 3-59, 4-158, 5-166, 6-196, 7-212, 8-246, 9-246

NOTTS	First Innings		Second Innings	
DJ Bicknell	c Foster b Cowan	0	lbw b Adams	13
JER Gallian (capt)	run out	74	not out	120
RJ Warren	lbw b Napier	14	c Foster b Middlebrook	8
KP Pietersen	lbw b Adams	167	not out	69
DJ Hussey	c Foster b Cowan	116		
*CMW Read	lbw b Adams	0		
MA Ealham	c Flower b Cowan	17		
PJ Franks	c Foster b Adams	0		
GJ Smith	b Adams	8		
SCG MacGill	c Middlebrook b Adams	18		
CE Dagnall	not out	1		
Extras	b 6, lb 3, w 3, nb 8	20	lb 2, w 6	8
	(103.4 overs)	435	(2 wkts 55.1 overs)	246

Bowling
Cowan 24-5-70-3. Brant 14-3-48-0. Napier 14-1-65-1. Middlebrook 18-1-102-0. Adams 22.4-1-93-5. Grayson 11-0-48-0.
Cowan 8-0-39-0. Adams 13-1-42-1. Brant 7-2-27-0. Middlebrook 15-3-62-1. Napier 4-0-24-0. Grayson 8.1-0-50-0.
Fall of Wickets: 1-0, 2-43, 3-171, 4-383, 5-384, 6-397, 7-408, 8-408, 9-432
1-31, 2-128

Nottinghamshire won by 8 wickets -
Essex (8pts), Nottinghamshire (22pts)

LEICESTERSHIRE v. DURHAM - at Leicester

LEICESTERSHIRE	First Innings		Second Innings	
DDJ Robinson	c Muchall b Plunkett	62		
DL Maddy	c Pratt b Blignaut	11		
BJ Hodge (capt)	c Breese b Killeen	262		
JL Sadler	lbw b Blignaut	21		
DI Stevens	lbw b Onions	84		
*PA Nixon	c sub b Onions	22		
OD Gibson	b Onions	21		
JM Dakin	not out	71		
MF Cleary	c North b Breese	38		
CW Henderson	c & b Breese	9		
CE Dagnall	not out	4		
Extras	b 1, lb 11, w 1, nb 16	29		
	(9 wkts dec 135.4 overs)	634		

Bowling
Plunkett 25.4-1-132-1. Blignaut 16-0-109-2. Killeen 24-4-81-1. Onions 23-4-110-3. Collingwood 14-4-52-0. Breese 27-4-114-2. Muchall 5-1-22-0. Coetzer 1-0-2-0.
Fall of Wickets: 1-32, 2-120, 3-179, 4-402, 5-478, 6-510, 7-510, 8-603, 9-615

DURHAM	First Innings		Second Innings	
JJB Lewis (capt)	b Gibson	9	b Dagnall	21
GR Breese	lbw b Gibson	0	c Nixon b Dagnall	43
GJ Muchall	c Stevens b Henderson	60	c Maddy b Henderson	95
PD Collingwood	c Maddy b Henderson	17	c Robinson b Gibson	57
MJ North	lbw b Dagnall	48	c Maddy b Gibson	5
KJ Coetzer	c Sadler b Henderson	33	c and b Henderson	38
*A Pratt	c Nixon b Henderson	9	c Nixon b Cleary	1
AM Blignaut	st Nixon b Henderson	12	b Gibson	56
LE Plunkett	not out	19	lbw b Cleary	26
N Killeen	c Sadler b Henderson	0	run out	4
G Onions	c Nixon b Henderson	0	not out	4
Extras	b 4, lb 8	12	lb 17, w 4, nb 18	39
	(63.4 overs)	219	(97.3 overs)	389

Bowling
Cleary 9-3-20-0. Gibson 19-4-62-2. Dakin 2-0-9-0. Henderson 25.4-7-74-7. Dagnall 8-1-42-1.
Cleary 13-2-50-2. Gibson 16.3-2-67-3. Dakin 9-2-33-0. Dagnall 14-1-64-2. Henderson 36-11-104-2. Hodge 5-0-35-0. Maddy 3-0-16-0. Robinson 1-0-3-0.
Fall of Wickets: 1-32, 2-11, 3-59, 4-140, 5-148, 6-162, 7-188, 8-205, 9-211
1-46, 2-97, 3-185, 4-193, 5-261, 6-265, 7-288, 8-380, 9-386

Leicestershire won by an innings and 26 runs -
Leicestershire (22pts), Durham (3pts)

DERBYSHIRE v. YORKSHIRE - at Derby

DERBYSHIRE	First Innings		Second Innings	
SD Stubbings	c Gray b Kirby	51	c Craven b Kirby	1
AI Gait	lbw b Kirby	7	b Blain	12
J Moss	lbw b Kirby	10	c Gray b Blain	56
Hassan Adnan	lbw b Kirby	86	c McGrath b Havell	41
CWG Bassano	b McGrath	100	(10) b Kirby	25
JDC Bryant	c Wood b McGrath	5	(5) c Dawood b Craven	20
*LD Sutton (capt)	lbw b McGrath	25	(6) Ibw b Craven	0
G Welch	lbw b McGrath	6	(7) c & b Dawson	24
AG Botha	c & b Blain	19	(8) c Wood b Dawson	49
MA Sheikh	c Dawood b Gray	42	(9) not out	36
PMR Havell	not out	8	not out	4
Extras	b 22, lb 8, w 10, nb 8	48	b 5, lb 10, w 8, nb 8	31
	(118 overs)	406	(9 wkts dec 92 overs)	305

Bowling
Kirby 21-1-76-2. Blain 19-5-58-2. Harvey 21-4-73-0. Craven 11-1-51-0. Dawson 5-1-23-0. McGrath 22-7-39-5. Gray 19-2-56-1.
Kirby 21-3-75-3. Harvey 15-4-38-0. Blain 11-1-58-2. McGrath 16-4-41-0. Craven 7-2-18-2. Dawson 16-5-45-2. Gray 5-0-13-0. Lumb 1-0-2-0.
Fall of Wickets: 1-14, 2-35, 3-163, 4-195, 5-205, 6-281, 7-293, 8-324, 9-350
1-4, 2-66, 3-79, 4-126, 5-134, 6-174, 7-176, 8-266, 9-300

YORKSHIRE	First Innings		Second Innings	
MJ Wood (capt)	c Welch b Sheikh	89	lbw b Welch	25
AW Gale	c Stubbings b Havell	10	c Bryant b Sheikh	174
A McGrath	lbw b Moss	18	c Welch b Sheikh	174
MJ Lumb	c Gait b Sheikh	21	run out	18
IJ Harvey	c Stubbings b Sheikh	19	st Sutton b Botha	12
VJ Craven	c Wood b Moss	81	b Moss	19
*I Dawood	lbw b Hassan Adnan	36	not out	46
RKJ Dawson	c Sutton b Moss	25	c Botha b Moss	26
AKD Gray	c Stubbings b Welch	27	b Welch	0
JAR Blain	c Gait b Botha	0	not out	1
SP Kirby	lbw b Botha	5		
Extras	b 5, lb 14, w 1, nb 2	22	b 6, lb 2, w 7, nb 2	17
	(109 overs)	354	(8 wkts 82.5 overs)	341

Bowling
Havell 14-0-85-1. Welch 23-7-54-1. Sheikh 20-4-68-3. Moss 30-7-73-2. Botha 20-6-51-2. Hassan Adnan 2-0-4-1.
Welch 22-2-101-2. Havell 7-0-33-1. Moss 18.5-2-66-2. Sheikh 9-1-33-1. Botha 24-2-88-1. Hassan Adnan 2-0-12-0.
Fall of Wickets: 1-19, 2-65, 3-125, 4-166, 5-173, 6-250, 7-312, 8-353, 9-354
1-8, 2-104, 3-129, 4-161, 5-208, 6-282, 7-329, 8-331

Match drawn - Derbyshire (12pts), Yorkshire (11pts)

respectively by David Hussey (116) and Kevin Pietersen (167) giving the innings a formidable look. Both players fell early on the third day, however, having put on 212, and good bowling from Andre Adams and Ashley Cowan meant that Notts' eventual lead was a mere four runs. Then came MacGill's decisive contribution of 7 for 109, and it took a 67-ball 60 from Irani and an unbeaten 44 from James Foster to give Essex any sort of total to defend. Darren Bicknell fell to Adams before the close of play on day three, but Gallian was unbeaten on 28 overnight and, the following morning, moved swifly on to an unbeaten 120 to see his side home. Pietersen also added further lustre to his own fine match by finishing on 69 not out, from 60 balls.

Brad Hodge's 262, the highest individual score made at Grace Road, was chiefly responsible for Leicestershire's innings-and-26-run victory against a Durham side badly missing the injured Mark Davies, the country's leading wicket-taker. Hodge, yet to win an Australian Test cap, scored 90 of his first 100 in boundaries and, overall, hit 46 fours and two sixes from the 299 balls he faced. Hodge was a class above anything else on view, although Darren Robinson and Darren Stevens both played ideal supporting roles and Jon Dakin enjoyed himself with an unbeaten 71 in the lead-up to a declaration on an intimidating 634 for 9. By the end of the second day, Durham were in dire straits at 194 for 7 in reply and, the next morning, they were soon

Shane Warne, inspirational for Hampshire at Cardiff.

following on as Claude Henderson wrapped up a seven-wicket haul. Gordon Muchall added a gutsy 95 to his first-innings 60, but that and half-centuries from Paul Collingwood and Andy Blignaut only served to delay the inevitable and only 23 minutes of play were required on the final day as Leicestershire wrapped up a comfortable victory.

Anthony McGrath had a match to remember at Derby, but even his heroics with both bat and ball could not quite inspire what would have been a memorable Yorkshire win. Ultimately, at the end of a closely fought and excellent four-day game, Yorkshire were just 17 runs short of their target at 341 for 8 when the draw was confirmed. Both sides could feel proud of their efforts, but McGrath's last-day 174 off 229 balls was exceptional and it almost dragged Yorkshire

across the finishing line. Derbyshire, however, would say that they did not deserve to lose, having built a first-innings total of 406 despite McGrath's career-best 5 for 39, and then stayed in control of proceedings until their perfectly timed second-innings declaration. Chris Bassano was the game's other century-maker, and he made a brave 25 in Derbyshire's second innings after dropping down to No. 10 due to injury, but there were also significant innings from Hassan Adnan, Matthew Wood and Vic Craven.

Round 14: 3–6 August 2004

Division One

In one of the classic matches of the summer, the power and the glory of four-day county championship cricket came packaged in a contest at Canterbury which ended – deep into the final session – with Kent beating Sussex by 236 runs. To appreciate the power of it, you had only to walk around the boundary and past all of the full marquees at the St Lawrence Ground on any one of the four sun-blessed days to see the contentment, the enjoyment and the age-range of large crowds several thousands strong. To appreciate the glory of it, you also had to consider the match in its context: only a week earlier, Kent had been beaten heavily by Sussex at Hove. The champions, still troubled by the threat of relegation, were clearly running back into form. The home county, however, suffering a miserable season in one-day cricket and the subject of rumours of dressing-room unrest both before and during this game, were not out of the relegation woods themselves in a tense division where only Warwickshire, the leaders, and Northamptonshire, the bottom club, seemed to have had their seasons defined. The greater part of the glory, of course, came in the quality and competitiveness of the play itself. On a fine pitch, that wore naturally and fairly, Kent won what David Fulton, their captain, later described as the most satisfying victory of his career. The strokeplay of Ed Smith and Matthew Walker, supported by the high promise of Alex Loudon, enabled Kent to score enough runs to control the match – but it was the tenacity of their predominantly young bowling attack, which blended effectively with the experience of Min Patel, that pleased Fulton most. Such a committed display in the field, and the sheer effort behind the successful acquisition of 20 Sussex wickets, also told of players that plainly wanted to do well for each other. Smith, one of the players reported to be at the centre of

Ed Smith: beautiful strokeplay in a classic at Canterbury.

Kent's dressing-room unrest, set the tone for what was to come with an innings of 166 on the first day that was fit, in style and effortless power, to follow the Canterbury tradition of Woolley, Ames, Cowdrey and Woolmer. Opening the batting for the first time this season, Smith scored his runs out of a total of 285 with 24 boundaries. Loudon made just 55 in a second-wicket stand worth 197, but looked like an apprentice with the talent to one day become the master, while the second half of the Kent first innings belonged to Walker. He hauled the total up above 500 by signing off with a withering assault on Mushtaq Ahmed, in which the Pakistani leg-spinning maestro was despatched for four, four, six in successive balls, and then another six soon afterwards, before eventually having Walker caught at long on for 157. A lovely 112 by Matthew Prior, one of the most eye-catching of young English batsmen on the circuit, lit up the rest of the second day, although three wickets apiece for Rob Joseph and Matt Dennington helped Kent to work their way through the Sussex order. Declining to enforce the follow-on, after the visitors had been bowled out for 332, Fulton then contributed just 13 to an opening partnership of 101 with the sparkling

Round 14: 3–6 August 2004 Division One

KENT v. SUSSEX - at Canterbury

KENT	First Innings		Second Innings	
DP Fulton (capt)	lbw b Kirtley	4	c Goodwin b Kirtley	13
ET Smith	c Goodwin b Akram	166	c Martin-Jenkins b Kirtley	93
AGR Loudon	c Montgomerie b Wright	55	c and b Mushtaq Ahmed	50
MG Bevan	lbw b Kirtley	0	b Akram	0
MJ Walker	c Akram b Mushtaq Ahmed	157	not out	100
MJ Dennington	lbw b Akram	0	lbw b Kirtley	0
*NJ O'Brien	run out	30	c Wright b Akram	20
MM Patel	b Mushtaq Ahmed	26		
A Khan	lbw b Mushtaq Ahmed	29		
RH Joseph	c Prior b Mushtaq Ahmed	7	(8) b Mushtaq Ahmed	6
SMJ Cusden	not out	12	(9) not out	3
Extras	b 13, lb 20, nb 8	41	b 8, lb 11, w 3, nb 4	26
	(136.5 overs)	527	(7 wkts dec 82.5 overs)	319

Bowling
Akram 28-5-100-2. Kirtley 30-6-99-2. Martin-Jenkins 17-0-95-0.
Mushtaq Ahmed 41.5-6-126-4. Wright 20-1-74-1.
Akram 19-3-85-2. Kirtley 16-1-52-3. Mushtaq Ahmed 35-3-119-2.
Wright 7.5-1-22-0. Martin-Jenkins 5-0-22-0.
Fall of Wickets: 1-15, 2-212, 3-215, 4-285, 5-285, 6-329, 7-362, 8-458, 9-506
1-101, 2-140, 3-195, 4-229, 5-229, 6-277, 7-296

SUSSEX	First Innings		Second Innings	
IJ Ward	b Khan	20	lbw b Joseph	14
RR Montgomerie	c O'Brien b Dennington	70	c Walker b Cusden	80
PA Cottey	c O'Brien b Joseph	0	c O'Brien b Dennington	49
MW Goodwin	c Bevan b Dennington	28	lbw b Patel	12
CJ Adams (capt)	c O'Brien b Dennington	5	lbw b Patel	2
*MJ Prior	st O'Brien b Patel	112	c Loudon b Patel	53
RSC Martin-Jenkins	lbw b Loudon	22	c Fulton b Patel	23
LJ Wright	c Walker b Patel	0	b Loudon	18
Mushtaq Ahmed	b Joseph	45	not out	2
RJ Kirtley	c O'Brien b Joseph	3	c Fulton b Loudon	0
M Akram	not out	6	b Loudon	4
Extras	b 2, lb 4, w 1, nb 14	21	b 10, lb 9, nb 2	21
	(69.2 overs)	332	(89 overs)	278

Bowling
Khan 9-0-47-1. Joseph 13.2-1-70-3. Cusden 10-1-61-0. Dennington 14-3-48-3.
Patel 11-1-44-2. Loudon 12-2-56-1.
Joseph 13-6-38-1. Dennington 12-2-41-1. Patel 35-9-75-4. Loudon 20-5-60-3.
Cusden 9-1-45-1.
Fall of Wickets: 1-32, 2-39, 3-70, 4-92, 5-231, 6-270, 7-270, 8-298, 9-313
1-22, 2-102, 3-145, 4-147, 5-209, 6-235, 7-268, 8-272, 9-274

Kent won by 236 runs - Kent (22pts), Sussex (5pts)

SURREY v. WORCESTERSHIRE - at The Oval

SURREY	First Innings		Second Innings	
SA Newman	c Hall b Malik	46	c Rhodes b Mason	59
RS Clinton	run out	73	lbw b Batty	27
MR Ramprakash	lbw b Mason	130	not out	100
R Clarke	c Batty b Hall	36	c Batty b Malik	47
*JN Batty (capt)	c Hick b Kabir Ali	8		
AD Brown	c Rhodes b Mason	22	(5) b Malik	25
JGE Benning	c Smith b Malik	6	not out	35
Azhar Mahmood	b Mason	25	(6) run out	22
AJ Tudor	lbw b Kabir Ali	0		
J Ormond	b Kabir Ali	0		
ND Doshi	not out	0		
Extras	b 2, lb 21, w 2, nb 4	29	b 5, lb 4, w 1, nb 4	14
	(103.2 overs)	375	(5 wkts dec 67.5 overs)	329

Bowling
Mason 25.2-10-89-3. Kabir Ali 25-5-93-3. Hall 21-6-55-1. Malik 19-4-71-2.
Batty 13-2-44-0.
Mason 11-4-38-1. Kabir Ali 12-1-73-0. Hall 12-3-33-0. Malik 12-0-76-2.
Batty 19-2-85-1. Solanki 1.5-0-15-0.
Fall of Wickets: 1-90, 2-176, 3-233, 4-254, 5-309, 6-332, 7-374, 8-375, 9-375
1-90, 2-106, 3-197, 4-233, 5-271

WORCS	First Innings		Second Innings	
SD Peters	c Batty b Azhar Mahmood	74	b Ormond	4
SC Moore	c Azhar Mahmood b Tudor	76	lbw b Ormond	5
GA Hick	c Clinton b Tudor	39	b Ormond	5
BF Smith (capt)	b Ormond	4	(5) b Ormond	8
VS Solanki	b Tudor	0	(6) lbw b Ormond	86
AJ Hall	c Brown b Tudor	5	(7) c Clarke b Azhar Mahmood	1
GJ Batty	b Clarke	12	(8) b Ormond	133
Kabir Ali	c Tudor b Azhar Mahmood	11	(4) c Clinton b Azhar Mahmood	0
*SJ Rhodes	not out	46	not out	59
MS Mason	c Tudor b Azhar Mahmood	13	b Azhar Mahmood	13
MN Malik	c Brown b Ormond	0	c Tudor b Azhar Mahmood	0
Extras	lb 2, w 2, nb 11	15	lb 22, w 1, nb 4	27
	(77.2 overs)	295	(85.2 overs)	341

Bowling
Ormond 23.2-4-63-2. Azhar Mahmood 19-4-83-3. Tudor 13-2-61-4.
Clarke 12-3-62-1. Doshi 9-2-15-0. Clinton 1-0-9-0.
Ormond 25-7-62-6. Azhar Mahmood 22.2-6-69-4. Tudor 9-2-57-0.
Clarke 10-2-45-0. Benning 3-0-17-0. Doshi 14-2-60-0. Ramprakash 2-0-9-0.
Fall of Wickets: 1-116, 2-159, 3-161, 4-167, 5-167, 6-189, 7-203, 8-253, 9-282
1-4, 2-13, 3-18, 4-18, 5-39, 6-44, 7-212, 8-318, 9-341

Surrey won by 68 runs - Surrey (21pts), Worcestershire (5pts)

MIDDLESEX v. GLOUCESTERSHIRE - at Lord's

GLOS	First Innings		Second Innings	
WPC Weston	c Dalrymple b Agarkar	98	c Nash b Agarkar	7
CM Spearman	c Nash b Cook	16	(1) lbw b Weekes	100
MEK Hussey	c Koenig b Agarkar	43	c Shah b Agarkar	0
CG Taylor (capt)	lbw b Agarkar	8	c Dalrymple b Weekes	91
APR Gidman	b Agarkar	1	b Dalrymple	56
*SJ Adshead	c Shah b Cook	19	b Dalrymple	37
JEC Franklin	c Compton b Cook	44	not out	39
ID Fisher	c Nash b Dalrymple	28	c Hutton b Dalrymple	28
MCJ Ball	c Cook b Agarkar	7	not out	2
JMM Averis	not out	28		
J Lewis	c Koenig b Weekes	21		
Extras	b 6, lb 3, nb 22	34	b 19, lb 5, nb 16	40
	(120.2 overs)	347	(7 wkts dec 92 overs)	400

Bowling
Cook 30-7-63-3. Agarkar 29-7-81-5. Betts 13-3-49-0. Hutchison 9-0-39-0.
Hutton 11-2-21-0. Weekes 17-2-21-0. Dalrymple 10-2-35-1.
Agarkar 9-1-28-2. Cook 8-0-31-0. Betts 7-2-20-0. Hutchison 6-0-37-0.
Dalrymple 25-0-141-3. Weekes 28-2-91-2. Hutton 6-2-8-0. Shah 3-0-20-0.
Fall of Wickets: 1-28, 2-107, 3-119, 4-121, 5-157, 6-250, 7-256, 8-268, 9-314
1-39, 2-39, 3-209, 4-224, 5-326, 6-333, 7-393

MIDDLESEX	First Innings	
BL Hutton (capt)	c Hussey b Franklin	1
SG Koenig	run out	36
NRD Compton	c Gidman b Lewis	2
OA Shah	lbw b Franklin	103
PM Hutchison	c Adshead b Lewis	3
PN Weekes	lbw b Franklin	4
JWM Dalrymple	b Averis	2
*DC Nash	not out	59
SJ Cook	c Gidman b Lewis	8
AB Agarkar	not out	4
MM Betts		
Extras	b 10, lb 3, w 1, nb 17	31
	(8 wkts dec 94.5 overs)	253

Bowling
Lewis 21.5-9-48-3. Franklin 18.2-7-42-3. Averis 16-3-40-1. Gidman 7-1-33-0.
Fisher 14-2-32-0. Ball 17-1-43-0. Hussey 1-0-2-0.
Fall of Wickets: 1-7, 2-20, 3-61, 4-67, 5-84, 6-98, 7-237, 8-249

Match drawn - Middlesex (9pts),
Gloucestershire (9pts)

Smith. It was perhaps the home crowd's only disappointment when Smith fell for 93 but, after Loudon had made another elegant 50, Walker did manage to complete a triumphant second hundred of the match, for the first time in his career. Sussex, 21 without loss overnight, then did their utmost to bat it out for a draw. Richard Montgomerie resisted for 67 overs to make 80 and, with Tony Cottey, added 80 for the second wicket. Perhaps the game was won and lost, though, when Prior was quite brilliantly caught at slip by Loudon off Patel, having again batted excellently for 53. Four wickets were still required by Kent at tea, but they were claimed in 13 overs of ratcheted-up tension afterwards. Those who regularly take a week's holiday to attend the Canterbury Festival each year had watched the undoubted bargain break of the summer.

At The Oval, Surrey looked like another team digging deep. At the heart of their fine 68-run win against Worcestershire was Mark Ramprakash, scoring the 71st and 72nd first-class centuries of his career and making two hundreds in a match for the fifth time. His first-innings 130 ensured a working total for Surrey, after Richard Clinton – a Loughborough University student formerly of Essex and the son of former Surrey batsman Grahame Clinton – had marked his debut for the club with a bright 73. Ramprakash's second-innings 100 not out set up a declaration which, when Worcestershire declined to 27 for 4 by the close of the third day, seemed to be over-cautious. The visitors were soon 44 for 6 the next morning, before Vikram Solanki and Gareth Batty fashioned one of the most dramatic counter-attacks of the season. They added 168 for the seventh wicket, before Solanki fell to Jimmy Ormond for 86, but then Batty was joined by Steve Rhodes in an eighth-wicket stand of 106 which, suddenly, even began to raise the possibility of an outrageous Worcestershire win. The persevering Ormond, however, produced a timely yorker in the third over after tea to end Batty's superb 160-ball 133, and Rhodes was left unbeaten on 59 when Azhar Mahmood took the last two wickets to clinch a well-earned victory to mark the announcement, by former captain Adam Hollioake, that he had retired from four-day cricket.

Just 45 overs were possible on the opening day at Lord's, because of localised showers, and further disruption on the third day also contributed to Middlesex's meeting with Gloucestershire fizzling

out into the dullest of draws. There was some good cricket, notably the batting of Phil Weston and Owais Shah and the bowling of Ajit Agarkar, but Gloucestershire's batting practice on the final day was devalued by the lack of a competitive edge.

Division Two

The Ricky Ponting factor was again in evidence at Taunton as Somerset continued their return to form with an eight-wicket victory over promotion-chasing

Ian Blackwell: career-best bowling figures for the Somerset left-arm spinner against Glamorgan at Taunton.

Glamorgan. Australia's captain raced to 71 not out on the first evening, after Simon Francis' 5 for 42 had been mainly responsible for Glamorgan's slide to 262 all out, to take command of the contest in Somerset's favour. He and Peter Bowler, who made an unbeaten 51 himself as the home side careered to 143 for 1 in the 28 overs available, then took their second-wicket stand to 210 on the following morning before Ponting was out top-edging a hook to long leg. Bowler scored 86 and Ian Blackwell – averaging almost 80 from his previous 19 championship innings – proved just the man to ensure a sizeable first-innings lead. Blackwell bludgeoned 98, despite some fiery fast bowling from Simon Jones, who had seen his first six overs disappear for 46 the previous evening, but who then underlined his tenacious temperament by taking 5 for 48 in his resulting 13.5 overs. Somerset were in danger of surrendering their advantage as Matthew Elliott, adding 85 to his first-innings century, and Mark Wallace (70) put on 126 for the first wicket to all but wipe out the deficit, but only Darren Thomas, with his second half-century of the match, could then withstand a confident Blackwell, who picked up a career-best 7 for 90 with his left-arm spin. A further half-century by Bowler, and 54 by John Francis, swept Somerset to their modest win target.

An 'unseemly altercation' between Shane Warne and Ronnie Irani on the second evening at the Rose Bowl resulted in the umpires giving the rival captains a ticking off before the match resumed the following morning. Perhaps the ever-combative Irani had touched a raw nerve, because Warne's Hampshire were by then on the way to their heaviest championship defeat since 1896. The home side's humbling by a massive 384-run margin was, conversely, Essex's biggest win for 71 years and Will Jefferson, the giant opener, had much to do with that. Jefferson took full advantage of Warne's strange decision to ask Essex to bat first by powering his way to a career-best 222. Essex's next best score, in a first-innings total of 416 that put them in the driving seat on a pitch of increasingly irregular bounce, was James Foster's 40. Jefferson hit 31 fours in his near-seven-hour effort, and then the four-pronged Essex seam attack got to work on the Hampshire first innings. Choosing not to ask the home side to follow on, Irani allowed Paul Grayson and James Middlebrook, with a cavalier 84-ball 93, to rub salt into Hampshire's wounds before Andre Adams – adding three more wickets to his earlier 4 for 46 – and Ashley Cowan made sure of the win. Only a violent, career-best 40 by last man Billy Taylor took Hampshire into three figures (he and Alan Mullally added 61 in nine overs after Mullally had been dropped on one), and Warne's misery was complete when he was out for a duck.

Round 14: 3–6 August 2004 Division Two

SOMERSET v. GLAMORGAN – at Taunton

GLAMORGAN	First Innings		Second Innings	
MTG Elliott	b McLean	103	[2] b Blackwell	85
*MA Wallace	c Turner b Johnson	0	[1] b Blackwell	70
DL Hemp	c Turner b Johnson	3	c Francis JD b Blackwell	6
MJ Powell	c Hildreth b Francis SRG	39	c Ponting b Blackwell	0
MP Maynard	c Ponting b Francis SRG	4	lbw b Johnson	25
J Hughes	c Ponting b Francis SRG	5	c Francis JD b Blackwell	1
RDB Croft (capt)	c Turner b Francis SRG	23	b Francis SRG	16
DS Harrison	c and b Francis SRG	4	c Turner b Johnson	5
SD Thomas	c Turner b McLean	54	b Blackwell	52
MS Kasprowicz	lbw b Blackwell	0	c Bowler b Blackwell	14
SP Jones	not out	0	not out	2
Extras	b 4, lb 2, nb 19	25	b 9, lb 5, w 5, nb 2	21
	(67.3 overs)	262	(78.5 overs)	294

Bowling
McLean 19.3-3-73-2. Johnson 16-4-82-2. Laraman 9-0-39-0. Francis SRG 15-6-42-5. Blackwell 8-2-20-1.
McLean 1.5-0-12-0. Johnson 23-2-102-2. Francis SRG 14.1-1-67-1. Blackwell 35.5-5-12-90-7. Laraman 4-0-9-0.
Fall of Wickets: 1-8, 2-14, 3-85, 4-99, 5-113, 6-166, 7-170, 8-262, 9-262
1-126, 2-136, 3-136, 4-188, 5-196, 6-196, 7-202, 8-263, 9-277

SOMERSET	First Innings		Second Innings	
PD Bowler	c Wallace b Jones	86	c Wallace b Harrison	55
JD Francis	c and b Kasprowicz	12	lbw b Croft	54
RT Ponting	c Jones b Thomas	117	not out	18
JC Hildreth	c Hemp b Jones	0	not out	32
M Burns (capt)	lbw b Harrison	10		
ID Blackwell	c Elliott b Jones	98		
AW Laraman	c Wallace b Harrison	1		
*RJ Turner	c Maynard b Croft	36		
RL Johnson	b Jones	9		
SRG Francis	not out	0		
NAM McLean	lbw b Jones	0		
Extras	b 1, lb 7, nb 16	24	b 1, lb 1, w 1, nb 2	5
	(104.5 overs)	394	(2 wkts 37.4 overs)	164

Bowling
Kasprowicz 21-3-81-1. Harrison 18-2-62-2. Jones 19.5-1-94-5. Croft 30-8-87-1. Thomas 16-1-62-1.
Kasprowicz 4-0-12-0. Croft 17.4-3-71-1. Jones 7-2-27-0. Thomas 4-0-25-0. Harrison 5-1-27-1.
Fall of Wickets: 1-19, 2-229, 3-231, 4-235, 5-267, 6-279, 7-364, 8-391, 9-394
1-103, 2-111

Somerset won by 8 wickets – Somerset (21pts), Glamorgan (5pts)

HAMPSHIRE v. ESSEX – at The Rose Bowl

ESSEX	First Innings		Second Innings	
WI Jefferson	c Pothas b Taylor	222	lbw b Mullally	4
AP Grayson	lbw b Bruce	7	c Clarke b Bruce	75
A Flower	c Warne b Mullally	32	c Pothas b Warne	33
A Habib	c Kenway b Warne	19	c Pothas b Mascarenhas	0
RC Irani (capt)	c Pothas b Taylor	17	c Pothas b Taylor	41
*JS Foster	c Brown b Warne	40	c Brown b Bruce	7
JD Middlebrook	c Pothas b Bruce	0	c Mascarenhas b Clarke	93
GR Napier	c sub b Bruce	8	not out	31
AR Adams	st Pothas b Warne	22		
AP Cowan	not out	21		
D Gough	lbw b Warne	0		
Extras	b 3, lb 9, w 2, nb 14	28	b 1, lb 1, w 2, nb 6	10
	(103 overs)	416	(7 wkts dec 79.1 overs)	294

Bowling
Mullally 20-6-72-1. Bruce 19-3-74-3. Mascarenhas 3-1-5-0. Taylor 23-3-111-2. Warne 32-1-118-4. Clarke 6-1-24-0.
Mullally 14-4-36-1. Bruce 13-1-62-2. Taylor 12-0-56-1. Mascarenhas 17-5-33-1. Warne 17-2-53-1. Clarke 6.1-0-52-1.
Fall of Wickets: 1-32, 2-154, 3-189, 4-222, 5-321, 6-322, 7-340, 8-385, 9-415
1-6, 2-83, 3-88, 4-144, 5-152, 6-212, 7-294

HAMPSHIRE	First Innings		Second Innings	
JHK Adams	b Napier	21	c Cowan b Adams	23
MJ Brown	c Adams b Gough	13	lbw b Gough	0
JP Crawley	c Flower b Cowan	55	c Jefferson b Napier	24
MJ Clarke	c Foster b Adams	18	b Adams	18
DA Kenway	c Foster b Adams	21	b Napier	5
*N Pothas	c Foster b Adams	0	c Foster b Cowan	12
AD Mascarenhas	b Adams	0	c Flower b Adams	0
SK Warne (capt)	c Irani b Napier	21	c Foster b Adams	0
JTA Bruce	b Gough	1	c Adams b Cowan	0
AD Mullally	b Cowan	15	not out	19
BV Taylor	not out	4	lbw b Gough	40
Extras	lb 2, nb 6	8	lb 4, nb 4	8
	(60 overs)	177	(33 overs)	149

Bowling
Gough 15-3-44-2. Cowan 17-3-45-2. Napier 14-2-40-2. Adams 14-1-46-4. Middlebrook 3-0-13-0.
Gough 8-2-39-2. Cowan 8-2-44-3. Napier 5-1-26-2. Adams 9-2-23-3.
Fall of Wickets: 1-25, 2-48, 3-75, 4-122, 5-122, 6-122, 7-149, 8-156, 9-164
1-9, 2-44, 3-50, 4-64, 5-84, 6-88, 7-88, 8-88, 9-88

Essex won by 384 runs – Hampshire (3pts), Essex (22pts)

Round 15: 10–16 August 2004

Division One

Mushtaq Ahmed took ten wickets in the match as Sussex beat a Middlesex team including Glenn McGrath by a comfortable 143-run margin. McGrath picked up three low-cost wickets in the Sussex first innings, but was overshadowed by Simon Cook's 5 for 51 when the visitors were bowled out for 196 on the third day. By then, however, Mushtaq – supported by his fellow Pakistani, Mohammad Akram – had put Sussex in charge, despite the fact that the champions had frittered away a powerful position, established by Ian Ward and Murray Goodwin, on a rain-shortened opening day. From 270 for 2, and 252 for 2 overnight, Sussex fell away alarmingly to 314 all out after Ward and Goodwin had put on 222 for the third wicket. Ward's 148 contained a six and 16 fours, but only Ed Joyce (69) made any headway against Mushtaq as Middlesex were bowled out for 212 in reply. The Sussex second innings followed a similar pattern to the first, with Chris Adams and Tony Cottey taking them to 167 for 3 before last season's champions slumped to 196 all out. However, Mushtaq, this time backed up chiefly by James Kirtley, was in no mood to allow Middlesex to get anywhere near their win target, leaving Owais Shah (60 not out) to play the lone hand of resistance.

Lancashire's season continued to go downhill and Surrey's fortunes continued to rise, as Mark Ramprakash's prolific run of form inspired a thumping innings win for the home side at the genteel Whitgift School. Lancashire were in trouble

Round 15: 10–16 August 2004 Division One

MIDDLESEX v. SUSSEX - at Lord's

SUSSEX	First Innings		Second Innings	
IJ Ward	lbw b Betts	148	run out	28
RR Montgomerie	lbw b Cook	4	lbw b Cook	34
PA Cottey	c Shah b Betts	25	c Shah b Cook	42
MW Goodwin	c and b Weekes	105	c Joyce b Hutton	6
CJ Adams (capt)	lbw b Cook	14	c Hutton b Cook	54
*MJ Prior	c Dalrymple b Hutton	4	lbw b Dalrymple	0
MJG Davis	c Scott b McGrath	5	c Hutton b Cook	6
Mushtaq Ahmed	b McGrath	1	c Shah b Cook	0
RJ Kirtley	c Hutton b Betts	0	c Hutton b McGrath	9
M Akram	not out	5	c Dalrymple b Betts	2
JD Lewry	b McGrath	1	not out	0
Extras	b 1, lb 3, w 1	5	b 8, lb 4, w 1, nb 2	15
	(106.2 overs)	314	(70.2 overs)	196

Bowling
McGrath 28.2-15-44-3. Cook 19-5-69-2. Betts 19-6-39-3. Hutton 8-2-31-1. Weekes 16-2-58-1. Dalrymple 12-1-43-0. Joyce 4-0-26-0.
McGrath 20.2-9-41-1. Cook 19-4-51-5. Betts 14-5-41-1. Hutton 10-2-24-1. Dalrymple 7-1-27-1.
Fall of Wickets: 1-4, 2-48, 3-270, 4-293, 5-300, 6-307, 7-310, 8-311, 9-313
1-51, 2-66, 3-83, 4-167, 5-167, 6-179, 7-179, 8-183, 9-196

MIDDLESEX	First Innings		Second Innings	
BL Hutton	c Prior b Akram	14	c Cottey b Mushtaq Ahmed	10
SG Koenig	c Prior b Kirtley	9	c Cottey b Mushtaq Ahmed	23
OA Shah	lbw b Mushtaq Ahmed	25	not out	60
EC Joyce (capt)	c Prior b Akram	69	c Cottey b Mushtaq Ahmed	4
JWM Dalrymple	lbw b Akram	8	c Adams b Akram	10
DC Nash	lbw b Mushtaq Ahmed	1	lbw b Mushtaq Ahmed	0
*BJM Scott	c Adams b Mushtaq Ahmed	13	(8) b Kirtley	7
SJ Cook	c sub b Mushtaq Ahmed	1	(9) b Mushtaq Ahmed	19
PN Weekes	b Kirtley	11	(7) b Akram	1
MM Betts	not out	4	c Montgomerie b Kirtley	5
GD McGrath	lbw b Mushtaq Ahmed	4	c Adams b Kirtley	0
Extras	b 4, lb 5	9	b 3, lb 2, w 3, nb 10	18
	(65.5 overs)	212	(61.2 overs)	155

Bowling
Akram 15-5-55-3. Kirtley 22-5-56-2. Lewry 4-0-26-0. Mushtaq Ahmed 24.5-3-66-5.
Akram 15-4-30-2. Kirtley 19.2-6-37-3. Mushtaq Ahmed 27-6-83-5.
Fall of Wickets: 1-24, 2-24, 3-96, 4-114, 5-137, 6-137, 7-163, 8-178, 9-206
1-28, 2-53, 3-57, 4-79, 5-80, 6-81, 7-111, 8-138, 9-151

Sussex won by 143 runs - Middlesex (4pts),
Sussex (20pts)

SURREY v. LANCASHIRE - at Whitgift School

LANCASHIRE	First Innings		Second Innings	
MJ Chilton	c Clarke b Bicknell	2	c Clinton b Bicknell	0
IJ Sutcliffe	b Ormond	0	c Murtagh b Ormond	17
*JJ Haynes	c Batty b Ormond	2	lbw b Bicknell	22
D Mongia	c ft b Bicknell	12	c Clarke b Ormond	0
CL Hooper (capt)	b Azhar Mahmood	51	c Batty b Azhar Mahmood	51
CP Schofield	c Clarke b Azhar Mahmood	69	b Ormond	2
G Chapple	c Azhar Mahmood b Bicknell	36	run out	5
DG Cork	c Newman b Murtagh	2	c Murtagh b Doshi	109
KW Hogg	c Bicknell b Azhar Mahmood	23	c Newman b Azhar Mahmood	12
SI Mahmood	c Clarke b Azhar Mahmood	15	c ft b Doshi	31
G Keedy	not out	0	not out	4
Extras	lb 15, nb 2	17	lb 3, nb 4	7
	(57.2 overs)	210	(66.4 overs)	260

Bowling
Bicknell 15-3-41-3. Ormond 15-2-72-2. Murtagh 14-5-42-1.
Azhar Mahmood 13.2-3-40-4.
Bicknell 14-3-61-2. Ormond 18-4-60-3. Azhar Mahmood 16-5-61-2.
Murtagh 12-4-25-0. Doshi 6.4-0-50-2.
Fall of Wickets: 1-6, 2-6, 3-17, 4-21, 5-71, 6-142, 7-164, 8-172, 9-209
1-0, 2-24, 3-28, 4-68, 5-73, 6-104, 7-113, 8-156, 9-231

SURREY	First Innings	
SA Newman	st Haynes b Keedy	61
RS Clinton	b Chilton b Cork	1
MR Ramprakash	c Hooper b Keedy	134
R Clarke	lbw b Cork	64
*JN Batty (capt)	c Keedy b Mahmood	15
AD Brown	b Cork	50
Azhar Mahmood	b Chapple	30
MP Bicknell	c Hooper b Mahmood	41
TJ Murtagh	c Chilton b Mongia	56
J Ormond	c Chapple b Hooper	10
ND Doshi	not out	29
Extras	b 1, lb 7, nb 26	34
	(129.3 overs)	525

Bowling
Chapple 26-8-72-1. Cork 24-2-110-3. Mahmood 29-3-131-2. Hogg 20-2-74-0.
Keedy 27-3-96-2. Hooper 3-0-27-1. Mongia 0.3-0-7-1.
Fall of Wickets: 1-20, 2-122, 3-246, 4-284, 5-330, 6-375, 7-399, 8-442, 9-464

Surrey won by an innings and 55 runs -
Surrey (22pts), Lancashire (4pts)

WARWICKSHIRE v. KENT - at Edgbaston

WARWICKSHIRE	First Innings		Second Innings	
NV Knight (capt)	b Butler	18	not out	63
MA Wagh	c O'Brien b Butler	5	b Loudon	33
IR Bell	b Loudon	121		
IJL Trott	c O'Brien b Patel	50	not out	1
MJ Powell	c Fulton b Butler	96		
DR Brown	c Fulton b Butler	49		
GB Hogg	c Smith b Patel	63		
HH Streak	b Joseph	2	(3) c O'Brien b Loudon	11
*T Frost	c Joseph b Trott	25		
NM Carter	c Fulton b Dennington	0		
N Tahir	not out	3		
Extras	b 6, lb 9, w 4, nb 6	25	b 1, nb 14	15
	(112.2 overs)	457	(2 wkts 36 overs)	123

Bowling
Butler 24-3-114-4. Joseph 18-4-83-1. Trott 13-0-67-1. Dennington 15-1-60-1.
Patel 23.2-5-57-2. Loudon 9-2-31-1. Walker 7-0-21-0. Bevan 3-0-9-0.
Butler 4-0-21-0. Joseph 6-0-24-0. Trott 6-3-13-0. Loudon 12-2-30-2.
Dennington 5-0-29-0. Walker 3-1-5-0.
Fall of Wickets: 1-22, 2-29, 3-167, 4-234, 5-339, 6-394, 7-397, 8-439, 9-439
1-79, 2-115

KENT	First Innings	
DP Fulton (capt)	st Frost b Wagh	100
ET Smith	c Wagh b Streak	95
AGR Loudon	c Frost b Carter	92
MG Bevan	lbw b Carter	0
MJ Walker	c Trott b Wagh	1
MJ Dennington	lbw b Streak	16
*NJ O'Brien	c Frost b Streak	69
MM Patel	c Wagh b Streak	0
IG Butler	c Frost b Streak	2
RH Joseph	not out	19
BJ Trott	c Frost b Bell	4
Extras	b 4, lb 9, w 1, nb 8	22
	(106.4 overs)	420

Bowling
Streak 23-4-85-4. Carter 19-4-85-2. Brown 11-1-52-0. Tahir 15-1-71-1.
Hogg 20-1-58-0. Wagh 18-4-55-2. Bell 0.4-0-1-1.
Fall of Wickets: 1-184, 2-229, 3-230, 4-231, 5-255, 6-382, 7-382, 8-390, 9-406

Match drawn - Warwickshire (12pts),
Kent (12pts)

WORCESTERSHIRE v. NORTHAMPTONSHIRE - at Worcester

NORTHANTS	First Innings		Second Innings	
TW Roberts	c Solanki b Bichel	53	lbw b Kabir Ali	10
RA White	c Moore b Kabir Ali	49	c Hall b Kabir Ali	0
ML Love	not out	133	not out	161
U Afzaal	c Rhodes b Mason	45	c Smith b Batty	22
DJG Sales (capt)	b Bichel	0	c Smith b Hall	13
GP Swann	lbw b Hall	16	c Peters b Hall	10
*GL Brophy	c Hall b Bichel	1	c Rhodes b Mason	94
J Louw	lbw b Bichel	1	not out	18
CM Goode	lbw b Bichel	0		
CJR Jennings	b Mason	6		
CG Greenidge	b Mason	0		
Extras	lb 7	7	b 14, lb 5, w 6, nb 6	31
	(98 overs)	311	(6 wkts 108 overs)	359

Bowling
Mason 20-9-37-3. Kabir Ali 15-3-52-1. Bichel 19-0-87-5. Hall 22-6-57-1.
Batty 16-0-49-0. Solanki 6-0-22-0.
Mason 23-4-55-1. Kabir Ali 22-5-48-2. Bichel 12-1-55-0. Hall 17-4-38-2.
Batty 20-6-76-1. Solanki 4-0-21-0. Moore 8-1-35-0. Peters 2-0-12-0.
Fall of Wickets: 1-87, 2-119, 3-251, 4-252, 5-283, 6-286, 7-290, 8-290, 9-311
1-11, 2-20, 3-95, 4-116, 5-130, 6-311

WORCS	First Innings	
SD Peters	c Afzaal b Louw	9
SC Moore	c Sales b Greenidge	0
Kabir Ali	b Louw	2
GA Hick	b Louw	66
BF Smith (capt)	c Roberts b Louw	13
VS Solanki	lbw b Goode	26
AJ Bichel	lbw b Louw	142
GJ Batty	c Love b Jennings	51
AJ Hall	c Roberts b Greenidge	12
*SJ Rhodes	not out	4
MS Mason	b Greenidge	1
Extras	b 1, lb 13, w 1, nb 20	35
	(97.2 overs)	361

Bowling
Louw 27-6-63-5. Greenidge 20.2-4-71-3. Goode 16-3-70-1. Jennings 14-3-64-1.
Swann 17-4-66-0. White 3-0-13-0.
Fall of Wickets: 1-4, 2-7, 3-22, 4-40, 5-81, 6-205, 7-328, 8-347, 9-349

Match drawn - Worcestershire (11pts),
Northamptonshire (10pts)

A fourth hundred in successive Surrey matches put Mark Ramprakash in the highest company.

The loss of three whole sessions of play – from after tea on the second day – consigned Warwickshire's meeting with Kent at Edgbaston to a draw. Both sides, however, took maximum points from the draw with David Fulton, Ed Smith and Alex Loudon all batting beautifully in response to a Warwickshire first-innings total of 457 that, once again, was centred on the high talent of Ian Bell. The 22-year-old's sixth hundred of the summer included 23 boundaries, while Michael Powell also showed up strongly with 96. Fulton's century was his fifth of the championship campaign, while Smith's 95 was stroked from 115 balls and Loudon gloved a pull to give the wicketkeeper a legside catch when only eight runs short of a maiden hundred. As the match drifted towards a draw on the final afternoon, Nick Knight completed his 1,000 first-class runs for the season.

right from the opening morning when Azhar Mahmood and Martin Bicknell, making his first championship appearance since June, had the visitors swaying at 71 for 5. Chris Schofield's unorthodox half-century fashioned a recovery of sorts, but Ramprakash was soon taking centre stage. Supported first by Scott Newman (61) and then by Rikki Clarke (64), Ramprakash became only the fourth Surrey batsman to score four hundreds in successive championship matches. The previous three were all illustrious names: Andy Ducat, Tom Hayward and Jack Hobbs. When he was finally out, for 134, it was left to Alistair Brown and Tim Murtagh, who was helped by Nayan Doshi, to add 61 for the last wicket and to push Surrey on past 500. By stumps on the second day, Lancashire were 57 for 3 and slipping away. Carl Hooper did make 51, but the total had declined further to 113 for 7 before Dominic Cork showed typical never-say-die spirit with seven sixes and ten fours in a hugely entertaining 81-ball 109. It was, nevertheless, all rather too late.

Andy Bichel's magnificent all-round performance at Worcester, and two wonderful unbeaten hundreds from Northamptonshire's Martin Love, were forced to take second billing as a result of the shock revelation, just before play was due to resume on the third morning, that Ben Smith had given up the Worcestershire captaincy. It was thought to be the first instance of a county captain resigning in the middle of a match, but Smith insisted that it was the right decision both for himself and the club. 'I am not mentally right to lead the team during the important run-in to the end of this season', said Smith, before handing over the reins temporarily to Steve Rhodes. Later that day, Bichel hit 142, to add to the 5 for 87 he had taken when Northants scored 311 on the opening day, to earn Worcestershire a handy 50-run lead. Love, though, who had remained 133 not out in the first innings, was dropped by Rhodes off Bichel when on 65 (and when the Northants lead was just 97) and went on to make an unbeaten 161. With Gerard Brophy keeping him company with 94, Northants encountered no further alarms as they batted out the game.

Division Two

The second instance of a 12th man scoring a first-class hundred provided one of the main talking points of a strange match at the Rose Bowl. Darren Thomas was the century-maker who followed in the footsteps of Sussex's Kevin Innes in 2003, although there was an element of controversy about the way his innings began. Glamorgan, who knew that England fast bowler Simon Jones would be arriving to replace Thomas after being left out of the Old Trafford Test squad, promoted Thomas up the order to No. 6 to take advantage of his superior batting ability. The rules state that a nominated player must be allowed to complete his innings if he is still batting when the replacement arrives at the ground, and Jones duly turned up to see Thomas fashioning a fine Glamorgan fightback from his elevated position in the order. At 72 for 4 in reply to Hampshire's 369, Thomas and Michael Powell took Glamorgan on to 257 for 4 by the end of the second day – with Thomas on 105 not out from just 121 balls. Thomas had been especially rough in his treatment of Shane Warne, reverse sweeping the Hampshire captain to distraction as the Australian leg spinner's nine overs cost him 51

runs, and also chalking up an eight when he hooked a no-ball by Alan Mullally for six! Before the resumption of play the following morning, however – which was to see Powell move on from his overnight 62 to 89 and Glamorgan fall away to

Round 15: 10–16 August 2004 Division Two

HAMPSHIRE v. GLAMORGAN - at The Rose Bowl

HAMPSHIRE	First Innings		Second Innings	
JHK Adams	run out	6	c Powell b Croft	42
MJ Brown	b Thomas	90	not out	109
JP Crawley	lbw b Croft	47	not out	70
MJ Clarke	c sub b Croft	5		
DA Kenway	c Wallace b Kasprowicz	64		
*N Pothas	b Croft	26		
AD Mascarenhas	c Elliott b Harrison	34		
SK Warne (capt)	c Hemp b Thomas	42		
SD Udal	b Thomas	40		
AD Mullally	c Wallace b Thomas	0		
BV Taylor	not out	2		
Extras	b 4, lb 5, nb 4	13	b 1, lb 13, nb 6	20
	(111.3 overs)	369	(1 wkt dec 40 overs)	241

Bowling
Kasprowicz 31-5-100-1. Harrison 20-4-51-1. Thomas 26.3-1-103-4. Dale 9-1-33-0. Croft 25-3-73-3.
Kasprowicz 14-2-37-0. Harrison 18-8-58-0. Jones 10-1-51-0. Croft 8-0-81-1.
Fall of Wickets: 1-6, 2-116, 3-146, 4-178, 5-235, 6-261, 7-302, 8-348, 9-348 1-111

GLAMORGAN	First Innings		Second Innings	
MTG Elliott	c Pothas b Taylor	8	(2) st Pothas b Warne	34
*MA Wallace	c Mullally b Mascarenhas	27	(7) lbw b Udal	9
DL Hemp	b Mascarenhas	4	b Warne	32
MJ Powell	lbw b Mascarenhas	89	c Brown b Udal	26
MP Maynard	c Udal b Mascarenhas	6	c Clarke b Warne	0
SD Thomas	retired not out	105		
J Hughes	c Pothas b Mascarenhas	0	(6) b Warne	0
A Dale	b Warne	15	not out	4
RDB Croft (capt)	not out	14	(1) b Mascarenhas	18
DS Harrison	b Taylor	0	(9) lbw b Udal	0
MS Kasprowicz	b Udal	18	(10) not out	20
SP Jones				
Extras	b 8, lb 7, nb 26	41	lb 1, nb 6	7
	(9 wkts 91.5 overs)	342	(8 wkts 58.5 overs)	150

Bowling
Mullally 16-3-64-0. Taylor 21-5-64-3. Mascarenhas 24-6-64-5. Udal 8.5-1-48-1. Warne 22-1-87-0.
Taylor 7-0-24-0. Mullally 3-0-16-0. Mascarenhas 14-4-44-1. Udal 16-6-39-3. Warne 18.5-12-26-4.
Fall of Wickets: 1-13, 2-55, 3-62, 4-72, 5-287, 6-290, 7-311, 8-311, 9-342 1-35, 2-85, 3-98, 4-98, 5-108, 6-119, 7-130, 8-130

Match drawn - Hampshire (11pts), Glamorgan (10pts)

NOTTINGHAMSHIRE v. LEICESTERSHIRE - at Trent Bridge

NOTTS	First Innings	
DJ Bicknell	b Cleary	2
JER Gallian (capt)	b Maddy	66
RJ Warren	b Gibson	134
KP Pietersen	lbw b Cleary	0
DJ Hussey	c Robinson b Masters	140
RJ Sidebottom	c Stevens b Hodge	62
*CMW Read	b Gibson	0
MA Ealham	run out	1
PJ Franks	not out	57
GJ Smith	b Gibson	1
SCG MacGill	b Gibson	2
Extras	b 2, lb 11, nb 12	25
	(125 overs)	490

Bowling
Cleary 22-3-66-2. Gibson 30-5-106-4. DeFreitas 29-5-107-0. Masters 22-3-97-1. Henderson 12-1-54-0. Maddy 6-0-30-1. Hodge 4-0-17-1.
Fall of Wickets: 1-2, 2-110, 3-111, 4-341, 5-342, 6-387, 7-396, 8-462, 9-464

LEICESTERSHIRE	First Innings		Second Innings	
DDJ Robinson	c Read b Smith	4	b Hussey	88
DL Maddy	c Pietersen b Ealham	51	b Franks	31
DI Stevens	b Ealham	13	(5) c sub b MacGill	5
JL Sadler	lbw b Ealham	4	b MacGill	7
BJ Hodge (capt)	b Ealham	9	(3) c Gallian b Franks	76
*PA Nixon	c Ealham b Franks	18	not out	17
PAJ DeFreitas	c Read b Franks	4	not out	8
OD Gibson	lbw b Sidebottom	26		
CW Henderson	c Pietersen b Sidebottom	37		
MF Cleary	c Read b Smith	14		
DD Masters	not out	9		
Extras	b 4, lb 9, w 2, nb 8	23	b 5, lb 5, nb 21	31
	(66.1 overs)	212	(5 wkts 74 overs)	263

Bowling
Smith 12.1-3-27-2. Sidebottom 16.4-4-37-2. Ealham 17-3-43-4. Franks 9-1-40-2. MacGill 10.2-1-48-0. Pietersen 1-0-4-0.
Smith 11-1-48-0. Ealham 14-5-40-0. MacGill 28-10-66-2. Franks 13-1-68-2. Pietersen 3-0-24-0. Hussey 5-1-7-1.
Fall of Wickets: 1-6, 2-28, 3-38, 4-54, 5-100, 6-104, 7-121, 8-183, 9-188 1-58, 2-203, 3-228, 4-238, 5-238

Match drawn - Nottinghamshire (12pts), Leicestershire (8pts)

YORKSHIRE v. DERBYSHIRE - at Headingley

YORKSHIRE	First Innings	
MJ Wood (capt)	c Havell b Sheikh	123
AW Gale	lbw b Moss	29
A McGrath	c Sutton b Welch	109
DS Lehmann	lbw b Havell	66
IJ Harvey	run out	16
VJ Craven	b Welch	11
*I Dawood	c Sutton b Welch	5
RKJ Dawson	c Hassan-Adnan b Sheikh	22
JAR Blain	not out	28
MAK Lawson	not out	6
SP Kirby		
Extras	b 3, lb 7, w 1, nb 16	27
	(8 wkts dec 109 overs)	442

Bowling
Havell 16-0-100-1. Welch 31-6-118-3. Sheikh 23-3-85-2. Moss 20-4-60-1. Paget 19-3-69-0.
Fall of Wickets: 1-64, 2-254, 3-289, 4-318, 5-347, 6-361, 7-393, 8-409

DERBYSHIRE	First Innings		Second Innings	
SD Stubbings	c Wood b Harvey	37	b Lehmann	58
AI Gait	lbw b Harvey	0	lbw b Blain	5
J Moss	b Blain	7	run out	87
Hassan Adnan	c Harvey b Kirby	86	c Wood b Blain	6
CWG Bassano	c Wood b Blain	35	not out	29
JDC Bryant	b Blain	1	lbw b Dawson	10
*LD Sutton (capt)	c Kirby b Lawson	35	not out	33
G Welch	b Blain	1		
MA Sheikh	lbw b Harvey	0		
CD Paget	lbw b Lehmann	7		
PMR Havell	not out	1		
Extras	b 5, lb 12, w 1, nb 12	30	b 4, lb 6, w 3, nb 4	17
	(79.2 overs)	240	(5 wkts 92 overs)	245

Bowling
Kirby 17-3-41-1. Harvey 17-4-38-3. Dawson 9-0-30-0. Blain 12-3-38-4. Lawson 11.2-1-39-1. McGrath 7-0-22-0. Lehmann 6-0-15-1.
Kirby 13-4-25-0. Blain 10-1-28-2. Harvey 11-1-28-0. McGrath 7-2-21-0. Dawson 26-7-53-1. Craven 2-0-10-0. Lawson 13-1-48-0. Lehmann 10-2-22-1.
Fall of Wickets: 1-20, 2-76, 3-76, 4-175, 5-187, 6-191, 7-202, 8-210, 9-232 1-24, 2-139, 3-159, 4-163, 5-190

Match drawn - Yorkshire (12pts), Derbyshire (7pts)

DURHAM v. SOMERSET - at The Riverside

DURHAM	First Innings		Second Innings	
JJB Lewis (capt)	b Francis SRG	8	lbw b Andrew	25
GR Breese	c Ponting b Laraman	10	lbw b Johnson	5
GJ Muchall	c Turner b Francis SRG	40	c Andrew b Francis SRG	4
MJ North	c Turner b Francis SRG	4	lbw b Laraman	7
KJ Coetzer	c sub b Francis SRG	16	c Burns b Andrew	6
GM Hamilton	c Francis JD b Francis SRG	41	c Ponting b Francis JD	12
*A Pratt	c Francis JD b Laraman	16	not out	24
GD Bridge	c Turner b Johnson	8	not out	0
LE Plunkett	c Turner b Andrew	38		
N Killeen	not out	35		
SW Tait	c Turner b Johnson	0		
Extras	b 4, w 3, nb 8	15	b 2	2
	(75.5 overs)	231	(6 wkts 37.3 overs)	85

Bowling
Johnson 20.5-2-71-2. Francis SRG 23-6-75-5. Laraman 19-7-30-2.
Andrew 10-1-39-1. Francis JD 3-0-12-0.
Johnson 7-3-11-1. Francis SRG 16-5-34-1. Laraman 4-2-8-1. Andrew 6-2-24-2. Francis JD 2.3-1-4-1. Bowler 2-1-2-0.
Fall of Wickets: 1-9, 2-29, 3-34, 4-86, 5-87, 6-129, 7-142, 8-164, 9-225 1-15, 2-26, 3-33, 4-46, 5-47, 6-83

SOMERSET	First Innings	
PD Bowler	b Hamilton	30
JD Francis	lbw b Killeen	14
RT Ponting	c Breese b Plunkett	50
MJ Wood	lbw b Hamilton	0
M Burns (capt)	b Bridge	8
AW Laraman	not out	66
ID Blackwell	lbw b Plunkett	0
*RJ Turner	c Pratt b Killeen	46
GM Andrew	c Breese b Muchall	15
RL Johnson	not out	101
SRG Francis		
Extras	lb 11, w 15, nb 44	70
	(8 wkts dec 71.3 overs)	400

Bowling
Tait 12-0-113-0. Plunkett 16-0-100-2. Killeen 18-4-62-2. Hamilton 12-2-28-2. Bridge 4-0-26-1. Muchall 3-1-15-1. Breese 4-1-42-0. North 0.3-0-3-0.
Fall of Wickets: 1-45, 2-103, 3-103, 4-119, 5-151, 6-151, 7-219, 8-243

Match drawn - Durham (7pts - 1.5pts deducted for slow over rate), Somerset (12pts)

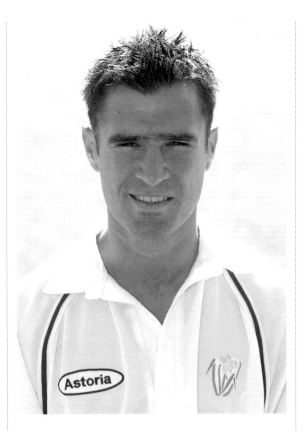

Super Sub: Darren Thomas, of Glamorgan, who savaged Shane Warne in a flamboyant hundred at the Rose Bowl before being retired from the match.

342 all out – Thomas was voluntarily retired out so that he could drive back to Llanelli to attend his grandfather's funeral. Dimitri Mascarenhas, who had taken three early wickets, finished up with 5 for 64 and Hampshire then flung the game wide open again by charging to 241 for 1 declared as Michael Brown and John Crawley plundered the last 113 runs of their unbroken stand of 130 in just ten overs. Warne, however, was then left to wish he had declared even earlier as – taking 4 for 26 himself and seeing Shaun Udal chip in with 3 for 39 – Hampshire had the Welsh county eight wickets down with more than half-an-hour left. The last 10.5 overs, though, were repelled by Adrian Dale – who took the responsibility of resisting Warne – and Michael Kasprowicz. Brown, with 90 and 109 not out, had enjoyed a particularly fine match but, at the end of it all, it was just a draw.

David Hussey's high-class strokeplay, and Russell Warren's return to form, should have resulted in a comfortable Nottinghamshire victory over Leicestershire at Trent Bridge. After the loss of the entire third day to the weather, however, the visitors hung on in their second innings through Darren Robinson (88) and Brad Hodge (76) after being forced to follow on. Hussey, who reached his century in 124 balls and passed 1,000 runs for the season in the process, struck two sixes and 13 fours.

There was a similar story at Headingley, where heavy weather interrupted the first two days and meant that Yorkshire only managed to declare on 442 for 8 after more than an hour's play on day three. Despite Hassan Adnan's 86, they then succeeded in bowling Derbyshire out for 240. Needing to bat out the final day, after being asked to follow on, Derbyshire managed to see it through at 245 for 5, with much of the hard graft being done by Steve Stubbings and Jon Moss in a second-wicket stand of 115. The Yorkshire innings had earlier been based on centuries from both Matthew Wood and Anthony McGrath, and a partnership between them of 190, besides also featuring the promising championship debut of Repton School pupil Chris Paget. At 16 years and 283 days old, Paget became the youngest championship player in Derbyshire's history and also caught the eye with a decent 12-over spell of off spin that cost him only 35 runs.

Durham's match against Somerset at the Riverside was always likely to be a draw once the first two days had been completely washed out by bad weather. In the end, however, the home side were left hanging on for a fortuitous draw at 85 for 6 following the whirlwind hitting of Richard Johnson. Somerset began the final day on a distinctly unpromising 127 for 4 in reply to a Durham first-innings total of 231, in which Simon Francis had snapped up 5 for 75. Ricky Ponting could add only 14 more runs before falling for 50, but when Johnson joined Aaron Laraman at the crease, the game was suddenly transformed into life. No. 10 Johnson smashed six sixes and nine fours to claim the season's fastest first-class century, off just 63 balls. Somerset's eventual 400 for 8 declared also contained the extraordinary struggles of Shaun Tait, the highly rated Australian fast bowler. Tait's 12 overs cost him 113 runs, with a good percentage of them made up by a sad tally of 21 no-balls. The drama, however, had not ended. In the 38 overs that remained, Durham's batting also collapsed – leaving Somerset to wonder what might have been had they not decided to claim the maximum batting points that Johnson's hitting suddenly brought into view.

Round 16: 18–22 August 2004

Division One

Mushtaq Ahmed bagged a match return of 13 for 140, his best for Sussex, as the champions' improving form continued with an excellent seven-wicket win against Worcestershire at Hove. A fifth-wicket stand of 144 between Murray Goodwin and Matthew Prior provided the basis for a good-sized first-innings total, with Mark Davis and James Kirtley also making useful lower-middle-order contributions. In reply, Worcestershire were all out for 202 and in all sorts of trouble against the leg breaks and googlies of Mushtaq. They were, don't forget, only in Division Two when the Pakistani bamboozled the rest of the championship top flight in 2003 and their early-season game with Sussex at Worcester had been abandoned without a ball being bowled. As a result, their batsmen were less-prepared than they might have been for Mushtaq's variations – their confidence also took a battering when Graeme Hick, a fine player of spin and an old Test adversary of Mushtaq's, fell to him for 47. Within half-an-hour of the start of the third day, Worcestershire were following on with Mushtaq having taken 6 for 67. By the end of the day, Mushtaq's second-innings figures were an almost-identical 6 for 73, with the visitors only still hanging on at 305 for 8 because of positive innings of 84

and 60 by Vikram Solanki and Andrew Hall. Ray Price also resisted sternly the next morning, but Mushtaq ended up with 7 for 73 to take his championship wicket tally to 66, the country's best. An 80-run second-wicket partnership between Tony

Round 16: 18–22 August 2004 Division One

SUSSEX v. WORCESTERSHIRE – at Hove

SUSSEX	First Innings		Second Innings	
IJ Ward	c Hick b Bichel	2	b Hall	1
RR Montgomerie	c Rhodes b Price	69	c Solanki b Batty	37
PA Cottey	c Hall b Mason	34	c Peters b Batty	45
MW Goodwin	c Hick b Hall	85	not out	8
CJ Adams (capt)	c Rhodes b Batty	34	not out	18
*MJ Prior	c Solanki b Hall	93		
RSC Martin-Jenkins	c Peters b Hall	7		
MJG Davis	c Rhodes b Mason	43		
Mushtaq Ahmed	c Hick b Mason	0		
RJ Kirtley	c Hick b Price	36		
M Akram	not out	18		
Extras	b 1, lb 8, w 2	11	b 2	2
	(136.3 overs)	432	(3 wkts 33.1 overs)	111

Bowling
Bichel 6.3-1-29-1. Mason 32.3-8-57-3. Hall 32.3-7-105-3. Batty 32-6-126-1. Price 28.5-5-91-2. Solanki 5-0-15-0.
Hall 6-1-18-1. Mason 4-0-18-0. Batty 13-2-55-2. Price 10.1-2-18-0.
Fall of Wickets: 1-7, 2-105, 3-109, 4-170, 5-314, 6-328, 7-329, 8-334, 9-391
1-2, 2-82, 3-86

WORCS	First Innings		Second Innings	
SD Peters	c Davis b Martin-Jenkins	28	c Prior b Akram	14
SC Moore	c Adams b Akram	4	lbw b Mushtaq Ahmed	32
GA Hick	c Et b Mushtaq Ahmed	47	c Montgomerie b M-Jenkins	12
BF Smith	c Hick b Mushtaq Ahmed	1	b Mushtaq Ahmed	40
VS Solanki	lbw b Mushtaq Ahmed	26	b Mushtaq Ahmed	84
GJ Batty	lbw b Mushtaq Ahmed	28	(7) lbw b Mushtaq Ahmed	6
AJ Bichel	c Prior b Akram	29	(6) lbw b Mushtaq Ahmed	0
AJ Hall	b Mushtaq Ahmed	11	c Prior b Mushtaq Ahmed	60
*SJ Rhodes (capt)	c Adams b Akram	7	c Goodwin b Akram	35
RW Price	lbw b Mushtaq Ahmed	6	not out	31
MS Mason	not out	0	c Davis b Mushtaq Ahmed	1
Extras	b 8, lb 5, nb 2	15	b 7, lb 11, w 1, nb 6	25
	(59.2 overs)	202	(109.2 overs)	340

Bowling
Akram 14.2-2-52-3. Kirtley 10-3-29-0. Mushtaq Ahmed 23-8-67-6.
Martin-Jenkins 12-4-41-1.
Akram 24-2-83-2. Kirtley 23-3-98-0. Mushtaq Ahmed 38.2-12-73-7.
Martin-Jenkins 14-1-37-1. Davis 10-1-31-0.
Fall of Wickets: 1-13, 2-49, 3-58, 4-105, 5-120, 6-171, 7-177, 8-190, 9-202
1-20, 2-63, 3-78, 4-145, 5-145, 6-155, 7-242, 8-265, 9-339

Sussex won by 7 wickets - Sussex (22pts),
Worcestershire (4pts)

GLOUCESTERSHIRE v. WARWICKSHIRE – at Bristol

WARWICKSHIRE	First Innings		Second Innings	
NV Knight (capt)	c Hardinges b Lewis	7	b Lewis	0
MA Wagh	c Gidman b Averis	17	c Adshead b Averis	73
MJ Powell	c Hussey b Lewis	10	(5) c Weston b Sillence	9
UL Trott	c Adshead b Hardinges	21	(3) c Spearman b Fisher	79
JO Troughton	c Spearman b Lewis	120	(4) lbw b Fisher	28
DR Brown	c Hussey b Sillence	91	c Taylor b Gidman	49
*T Frost	c Taylor b Sillence	2	b Lewis	28
HH Streak	c Spearman b Fisher	29	c Hardinges b Lewis	4
NM Carter	c Hardinges b Fisher	0	(10) not out	1
N Tahir	not out	18	(9) not out	11
D Pretorius	c Weston b Lewis	9		
Extras	b 1, lb 10, w 1, nb 14	26	b 5, lb 3, w 2, nb 24	34
	(97 overs)	350	(8 wkts 122 overs)	308

Bowling
Lewis 23-7-59-3. Averis 18-3-89-1. Hardinges 17-2-78-1. Gidman 5-1-21-0.
Sillence 14-4-50-2. Fisher 20-5-42-3.
Lewis 27-6-89-3. Averis 15-4-57-1. Hardinges 13-2-42-0. Sillence 17-8-33-1.
Fisher 36-20-50-2. Hussey 1-0-1-0. Taylor 1-0-2-0. Gidman 12-4-26-1.
Fall of Wickets: 1-10, 2-38, 3-38, 4-78, 5-260, 6-266, 7-300, 8-300, 9-313
1-0, 2-163, 3-164, 4-202, 5-202, 6-263, 7-281, 8-306

GLOS	First Innings	
CM Spearman	c Et b Troughton	237
WPC Weston	c Trott b Tahir	30
MEK Hussey	lbw b Troughton	26
ID Fisher	c Frost b Pretorius	13
APR Gidman	c Powell b Wagh	47
CG Taylor (capt)	b Brown	30
*SJ Adshead	b Brown	32
MA Hardinges	not out	68
RJ Sillence	lbw b Trott	92
JMM Averis	not out	0
J Lewis		
Extras	b 3, lb 11, w 1, nb 2	17
	(8 wkts 161 overs)	592

Bowling
Pretorius 20-2-84-1. Carter 21-3-93-0. Brown 31-9-84-2. Tahir 5-0-43-1.
Wagh 28-3-107-1. Troughton 37-9-106-2. Powell 7-0-36-0. Streak 8-1-24-0.
Trott 2-1-1-1.
Fall of Wickets: 1-99, 2-190, 3-229, 4-363, 5-368, 6-427, 7-434, 8-588

Match drawn - Gloucestershire (12pts),
Warwickshire (10pts)

KENT v. SURREY – at Canterbury

KENT	First Innings		Second Innings	
DP Fulton (capt)	c Clarke b Azhar Mahmood	57	c Clarke b Murtagh	42
ET Smith	c Brown b Bicknell	0	c Batty b Ormond	0
AGR Loudon	c Azhar Mahmood b Bicknell	18	lbw b Ormond	8
MG Bevan	b Bicknell	7	c Clarke b Ormond	0
MJ Walker	b Azhar Mahmood	14	c sub b Azhar Mahmood	57
*NJ O'Brien	c Batty b Azhar Mahmood	20	lbw b Bicknell	5
MJ Dennington	c Batty b Murtagh	3	not out	50
RS Ferley	b Ormond	29	b Azhar Mahmood	0
MM Patel	b Azhar Mahmood	10	c sub b Azhar Mahmood	14
IG Butler	c Batty b Azhar Mahmood	68	not out	48
RH Joseph	not out	2		
Extras	b 3, lb 5, nb 2	10	b 3, lb 6, w 1, nb 12	22
	(74.1 overs)	226	(8 wkts 78 overs)	234

Bowling
Bicknell 22-3-72-3. Ormond 20-6-57-1. Azhar Mahmood 20.1-7-54-5.
Murtagh 12-4-35-1.
Bicknell 18-2-67-1. Ormond 22-6-65-3. Azhar Mahmood 20-8-55-3.
Murtagh 12-6-25-1. Doshi 4-1-13-0. Brown 2-2-0-0.
Fall of Wickets: 1-9, 2-43, 3-71, 4-85, 5-94, 6-99, 7-111, 8-121, 9-224
1-6, 2-26, 3-34, 4-107, 5-120, 6-134, 7-134, 8-142

SURREY	First Innings	
SA Newman	b Walker b Dennington	111
RS Clinton	lbw b Dennington	58
*JN Batty (capt)	b Patel	46
R Clarke	c Loudon b Patel	33
MR Ramprakash	b Dennington	9
J Ormond	b Joseph	4
AD Brown	c O'Brien b Butler	85
Azhar Mahmood	c Butler b Patel	24
MP Bicknell	not out	14
TJ Murtagh	not out	1
ND Doshi		
Extras	b 2, lb 8, w 1, nb 2	13
	(8 wkts 98 overs)	402

Bowling
Butler 14-2-71-1. Joseph 16-2-76-1. Patel 30-2-96-3. Dennington 18-2-88-3.
Loudon 16-1-47-0. Ferley 4-0-14-0.
Fall of Wickets: 1-170, 2-179, 3-234, 4-247, 5-256, 6-309, 7-367, 8-397

Match drawn - Kent (7pts),
Surrey (12pts)

NORTHAMPTONSHIRE v. MIDDLESEX – at Northampton

MIDDLESEX	First Innings		Second Innings	
BL Hutton	c Swann b Louw	100	c Swann b Louw	1
SG Koenig	lbw b Rofe	28	c Brophy b Swann	22
OA Shah	c Brophy b Swann	62	c Phillips b Rofe	100
CT Peploe	lbw b Swann	4		
EC Joyce (capt)	c Afzaal b Phillips	23	(4) lbw b Louw	5
PN Weekes	c Sales b Phillips	44	(5) b Louw	51
JWM Dalrymple	lbw b Louw	2	(6) b Louw	11
*BJM Scott	c Brophy b Brown	31	(7) not out	22
SJ Cook	c Swann b Louw	34		
SR Clark	c Afzaal b Louw	34		
M Hayward	not out	0		
Extras	lb 4	4	b 2, lb 5, nb 2	9
	(124.3 overs)	345	(6 wkts dec 62.5 overs)	216

Bowling
Louw 31.3-7-110-4. Rofe 24-6-66-1. Phillips 23-7-38-2. Brown 24-5-76-1.
Swann 20-5-49-2. White 2-1-2-0.
Rofe 12-5-38-1. Louw 12.5-2-44-5. Brown 17-3-50-0. Swann 12-0-50-0.
Phillips 9-2-27-0.
Fall of Wickets: 1-45, 2-182, 3-194, 4-198, 5-257, 6-260, 7-272, 8-303, 9-337
1-3, 2-56, 3-56, 4-159, 5-185, 6-216

NORTHANTS	First Innings		Second Innings	
TW Roberts	c Joyce b Hayward	1	run out	46
RA White	b Cook	0	c Shah b Hayward	3
MJ Powell	c Et b Peploe	14	b Peploe	0
U Afzaal	lbw b Hayward	111	(8) c Joyce b Peploe	6
DJG Sales (capt)	c Shah b Peploe	57	(4) not out	73
*GL Brophy	b Dalrymple	1	st Scott b Cook	11
GP Swann	c Hutton b Clark	32	c Hutton b Hayward	2
BJ Phillips	c Scott b Clark	34	(9) not out	0
J Louw	b Hayward	63	(5) b Dalrymple	8
PC Rofe	not out	0		
JF Brown	b Hayward	0		
Extras	lb 6	6	b 4, nb 2	6
	(109.3 overs)	295	(7 wkts 47.4 overs)	155

Bowling
Cook 23-6-53-1. Hayward 19.3-4-62-4. Peploe 28-10-66-2. Clark 15-9-47-2.
Dalrymple 18-6-48-1. Weekes 2-0-13-0.
Cook 9-2-16-1. Hayward 13-5-36-2. Peploe 10.4-2-43-2. Clark 7-1-21-0.
Dalrymple 8-0-35-1.
Fall of Wickets: 1-1, 2-1, 3-24, 4-131, 5-132, 6-173, 7-185, 8-286, 9-295
1-20, 2-31, 3-80, 4-112, 5-133, 6-138, 7-153

Match drawn - Northamptonshire (9pts), Middlesex (10pts)

Cottey and Richard Montgomerie, who added 37 to his first-innings half-century, ensured no serious alarms as Sussex cruised to victory.

Warwickshire's strong claims on the county championship title looked hard to digest at Bristol where their bowling attack was thoroughly exposed by both the brilliant batting of Craig Spearman and the considerable wagging of the Gloucestershire tail. In the end, with Dougie Brown battling through three-and-a-half hours on the last afternoon for 49 and with Tony Frost also making a vital late contribution, Warwickshire could do no more than hang on for a draw. Brown had scored 91 from 117 balls on the first day, too, when he came in at 78 for 4 and helped Jim Troughton, playing his first championship innings for eight weeks, to pull Warwickshire's first innings around. Troughton hit 19 fours in his 120, with the championship leaders adding a further four batting bonus points to their already impressive collection. By stumps on day two, however, it was Gloucestershire who were in complete command, as Spearman shredded the bowling of the champions-elect. Four sixes decorated his boundary blitz and 232 not out was up on the scoreboard alongside the end-of-day total of 352 for 3. It was, remarkably, the first double-hundred by a Gloucestershire player at their Bristol headquarters since Walter Hammond made 214 against Somerset in 1946. Spearman, however, could add only five more runs the following day – leaving the stage free for the bit-part all-rounders, Mark Hardinges and Roger Sillence, to humiliate the Warwickshire attack. Hardinges made an unbeaten 68 and Sillence a flamboyant 92 before a declaration finally came at 592 for 8. Nick Knight was bowled by Jon Lewis without scoring, but Mark Wagh and Jon Trott then scored valuable half-centuries to rally Warwickshire to 111 for 1 at the close. The remaining 90 overs bowled on the final day represented a real test of character for Warwickshire and, to their credit, they passed it.

Kent looked like plunging to defeat against Surrey at Canterbury until Matt Dennington and Ian Butler, their ninth-wicket pair, added an

Whirling dervish: Mushtaq Ahmed was back to his best with 13 wickets in the match as Sussex beat Worcestershire at Hove.

unbroken 92 to see out time and thwart the visiting attack. Azhar Mahmood, Jimmy Ormond and Martin Bicknell ran out of steam towards the end, but they had put in a valiant effort to make up for the day-and-a-half's playing time lost to the weather. Butler added an unbeaten 48 to his career-best 68 in the first innings, and Kent were most grateful for his runs. Only David Fulton, with 57 and 42, and Matthew Walker, with a second-innings half-century, looked the part in the home side's top order and Kent were always destined to be hanging on for the draw once they had underperformed with the bat by collapsing to 136 for 8 in the 46 overs possible on the opening day and then saw Butler's counter-attack trumped by a first-wicket stand of 170 between Scott Newman (111) and Richard Clinton (58). Alistair Brown's typically aggressive 85 ensured a potentially match-winning lead, but the combination of Dennington, Butler and time conspired against a rejuvenated Surrey.

Middlesex had much the better of their fixture against Northamptonshire at Wantage Road – and might even have snatched victory had they been a touch more adventurous with their second-innings declaration. Caution, unfortunately, is the watchword in Division One and Middlesex, having given themselves only 48 overs to bowl at Northants on the last afternoon – and set them a target of 267 – proceeded to reduce them to 155 for 7. Indeed, the home side had skipper David Sales' unbeaten 73 to thank for their survival. Johann Louw impressed with both bat and ball for Northants, while Usman Afzaal ground out a valuable, but sometimes tortuous, 111 on the third day. Ben Hutton completed 1,000 first-class runs for the season for the first time during his fifth championship hundred of the campaign, while Owais Shah continued his sparkling late-summer form with delightful knocks of 62 and 100.

Division Two

Shane Warne and Mike Burns, the two captains, conjured up a magnificent contest at Taunton despite the loss of huge chunks of play to the weather during the previous three days. In the end, it was Warne's

Round 16: 18–22 August 2004 Division Two

SOMERSET v. HAMPSHIRE - at Taunton

HAMPSHIRE	First Innings			Second Innings	
JHK Adams	c Hildreth b Johnson	31		not out	21
MJ Brown	c Wood b Caddick	17		c Bowler b Hildreth	5
JP Crawley	c Burns b Johnson	34			
SM Katich	c Johnson b Caddick	38			
DA Kenway	c Turner b Caddick	37		(4) not out	21
*N Pothas	c Bowler b Caddick	5			
LR Prittipaul	c Bowler b Johnson	44		(3) c Caddick b Hildreth	49
AD Mascarenhas	c Turner b Caddick	1			
SK Warne (capt)	c Francis JD b Laraman	47			
BV Taylor	c Turner b Laraman	14			
JTA Bruce	not out	0			
Extras	b 8, lb 6, w 1, nb 18	33		w 3	3
	(92 overs)	301		(2 wkts dec 25.4 overs)	99

Bowling
Johnson 26-9-81-3. Caddick 29-4-97-5. Laraman 17-3-67-2. Burns 20-5-62-0.
Burns 10.4-0-40-0. Hildreth 10-1-39-2. Francis JD 1-1-14-0. Wood 2-0-6-0.
Fall of Wickets: 1-31, 2-72, 3-116, 4-167, 5-177, 6-190, 7-196, 8-271, 9-293
1-7, 2-67

SOMERSET	First Innings			Second Innings	
PD Bowler	not out	22		b Mascarenhas	25
JD Francis	c Bruce b Taylor	4		c Katich b Warne	110
J Cox	not out	12		c Pothas b Warne	20
JC Hildreth				c Prittipaul b Warne	40
M Burns (capt)				run out	79
RL Johnson				b Warne	4
MJ Wood				run out	18
AW Laraman				c Pothas b Warne	3
*RJ Turner				lbw b Warne	11
AR Caddick				run out	0
SRG Francis				not out	1
Extras	nb 12	12		b 2, lb 3, w 2, nb 22	29
	(1 wkt dec 26 overs)	50		(83.4 overs)	340

Bowling
Bruce 5-0-13-0. Taylor 4-2-7-1. Prittipaul 4-2-13-0. Katich 6-0-11-0. Adams 5-2-6-0.
Kenway 2-2-0-0.
Taylor 15-2-55-0. Bruce 16-3-77-0. Mascarenhas 17-4-46-1. Prittipaul 2-1-9-0.
Warne 30.4-1-127-6. Katich 3-0-21-0.
Fall of Wickets: 1-10
1-48, 2-93, 3-155, 4-300, 5-306, 6-313, 7-324, 8-336, 9-336

Hampshire won by 10 runs - Somerset (3pts), Hampshire (17pts)

DERBYSHIRE v. NOTTINGHAMSHIRE - at Derby

DERBYSHIRE	First Innings			Second Innings	
SD Stubbings	c Singh b Franks	31		b Harris	23
BJ France	c Read b Harris	9		b Smith	12
J Moss	c Bicknell b Franks	30		c Read b Smith	1
Hassan Adnan	b Smith	140		lbw b Smith	28
CWG Bassano	not out	123		lbw b Harris	7
JDC Bryant	b Harris	8		c Singh b MacGill	0
*LD Sutton (capt)	b Harris	6		b Harris	0
G Welch	c Gallian b Harris	12		b Harris	0
MA Sheikh	not out	5		not out	17
CD Paget				lbw b Smith	0
PMR Havell				b Smith	1
Extras	b 2, lb 23, w 1, nb 10	36		b 4, lb 1	5
	(7 wkts dec 108.5 overs)	400		(39.1 overs)	96

Bowling
Smith 20-2-95-1. Harris 24-4-61-4. Franks 16.5-3-67-2. Ealham 17-5-44-0.
MacGill 26-4-82-0. Pietersen 1-0-5-0. Hussey 4-0-21-0.
Smith 11.1-2-35-5. Harris 13-6-22-4. MacGill 11-1-26-1. Franks 4-1-8-0.
Fall of Wickets: 1-21, 2-42, 3-341, 4-371, 5-419, 6-420, 7-420, 8-524, 9-539
1-33, 2-35, 3-47, 4-61, 5-64, 6-65, 7-65, 8-90, 9-90

NOTTS	First Innings	
DJ Bicknell	c and b Havell	175
JER Gallian (capt)	c Hassan Adnan b Welch	8
A Singh	b Welch	14
KP Pietersen	c Hassan Adnan b Havell	153
DJ Hussey	b Sheikh	15
*CMW Read	not out	90
MA Ealham	b Welch	1
PJ Franks	lbw b Welch	0
GJ Smith	run out	35
SCG MacGill	c France b Welch	9
AJ Harris	not out	1
Extras	b 15, lb 9, w 1, nb 26	51
	(9 wkts dec 127 overs)	552

Bowling
Welch 29-7-101-5. Havell 24-1-137-2. Sheikh 31-7-99-1. Moss 13-0-65-0.
Paget 17-1-68-0. Hassan Adnan 13-0-58-0.
Fall of Wickets: 1-21, 2-44, 3-341, 4-371, 5-419, 6-420, 7-420, 8-524, 9-539

Nottinghamshire won by an innings and 56 runs - Derbyshire (8pts), Nottinghamshire (21pts)

LEICESTERSHIRE v. YORKSHIRE - at Leicester

LEICESTERSHIRE	First Innings			Second Innings	
DDJ Robinson	lbw b McGrath	154		c Wood b Bresnan	14
DL Maddy	lbw b Bresnan	27		b Bresnan	1
JK Maunders	b Kirby	20		lbw b Kirby	3
BJ Hodge (capt)	b McGrath	24		c Dawood b Blain	60
DI Stevens	c Dawson b Kirby	48		lbw b Kirby	2
JN Snape	c Gale b Kirby	0		c McGrath b Blain	15
*PA Nixon	c & b McGrath	1		not out	22
PAJ DeFreitas	c Jaques b Bresnan	15		not out	19
OD Gibson	not out	60			
CW Henderson	b Bresnan	1			
CE Dagnall	lbw b Blain	6			
Extras	b 3, lb 6, w 3, nb 18	30		b 4, lb 6, nb 20	30
	(113 overs)	382		(6 wkts dec 48.4 overs)	166

Bowling
Kirby 25-5-87-3. Blain 13-1-65-1. Bresnan 22-7-42-2. Craven 8-1-30-1.
Dawson 23-3-84-0. McGrath 21-1-65-3.
Bresnan 15-2-41-2. Kirby 16-5-60-2. Blain 6-0-19-2. McGrath 6-2-13-0.
Dawson 5-1-18-0. Craven 0.4-0-5-0.
Fall of Wickets: 1-90, 2-126, 3-177, 4-289, 5-293, 6-294, 7-295, 8-334, 9-346
1-17, 2-18, 3-38, 4-44, 5-117, 6-118

YORKSHIRE	First Innings			Second Innings	
MJ Wood (capt)	c Maddy b Henderson	20		(2) b Gibson	14
PA Jaques	c Gibson b DeFreitas	11		(1) c Robinson b Gibson	1
A McGrath	c Nixon b DeFreitas	2		lbw b Dagnall	6
JJ Sayers	c Maddy b Henderson	35		lbw b DeFreitas	18
AW Gale	c Dagnall b Henderson	13		c Robinson b Henderson	14
VJ Craven	lbw b Hodge	24		lbw b Henderson	11
*I Dawood	c & b Hodge	2		not out	42
RKJ Dawson	c Nixon b DeFreitas	76		c Maunders b Maddy	19
TT Bresnan	c Maunders b Henderson	35		b DeFreitas	4
JAR Blain	not out	3		not out	0
SP Kirby	c Stevens b DeFreitas	0			
Extras	b 5, lb 11, nb 2	18		lb 14, nb 4	18
	(94.1 overs)	239		(8 wkts 68.5 overs)	147

Bowling
Gibson 20-5-55-0. DeFreitas 17.1-3-49-4. Henderson 32-16-41-4. Hodge 8-3-18-2.
Dagnall 5-0-23-0. Maddy 6-3-19-0. Snape 6-1-18-0.
Gibson 16-5-39-2. Henderson 23.5-10-26-2. Dagnall 7-3-11-1. DeFreitas 16-5-48-2.
Hodge 3-0-7-0. Maddy 3-1-2-1.
Fall of Wickets: 1-28, 2-36, 3-36, 4-59, 5-98, 6-102, 7-154, 8-232, 9-237
1-2, 2-23, 3-35, 4-63, 5-73, 6-90, 7-125, 8-145

Match drawn - Leicestershire (11pts), Yorkshire (8pts)

ESSEX v. DURHAM - at Colchester

DURHAM	First Innings	
JJB Lewis (capt)	st Foster b Danish Kaneria	127
GR Breese	c Adams b Cowan	34
GJ Muchall	c Foster b Cowan	0
MJ North	c Habib b Cowan	7
KJ Coetzer	lbw b Danish Kaneria	29
GM Hamilton	c Middlebrook b Adams	9
*A Pratt	lbw b Danish Kaneria	10
GD Bridge	c Jefferson b Danish Kaneria	26
LE Plunkett	lbw b Middlebrook	7
N Killeen	not out	6
SW Tait	c Adams b Middlebrook	4
Extras	b 3, lb 4, nb 2	9
	(101.5 overs)	268

Bowling
Gough 13-3-34-1. Cowan 21-8-42-2. Adams 25-5-77-1. Danish Kaneria 33-11-70-4.
Middlebrook 9.5-2-38-2.
Fall of Wickets: 1-60, 2-64, 3-77, 4-135, 5-156, 6-169, 7-237, 8-258, 9-258

ESSEX	First Innings	
WI Jefferson	lbw b Breese	134
AP Grayson	c Breese b Bridge	26
A Flower	c Plunkett b Hamilton	72
A Habib	b Bridge	17
RC Irani (capt)	not out	7
*JS Foster	not out	0
JD Middlebrook		
AP Cowan		
AR Adams		
D Gough		
Danish Kaneria		
Extras	lb 8, nb 10	18
	(4 wkts 52 overs)	274

Bowling
Tait 6-0-63-0. Plunkett 11-1-49-0. Killeen 14-4-31-0. Hamilton 9-0-57-1.
Bridge 9-2-49-2. Breese 6-2-17-1.
Fall of Wickets: 1-104, 2-247, 3-254, 4-274

Match drawn - Essex (9pts), Durham (7pts)

Hampshire who gained the maximum reward of 14 win points – but it was mighty close. Indeed, Burns' Somerset, chasing 351, should surely have won the game themselves once they had reached 300 for the loss of just four wickets, but then Warne himself fiddled out John Francis, for 110, and panic set in. Three run outs later, plus a Warne haul of 6 for 127, and Hampshire had won by ten runs. Burns, who played a brave innings of 79 in the thrilling chase, should take his share of the credit for producing such a compelling conclusion to a match which also marked the return from injury of Andrew Caddick, who responded with a first-innings haul of 5 for 97 in his first appearance since June.

Derbyshire were probably feeling quite pleased with themselves when they were able to declare, three balls into the third day, on 400 for 7. Rain had decimated the second day, but they had achieved maximum batting points against the division leaders and neighbourly rivals Nottinghamshire and both Hassan Adnan and Chris Bassano had made excellent hundreds. Adnan's 140, moreover, was a career best and took him past 1,000 runs for the season. Luke Sutton's team, however, were about to feel the full force of Kevin Pietersen's talent – 24 hours after he had been offered a new three-year contract by the club he had all but left following a dressing-room dispute in 2003. At 42 for 2, Notts were looking a little wobbly, but then Pietersen joined Darren Bicknell and the whole tenor of the match quickly changed. By the close they had added 299, with Bicknell still there on 159 and Pietersen having gone for a brilliant 153. It had taken him only 194 balls, had included a six and 21 fours and was his fifth championship century against Derbyshire. The next morning brought no respite for the home attack either. Bicknell moved on to a valiant 175 and Chris Read stroked his way to an unbeaten 90 before Notts declared with a 152-run lead. It was enough – with Greg Smith picking up 5 for 35 and Andrew Harris adding another 4 for 22 to his first-innings four-wicket haul, Derbyshire slid ignominiously to 96 all out and defeat by an innings and 56 runs. There were still more than 20 overs left to be bowled, too, just to add to Derbyshire's humbling experience.

Kevin Pietersen, who hit a brilliant 153 against Derbyshire after being offered a new three-year contract by Nottinghamshire.

Leicestershire captain Brad Hodge paid the price for declaring his side's second innings too late when Yorkshire managed to limp to a draw at 147 for 8 at Grace Road. The home side's lead was over 300 before Hodge finally decided to have a go at the visitors. They had soon slipped to 90 for 6, but Ismael Dawood held on determinedly for an unbeaten 42 and Richard Dawson, who had made 76 the previous day, also occupied the crease for an important period of time. The match had begun with Darren Robinson plundering some wayward Yorkshire seam bowling on his way to 154, his first hundred for Leicestershire, while Phil DeFreitas and Claude Henderson combined to keep the home side on top following a rain-ravaged second day.

The outfield at Colchester's Castle Park could not cope with a succession of heavy downpours both before and during Essex's match against Durham. No play at all was possible on days two and four and, in the cricket that was played before the match was abandoned as a draw, Jon Lewis made a resolute, if occasionally strokeless, century against his former county, while both Will Jefferson and Andy Flower emphasised the growing gulf between the top and bottom halves of Division Two by thrashing the Durham attack to all corners

of the ground in a stand of 143 in just 21 overs. Jefferson's hundred took him only 112 balls and he hit 17 fours, and Flower twice hit left-arm spinner Graeme Bridge for six in his own classy innings of 72.

Round 17: 24–27 August 2004

Division One

With a great deal of help from the weather, Warwickshire held off the determined challenge of holders Sussex at Edgbaston to grab the draw which, in effect, confirmed the championship's succession. Tony Frost and Heath Streak, Warwickshire's eighth-wicket pair, defied an increasingly weary and frustrated Mushtaq Ahmed – and the rest of the Sussex attack – for 28 overs and two hours. It was the partnership that clinched Warwickshire's successful, if weakening, defence of the sizeable lead they had built up in the first half of the summer. The draw meant that Nick Knight's team were left requiring only a further 20 points (and probably less) from their last two matches to be sure of the title; Sussex, finishing the strongest of all of the Division One sides, were denied a victory that would have taken them to within

Round 17: 24–27 August 2004 Division One

WARWICKSHIRE v. SUSSEX - at Edgbaston

WARWICKSHIRE	First Innings			Second Innings	
NV Knight (capt)	c Ward b Akram	65		b Mushtaq Ahmed	23
MA Wagh	c Ward b Akram	6		b Kirtley	0
IR Bell	b Kirtley	87		b Akram	6
IJL Trott	b Martin-Jenkins	90		c Goodwin b Akram	0
MJ Powell	c Prior b Akram	5		lbw b Akram	39
JO Troughton	c Martin-Jenkins b Kirtley	2		c Davis b Martin-Jenkins	33
DR Brown	c Adams b Martin-Jenkins	12		c Prior b Mushtaq Ahmed	14
*T Frost	lbw b Mushtaq Ahmed	48		not out	45
HH Streak	c Goodwin b Martin-Jenkins	2		not out	27
N Tahir	not out	3			
D Pretorius	lbw b Martin-Jenkins	14			
Extras	b 2, lb 6, nb 4	12		b 4, lb 9, p 5	18
	(120 overs)	346		(7 wkts 89 overs)	205

Bowling
Akram 27-5-94-3. Kirtley 32-7-75-2. Mushtaq Ahmed 27-3-74-1. Martin-Jenkins 21-5-62-4. Davis 13-0-33-0.
Akram 20-6-45-3. Kirtley 21-5-68-1. Martin-Jenkins 14-6-20-1. Mushtaq Ahmed 31-13-52-2. Davis 3-2-2-0.
Fall of Wickets: 1-11, 2-141, 3-184, 4-195, 5-198, 6-226, 7-325, 8-327, 9-330 1-6, 2-15, 3-15, 4-66, 5-98, 6-121, 7-132

SUSSEX	First Innings	
IJ Ward	lbw b Tahir	34
RR Montgomerie	lbw b Streak	78
PA Cottey	run out	30
MW Goodwin	lbw b Streak	75
CJ Adams (capt)	c Trott b Pretorius	7
*MJ Prior	b Bell	95
RSC Martin-Jenkins	c Frost b Tahir	26
MJG Davis	c Frost b Tahir	8
Mushtaq Ahmed	c Tahir b Pretorius	21
RJ Kirtley	not out	53
M Akram	not out	35
Extras	b 6, lb 14	20
	(9 wkts dec 143 overs)	482

Bowling
Streak 31-8-92-2. Pretorius 22-1-99-2. Brown 26-8-71-0. Tahir 24-4-81-3. Bell 24-4-57-1. Troughton 10-3-29-0. Powell 1-0-15-0. Wagh 5-0-23-0.
Fall of Wickets: 1-106, 2-135, 3-181, 4-190, 5-293, 6-343, 7-363, 8-372, 9-412

Match drawn - Warwickshire (10pts), Sussex (12pts)

NORTHANTS v. GLOUCESTERSHIRE - at Northampton

NORTHANTS	First Innings			Second Innings	
TW Roberts	b Lewis	7		c Adshead b Lewis	33
JW Cook	c Hussey b Averis	2		c Adshead b Sillence	23
TB Huggins	lbw b Averis	0		c Spearman b Ball	45
U Afzaal	c Adshead b Lewis	96		not out	100
DJG Sales (capt)	c Fisher b Sillence	10		not out	82
*GL Brophy	c Lewis b Fisher	34			
GP Swann	c Averis b Fisher	29			
J Louw	c Hussey b Fisher	13			
BJ Phillips	c Adshead b Averis	1			
PC Rofe	not out	0			
JF Brown	c Adshead b Lewis	0			
Extras	b 3, lb 8, w 1, nb 18	30		b 5, lb 9, nb 10	24
	(95.4 overs)	222		(3 wkts dec 76 overs)	307

Bowling
Lewis 23.2-7-64-3. Averis 13-7-25-3. Sillence 14-4-33-1. Gidman 2.2-1-5-0. Fisher 31-11-63-3. Hussey 2-1-6-0. Ball 10-3-15-0.
Lewis 12-0-62-1. Averis 18-1-84-0. Sillence 7-3-19-1. Fisher 16-2-55-0. Gidman 11-3-33-0. Ball 12-2-40-1.
Fall of Wickets: 1-14, 2-14, 3-24, 4-45, 5-133, 6-190, 7-216, 8-222, 9-222 1-56, 2-64, 3-166

GLOS	First Innings			Second Innings	
WPC Weston	lbw b Swann	2		(2) c Sales b Louw	6
CM Spearman	c Brophy b Louw	20		(1) c Afzaal b Brown	69
MEK Hussey	c Sales b Cook	78		not out	49
CG Taylor (capt)	c Huggins b Phillips	20		c Brophy b Brown	2
*SJ Adshead	c Swann b Louw	6		(6) not out	13
ID Fisher	lbw b Brown	17			
JMM Averis	c Bt b Brown	23			
APR Gidman	c Brophy b Cook	1		(5) lbw b Swann	13
RJ Sillence	c Brophy b Cook	4			
MCJ Ball	not out	31			
J Lewis	c Brophy b Phillips	29			
Extras	lb 3, nb 6	9		b 3, lb 1, nb 4	8
	(92.2 overs)	240		(4 wkts 62 overs)	160

Bowling
Louw 27-4-90-3. Rofe 17-4-58-0. Phillips 21.2-11-32-2. Cook 12-4-42-3. Brown 14-8-14-2. Swann 9-2-14-1. Cook 1-1-0-0.
Louw 11-1-35-1. Rofe 11-6-20-0. Phillips 7-1-37-0. Brown 23-4-50-2. Swann 9-2-14-1. Cook 1-1-0-0.
Fall of Wickets: 1-12, 2-29, 3-79, 4-92, 5-123, 6-171, 7-176, 8-180, 9-185 1-33, 2-96, 3-105, 4-138

Match drawn - Northamptonshire (8pts), Gloucestershire (8pts)

LANCASHIRE v. KENT - at Old Trafford

KENT	First Innings			Second Innings	
DP Fulton (capt)	c Sutcliffe b Chapple	18		c Haynes b Chapple	0
RWT Key	lbw b Mahmood	52		st Haynes b Keedy	18
ET Smith	c Haynes b Chapple	0		not out	35
AGR Loudon	c Mongia b Keedy	45		lbw b Mongia	34
MJ Walker	c Haynes b Hooper	61			
*NJ O'Brien	lbw b Keedy	19			
MJ Dennington	c Haynes b Keedy	15			
A Khan	lbw b Keedy	0			
MM Patel	c Hooper b Cork	17			
IG Butler	b Cork	9			
RH Joseph	not out	7			
Extras	b 2, lb 6, w 1, nb 4	13		lb 3, nb 2	5
	(75 overs)	266		(3 wkts 33.1 overs)	92

Bowling
Martin 15-6-41-0. Chapple 16-3-79-2. Cork 11-3-18-2. Mahmood 8-0-45-1. Keedy 21-4-62-4. Hooper 4-1-13-1.
Chapple 5-0-18-1. Mahmood 6-0-20-0. Keedy 11-1-30-1. Cork 2-0-4-0. Hooper 6-0-16-0. Mongia 1.1-0-1-1.
Fall of Wickets: 1-34, 2-34, 3-92, 4-162, 5-195, 6-213, 7-218, 8-229, 9-237 1-0, 2-32, 3-92

LANCASHIRE	First Innings	
MJ Chilton	c Fulton b Patel	26
IJ Sutcliffe	b Butler	5
MB Loye	b Patel	4
D Mongia	c Bt b Dennington	41
CL Hooper (capt)	lbw b Patel	0
*JJ Haynes	c Dennington b Joseph	2
G Chapple	c Fulton b Joseph	18
DG Cork	b Joseph	28
SI Mahmood	c Loudon b Butler	10
PJ Martin	not out	33
G Keedy	c Joseph b Butler	2
Extras	b 5, lb 6, nb 6	17
	(52.3 overs)	184

Bowling
Butler 6.3-2-10-3. Joseph 15-1-70-3. Khan 6-1-32-0. Patel 20-4-51-3. Loudon 3-0-31-0. Dennington 2-0-10-1.
Fall of Wickets: 1-23, 2-38, 3-47, 4-47, 5-50, 6-84, 7-130, 8-134, 9-174

Match drawn - Lancashire (7pts), Kent (9pts)

Usman Afzaal did his best to set up a Northamptonshire victory with scores of 96 and 100 not out at Wantage Road, but Gloucestershire refused to go for a final afternoon run chase.

33 points of Warwickshire, and with a game in hand over them. In the 60 overs possible on the opening day, Warwickshire reached 177 for 2 with Knight making 65 and Ian Bell continuing his remarkable run of form to score an unbeaten 84. He added just three more runs the next morning, however, and Warwickshire needed a seventh-wicket stand of 99 between Jon Trott (90) and Frost (48) to haul them up to 346. Sussex, initially through Richard Montgomerie's 78, then the middle-order strokeplay of Murray Goodwin (75) and Matthew Prior (95), and finally an unbroken tenth-wicket alliance of 70 between James Kirtley and Mohammad Akram, built a lead of 136. Time was running out, but it was enough to put the home side under pressure. Kirtley further yanked up the pressure by quickly yorking Mark Wagh to seize his 500th first-class wicket and, with Mushtaq bowling like a cricketing whirling dervish, Warwickshire were soon staring defeat in the face. They slumped to 98 for 5 and, when Streak joined the underrated Frost, they were still four runs behind. At last, though, a Warwickshire partnership held firm and Mushtaq's screeching appeals went unanswered.

Sussex captain Chris Adams called it a day with seven overs still remaining.

Gloucestershire, clearly with more than one eye on their rematch with Worcestershire in the following day's Cheltenham & Gloucester Trophy final at Lord's, declined to accept Northamptonshire's run chase offer of scoring 290 on the final afternoon at Wantage Road. Craig Spearman, ever-positive, was tempted enough to hit 69 from 81 balls but, when he was out with the score on 96 for 2 in the 25th over, Gloucestershire shut up shop. Mike Hussey added 49 not out to his first-innings 78 to frustrate his former county, although Northants fans did have the pleasure of watching Usman Afzaal score 96 and 100 not out, while David Sales thumped two sixes and seven fours to race to 82 not out from 93 balls early on the final day. Kepler Wessels, the Northants cricket manager, also signed a new three-year contract during this game and was left wondering if his side could have forced a victory if Jon Lewis, on his 29th birthday, and Martyn Ball had not held them up with a last-wicket stand of 55 midway through the third day.

Lancashire's relegation fears intensified during a rain-ruined match against Kent at Old Trafford. Just 6.3 overs were bowled on the first two days, with the second day a complete washout, and Lancashire's batting looked bereft of confidence when they slid to 184 all out in reply to Kent's less-than-convincing 266.

Division Two

All three games in this division were ravaged by the heavy storms sweeping across Britain, although Durham's highly promising England Under 19 all-rounder Liam Plunkett did have time to record a career-best 6 for 74 against Shane Warne's Hampshire at the Riverside. Four of his wickets came in an eight-over new-ball spell as Hampshire initially crumbled to 50 for 5 by the end of the third day (effectively, the first) in reply to Durham's first innings of 217. However, Dimitri Mascarenhas, with a fine hundred, led a recovery that also featured valuable contributions from Nic Pothas and Warne himself and resulted in a 63-run lead for the visitors.

The first, second and fourth days were washed away at both Colwyn Bay and Derby. The abandonment of Glamorgan's game against Yorkshire confirmed that Nottinghamshire became the first team to be promoted to Division One, while in the mere 43 overs that were possible on day three at the Racecourse Ground, there was at least a half-century for 22-year-old opener Ben France to celebrate in only his second championship appearance.

Round 17: 24–27 August 2004 Division Two

DURHAM v. HAMPSHIRE – at The Riverside

DURHAM	First Innings		Second Innings	
JJB Lewis (capt)	b Adams	29	lbw b Mascarenhas	37
GR Breese	c Pothas b Mascarenhas	6	lbw b Bruce	6
GJ Muchall	lbw b Warne	47	c Pothas b Mascarenhas	4
MJ North	c and b Mascarenhas	0	not out	23
KJ Coetzer	c Taylor b Adams	6	c Pothas b Warne	12
GM Hamilton	c Adams b Mascarenhas	25	not out	9
*P Mustard	st Pothas b Warne	7		
GD Bridge	not out	51		
LE Plunkett	b Udal	14		
N Killeen	c Kenway b Warne	0		
G Onions	b Udal	11		
Extras	b 7, lb 5, w 1, nb 8	21	lb 2, nb 16	18
	(76.1 overs)	**217**	(4 wkts 29 overs)	**109**

Bowling
Taylor 12-5-28-0. Bruce 6-1-33-0. Mascarenhas 21-5-48-3. Adams 8-4-16-2. Udal 8.1-0-27-2. Warne 21-8-53-3.
Taylor 6-1-26-0. Bruce 5-0-27-1. Mascarenhas 9-4-21-2. Adams 2-0-10-0. Warne 7-1-23-1.
Fall of Wickets: 1-26, 2-56, 3-57, 4-68, 5-107, 6-119, 7-147, 8-193, 9-196
1-42, 2-64, 3-75, 4-94

HAMPSHIRE	First Innings	
JHK Adams	c Breese b Plunkett	16
MJ Brown	lbw b Killeen	0
JP Crawley	c Mustard b Plunkett	1
SM Katich	c Mustard b Plunkett	27
DA Kenway	c Mustard b Plunkett	0
*N Pothas	b Hamilton	54
AD Mascarenhas	b Bridge	104
SK Warne (capt)	c Breese b Plunkett	41
SD Udal	b Plunkett	0
BV Taylor	not out	17
JTA Bruce	b Bridge	0
Extras	b 6, lb 6, nb 8	20
	(66 overs)	**280**

Bowling
Plunkett 20-1-74-6. Killeen 14-3-64-1. Onions 5-0-46-0. Hamilton 7-0-26-1. Bridge 20-5-58-2.
Fall of Wickets: 1-4, 2-7, 3-32, 4-36, 5-49, 6-136, 7-210, 8-210, 9-280

Match drawn – Durham (8pts), Hampshire (9pts)

GLAMORGAN v. YORKSHIRE – at Colwyn Bay

YORKSHIRE	FIRST INNINGS	
MJ Wood (capt)	c Wallace b Lewis	5
PA Jaques	lbw b Thomas	21
A McGrath	c Maynard b Jones	46
JJ Sayers	c Powell b Harrison	18
RM Pyrah	not out	25
VJ Craven	c Wallace b Harrison	10
*I Dawood	not out	11
RKJ Dawson		
JAR Blain		
TT Bresnan		
SP Kirby		
Extras	b 4, lb 1, w 1, nb 16	22
	(5 wkts 51 overs)	**158**

Bowling
Harrison 12-5-36-2. Lewis 7-0-25-1. Thomas 10-2-24-1. Jones 9-1-49-1. Croft 10-5-11-0. Maynard 3-0-8-0.
Fall of Wickets: 1-9, 2-61, 3-96, 4-131, 5-145

GLAMORGAN		
MTG Elliott		
*MA Wallace		
DL Hemp		
MJ Powell		
MP Maynard		
J Hughes		
RDB Croft (capt)		
SD Thomas		
ML Lewis		
DS Harrison		
SP Jones		

Match drawn – Glamorgan (5pts), Yorkshire (4pts)

DERBYSHIRE v. LEICESTERSHIRE – at Derby

DERBYSHIRE	First Innings	
SD Stubbings	b Gibson	0
BJ France	c Maddy b Henderson	56
JDC Bryant	st New b Hodge	25
Hassan Adnan	not out	30
J Moss	not out	13
CWG Bassano		
*LD Sutton (capt)		
G Welch		
MA Sheikh		
CD Paget		
NGE Walker		
Extras	lb 5, w 7, nb 2	14
	(3 wkts 43 overs)	**138**

Bowling
Gibson 6-3-10-1. Dagnall 7-2-19-0. Cleary 2-0-17-0. DeFreitas 7.4-2-19-0. Maddy 2-0-16-0. Hodge 5-2-13-1. Henderson 9-2-25-1. Snape 4.2-1-14-0.
Fall of Wickets: 1-0, 2-78, 3-103

LEICESTERSHIRE		
DDJ Robinson		
DL Maddy		
BJ Hodge (capt)		
DI Stevens		
JN Snape		
*TJ New		
OD Gibson		
PAJ DeFreitas		
MF Cleary		
CW Henderson		
CE Dagnall		

Match drawn – Derbyshire (4pts), Leicestershire (5pts)

Round 18:
31 August–7 September 2004

Division One

Surrey continued their march up the championship table by beating Lancashire by 147 runs at Old Trafford and in the process pushed the home side nearer to relegation. On a pitch that, by the end, was very spin-friendly, Lancashire collapsed to 129 all out as Nayan Doshi celebrated an 11-wicket match haul and the second of his first two five-wicket hauls for Surrey. The left-arm spinner was well supported on the third afternoon by Jimmy Ormond, bowling in his off-cutters role. Earlier in the day, on which 20 wickets fell, Surrey slid to 185 all out in their own second innings, with Gary Keedy and Carl Hooper the successful spin pairing. The man who set up the Surrey victory, however, was Alistair Brown – and in reaching a brilliant 154, he completed his full set of first-class hundreds against the 17 other counties. Fast bowler Sajid Mahmood had produced beauties to dismiss both Mark Butcher and Mark Ramprakash and, at 225 for 7, Surrey were in danger of wasting the opportunity given to them by batting first. Then Tim Murtagh arrived at the crease to give Brown the sort of support he wanted and, by the close, the pair had put on 121. Only three more runs were added the next morning before Murtagh fell for 65, but Surrey's total had been boosted up to 369 by the time that Brown was lbw to Mahmood for 154. Lancashire's first innings struggled to 278, thanks in the main to a 114-run sixth-wicket stand between Chris Schofield and Glen Chapple, but Doshi's 5 for 125, backed up earlier good work by Martin Bicknell, put Surrey firmly in control of the game.

Kent bullied bottom club Northamptonshire into a 194-run defeat at Canterbury, despite losing both Matt Dennington and Niall O'Brien to injury on the opening day. Dennington had his right hand broken by a ball from Johann Louw, who also forced O'Brien to retire hurt needing seven stitches in a cut over his right eye after the Kent wicketkeeper had been struck by another short delivery. Richard Piesley, the Kent Academy keeper, deputised for the rest of the match, but Kent also had to operate with an attack missing its fourth seamer. That they did so successfully was largely down to the promise of two of their youngest bowlers – 19-year-old Simon Cusden and 22-year-old Rob Joseph – and the long-overdue return to form of Amjad Khan. A blitz by the Kent top order on the opening day also left

Northants reeling, and must have contributed to their first-innings decline to 151 all out, in which Khan took 4 for 47 and both Joseph and Cusden snapped up two wickets. Kent had declared their own first innings on 414 for 8 just 15 balls into the second day, due to the absence through injury of both Dennington and O'Brien, and by then had already fully justified the decision to leave out Michael Bevan, their out-of-sorts overseas batsman. David Fulton and Rob Key had opened up with a sparkling partnership of 118, and then Key was joined by the equally assertive and even more elegant Ed Smith in a second-wicket stand worth 142. Key's seventh first-class hundred of the season had taken him just 118 balls, while Smith's 70 had occupied only 88 balls. As Kent romped to 409 for 7 by the close, Alex Loudon and Matthew Walker both hit further half-centuries as 131 more runs were added for the fourth wicket. More was to come from Kent's batsmen, especially Smith, after Northants' first-innings collapse. Fulton opted not to enforce the follow-on, and Smith stroked his way

With his future at the club in doubt, Ed Smith spearheaded Kent's win over Northamptonshire with scores of 70 and 156.

to a wonderful 156, from 216 balls, while hitting three sixes and 19 fours. An eventual declaration at 318 for 5 set Northants 582 to win and, initially, they made a good fist of it. Jeff Cook's first championship hundred for four years propelled them to 281 for 3 by the end of the third day, but Kent's attack roused themselves following a good night's sleep to close out the game by lunchtime. David Sales, the last man out for 92, provided the only real resistance, but Cusden's career-best 4 for 68 was a particularly worthy performance.

The class of Middlesex's Owais Shah ultimately decided a peculiar sort of game at Hove, where Sussex had looked like being comfortable winners for long periods of the match. In the end, though, Shah's fourth championship hundred in six matches prevented even the leg-spin genius of Mushtaq Ahmed from pulling the match out of the fire for Sussex. The champions had only themselves to blame, as they collapsed to 141 in their second innings in which only Mushtaq emerged with credit. Coming in at 68 for 7, he thumped a merry unbeaten 49 to ensure that Middlesex at least had to make the highest score of the game to win. Starting the day at 4 for 1, with the unhappy Ben Hutton already dismissed by James Kirtley, Middlesex soon lost nightwatchman Chris Peploe, but Sven Koenig hung on grimly against Mushtaq and Shah began to play with massive certainty and maturity at the other end. When Koenig finally fell

to his tormentor, toe-ending a sweep, and Ed Joyce was also beaten, Paul Weekes arrived to lend a calm hand. Mushtaq and Kirtley had previously destroyed the Middlesex first innings for 135, at

Round 18: 31 August–7 September 2004 Division One

LANCASHIRE v. SURREY - at Old Trafford

SURREY	First Innings		Second Innings	
SA Newman	lbw b Keedy	17	lbw b Hooper	8
RS Clinton	b Chapple	4	c Mahmood b Hooper	35
MA Butcher	c Hegg b Mahmood	30	lbw b Keedy	33
MR Ramprakash	lbw b Mahmood	3	c Hooper b Keedy	0
*JN Batty (capt)	c Chapple b Hooper	36	c Sutcliffe b Keedy	3
AD Brown	lbw b Mahmood	154	b Hooper	58
Azhar Mahmood	c Clark b Keedy	18	not out	14
MP Bicknell	b Mahmood	14	lbw b Keedy	2
TJ Murtagh	c Hooper b Cork	65	c Law b Hooper	17
J Ormond	not out	4	c Cork b Keedy	1
ND Doshi	c Loye b Keedy	4	c Law b Keedy	2
Extras	b 7, lb 13	20	b 6, lb 6	12
	(130.4 overs)	369	(63.2 overs)	185

Bowling
Chapple 16-3-46-1. Cork 16-4-37-1. Mahmood 20-4-59-4. Keedy 44.4-7-112-3. Hooper 25-3-66-1. Schofield 9-2-29-0.
Mahmood 5-0-22-0. Keedy 31.2-7-95-6. Hooper 27-8-56-4.
Fall of Wickets: 1-11, 2-50, 3-58, 4-58, 5-177, 6-206, 7-225, 8-349, 9-362
1-12, 2-69, 3-69, 4-105, 5-105, 6-111, 7-115, 8-162, 9-167

LANCASHIRE	First Innings		Second Innings	
MJ Chilton	lbw b Bicknell	6	c Murtagh b Doshi	21
IJ Sutcliffe	c Clinton b Doshi	6	c Batty b Doshi	11
MB Loye	b Ormond	54	b Doshi	9
SG Law	c Batty b Doshi	34	lbw b Doshi	24
CL Hooper	st Batty b Doshi	0	c Azhar Mahmood b Doshi	10
CP Schofield	st Batty b Doshi	65	c Batty b Ormond	4
G Chapple	c Batty b Bicknell	67	st Batty b Ormond	8
DG Cork	b Bicknell	0	c Clinton b Ormond	3
*WK Hegg (capt)	st Batty b Doshi	18	not out	17
SI Mahmood	not out	11	st Batty b Doshi	4
G Keedy	c Batty b Azhar Mahmood	4	b Ormond	17
Extras	b 2, lb 9, nb 2	13	b 5, lb 4	9
	(81 overs)	278	(40.5 overs)	129

Bowling
Bicknell 15-4-38-3. Ormond 15-4-47-1. Azhar Mahmood 18-4-56-1.
Doshi 31-6-125-5. Ramprakash 2-1-1-0.
Bicknell 7-1-19-0. Doshi 20-3-57-6. Azhar Mahmood 7-0-22-0. Ormond 6.5-1-22-4.
Fall of Wickets: 1-8, 2-28, 3-100, 4-100, 5-112, 6-226, 7-226, 8-258, 9-261
1-22, 2-24, 3-45, 4-66, 5-75, 6-85, 7-90, 8-99, 9-104

Surrey won by 147 runs - Lancashire (5pts),
Surrey (21pts)

KENT v. NORTHAMPTONSHIRE - at Canterbury

KENT	First Innings		Second Innings	
DP Fulton (capt)	c Sales b Rofe	57	b Phillips	39
RWT Key	c Louw b Swann	131	c Brophy b Louw	17
ET Smith	c Roberts b Phillips	70	lbw b Louw	156
AGR Loudon	c Swann b Louw	60	b Cook	51
MJ Walker	c Swann b Louw	63	b Rofe	34
*NJ O'Brien	retired hurt	10		
MJ Dennington	retired hurt	1		
MM Patel	b Phillips	1	(6) not out	9
A Khan	lbw b Louw	3		
RH Joseph	c Cook b Louw	0		
SMJ Cusden	not out	5		
Extras	nb 4	13	b 5, lb 5, nb 2	12
	(8 wkts dec 105.5 overs)	414	(5 wkts dec 75.4 overs)	318

Bowling
Louw 22.5-4-92-4. Rofe 19-2-78-1. Jones 11-1-67-0. Phillips 21-9-58-2.
Swann 21-2-65-1. Cook 7-0-45-0.
Louw 9.4-0-66-2. Rofe 11-1-48-1. Phillips 9-1-21-1. Jones 14-0-66-0.
Swann 14-3-41-0. Cook 18-1-66-1.
Fall of Wickets: 1-118, 2-260, 3-262, 4-393, 5-400, 6-409, 7-409, 8-414, 9-414
1-29, 2-95, 3-184, 4-292, 5-318

NORTHANTS	First Innings		Second Innings	
TW Roberts	b Cusden	16	b Khan	0
JW Cook	b Khan	4	(3) b Loudon	114
TB Huggins	c sub b Joseph	1	(2) c Cusden b Joseph	44
U Afzaal	b Khan	34	lbw b Patel	41
DJG Sales (capt)	lbw b Walker	3	c Key b Cusden	92
*GL Brophy	lbw b Khan	10	lbw b Khan	20
GP Swann	b Khan	16	c sub b Joseph	9
J Louw	c Fulton b Joseph	1	(9) c sub b Cusden	0
BJ Phillips	b Cusden	12	(8) b Cusden	4
PS Jones	c sub b Patel	37	b Cusden	4
PC Rofe	not out	0	not out	15
Extras	lb 3, w 2, nb 12	17	b 10, lb 12, w 12, nb 10	44
	(44.1 overs)	151	(111.3 overs)	387

Bowling
Joseph 13-6-38-2. Khan 11-3-47-4. Cusden 8-3-18-2. Walker 7-2-24-1.
Patel 5.1-1-21-1.
Joseph 22-4-71-2. Khan 16-2-53-2. Patel 33-8-102-1. Cusden 15.3-3-68-4.
Walker 7-0-24-0. Loudon 18-3-47-1.
Fall of Wickets: 1-6, 2-25, 3-27, 4-45, 5-58, 6-92, 7-99, 8-106, 9-151
1-1, 2-162, 3-223, 4-284, 5-315, 6-330, 7-334, 8-334, 9-344

Kent won by 194 runs - Kent (22pts), Northamptonshire (2pts)

SUSSEX v. MIDDLESEX - at Hove

SUSSEX	First Innings		Second Innings	
IJ Ward	b Hayward	3	lbw b Cook	0
RR Montgomerie	c Shah b Hayward	40	c Shah b Clark	12
PA Cottey	lbw b Clark	23	c Scott b Cook	12
MW Goodwin	c Joyce b Weekes	5	b Clark	16
CJ Adams (capt)	b Clark	26	b Clark	25
*MJ Prior	c Dalrymple b Peploe	11	c Shah b Peploe	12
MH Yardy	c Hutton b Peploe	11	lbw b Weekes	3
RSC Martin-Jenkins	not out	64	c Shah b Peploe	0
Mushtaq Ahmed	c Peploe b Weekes	48	not out	49
RJ Kirtley	c Joyce b Peploe	3	b Hayward	15
M Akram	c Hayward b Peploe	18	lbw b Weekes	7
Extras	b 6, lb 5, w 3, nb 6, p 5	25	nb 2	2
	(86.3 overs)	277	(57.4 overs)	141

Bowling
Cook 16-4-46-0. Hayward 17-5-59-2. Clark 21-5-46-2. Hutton 4-0-16-0.
Peploe 18.3-4-65-4. Weekes 10-3-29-2.
Cook 14-3-38-2. Hayward 12-3-20-1. Clark 10-1-28-3. Peploe 15-6-41-2.
Weekes 6.4-1-14-2.
Fall of Wickets: 1-3, 2-56, 3-70, 4-84, 5-97, 6-129, 7-129, 8-213, 9-239
1-0, 2-0, 3-24, 4-31, 5-58, 6-67, 7-68, 8-94, 9-132

MIDDLESEX	First Innings		Second Innings	
BL Hutton	lbw b Akram	0	lbw b Kirtley	0
SG Koenig	lbw b Mushtaq Ahmed	26	c Cottey b Mushtaq Ahmed	49
OA Shah	c Mushtaq Ahmed b Kirtley	4	(4) lbw b Mushtaq Ahmed	108
EC Joyce (capt)	lbw b Martin-Jenkins	12	(5) c Prior b Martin-Jenkins	18
PN Weekes	b Kirtley	19	(6) not out	50
CT Peploe	c and b Mushtaq Ahmed	16	(3) lbw b Mushtaq Ahmed	7
JWM Dalrymple	not out	39	not out	14
*BJM Scott	c Cottey b Mushtaq Ahmed	5		
SJ Cook	b Mushtaq Ahmed	5		
SR Clark	c Mushtaq Ahmed b Kirtley	1		
M Hayward	b Kirtley	9		
Extras	b 1, lb 2	3	b 12, lb 17, w 8, nb 2	39
	(51.3 overs)	135	(5 wkts 90.3 overs)	285

Bowling
Akram 1-0-4-1. Kirtley 18.3-7-32-4. Martin-Jenkins 11-3-30-1.
Mushtaq Ahmed 21-5-66-4.
Kirtley 20-7-34-1. Martin-Jenkins 15.3-6-29-1. Mushtaq Ahmed 37-5-137-3.
Akram 9-1-33-0. Yardy 9-2-23-0.
Fall of Wickets: 1-0, 2-5, 3-8, 4-31, 5-64, 6-75, 7-75, 8-87, 9-114
1-0, 2-17, 3-113, 4-176, 5-259

Middlesex won by 5 wickets - Sussex (5pts), Middlesex (17pts)

WORCESTERSHIRE v. WARWICKSHIRE - at Worcester

WARWICKSHIRE	First Innings		Second Innings	
NV Knight (capt)	c Smith b Price	37	c Hick b Price	39
MA Wagh	c Peters b Bichel	15	b Price	69
IR Bell	c Hick b Price	54	c Kadeer Ali b Price	17
IJL Trott	c Smith b Mason	63	(5) c Rhodes b Hall	51
MJ Powell	c Price b Malik	69	(6) b Malik	43
JO Troughton	c Rhodes b Malik	64	(7) c Rhodes b Price	6
DR Brown	c Hall b Bichel	3	(8) not out	27
N Tahir	c Rhodes b Bichel	49	(4) b Hick	0
*T Frost	lbw b Bichel	19	c Hall b Malik	20
HH Streak	not out	30		
NM Carter	b Hall	13	(10) not out	1
Extras	b 10, lb 19, w 9, nb 6	44	b 4, lb 5, w 1	10
	(159 overs)	460	(8 wkts dec 83 overs)	254

Bowling
Mason 33-10-84-1. Bichel 29-5-108-4. Hall 24-7-74-1. Malik 13-6-68-2.
Price 56-24-95-2. Kadeer Ali 1-0-2-0.
Mason 12-4-36-0. Bichel 11-1-47-0. Malik 13-1-54-2. Price 35-9-83-4.
Hick 2-1-1-1. Hall 10-1-24-1.
Fall of Wickets: 1-26, 2-108, 3-117, 4-248, 5-271, 6-274, 7-388, 8-409, 9-426
1-66, 2-93, 3-94, 4-108, 5-186, 6-193, 7-213, 8-243

WORCS	First Innings		Second Innings	
SD Peters	lbw b Streak	19	c Troughton b Streak	9
SC Moore	lbw b Brown	0	not out	83
GA Hick	b Brown	93	not out	56
BF Smith	c Powell b Streak	2		
Kadeer Ali	c Frost b Brown	66		
AJ Bichel	c Frost b Troughton	36		
*SJ Rhodes (capt)	not out	44		
RW Price	b Brown	32		
MS Mason	b Streak	63		
MN Malik	b Streak	0		
Extras	b 8, lb 14, nb 13	35	lb 1, w 1, nb 6	8
	(123.2 overs)	416	(1 wkt 29 overs)	156

Bowling
Streak 29.2-8-81-4. Brown 32-3-89-5. Tahir 8-0-48-0. Wagh 7-2-11-0.
Carter 20-2-71-0. Troughton 25-6-76-1. Bell 2-0-18-0.
Streak 7-0-20-1. Brown 4-0-20-0. Tahir 2-0-16-0. Carter 3-0-35-0.
Troughton 6-0-21-0. Wagh 6-1-33-0. Trott 1-0-10-0.
Fall of Wickets: 1-12, 2-30, 3-38, 4-195, 5-202, 6-254, 7-286, 8-322, 9-410
1-14

Match drawn - Worcestershire (11pts), Warwickshire (11pts)

which point Sussex looked odds-on favourites after counter-attacking batting from Robin Martin-Jenkins (64) and Mushtaq (48) had helped to boost their faltering first innings up to a respectable 277.

Nick Knight knew what he had to do on the final day of a hard-fought West Midlands derby against Worcestershire at New Road: given the choice of giving the hosts the chance of a run chase or settling for the four extra points available from the draw, he chose the draw. And why not? With Worcestershire ending up at 156 for 1, after being asked to score an unrealistic 299 from 38 overs, Knight's Warwickshire edged ever closer to the championship title with the 11 points they gathered up from this game. Worcestershire's only real chance, on the final day, was to finish off a Warwickshire second innings that looked a little vulnerable at 94 for 3 overnight, but Jonathan Trott scored his second half-century of the game as Ray Price wheeled away from one end and the draw was made certain long before Knight's eventual declaration with the score on 254 for 8. Batting first for the 11th time in 15 matches, Warwickshire had earlier begun the match by passing 400, also for the 11th time in the summer. Michael Powell's 69 was the top score, testimony to the all-round strength of an order in which players as capable as Heath Streak and Neil Carter came in at Nos. 10 and 11. Dougie Brown and Streak then ensured maximum bowling points, despite Worcestershire reaching 416 themselves thanks to a stand of 157 between Graeme Hick and Kadeer Ali and some big hitting at the end of the innings by Matt Mason, who included three sixes in his 63.

Division Two

One of the most remarkable championship matches in history ended with Glamorgan beating Essex by four wickets at Chelmsford, with 22 balls to spare, to take themselves to the brink of promotion. Essex, who had begun the game 24.5 points behind their third-placed opponents, were left shell-shocked. Ronnie Irani's team might take a while to acknowledge it, given the manner of their defeat, but that such a result was even possible was a huge vindication of the four-day game. The bare facts are that Essex, batting first, ran up a massive 642 – and still lost. It was, unsurprisingly, the highest score ever made by a first-class side that has gone on to lose, but tremendous credit should also be given to the fighting spirit of Glamorgan, and their captain Robert Croft. Will Jefferson was bowled by the third ball of the match, earning David Harrison

his 50th wicket of the season, but then Paul Grayson and Andy Flower built the base of Essex's total with a second-wicket stand of 122. Flower went on to score 119, adding a further 146 with Irani, but the Glamorgan attack began to feel real pressure when Irani was joined by James Foster. They added 167 runs from the last 29 overs of the opening day, taking the Essex score on to 445 for 4, and by then Irani was on 145 and Foster already on 95 not out. Their stand eventually realised 210, before Irani fell for 164, but Foster – supported by a quick 50 from Graham Napier – blazed his way on to 188 before being the last man out. It was an eye-catching innings, from 284 balls and with three sixes and 27 fours, and it underlined his claims for an England recall should anything happen to Geraint Jones. Croft's figures of 3 for 203 were the most expensive in Glamorgan history, but the off spinner never shirked his workload and – when Glamorgan replied – he steeled himself to exact retribution. The chance came when he walked out to bat at No. 9, with Danish Kaneria threatening to

Crafty Crofty: the Glamorgan captain inspired his side to an astonishing comeback victory against Essex at Chelmsford.

bowl Essex into an impregnable position. Matthew Maynard, however, was going well and Croft gritted his teeth and stayed with the former captain until Maynard was out for 136 and 163 had been added for the eighth wicket. Croft's fun, though, was just about to start. With Harrison proving to be an aggressive ally against the wilting home attack, a further 138 was put on for the ninth wicket. Croft scored 125, Harrison a booming 88 and, by the time the Glamorgan lower order had finished, the Welsh county's first-innings total stood at 587. Yet more drama was to come on that third afternoon, however, with Mick Lewis snapping up three wickets with the new ball to plunge Essex to 22 for 4. They rallied to 67 for 4 by the close, through Flower and Foster, but when the fifth-wicket pair were split the next morning, having put on 84, Croft led Glamorgan's renewed charge for glory. He sent back both Flower and Foster in a spell of 4 for 13 in 44 balls and, suddenly, Glamorgan needed 221 for victory. It was not going to be easy, on a dusting pitch seemingly made for both Kaneria and James Middlebrook, and at 153 for 6 the match was in the balance. Enter Croft, again. With an unbeaten 28, he helped the excellent David Hemp to close out the game with Hemp adding a skilful 83 not out to his first-innings 67. 'This is one of the greatest victories in my time at the club', said a beaming Croft afterwards.

At Trent Bridge, Somerset inflicted defeat on Nottinghamshire for the first time in ten matches and, in the process, moved from seventh up to fourth in the table. The leaders looked to be on solid

Round 18: 31 August–7 September 2004
Division Two

ESSEX v. GLAMORGAN - at Chelmsford

ESSEX	First Innings		Second Innings	
WI Jefferson	b Harrison	0	lbw b Lewis	8
AP Grayson	c Hemp b Croft	57	c Hemp b Jones	5
A Flower	c Lewis b Jones	119	c Hughes b Croft	48
RC Irani (capt)	c Wallace b Croft	164	b Lewis	3
RS Bopara	c Hemp b Jones	4	c Wallace b Lewis	0
*JS Foster	c Wallace b Jones	188	c Hughes b Croft	45
JD Middlebrook	lbw b Harrison	3	b Lewis	34
GR Napier	b Croft	50	c Wallace b Jones	6
AR Adams	lbw b Lewis	3	c Harrison b Croft	6
AP Cowan	b Jones	25	b Croft	0
Danish Kaneria	not out	2	not out	2
Extras	b 8, lb 7, nb 12	27	lb 1, w 1, nb 10	12
	(154.2 overs)	642	(50.1 overs)	165

Bowling
Harrison 25-3-101-2. Jones 25.2-3-100-4. Lewis 25.2-3-126-1. Thomas 21-3-86-0. Croft 58-9-203-3. Maynard 1-0-11-0.
Jones 16-2-50-2. Lewis 9.1-0-39-4. Croft 19-1-52-4. Harrison 2-0-7-0. Thomas 4-0-16-0.
Fall of Wickets: 1-0, 2-122, 3-268, 4-278, 5-488, 6-495, 7-566, 8-583, 9-625
1-17, 2-17, 3-22, 4-22, 5-106, 6-119, 7-124, 8-135, 9-138

GLAMORGAN	First Innings		Second Innings	
DD Cherry	c Bopara b Danish Kaneria	22	(2) lbw b Danish Kaneria	17
*MA Wallace	c Foster b Danish Kaneria	42	(1) c Flower b Middlebrook	19
DL Hemp	c Flower b Middlebrook	67	not out	83
MJ Powell	c Bopara b Middlebrook	31	run out	10
MP Maynard	c Bopara b Adams	136	lbw b Napier	32
ML Lewis	lbw b Danish Kaneria	0		
J Hughes	c Foster b Cowan	11	(6) st Foster b Danish Kaneria	24
SD Thomas	c Bopara b Masters	22	(7) c Middlebrook b Danish Kaneria	0
RDB Croft (capt)	b Napier	125	(8) not out	28
DS Harrison	c Flower b Danish Kaneria	88		
SP Jones	not out	0		
Extras	b 6, lb 16, w 2, nb 14, p 5	43	b 4, lb 6	10
	(127.2 overs)	587	(6 wkts dec 65.2 overs)	223

Bowling
Cowan 21-5-79-1. Adams 22-1-107-1. Danish Kaneria 47.2-6-193-5.
Napier 12-0-82-1. Middlebrook 18-5-81-2. Grayson 5-1-5-0. Bopara 2-0-13-0.
Cowan 6-3-15-0. Danish Kaneria 26.2-5-80-3. Middlebrook 18-3-60-1.
Napier 7-0-26-1. Adams 5-1-19-0. Grayson 3-0-13-0.
Fall of Wickets: 1-73, 2-74, 3-182, 4-187, 5-188, 6-235, 7-286, 8-449, 9-587
1-36, 2-40, 3-58, 4-113, 5-153, 6-153

Glamorgan won by 4 wickets - Essex (8pts), Glamorgan (21pts)

NOTTINGHAMSHIRE v. SOMERSET - at Trent Bridge

NOTTS	First Innings		Second Innings	
DJ Bicknell	c Turner b Johnson	6	c Burns b Blackwell	142
JER Gallian (capt)	c Turner b Blackwell	68	c Durston b Blackwell	55
A Singh	c Burns b Johnson	7	(4) lbw b Johnson	1
DJ Hussey	c Caddick b Blackwell	25	(5) c Bowler b Blackwell	7
BM Shafayat	c Turner b Johnson	13	(6) c Durston b Blackwell	3
*CMW Read	c Hildreth b Francis	59	(7) c Cox b Durston	24
MA Ealham	c Durston b Johnson	104	(8) c Durston b Blackwell	44
PJ Franks	c Hildreth b Johnson	11	(9) b Blackwell	6
GJ Smith	c Bowler b Caddick	8	(10) not out	13
AJ Harris	lbw b Caddick	13	(3) c Turner b Johnson	10
PJ McMahon	not out	0	c Turner b Blackwell	0
Extras	lb 10, w 5, nb 8	23	b 4, lb 4, nb 4	12
	(114.4 overs)	337	(108.3 overs)	317

Bowling
Caddick 25.4-8-97-2. Johnson 25-9-69-5. Francis 19-3-66-1. Burns 2-0-8-0.
Blackwell 38-16-64-2. Durston 5-1-23-0.
Caddick 8-1-55-0. Johnson 21-5-64-2. Blackwell 43.3-17-90-7. Francis 17-2-50-0.
Durston 19-5-50-1.
Fall of Wickets: 1-13, 2-29, 3-77, 4-122, 5-143, 6-273, 7-297, 8-322, 9-329
1-121, 2-164, 3-172, 4-201, 5-207, 6-242, 7-256, 8-288, 9-317

SOMERSET	First Innings		Second Innings	
PD Bowler	c Read b Smith	2	not out	1
MJ Wood	lbw b McMahon	113	not out	0
J Cox	c Gallian b McMahon	250		
JC Hildreth	c Hussey b Harris	108		
M Burns (capt)	run out	34		
ID Blackwell	c & b McMahon	0		
*RJ Turner	not out	41		
WJ Durston	b Bicknell	47		
RL Johnson	c Ealham b Bicknell	8		
SRG Francis				
AR Caddick				
Extras	b 5, lb 13, w 9, nb 24	51		0
	(8 wkts dec 162.1 overs)	654	(0 wkts 0.4 overs)	1

Bowling
Smith 22-4-99-1. Harris 30-5-113-1. Franks 22-2-80-0. McMahon 43-4-169-3.
Ealham 18-4-64-0. Shafayat 2-0-16-0. Hussey 14-1-63-0. Bicknell 11.1-0-32-2.
Bicknell 0.4-0-1-0.
Fall of Wickets: 1-2, 2-205, 3-412, 4-499, 5-500, 6-581, 7-646, 8-654

Somerset won by 10 wickets - Nottinghamshire (4pts), Somerset (22pts)

LEICESTERSHIRE v. HAMPSHIRE - at Leicester

HAMPSHIRE	First Innings		Second Innings	
JHK Adams	c New b Maddy	16	b Gibson	20
MJ Brown	c Stevens b Dakin	0	b Masters	51
JP Crawley	b Dakin	4	b Masters	61
SM Katich	c Dakin b Gibson	30	c New b Gibson	66
LR Prittipaul	c Masters b Henderson	9	b Masters	4
*N Pothas	b Henderson	107	lbw b Maddy	7
AD Mascarenhas	c Maddy b Henderson	0	c Maunders b Henderson	4
SK Warne (capt)	c New b Hodge	22	c Stevens b Henderson	42
SD Udal	c New b Hodge	22	c Stevens b Masters	39
CT Tremlett	c Hodge b Henderson	48	b Dakin	7
BV Taylor	not out	8	not out	4
Extras	lb 9, w 3, nb 8	20	b 3, lb 6, nb 6	15
	(92.4 overs)	321	(104 overs)	329

Bowling
Gibson 21-4-72-66-2. Masters 16-2-59-1. Maddy 12-3-28-1.
Henderson 25.4-4-103-4. Hodge 4-1-14-1.
Gibson 20-8-38-2. Dakin 17-3-72-2. Maunders 21-5-40-6. Maddy 5-0-23-0.
Henderson 37-9-88-2. Masters 20-3-74-4. Hodge 2-0-14-0. Sadler 1-0-2-0.
Fall of Wickets: 1-0, 2-5, 3-31, 4-68, 5-74, 6-78, 7-189, 8-231, 9-278
1-24, 2-138, 3-155, 4-163, 5-185, 6-210, 7-270, 8-270, 9-317

LEICESTERSHIRE	First Innings		Second Innings	
JK Maunders	lbw b Mascarenhas	13	lbw b Mascarenhas	0
DL Maddy	b Taylor	41	b Udal	4
BJ Hodge (capt)	lbw b Tremlett	26	(5) lbw b Tremlett	74
DI Stevens	c Mascarenhas b Tremlett	105	c Pothas b Warne	70
JL Sadler	c Udal b Mascarenhas	5	(6) c Crawley b Warne	15
DG Brandy	b Warne	7	(3) c Katich b Tremlett	4
*TJ New	lbw b Udal	0	(8) not out	22
OD Gibson	c Pothas b Tremlett	50	(7) b Warne	27
JM Dakin	not out	21	b Taylor	4
CW Henderson	c Warne b Taylor	3	lbw b Taylor	1
DD Masters	st Pothas b Udal	1	lbw b Taylor	0
Extras	b 8, lb 9, w 1, nb 12	30	b 7, lb 12, w 4, nb 12	35
	(88.5 overs)	282	(75.5 overs)	282

Bowling
Tremlett 14-3-49-3. Taylor 15-2-55-2. Warne 12-0-31-1. Mascarenhas 19-7-40-2.
Udal 13.5-3-44-2. Prittipaul 6-1-17-0. Katich 9-1-29-0.
Mascarenhas 14-5-38-1. Tremlett 14-1-46-1. Taylor 15.5-2-53-3. Udal 12-0-51-1.
Warne 18-3-62-3. Adams 2-0-15-0.
Fall of Wickets: 1-39, 2-41, 3-87, 4-105, 5-137, 6-198, 7-254, 8-256, 9-276
1-3, 2-18, 3-70, 4-201, 5-201, 6-239, 7-257, 8-274, 9-282

Hampshire won by 86 runs - Leicestershire (5pts), Hampshire (20pts)

YORKSHIRE v. DURHAM - at Scarborough

DURHAM	First Innings		Second Innings	
JJB Lewis (capt)	c & b Bresnan	12	c Dawood b Kirby	15
JA Lowe	c Wood b Hoggard	31	lbw b Hoggard	41
GJ Muchall	not out	142	lbw b Dawson	18
MJ North	c Dawood b Bresnan	24	lbw b Kirby	62
GR Breese	lbw b Bresnan	35	c Dawood b Lawson	68
GM Hamilton	lbw b Lawson	2	b Dawson	58
*P Mustard	c Dawood b Lawson	15	c Lawson b Kirby	46
GD Bridge	lbw b Lawson	8	not out	46
LE Plunkett	b Lawson	5	c Dawood b Dawson	0
N Killeen	c Wood b Lawson	6	c Dawood b Hoggard	20
G Onions	st Dawood b Dawson	16		
Extras	lb 6, w 1, nb 22	29	b 5, lb 7, w 5, nb 4	21
	(82 overs)	325	(9 wkts dec 94.4 overs)	375

Bowling
Hoggard 13-1-53-2. Kirby 14-0-80-0. Bresnan 11-1-32-3. Dawson 25-3-92-1.
Lawson 19-2-62-5.
Hoggard 16.4-1-47-2. Kirby 20-1-64-3. Dawson 29-6-115-3. Bresnan 13-4-52-0.
Lawson 15-1-84-1. Wood 1-0-1-0.
Fall of Wickets: 1-47, 2-81, 3-119, 4-203, 5-208, 6-236, 7-264, 8-270, 9-278
1-23, 2-150, 3-195, 4-203, 5-228, 6-303, 7-306, 8-306, 9-375

YORKSHIRE	First Innings		Second Innings	
MJ Wood (capt)	b Killeen	22	c Onions b Breese	42
PA Jaques	b Plunkett	66	c North b Breese	53
JJ Sayers	c Lowe b Breese	54	c Mustard b Breese	17
RM Pyrah	b Plunkett	4	b Breese	34
MJ Lumb	lbw b Breese	17	c Muchall b Bridge	4
*I Dawood	not out	21	c Mustard b Plunkett	75
RKJ Dawson	c Muchall b Breese	6	c Mustard b Bridge	6
TT Bresnan	lbw b Bridge	0	lbw b Bridge	6
MJ Hoggard	b Bridge	4	c & b Breese	6
MAK Lawson	c Lowe b Breese	1	lb b Breese	5
SP Kirby	c Bridge b Breese	0	not out	14
Extras	lb 2, w 1	3	b 1, lb 6, w 1, nb 10	18
	(63.3 overs)	200	(80.5 overs)	290

Bowling
Plunkett 15-3-55-2. Killeen 16-6-39-2. Onions 2-0-22-0. Breese 13.3-1-41-5.
Bridge 17-1-41-1.
Plunkett 10.5-3-57-1. Killeen 7-2-34-0. Breese 35-3-110-5. Hamilton 7-1-18-0.
Bridge 21-7-64-4.
Fall of Wickets: 1-56, 2-120, 3-126, 4-155, 5-170, 6-176, 7-177, 8-199, 9-200
1-98, 2-113, 3-137, 4-142, 5-174, 6-203, 7-213, 8-225, 9-250

Durham won by 210 runs - Yorkshire (4pts), Durham (20pts)

enough ground after half-centuries from Jason Gallian and Chris Read, and a fine 104 from Mark Ealham, had taken them to 337 in their first innings. By the close of the second day, however, the visitors were already two runs ahead with only two wickets down, following a 203-run stand between Matthew Wood (113) and Jamie Cox, who remained on 128 not out and who had already been joined by James Hildreth in a classy third-wicket partnership. The 19-year-old Hildreth took his overnight 67 on to 108 the following day, but Cox went on to score a wonderful career-best 250 – hitting a six and 35 fours from the 428 balls he faced. Cox's great effort allowed Somerset to declare on 654 for 8 and Notts, despite Darren Bicknell's 43rd first-class hundred, and his century opening stand with Gallian, were unable to resist the slow left-arm spin of Ian Blackwell. His 7 for 90 equalled the career-best figures he had produced against Glamorgan a month earlier and, when Notts were all out for 317, Somerset required just a single run to clinch a morale-boosting win.

Leicestershire, with Darren Stevens and Brad Hodge both flowing into the 70s on the final morning, found themselves requiring just another 174 with seven wickets in hand to beat Hampshire at Grace Road. Then, however, both were dismissed in successive balls and, with Shane Warne picking up three wickets and Billy Taylor blowing away the tail, Hampshire ran out 86-run winners. It was a good all-round performance by Hampshire, once Nic Pothas (107) and Warne (57) had rallied them from the depths of 78 for 6 on the opening day by adding 111 for the seventh wicket at five runs an over. Stevens also impressed in the Leicestershire first innings, hitting 105, while Ottis Gibson struck three big sixes in a seventh-wicket stand of 116. However, Hampshire's solid second-innings batting performance kept them well in control of affairs.

Gordon Muchall and Gareth Breese were the inspirations behind Durham's famous 210-run beating of Yorkshire at Scarborough. Muchall's opening-day 142 not out, batting at No. 3, sustained a Durham first innings in which Mark Lawson, an 18-year-old leg spinner in only his third first-class match, took 5 for 62. Phil Jaques and Joe Sayers, with a maiden championship half-century, then took Yorkshire swiftly to 120 for 1 in reply to Durham's 325, but that was as good as it got. Breese's off spin brought him 5 for 18 in the space of 41 balls and Yorkshire were suddenly 200 all out. Breese then top scored with 68 as Durham rammed home their advantage with a confident march to 375 for 9 in their second innings – Gavin Hamilton also contributed 58 against his

former county – and Yorkshire soon fell away once Jaques and Matthew Wood's 98-run opening partnership had been broken. Ismael Dawood could also hold his head high after a battling 75, but, otherwise, this was a woeful batting display by a side searching for promotion. Breese, though, after adding 5 for 110 to his first-innings 5 for 41, led the Durham celebrations.

Round 19: 9–13 September 2004

Division One

Lancashire, staring relegation in the face, were still unwilling to take the greater risk of defeat at Worcester in search of the victory that might have kept them in Division One. Warren Hegg, their captain, clearly felt that he could not offer Worcestershire any tastier a target than a rather unappetising 294 from 47 overs. If Worcestershire had won, mind you, Lancashire would definitely have gone down, but even so, Hegg must have been left wishing he had shown just a little more faith in his bowlers. After the 47 overs had been delivered, the home side were hanging on for the draw at 199 for 8 – leaving Mark Newton, the Worcestershire chief executive, more than a little peeved at the Lancashire conservatism that, in the end, confirmed his own county's relegation. 'I was very unimpressed by it, and I hope they come down with us', he said afterwards. Lancashire, as a result of their failure to win here, were left needing to beat Gloucestershire by a margin of at least 17 points in their final match at Old Trafford – a tall order. Hegg's side, however, could feel aggrieved at the loss of all but 15.4 overs on the second day, in which they moved from an overnight 350 for 8 to a full complement of batting points at 403 for 9. Stuart Law's 68th first-class hundred, a chanceless five-hour effort containing 24 fours and a six smashed over midwicket off Matt Mason, was the basis of the Lancashire first innings and, at 77 for 5 in reply, Worcestershire were in serious trouble early on day three. Andrew Hall, however, hit back with a fighting 70 and the 40-year-old Steve Rhodes, in his 440th and final first-class appearance, followed up his earlier quicksilver stumping of Iain Sutcliffe by battling to 53. Coming in at 149 for 6, he helped Hall to put on 63 for the seventh wicket and then, with an increasingly belligerent Ray Price, he occupied the crease long enough for another 115 to be added. Price's unbeaten 76 enabled Worcestershire to declare at 352 for 9, challenging Lancashire to make a game of it on the final day. Lancashire, though, delayed their declaration until they had reached 242 for 6 and, after Ben Smith and Hall had raised faint hopes of some sort of meaningful chase to stave off relegation, it was left to Rhodes to march out with applause ringing around New Road to deny Lancashire in the final overs with 19 not out. The former England wicketkeeper then left the first-class stage to more heartfelt applause at the end of a distinguished career that featured almost 15,000 runs at an average of 32, including 12 hundreds, and a tally of 1,263 victims which puts him eighth in the all-time wicketkeeping list. Yorkshireman Rhodes will not be leaving his beloved Worcestershire, though, as he has accepted an invitation to be the county's assistant coach to Tom Moody.

Gloucestershire's failure to gain any batting points against Sussex at Bristol, plus the bad weather that ultimately caused the match to be drawn, left them sweating on the possibility of relegation. Tim Hancock was also peeved at the return of the rain just after lunch on the final day. He had been the only home batsman to make any headway against James Kirtley and Jason Lewry on the opening day, and he was in sight of a first hundred at Bristol in 14 seasons with Gloucestershire, when the match was abandoned as a

Farewell: English cricket bids goodbye to one of its best servants, Worcestershire's wicketkeeper and captain Steve Rhodes.

Round 19: 9–13 September 2004 Division One

WORCESTERSHIRE v. LANCASHIRE - at Worcester

LANCASHIRE	First Innings			Second Innings	
MJ Chilton	b Bichel	3	c Hick b Hall		30
IJ Sutcliffe	st Rhodes b Price	51	c Rhodes b Hall		29
MB Loye	c Rhodes b Mason	17	lbw b Bichel		0
SG Law	lbw b Bichel	159	lbw b Hall		0
CL Hooper	lbw b Hall	8	not out		75
AR Crook	c Rhodes b Khalid	27	c Hall b Mason		24
G Chapple	c Peters b Price	50	c Smith b Moore		63
*WK Hegg (capt)	c Hick b Bichel	43			
DG Cork	c Et b Bichel	8			
SI Mahmood	not out	24			
G Keedy	not out	10			
Extras	lb 3	3	b 4, lb 8, w 1, nb 8		21
	(9 wkts dec 119.4 overs)	403	(6 wkts dec 52.3 overs)		242

Bowling
Mason 29-5-102-1. Bichel 26.4-8-91-4. Hall 23-1-92-1. Price 31-10-79-2. Khalid 6-0-28-1. Kadeer Ali 4-0-8-0.
Bichel 13-2-42-1. Hall 13-4-41-3. Khalid 8-0-46-0. Kadeer Ali 4-0-26-0. Price 9-0-54-0. Mason 4-2-8-1. Moore 1.3-0-13-1.
Fall of Wickets: 1-5, 2-47, 3-101, 4-128, 5-183, 6-291, 7-326, 8-348, 9-381
1-68, 2-71, 3-71, 4-71, 5-124, 6-242

WORCS	First Innings			Second Innings	
SD Peters	c Hooper b Cork	27	lbw b Cork		3
SC Moore	c Hooper b Chapple	14	b Chapple		19
GA Hick	lbw b Cork	6	lbw b Chapple		7
BF Smith	c Law b Cork	0	b Mahmood		50
Kadeer Ali	b Cork	11	b Mahmood		27
AJ Bichel	b Mahmood	31	c Et b Keedy		10
AJ Hall	lbw b Keedy	70	c Hegg b Keedy		39
*SJ Rhodes (capt)	c Hegg b Keedy	53	not out		19
RW Price	not out	76	b Crook		1
MS Mason	c Hegg b Keedy	0	not out		0
SA Khalid	not out	6			
Extras	b 15, lb 10, nb 33	58	b 4, lb 9, w 1, nb 10		24
	(9 wkts dec 87 overs)	352	(8 wkts 47 overs)		199

Bowling
Mahmood 12-0-78-1. Cork 17-5-61-4. Chapple 14-6-30-1. Keedy 17-1-74-3. Hooper 16-4-39-0. Crook 11-1-45-0.
Chapple 10-1-35-2. Cork 11-2-62-1. Mahmood 8-0-41-2. Hooper 3-0-21-0. Keedy 11-3-19-2. Crook 4-1-8-1.
Fall of Wickets: 1-43, 2-49, 3-55, 4-70, 5-77, 6-149, 7-212, 8-327, 9-327
1-9, 2-24, 3-41, 4-103, 5-120, 6-134, 7-188, 8-191

Match drawn - Worcestershire (11pts), Lancashire (12pts)

GLOUCESTERSHIRE v. SUSSEX - at Bristol

GLOUCS	First Innings			Second Innings	
CM Spearman	lbw b Martin-Jenkins	12	(2) lbw b Mushtaq Ahmed		65
WPC Weston	lbw b Kirtley	1	(1) lbw b Kirtley		13
MEK Hussey	lbw b Lewry	1	lbw b Davis		37
CG Taylor (capt)	lbw b Lewry	0	run out		15
THC Hancock	c Ward b Martin-Jenkins	44	not out		77
APR Gidman	c Goodwin b Lewry	22	c Martin-Jenkins b Davis		82
*SJ Adshead	b Mushtaq Ahmed	19	not out		0
ID Fisher	lbw b Kirtley	17			
JMM Averis	b Mushtaq Ahmed	14			
J Lewis	not out	27			
NW Bracken	b Kirtley	8			
Extras	b 6, lb 3, nb 4	13	b 2, lb 7, w 1, p 5		15
	(69.3 overs)	178	(5 wkts 95.2 overs)		304

Bowling
Kirtley 18.3-4-52-3. Lewry 13-6-27-3. Mushtaq Ahmed 23-5-64-2.
Martin-Jenkins 12-6-24-2. Davis 3-1-2-0.
Kirtley 17-4-46-1. Lewry 10-2-35-0. Martin-Jenkins 17-3-74-0.
Mushtaq Ahmed 34-10-68-1. Davis 17.2-0-67-2.
Fall of Wickets: 1-7, 2-12, 3-12, 4-31, 5-69, 6-110, 7-110, 8-135, 9-169
1-22, 2-109, 3-129, 4-142, 5-304

SUSSEX	First Innings		
IJ Ward	b Averis	16	
RR Montgomerie	b Averis	7	
PA Cottey	lbw b Averis	21	
MW Goodwin	c Hussey b Averis	5	
CJ Adams (capt)	b Gidman	9	
*MJ Prior	c Adshead b Gidman	27	
RSC Martin-Jenkins	b Bracken	6	
MJG Davis	c Adshead b Lewis	11	
Mushtaq Ahmed	c Gidman b Bracken	13	
RJ Kirtley	not out	20	
JD Lewry	c Hussey b Averis	32	
Extras	b 2, lb 7, w 1, nb 28	32	
	(52.2 overs)	199	

Bowling
Lewis 18-4-81-1. Bracken 17-6-58-2. Averis 10.2-1-45-5. Gidman 7-2-12-2.
Fall of Wickets: 1-30, 2-37, 3-57, 4-62, 5-78, 6-105, 7-109, 8-135, 9-149

Match drawn - Gloucestershire (7pts), Sussex (7pts)

MIDDLESEX v. NORTHAMPTONSHIRE - at Lord's

MIDDLESEX	First Innings			Second Innings	
BL Hutton	c Brophy b Louw	7	(2) st Brophy b Brown		31
SG Koenig	c Brophy b Rofe	6	(1) c Afzaal b Brown		51
OA Shah	c Afzaal b Rofe	85	c Cook b Brown		24
EC Joyce (capt)	c Roberts b Rofe	71	c Sales b Rofe		59
PN Weekes	c Rofe b Louw	54	c Cook b Rofe		38
JWM Dalrymple	lbw b Louw	1	c Brown b Rofe		2
*BJM Scott	not out	101	not out		1
SJ Cook	lbw b Rofe	40			
CT Peploe	c Brophy b Louw	21			
SR Clark	b Brown	24			
M Hayward	c Louw b Brown	0			
Extras	lb 10, w 5	15	b 1, lb 3, w 2		6
	(139.4 overs)	425	(6 wkts dec 54.5 overs)		212

Bowling
Louw 34-8-112-4. Rofe 35-7-109-4. Phillips 23-7-78-0. Cook 8-2-19-0.
Brown 36.4-8-87-2. White 3-0-10-0.
Louw 9-3-35-0. Rofe 7.5-2-23-3. Phillips 7-1-22-0. Brown 18-2-65-3.
White 5-0-23-0. Cook 5-0-28-0. Afzaal 3-0-12-0.
Fall of Wickets: 1-12, 2-14, 3-170, 4-177, 5-182, 6-259, 7-320, 8-352, 9-415
1-82, 2-87, 3-122, 4-202, 5-207, 6-212

NORTHANTS	First Innings			Second Innings	
TB Huggins	c Joyce b Cook	4	(2) not out		82
TW Roberts	lbw b Clark	0	(1) c Hayward b Cook		11
JW Cook	c Scott b Clark	8	lbw b Cook		0
U Afzaal	b Hayward	62	c Joyce b Hayward		12
DJG Sales (capt)	b Clark	22	c Cook b Hutton		90
*GL Brophy	c Et b Hutton	81	not out		5
AR White	c Shah b Dalrymple	22			
BJ Phillips	c Et b Hutton	30			
J Louw	c Scott b Hayward	32			
PC Rofe	c Peploe b Hutton	0			
JF Brown	not out	0			
Extras	b 6, lb 7, w 1, nb 6	20	b 8, lb 12, nb 4		24
	(105.3 overs)	282	(4 wkts 74 overs)		224

Bowling
Cook 20-4-68-1. Clark 22-6-51-3. Peploe 14-5-54-0. Hayward 21.3-5-54-2.
Dalrymple 17-5-35-1. Hutton 9-6-14-3. Shah 2-1-1-0.
Cook 12-8-11-2. Clark 10-5-24-0. Hayward 14-5-30-1. Hutton 13-3-47-1.
Peploe 7-3-14-0. Dalrymple 10-0-45-0. Weekes 7-1-27-0. Koenig 1-0-6-0.
Fall of Wickets: 1-4, 2-8, 3-12, 4-117, 5-161, 6-210, 7-210, 8-272, 9-282
1-14, 2-18, 3-43, 4-212

Match drawn - Middlesex (11pts), Northamptonshire (8pts)

draw. Sussex had fared little better in their own first innings, which was interrupted by a washed-out second day, but Hancock, Craig Spearman and Alex Gidman were all in the runs as Gloucestershire then built a sizeable lead. Nathan Bracken, the left-arm quick bowler making his championship debut in this match, became the 31st Australian out of 59 official overseas players to be used in county cricket in 2004.

Tom Huggins, the 21-year-old Northamptonshire batsman, defied both toothache and a fiery spell from Nantie Hayward to lead his side to a draw against Middlesex at Lord's. Huggins' unbeaten 82 was not just his best score in a fledgling career, it also threatened to earn him a fresh Northants contract despite the shake-up at the club being planned by manager Kepler Wessels. David Sales, the Northants captain, struck three sixes in his 90 and helped Huggins to add 169 for the fourth wicket following the loss of three early wickets. Middlesex, despite not being able to force victory on the last afternoon, controlled the game once wicketkeeper Ben Scott had added a most promising maiden first-class hundred, from 156 balls and with 15 fours, to earlier half-centuries from Owais Shah, Ed Joyce and Paul Weekes.

Division Two

Twenty wickets fell on the opening day at Chelmsford but, after reserving judgement until Essex had wrapped up an eight-wicket win over Derbyshire inside two days, ECB pitch officer Tony Brown decided that it was a lack of technique by the batsmen and not a sub-standard surface which had produced the early finish. The ball turned for the spinners, among whom Essex's Danish Kaneria was a class apart, and Will Jefferson then struck 60 off 81 balls in an opening stand worth 103 with Alastair Cook to ensure that the home side made scoring the highest total of the match to win look easy.

Durham's six-wicket loss to Leicestershire at the Riverside was their fifth home defeat of the season, and it was a comprehensive one, despite three wickets with the new ball for Liam Plunkett, as the visitors rushed to their modest target on the final morning. A combative 60 from Phil Mustard and a career-best 52 by Graeme Bridge, plus a 47-run last-wicket stand, could not prevent Durham from being bowled out for an all-too-familiar below-par first-innings total on day one. A solid start from Darren Robinson and Darren Maddy then provided Leicestershire with the base to build a match-winning total of their own, and timely knocks from John Maunders and Darren Stevens took the game away from Durham. Maunders

completed an important century, in terms of his career as much as this match, while 52 of Stevens' first 53 runs came in boundaries. A partnership of 93 for the fifth wicket between Gareth Breese and Gavin Hamilton, who both scored half-centuries, did at least save the home team from the ignominy of an innings defeat, but it was scant consolation.

A rain-ravaged first three days was followed by a total washout on the fourth, forcing Somerset and Yorkshire to be content with a draw at Taunton. Only 16 overs were possible on day one – although in that time Phil Jaques plundered six fours off Andy Caddick to race to 48 not out. Yorkshire's opening partnership of Jaques and Joe Sayers then converted the overnight 60 without loss into a stand of 162, with Jaques' 95 the undoubted highlight.

Leg-spin wizard: Danish Kaneria, of Pakistan and Essex.

Somerset's failure to beat Yorkshire, however, with the weather ultimately frustrating even their efforts at generating a last-day run chase by declaring their first

Round 19: 9–13 September 2004
Division Two

```
           ESSEX v. DERBYSHIRE - at Chelmsford

DERBYSHIRE       First Innings                    Second Innings
SD Stubbings     c Bopara b Palladino      0      lbw b Napier                   7
BJ France        b Napier                  2      b Danish Kaneria              33
J Moss           lbw b Adams              28      lbw b Adams                   11
Hassan Adnan     c Cook b Middlebrook     58      c Flower b Adams               3
CWG Bassano      c Foster b Adams          0      c Cook b Middlebrook          34
*LD Sutton (capt) lbw b Middlebrook       48      c Bopara b Danish Kaneria     44
G Welch          c Jefferson b Adams       5      c Cook b Middlebrook           0
MA Sheikh        c Foster b Middlebrook   23      lbw b Middlebrook              8
NRC Dumelow      c Cook b Middlebrook      6      lbw b Danish Kaneria           0
ID Hunter        b Middlebrook             0      c Jefferson b Middlebrook      6
PMR Havell       not out                   2      not out                       2
Extras           b 6, lb 2, w 1, nb 8     17      b 4, lb 9, w 1, nb 4          18
                 (58.3 overs)            192      (55.4 overs)                 166
Bowling
Palladino 7-1-28-1. Napier 5-0-46-1. Adams 14-5-44-3. Bopara 6-0-20-0.
Danish Kaneria 12-4-20-0. Middlebrook 14.3-5-26-5.
Palladino 3-0-17-0. Napier 5-1-14-1. Adams 11-1-39-2. Danish Kaneria 22.4-9-36-4.
Middlebrook 14-3-47-3.
Fall of Wickets: 1-0, 2-11, 3-58, 4-58, 5-136, 6-141, 7-153, 8-163, 9-163
1-11, 2-26, 3-42, 4-91, 5-95, 6-99, 7-120, 8-120, 9-129

ESSEX            First Innings                    Second Innings
WI Jefferson     c Sutton b Hunter         0      c Sutton b Moss               60
AN Cook          c Sutton b Dumelow       22      not out                       68
A Flower         c Sutton b Havell         5      c Sutton b Moss                0
RC Irani (capt)  c Bassano b Havell        0      not out                       43
RS Bopara        lbw b Sheikh             29
*JS Foster       b Welch                  22
JD Middlebrook   c Sutton b Welch          7
GR Napier        b Hunter                 52
AR Adams         run out                  10
AP Palladino     b Hunter                  0
Danish Kaneria   not out                   1
Extras           b 1, lb 7, nb 11         19      b 8, lb 6, w 1, nb 8          23
                 (40.3 overs)            167      (2 wkts 39.3 overs)          194
Bowling
Hunter 8.3-1-32-3. Havell 8-1-23-2. Dumelow 12-2-52-1. Welch 8-2-28-2.
Sheikh 4-1-24-1.
Hunter 6-0-20-0. Havell 7-0-38-0. Welch 7-1-21-0. Dumelow 10-1-58-0.
Sheikh 3.3-0-24-0. Moss 6-2-19-2.
Fall of Wickets: 1-0, 2-13, 3-21, 4-35, 5-66, 6-82, 7-145, 8-159, 9-166
1-103, 2-103

            Essex won by 8 wickets - Essex (17pts),
                      Derbyshire (3pts)
```

innings on 141 without loss, meant that Glamorgan were promoted to Division One. 'It doesn't matter how you get there', said Glamorgan's Matthew Maynard. 'What counts is that we've achieved what we set out to do this summer'. The Welsh county, therefore, could celebrate, despite taking just six points from a home fixture against Nottinghamshire at Cardiff that was decimated by rain. There was no play at all on both the first and last days, and, in between, there was only just enough time for Anurag Singh to reach an unbeaten century for the visitors.

Round 20:
16–19 September 2004

Division One

Kent made sure of the runners-up cheque from Frizzell by trouncing Middlesex by an innings and 49 runs at Canterbury. It was their seventh win of the season – two more than champions Warwickshire. The victory was also a triumph for Ed Smith, who scored a wonderful 189 with 23 fours in what was thought to be his last innings for Kent … and against the county reportedly most interested in signing him. Smith and Rob Key added 255 for the second wicket to press home Kent's advantage following their dismissal of Middlesex for only 235 on the opening day. Kent were already 163 for 1 by the close of the first day, and then moved on to 473 for 6 by the end

```
          DURHAM v. LEICESTERSHIRE - at The Riverside

DURHAM           First Innings                    Second Innings
JJB Lewis (capt) lbw b Maunders           27      b Gibson                      14
JA Lowe          c Stevens b Dagnall       9      b Gibson                      10
GJ Muchall       c Gibson b Dagnall       35      lbw b Masters                 43
MJ North         c Maddy b Masters        11      c New b Dagnall               11
GR Breese        c Robinson b Masters      5      c Stevens b Henderson         65
GM Hamilton      c New b Gibson           29      lbw b Gibson                  53
*P Mustard       c Robinson b Gibson      60      lbw b Dagnall                 40
GD Bridge        c Sadler b Hodge         52      c Dagnall b Henderson          5
LE Plunkett      b Maddy                   7      not out                       17
N Killeen        b Gibson                 30      b Henderson                    0
G Onions         not out                  20      lbw b Henderson                0
Extras           b 2, lb 6, nb 8          16      b 1, lb 17, nb 4              22
                 (80.2 overs)            298      (73.4 overs)                 280
Bowling
Gibson 14.2-1-69-3. Dagnall 14-5-42-2. Maunders 9-6-11-1. Masters 16-5-62-2.
Maddy 7-0-26-1. Henderson 18-5-62-0. Hodge 2-0-18-1.
Gibson 19-1-70-3. Dagnall 18-3-73-2. Masters 19-5-54-1. Henderson 13.4-2-44-4.
Maunders 2-0-12-0. Maddy 2-0-9-0.
Fall of Wickets: 1-33, 2-51, 3-62, 4-68, 5-114, 6-143, 7-200, 8-224, 9-251
1-18, 2-41, 3-75, 4-95, 5-188, 6-246, 7-259, 8-263, 9-272

LEICESTERSHIRE   First Innings                    Second Innings
DDJ Robinson     run out                  65      lbw b Muchall                 38
DL Maddy         lbw b Breese             70      c Muchall b Plunkett          10
JK Maunders      b Plunkett              116      c Muchall b Plunkett           0
DI Stevens       c Hamilton b Bridge      92      not out                       19
BJ Hodge (capt)  c Mustard b Plunkett     46
JL Sadler        lbw b Breese             28      (5) b Plunkett                 0
*TJ New          not out                  51      (6) not out                    0
OD Gibson        lbw b Breese              0
CW Henderson     c Mustard b Killeen       4
DD Masters       b Plunkett                1
CE Dagnall       b Breese                 16
Extras           b 2, lb 16, w 1, nb 6    19      b 1, lb 1, nb 2                4
                 (139.2 overs)           508      (4 wkts 12.5 overs)           71
Bowling
Plunkett 33.9-9-104-3. Killeen 35-9-93-1. Onions 20-3-93-0. Muchall 7-1-21-0.
Bridge 20-3-92-1. Breese 24.2-6-93-4.
Plunkett 6.5-1-27-3. Onions 5-1-41-0. Muchall 1-0-1-1.
Fall of Wickets: 1-101, 2-161, 3-311, 4-402, 5-405, 6-454, 7-454, 8-468, 9-469
1-31, 2-31, 3-65, 4-70

         Leicestershire won by 6 wickets -
       Durham (5pts), Leicestershire (22pts)
```

```
         SOMERSET v. YORKSHIRE - at Taunton

YORKSHIRE        First Innings                    Second Innings
PA Jaques        c Bowler b Caddick       95      c Johnson b Francis           27
JJ Sayers        c Wood b Caddick         62      c Francis b Laraman           46
MJ Lumb          lbw b Blackwell           4      c Blackwell b Francis          0
MJ Wood (capt)   c Turner b Johnson       46      not out                       26
RM Pyrah         lbw b Johnson            39      run out                        8
*I Dawood        c Francis b Blackwell    31      not out                        6
RKJ Dawson       c Bowler b Laraman        0
TT Bresnan       c Hildreth b Caddick     13
DJ Wainwright    c Burns b Laraman         5
MJ Hoggard       c Cox b Caddick           7
SP Kirby         not out                   0
Extras           b 8, lb 4, nb 10         22      lb 4, nb 8                    12
                 (93.3 overs)            324      (4 wkts 16 overs)           125
Bowling
Caddick 19.3-1-94-4. Johnson 22-4-78-2. Francis 8-1-22-0. Blackwell 31-4-75-2.
Laraman 13-3-43-2.
Caddick 3-0-23-0. Johnson 3-0-30-0. Laraman 5-0-33-1. Francis 5-0-35-2.
Fall of Wickets: 1-162, 2-167, 3-171, 4-246, 5-273, 6-277, 7-299, 8-304, 9-323
1-69, 2-69, 3-93, 4-103

SOMERSET         First Innings
PD Bowler        not out                  75
MJ Wood          not out                  62
J Cox
JC Hildreth
M Burns (capt)
ID Blackwell
AW Laraman
*RJ Turner
RL Johnson
AR Caddick
SRG Francis
Extras           nb 4                      4
                 (0 wkts dec 33 overs)   141
Bowling
Hoggard 8-1-44-0. Kirby 10-2-38-0. Bresnan 4-0-25-0. Dawson 8-1-29-0.
Wainwright 3-1-5-0.

         Match drawn - Somerset (7pts),
                 Yorkshire (7pts)
```

```
        GLAMORGAN v. NOTTINGHAMSHIRE - at Cardiff

NOTTS            First Innings
DJ Bicknell      c Wallace b Jones         3
JER Gallian (capt) lbw b Harrison         10
A Singh          not out                 112
KP Pietersen     b Croft                  20
DJ Hussey        b Croft                  11
*CMW Read        not out                  15
MA Ealham        lbw b Harrison           30
PJ Franks        not out                  52
GJ Smith
RJ Sidebottom
SCG MacGill
Extras           lb 4, nb 16              20
                 (6 wkts 74 overs)       273
Bowling
Harrison 14-7-23-2. Jones 19-3-83-1. Lewis 13-2-63-0. Croft 23-2-77-2.
Thomas 5-0-23-0.
Fall of Wickets: 1-7, 2-13, 3-49, 4-77, 5-103, 6-162

GLAMORGAN
MTG Elliott
*MA Wallace
DL Hemp
MJ Powell
MP Maynard
J Hughes
SD Thomas
RDB Croft (capt)
DS Harrison
SP Jones
ML Lewis

         Match drawn - Glamorgan (6pts),
              Nottinghamshire (6pts)
```

of an abbreviated day two. Matthew Walker, 86 not out overnight, went on to complete (like Smith) his fourth hundred of the season, and Kent completed their victory inside three days, as Alex Loudon underlined his growing maturity as an all-rounder by snapping up 6 for 47 with his off breaks.

Third place went to Surrey, who pipped Sussex to it by beating them by 37 runs in a fine contest at Hove. Rikki Clarke's 90-ball 112 was the highlight of the first day, helping Surrey to rally well from the shock of having slipped to 14 for 4 against the new ball, while the second day belonged to Mike Yardy, who scored his maiden championship hundred. Sussex, however, collapsed alarmingly from 239 for 4 to 271 all out, and Alastair Brown gave Surrey the upper hand by hitting his fourth century of the season. He passed his 1,000 first-class runs for the summer during the early part of his fine innings of 123, but Jason Lewry then gave Sussex renewed hope by wrapping up the Surrey second innings with three wickets in four balls. When Murray Goodwin was cruising to 119, with good support first from Chris Adams and then from the fluent Matthew Prior, it seemed as though dethroned

champions Sussex would end their 2004 campaign with a flourish. From 242 for 4, however, they fell away to 286 all out. Prior's mishit to mid-off was followed, in James Ormond's next over, by the yorking of Goodwin and Sussex could not keep their chase for 324 in 80 overs after that. Nayan Doshi then wrapped up the tail to finish with career-best figures of 7 for 110, taking his wicket-tally for Surrey to 33 from his first nine matches.

Lancashire, meanwhile, had their relegation place confirmed as Gloucestershire won through a tense first two days at Old Trafford. The ECB had appointed former England batsman Phil Sharpe as a match referee, such was the potential for skulduggery in a game which began with Gloucestershire, themselves not out of the relegation mire, needing to prevent Lancashire from winning the game by a margin of 17 points. The match was eventually drawn, with rain washing away the entire third day, but all the drama had by then been played out. On the opening day, half-centuries from Chris Taylor, Tim Hancock and Steve Adshead had enabled Gloucestershire to get three batting bonus points on to the board. Then, at 331 for 8, and apparently having first consulted with Sharpe, they declared to deny Lancashire a third bowling point. In effect, it left the Lancastrians needing to score at least 400 in reply inside the 130-over bonus point cut-off limit, for the loss of no more than five wickets, and then go on to win the match. At

Matthew Walker, voted Kent's player of the season by the supporters, says his thanks with 108 against Middlesex in the county's final match ... and seventh win of the summer.

Round 20: 16–19 September 2004
Division One

KENT v. MIDDLESEX - at Canterbury

MIDDLESEX

	First Innings		Second Innings	
SG Koenig	c O'Brien b Cusden	39	c O'Brien b Cusden	28
BL Hutton	c O'Brien b Cusden	16	c Fulton b Patel	32
OA Shah	c O'Brien b Walker	25	c Joseph b Patel	14
EC Joyce (capt)	c O'Brien b Trott	20	c Trott b Loudon	74
PN Weekes	c O'Brien b Walker	12	c Fulton b Loudon	29
JWM Dalrymple	not out	52	st O'Brien b Loudon	20
*BJM Scott	c O'Brien b Cusden	4	lbw b Loudon	0
SJ Cook	b Joseph	30	b Loudon	15
CT Peploe	lbw b Joseph	0	c Cusden b Loudon	6
MM Betts	b Joseph	0	st O'Brien b Patel	5
M Hayward	b Loudon	0	not out	0
Extras	lb 9, w 2, nb 26	37	b 14, lb 5, w 1, nb 8	28
	(72 overs)	235	(69.5 overs)	251

Bowling
Joseph 11-2-47-3. Trott 14-4-37-1. Stiff 9-2-31-0. Cusden 12-1-37-3. Loudon 7-1-31-1. Walker 10-2-21-2. Patel 9-3-22-0.
Joseph 7-1-26-0. Trott 10-1-31-0. Patel 31-5-89-3. Cusden 5-1-21-1. Stiff 2-1-18-0. Loudon 14.5-1-47-6.
Fall of Wickets: 1-60, 2-91, 3-115, 4-143, 5-147, 6-177, 7-230, 8-232, 9-234
1-67, 2-85, 3-100, 4-155, 5-183, 6-183, 7-213, 8-223, 9-251

KENT

	First Innings	
DP Fulton (capt)	c Weekes b Cook	17
RWT Key	c Betts b Weekes	131
ET Smith	lbw b Betts	189
AGR Loudon	b Dalrymple	8
MJ Walker	st Scott b Dalrymple	108
*NJ O'Brien	c Scott b Cook	2
MM Patel	c Koenig b Cook	5
RH Joseph	c Hutton b Weekes	26
SMJ Cusden	c Hutton b Dalrymple	0
DA Stiff	c Hutton b Dalrymple	5
BJ Trott	not out	4
Extras	b 14, lb 15, w 5, nb 6	40
	(128.4 overs)	535

Bowling
Cook 28-3-107-3. Hayward 19-0-81-0. Betts 21-2-72-1. Hutton 2-0-9-0. Weekes 23-1-91-2. Peploe 13-0-73-0. Dalrymple 19.4-1-66-4. Shah 3-0-7-0.
Fall of Wickets: 1-18, 2-273, 3-293, 4-448, 5-451, 6-459, 7-522, 8-525, 9-526

Kent won by an innings and 49 runs –
Kent (22pts), Middlesex (4pts)

Nick Knight, the Warwickshire captain, brandishes the Frizzell County Championship trophy, to the delight of his team-mates.

SUSSEX v. SURREY - at Hove

SURREY

	First Innings			Second Innings	
SA Newman	b Kirtley	0		b Lewry	25
RS Clinton	lbw b Kirtley	4		lbw b Lewry	5
MA Butcher	c Prior b Lewry	6		c Prior b Martin-Jenkins	24
MR Ramprakash	c Montgomerie b Kirtley	3		lbw b Mushtaq Ahmed	51
*JN Batty (capt)	c Prior b Lewry	8		c Prior b Davis	42
AD Brown	c M-Jenkins b Mushtaq Ahmed	54		b Lewry	123
R Clarke	b Mushtaq Ahmed	112		lbw b Martin-Jenkins	5
MP Bicknell	c Goodwin b Davis	40		lbw b Kirtley	9
TJ Murtagh	c Goodwin b Davis	13		not out	14
J Ormond	c Adams b Davis	22		b Lewry	0
ND Doshi	not out	11		b Lewry	0
Extras	b 1, lb 2, w 1, nb 6	10		b 2, lb 6, w 1, nb 4	13
	(70 overs)	283		(82 overs)	311

Bowling
Kirtley 15-2-80-3. Lewry 16-7-30-2. Martin-Jenkins 5-0-40-0.
Mushtaq Ahmed 21-3-81-2. Yardy 4-0-23-0. Davis 9-2-26-3.
Kirtley 20-2-87-1. Lewry 16-3-66-5. Martin-Jenkins 19-4-67-2.
Mushtaq Ahmed 17-2-51-1. Davis 10-1-32-1.
Fall of Wickets: 1-0, 2-5, 3-13, 4-14, 5-60, 6-142, 7-228, 8-239, 9-256
1-31, 2-32, 3-82, 4-128, 5-223, 6-230, 7-268, 8-311, 9-311

SUSSEX

	First Innings			Second Innings	
MH Yardy	c Batty b Doshi	115		c Clinton b Doshi	25
RR Montgomerie	lbw b Bicknell	25		c Batty b Murtagh	0
PA Cottey	c Butcher b Murtagh	8		c Murtagh b Doshi	4
MW Goodwin	lbw b Doshi	16		b Ormond	119
CJ Adams (capt)	b Doshi	40		c B b Doshi	41
*MJ Prior	run out	12		c Brown b Ormond	39
RSC Martin-Jenkins	c Batty b Ormond	23		c Clinton b Doshi	12
MJG Davis	c Ramprakash b Ormond	9		lbw b Doshi	1
Mushtaq Ahmed	c Murtagh b Ormond	4		c Batty b Doshi	16
RJ Kirtley	not out	0		c Murtagh b Doshi	11
JD Lewry	c Clinton b Ormond	0		not out	1
Extras	b 5, lb 7, nb 6, p 5	23		b 3, lb 9, w 1, nb 4	17
	(79.5 overs)	271		(72.4 overs)	286

Bowling
Bicknell 13-7-26-1. Ormond 23.5-6-69-4. Clarke 8-0-49-0. Murtagh 10-1-37-1.
Doshi 25-5-73-3.
Ormond 28-6-98-2. Murtagh 12-1-35-1. Doshi 27.4-3-110-7. Clarke 5-0-31-0.
Fall of Wickets: 1-47, 2-83, 3-126, 4-210, 5-239, 6-239, 7-266, 8-266, 9-271
1-2, 2-12, 3-49, 4-158, 5-242, 6-243, 7-246, 8-263, 9-281

*Surrey won by 37 runs - Sussex (5pts),
Surrey (19pts)*

LANCASHIRE v. GLOUCESTERSHIRE - at Old Trafford

GLOS

	First Innings			Second Innings	
CM Spearman	st Hegg b Keedy	34		(2) c Chilton b Mahmood	5
WPC Weston	b Keedy	19		(1) c Hegg b Keedy	27
MEK Hussey	c Law b Keedy	46		b Keedy	45
CG Taylor (capt)	st Hegg b Keedy	60		c Hooper b Crook	109
THC Hancock	c Law b Keedy	61		c Cork b Keedy	1
APR Gidman	lbw b Keedy	0		c Mahmood b Keedy	28
*SJ Adshead	not out	52		c and b Hooper	8
ID Fisher	c Law b Keedy	5		c Hegg b Keedy	34
MCJ Ball	b Chapple	6		lbw b Keedy	0
J Lewis				b Keedy	8
NW Bracken				not out	13
Extras	b 7, lb 4, w 1, nb 16	28		b 3, lb 3, nb 4	10
	(8 wkts dec 100.2 overs)	311		(73 overs)	289

Bowling
Chapple 13.2-1-35-1. Cork 8-0-29-0. Mahmood 6-0-34-0. Keedy 42-9-95-7.
Crook 14-1-67-0. Hooper 17-4-40-0.
Cork 2-0-7-0. Mahmood 5-0-14-1. Keedy 35-2-132-7. Crook 21-3-92-1.
Hooper 10-0-38-1.
Fall of Wickets: 1-55, 2-60, 3-171, 4-181, 5-181, 6-278, 7-288, 8-311
1-10, 2-72, 3-97, 4-105, 5-169, 6-177, 7-248, 8-252, 9-272

LANCASHIRE

	First Innings			Second Innings	
MJ Chilton	c Weston b Fisher	47		c Taylor b Bracken	3
IJ Sutcliffe	c Et b Ball	28		c Adshead b Gidman	3
MB Loye	c Hancock b Ball	4		not out	45
SG Law	c Weston b Fisher	11			
CL Hooper	c Hussey b Fisher	77		not out	43
G Chapple	b Ball	10			
AR Crook	c Fisher b Lewis	17		(4) c Hancock b Bracken	0
*WK Hegg (capt)	c Adshead b Fisher	5			
DG Cork	not out	77			
SI Mahmood	c Spearman b Fisher	3			
G Keedy	c Adshead b Bracken	9			
Extras	b 10, lb 7, nb 6	23		b 4, lb 4	8
	(86 overs)	311		(3 wkts 29 overs)	99

Bowling
Lewis 11-1-38-1. Bracken 15-4-36-1. Gidman 3-2-10-0. Fisher 29-6-114-5.
Ball 28-8-96-3.
Bracken 7-2-12-2. Gidman 5-1-16-1. Fisher 5-0-20-0. Ball 5-0-14-0.
Hussey 4-1-13-0. Hancock 2-0-16-0. Weston 1-1-0-0.
Fall of Wickets: 1-87, 2-87, 3-102, 4-110, 5-154, 6-209, 7-217, 8-218, 9-231
1-2, 2-12, 3-12

Match drawn - Lancashire (9pts), Gloucestershire (10pts)

NORTHANTS v. WARWICKSHIRE - at Northampton

WARWICKSHIRE

	First Innings			Second Innings	
MA Wagh	c Brophy b Louw	7		b Phillips	19
IJ Westwood	c Brophy b Louw	3		c Louw b White	38
IR Bell	c Cook b Rofe	24		(4) lbw b Brown	1
IJL Trott	b Brown	15		(5) not out	38
NV Knight (capt)	b Louw	20		(6) b White	3
MJ Powell	lbw b Cook	49		(7) not out	5
JO Troughton	c Sales b Brown	27			
DR Brown	not out	108		(3) c Afzaal b Phillips	0
*T Frost	b Phillips	23			
HH Streak	b Louw	14			
NA Warren	b Louw	0			
Extras	b 3, nb 2	5		lb 3, nb 2	5
	(112.4 overs)	295		(5 wkts 65.3 overs)	109

Bowling
Louw 20.4-2-93-5. Rofe 28-9-63-1. Phillips 19-11-36-1. Brown 35-11-67-2.
Cook 7-1-23-1. White 3-0-10-0.
Louw 7-2-18-0. Rofe 3-2-2-0. Brown 26-8-47-1. Phillips 8-3-10-2. White 15-3-19-2.
Sales 2-1-2-0. Afzaal 2.3-1-7-0. Roberts 1-1-0-0. Brophy 1-0-1-0.
Fall of Wickets: 1-5, 2-18, 3-43, 4-69, 5-69, 6-115, 7-197, 8-246, 9-295
1-36, 2-36, 3-37, 4-87, 5-96

NORTHANTS

	First Innings		
TW Roberts	c Wagh b Brown	46	
TB Huggins	b Brown	34	
JW Cook	lbw b Trott	51	
U Afzaal	c Frost b Wagh	19	
DJG Sales (capt)	not out	72	
*GL Brophy	b Warren	23	
AR White	lbw b Warren	0	
BJ Phillips	c Frost b Warren	0	
J Louw	c Frost b Brown	5	
PC Rofe	c Bell b Brown	4	
JF Brown	lbw b Brown	0	
Extras	lb 6, w 1, nb 4	11	
	(80.3 overs)	265	

Bowling
Streak 17-2-62-0. Brown 20.3-3-53-5. Warren 17-3-60-3. Bell 5-2-17-0.
Wagh 10-2-37-1. Troughton 3-0-10-0. Trott 8-1-20-1.
Fall of Wickets: 1-79, 2-84, 3-129, 4-189, 5-230, 6-230, 7-232, 8-255, 9-265.

*Match drawn - Northamptonshire (9pts),
Warwickshire (9pts)*

4.35 pm on the second day, when Lancashire lost their sixth wicket as Andrew Crook hooked Jon Lewis straight to deep square leg, it was all over. All that remained was for Dominic Cork to show some late-order defiance, for Gloucestershire captain Taylor to set the seal on his personally satisfying debut season as skipper with a fourth hundred of the championship campaign, and for Gary Keedy to take his second seven-wicket haul of the game to claim the competition's best match figures (14 for 227) of 2004.

Warwickshire maintained their unbeaten record, for the first time since their 1972 championship-winning season, in a rain-ruined match at Northampton. Dougie Brown reached 95 not out on the opening day, during which the Frizzell championship trophy was presented to Nick Knight's team, but the all-rounder of the season was made to wait by a washed-out second day before he could reach three figures. Brown then took 5 for 53 – the first time in his long career that he had hit a century and taken five wickets in the same match – as Northants were bowled out 30 runs short of Warwickshire's first-innings 295. The champions then saw out time in a rather undignified plod to 109 for 5 from 65.3 overs.

Division Two

Nottinghamshire, the Division Two champions, capped their successful season in magnificent style by beating Essex by three wickets off the very last ball of the match at Trent Bridge. In a dazzling contest, in which 1,359 runs were scored, despite the loss of the second day to rain, Paul Franks straight drove Graham Napier for two to clinch victory. It had been a tremendous run chase on the final afternoon, set up by Darren Bicknell's 110 from 135 balls, in which he had put on 121 for the first wicket with Jason Gallian and then a further 85 for the second with Anurag Singh, who went on to score a stylish 89. Chris Read also played his part, hitting a robust 49, before Franks and Greg Smith put together the decisive 40-run partnership at the end. Franks had also hit an unbeaten 50 in the Notts first innings, helping century-maker David Hussey to rebuild the home side's innings after they had slipped to 172 for 6, while Essex earned plaudits for making a game of it with a second-innings declaration. Will Jefferson scored his fourth and fifth centuries of a productive season, Andy Flower was content to play second fiddle with two half-centuries, and Napier thumped three sixes and 14 fours in a 78-ball hundred as he and Tony Palladino added 143 for the eighth wicket in Essex's first innings of 500.

A stubborn 89 not out from Matthew Hoggard,

illustrating just what strides the former England No. 11 has made with the bat since coming under Duncan Fletcher's guidance at national level, saved Yorkshire from probable defeat against Glamorgan at Headingley. However, Hoggard's heroics, as second-innings nightwatchman, could not prevent his county from finishing third from bottom of the division – in effect 16th, and their lowest championship position for

A five-wicket haul against Yorkshire enabled Simon Jones to finish the season in fine style for Glamorgan.

12 years. Hoggard was joined by Richard Dawson in a seventh-wicket stand of 85, and he also put on 53 with last man Steve Kirby, who had come to the crease with Yorkshire still just 225 ahead and with a scheduled 40 overs of the match remaining. The match had begun well for Yorkshire, with Phil Jaques hammering 173 off 197 balls and dominating stands of 171 and 116 with Joe Sayers and Michael Lumb. Simon Jones then led a Glamorgan fightback by taking 5 for 77, his best county figures for more than two years, and the Welsh county totalled just over 400 to put the home side back under pressure. They began the last day on 104 for 4, but, in Hoggard, they found an unlikely saviour.

Two declarations early on the last day, following a second-day washout and more third-day disruption, saw Derbyshire being set 321 in 85 overs for victory. They did not get near it, thanks to Shaun Udal's season's-best haul of 6 for 79, despite an excellent unbeaten 64 by Chris Bassano. Hampshire, for whom young Chris Benham had scored 74 on debut and Greg Lamb a promising 94 in their first innings, ran out winners by 91 runs.

Similar collusion at Grace Road allowed a positive result to be reached despite the loss of both the second and third days to bad weather. Somerset had been bowled out for just 213 on the opening day, with Ottis Gibson doing much of the damage, but were let back into the match by two declarations early on the final day. Leicestershire, who had left out the apparently Lancashire-bound Brad Hodge, then slipped to 199 all out after being set a generous 275 from 65 overs.

Gibson thrashed 50 of his 57 runs in boundaries, but Andy Caddick ended a frustrating season by taking 4 for 69 to spearhead a 75-run win that propelled Somerset into fourth place in the division.

Round 20: 16–19 September 2004
Division Two

NOTTINGHAMSHIRE v. ESSEX – at Trent Bridge

ESSEX	First Innings		Second Innings	
WI Jefferson	b Bicknell	167	not out	100
AN Cook	c Read b Sidebottom	7	lbw b Sidebottom	11
A Flower	c Read b Smith	56	not out	61
RC Irani (capt)	lbw b Franks	16		
RS Bopara	lbw b Ealham	34		
*JS Foster	b Smith	23		
JD Middlebrook	c Read b Franks	14		
GR Napier	not out	106		
AP Palladino	lbw b Bicknell	41		
Danish Kaneria	b Bicknell	0		
AR Adams	absent hurt			
Extras	b 6, lb 12, nb 18	36	lb 3, w 2, nb 2	7
	(9 wkts dec 117.5 overs)	500	(1 wkt dec 34.2 overs)	179

Bowling
Smith 25-6-97-2. Sidebottom 21-3-103-1. Franks 19-4-77-2. Ealham 13-4-37-1. MacGill 20-3-72-0. Pietersen 11-0-58-0. Bicknell 6.5-0-33-3. Hussey 2-0-5-0. Sidebottom 6-0-22-1. Smith 3-0-17-0. Bicknell 8-0-37-0. Hussey 10-0-69-0. MacGill 5.2-0-24-0. Pietersen 2-0-7-0.
Fall of Wickets: 1-20, 2-152, 3-180, 4-261, 5-298, 6-339, 7-357, 8-500, 9-500
1-31

NOTTS	First Innings		Second Innings	
DJ Bicknell	lbw b Palladino	24	c Foster b Napier	110
JER Gallian (capt)	lbw b Danish Kaneria	13	c Eb b Danish Kaneria	57
A Singh	lbw b Danish Kaneria	21	lbw b Danish Kaneria	89
KP Pietersen	b Middlebrook	37	b Napier	0
DJ Hussey	not out	124	b Napier	1
*CMW Read	c Flower b Danish Kaneria	7	b Palladino	49
MA Ealham	b Danish Kaneria	1	lbw b Napier	10
PJ Franks	not out	50	not out	22
GJ Smith			not out	16
SCG MacGill				
RJ Sidebottom				
Extras	b 14, lb 7, w 1, nb 2	24	b 12, lb 10, w 1, nb 2	25
	(6 wkts dec 63.4 overs)	301	(7 wkts 71 overs)	379

Bowling
Palladino 9-2-38-1. Napier 10-1-43-0. Danish Kaneria 26-2-102-4. Bopara 6-1-24-0. Middlebrook 12.4-1-73-1.
Palladino 15-2-75-1. Napier 17-0-105-3. Danish Kaneria 24-1-92-3. Middlebrook 6-0-37-0. Bopara 9-0-48-0.
Fall of Wickets: 1-34, 2-46, 3-97, 4-107, 5-164, 6-172
1-121, 2-206, 3-206, 4-216, 5-299, 6-316, 7-339

Nottinghamshire won by 3 wickets - Nottinghamshire (20pts), Essex (7pts)

YORKSHIRE v. GLAMORGAN – at Headingley

YORKSHIRE	First Innings		Second Innings	
PA Jaques	b Jones	173	c Thomas b Harrison	9
JJ Sayers	lbw b Croft	56	lbw b Harrison	5
MJ Lumb	c Wallace b Jones	55	c Harrison b Thomas	13
MJ Wood (capt)	c Wallace b Jones	3	b Croft	30
RM Pyrah	c Elliott b Croft	12	c Wallace b Croft	36
*I Dawood	c Wallace b Davies	24	(7) st Wallace b Croft	2
RKJ Dawson	c Thomas b Croft	16	(8) c Wallace b Thomas	58
TT Bresnan	lbw b Davies	17	(9) c Wallace b Jones	1
JAR Blain	c Elliott b Jones	4	(10) b Harrison	10
MJ Hoggard	c Wallace b Jones	1	(6) not out	89
SP Kirby	not out	9	lbw b Harrison	7
Extras	b 7, lb 12, w 2, nb 10	31	b 4, lb 9, w 1, nb 12	26
	(106 overs)	401	(102.5 overs)	286

Bowling
Harrison 17-3-75-0. Jones 24-5-77-5. Davies 24-3-95-2. Croft 31-8-93-3. Thomas 10-0-42-0.
Harrison 20.5-2-73-4. Jones 26-5-60-1. Davies 7.4-1-35-0. Thomas 14.2-3-44-2. Croft 34-9-61-3.
Fall of Wickets: 1-171, 2-287, 3-294, 4-323, 5-325, 6-363, 7-367, 8-383, 9-385
1-13, 2-20, 3-34, 4-101, 5-112, 6-114, 7-199, 8-203, 9-233

GLAMORGAN	First Innings		Second Innings	
MTG Elliott	c Hoggard b Dawson	125	(2) c Wood b Dawson	23
DD Cherry	b Hoggard	21	(1) not out	18
DL Hemp	b Blain	60	not out	0
MJ Powell	c Dawood b Blain	5		
J Hughes	b Bresnan	20		
*MA Wallace	lbw b Dawson	25		
SD Thomas	b Kirby	41		
RDB Croft (capt)	not out	31		
DS Harrison	b Blain	15		
AP Davies	c Bresnan b Blain	6		
SP Jones	c Dawson b Hoggard	20		
Extras	b 5, lb 6, w 1, nb 29	41	lb 1, lb 7, w 2, nb 4	14
	(111.3 overs)	410	(1 wkt 15 overs)	55

Bowling
Hoggard 23.3-6-67-2. Kirby 18-2-65-1. Blain 19-1-110-4. Bresnan 12-3-40-1. Dawson 31-4-97-2. Jaques 2-0-18-0. Pyrah 6-4-2-0.
Kirby 6-0-21-0. Hoggard 3-1-8-0. Blain 4-0-16-0. Dawson 2-0-2-1.
Fall of Wickets: 1-92, 2-217, 3-223, 4-233, 5-276, 6-301, 7-341, 8-371, 9-383
1-50

Match drawn - Yorkshire (12pts),
Glamorgan (12pts)

DERBYSHIRE v. HAMPSHIRE – at Derby

HAMPSHIRE	First Innings		Second Innings	
JHK Adams	c Goddard b Welch	27	not out	10
MJ Brown	c Goddard b Sheikh	57		
JP Crawley	b Stubbings b Havell	18		
SM Katich	c Goddard b Welch	22		
CC Benham	c Sheikh b Havell	74		
*N Pothas	c France b Havell	12		
GA Lamb	c Goddard b Welch	94	(2) not out	7
AD Mascarenhas	c Goddard b Welch	22		
SD Udal (capt)	c Stubbings b Sheikh	1		
CT Tremlett	b Welch	0		
JA Tomlinson	not out	12		
Extras	b 8, lb 8, w 9, nb 32	57	nb 2	2
	(126.1 overs)	396	(0 wkts dec 8.3 overs)	19

Bowling
Havell 24-2-113-3. Sheikh 28-5-76-2. Welch 31.1-7-57-5. Moss 26-5-75-0. Dumelow 13-2-39-0. France 4-0-20-0.
Sheikh 1-0-1-0. Dumelow 4-0-5-0. Hassan Adnan 3.3-0-13-0.
Fall of Wickets: 1-56, 2-93, 3-157, 4-157, 5-196, 6-309, 7-363, 8-364, 9-387

DERBYSHIRE	First Innings		Second Innings	
SD Stubbings	not out	35	lbw b Udal	34
BJ France	c Pothas b Tomlinson	4	c Tremlett b Udal	12
JDC Bryant	b Tremlett	1	c sub b Tremlett	23
Hassan Adnan	not out	41	lbw b Tremlett	5
J Moss			c Tomlinson b Udal	20
CWG Bassano			not out	64
*L Goddard			lbw b Mascarenhas	8
G Welch (capt)			b Mascarenhas	12
MA Sheikh			c Katich b Udal	14
NRC Dumelow			lbw b Udal	12
PMR Havell			c Mascarenhas b Udal	3
Extras	b 3, lb 2, w 1, nb 10	16	b 8, lb 12, nb 2	22
	(2 wkts dec 35 overs)	95	(65.5 overs)	229

Bowling
Tremlett 9-1-24-1. Tomlinson 8-4-9-1. Mascarenhas 6-1-18-0. Adams 2-0-14-0. Udal 7-2-24-0. Lamb 3-2-11-0.
Tremlett 16-1-60-2. Tomlinson 12-3-34-0. Udal 26.5-8-79-6. Mascarenhas 9-2-22-2. Lamb 2-0-14-0.
Fall of Wickets: 1-8, 2-19
1-38, 2-52, 3-79, 4-80, 5-110, 6-148, 7-164, 8-203, 9-221

Hampshire won by 91 runs - Derbyshire (3pts),
Hampshire (18pts)

LEICESTERSHIRE v. SOMERSET – at Leicester

SOMERSET	First Innings		Second Innings	
MJ Wood	c Maddy b Gibson	35	c New b Maunders	3
NJ Edwards	c Sadler b Masters	45	c New b Stevens	33
M Burns (capt)	c Maunders b DeFreitas	12	b Stevens	26
JC Hildreth	b DeFreitas	0	not out	52
ID Blackwell	c Maddy b Gibson	38	not out	46
AV Suppiah	c New b Masters	0		
AW Laraman	c Dagnall b Gibson	12		
*RJ Turner	lbw b Gibson	1		
RL Johnson	c Maddy b Henderson	11		
AR Caddick	not out	19		
SRG Francis	lbw b Gibson	15		
Extras	lb 6, w 1, nb 18	25	b 4, lb 2, nb 18	24
	(56 overs)	213	(3 wkts dec 30.2 overs)	184

Bowling
Gibson 18-4-44-5. Dagnall 6-1-36-0. DeFreitas 7-1-44-2. Masters 10-2-28-2. Henderson 15-2-55-1.
DeFreitas 3-0-19-0. Maunders 8-0-45-1. Stevens 13.2-1-50-2. Robinson 2-0-30-0. Sadler 4-0-34-0.
Fall of Wickets: 1-52, 2-77, 3-78, 4-125, 5-125, 6-164, 7-166, 8-177, 9-183
1-25, 2-59, 3-72

LEICESTERSHIRE	First Innings		Second Innings	
DDJ Robinson	c Wood b Johnson	59	lbw b Caddick	20
DL Maddy (capt)	b Johnson	52	b Johnson	21
JK Maunders	c Laraman b Johnson	9	b Francis	29
DI Stevens	not out	0	c Turner b Johnson	1
JL Sadler	not out	1	st Turner b Suppiah	27
*TJ New			run out	1
OD Gibson			st Turner b Suppiah	57
PAJ DeFreitas			c Blackwell b Caddick	6
CW Henderson			lbw b Caddick	1
DD Masters			b Caddick	31
CE Dagnall			not out	9
Extras	nb 2	2	lb 4, lb 7, w 2, nb 2	15
	(3 wkts dec 38 overs)	123	(46.2 overs)	199

Bowling
Caddick 3-0-14-0. Johnson 14-4-33-3. Blackwell 10-2-28-0. Francis 5-1-24-0. Laraman 3-0-26-0.
Johnson 10-3-42-1. Caddick 16.2-1-69-4. Blackwell 8-2-25-0. Francis 5-2-27-1. Suppiah 7-0-36-2.
Fall of Wickets: 1-89, 2-121, 3-122
1-3, 2-41, 3-46, 4-73, 5-76, 6-138, 7-158, 8-159, 9-162

Somerset won by 75 runs - Leicestershire (3pts), Somerset (16pts)

DIVISION ONE FINAL POSITIONS

	P	W	L	D	Bat	Bowl	Pts
Warwickshire	16	5	0	11	65	43	222.00
Kent	16	7	3	6	43	41	206.00
Surrey	16	5	5	6	60	42	195.50
Middlesex	16	4	4	8	48	43	179.00
Sussex	16	4	5	7	46	42	172.00
Gloucestershire	16	3	3	10	49	41	172.00
Worcestershire	16	3	6	7	51	40	161.00
Lancashire	16	2	4	10	44	44	154.00
Northants	16	1	4	11	35	41	134.00

Slow Over Rate Deductions

Lancashire	2.00	v. Sussex (Hove, 21 April)
Surrey	0.50	v. Worcestershire (Worcester, 23 June)

DIVISION TWO FINAL POSITIONS

	P	W	L	D	Bat	Bowl	Pts
Nottinghamshire	16	9	2	5	66	40	252.00
Hampshire	16	9	2	5	42	40	228.00
Glamorgan	16	5	2	9	48	44	196.50
Somerset	16	4	5	7	47	44	175.00
Essex	16	3	6	7	50	45	165.00
Leicestershire	16	4	5	7	39	42	163.50
Yorkshire	16	3	4	9	44	40	162.00
Derbyshire	16	1	6	9	36	40	126.00
Durham	16	2	8	6	28	41	118.50

Slow Over Rate Deductions

Durham	1.00	v. Hampshire (Rose Bowl, 16 April)
Glamorgan	1.50	v. Essex (Cardiff, 12 May)
Leicestershire	1.50	v. Somerset (Taunton, 23 June)
Durham	1.50	v. Somerset (Riverside, 13 August)

COUNTY CHAMPIONSHIP FEATURES 2004

INDIVIDUAL SCORES OVER 200

CM Spearman	341	Gloucestershire v. Middlesex	at Gloucester
NV Knight	303*	Warwickshire v. Middlesex	at Lord's
JP Crawley	301*	Hampshire v. Nottinghamshire	at Trent Bridge
IR Bell	262*	Warwickshire v. Sussex	at Horsham
GA Hick	262	Worcestershire v. Gloucestershire	at Worcester
BJ Hodge	262	Leicestershire v. Durham	at Leicester
J Cox	250	Somerset v. Nottinghamshire	at Trent Bridge
JWM Dalrymple	244	Middlesex v. Surrey	at The Oval
PA Jaques	243	Yorkshire v. Hampshire	at The Rose Bowl
BJ Hodge	240	Leicestershire v. Essex	at Chelmsford
CM Spearman	237	Gloucestershire v. Warwickshire	at Bristol
WI Jefferson	222	Essex v. Hampshire	at The Rose Bowl
BJ Hodge	221	Leicestershire v. Derbyshire	at Oakham School
MJ North	219	Durham v. Glamorgan	at Cardiff
JS Foster	212	Essex v. Leicestershire	at Chelmsford
CJ Adams	200	Sussex v. Northamptonshire	at Hove

BEST INNINGS BOWLING (7 WICKETS OR MORE)

GJ Batty	7-52	Worcestershire v. Northamptonshire	at Northampton
JEC Franklin	7-60	Gloucestershire v. Lancashire	at Cheltenham
Danish Kaneria	7-65	Essex v. Yorkshire	at Chelmsford
RL Johnson	7-69	Somerset v. Durham	at Taunton
J Lewis	7-72	Gloucestershire v. Surrey	at Bristol
PJ Franks	7-72	Nottinghamshire v. Somerset	at Bath
Mushtaq Ahmed	7-73	Sussex v. Worcestershire	at Hove
CW Henderson	7-74	Leicestershire v. Durham	at Leicester
MF Cleary	7-80	Leicestershire v. Derbyshire	at Oakham School
HH Streak	7-80	Warwickshire v. Northamptonshire	at Edgbaston
ID Blackwell	7-90	Somerset v. Glamorgan	at Taunton
ID Blackwell	7-90	Somerset v. Nottinghamshire	at Trent Bridge
G Keedy	7-95	Lancashire v. Gloucestershire	at Old Trafford
SCG MacGill	7-109	Nottinghamshire v. Essex	at Southend-on-Sea
ND Doshi	7-110	Surrey v. Sussex	at Hove
DG Cork	7-120	Lancashire v. Middlesex	at Lord's
G Keedy	7-132	Lancashire v. Gloucestershire	at Old Trafford

BEST MATCH BOWLING

G Keedy	14/227	Lancashire v. Gloucestershire	at Old Trafford
Mushtaq Ahmed	13/140	Sussex v. Worcestershire	at Hove
HH Streak	13/158	Warwickshire v. Northamptonshire	at Edgbaston
Danish Kaneria	13/186	Essex v. Yorkshire	at Chelmsford
NAM McLean	11/124	Somerset v. Yorkshire	at Scarborough
OD Gibson	11/141	Leicestershire v. Nottinghamshire	at Leicester
ND Doshi	11/182	Surrey v. Lancashire	at Old Trafford
JM Anderson	10/81	Lancashire v. Worcestershire	at Old Trafford
GJ Batty	10/113	Worcestershire v. Northamptonshire	at Northampton
Mohammad Sami	10/138	Kent v. Northamptonshire	at Northampton
OD Gibson	10/147	Leicestershire v. Essex	at Leicester
Mushtaq Ahmed	10/149	Sussex v. Middlesex	at Lord's
GR Breese	10/151	Durham v. Yorkshire	at Scarborough
ND Doshi	10/183	Surrey v. Sussex	at Hove
SCG MacGill	10/233	Nottinghamshire v. Essex	at Southend-on-Sea
G Keedy	9/82	Lancashire v. Worcestershire	at Old Trafford
M Davies	9/87	Durham v. Hampshire	at The Rose Bowl
RKJ Dawson	9/115	Yorkshire v. Durham	at The Riverside
SCG MacGill	9/135	Nottinghamshire v. Durham	at Trent Bridge
CE Shreck	9/138	Nottinghamshire v. Durham	at The Riverside

COUNTY CHAMPIONSHIP FEATURES 2004

HIGHEST TEAM TOTALS

708 for 9d	Essex v. Leicestershire	at Chelmsford
695 for 9d	Gloucestershire v. Middlesex	at Gloucester
654 for 8d	Somerset v. Nottinghamshire	at Trent Bridge
642	Essex v. Glamorgan	at Chelmsford
641 for 4d	Hampshire v. Nottinghamshire	at Trent Bridge
634 for 9d	Leicestershire v. Durham	at Leicester
619 for 6d	Worcestershire v. Gloucestershire	at Worcester
618	Sussex v. Kent	at Hove
615	Kent v. Lancashire	at Tunbridge Wells
612	Nottinghamshire v. Hampshire	at Trent Bridge
608 for 7d	Warwickshire v. Middlesex	at Lord's
600 for 6d	Warwickshire v. Sussex	at Horsham
598	Surrey v. Gloucestershire	at The Oval
592 for 8d	Gloucestershire v. Warwickshire	at Bristol
587	Glamorgan v. Essex	at Chelmsford
570	Northamptonshire v. Sussex	at Hove
562	Sussex v. Warwickshire	at Horsham
552 for 9d	Nottinghamshire v. Derbyshire	at Derby
551 for 7d	Nottinghamshire v. Derbyshire	at Trent Bridge
546	Warwickshire v. Surrey	at Edgbaston

LOWEST TEAM TOTALS

91	Durham v. Derbyshire	at The Riverside
93	Durham v. Nottinghamshire	at The Riverside
96	Derbyshire v. Nottinghamshire	at Derby
106	Sussex v. Gloucestershire	at Arundel Castle
111	Leicestershire v. Hampshire	at The Rose Bowl
113	Hampshire v. Nottinghamshire	at The Rose Bowl
116	Essex v. Yorkshire	at Chelmsford
127	Worcestershire v. Lancashire	at Old Trafford
128	Durham v. Hampshire	at The Rose Bowl
129	Kent v. Gloucestershire	at Canterbury
129	Lancashire v. Surrey	at Old Trafford
135	Middlesex v. Sussex	at Hove
137	Leicestershire v. Glamorgan	at Cardiff
139	Leicestershire v. Hampshire	at The Rose Bowl
141	Sussex v. Middlesex	at Hove
146	Worcestershire v. Lancashire	at Old Trafford
146	Somerset v. Hampshire	at The Rose Bowl
147	Surrey v. Northamptonshire	at Northampton
149	Hampshire v. Essex	at The Rose Bowl
150	Durham v. Yorkshire	at The Riverside

COUNTY CHAMPIONSHIP FEATURES 2004

LEADING RUN SCORERS

Player	Runs	Matches
BJ Hodge (Leicestershire)	1548	15
IR Bell (Warwickshire)	1498	15
MR Ramprakash (Surrey)	1451	16
CM Spearman (Gloucestershire)	1424	16
WI Jefferson (Essex)	1411	16
U Afzaal (Northamptonshire)	1365	16
GA Hick (Worcestershire)	1349	16
OA Shah (Middlesex)	1280	16
RWT Key (Kent)	1274	10
ET Smith (Kent)	1269	16
NV Knight (Warwickshire)	1256	15
Hassan Adnan (Derbyshire)	1247	16
MTG Elliott (Glamorgan)	1245	14
MJ Walker (Kent)	1234	16
DJG Sales (Northamptonshire)	1230	16
DJ Hussey (Nottinghamshire)	1208	16
SA Newman (Surrey)	1162	16
BL Hutton (Middlesex)	1129	16
IJL Trott (Warwickshire)	1126	16
PA Jaques (Yorkshire)	1118	11

MOST SIXES

Player	Sixes	Matches
DJ Hussey (Nottinghamshire)	25	16
MA Ealham (Nottinghamshire)	20	15
DJG Sales (Northamptonshire)	20	16
ID Blackwell (Somerset)	19	10
GR Napier (Essex)	19	14
GA Hick (Worcestershire)	18	16
BJ Hodge (Leicestershire)	17	15
KP Pietersen (Nottinghamshire)	15	14
CM Spearman (Gloucestershire)	15	16
RWT Key (Kent)	14	10
AJ Bichel (Worcestershire)	14	14
MJ Brown (Hampshire)	14	16
AD Brown (Surrey)	13	14
PA Jaques (Yorkshire)	12	11
DG Cork (Lancashire)	12	14
CJ Adams (Sussex)	12	16
RL Johnson (Somerset)	11	13
MTG Elliott (Glamorgan)	11	14
MR Ramprakash (Surrey)	11	16
CL Hooper (Lancashire)	10	13

COUNTY CHAMPIONSHIP FEATURES 2004

MOST FOURS

Player	Fours	Matches
WI Jefferson (Essex)	225	16
BJ Hodge (Leicestershire)	203	15
IR Bell (Warwickshire)	192	15
GA Hick (Worcestershire)	191	16
MR Ramprakash (Surrey)	187	16
MTG Elliott (Glamorgan)	182	14
SA Newman (Surrey)	180	16
ET Smith (Kent)	175	16
RWT Key (Kent)	170	10
CM Spearman (Gloucestershire)	166	16
PA Jaques (Yorkshire)	165	11
DJ Hussey (Nottinghamshire)	162	16
DJ Bicknell (Nottinghamshire)	161	16
NV Knight (Warwickshire)	159	15
Hassan Adnan (Derbyshire)	154	16
JER Gallian (Nottinghamshire)	153	16
DJG Sales (Northamptonshire)	150	16
IJL Trott (Warwickshire)	147	16
DL Hemp (Glamorgan)	144	16
DDJ Robinson (Leicestershire)	143	15

LEADING WICKET-TAKERS

Player	Wickets	Matches
Mushtaq Ahmed (Sussex)	82	16
G Keedy (Lancashire)	72	16
Danish Kaneria (Essex)	63	11
OD Gibson (Leicestershire)	60	15
J Louw (Northamptonshire)	60	16
J Lewis (Gloucestershire)	57	16
A D Mascarenhas (Hampshire)	56	16
AR Caddick (Somerset)	54	13
RDB Croft (Glamorgan)	54	16
DS Harrison (Glamorgan)	53	16
SK Warne (Hampshire)	51	12
MS Mason (Worcestershire)	51	16
M Davies (Durham)	50	10
J Ormond (Surrey)	48	16
GJ Batty (Worcestershire)	45	12
G Welch (Derbyshire)	45	16
NAM McLean (Somerset)	43	10
M Akram (Sussex)	43	13
PJ Franks (Nottinghamshire)	42	16
MM Patel (Kent)	41	11

COUNTY CHAMPIONSHIP FEATURES 2004

LEADING CATCHES (EXCLUDING WICKETKEEPERS)

Player	Catches	Matches
GA Hick (Worcestershire)	25	16
MJ Wood (Yorkshire)	24	16
DJ Hussey (Nottinghamshire)	24	16
DL Maddy (Leicestershire)	23	16
BL Hutton (Middlesex)	23	16
MJ Clarke (Hampshire)	20	12
DP Fulton (Kent)	20	15
CL Hooper (Lancashire)	19	13
AN Cook (Essex)	18	12
WPC Weston (Gloucestershire)	18	16
A Flower (Essex)	18	16
DJG Sales (Northamptonshire)	18	16
OA Shah (Middlesex)	18	16
SG Law (Lancashire)	17	12
DG Cork (Lancashire)	17	14
KP Pietersen (Nottinghamshire)	17	14
BF Smith (Worcestershire)	17	15
M Burns (Somerset)	17	15
JER Gallian (Nottinghamshire)	16	16
MJ Walker (Kent)	16	16

LEADING DISMISSALS (WICKETKEEPERS)

Player	Dismissals	Matches
RJ Turner (Somerset)	65	15
JN Batty (Surrey)	52	16
N Pothas (Hampshire)	50	16
T Frost (Warwickshire)	48	16
SJ Rhodes (Worcestershire)	46	16
JS Foster (Essex)	44	16
SJ Adshead (Gloucestershire)	41	15
MA Wallace (Glamorgan)	41	16
PA Nixon (Leicestershire)	40	12
CMW Read (Nottinghamshire)	38	13
NJ O'Brien (Kent)	38	14
LD Sutton (Derbyshire)	33	15
A Pratt (Durham)	32	13
GL Brophy (Northamptonshire)	29	14
DC Nash (Middlesex)	28	10
WK Hegg (Lancashire)	28	12
SM Guy (Yorkshire)	23	8
TR Ambrose (Sussex)	21	8
MJ Prior (Sussex)	18	8
JJ Haynes (Lancashire)	14	4

COUNTY CHAMPIONSHIP FEATURES 2004

MOST HUNDREDS

Player	Hundreds	Matches
RWT Key (Kent)	6	10
IR Bell (Warwickshire)	6	15
MR Ramprakash (Surrey)	6	16
DJ Hussey (Nottinghamshire)	6	16
DP Fulton (Kent)	5	15
BJ Hodge (Leicestershire)	5	15
DJ Bicknell (Nottinghamshire)	5	16
BL Hutton (Middlesex)	5	16
WI Jefferson (Essex)	5	16
AD Brown (Surrey)	4	14
MTG Elliott (Glamorgan)	4	14
KP Pietersen (Nottinghamshire)	4	14
IJ Ward (Sussex)	4	15
CJ Adams (Sussex)	4	16
MJ Walker (Kent)	4	16
U Afzaal (Northamptonshire)	4	16
OA Shah (Middlesex)	4	16
ET Smith (Kent)	4	16
CG Taylor (Gloucestershire)	4	16
CM Spearman (Gloucestershire)	4	16

MOST FIFTIES (INCLUDING HUNDREDS)

Player	Fifties	Matches
DJG Sales (Northamptonshire)	13	16
MR Ramprakash (Surrey)	12	16
MJ Walker (Kent)	12	16
OA Shah (Middlesex)	12	16
PN Weekes (Middlesex)	11	16
U Afzaal (Northamptonshire)	11	16
SA Newman (Surrey)	11	16
IJL Trott (Warwickshire)	11	16
NV Knight (Warwickshire)	10	15
DDJ Robinson (Leicestershire)	10	15
IR Bell (Warwickshire)	10	15
JER Gallian (Nottinghamshire)	10	16
DL Hemp (Glamorgan)	10	16
WI Jefferson (Essex)	10	16
Hassan Adnan (Derbyshire)	10	16
AD Brown (Surrey)	9	14
MTG Elliott (Glamorgan)	9	14
BJ Hodge (Leicestershire)	9	15
GA Hick (Worcestershire)	9	16
ET Smith (Kent)	9	16

COUNTY CHAMPIONSHIP FEATURES 2004

LEADING DUCK-MAKERS

Player	Ducks	Matches
SP Kirby (Yorkshire)	8	13
MN Malik (Worcestershire)	5	7
AG Wharf (Glamorgan)	5	10
JK Maunders (Leicestershire)	5	10
JF Brown (Northamptonshire)	5	13
KP Pietersen (Nottinghamshire)	5	14
MJ Brown (Hampshire)	5	16
MS Kasprowicz (Glamorgan)	4	7
N Peng (Durham)	4	9
AJ Hollioake (Surrey)	4	10
N Killeen (Durham)	4	12
DG Cork (Lancashire)	4	14
SD Stubbings (Derbyshire)	4	14
IJ Ward (Sussex)	4	15
MA Wagh (Warwickshire)	4	16
ET Smith (Kent)	4	16
AD Mascarenhas (Hampshire)	4	16
TW Roberts (Northamptonshire)	4	16
JS Foster (Essex)	4	16
MG Bevan (Kent)	3	4

HUNDREDS IN EACH INNINGS

Name	For	Against	Venue	Date	1st	2nd
BJ Hodge	Leics	v. Glamorgan	Leicester	21 April	105	158
SD Peters	Worcs	v. Kent	Worcester	9 June	123	117
MJ Clarke	Hants	v. Notts	Trent Bridge	23 July	140	103
BL Hutton	Middlesex	v. Kent	Southgate	28 July	100	107
IR Bell	Warwicks	v. Lancs	Old Trafford	28 July	112	181
MJ Walker	Kent	v. Sussex	Canterbury	3 August	157	100*
MR Ramprakash	Surrey	v. Worcs	The Oval	3 August	130	100*
ML Love	Northants	v. Worcs	Worcester	11 August	133*	161*
WI Jefferson	Essex	v. Notts	Trent Bridge	16 Sept	167	100*

FASTEST COUNTY CHAMPIONSHIP HUNDREDS

RL Johnson	63 balls	Somerset v. Durham at Taunton		16 August
GR Napier	78 balls	Essex v. Notts	at Trent Bridge	18 September
AR Adams	80 balls	Essex v. Leics	at Grace Road	21 July
D G Cork	81 balls	Lancs v. Surrey	at Whitgift	13 August
G Chapple	82 balls	Lancs v. Warwicks	at Old Trafford	30 July

FESTIVAL CRICKET

DAVID GREEN, the former Lancashire and Gloucestershire batsman who now writes on cricket for the *Daily Telegraph*, examines the continuing appeal of festival cricket and the way it seems to be gathering strength again as a vital heartbeat of the English sporting summer.

Festival cricket has been adding spice to the English game for more than 150 years. By the time the counties had begun to play each other with any regularity, around the mid-1860s, Canterbury Week, the oldest of all the festivals, had been established for a quarter of a century.

Today, the public still values county cricket's festivals, some of which, like Canterbury, Cheltenham and Bath, are long-established while others, such as Arundel and Oakham School, are comparatively recent.

Two venues were used for the first time last season, Beckenham and Stratford-upon-Avon, an encouraging development after a period, beginning in the mid-1980s, when out-grounds were struck off fixture lists in large numbers. Takings at festivals, moreover, were particularly healthy last summer, with record receipts at Tunbridge Wells, Cheltenham and also Scarborough – despite Yorkshire's match with Durham not making it into the fourth day.

This situation would have been scarcely credible ten or 15 years ago when the generally held view among cricket administrators was that festival cricket, indeed all cricket played at out-grounds (ie away from the headquarters ground), was a dead duck. For one thing, it was argued, with only eight home championship fixtures, it was difficult to justify taking matches away from those headquarters that are generally situated in the most densely populated area of the county and that serve the bulk of the membership.

Things were, of course, very different before the introduction of one-day cricket and the subsequent drastic additional cutback of championship fixtures due to the launch of four-day championship cricket. In 1968, before the Sunday League was introduced, there were 28 championship games of three days' duration. This meant 14 home games, plus one against the tourists and possibly another against one of the Universities. The cake was then big enough to allow two or three slices or more to go to out-grounds.

From 1969, the championship was reduced to 24 matches. From 1988, when some four-day championship matches were played alongside three-day games as an experiment, that figure became 22.

The eight home matches now played are no longer regularly supplemented by a tourist game, owing to the proliferation of one-day internationals which, in turn, means that Test matches are frequently played back-to-back. As for the Universities, it is many years since they played away matches against counties, and many years since they were strong enough to provide credible opposition. The cake, it was said, was now clearly not big enough to be shared around.

Another factor which told against festival cricket was the increasing expense of setting up what are basically club or school grounds for first-class cricket. This had always been considerable, what with the transport of seating, the putting-up of temporary stands and the hiring of marquees, but it escalated with the advance of Health and Safety regulations.

These insisted on such things as specialised disabled access, a minimum number of points with running water available, hot and cold water for washing up and, not before time, minimum standards for the quantity and quality of lavatories. I remember attending the second match of a two-match festival in the early 1980s where the gents' toilets consisted of a small marquee containing half a dozen oil drums that had started the week empty. That festival was played in a heat wave, crowds were big, lots of beer was drunk; by day six, conditions in that marquee beggared belief.

A further argument against the use of out-grounds, whether for festivals or single one-day matches, was the fact that by 1980 most headquarters grounds had been significantly and expensively upgraded in terms of seating and general spectator facilities. Several grounds had invested in purpose-built indoor nets, which contrasted sharply with the converted dining rooms, permitting only a few paces of run-up, which my generation grew up with.

By then, too, fitness centres were by no means uncommon; therefore, it seemed nonsensical to possess all these facilities and then ignore them for many weeks by going off and playing somewhere else.

Given all of this, it is not altogether surprising that so many festivals were terminated. A glance at the 1985 fixture list reveals just how many have gone under during the last 20 years. In that year, championship cricket was still being played at Bradford, Chesterfield, Sheffield (Abbeydale Park), Basingstoke, Middlesbrough, Ilford, Abergavenny, Neath, Bournemouth, Portsmouth, Harrogate, Hastings, Nuneaton, Maidstone, Eastbourne, Uxbridge, Weston-super-Mare, Buxton and Folkestone. A couple of these grounds still host limited-overs matches but, in festival terms, they are at one with Nineveh and Tyre.

So far I have only concentrated on festivals that are, or were, part of the championship season, but the end-of-season festival, which for most of us means Scarborough, has also been under pressure. People of my advanced years will be aware that there were end-of-season festivals at Hastings, Torquay and also at Kingston-upon-Thames; indeed, Hastings was the setting for one of Gilbert Jessop's most celebrated innings.

Playing for the Gentlemen of the South against the Players of the South, in 1907, he reached his century in 42 minutes and was finally dismissed after 90 minutes at the crease ... for 191.

Scarborough, who hosted their first festival in 1896, consisted of three matches for most of its existence – Yorkshire v. the MCC, HDG Leveson-Gower's XI (later TN Pearce's XI) against the tourists, and Gents v. Players. When the amateur-professional distinction was abolished after 1962, the third game would often be an England XI v. The Rest of the World XI.

Given good weather, Scarborough attracted very big crowds (I played there for Lancashire 2nd XI against Yorkshire 2nd XI in 1960 in front of a crowd of 8,000). Many of the spectators were children, some of whom were encouraged by the genial and relaxed atmosphere of the place to pluck up courage to ask, for the first time, for a famous player's autograph.

I can remember Hastings and Torquay putting on matches between North and South, and between an England XI and a Commonwealth XI. These latter sides would consist of Australian cricketers playing for English counties – such as Bruce Dooland of Notts, George Tribe and Jock Livingston of Northants, Vic Jackson of Leicestershire – and leavened by Indian, Pakistani and West Indian Test players engaged in the Northern Leagues

(hence these matches always took place midweek).

Though Scarborough had first pick, some pretty useful English players turned out at Hastings and Torquay. In 1954 at Hastings, for instance, the Commonwealth XI was Ken Archer, Roy Marshall, Gul Mahomed, Frank Worrell, Clyde Walcott, Bruce Dooland, Vinoo Mankad, GS Ramchand, George Tribe, Ben Barnett and Sonny Ramadhin, while the English XI included talents like Don Kenyon, Allan Watkins, Jim Laker, Derek Shackleton, Tony Lock and Peter Loader. I would happily have forked out a few shillings to loll in a deckchair for three days and watch that lot play cricket.

Torquay and Hastings did not survive as end-of-season festival venues beyond the mid-1960s, although the latter continued to host county championship games in festival style until the field was sold as building land a decade or so ago.

Scarborough continued to thrive, until the extension of the championship season to mid-September and beyond forced an adjustment. It would have been pointless to put on games after the championship had ended, since by mid-September the bulk of the potential audience, holidaying people, would have departed; the adults to go back to work and the children to return to school. Accordingly, the festival now consists of a four-day match and a one-day league game, played at the traditional time in early September. It remains hugely popular.

When the moneymen were issuing their dire warnings about the ruinous cost of running festivals, a few counties capitulated. Some individuals in positions of influence dug in their heels, however. Among that number was Peter Edwards, under whose shrewd guidance as secretary/manager Essex

Since hosting its first first-class match in 1990, Arundel has become an increasingly popular out-ground venue.

were prosperous and successful from the 1970s until his untimely death five years ago. By 1984, as well as playing at their Chelmsford headquarters, Essex also staged fixtures at Ilford, Southend and Colchester.

This was a reduction from the number of games they had played at out-grounds 20 years previously, when they also appeared at Romford, Clacton, Westcliff, Brentwood and Leyton. However, with extensive – and expensive – development work taking place at Chelmsford, Edwards inevitably came under pressure to concentrate Essex cricket there. I remember discussing the issue with him at the time.

'With little cricket being played in state schools these days', he said, 'we need to find a way to introduce the next generation to the first-class game. We won't be able to do this if people have to make round trips of anything from 70 to 100 miles to Chelmsford to see a game. Essex is a big county and we have to take the game to the spectators. We have rationalised considerably since the 1960s, when we regularly played on eight different grounds, but if we go further we risk losing the broad base of our support – and that will be a lot more expensive than continuing to play at our three out-grounds.'

Somerset chief executive Peter Anderson has also recently told me that a few years ago the county were looking hard at the economics of continuing to have a festival at Bath, especially with Weston-super-Mare having hosted its last championship match in 1996.

'On paper', he said, 'there is only one course of action. When we get good weather at Bath we take plenty of money, but when you put the setting-up costs against those receipts plus, something that is often forgotten, the money we would have taken without any hassle if the game was played at Taunton, you get a very different picture.

'Of course, other factors have to be considered, and that means not just keeping our members in the north of the county happy. Tradition is important to cricket, and that is why we continue to play matches at venues like Bath.'

Mike Fatkin, the Glamorgan chief executive, also expresses views about Colwyn Bay that – at face value – are not entirely the best from a commercial angle. It is the county's outpost in North Wales and, having played there once in 1970, they returned 20 years later and have staged matches at the ground almost every year since.

'Colwyn Bay is four hours from Cardiff by car', said Fatkin, 'so it isn't the most sensible place for us to play. But we have development officers working away diligently in North Wales, as well as everywhere else in the country, and we can hardly claim to represent the whole of Wales if we are not prepared to move away from the South for the odd game. Apart from that, the people up there are most efficient, it is a lovely spot and if we get decent weather we make money.'

It would appear, therefore, that festival cricket, if not so robust as it was 50 years ago, is in very reasonable health. Some venues have gone for ever, but some, like Chesterfield, could yet return. There certainly seems to be a willingness among the counties to ignore the cheeseparing blandishments of the accountants.

New venues, indeed, are popping up. Arundel, which started, I believe, in 1990, was against the trend of the time, but more recent newcomers, such as Oakham School, Whitgift School, Beckenham and Southgate, offer welcome reinforcement of the old established festivals.

Moreover, those counties now beginning to make an effort to offer new festivals are only giving the customers what they want. The fact is, we like our festivals. Some county headquarters, such as Trent Bridge, Worcester or Hove, have a distinct aesthetic appeal – but a good many others are distinctly uninspiring. The playing surfaces may be excellent, the seats more comfortable, and there may be plenty of cover

Scarborough fare: Yorkshire's traditional late-summer festival in the seaside town remains as popular as ever, and in 2004 generated record receipts.

for when it rains, but out-grounds such as Cheltenham, Arundel and Bath, which have views and lawns and trees to please even the jaundiced eye, offer something special.

There is, though, more to it than mere aesthetics. I believe the main thing that gives the English festival ground its particular appeal is the spectators themselves. Very few people at a festival ground have wandered in on spec or to while away a couple of hours in the sun. They go because they love cricket.

Of course, at places such as Bath and Cheltenham, or at Horsham or at Canterbury Week, there is also a strong element of local support. However, there is also a powerful presence of those who are not partisan, but who are there for the game itself.

Such people plan their holidays so that they – and often their equally besotted families – can enjoy their week or ten days at the festival. If you don't believe me, try to book a hotel room, or even a modest bed and breakfast, within five miles of Cheltenham during the festival.

Crowds composed largely of such people have seemed to me, since my own first playing experience of festival cricket at Cheltenham in 1961, to be clearly more knowledgeable than others. They are more appreciative, less likely to applaud an edged boundary and more likely to applaud a bowler at the end of the over – even though it wasn't a maiden. Players react to this kind of support, their spirits lift and their performance is enhanced.

Cricket can be boring and cricketers can get cross with each other, but such things are as rare as hen's teeth at festivals. For various reasons, some clear, some inscrutable, the future of festival cricket seems to be secure and the English game is stronger and more vibrant for its continued existence.

TOTESPORT LEAGUE
By Mark Baldwin

25 April 2004: Division One

at The Oval
Surrey 146 (42.3 overs) (IDK Salisbury 59*,
AP Davies 4 for 29)
Glamorgan 147 for 3 (22.3 overs) (MTG Elliott 69*,
MJ Powell 64)
Glamorgan (4pts) won by 7 wickets

at Canterbury
Kent 175 for 9 (45 overs)
Gloucestershire 174 (44.3 overs) (CM Spearman 63,
Mohammad Sami 6 for 20)
Kent (4pts) won by 1 run

at Edgbaston
Hampshire 215 for 6 (45 overs) (MJ Clarke 68)
Warwickshire 189 (42.4 overs)
Hampshire (4pts) won by 26 runs

at Northampton
Northamptonshire 161 for 9 (45 overs) (GL Brophy 50*)
Lancashire 162 for 5 (41 overs) (MB Loye 70)
Lancashire (4pts) won by 5 wickets

Within an hour of kicking off their defence of the one-day league title, Surrey were in disarray at 36 for 7 against Glamorgan at The Oval. Even the presence of a new coach and captain, Steve Rixon and Jon Batty, could not prevent Surrey from plunging to a seven-wicket defeat. The Glamorgan new-ball bowlers, Mike Kasprowicz and Andrew Davies, were the chief architects of Surrey's destruction – Kasprowicz took 3 for 23 in his opening spell and Davies wreaked yet more havoc in a remarkable burst. In 18 balls, he produced eight wides, a no-ball, and four wicket-taking deliveries. Surrey managed to reach 146 thanks to Ian Salisbury's unbeaten 59 and his 64-run eighth-wicket stand with Saqlain Mushtaq. Glamorgan were inspired by Michael Powell's aggressive 64 off just 40 balls, with 14 fours, while opener Matthew Elliott finished on 69 not out. For Surrey, however, it was a demoralising day. Rixon and Batty looked to be in for a difficult first half of the season as they sought to stabilise the side again following the resignations of Adam Hollioake and Keith Medlycott, as captain and coach, the retirement of Alec Stewart and the loss to Sussex of Ian Ward at the end of the 2003 season. The absences of Graham Thorpe and Mark Butcher, rested by England's

management, and Martin Bicknell, injured, did not help the Surrey cause either, but the champions were still left heavily bruised by this opening defeat.

Mohammad Sami stole the show at Canterbury, as last season's runners-up, Gloucestershire, fell an agonising one run short in a dramatic final over. The Pakistan fast bowler, generating breathtaking pace, completed a six-wicket haul just 12 hours after arriving at Heathrow, following an 11-hour overnight flight from Karachi. Sami had already taken three wickets in his initial five-over spell – after Gloucestershire had reached 51 without loss – plus the important wicket of Craig Spearman, yorked, with the tenth ball of a two-over second spell. The real drama was still to come, however. Sami began the final over with Gloucestershire needing only two more runs to win, and with two wickets still in hand. He immediately had Jon Lewis caught behind and, two balls later, plucked out No. 11 Mike Smith's off stump.

At Edgbaston, three days before his 21st birthday, Graham Wagg hit Shane Warne for three successive sixes in an over – and still ended up on the losing side as promoted Hampshire began their Division One campaign with a 26-run win against Warwickshire. Wagg's hitting came too late to save his side after they had collapsed to 137 for 7 in reply to Hampshire's 215 for 6. That total was made possible by Michael Clarke's elegant 68 and especially by a late onslaught from Shaun Udal. The former England one-day

The pace of Kent's Mohammad Sami was too much for Gloucestershire at Canterbury.

international struck a six and five fours in an unbeaten 30 that took him just nine balls. In all, Hampshire plundered 54 from their last four overs. In the end this proved to be the difference between the two sides – despite Wawickshire's Wagg of the tail.

Division One new boys, Lancashire and Northamptonshire, met at Wantage Road with 2003 Division Two champions Lancashire running out comfortable five-wicket winners. The Northants batting proved as wobbly as their accounts, as the team slid to 71 for 6 on the weekend that it was revealed that the county had lost a staggering £247,000 through 'accounting irregularities'. Gerard Brophy's unbeaten 50 eventually took Northants to 161 for 9 from their 45 overs, but Lancashire were virtually home and dry by the time Mal Loye and Iain Sutcliffe had put on 93 for the first wicket. Sutcliffe had a stroke of fortune when he played the ball onto his own stumps without dislodging a bail, while Loye's brutal 53-ball innings of 70 against his former county included 14 fours.

Division Two

at Headingley
Leicestershire 257 for 7 (45 overs) (JL Sadler 88, JN Snape 69)
Yorkshire 112 (28 overs) (CW Henderson 5 for 24)
Leicestershire (4pts) won by 145 runs

at Taunton
Somerset 278 for 7 (45 overs) (M Burns 97, KA Parsons 51)
Derbyshire 169 (36.1 overs)
Somerset (4pts) won by 109 runs

at Lord's
Middlesex 140 (37.4 overs)
Sussex 143 for 2 (30.1 overs) (MJ Prior 70, IJ Ward 56*)
Sussex (4pts) won by 8 wickets

at The Riverside
Durham 200 for 7 (45 overs) (MJ North 53)
Nottinghamshire 174 (42 overs)
Durham (4pts) won by 26 runs

A record stand of 165 between Leicestershire's middle-order batsmen John Sadler and Jeremy Snape was the major difference between two of last year's relegated sides at Headingley, where Yorkshire later slumped to 22 for 5. Leicestershire looked to be in trouble themselves at 44 for 4 before 22-year-old Sadler, a former Yorkshire player, was joined by

Snape. Sadler was eventually stumped for 88, while Snape struck three sixes in his innings of 69. In all, 95 runs flowed from the last ten overs and, at 257 for 7, a full recovery had been made. Yorkshire's own early-order collapse, however, proved terminal. Bowled out for just 112, they also saw their two Australians, Darren Lehmann and Ian Harvey, suffer worrying leg injuries. Mark Cleary and Ottis Gibson did the initial damage, and left-arm spinner Claude Henderson finished things off with 5 for 24. Before the game, a minute's silence was observed in memory of Willie Watson, who played both cricket and football for England and, like Sadler in this match, joined Leicestershire from his native Yorkshire.

Somerset built three key run-scoring partnerships as they claimed a morale-boosting early-season victory over Derbyshire at Taunton. Skipper Mike Burns featured in two of them, adding 97 for the first wicket with John Francis and 69 for the second with Carl Gazzard, before being stumped for 97 as he attempted a big hit to complete a century in style. Keith Parsons and Rob Turner then added a further 41 in the last four overs, with Parsons reaching an entertaining 51 from 49 balls. Derbyshire needed a stiff 6.2 runs per over and, despite a promising start, they soon found the task beyond them. The last eight wickets fell for just 120 runs, with a fiery Nixon McLean almost taking a hat-trick. Chris Bassano and Nathan Dumelow fell to his tenth and 11th deliveries, but Hassan Adnan survived the next ball – much to the crowd's disappointment.

A startling collapse from 47 for 1 to 98 for 8, in the space of only 17 overs, condemned Middlesex to a heavy defeat against Sussex at Lord's. The four Sussex seamers shared the wickets, with Jason Lewry emerging with the best figures by taking 3 for 26. The home side's underachievement was put into sharp relief by the 126-run opening partnership with which Ian Ward and Matt Prior launched the Sussex reply to Middlesex's eventual 140 all out. Prior, aiming for further representative honours in 2004 after his winter stint with the National Academy, hit 70 from 77 balls – but only after he had been dropped on 11. He reached his half-century with a flat six back over the head of Paul Weekes, the off spinner.

Durham made a winning start to the season, thanks, in large part, to the malfunctioning of the Nottinghamshire top order. The fall of Kevin Pietersen, for 23, was a severe loss for Notts, who slid to 64 for 4 and then 131 for 9 in reply to Durham's seemingly unthreatening total of 200 for 7. That they eventually got to within 26 runs was due to a last-wicket stand of 43 between Stuart MacGill and Greg

Smith. Durham's score was built around a third-wicket partnership of 65, with Marcus North hitting 53 and Gary Pratt 42. Gareth Breese, the Jamaican making his debut, immediately endeared himself to the Riverside crowd with a huge straight six during his innings of 25, and later took three wickets to underline his worth as an off-spinning all-rounder.

2 May 2004: Division One

at Old Trafford
Kent 203 (44 overs)
Lancashire 207 for 7 (44.2 overs)
Lancashire (4pts) won by 3 wickets

at Bristol
Gloucestershire 213 for 8 (45 overs)
(MGN Windows 79)
Glamorgan 216 for 2 (37.2 overs) (MTG Elliott 91*,
RDB Croft 56)
Glamorgan (4pts) won by 8 wickets

at The Rose Bowl
Hampshire 184 for 7 (45 overs) (N Pothas 64,
WS Kendall 55*)
Essex 153 (43.1 overs)
Hampshire (4pts) won by 31 runs

When 20-year-old Kyle Hogg came out to bat at No. 8 at Old Trafford, Lancashire still needed 62 from 11 overs to beat Kent. In the end, with Hogg unbeaten on 37 from 35 balls, victory was achieved with just four balls to spare. It was a gutsy effort, and Hogg's composure in a tight situation put some of his more senior colleagues to shame. Kent's total of 203 was below par on a good pitch; they would not have got there at all if it had not been for Rob Ferley's 42 from No. 8. Three top-order wickets from Sajid Mahmood added to the good reputation he had gained for himself during his time at the National Academy during the winter. At 93 for no wicket, with openers Mal Loye and Iain Sutcliffe in control, Lancashire seemed to be cruising. However, six wickets were then lost in 14 overs, with spinners Ferley and James Tredwell sharing four of them, and it needed the entry of Hogg to re-ignite Lancashire's run chase.

Matthew Elliott's elegant, yet aggressive, unbeaten 91, from 116 balls, earned Glamorgan a comfortable eight-wicket victory against Gloucestershire at Bristol. Glamorgan's performance with the bat was in direct contrast to Gloucestershire's, apart from the efforts of Matt Windows and Craig Spearman. Windows

made 79, dominating a fifth-wicket stand of 66 with Chris Taylor, and hitting a six and four boundaries. Elliott struck a six and 11 fours and was joined in a first-wicket partnership of 98 by Robert Croft, who played the pinch-hitting role to perfection with 56. Mike Powell then helped Elliott to add a further 92 for the second wicket, and victory arrived with 7.4 overs to spare.

Gritty half-centuries from Nic Pothas and Will Kendall gave Hampshire enough runs to see off Essex's challenge on a bowler-friendly surface at the Rose Bowl. Only two Essex batsmen passed 20 as they fell 31 runs short of Hampshire's 184 for 7, with Shane Warne picking up three cheap wickets and fellow Australian Michael Clarke two in their last match before their temporary absence on international duty. The Essex top three fell to the seamers, with Nasser Hussain top scoring with 24, before the Hampshire spinners took over and squeezed any remaining life out of the visitors. Pothas swung Danish Kaneria – Essex's Pakistani leg spinner – for six in his innings of 64, while Kendall finished unbeaten on 55, but, in truth, this was the sort of pitch on which no one could bat with any conviction.

Division Two

at Leicester
Scotland 86 (37.4 overs)
Leicestershire 87 for 1 (19.5 overs)
Leicestershire (4pts) won by 9 wickets

at Trent Bridge
Nottinghamshire 291 for 6 (45 overs) (DJ Hussey 87*,
RJ Warren 81)
Yorkshire 187 (34.4 overs) (C White 59)
Nottinghamshire (4pts) won by 104 runs

at Worcester
Worcestershire 239 for 5 (45 overs) (BF Smith 77,
GA Hick 63)
Sussex 218 (44.2 overs) (IJ Ward 50, MN Malik 4 for 42,
AJ Bichel 4 for 60)
Worcestershire (4pts) won by 21 runs

at Derby
Durham 207 (44.5 overs) (A Pratt 53, G Welch 4 for 26)
Derbyshire 208 for 4 (42.3 overs) (Hassan Adnan 50*)
Derbyshire (4pts) won by 6 wickets

Leicestershire moved into an early lead in Division Two by trouncing Scotland by nine wickets at Grace Road. The Saltires looked as though they were going to have a long season ahead of them when they were brushed aside for 86 in 37.4 overs – their lowest score in the competition. Six home bowlers shared the wickets and then Darren Robinson eased his way to 43 not out.

David Hussey announced himself to the Trent Bridge regulars by thumping an unbeaten 87 from just 75 balls to propel Nottinghamshire to the sort of total that was always going to be well beyond a disjointed Yorkshire side. The Australian was particularly severe on England's Matthew Hoggard and the youngster Tim Bresnan while adding 106 in 18 overs with Russell Warren, whose 81 came off 105 balls and contained seven fours. Craig White charged to 50 from 40 balls in reply, but when he hit across a straight one from Paul Franks, the Yorkshire innings fell away, apart from some brief defiance by Ian Harvey.

Worcestershire kicked off their totesport League season by disposing of Sussex by 21 runs at New Road. The win was based, as has so often been the case in the past, on a fine stand between Graeme Hick and Ben Smith. Hick's 63 took him 73 balls, while Smith's 77 off 79 balls was his 50th one-day half-century. Stephen Moore's unbeaten 46 made sure of a decent total and Sussex were only ever really in the hunt when Ian Ward was blazing his way to 50 off 43 balls at the top of the order.

A sixth-wicket partnership of 94 between Gareth Breese and Andy Pratt, launched from the shaky position of 63 for 5, was not enough in the end for Durham. Their total of 207 was below par, despite a slow pitch, and Derbyshire's top order paced their run chase perfectly. Andrew Gait and Chris Bassano added 80 for the second wicket, and Hassan Adnan saw Derbyshire past the winning post with an unbeaten 50.

3 May 2004: Division One

at Cardiff
Northamptonshire 233 for 7 (45 overs) (GP Swann 66, U Afzaal 61, DJG Sales 53)
Glamorgan 234 for 3 (39.5 overs) (MTG Elliott 112*, MP Maynard 71*)
Glamorgan (4pts) won by 7 wickets

at The Oval
Surrey v. **Hampshire**
Match abandoned – 2pts each

at Chelmsford
Essex 89 for 2 (10 overs)
Warwickshire 83 for 6 (10 overs)
Essex (4pts) won by 6 runs

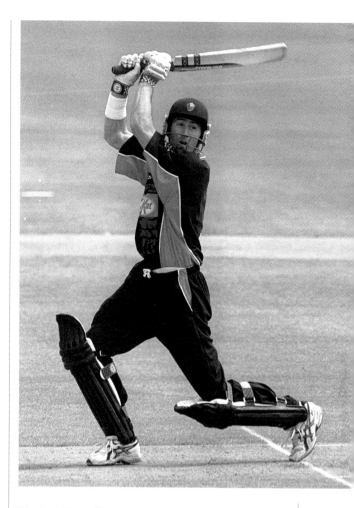

Matthew Elliott, Glamorgan's Australian opener, was in prolific early-season form.

Matthew Elliott took his season's totesport League run aggregate to 272 with a brilliant unbeaten 112 from 116 balls against Northamptonshire at Cardiff as Glamorgan extended their 100 per cent record to three games; Elliott had yet to be dismissed in his first three innings. Matthew Maynard supported Elliott with 71 not out in an unbroken fourth-wicket stand of 169 that swept Glamorgan to victory with 5.1 overs to spare. Earlier, Graeme Swann had opened up with 66 off 70 balls and David Sales had scored a 44-ball 53.

There was no play at The Oval, where rain forced Surrey and Hampshire to share the points, while Essex overcame Warwickshire by six runs in a ten-over slog at Chelmsford. Nasser Hussain took just 21 balls to reach 40 not out in Essex's 89 for 2, hitting Graham Wagg for one straight six, and Warwickshire never got going in reply.

Division Two

at Leicester
Leicestershire 131 for 8 (20 overs)
Derbyshire 98 (19.1 overs) (CW Henderson 4 for 9)
Leicestershire (4pts) won by 33 runs

at Lord's
Durham 120 for 7 (20 overs)
Middlesex 121 for 3 (18.5 overs) (BL Hutton 70*)
Middlesex (4pts) won by 7 wickets

at Headingley
Yorkshire 240 for 5 (45 overs) (DS Lehmann 88*)
Scotland 165 (37.5 overs)
Yorkshire (4pts) won by 75 runs

Claude Henderson picked up four wickets for only nine runs to bewitch the Derbyshire batting in a match reduced to 20 overs per side at Leicester. Paul Nixon's four sixes had boosted the Leicestershire total to 131 for 8 and, from 44 without loss, Derbyshire fell away against Henderson and Brad Hodge.

In another 20-over contest at Lord's, there was joy for Middlesex, who did well to restrict Durham to 120 for 7 and then romped home thanks to a first-wicket stand of 92 between Paul Weekes and Ben Hutton, who ended up on 70 not out.

Scotland endured more misery at Headingley, where Darren Lehmann rose above the general mediocrity on show to anchor Yorkshire's 240 for 5 with a sensible and controlled innings of 88 not out. Hitting out towards the end of the innings, Lehmann included nine fours from the 95 balls he faced, and, in all, 97 runs came from the last ten overs as Vic Craven and Tim Bresnan (with two sixes and two fours in a 14-ball 29 not out) also enjoyed themselves. The Saltires, in reply, could find no answer to Lehmann's slow left-armers and after the Australian had taken 3 for 34 it was left to John Blain, ironically a Scot, to pick up the last three wickets.

4 May 2004: Division Two

at Worcester
Worcestershire v. **Nottinghamshire**
Match abandoned – 2pts each

The game between Worcestershire and Nottinghamshire fell victim to the bad weather with the points being shared between the two sides.

7 May 2004: Division Two

at The Grange
Somerset 248 for 7 (45 overs) (KA Parsons 53, J Cox 51)
Scotland 193 (40.1 overs)
Somerset (4pts) won by 55 runs

Somerset made it three defeats out of three for the Scottish Saltires when they went to Edinburgh and avenged their embarrassing 2003 defeat with a comfortable 55-run win. Ryan Watson had struck an astonishing 42-ball hundred on the previous occasion the two sides had met north of the border, and although he made 45 this time, he was also guilty of running out Indian batsman Sridharan Sriram for 35 just when the two of them, having added 74, had looked capable of mounting a serious challenge to Somerset's calmly-constructed 248 for 7.

9 May 2004: Division One

at Edgbaston
Warwickshire 240 (45 overs) (Azhar Mahmood 5 for 24)
Surrey 195 (41 overs) (JN Batty 52, D Pretorius 4 for 36)
Warwickshire (4pts) won by 45 runs

Dewald Pretorius took three wickets in six balls as Surrey's top order fell apart in reply to Warwickshire's 240 at Edgbaston. The ball had moved lavishly off the seam for Azhar Mahmood earlier, when he picked up 5 for 24, but he found little support from the other Surrey quicks. For Warwickshire, Neil Carter initially gave Pretorius excellent back-up with the wickets of Rikki Clarke and Mark Ramprakash as Surrey slumped to 7 for 4 and then 86 for 7. Jon Batty's 52 led a Surrey fightback of sorts, but, by then, the damage had already been done and the visitors fell to a 45-run defeat.

Division Two

at Taunton
Yorkshire 284 for 9 (45 overs) (A McGrath 58, MJ Wood 51)
Somerset 139 (34.5 overs) (J Cox 69)
Yorkshire (4pts) won by 145 runs

Somerset put Yorkshire into bat on another flat Taunton wicket, and then watched in dismay as the visitors ran up 284 for 9 to overwhelm them. Matthew Wood (51) and Craig White provided the ideal start, with a stand of 68 in 11 overs, and Anthony McGrath (58) and Tim Bresnan turned on the late-innings power. Bresnan took 14 runs off three successive balls from Nixon McLean in the penultimate over on his way to 49. In reply, only Jamie Cox, with 69 from 83 balls, made any headway before he lofted Richard Dawson to long on.

16 May 2004: Division One

at Old Trafford
Hampshire 189 for 9 (45 overs) (MJ Clarke 54)
Lancashire 192 for 3 (31.5 overs) (SG Law 83, MJ Chilton 58*)
Lancashire (4pts) won by 7 wickets

at Bristol
Gloucestershire 257 for 6 (45 overs) (APR Gidman 70, WPC Weston 53)
Surrey 215 for 9 (45 overs) (MR Ramprakash 73)
Gloucestershire (4pts) won by 42 runs

at Cardiff
Essex 162 for 9 (45 overs)
Glamorgan 163 for 4 (37.5 overs)
Glamorgan (4pts) won by 6 wickets

Lancashire stepped up their challenge for one-day league honours by making it three wins out of three when they overpowered Hampshire by seven wickets at Old Trafford. Magnificent strokeplay from Stuart Law eased them to victory, and the Australian received a deserved standing ovation for his innings of 83 off 74 balls that simply toyed with the Hampshire bowlers. He twice drove Shaun Udal for six, hitting eight other fours, and was then joined by Mark Chilton, who finished on 58 not out, in a match-winning partnership of 98 for the third wicket. Hampshire had earlier collapsed dreadfully from 150 for 3, with Sajid Mahmood's pace and movement bringing him three middle-order scalps.

Mark Ramprakash did his best with 73 but, after he had gone – bowled behind his legs by Shoaib Malik – Surrey lost five wickets for the addition of only 19 runs and fell to a 42-run defeat against Gloucestershire at Bristol. Alex Gidman's 70 from 89 balls, and significant contributions from both Phil Weston and Matt Windows, ensured an excellent home total, but Surrey had looked in a position to strike once Ramprakash and Adam Hollioake had taken them to 163 for 3. Self-belief, however, had been affected by the county's failure to win any of their previous nine matches: this slide to 215 for 9, sadly, made it ten in a row.

Glamorgan maintained their fast pace at the top of the division by defeating Essex by six wickets at Cardiff. Their fourth win from four matches was

based on some excellent swing-and-seam bowling from Andrew Davies, David Harrison and Alex Wharf, who then made a hard-hit 41 from 53 balls to complete a significant all-round display. Matthew Maynard and David Hemp wrapped things up with an unbroken stand of 70.

Division Two

at Headingley
Sussex 267 for 9 (45 overs) (MJ Prior 72, MW Goodwin 64, CJ Adams 56)
Yorkshire 271 for 5 (44.2 overs) (PA Jaques 105)
Yorkshire (4pts) won by 5 wickets

at Leicester
Nottinghamshire 252 for 5 (45 overs) (JER Gallian 68)
Leicestershire 209 (44.2 overs) (JN Snape 64)
Nottinghamshire (4pts) won by 43 runs

at Worcester
Durham 319 for 3 (45 overs) (MJ North 110, PD Collingwood 102*, N Peng 65)
Worcestershire 225 for 8 (45 overs) (SJ Rhodes 71*, SC Moore 51)
Durham (4pts) won by 94 runs

at The Grange
Scotland 218 for 5 (45 overs) (S Sriram 88*)
Middlesex 221 for 1 (28 overs) (AJ Strauss 107*, PN Weekes 83)
Middlesex (4pts) won by 9 wickets

Yorkshire moved alongside Leicestershire at the head of the Division Two table by chasing down Sussex's challenging total of 267 for 9 at Headingley to win with four balls to spare. Phil Jaques, on his one-day debut for the county as Darren Lehmann's stand-in, launched his Yorkshire limited-overs career in the best possible way with a brilliant 105 off just 82 balls. He hit three sixes and nine fours and was joined by Anthony McGrath in a fourth-wicket stand of 100 that took the home side to within 64 runs of victory. Jaques was caught in the penultimate over, but Ian Harvey's unbeaten 27 from 17 balls saw Yorkshire home. Matthew Prior, Murray Goodwin and Chris Adams all enjoyed the fine surface during the Sussex innings with fluent half-centuries.

Nottinghamshire inflicted a first defeat of the one-day league season on Leicestershire, with a virtuoso all-round performance by Mark Ealham at the centre of their 43-run win at Grace Road. Ealham's thumping unbeaten 40, containing four sixes and two fours off just 20 balls, set the seal on a Notts innings of 252 for 5, and then the canny medium pacer produced two early strikes in a typically controlled new-ball spell to undermine the Leicestershire reply. At 54 for 5, with the other Notts seamers getting into the act, there was no way back for the home side and Jeremy Snape's late-order 64 merely delayed the inevitable.

Durham moved up into fourth place by shocking Worcestershire in front of their own fans at New Road. Hot on the heels of making 453 to beat Somerset in the championship at Taunton the previous afternoon, they really made it a weekend to remember by thrashing the Worcestershire bowling to all parts. Their 319 for 3, the first one-day score above 300 in their short history as a first-class county,

A 72-ball hundred by Paul Collingwood was the fastest one-day century scored by a Durham batsman.

was based on superb hundreds by Paul Collingwood and Marcus North and a fine 65 with 11 fours by Nicky Peng. Collingwood was particularly disdainful of the bowling on offer, completing the fastest one-day century by a Durham batsman off just 72 balls. North, meanwhile, studded his run-a-ball 110 with five sixes and put on 137 with Peng for the first wicket and then another 156 with Collingwood, who remained 102 not out at the end. In reply, Worcestershire lost Stephen Peters and Graeme Hick early to Shoaib Akhtar and, at 90 for 6, they only had their dignity to play for, and that was saved, to some extent, in the shape of a seventh-wicket stand of 68 between Stephen Moore and Steve Rhodes, who went on to make a defiant unbeaten 71.

Andrew Strauss hit 107 not out from only 80 balls as Middlesex brushed aside Scotland by nine wickets in Edinburgh. Sridharan Sriram, their Indian professional, ensured a decent home total with an unbeaten 88, but Paul Weekes helped his captain to put on 196 for the first wicket. When Weekes spooned up a catch on 83, all that remained was for Strauss to reach three figures and then to finish the match with a straight six.

23 May 2004: Division One

at The Oval
Surrey 268 (43.3 overs) (SA Newman 106, JN Batty 66, GR Napier 4 for 45)
Essex 237 (42.5 overs) (A Flower 70)
Surrey (4pts) won by 31 runs

at Bristol
Gloucestershire 240 for 5 (45 overs) (WPC Weston 75, CM Spearman 57, Shoaib Malik 51, SK Warne 4 for 27)
Hampshire 244 for 6 (43.3 overs) (MG Dighton 74)
Hampshire (4pts) won by 4 wickets

at Old Trafford
Glamorgan 210 (42.1 overs) (AG Wharf 72, SI Mahmood 4 for 39)
Lancashire 211 for 5 (34.5 overs)
Lancashire (4pts) won by 5 wickets

at Northampton
Northamptonshire 211 for 5 (45 overs) (U Afzaal 66, DJG Sales 51*)
Kent 146 (40.1 overs)
Northamptonshire (4pts) won by 65 runs

A Test-class fast bowler appearing as an amateur took a wicket with his first ball at The Oval, and then another with his sixth. It was the spark of inspiration that Surrey needed to record their first victory of a wretched early season, in their 11th competitive match. Complications obtaining a work visa looked to have scuppered the county's plans to replace the injured Saqlain Mushtaq with, temporarily, India's Zaheer Khan, but then the player himself offered to play for nothing – meaning that all Surrey had to do was to register him in time for the start of the game. Both Zaheer and the Indian selectors were keen for him to test his recovery from a groin muscle injury ahead of the Asia Cup – and so a short break spent with friends in Britain became an unlikely working holiday. Will Jefferson and Alastair Cook, the young Essex openers, will not forget their own brief encounter with an international paceman playing for fun. Jefferson was cleaned up by Zaheer's first ball, a rapid in-swinger, and Cook was lbw at the end of a dramatic over in which Andy Flower had survived a leg-before shout from the third ball. Essex, in reply to Surrey's 268, were 1 for 2 and, despite Flower's fighting 70, they never really recovered. Surrey's innings was based on 106 from 104 balls by the often-flamboyant Scott Newman, a determined 66 by skipper Jon Batty and the bonus of 12 penalty runs donated by Essex because of their slow over rate.

Shane Warne, who had returned 24 hours earlier from Australia's aborted tour of Zimbabwe, was clearly delighted to be concentrating on playing some cricket again when he led Hampshire to a four-wicket win over Gloucestershire at Bristol. It was a rare defeat for Mark Alleyne's side in a one-dayer on home soil, but then Warne has a rare talent of achieving the unexpected. Here he took four of Gloucestershire's five wickets to fall, at minimal cost, and then helped to launch the overhaul of their 240 for 5 by promoting himself to No. 3 and thumping 47 off 49 balls with four fours and a six. Warne was also joined in a third-wicket stand of 68 in 11 overs by fellow Aussie Michael Dighton, a temporary replacement for Michael Clarke, who went on to strike five fours and two sixes in a 64-ball 74.

Lancashire won the battle between the only two undefeated teams in the division by overcoming Glamorgan with considerable ease at Old Trafford. Sajid Mahmood recorded his best one-day figures, 4 for 39, to spearhead an excellent home attack, while Carl Hooper added to his two wickets with a calm unbeaten 49 to steer Lancashire home with one ball more than ten overs to spare.

Half-centuries from Usman Afzaal and David Sales gave Northamptonshire a total which proved beyond

Kent at Wantage Road. On a sluggish surface, the visitors slid to an unhappy 33 for 5, and then 73 for 7, and the end was only delayed by some late-order defiance from Rob Ferley and Min Patel.

Division Two

at Derby
Somerset 316 for 5 (45 overs) (CM Gazzard 157, M Burns 73)
Derbyshire 202 (35.5 overs) (CWG Bassano 85, KA Parsons 5 for 39)
Somerset (4pts) won by 114 runs

at Horsham
Leicestershire 324 for 4 (45 overs) (BJ Hodge 154*, DL Maddy 95)
Sussex 323 for 5 (45 overs) (IJ Ward 136, MW Goodwin 66)
Leicestershire (4pts) won by 1 run

at Trent Bridge
Nottinghamshire 207 for 7 (45 overs)
Middlesex 211 for 7 (45 overs) (PN Weekes 57, L Klusener 56*, SCG MacGill 4 for 55)
Middlesex (4pts) won by 3 wickets

at Headingley
Worcestershire 238 for 6 (45 overs) (VS Solanki 68, GA Hick 54, Kadeer Ali 51)
Yorkshire 199 (43.3 overs)
Worcestershire (4pts) won by 39 runs

Carl Gazzard, a 22-year-old Cornishman, struck 157 off 136 balls to overwhelm a Derbyshire side missing six first-choice players through injury. Chris Bassano's 85 in reply was a brave gesture for the home team, but Somerset were always going to achieve the win which kept them hard on the heels of leaders Leicestershire once Gazzard accelerated with an impressive range of strokes following the fall, for 73, of Mike Burns, his partner in an opening stand worth 125.

Brad Hodge, meanwhile, set a Leicestershire record for one-day cricket when he hit 154 not out off only 122 balls at Horsham – and yet he still only ended up on the winning side by the narrowest of margins. Sussex, with Ian Ward hitting 136 from 120 balls, fell, agonisingly, just one run short of Leicestershire's own huge total of 324 for 4 when their 45-over allocation ran out. The game was probably settled by the fact that Leicestershire plundered 116 from their last ten overs, while

Hodge hurtled from 100 to 150 in only 17 balls, whereas Sussex could not quite make the 93 they required from their own final ten overs. Hodge, in all, hit 14 fours and six sixes, and put on 165 in 26 overs for the second wicket with Darren Maddy (95 off 92 balls) while Ward was out with 56 still needed from six overs.

Middlesex won a thrilling last-ball victory against Nottinghamshire at Trent Bridge when Lance Klusener launched a ferocious final-over assault on leg spinner Stuart MacGill. Klusener even failed to score off MacGill's first ball, with 19 still needed, but then smote a four, two on-driven sixes, a two and finally a pulled four. He ended up on 56 not out from 58 balls and ruined MacGill's figures. At the start of the last over he had taken 4 for 33 and had bowled Notts to the brink of victory in what had been an enthralling encounter.

Poor batting cost Yorkshire dearly at Headingley where, chasing 239 on a perfectly reasonable pitch, they raced to 86 for 1 in the first 15 overs before throwing away a succession of cheap wickets. Worcestershire, however, also fielded brilliantly and, in off spinner Gareth Batty, they had the perfect man for the job of imposing a stranglehold on the home batsmen. Ajmal Shahzad, meanwhile, an 18-year-old schoolboy seamer from Bradford, became the first Yorkshire-born player of Asian descent to play for the county. He did not take a wicket, but he bowled tidily with the new ball and could be proud of his historic debut performance.

31 May 2004: Division One

at Edgbaston
Glamorgan 243 for 9 (45 overs) (MJ Powell 73, RDB Croft 54, MA Wagh 4 for 35)
Warwickshire 230 (44 overs) (NV Knight 111, AG Wharf 4 for 35)
Glamorgan (4pts) won by 13 runs

at The Rose Bowl
Kent 169 for 9 (45 overs)
Hampshire Did not bat
Match abandoned – 2pts each

Leaders Glamorgan had a brilliant hat-trick from Alex Wharf to thank for an eventual 13-run win against Warwickshire at Edgbaston. With 16 runs needed from the last two overs, and with Nick Knight still there with a century to his name, Warwickshire were closing in on a Glamorgan total of 243 for 9 that was built on half-centuries by Robert Croft and Michael

Alex Wharf ... hat-trick hero for Glamorgan against Warwickshire.

Powell. From the fourth, fifth and sixth balls of the penultimate over, however, Wharf removed Graham Wagg, Knight and last man Dewald Pretorius to stun a 5,000-strong home crowd. Wagg skied to mid-off, Knight swept to deep backward square – after reaching a 118-ball 111 – and Pretorius swung and missed.

Kent struggled to 169 for 9 from their 45 overs against Hampshire at the Rose Bowl before rain intervened and prevented the home side from replying. David Fulton's unbeaten 39 off 37 balls was the only batting display that could be described as free-flowing in conditions which encouraged both seam and spin.

Division Two

at The Riverside
Derbyshire 82 (44.3 overs) (Shoaib Akhtar 4 for 15)
Durham 83 for 3 (26.3 overs)
Durham (4pts) won by 7 wickets

at Lord's
Somerset 249 for 6 (45 overs) (ID Blackwell 69, KA Parsons 62*)
Middlesex 250 for 4 (43.4 overs) (PN Weekes 119*, OA Shah 54)
Middlesex (4pts) won by 6 wickets

at Trent Bridge
Sussex 176 (44.5 overs) (CJ Adams 56, GJ Smith 4 for 28)
Nottinghamshire 180 for 3 (37.4 overs) (KP Pietersen 80*)
Nottinghamshire (4pts) won by 7 wickets

at The Grange
Yorkshire 199 for 8 (45 overs)
Scotland 140 (39.4 overs) (RKJ Dawson 4 for 20)
Yorkshire (4pts) won by 59 runs

A bouncy pitch at the Riverside was exploited with relish by Shoaib Akhtar, who took 4 for 15 from his nine overs as Derbyshire were routed. Indeed, only a fighting 43 from captain Luke Sutton, and a last-wicket stand with Daren Powell which doubled the score, allowed them to reach even the comparative riches of 82 all out. Two unnecessary run outs only added to Derbyshire's woes and Durham had little bother completing a seven-wicket win.

Middlesex moved alongside Leicestershire at the head of the table by chasing down a Somerset total of 249 for 6 at Lord's. Big hitting by Ian Blackwell and Keith Parsons had ensured a competitive total, but Paul Weekes played the anchor role to perfection with an unbeaten 119 and was joined by Ben Hutton, Owais Shah and Ed Joyce in successive partnerships of 68, 127 and 51 that took Middlesex to the brink of victory.

Superb wicketkeeping from Chris Read was at the heart of Nottinghamshire's victory against Sussex at Trent Bridge. The discarded England gloveman once again demonstrated his peerless skills with two superlative legside stumpings and three catches – all standing up to the stumps against the medium pace of Mark Ealham and Gareth Clough as well as the spin of Stuart MacGill – as Sussex were held to 176 all out. Kevin Pietersen's first one-day 50 of the season, an unbeaten 80 from 85 balls, then breezed Notts home.

England captain Michael Vaughan successfully tested out the knee injury that had ruled him out of the opening Test match against New Zealand by scoring 32 as Yorkshire overcame the Scottish Saltires by 59 runs at Edinburgh. Vaughan even bowled a couple of overs in support of Richard Dawson's excellent spell of 4 for 20 as the Scots could only reach 140 in reply to Yorkshire's far-from-fluent progress to 199 for 8.

6 June 2004: Division One

at Swansea
Glamorgan 250 (45 overs) (RDB Croft 68,
MP Maynard 67)
Gloucestershire 217 (39.3 overs) (MGN Windows 55,
Shoaib Malik 52)
Glamorgan (4pts) won by 33 runs

at The Rose Bowl
Hampshire 241 for 7 (45 overs) (JP Crawley 68,
AD Mascarenhas 55, MJ Clarke 54)
Warwickshire 213 (43.4 overs) (CT Tremlett 4 for 37)
Hampshire (4pts) won by 28 runs

at Tunbridge Wells
Kent 301 (44.5 overs) (A Symonds 146, MJ Walker 61,
SI Mahmood 4 for 42)
Lancashire 245 (42.2 overs) (SG Law 51)
Kent (4pts) won by 56 runs

at Northampton
Essex 151 (41.4 overs)
Northamptonshire 155 for 2 (32.2 overs)
(M van Jaarsveld 96*)
Northamptonshire (4pts) won by 8 wickets

Glamorgan maintained their lead with a solid all-round performance to beat Gloucestershire at Swansea that was kicked off by an explosive 68 by Robert Croft. The skipper hit 14 fours in his 45-ball innings, after Glamorgan had been put into bat, and when he was caught behind in the 12th over the total had already reached 95. Given that start, and the way Matthew Maynard built on it with a responsible 67, Glamorgan were able to defend an eventual total of 250. Only the late hitting of tail-ender Shabbir Ahmed, whose 42 took just 20 balls, hauled Gloucestershire above 200 in reply.

Hampshire maintained their title challenge with a highly competent 28-run win against Warwickshire at the Rose Bowl. Dimitri Mascarenhas struck 55 from 31 balls to inspire a late Hampshire charge that produced 91 runs from the final eight overs. In reply, seven visiting batsmen got to 20, but only one of them, Brad Hogg with 39, got into the 30s.

Brutal hitting by Andrew Symonds, whose 146 took just 110 balls, thrilled a 4,500 crowd enjoying a beautiful early-summer day at the lovely Nevill Ground in Tunbridge Wells. Symonds claimed Kent's highest individual one-day league innings from Carl Hooper, who was prevented by injury from appearing in a Lancashire team who soon found the Australian impossible to bowl at. Seventeen fours and four sixes flew from his bat, and his first league hundred came up in 81 deliveries. Matthew Walker then made 61 to take Kent just beyond 300 and also picked up three late wickets as Lancashire fell well short.

Kent's Australian one-day all-rounder Andrew Symonds thrilled a Tunbridge Wells full house with a brutal 146.

Essex failed to get off the bottom of the Division One table, sliding to 151 all out and an eight-wicket defeat at Northampton. Graham Napier quickly removed Tom Huggins when Northants began their reply, but Martin van Jaarsfeld then hit an imperious 96 not out and dominated a second-wicket stand of 124 with Tim Roberts.

Division Two

at Derby
Derbyshire 161 (40.1 overs)
Middlesex 162 for 2 (32.1 overs) (EC Joyce 74*, PN Weekes 60*)
Middlesex (4pts) won by 8 wickets

at The Riverside
Durham 203 for 9 (45 overs) (GJ Pratt 54)
Scotland 178 (43.4 overs) (N Killeen 4 for 24)
Durham (4pts) won by 25 runs

at Oakham School
Worcestershire 261 for 8 (45 overs)
(VS Solanki 101)
Leicestershire 137 (36.4 overs) (AJ Hall 4 for 26)
Worcestershire (4pts) won by 124 runs

at Hove
Sussex 230 for 7 (45 overs) (MW Goodwin 81)
Somerset 224 for 7 (45 overs)
(J Cox 71, M Burns 62)
Sussex (4pts) won by 6 runs

Middlesex recorded their fifth win in six matches – a straightforward eight-wicket success against Derbyshire at the Racecourse Ground – to stay out in front in Division Two. Derbyshire briefly looked as though they might cause an upset when the leaders slipped to 24 for 2 in reply to their modest total of 161, but then Ed Joyce joined Paul Weekes in an unbroken stand of 138 to complete victory with almost 13 overs to spare.

Durham moved alongside Leicestershire and Yorkshire in joint second place by inflicting a sixth successive defeat on the sorry Scottish Saltires. There was not much for the Riverside faithful in terms of entertainment value, however, on a sluggish pitch. Shoaib Akhtar was promoted to No. 3 in the order in a bid to inject some unorthodox hitting into the early overs, but he soon departed for 15 and it took a half-century from the more understated Gary Pratt to take Durham up past 200. The Scotland reply always looked like coming up short, especially with Neil Killeen picking up four cheap wickets, although Cedric English did at least succeed in producing a flurry of strokes in his 45.

Leicestershire tumbled to defeat by 124 runs at Oakham School, with their bowlers unable to contain the wristy strokeplay of Vikram Solanki and their batsmen quite unable to accept the challenge of matching it. Solanki's 101 came off 102 balls, with four sixes and eight fours, and Andrew Hall then undermined the home side's response with four wickets out of the top seven.

Somerset threw away the chance of beating Sussex at Hove in spectacular fashion, collapsing from 168 for 2 in the 34th over as they chased 231 for victory. Mike Burns and Jamie Cox set up what should have been a comfortable win with a second-wicket stand of 140, but then Somerset lost their way. A partial recovery was crafted by Keith Parsons and Rob Turner, but Parsons was then bowled by Luke Wright trying to repeat an earlier six over long on and Turner was forced to look on helplessly as, with seven needed, Andy Caddick swung and missed at all five of the last balls of the match, which were bowled by James Kirtley.

8 June 2004: Division One

at Chelmsford
Essex 211 for 4 (45 overs)
Hampshire 176 (41 overs) (JP Crawley 70*)
Essex (4pts) won by 35 runs

Two young English cricketers made hay against Shane Warne as Essex beat Hampshire by 35 runs at Chelmsford. James Foster and Ravi Bopara added 68 for the fifth wicket, scoring 46 and 40 not out respectively, to take Essex to 211 for 4 and leave Warne nursing figures of 0 for 62 from his nine overs. There was a comic moment when Ronnie Irani, two balls after calling for a runner because of cramp, was run out for 31 when he charged up the pitch looking for a sharp single and then failed to get back into his crease – with his runner already safe. Bopara then took two cheap wickets as Hampshire, despite John Crawley's unbeaten 70, fell away to 176 all out.

Division Two

at Derby
Derbyshire 182 (44.5 overs) (MA Sheikh 50*)
Scotland 154 (39.4 overs)
Derbyshire (4pts) won by 28 runs

Mo Sheikh was the all-round star as Derbyshire beat the Scottish Saltires by 28 runs at Derby. First he hit an unbeaten 50 from 58 balls to revive an innings which had gone into decline after an initial assault of 43 in 26 balls by Nick Walker, and then he took 3 for 26 to help undermine a Scotland reply in which only Fraser Watts made any headway with 45.

13 June 2004: Division One

at Gloucester
Northamptonshire 266 for 6 (45 overs)
(TW Roberts 88, U Afzaal 69)
Gloucestershire 157 (36.4 overs) (GP Swann 4 for 21)
Northamptonshire (4pts) won by 109 runs

at The Oval
Surrey 230 for 8 (45 overs) (N Shahid 61*)
Kent 234 for 5 (43.5 overs) (AGR Loudon 51, MJ Walker 51*, MA Carberry 50)
Kent (4pts) won by 5 wickets

at Edgbaston
Warwickshire 310 for 5 (45 overs) (NV Knight 92, MA Wagh 69)
Lancashire 198 (39.3 overs)
Warwickshire (4pts) won by 112 runs

Gloucestershire, for some years the undisputed kings of English domestic one-day cricket, fell to the foot of the Division One table when they lost their fifth game in six matches. Northamptonshire came to Archdeacon Meadow in Gloucester and fully deserved a 109-run victory, built upon Tim Roberts' 88 off 94 balls and a measured 69 from Usman Afzaal. No home batsman could match those efforts and, with Graeme Swann picking up 4 for 21 and Jason Brown 3 for 27, Gloucestershire were undone by the Northants spinners.

Rikki Clarke conceded 24 runs from a single over as Kent recovered from 19 for 2 to beat Surrey by five wickets at The Oval. Alex Loudon did the damage to Clarke's figures with four boundaries and a six over long on after the bowler had no-balled and thus presented the young Kent batsman with a free hit. Loudon went on to make 51 and added 85 for the third wicket with fellow half-centurion Michael Carberry. A further stand of 95 between Matthew Walker – who finished on 51 not out – and David Fulton eased Kent past a Surrey total boosted by Nadeem Shahid's late-order 61 not out from 55 balls.

Warwickshire's in-form batting line-up was far too strong for Lancashire at Edgbaston, running up a total of 310 for 5 that proved far too intimidating for the visitors as they slid to a 112-run defeat. Nick Knight, the Warwickshire captain, led the way with 92 from 87 balls – an innings which meant he had scored 846 runs from eight visits to the crease in 18 days, at an average of 169.20. Mark Wagh made 69 and, at the end of an even batting display, Brad

Hogg took Warwickshire past their previous best one-day league total, 307, by blasting a 27-ball unbeaten 41.

Division Two

at Worcester
Worcestershire 189 (44.5 overs) (VS Solanki 52)
Yorkshire 190 for 4 (43 overs) (PA Jaques 62)
Yorkshire (4pts) won by 6 wickets

at Lord's
Nottinghamshire 294 for 6 (45 overs)
(JER Gallian 109, DJ Hussey 75)
Middlesex 200 (36.4 overs) (PN Weekes 65)
Nottinghamshire (4pts) won by 94 runs

at Bath
Leicestershire 263 for 7 (45 overs) (DI Stevens 83, JN Snape 50)

Jason Gallian hit his first one-day hundred since 1999 as Nottinghamshire overpowered Middlesex at Lord's.

Somerset 265 for 7 (44.1 overs) (KA Parsons 73)
Somerset (4pts) won by 3 wickets

Yorkshire moved joint top of the table with a comfortable six-wicket win over Worcestershire at New Road. Vikram Solanki and Graeme Hick both threatened, but, overall, Yorkshire's bowling attack kept a disciplined lid on the home side's strokeplay. Then, when they chased a target of 190, Phil Jaques overcame the loss of two early wickets to hit an aggressive 62 from 65 balls.

Middlesex lost only their second game of the one-day league season when they were overpowered by 94 runs by Nottinghamshire at Lord's. Nottinghamshire were helped by Jason Gallian's first one-day hundred since 1999 and a highly impressive 75 from 44 balls by David Hussey. Middlesex reached 164 for 3 by the 29th over, but then lost three wickets in three balls and all of their forward momentum was lost.

After losing their previous five matches in all competitions, Somerset were at least able to enjoy a fine end to the Bath festival when they successfully chased down Leicestershire's challenging 263 for 7 to win by three wickets and with five balls in hand. Keith Parsons, the Somerset beneficiary, played the match-winning innings by reaching his 50 from 39 balls and going on to make 73 off 70 balls with ten fours and a six. Overall, there was excellent entertainment for a crowd basking in fine weather and the beautiful Georgian setting, and an early highlight was the uppercut six over cover off Andy Caddick by Darren Stevens, who top scored for the visitors with 83 from 90 balls.

20 June 2004: Division Two

at The Grange
Durham 189 for 7 (41 overs)
Scotland 190 for 4 (39.3 overs) (CJO Smith 79*, CV English 53*)
Scotland (4pts) won by 6 wickets

The biggest fifth-wicket partnership in Scotland's one-day cricket history inspired the Saltires as they beat Durham at Edinburgh to record their first win of the season in the totesport League. Wicketkeeper Colin Smith hit 79 not out and was joined by Cedric English, unbeaten on 55, in an unbroken stand worth 146. Earlier, in a match reduced to 41 overs per side, Jon Lewis and Gary Pratt had added 83 for Durham as the visitors largely struggled to reach a total of 189 for 7.

25 June 2004: Division One

at Old Trafford
Lancashire 176 (44.1 overs) (MJ Chilton 51,
JF Brown 4 for 33)
Northamptonshire 180 for 3 (27.1 overs)
(GP Swann 78, M van Jaarsveld 65*)
Northamptonshire (4pts) won by 7 wickets

Being hit on the head by a John Wood bouncer
seemed to have a galvanising effect on Graeme Swann
under the Old Trafford floodlights. On 24 at the
time, as Northamptonshire attempted to overhaul
Lancashire's 176, Swann proceeded to smash 54 more
runs from the next 30 balls he received before being
dismissed for 78. Martin van Jaarsfeld, though,
finished up on 65 not out, having helped Swann to
add 138, as Northants romped to a crushing seven-
wicket win. Earlier, Swann had taken a brilliant diving
catch to dismiss his elder brother Alec for 22 in a
Lancashire innings that foundered on the off breaks
of Jason Brown who took 4 for 33.

27 June 2004: Division One

at Beckenham
Warwickshire 233 for 9 (45 overs) (MA Wagh 83)
Kent 140 for 2 (30 overs) (ET Smith 81)
*Kent (4pts) won by 10 runs – DL Method: target 131
from 30 overs*

at Cardiff
Surrey 197 for 8 (45 overs) (JN Batty 51)
Glamorgan 94 for 1 (8.2 overs)
*Glamorgan (4pts) won by 9 wickets – DL Method: target
94 from 15 overs*

Ed Smith, recalled to Kent's one-day side in the
absence on England duty of Rob Key, began to play
himself back into form with a fluent innings of 81 at
Beckenham. Smith was run out, after hitting a six
and 11 fours from 100 balls, just before the advent of
rain that forced the players off and confirmed Kent
as winners under the Duckworth-Lewis regulations.

Glamorgan, meanwhile, stretched their lead in the
division to eight points when they beat Surrey by nine
wickets at Cardiff. Needing 94 off 15 overs under
Duckworth-Lewis computations – a period of rainfall
having followed their restriction of Surrey's innings to
197 for 8 in 45 overs – the Welsh county romped
home in a mere 8.2. Robert Croft hit 46 off just 25
balls and Ian Thomas an unbeaten 38 from the same
number of deliveries.

Division Two

at Arundel
Sussex 118 (32.1 overs)
Yorkshire 119 for 2 (26.5 overs)
Yorkshire (4pts) won by 8 wickets

at Taunton
Durham 278 for 4 (45 overs) (GJ Pratt 67*, N Peng 62)
Somerset 210 for 9 (33.2 overs) (JD Francis 75)
*Durham (4pts) won by 16 runs – DL Method: target
227 from 32.2 overs*

at Derby
Derbyshire 215 for 8 (45 overs) (J Moss 104,
LD Sutton 58*)
Worcestershire 159 for 9 (32 overs)
*Derbyshire (4pts) won by 18 runs – DL Method: target
178 from 32 overs*

at Leicester
Leicestershire 205 (44.5 overs) (SJ Cook 6 for 37)
Middlesex 187 for 4 (40.3 overs) (PN Weekes 90)
*Middlesex (4pts) won by 6 wickets – DL Method: target
187 from 42 overs*

at The Grange
Nottinghamshire 205 for 8 (45 overs)
(KP Pietersen 51)
Scotland Did not bat
Match abandoned – 2pts each

Superb new-ball bowling by Matthew Hoggard and
Tim Bresnan ripped out the Sussex top order at
Arundel and set up a simple eight-wicket win for
Yorkshire. Hoggard's three wickets and Bresnan's two
reduced Sussex to 43 for 5 and, from there, they
could only reach 118 all out. Andrew Gale, a 20-year-
old left-hander playing in only his second league
match, then unveiled some thumping drives while
scoring 46 in a second-wicket partnership of 92 with
Matthew Wood.

Durham deservedly beat Somerset by 16 runs at
Taunton, under Duckworth-Lewis, despite an
exciting middle-order rally from the home side led
by John Francis and James Hildreth. In truth,
however, the rain interruption gave new hope to
Somerset, who had earlier struggled to contain a
consistent Durham batting order in which Nicky
Peng and Gary Pratt stood out.

Jon Moss, their new Australian all-rounder,
scored his first century for Derbyshire as the
county beat Worcestershire to record their third

Simon Cook, the Middlesex seamer, took a six-wicket haul at Grace Road.

victory of the season in the competition. Moss reached three figures from 109 balls, hitting two sixes and six fours, and Luke Sutton also contributed an excellent unbeaten 58 to an eventual total of 215 for 8. After a teatime downpour, Worcestershire's target was brought down to 178 from 32 overs, but the run out of Vikram Solanki (for 32) hit the visitors hard.

Simon Cook saw his first two overs go for 16 runs against Leicestershire at Grace Road. He bounced back so well that, by the end of the innings, he had taken six for 37 in two spells as Leicestershire, 77 for 0 at one stage, fell away to 205 all out. Paul Weekes, one of the league's most in-form batsmen, then ensured that Middlesex did not fall behind their Duckworth-Lewis target by hitting 90.

The Scottish Saltires were sorry to see rain arrive at the halfway point of their match against

Nottinghamshire at Edinburgh. By then they had restricted the county to 205 for 8, with only Paul Franks and Kevin Pietersen flourishing against some tidy bowling.

28 June 2004: Division One

at Chelmsford
Gloucestershire 234 for 7 (45 overs) (WPC Weston 65, CG Taylor 56)
Essex 234 for 8 (45 overs) (RS Bopara 55)
Match tied - 2pts each

A bottom-of-the-table encounter under the Chelmsford lights produced an exciting tie as Essex's Ashley Cowan hit the last ball to long on but saw Chris Taylor throw in accurately enough to the bowler to run out Paul Grayson, his partner, as he tried to get back for the second run. Taylor and Matt Windows had earlier scored good fifties in Gloucestershire's 234 for 7, but Ravi Bopara replied with a classy 55 before Grayson and Graham Napier added a quick-fire 50 for the sixth wicket to take the game to the wire.

30 June 2004: Division Two

at Hove
Sussex 261 for 4 (45 overs) (MJ Prior 119, CJ Adams 81)
Durham 162 for 8 (45 overs)
(GJ Pratt 58*)
Sussex (4pts) won by 99 runs

at The Grange
Worcestershire 128 (22 overs)
Scotland 119 for 7 (22 overs)
Worcestershire (4pts) won by 9 runs

Matthew Prior's first one-day hundred for Sussex, plus a forthright 81 off 69 balls by Chris Adams, powered Sussex to victory by 99 runs over Durham under the Hove floodlights. Prior and Adams added 135 in 20 overs for the third wicket, with the wicketkeeper's 119 taking him 135 balls, with 14 fours. Durham's reply was almost immediately undermined by Robin Martin-Jenkins' three wickets in four overs.

Rain forced a 22-overs-per-side match to be played at Edinburgh, with Worcestershire running out narrow victors by nine runs thanks, in the main, to some productive late hitting by Kabir Ali, whose 33 boosted the county up to 128.

Matt Prior of Sussex plundered Durham's bowlers to reach a maiden one-day hundred.

at Maidstone
Kent 168 for 2 (27 overs) (MA Carberry 76, ET Smith 58*)
Essex Did not bat
Match abandoned – 2pts each

A fine 112 by Tim Roberts looked as though it would bring Northamptonshire victory over Warwickshire at Edgbaston, but then Mark Wagh held the home reply together for long enough to allow Brad Hogg to march in and play the match-winning innings of 74 from 71 balls. Roberts' runs had come from 129 balls and it was his second league hundred.

Gloucestershire hauled themselves off the bottom of the Division One table with a hard-fought 18-run win over Lancashire at Old Trafford. They were given early impetus by Craig Spearman's 89 off 66 balls, and a late injection of runs by Tim Hancock's unbeaten 53. Mal Loye made 65 in reply, but Gloucestershire's attack maintained their discipline well – none more so than Jon Lewis, who cut short a late Lancashire rally with three wickets to add to his important early scalp of Stuart Law.

Michael Carberry and Ed Smith provided rich entertainment for a 3,000 crowd at Maidstone before rain brought a premature end to proceedings and forced Kent and Essex to share the points. Carberry's 76 took him just 57 balls and Smith included some beautiful strokes in his 58 not out.

4 July 2004: Division One

at Edgbaston
Northamptonshire 233 (44.5 overs) (TW Roberts 112)
Warwickshire 235 for 6 (43.4 overs) (GB Hogg 74, MA Wagh 70)
Warwickshire (4pts) won by 4 wickets

at Old Trafford
Gloucestershire 237 for 9 (45 overs) (CM Spearman 89, THC Hancock 53*)
Lancashire 219 (43.1 overs) (MB Loye 65, J Lewis 4 for 30)
Gloucestershire (4pts) won by 18 runs

Division Two

at Trent Bridge
Nottinghamshire 211 for 8 (45 overs) (JER Gallian 56, J Moss 4 for 45)
Derbyshire 212 for 1 (40.2 overs) (CWG Bassano 100*, J Moss 92)
Derbyshire (4pts) won by 9 wickets

at Headingley
Middlesex 209 for 7 (24 overs) (OA Shah 81, VJ Craven 4 for 50)

Yorkshire 180 for 9 (23.5 overs) (PA Jaques 70)
Middlesex (4pts) won by 29 runs

at Worcester
Worcestershire 238 for 7 (39 overs) (VS Solanki 59,
GA Hick 52)
Somerset 179 (35.5 overs) (KP Dutch 79*)
Worcestershire (4pts) won by 64 runs

at Hove
Sussex 57 for 2 (10.2 overs)
Scotland Did not bat
Match abandoned – 2pts each

at The Riverside
Durham v. **Leicestershire**
Match abandoned - 2pts each

A superb opening stand of 184 between Chris
Bassano and Jon Moss swept Derbyshire to a
highly satisfying nine-wicket win over
Nottinghamshire in a local derby encounter at
Trent Bridge. Moss had earlier taken 4 for 45 in a
Notts innings that had fallen away from 96 for 1 –
following a fine stand between Jason Gallian and
Russell Warren – to 211 for 8. Neither Bassano nor
Moss gave a chance in their great partnership, until
Moss hoicked a long hop to deep square leg after
hitting 92 from 117 balls, with ten fours and a six.
There was just time, though, for Bassano to
complete his hundred with his 13th four to set
beside two huge sixes.

A top-of-the-table match reduced to 24 overs
per side was won by Middlesex, for whom Owais
Shah played the most influential innings with 81
from 56 balls, an innings that contained three sixes
and eight fours. A total of 209 for 7 was always
going to be tough for Yorkshire, and so it proved,
despite a fine 70 off just 46 balls by Phil Jaques,
who hit three sixes and five fours. Falling away
from 132 for 2, they eventually finished 29 runs
short.

Worcestershire rose to third in the table after
overpowering an injury-ravaged Somerset side by 64
runs in a 39-overs-per-side match at Worcester.
Vikram Solanki, Stephen Moore and Graeme Hick
all made valuable contributions in the upper order,
before falling to Gareth Andrew, but Somerset were
never in the hunt in reply to the home side's 238 for
7, despite a gutsy unbeaten 79 from Keith Dutch.

A young Scottish member of the Sussex groundstaff
at Hove could have made his totesport League debut
for the visiting Scotland team, if Chris Adams had

allowed it. As it was, 23-year-old Greig Peal, who hails
from Arbroath, was only able to act as a substitute
fielder after Stewart Bruce had broken a finger in the
warm-up and Adams, the Sussex captain, had ruled
against Peal being drafted in to bat and bowl. The
ECB had been happy for Peal to be registered for the
match, but, in the end, he was required more for his
day job – under head groundsman Derek Traill – after
rain caused proceedings to be abandoned after just
10.2 overs of the Sussex innings. Rain also caused the
abandonment of Durham's fixture against
Leicestershire at the Riverside.

5 July 2004: Division Two

at Richmond
Middlesex 216 for 4 (45 overs) (OA Shah 105*)
Scotland 89 (25.4 overs)
Middlesex (4pts) won by 127 runs

Owais Shah cut short any thoughts of an upset at Old
Deer Park in Richmond by hitting the Scottish
Saltires attack for an unbeaten 105 from 121 balls.
This was enough to take Middlesex to 216 for 4 on a
slow, low pitch and, in reply, the Saltires fell away to
89 all out and defeat by 127 runs. The home side's
win stretched their lead in Division Two to eight
points over second-placed Yorkshire.

11 July 2004: Division One

at Northampton
Northamptonshire 267 for 8 (45 overs) (RA White 101,
TW Roberts 68)
Glamorgan 250 (44.3 overs) (MP Maynard 117)
Northamptonshire (4pts) won by 17 runs

at The Rose Bowl
Lancashire 182 for 8 (45 overs) (DG Cork 57)
Hampshire 181 for 7 (45 overs) (SR Watson 54*)
Lancashire (4pts) won by 1 run

at The Oval
Surrey 176 (43.5 overs) (MW Alleyne 4 for 39)
Gloucestershire 180 for 6 (38.1 overs)
(MGN Windows 63, R Clarke 4 for 50)
Gloucestershire (4pts) won by 4 wickets

at Edgbaston
Warwickshire 223 (43.5 overs) (NV Knight 51,
SA Brant 4 for 49)
Essex 169 (36.4 overs) (GB Hogg 5 for 23)
Warwickshire (4pts) won by 54 runs

Leaders Glamorgan lost for only the second time when a Northamptonshire side inspired by their two young openers, Tim Roberts and Rob White, beat them by 17 runs at Wantage Road. Roberts hit 68 in a first-wicket stand of 124, but White went on to reach 101 from 120 balls. Glamorgan looked out of contention at 125 for 7, but then Alex Wharf joined Matthew Maynard in an eighth-wicket partnership of 113 in only 17 overs. Maynard, playing as well at 38 as he ever did, scored 117 from 108 balls to take the Welsh county to within sight of a dramatic victory. Thirty runs were required from the last two overs, but Maynard had already hit four sixes and eight fours and – at the last – his heroics could not quite take his side home. He was bowled swinging at Jason Brown, and, when Wharf also missed an attempted big hit later in the same over, the contest was decided.

Shane Watson and Nic Pothas, who had revived Hampshire with a seventh-wicket stand of 66 on a difficult pitch at the Rose Bowl, could not make the seven runs required for victory from the final over of the match, bowled by Carl Hooper, and, in a thrilling finish, Lancashire held on to win by one run. It had taken a determined seventh-wicket alliance of 79 between Dominic Cork and Warren Hegg, that doubled the score, to haul Lancashire's total up to 182 for 8, and then excellent seam and swing bowling by James Anderson, Sajid Mahmood and Cork reduced Hampshire to 110 for 6. Pothas then hit 29 for the home side and a frustrated Watson was 54 not out at the end.

A third-wicket stand of 106 between Phil Weston and Matt Windows, who scored the game's only half-century, saw Gloucestershire to a much-needed win over fellow strugglers Surrey at The Oval. Earlier, in a disappointing Surrey total of 176, Mark Alleyne had picked up 4 for 39.

Nick Knight hit 51 on his return from injury and a 42-ball 41 at the death from Dougie Brown enabled Warwickshire to set Essex the task of making 224 for victory at Edgbaston. However, it was the bowling of left-arm spinner Brad Hogg, supported by Ian Bell's medium pace, which sent Essex into a downward spiral from the promising position of being 99 for 2 in reply. Hogg's 5 for 23 represented the best one-day figures of his career and it was the first two wickets of his accurate and impressive spell, those of Andy Flower and Ronnie Irani, which were the most important.

Brad Hogg, a World Cup winner with Australia in 2003, took the best one-day bowling figures of his career in Warwickshire's win over Essex.

Division Two

at Southgate
Derbyshire 182 for 8 (45 overs) (Hassan Adnan 57, M Hayward 4 for 21)
Middlesex 183 for 1 (38.5 overs) (PN Weekes 80*, AJ Strauss 59*)
Middlesex (4pts) won by 9 wickets

at Leicester
Leicestershire 234 for 6 (45 overs)
Sussex 186 (42.1 overs)
Leicestershire (4pts) won by 48 runs

at Trent Bridge
Somerset 204 for 9 (45 overs) (JC Hildreth 85)
Nottinghamshire 208 for 7 (43.5 overs) (KP Pietersen 82*)
Nottinghamshire (4pts) won by 3 wickets

at The Riverside
Yorkshire 40 for 0 (9 overs)
Durham Did not bat
Match abandoned – 2pts each

Middlesex went ten points clear at the top of Division Two when they cruised to a nine-wicket win over Derbyshire at Southgate. Only Hassan Adnan's 57 blunted an attack spearheaded by Nantie Hayward's 4 for 21 for long, and then Paul Weekes and Andrew Strauss made short work of a target of 183 with an unbroken second-wicket stand of 108. The only downside for Middlesex was a serious back injury suffered by Chad Keegan, who broke down after delivering just three overs with the new ball.

John Sadler, with 49, was the game's top scorer, but Leicestershire's batsmen, collectively, had a much better day of it than Sussex's in a colourless affair at Grace Road. A total of 234 for 6 was a demanding one for Sussex to chase and the spinners, Claude Henderson and Jeremy Snape, shared six wickets after Charlie Dagnall had taken the first three visiting wickets in a lively new-ball spell.

Two of the best young batsmen in the country lit up a fascinating contest at Trent Bridge, won in the end by three wickets by Nottinghamshire. Kevin Pietersen, the South African just three months short of qualifying for England, finished on 82 not out from 99 balls to lead his side across the winning line. Earlier, Somerset's James Hildreth, 19, had won approving nods from many boundary-edge judges for his 90-ball 85.

Just nine overs of play were possible at the Riverside, with second-placed Yorkshire reaching 40 without loss before the rains came and the match was abandoned.

18 July 2004: Division One

at Canterbury
Kent 192 for 8 (34 overs) (ET Smith 61)
Surrey 193 for 6 (33.4 overs) (MR Ramprakash 66)
Surrey (4pts) won by 4 wickets

at Old Trafford
Essex 185 for 7 (45 overs) (RC Irani 102*)
Lancashire 186 for 3 (38.4 overs) (MJ Chilton 59*, CL Hooper 50*)
Lancashire (4pts) won by 7 wickets

at The Rose Bowl
Hampshire 153 (45 overs)
Northamptonshire 157 for 5 (43.1 overs) (DJG Sales 63)
Northamptonshire (4pts) won by 5 wickets

Surrey beat Kent by four wickets in a thrilling finish at Canterbury, achieving the 36 they still required from the last 24 balls in a match reduced to 34 overs per side. Adam Hollioake – with 41 not out off 31 balls – and Alex Tudor were responsible for the successful late assault, after Mark Ramprakash and Jon Batty had rallied the side from 45 for 3 in reply to Kent's 192 for 8. Ed Smith earlier scored his fifth consecutive one-day half-century at the head of the Kent order, but the home side ultimately paid dearly for dawdling in the middle of their innings after three wickets had fallen for 15 runs.

Unbeaten half-centuries from Mark Chilton and Carl Hooper took Lancashire to an easy seven-wicket win over Essex at Old Trafford. The result was hard to bear for Ronnie Irani, the captain of Essex, who steeled himself to play the anchor role once three early wickets were lost for 13 and ended up scoring 102 not out from 129 balls, with three sixes and seven fours, against the club with which he began his career.

Another low-scoring and attritional affair at the Rose Bowl was settled in Northamptonshire's favour by their captain, David Sales, who made 63 in an innings that included two sixes. Indeed, the match was effectively over when Sales greeted the arrival into the attack of Shane Warne and Shaun Udal by pulling and mowing them for sixes. He also took two boundaries off Warne's first two overs.

Division Two

at The Riverside
Middlesex 191 for 6 (45 overs) (EC Joyce 70*, JWM Dalrymple 58)
Durham 193 for 9 (44.5 overs) (MJ North 59, GR Breese 52*)
Durham (4pts) won by 1 wicket

at Derby
Sussex 185 (44.4 overs)
Derbyshire 166 (40.1 overs) (Hassan Adnan 51, MJG Davis 4 for 40)
Sussex (4pts) won by 10 runs − DL Method: target 177 from 41 overs

Durham had the rare chance to play both Steve Harmison and Paul Collingwood in their fixture against Middlesex, the division leaders, at the Riverside, and what a difference it made. Harmison, in fact, ended up by squeezing out two important singles in a thrilling finish as Durham just managed to chase down Middlesex's 191 for 6, in which Ed Joyce had made a stylish 70 not out and Jamie Dalrymple an enterprising 58. Harmison's nine overs had cost just 22 runs, and included the prized wicket of Owais Shah, and half-centuries from Marcus North and Gareth Breese also helped to make it a memorable day for the Durham supporters. Breese was faced with needing three for victory when he swept the penultimate ball of the match, from Dalrymple, to the boundary.

Sussex won a low-scoring game on a slow surface at Derby by just ten runs, after Derbyshire's target had been adjusted to 177 from 41 overs under Duckworth-Lewis regulations, following a sharp shower. Mark Davis, the off spinner, took four vital wickets, while both Hassan Adnan and Graeme Welch, who shared a sixth-wicket stand of 85 in 16 overs, were both run out as the match reached a gripping conclusion.

20 July 2004: Division One

at Canterbury
Hampshire 146 (42.3 overs) (AD Mascarenhas 79)
Kent 124 (35.4 overs)
Hampshire (4pts) won by 22 runs

Shane Warne's magic was sprinkled under the Canterbury floodlights as Hampshire pulled off a dramatic 22-run win over a shocked Kent. Initially, only a 93-ball 79 by Dimitri Mascarenhas, with two sixes and ten fours, had kept Hampshire in the game after they had slumped to 47 for 5 in the 18th over.

Then Kent progressed smoothly to 75 for 2 in reply, first through the elegant strokeplay of Ed Smith and subsequently through a determined partnership between Alex Loudon and Andrew Symonds. When Warne brought himself on in the 16th over, though, everything changed. Symonds was almost immediately held at slip and, when Shaun Udal was introduced at the other end, Matthew Walker was held at silly point and David Fulton caught off bat and pad from the very next ball. Warne continued to turn the game on its head by bowling both Loudon and Niall O'Brien, and two run outs by Michael Clarke completed the home side's bewilderment.

21 July 2004: Division Two

at Hove
Nottinghamshire 260 for 4 (45 overs) (RJ Warren 78, JER Gallian 77)
Sussex 260 (45 overs) (CJ Adams 93, RJ Logan 4 for 50)
Match tied − 2pts each

at Worcester
Worcestershire 252 for 4 (45 overs) (GA Hick 107*, VS Solanki 55)
Middlesex 182 (42.3 overs) (EC Joyce 65)
Worcestershire (4pts) won by 70 runs

The seventh tie in Sussex's one-day history provided a pulsating finish at Hove but, in the end, it was Nottinghamshire's players who were jubilant. What this revealed, accurately, was that Sussex had simply thrown the game away. Replying to Notts' 260 for 4, which was built on an opening stand of 147 between Jason Gallian and Russell Warren, Sussex were cruising to victory on the back of a superb innings by Chris Adams, their captain. The 42nd over began with Sussex needing 35, but Adams thumped Richard Logan for two fours and a six as 21 runs came from it. When Mark Davis also struck the first ball of the next over to the boundary, off Ryan Sidebottom; Sussex were cantering to the line. From the first ball of the 44th over, however, and with only six more runs required, Adams holed out to deep cover for 93 to be sixth out. Logan then had Davis caught at the wicket from the next ball and although Robin Martin-Jenkins clipped the hat-trick ball for a single, he was bowled later in the same over. Four runs were now needed from the final over and Luke Wright, attempting a second to wide third man, was run out by inches. Two frantic singles followed − before Sidebottom bowled James Kirtley with the last ball of the match.

Middlesex had Glenn McGrath and Ajit Agarkar, with 315 one-day international appearances between them, to open the bowling at Worcester – but both were upstaged by Graeme Hick as the division leaders were beaten by 71 runs. Hick hit an unbeaten 107 off 109 balls, yet at first was content to play second fiddle to the exuberant strokeplay of Vikram Solanki, who scored 55. A total of 252 for 4 was soon shown to be out of Middlesex's reach, despite a 107-run stand for the third wicket between Owais Shah and Ed Joyce, who top scored for the visitors with 65.

25 July 2004: Division One

at Guildford
Surrey 315 for 8 (45 overs) (JGE Benning 71, R Clarke 70, Azhar Mahmood 56*)
Warwickshire 225 for 9 (34.3 overs) (IR Bell 89)
Surrey (4pts) won by 90 runs

at Cheltenham
Gloucestershire 211 for 9 (36 overs) (MEK Hussey 60)
Lancashire 114 (29.2 overs) (J Lewis 5 for 23)
Gloucestershire (4pts) won by 102 runs – DL Method: target 217 from 36 overs

at Southend-on-Sea
Essex 168 (44.2 overs) (J Louw 4 for 30)
Northamptonshire 138 (42.3 overs) (GR Napier 4 for 23)
Essex (4pts) won by 30 runs

Surrey stayed bottom of Division One, but still felt a lot better about themselves after mauling Warwickshire by a 90-run margin at Guildford. James Benning hit 71 off 53 balls, with 13 fours, and Rikki Clarke's 70 took him 69 balls, with ten fours. However, Surrey's rapid progress to 315 for 8 was really accelerated by Alistair Brown's brutal 46 and a remarkable innings of 56 not out from Azhar Mahmood which included five sixes and four fours and occupied a mere 27 balls. Warwickshire only had a slim chance of matching Surrey's score when Ian Bell was at the crease, hitting five sixes himself in a 70-ball 89, but when he was held at deep square leg their faint hopes went with him.

Gloucestershire lifted themselves out of the relegation zone by inflicting a heavy defeat on Lancashire at Cheltenham. The margin in the end was 102 runs, under Duckworth-Lewis, as Lancashire were dismissed for just 114. Rain had reduced the match to 36 overs per side, and following a savage early assault by Craig Spearman on Glen Chapple, the visitors found themselves having to chase 217 in reply to Gloucestershire's 211 for 9. They also found their top order ripped to shreds by Jon Lewis' opening burst of 4 for 23 in six overs, and the seamer later returned to finish things off to great acclaim from the locals.

James Foster came in at 73 for 6 to score a fine 39 and pull round an Essex innings in seemingly terminal decline. He later took two good catches standing up to the stumps and, with Graham Napier also enjoying an excellent all-round day, the home side did just enough to send the Southend festival crowd away in a happy mood. Only Tim Roberts, with a quick-fire 33 at the top of the order, threatened to win the game for Northamptonshire, who were bowled out for 138 with Napier finishing with figures of 4 for 23.

Division Two

at Leicester
Leicestershire 176 for 7 (39 overs)
Durham 161 for 8 (39 overs) (GJ Pratt 55*)
Leicestershire (4pts) won by 15 runs

at Scarborough
Somerset 252 for 6 (41 overs) (RT Ponting 113)
Yorkshire 255 for 4 (38.4 overs) (MJ Lumb 71, AW Gale 70*, MJ Wood 56)
Yorkshire (4pts) won by 6 wickets

Another slow and lifeless pitch at Leicester produced a similarly low-scoring match between Leicestershire and Durham, which was won by the home team by just 15 runs as the visitors subsided in a rash of run outs. Brad Hodge and Darren Stevens put on 95 in 21 overs for Leicestershire, while Gary Pratt did his best to keep the game alive for Durham with a brave unbeaten 55 from 63 balls.

Andrew Gale, the 20-year-old Yorkshire left-hander, received a congratulatory handshake from Ricky Ponting as he left the field unbeaten on 70 at Scarborough. His 84-ball innings had just helped to trump Ponting's earlier 113, with Michael Lumb also weighing in with 71 as Yorkshire chased down 253 – a total that was one run more than Somerset's 252 for 6 following a short weather interruption and a Duckworth-Lewis recalculation. Ponting's hundred took him 101 balls, but Yorkshire always looked capable of winning once Matthew Wood had raced to a half-century in 35 balls. The poise and promise of young Gale, however, set the seal on a richly entertaining day at ever-popular North Marine Road.

Australian captain Ricky Ponting's arrival could not initially improve Somerset's totesport League fortunes.

27 July 2004: Division One

at Old Trafford
Warwickshire 251 for 5 (45 overs) (NV Knight 122*)
Lancashire 255 for 8 (44 overs) (D Mongia 104*, IJ Sutcliffe 68)
Lancashire (4pts) won by 2 wickets

at The Oval
Surrey 265 for 6 (45 overs) (AJ Hollioake 80*, JN Batty 66, JGE Benning 50)
Northamptonshire 226 (41.3 overs) (J Ormond 4 for 48)
Surrey (4pts) won by 39 runs

In an extraordinary finish at almost 10.30 pm, a magnificent unbeaten century by Dinesh Mongia upstaged an equally outstanding hundred from Nick Knight and brought Lancashire the victory that took them into second place in the division table. Knight had scored 122 not out, from 116 balls, and it was an innings that deserved to win the match. However, Mongia's own effort, following a Lancashire collapse of five wickets for 25 runs in five overs, was boosted when the umpires awarded the home side six penalty runs as a result of Warwickshire not bowling their 45 overs in the allotted time. This left Lancashire needing just two runs from eight balls, and not eight, and Mongia drove the winning boundary two deliveries later.

Adam Hollioake bludgeoned 80 not out from 66 balls to spearhead a Surrey charge to 265 for 6, and a winning total, against Northamptonshire at The Oval. Hollioake hit three sixes in a stand with Jon Batty of

26 July 2004: Division Two

at Taunton
Worcestershire 225 (44.2 overs) (VS Solanki 122, NAM McLean 4 for 35)
Somerset 191 (41.4 overs)
Worcestershire (4pts) won by 34 runs

A masterful innings by Vikram Solanki saw Somerset slide to their second defeat in two days as Worcestershire ran out 34-run winners at Taunton. Solanki withstood a fiery spell of bowling from Nixon McLean to score a magnificent unbeaten 122 out of the visitors' total of 225. Somerset's reply never got going and they were bowled out with 3.5 of their 45-over allocation still to go.

151 in just 18 overs. Earlier, James Benning's 50 had come off 57 balls and he and Rikki Clarke rallied Surrey after they had lost their first two wickets for 18.

28 July 2004: Division One

at Cardiff
Hampshire 174 for 9 (45 overs) (AP Davies 4 for 30)
Glamorgan 176 for 3 (34.4 overs) (MTG Elliott 81*)
Glamorgan (4pts) won by 7 wickets

Glamorgan's crushing seven-wicket victory over Hampshire at Cardiff followed the news that the club is planning to instal permanent floodlights at Sophia Gardens. It also put them four points clear of Lancashire at the top of the totesport League with two games in hand. Andrew Davies set up this win with a damaging four-wicket new-ball burst, and although Hampshire scrapped their way from 41 for 4 to 174 for 9, it was nowhere near enough. Matthew Elliott's unbeaten 81 ensured no alarms, and Michael Powell included a six off Shane Warne in his breezy innings of 36.

1 August 2004: Division One

at Cheltenham
Kent 226 for 8 (45 overs) (ET Smith 70)
Gloucestershire 230 for 4 (37.4 overs)
(MEK Hussey 107*, CG Taylor 60)
Gloucestershire (4pts) won by 6 wickets

Mike Hussey stood head and shoulders above everyone else on display as Gloucestershire ended the most financially successful of all the Cheltenham festivals with a thumping six-wicket win against Kent. Hussey's unbeaten 107 took him just 105 balls, with a six and 11 fours, and he was joined by Chris Taylor – who made 60 off 58 deliveries – in a match-winning stand of 139 in 22 overs. Ed Smith's 70 was the highlight of Kent's innings, but their bowling attack was quite unable to withstand Hussey and Taylor after a good opening spell from Rob Joseph. Overall receipts for Cheltenham's cricket week passed £100,000 for the first time, and it attracted more than 27,000 spectators over its duration.

Division Two

at Southgate
Middlesex 273 for 6 (45 overs) (OA Shah 125*)
Yorkshire 257 for 9 (45 overs) (A McGrath 96*)
Middlesex (4pts) won by 16 runs

at Cleethorpes
Nottinghamshire 229 for 7 (45 overs) (MA Ealham 56)
Durham 233 for 4 (42.4 overs) (MJ North 121*)
Durham (4pts) won by 6 wickets

at The Grange
Scotland 222 for 9 (45 overs) (DR Lockhart 63)
Leicestershire 223 for 4 (42 overs) (DDJ Robinson 109*)
Leicestershire (4pts) won by 6 wickets

at Taunton
Sussex 274 for 9 (45 overs) (MW Goodwin 50, PA Cottey 50)
Somerset 268 for 9 (45 overs) (JD Francis 79, RT Ponting 56, KA Parsons 54, PA Cottey 5 for 49)
Sussex (4pts) won by 6 runs

at Worcester
Worcestershire 248 for 7 (45 overs) (AJ Hall 70*, BF Smith 50)
Derbyshire 137 (33.4 overs) (SA Selwood 55)
Worcestershire (4pts) won by 111 runs

Middlesex remained on course for the Division Two title with a 16-run victory over Yorkshire in a high-scoring contest at Southgate. Owais Shah was the home star, hitting each of the last three balls of the innings from Tim Bresnan for six over long on. In all, 25 runs were plundered from this over, and that, in the end, made all the difference. Shah's unbeaten 125 took him 126 balls and left the 3,000 crowd breathless. In reply, Anthony McGrath did his best to trump Shah's effort, but he finished on 96 not out and could not repeat Shah's final flourish when faced with scoring 24 from Simon Cook's last over.

Marcus North's 121 not out swept Durham to a six-wicket win over Nottinghamshire at Cleethorpes that boosted their hopes of promotion. North faced just 114 balls and none of the home bowlers could match the accuracy and success enjoyed by Durham's left-arm spinner Graeme Bridge, who returned the splendid figures of 9–4–14–3.

Dougie Lockhart hit an excellent 63 for the Scottish Saltires at Edinburgh, but still finished up on the losing side as Leicestershire opener Darren Robinson responded with 109 not out. At 140 for 4, the visitors remained uncertain of victory, but an unbroken stand of 83 between Robinson and Jeremy Snape soon put them at their ease.

Tony Cottey's best bowling figures in any cricket, 5 for 49, emerged as the remarkable reason behind Sussex's narrow six-run win over Somerset at

Owais Shah hit each of the last three balls of Middlesex's innings at Southgate for six as he finished 125 not out against Yorkshire.

Taunton. Cottey also caught Ricky Ponting at slip, to give a joyous Mushtaq Ahmed the prize scalp of the innings, and provide his team with the wicket that probably tipped the balance of the scales in their favour. Somerset, however, were still overwhelming favourites at 230 for 3 as they chased Sussex's 274 for 9, with John Francis and Keith Parsons also going past fifty. However, Cottey's very occasional off breaks then came up trumps and, to go with his earlier 50, made it very much his day.

Andrew Hall – who finished on 70 not out – and Kabir Ali plundered 42 runs from the last two overs of the Worcestershire innings against Derbyshire at New Road. The result was the transformation of a useful total into a very good one, and, in reply, Derbyshire slipped to 137 all out and defeat by 111 runs with only Steve Selwood, with 55 from 68 balls in his first one-day appearance of the season, making any headway.

3 August 2004: Division Two

at Derby
Leicestershire 201 for 8 (37.1 overs)
(DL Maddy 78)
Derbyshire Did not bat
Match abandoned – 2pts each

Darren Maddy hit two sixes and 12 fours in a 70-ball 78, and Darren Stevens was bowled by a double-bouncing off break that went wrong from Nathan Dumelow, before rain washed out Leicestershire's visit to Derby. The home side were preparing to chase a revised target of 96 from 13 overs when a further, decisive, shower hit the ground. Two points from the no result were, however, enough to lift Leicestershire into third place.

4 August 2004: Division One

at Northampton
Northamptonshire 172 (44.5 overs)
Warwickshire 176 for 9 (44.5 overs) (IR Bell 58, J Louw 5 for 27)
Warwickshire (4pts) won by 1 wicket

Tony Frost swung the penultimate ball of the match into the leg side for a single to earn Warwickshire a thrilling one-wicket win over Northamptonshire at Wantage Road. It could easily have been a victory for the home side, though, when Graeme Swann missed the bowler's stumps by what seemed a fraction of an inch as last man Alan Richardson tried to lunge for safety after calling for a sharp single from the previous ball. Dougie Brown had perished to the third ball of that dramatic over, and for a moment it looked as if Ian Bell's 58 would be in vain. In difficult, sultry conditions, Johann Louw had taken 5 for 27 from his nine overs to bowl Northants back into the game after the home side had initially been boosted by a sixth-wicket stand of 69 between Swann and Gerard Brophy.

8 August 2004: Division One

at Northampton
Gloucestershire 200 (45 overs) (J Louw 4 for 41)
Northamptonshire 109 (35 overs)
Gloucestershire (4pts) won by 91 runs

Mike Hussey top scored with 44 against his former county, at Northampton, and, in the process, handed Gloucestershire an early advantage that they never relinquished. Having totalled 200 on a difficult, wearing pitch, Gloucestershire's bowlers then exerted such a grip that Northamptonshire were bowled out for just 109 in reply. Ian Fisher, the slow left-armer, took 3 for 18 from his nine overs.

Division Two

at The Riverside
Worcestershire 205 for 7 (45 overs) (SC Moore 93*)
Durham 209 for 5 (43 overs) (PD Collingwood 63*)
Durham (4pts) won by 5 wickets

at Hove
Sussex 271 for 7 (45 overs) (MH Yardy 88*, MJ Prior 59)
Derbyshire 187 (39 overs) (G Welch 82, RSC Martin-Jenkins 4 for 39)
Sussex (4pts) won by 84 runs

Led by Paul Collingwood's unbeaten 63, Durham leapt into second place in the division with a convincing five-wicket win over Worcestershire at the Riverside. Stephen Moore's unbeaten 93 anchored the visitors' sometimes-hesitant progress to 205 for 7, but then Collingwood joined Jon Lewis to add 62 for the third wicket and, later, was able to sit back as Gary Pratt arrived to score the lion's share of an unbroken partnership of 52 which clinched the match.

Mike Yardy's highest one-day score, an unbeaten 88 from 74 balls, helped Sussex to a commanding victory against Derbyshire at Hove which continued their climb up the Division Two table. Ian Ward hit three sixes in his 49 and, with Matthew Prior, added 102 for the opening wicket. Prior went on to 59 off 69 balls before leaving the stage to Yardy. Derbyshire's chances of overhauling Sussex's 271 for 7 were non-existent once James Kirtley – with a spell of 3 for 3 in 25 balls – had made a mess of their top order, and Robin Martin-Jenkins then set about dismantling the middle order.

9 August 2004: Division One

at Canterbury
Glamorgan 250 for 6 (42 overs) (MTG Elliott 112, MP Maynard 66)
Kent 93 for 2 (20 overs)
Glamorgan (4pts) won by 10 runs – DL Method: target 104 from 20 overs

at Chelmsford
Essex 107 for 0 (21 overs)
Lancashire Did not bat
Match abandoned – 2pts each

at The Rose Bowl
Hampshire v. **Surrey**
Match abandoned – 2pts each

Kent felt like losers twice over when they were beaten by Glamorgan at Canterbury. First, the game had been pushed back 24 hours to the Monday, due to Glamorgan's presence in the Twenty20 Cup semi-finals two days earlier, costing the club an estimated £12,000 in lost gate receipts and corporate hospitality bookings. Secondly, the match did not even run its full course, with rain arriving a third of the way through the Kent reply and forcing the contest to be decided by a Duckworth-Lewis calculation. Alex Loudon, desperately trying to up the pace with rain already falling, only made matters worse for Kent by getting himself out, lbw, shortly before the players came off. Glamorgan, to be fair, may have made enough runs anyway, after Matthew Elliott had scored 112 from 122 balls and Matthew Maynard had struck a 61-ball 66 that included a remarkable on-driven six off Rob Ferley with his bottom hand off the bat. The result, meanwhile, left Glamorgan needing only another two victories to make sure of the totesport League title.

Essex were left to rue the bad weather as Will Jefferson and Ronnie Irani were both going well on 49 not out when rain cut short their home fixture with Lancashire at Chelmsford. The no result was highly frustrating for both teams – Essex remained bottom of the table, while Lancashire's pursuit of Glamorgan was weakened with the Welsh county beating both the weather and Kent.

The match between Hampshire and Surrey at the Rose Bowl also fell foul of the bad weather without a ball being bowled. Both sides picked up two points.

Division Two

at Lord's
Middlesex 215 for 9 (41.5 overs)
(CW Henderson 4 for 45)
Leicestershire 117 (18.4 overs)
Middlesex (4pts) won by 17 runs – DL Method:
target 135 from 20 overs

Twenty20 Cup champions Leicestershire were
given the opportunity to continue their 20-over
form 48 hours later when their rearranged match
against Middlesex at Lord's was interrupted by the
weather. After restricting Middlesex to 215 for 9,
their target became 135 from 20 overs, but the
short-form experts were found wanting this time
as, in fading light, they fell apart against the home
seamers. In truth, it was a scruffy performance
from Leicestershire; earlier, their own bowlers had
given away 31 runs in wides.

10 August 2004: Division Two

at Headingley
Derbyshire 128 for 5 (17 overs) (J Moss 54*)
Yorkshire 99 for 7 (17 overs)
Derbyshire (4pts) won by 29 runs

A floodlit match at Headingley became something of a
damp squib as Yorkshire floundered to a mere 99 for 7
in reply to Derbyshire's 128 for 5 in a contest reduced
to 17 overs per side because of bad weather. Jon Moss
carried his bat for 54 from 49 balls for Derbyshire,
adding 71 in nine overs with Hassan Adnan, but the
Yorkshire batsmen could not deal with conditions in
which the ball darted around under the lights.

11 August 2004: Division Two

at The Riverside
Durham 162 for 9 (45 overs) (GM Hamilton 66*)
Somerset 147 for 4 (31.2 overs) (RT Ponting 83*)
Somerset (4pts) won by 6 wickets – DL Method:
target 146 from 37 overs

Ricky Ponting hit a brilliant unbeaten 83 in surreal
conditions at the Riverside to guide Somerset to a
six-wicket win over Durham. A mist rolling down
from the ramparts of the nearby Lumley Castle
mingled with the beams from occasionally faltering
floodlights to produce an eerie atmosphere.
Through the evening gloom, however, emerged a
knight in shining armour, as Ponting pulled and cut

his way to a revised target of 146 from 37 overs,
following a break for drizzle that only added to the
bizarre conditions for a cricket match.

13 August 2004: Division One

at Bristol
Gloucestershire 150 for 6 (33 overs)
Essex 164 for 4 (32 overs) (A Flower 58,
AP Grayson 58*)
Essex (4pts) won by 6 wickets – DL Method:
target 164 from 33 overs

Canny half-centuries from both Andy Flower and
Paul Grayson – who put on a decisive 113 in 22 overs
– meant a rare failure for Gloucestershire in
defending a decent total at Bristol. The home side
had added 32 runs from three overs, following a rain
break, leaving Essex to score 164 in 33 overs for
victory. So close were the teams in Division One at
this stage of the summer that Essex, bottom of the
table before this game, moved to within four points of
third-placed Gloucestershire as a result of this win.

15 August 2004: Division One

at Whitgift School
Surrey 235 for 8 (45 overs) (AJ Hollioake 66,
AJ Tudor 56)
Lancashire 238 for 2 (38.1 overs) (MJ Chilton 115,
IJ Sutcliffe 102*)
Lancashire (4pts) won by 8 wickets

at Edgbaston
Kent 135 (37.5 overs)
Warwickshire 139 for 4 (24.1 overs) (IR Bell 51)
Warwickshire (4pts) won by 6 wickets

at The Rose Bowl
Hampshire 208 (37 overs)
(JP Crawley 56)
Glamorgan 209 for 7 (36 overs)
(MTG Elliott 79*, RDB Croft 52)
Glamorgan (4pts) won by 3 wickets

Surrey's depleted bowling resources were self-
evident at Whitgift School when Lancashire had
little trouble in overhauling a target of 236. In fact,
with Mark Chilton and Iain Sutcliffe both making
hundreds and putting on a county record 223 for
the first wicket, they did so for the loss of just two
wickets and with almost seven overs to spare.
Earlier, Surrey had collapsed to 72 for 6 before

Adam Hollioake, in his last home game for the club, was joined by Alex Tudor in a seventh-wicket stand of 128 in 21 overs.

A superb new-ball spell by Heath Streak, who took 3 for 7 in six overs, undermined Kent to such an extent that they went on to be bowled out for only 135 at Edgbaston. In reply, with Ian Bell easing his way to 51, Warwickshire cantered to a six-wicket win that increased their survival chances, at the expense of Kent's.

Glamorgan put one hand on to the totesport League tophy by seeing off Hampshire at the Rose Bowl. Robert Croft, taken for 60 runs from his six overs, exacted swift revenge by belting a 34-ball half-century as Glamorgan set out in pursuit of Hampshire's 208. Croft's early salvo, in a first-wicket stand of 79, put the Welsh county in control – and that advantage was maintained, despite a steady fall of wickets at the other end, by Matthew Elliott's 79 not out in a perfect anchor role.

Division Two

at Trent Bridge
Nottinghamshire 249 for 6 (45 overs) (JER Gallian 73, KP Pietersen 51)
Leicestershire 229 (44.5 overs) (DL Maddy 75)
Nottinghamshire (4pts) won by 20 runs

at Lord's
Worcestershire 261 for 7 (45 overs) (GA Hick 120, DA Leatherdale 63, SJ Cook 5 for 34)
Middlesex 178 (37 overs) (OA Shah 55)
Worcestershire (4pts) won by 83 runs

at The Grange
Sussex 263 for 6 (45 overs) (MH Yardy 83)
Scotland 149 (34.5 overs) (Mushtaq Ahmed 4 for 46)
Sussex (4pts) won by 114 runs

Nottinghamshire bolstered their promotion hopes by beating Leicestershire by 20 runs in a closely fought affair at Trent Bridge. Jason Gallian and Anurag Singh opened up with a 112-run partnership and Kevin Pietersen hit 51, but perhaps the match turned on Chris Read's quick-fire 31 at the end of the Notts innings and then his three fine stumpings off Stuart MacGill – one of them to get rid of Leicestershire dangerman Darren Maddy, who had made 75 from 72 balls.

Worcestershire moved into second place by beating the leaders, Middlesex, by 83 runs at Lord's. Graeme Hick's 120, and his 160-run

Still dangerous after all these years: Graeme Hick's 120 helped Worcestershire to see off Middlesex at Lord's.

alliance with David Leatherdale, was the major reason Worcestershire were able to shrug off Simon Cook's 5 for 34 and then a stomach injury to their own opening bowler, Kabir Ali, which prevented him from completing his second over.

The Scottish Saltires found themselves totally bemused by Mushtaq Ahmed's box of tricks as they went down to defeat by 114 runs at Edinburgh. The Pakistan leg spinner took 4 for 46 after Sussex's 263 for 6 had been based upon Mike Yardy's 83 and a quick-fire 44 from 39 balls by Matt Prior.

16 August 2004: DivisionTwo

at Headingley
Nottinghamshire 141 for 4 (25 overs)
Yorkshire 9 for 3 (4 overs)
Match abandoned – 2pts each

Yorkshire were in deep trouble at 9 for 3 chasing 142 for victory when rain brought a premature halt to proceedings at Headingley.

17 August 2004: Division One

at Edgbaston
Gloucestershire 192 for 7 (42 overs)
Warwickshire 31 for 2 (7.2 overs)
Match abandoned – 2pts each

A frustrating no result at Edgbaston, confirmed when just another 16 balls were needed to bring the match into Duckworth-Lewis territory, failed to lift relegation fears for both Gloucestershire and Warwickshire. Brad Hogg bowled well to peg back Gloucestershire, after Phil Weston and Craig Spearman had given them a brisk start, but Warwickshire had slipped to 31 for 2 in reply as they chased 205 from 42 overs before rain intervened for the final time.

Division Two

at Hove
Worcestershire 203 for 8 (45 overs) (SC Moore 76)
Sussex 99 for 2 (15.1 overs) (MJ Prior 56*)
Sussex (4pts) won by 8 wickets – DL Method: target 96 from 16 overs

Sussex won a farcical match under Duckworth-Lewis regulations at Hove, keeping alive their own promotion hopes but wrecking Worcestershire's Division Two title aspirations. The rain first swept in off the sea with Sussex on 6 for no wicket after two overs. A lengthy delay meant that the home side's target became 117 off 20 overs, and Matt Prior set about the Worcestershire attack with a string of fine shots. More rain arrived with Sussex on 94 for 2 from 15.1 overs and, when play resumed for the final time after 10 pm, they required just another two runs from a further 11 balls. Andrew Hall's first ball back then went for four wides, and that was it.

18 August 2004: Division Two

at Derby
Derbyshire 172 for 7 (39 overs) (Hassan Adnan 57)
Nottinghamshire 82 for 1 (17 overs)
Nottinghamshire (4pts) won by 24 runs – DL Method: target 58 from 17 overs

at Leicester
Yorkshire 177 for 8 (32 overs) (DS Lehmann 56)
Leicestershire 145 (30.3 overs)
Yorkshire (4pts) won by 34 runs

Derbyshire's new £200,000 permanent floodlights were switched on for the first time at Derby's Racecourse Ground, and drew immediate praise from the Nottinghamshire batsmen who raced to 82 for 1 from 17 overs before rain brought a premature end to proceedings. Anurag Singh's unbeaten 47 from 52 balls, and 30 not out from David Hussey, meant that Notts were declared the winners under the Duckworth-Lewis regulations. Earlier, Derbyshire had struggled to reach 172 for 7 from 39 overs, with only Hassan Adnan and Luke Sutton flourishing.

In a tense contest that was effectively a promotion eliminator, Yorkshire beat Leicestershire by 34 runs at Grace Road with spinners Richard Dawson and Darren Lehmann proving the match-winners on a slow pitch. Lehmann also hit 56 from 61 balls during the Yorkshire innings.

22 August 2004: Division One

at Colwyn Bay
Lancashire 218 for 7 (45 overs) (D Mongia 58)
Glamorgan 219 for 5 (40.2 overs) (RDB Croft 106, MP Maynard 63)
Glamorgan (4pts) won by 5 wickets

at Colchester
Essex 267 for 6 (45 overs) (RC Irani 98, WI Jefferson 97, AGR Loudon 4 for 48)
Kent 232 for 7 (45 overs) (ET Smith 61, AGR Loudon 52, MG Bevan 52, GR Napier 4 for 25)
Essex (4pts) won by 35 runs

at Campbell Park
Hampshire 238 for 9 (45 overs) (N Pothas 70*, SM Katich 58, GA Lamb 54)
Northamptonshire 171 (41.5 overs) (GP Swann 59, SD Udal 4 for 46)
Hampshire (4pts) won by 67 runs

Glamorgan made sure of the totesport League title in fitting style at Colwyn Bay: they thumped Lancashire, their only surviving challengers, by five wickets with Robert Croft and Matthew Maynard their chief inspirations. A third one-day league triumph in their history was clinched with three matches still to play – an indication of just how dominant they had been throughout the campaign. After skipper Croft had spoken of his pleasure at the achievement, he and Maynard sprayed champagne on a delirious North Wales crowd. Earlier, Croft had scored a brilliant 106 to lead Glamorgan's charge towards a Lancashire total of 218 for 7. He rushed to his half-century in just 35 balls, but then settled down once the fielding restrictions had been lifted and reached his hundred from 103 deliveries, with 16 fours. He was joined by Maynard, who scored 63, in a match-winning fourth-wicket stand of 121.

An opening stand of 196 between Will Jefferson and Ronnie Irani, who, respectively, perished just three and two runs short of hundreds, paved the way for Essex to enhance their own chances of avoiding relegation at the expense of Kent's. In the end, and despite Kent getting to 217 for 2 at one stage in reply, they won by 35 runs at Colchester. Irani hit six sixes and six fours in his 111-ball innings, while Jefferson faced 94 balls and hit 11 fours and two sixes.

A return to Milton Keynes for the first time for seven years did not bring Northamptonshire any luck against Shane Warne's Hampshire. Warne did not take a wicket, but Shaun Udal took four as Northants were bundled out for 171 in response to a Hampshire total of 238 for 9 that was built upon half-centuries from Simon Katich, Greg Lamb and Nic Pothas.

Division Two

at Taunton
Somerset 253 for 8 (45 overs) (J Cox 63, MJ Wood 56, JC Hildreth 53, CM Wright 5 for 44)
Scotland 246 (44.2 overs) (CV English 55, Yasir Arafat 55*, GM Andrew 4 for 48)
Somerset (4pts) won by 7 runs

Only 1,000 or so (one of Somerset's sparsest-ever one-day crowds at Taunton) turned up to see the home side hang on to win a high-scoring contest against the Scottish Saltires by seven runs. In fact, the Scots began the final over needing only eight for victory, but they lost their last two wickets to the first two balls of it, delivered by Gareth Andrew.

24 August 2004: Division Two

at Taunton
Somerset 179 (39.3 overs)
Middlesex 153 for 2 (28 overs) (PN Weekes 76*, AJ Strauss 68)
Middlesex (4pts) won by 57 runs – DL Method: target 97 from 28 overs

at Worcester
Worcestershire 131 (40.4 overs) (BF Smith 50*, Yasir Arafat 4 for 22)
Scotland 130 (39.3 overs)
Worcestershire (4pts) won by 1 run

Somerset members, who, yet again, were denied the chance to see their own Marcus Trescothick in action at Taunton because of the constraints of his ECB central contract, had to endure the sight of Andrew Strauss hitting 68 from 78 balls to lead Middlesex to an easy eight-wicket win. Strauss, an England regular alongside Trescothick all season but not on a central contract, relished the rare chance of turning out for his county and helped Paul Weekes to fashion a second-wicket stand of 143 in 26 overs which more than made up for the early loss of Ben Hutton in response to Somerset's inadequate total of 179 all out.

An attack of lower-order nerves condemned the Scottish Saltires to a one-run defeat at Worcester, and allowed the home side to keep their promotion ambitions intact. After bowling Worcestershire out on a green seamer – with Yasir Arafat picking up 4 for 22 – the Scots seemed well on course for victory at 79 for 2 in the 20th over. However, Ryan Watson, who had struck 44 from 55 balls, was then caught at the wicket off Andrew Hall, and the innings disintegrated with only Arafat, eventually left high and dry on 22 not out, keeping his composure as the wickets tumbled around him.

25 August 2004: Division One

at Chelmsford
Essex 135 for 5 (25.1 overs) (WI Jefferson 61*)
Surrey Did not bat
Match abandoned – 2pts each

at Trent Bridge
Nottinghamshire v. **Worcestershire**
Match abandoned – 2pts each

A controversial decision to call this match off at 9.10 pm – an hour after the rain which had interrupted the contest at Chelmsford had stopped – left Essex marginally more happy than Surrey. Holding a six-point advantage over the visiting side, and with both teams languishing in the lower reaches of the division, Essex were more than content to take the two points on offer for a no result after struggling somewhat to score 135 for 5 in 25.1 of the original 32-overs-per-side game. Will Jefferson, with an unbeaten 61, was the only batsman who looked comfortable in the damp conditions.

The game between Nottinghamshire and Worcestershire also fell foul of the weather with both sides picking up two points.

Stuart MacGill's leg breaks and googlies were too hot for the Scots to handle at Trent Bridge.

26 August 2004: Division Two

at Trent Bridge
Scotland 143 (38.5 overs) (SCG MacGill 4 for 18)
Nottinghamshire 144 for 7 (36 overs) (A Singh 67)
Nottinghamshire (4pts) won by 3 wickets

Nottinghamshire took another big step towards the totesport League's top division by overcoming the Scottish Saltires by three wickets at Trent Bridge. The Scots made Notts work hard for their runs, but the visitors were always up against it after being bewitched by Stuart MacGill's leg breaks and googlies. The Australian took 4 for 18 from his nine-over allocation as the Saltires were bowled out for 143.

29 August 2004: Division One

at Cardiff
Glamorgan 142 for 7 (25 overs)
Kent 143 for 9 (25 overs) (AG Wharf 6 for 5)
Kent (4pts) won by 1 wicket

at Northampton
Surrey 179 for 7 (41 overs) (Azhar Mahmood 67, AD Brown 54)
Northamptonshire 191 for 5 (39.5 overs) (U Afzaal 86*)
Northamptonshire (4pts) won by 5 wickets – DL Method: target 189 from 41 overs

As a result of the rain, it may only have been a 25-overs-per-side affair in the end, but Glamorgan's

chance to show off the totesport trophy in front of the Sky television cameras and their own fans at Cardiff had everything … bar a home win! Ian Butler, Kent's New Zealand fast bowler, swung the final ball of the match – bowled by Adrian Dale in his last game for Glamorgan – high over the square-leg boundary for six to provide an extraordinary climax to an action-packed few hours. Matthew Elliott and David Hemp both played fluently to ensure a competitive home total and, although Ed Smith launched the reply with some superlative strokes, Kent were soon in trouble. Most of the damage was done by Alex Wharf in an incredible spell of fast-medium bowling. After having Smith caught at long leg for 36, he went on to take 6 for 5 in his five overs. Dale then bowled Matt Dennington and Mick Lewis ended Matthew Walker's defiance, to leave Kent staring defeat in the face on 115 for 9. The last over began with 15 runs still needed, but four byes helped the visitors' cause and, with six still needed from the final ball, Dale bowled a shin-high full toss in his anxiety to find a yorker – and saw Butler pick it up effortlessly with a dramatic swing of his bat. The Glamorgan players, however, were still able to pose for pictures with the trophy afterwards.

While Kent hung on by a thread to their Division One status, Surrey found themselves relegated after they were defeated by five wickets by Northamptonshire at Wantage Road. It was 12 months almost to the day that they had become the 2003 one-day league champions. Surrey fell to 50 for 5 before Alistair Brown and Azhar Mahmood reconstructed the innings and hauled it up to 179 for 7. Usman Afzaal, however, was more than up to the task of guiding Northants to their revised Duckworth-Lewis target of 189 in 41 overs, finishing on 86 not out from 112 balls to give his county a chance of beating the drop.

Division Two

at Derby
Derbyshire 168 for 6 (34 overs) (J Moss 75*)
Yorkshire 175 for 5 (32.4 overs) (PA Jaques 62, MP Vaughan 57)
Yorkshire (4pts) won by 5 wickets

at The Riverside
Sussex 214 for 7 (45 overs) (IJ Ward 72)
Durham 159 for 8 (27.4 overs)
Durham (4pts) won by 2 wickets – DL Method: target 159 from 28 overs

Glamorgan's Alex Wharf produced the remarkable figures of 5-3-5-6 against Kent at Cardiff ... and still ended up on the losing side!

at Leicester
Somerset 205 for 7 (45 overs)
Leicestershire Did not bat
Match abandoned – 2pts each

Michael Vaughan warmed up for the NatWest Challenge internationals against India by hitting 57 and sharing in a match-winning stand of 105 from 13 overs with Phil Jaques as Yorkshire brushed aside Derbyshire by five wickets at Derby. In a match reduced to 34 overs per side, the home team's 168 for 6 was based on an unbeaten 75 from their Australian all-rounder Jon Moss, from 94 balls, but off spinner Richard Dawson showed up well as he took 3 for 22.

Sussex saw their last hope of promotion undermined by Durham's Liam Plunkett at the Riverside. The 19-year-old all-rounder struck Robin Martin-Jenkins for a four and a six to midwicket and then straight for another four to give his side an unlikely victory in a rain-affected match. A rain interruption midway through their innings left Durham, on 69 for 3 at the time, with a recalculated target of 159 in 28 overs. That meant scoring another 90 from the remaining 13.3 overs, and 14 were still required when Martin-Jenkins ran in to bowl the final over. Plunkett, however, needed only the first four deliveries to score

the runs and Sussex, who earlier had totalled 214 for 7 with Ian Ward top scoring with 72, walked from the field in shock.

Two of Somerset's young bloods, James Hildreth and Arul Suppiah, caught the eye with some pleasing strokes before their match against Leicestershire at Grace Road fell victim to the weather. Hildreth hit 42 from 47 balls and Suppiah 30 from 33 balls, and they added 67 in 10 overs for the fifth wicket after Marcus Trescothick had helped give the Somerset innings a sound start by making 36.

30 August 2004: Division One

at The Rose Bowl
Gloucestershire 230 for 6 (45 overs)
Hampshire 234 for 5 (44.3 overs) (N Pothas 83*, JP Crawley 62)
Hampshire (4pts) won by 5 wickets

at Cardiff
Glamorgan 211 for 7 (45 overs) (MP Maynard 63)
Warwickshire 213 for 6 (41 overs)
Warwickshire (4pts) won by 4 wickets

Nic Pothas hit an unbeaten 83 off 79 balls at the Rose Bowl, an innings that contained a six and eight fours, to confirm Hampshire's place in Division One and to leave Gloucestershire in danger of relegation. Nathan Bracken, the Australian left-arm quick bowler, took two wickets in his second over on debut, and later returned to bowl John Crawley, whose 62 had initially held the Hampshire reply to Gloucestershire's 230 for 6 together. But Pothas then plundered 16 runs off one Ian Fisher over and was joined by Dimitri Mascarenhas in an unbroken stand of 55 in seven overs that swept Hampshire home.

Warwickshire, battling to survive the log-jam at the foot of the Division One table, eased the pressure off themselves with a four-wicket win over newly-crowned champions Glamorgan at Cardiff. Once again, it was the steady batting of their top order – in this instance, Nick Knight, Jonathan Trott, Ian Bell and Brad Hogg – that hurried them to victory.

31 August 2004: Division One

at Old Trafford
Lancashire 244 for 9 (45 overs) (SG Law 73, CP Schofield 69*, MJ Chilton 52)
Surrey 196 (40.2 overs)
Lancashire (4pts) won by 48 runs

Adam Hollioake's farewell match for Surrey ended in a defeat against Lancashire under the Old Trafford lights. For a man who has achieved so much for the county, both as a captain and a player, it was a low-key goodbye: his three overs cost 27 runs and he was later stumped for 12. Hollioake, however, will go down in Surrey's history as one of their most charismatic and important figures, as well as one of their most successful captains and, no doubt bearing that in mind, he appeared to be content enough to leave this particular stage to Lancashire. After running up a total of 244 for 9, thanks in the main to Stuart Law's comeback innings of 73 following a seven-week lay-off through illness and a typically punchy 69 not out from Chris Schofield, Lancashire's bowlers performed with distinction to confirm the county's runners-up position and a cheque from totesport for £27,000.

2 September 2004: Division Two

at Hove
Sussex 217 for 8 (45 overs) (MW Goodwin 91, SJ Cook 4 for 37)
Middlesex 85 (27.5 overs) (LJ Wright 4 for 12)
Sussex (4pts) won by 132 runs

A balmy night in Hove became a bittersweet one for Middlesex as the smiles between the innings, when the Division Two trophy was presented to Ed Joyce, quickly vanished as the champions fell apart against Sussex. They were 35 for 6 inside 15 overs, and later fell away to 85 all out as Sussex completed a 132-run victory. Murray Goodwin's 93-ball 91, with a six and 12 fours, provided the basis of Sussex's total of 217 for 8 – although the Zimbabwean was dropped on nought by David Nash at midwicket. Luke Wright and Robin Martin-Jenkins did most of the damage to the Middlesex batting with excellent spells of seam bowling, while Simon Cook was the only visiting player to take something worthwhile out of the experience: by taking 4 for 37 in the Sussex innings he equalled Adam Hollioake's 1996 record of 39 wickets in a one-day league season.

4 September 2004: Division One

at Bristol
Warwickshire 248 for 7 (45 overs) (IR Bell 76, IJL Trott 70)
Gloucestershire 250 for 7 (44.2 overs) (MEK Hussey 82)
Gloucestershire (4pts) won by 3 wickets

Gloucestershire made sure of their Division One survival by beating Warwickshire at Bristol. Ian Bell

and Jonathan Trott scored 76 and 70 respectively for the visitors, and added 126 for the third wicket in a total of 248 for 7. However, Mike Hussey's 82 then took the game away from Warwickshire, and Mark Alleyne calmly oversaw the culmination of Gloucestershire's successful chase over the tense final overs.

5 September 2004: Division Two

at Worcester
Leicestershire 107 (26.4 overs) (DH Wigley 4 for 37)
Worcestershire 111 for 5 (18.4 overs)
Worcestershire (4pts) won by 5 wickets

at The Grange
Derbyshire 179 (42.3 overs) (Hassan Adnan 50)
Scotland 182 for 2 (36.1 overs) (DR Lockhart 58)
Scotland (4pts) won by 8 wickets

at Scarborough
Durham 178 for 9 (45 overs) (GM Hamilton 76)
Yorkshire 181 for 7 (41.4 overs)
Yorkshire (4pts) won by 3 wickets

Steve Rhodes captained Worcestershire to the runners-up position in Division Two, and a cheque for £11,000, and left the field for the final time in a one-day league match to a standing ovation midway through this thumping victory over Leicestershire. Rhodes, retiring to a coaching role at New Road at the end of the season, finished off the visitors' hapless slide to 107 all out with a catch and a stumping – and then watched from the pavilion as Worcestershire's batsmen knocked off the required runs in just 18.4 overs. Former skipper Ben Smith also won generous applause for his unbeaten 33, as did 22-year-old pace bowler David Wigley for his four-wicket haul earlier in the day.

Perhaps their most impressive all-round performance of the season earned the Scottish Saltires a victory over Derbyshire to take with them into the long winter months. Paul Hoffmann spearheaded a fine display in the field with three wickets and the Scots, who the previous week had beaten Bangladesh in a pre-Champions Trophy warm-up fixture, then swept to an eight-wicket win with opener Dougie Lockhart scoring 58 and Ryan Watson finishing on 42 not out and adding an unbroken 68 with Fraser Watts. It was only the Saltires' second victory of the league season, but at least it was evidence that the experience of playing in the competition was doing them good.

Yorkshire, meanwhile, kept alive their hopes of promotion by beating Durham at Scarborough, with

England fast bowler Matthew Hoggard taking three wickets with the new ball to give his side early control of the game. Gavin Hamilton, the former Yorkshire all-rounder, fought back with a gutsy 76 but, in front of a 5,000-strong crowd, the home side would not be denied and victory was all but assured by a 66-run sixth-wicket stand between Matthew Wood and Richard Pyrah.

6 September 2004: Division One

at Chelmsford
Essex 316 for 4 (45 overs) (RC Irani 158*, A Flower 54)
Glamorgan 153 (26.3 overs) (MJ Powell 54)
Essex (4pts) won by 163 runs

Glamorgan were put to the sword by Ronnie Irani at Chelmsford. Essex skipper Irani hit 158 not out off just 141 balls and his side's 316 for 4 was well out of the reach of the Welsh county as both openers fell to Ashley Cowan for ducks.

Robert Croft smiles happily, and Matthew Maynard leads the singing, as Glamorgan begin to celebrate winning the 2004 totesport League title.

7 September 2004: Division One

at Canterbury
Northamptonshire 219 for 7 (45 overs)
Kent 215 for 7 (45 overs) (ET Smith 106)
Northamptonshire (4pts) won by 4 runs

In a thrilling floodlit finale to the season in the top tier of the one-day league, Northamptonshire beat Kent in dramatic fashion at Canterbury to save themselves from relegation – and, in the process, condemned Warwickshire, who had been crowned as county champions just 24 hours earlier, to relegation. Ben Phillips hit three sixes in the last over against his former county to boost the Northants 45-over total to 219 for 7, but Kent looked well on course for victory when Alex Loudon and Rob Key helped Ed Smith to put on 68 and 51 respectively for the second and third wickets. However, Graeme Swann fiddled both of them out with his off breaks and, in the end, it was down to Smith to play a lone hand. He looked like doing so, taking 16 off the penultimate over and going to a brilliant hundred. However, from the last ball of that same over, he lifted a catch to long on and Kent

were left to make seven from Johann Louw's final over. Niall O'Brien and Rob Ferley could not do it as Louw sent down a superb, full-length over and Northants emerged winners by four runs.

8 September 2004: Division Two

at Taunton
Nottinghamshire 259 for 7 (45 overs) (JER Gallian 68, PJ Franks 64)
Somerset 225 (42.5 overs) (KA Parsons 115*)
Nottinghamshire (4pts) won by 34 runs

Nottinghamshire, inspired in particular by Jason Gallian and Paul Franks, won promotion to Division One as they beat Somerset by 34 runs at Taunton. Gallian's 68 at the head of the order included ten fours in his first 50 runs, while Franks came in at No. 7 to biff four sixes and five fours in a rapid 64. In reply, Somerset lost far too many early wickets and were only kept in the match for any length of time by Keith Parsons' battling 116 not out, which came from 114 balls.

FINAL TABLES

Division One

	P	W	L	Tie	NR	RR	Pts
Glamorgan	16	11	5	0	0	4.08	44
Lancashire	16	9	6	0	1	-3.39	38
Hampshire	16	7	6	0	3	0.81	34
Northamptonshire	16	8	8	0	0	1.85	32
Gloucestershire	16	7	7	1	1	3.34	32
Essex	16	6	6	1	3	1.00	32
Warwickshire	16	7	8	0	1	4.60	30
Kent	16	5	9	0	2	-6.46	24
Surrey	16	4	9	0	3	-7.26	22

Division Two

	P	W	L	T	NR	RR	Pts
Middlesex	18	12	6	0	0	-0.11	48
Worcestershire	18	11	5	0	2	14.17	48
Nottinghamshire	18	9	4	1	4	9.74	46
Yorkshire	18	10	6	0	2	2.76	44
Sussex	18	9	7	1	1	7.90	40
Durham	18	9	7	0	2	2.49	40
Leicestershire	18	7	8	0	3	-0.10	34
Somerset	18	6	11	0	1	-1.66	26
Derbyshire	18	5	12	0	1	-16.04	22
Scotland	18	2	14	0	2	-17.56	12

FEATURES OF TOTESPORT LEAGUE 2004

HIGHEST TOTAL

324 for 4 (45 overs)	Leicestershire v. Sussex at Hove	23 May

HIGHEST TOTAL BATTING SECOND

323 for 5 (45 overs)	Sussex v. Leicestershire at Hove	23 May

LOWEST TOTAL

82 (44.3 overs)	Derbyshire v. Durham at The Riverside	31 May

HIGHEST INDIVIDUAL SCORE

158*	RC Irani	Essex v. Glamorgan at Chelmsford	6 September

39 centuries were scored in the competition

SIX WICKETS IN AN INNINGS

6-5	AG Wharf	Glamorgan v. Kent at Cardiff	29 August
6-20	M Sami	Kent v. Gloucestershire at Canterbury	25 April
6-37	SJ Cook	Middlesex v. Leicestershire at Leicester	27 June

There were 9 instances of five wickets in an innings

TIED MATCHES

Gloucestershire tied with Essex at Chelmsford	28 June
Nottinghamshire tied with Sussex at Hove	21 July

WINNING BY ONE WICKET

Durham beat Middlesex at The Riverside	18 July
Warwickshire beat Northamptonshire at Northampton	4 August
Kent beat Glamorgan at Cardiff	29 August

WINNING BY MORE THAN 150 RUNS

163	Essex beat Glamorgan at Chelmsford	6 September

There were 14 instances of a side winning by 100 runs or more

WINNING BY ONE RUN

Kent beat Gloucestershire by 1 run at Canterbury	25 April
Lancashire beat Hampshire by 1 run at The Rose Bowl	11 July
Leicestershire beat Sussex by 1 run at Horsham	23 May
Worcestershire beat Scotland by 1 run at Worcester	24 August

NO PLAY POSSIBLE

Surrey v. Hampshire at The Oval	3 May
Worcestershire v. Nottinghamshire at Worcester	4 May
Durham v. Leicestershire at The Riverside	4 July
Hampshire v. Surrey at The Rose Bowl	9 August
Nottinghamshire v. Worcestershire at Trent Bridge	25 August

TOTESPORT LEAGUE: DIVISION ONE FEATURES 2004

BATTING: LEADING AVERAGES

	M	Inns	NO	Runs	HS	Av	100	50
MTG Elliott (Glam)	12	12	5	686	112*	98.00	2	4
MP Maynard (Glam)	15	14	5	612	117	68.00	1	5
MEK Hussey (Glos)	7	7	1	357	107*	59.50	1	2
RC Irani (Essex)	14	13	3	546	158*	54.60	2	1
M v Jaarsveld (N'hants)	7	7	2	246	96*	49.20	-	2
D Mongia (Lancs)	8	7	2	241	104*	48.20	1	1
ET Smith (Kent)	14	14	1	618	106	47.53	1	5
NV Knight (Warwicks)	14	14	2	568	122*	47.33	2	2
N Pothas (Hants)	13	13	4	395	83*	43.88	-	3
MJ Chilton (Lancs)	16	15	3	498	115	41.50	1	4
WI Jefferson (Essex)	14	13	2	415	97	37.72	-	2
A Symonds (Kent)	7	7	1	225	146	37.50	1	-
JP Crawley (Hants)	10	9	1	296	70*	37.00	-	4
AD Mascarenhas (Hants)	13	12	3	308	79	34.22	-	2
U Afzaal (Northants)	15	15	2	444	86*	34.15	-	4
GL Brophy (Northants)	13	10	3	238	50*	34.00	-	1
MGN Windows (Glos)	13	13	0	434	79	33.38	-	3
CP Schofield (Lancs)	10	7	1	197	69*	32.83	-	1
CM Spearman (Glos)	16	16	0	518	89	32.37	-	3
GB Hogg (Warwicks)	15	14	3	355	74	32.27	-	1
IJ Sutcliffe (Lancs)	14	13	1	380	102*	31.66	1	1
RDB Croft (Glam)	16	16	0	490	106	30.62	1	4
IJL Trott (Warwicks)	16	16	3	398	70	30.61	-	1
SG Law (Lancs)	9	9	0	275	83	30.55	-	3
A Flower (Essex)	16	14	1	394	70	30.30	-	3
RS Bopara (Essex)	8	7	2	149	55	29.80	-	1
GP Swann (Northants)	16	15	2	384	78	29.53	-	3
JN Batty (Surrey)	14	13	1	351	66	29.25	-	4
MA Wagh (Warwicks)	15	13	1	349	83	29.08	-	3
MJ Clarke (Hants)	11	10	0	285	68	28.50	-	3
AJ Hollioake (Surrey)	14	13	2	312	80*	28.36	-	2
IR Bell (Warwicks)	15	15	0	424	89	28.26	-	4
CG Taylor (Glos)	16	16	2	392	60	28.00	-	2
WPC Weston (Glos)	16	16	0	444	75	27.75	-	3
WK Hegg (Lancs)	9	6	1	138	37	27.60	-	-
MJ Powell (Glam)	16	16	1	411	73	27.40	-	3
MB Loye (Lancs)	11	11	0	297	70	27.00	-	2
TW Roberts (Northants)	16	16	0	431	112	26.93	1	2
Azhar Mahmood (Surrey)	10	9	2	187	67	26.71	-	2
RS Ferley (Kent)	10	9	3	156	42	26.00	-	-
CL Hooper (Lancs)	12	10	3	181	50*	25.85	-	1
DR Brown (Warwicks)	16	10	2	202	41	25.25	-	-

Qualification: average 25 or above (minimum of five innings)

LEADING RUN SCORERS – TOP 20

	Runs	Inns
MTG Elliott (Glam)	686	12
ET Smith (Kent)	618	14
MP Maynard (Glam)	612	14
NV Knight (Warwicks)	568	14
RC Irani (Essex)	546	13
CM Spearman (Glos)	518	16
MJ Chilton (Lancs)	498	15
RDB Croft (Glam)	490	16
U Afzaal (Northants)	444	15
WPC Weston (Glos)	444	16
MGN Windows (Glos)	434	13
TW Roberts (Northants)	431	16
IR Bell (Warwicks)	424	15
WI Jefferson (Essex)	415	13
MJ Powell (Glam)	411	16
IJL Trott (Warwicks)	398	16
N Pothas (Hants)	395	13
A Flower (Essex)	394	14
CG Taylor (Glos)	392	16
GP Swann (Northants)	384	15

BOWLING: LEADING AVERAGES

	O	M	Runs	W	Av	Best	4i	Econ
JM Anderson (Lancs)	39.1	6	172	12	14.33	3-26	-	4.39
GR Napier (Essex)	94.3	6	391	25	15.64	4-23	3	4.13
J Louw (Northants)	135.2	14	533	34	15.67	5-27	3	3.93
A Symonds (Kent)	45	2	181	11	16.45	3-28	-	4.02
AG Wharf (Glam)	104.5	9	462	26	17.76	6-5	2	4.40
J Lewis (Glos)	98.3	7	440	24	18.33	5-23	2	4.46
MS Kasprowicz (Glam)	57.3	7	210	11	19.09	3-27	-	3.65
CT Tremlett (Hants)	56	3	270	14	19.28	4-37	1	4.82
ID Fisher (Glos)	52	3	219	11	19.90	3-18	-	4.21
Azhar Mahmood (Surrey)	72	6	299	15	19.93	5-24	1	4.15
SI Mahmood (Lancs)	104.2	12	486	24	20.25	4-39	2	4.65
AP Davies (Glam)	86.1	4	471	23	20.47	4-29	2	5.46
MA Wagh (Warwicks)	58.4	0	252	12	21.00	4-35	1	4.29
D Gough (Essex)	62.3	3	262	12	21.83	3-19	-	4.19
GP Swann (Northants)	136.4	7	516	23	22.43	4-21	1	3.77
D Pretorius (Warwicks)	48	5	249	11	22.63	4-36	1	5.18
NM Carter (Warwicks)	103.5	5	494	21	23.52	3-37	-	4.75
GB Hogg (Warwicks)	106.2	4	456	19	24.00	5-23	1	4.28
BV Taylor (Hants)	80.5	11	348	14	24.85	3-51	-	4.30
SK Warne (Hants)	103	4	450	18	25.00	4-27	1	4.36
JMM Averis (Glos)	84.4	10	425	17	25.00	3-28	-	5.01
AD Mullally (Hants)	108.1	16	452	18	25.11	2-18	-	4.17
BJ Phillips (Northants)	124	12	534	20	26.70	3-21	-	4.30
SA Brant (Essex)	60.5	1	330	12	27.50	4-49	1	5.42
G Chapple (Lancs)	98.5	12	464	16	29.00	3-32	-	4.69
J Ormond (Surrey)	60.3	3	319	11	29.00	4-48	1	5.27
MW Alleyne (Glos)	95	3	501	17	29.47	4-39	1	5.27
SD Udal (Hants)	95	2	429	14	30.64	4-46	1	4.51
RS Ferley (Kent)	78.4	0	338	11	30.72	2-20	-	4.29
DG Cork (Lancs)	112	13	494	16	30.87	3-35	-	4.41
RDB Croft (Glam)	123	1	595	19	31.31	3-30	-	4.83
AD M'carenhas (Hants)	90.4	7	349	11	31.72	3-54	-	3.84
JF Brown (Northants)	133.5	3	562	17	33.05	4-33	1	4.19
DR Brown (Warwicks)	111	5	639	19	33.63	3-48	-	5.75
MCJ Ball (Glos)	85	2	405	12	33.75	3-59	-	4.76
IR Bell (Warwicks)	73	3	346	10	34.60	2-17	-	4.73
JC Tredwell (Kent)	92.1	4	389	11	35.36	3-35	-	4.22
AM Smith (Glos)	73	7	378	10	37.80	2-42	-	4.78

Qualification: average of 38 or less (minimum of ten wickets)

LEADING WICKET-TAKERS – TOP 20

	W	O
J Louw (Northants)	34	135.2
AG Wharf (Glam)	26	104.5
GR Napier (Essex)	25	94.3
J Lewis (Glos)	24	98.3
SI Mahmood (Lancs)	24	104.2
AP Davies (Glam)	23	86.1
GP Swann (Northants)	23	136.4
NM Carter (Warwicks)	21	103.5
BJ Phillips (Northants)	20	124
GB Hogg (Warwicks)	19	106.2
DR Brown (Warwicks)	19	111
RDB Croft (Glam)	19	123
SK Warne (Hants)	18	103
AD Mullally (Hants)	18	108.1
JMM Averis (Glos)	17	84.4
MW Alleyne (Glos)	17	95
JF Brown (Northants)	17	133.5
G Chapple (Lancs)	16	98.5
DG Cork (Lancs)	16	112
Azhar Mahmood (Surrey)	15	72

FIELDING: LEADING DISMISSALS – TOP 20

SJ Adshead (Glos) - 24 (18 ct, 6 st); JS Foster (Essex) - 22 (20 ct, 2 st); MA Wallace (Glam) - 19 (16 ct, 3 st); JN Batty (Surrey) - 17 (17 ct); T Frost (Warwicks) - 17 (11 ct, 6 st); N Pothas (Hants) - 17 (11 ct, 6 st); GL Brophy (Northants) - 15 (12 ct, 3 st); DJG Sales (Northants) - 12 (12 ct); NJ O'Brien (Kent) - 12 (9 ct, 3 st); G Chapple (Lancs) - 11 (11 ct); WK Hegg (Lancs) - 11 (11 ct); TMB Bailey (Northants) - 11 (9 ct, 2 st); JJ Haynes (Lancs) - 11 (7 ct, 4 st); DA Cosker (Glam) - 9 (9 ct); JC Tredwell (Kent) - 9 (9 ct); DL Hemp (Glam) - 8 (8 ct); CM Spearman (Glos) - 8 (8 ct); AG Wharf (Glam) - 8 (8 ct); KJ Piper (Warwicks) - 8 (5 ct, 3 st); DA Kenway (Hants) - 7 (7 ct)

TOTESPORT LEAGUE: DIVISION TWO FEATURES 2004

BATTING: LEADING AVERAGES

	M	Inns	NO	Runs	HS	Av	100	50
PN Weekes (Middx)	18	18	4	807	119*	57.64	1	7
PA Jaques (Yorks)	9	8	1	366	105	52.28	1	3
PD Collingwood (Durham)	7	7	2	257	102*	51.40	1	1
A Singh (Notts)	6	6	1	237	67	47.40	–	1
VS Solanki (Worcs)	14	14	0	653	122	46.64	2	4
EC Joyce (Middx)	14	12	3	400	74*	44.44	–	3
OA Shah (Middx)	18	16	3	562	125*	43.23	2	3
A McGrath (Yorks)	12	11	3	327	96*	40.87	–	2
KP Pietersen (Notts)	16	15	2	531	82*	40.84	–	4
MJ Prior (Sussex)	18	18	2	641	119	40.06	1	4
JN Snape (Leics)	18	14	4	391	69	39.10	–	3
IJ Ward (Sussex)	15	15	1	538	136	38.42	1	3
DJ Hussey (Notts)	16	16	4	444	87*	37.00	–	2
J Moss (Derbys)	15	14	2	439	104	36.58	1	3
GA Hick (Worcs)	16	16	1	544	120	36.26	2	3
JER Gallian (Notts)	16	16	0	580	109	36.25	1	5
RJ Warren (Notts)	11	11	0	398	81	36.18	–	2
MH Yardy (Sussex)	12	12	2	361	88*	36.10	–	2
GJ Pratt (Durham)	18	15	4	396	67*	36.00	–	4
KA Parsons (Somerset)	17	17	2	530	115*	35.33	1	5
MW Goodwin (Sussex)	18	18	1	600	91	35.29	–	5
CM Gazzard (Somerset)	9	9	1	282	157	35.25	1	–
BJ Hodge (Leics)	17	15	2	454	154*	34.92	1	–
CJ Adams (Sussex)	18	18	2	557	93	34.81	–	4
C White (Yorks)	9	9	1	278	59	34.75	–	1
MJ North (Durham)	16	16	1	511	121*	34.06	2	2
MA Ealham (Notts)	15	13	5	269	56	33.62	–	1
SC Moore (Worcs)	13	13	2	367	93*	33.36	–	3
DS Lehmann (Yorks)	8	8	2	194	88*	32.33	–	2
JC Hildreth (Somerset)	14	14	2	384	85	32.00	–	2
S Sriram (Scotland)	12	10	2	256	88*	32.00	–	1
Yasir Arafat (Scotland)	15	11	4	218	55*	31.14	–	1
J Cox (Somerset)	12	12	0	356	71	29.66	–	4
JD Francis (Somerset)	13	12	0	342	79	28.50	–	2
DDJ Robinson (Leics)	13	11	2	246	109*	27.33	1	–
DL Maddy (Leics)	18	15	0	408	95	27.20	–	3
MJ Wood (Somerset)	10	10	2	213	56	26.62	–	1
AW Gale (Yorks)	9	9	1	213	70*	26.62	–	1
M Burns (Somerset)	15	15	0	398	97	26.53	–	3
Hassan Adnan (Derbys)	18	17	2	395	57	26.33	–	5
MJ Wood (Worcs)	18	18	3	386	56	25.73	–	2
CJO Smith (Scotland)	11	11	1	253	79*	25.30	–	1
JJB Lewis (Durham)	17	15	2	327	48	25.15	–	–

Qualification: average 25 or above (minimum of five innings)

LEADING RUN SCORERS – TOP 20

	Runs	Inns
PN Weekes (Middx)	807	18
VS Solanki (Worcs)	653	14
MJ Prior (Sussex)	641	18
MW Goodwin (Sussex)	600	18
JER Gallian (Notts)	580	16
OA Shah (Middx)	562	16
CJ Adams (Sussex)	557	18
GA Hick (Worcs)	544	16
IJ Ward (Sussex)	538	15
KP Pietersen (Notts)	531	15
KA Parsons (Somerset)	530	17
MJ North (Durham)	511	16
BJ Hodge (Leics)	454	15
DJ Hussey (Notts)	444	16
J Moss (Derbys)	439	14
DL Maddy (Leics)	408	15
EC Joyce (Middx)	400	12
RJ Warren (Notts)	398	11
M Burns (Somerset)	398	15
GJ Pratt (Durham)	396	15

BOWLING: LEADING AVERAGES

	O	M	Runs	W	Av	Best	4i	Econ
SJ Cook (Middx)	133.4	6	599	39	15.35	6-37	3	4.48
Shoaib Akhtar (Durham)	47.3	8	215	13	16.53	4-15	1	4.52
GJ Smith (Notts)	79.1	6	317	19	16.68	4-28	1	4.00
CW Henderson (Leics)	109.1	8	473	28	16.89	5-24	3	4.33
MA Ealham (Notts)	112.5	12	378	22	17.18	3-22	–	3.35
Kabir Ali (Worcs)	40.3	6	190	11	17.27	3-28	–	4.69
AJ Hall (Worcs)	88	7	376	21	17.90	4-26	1	4.27
IJ Harvey (Yorks)	61.3	5	289	16	18.06	3-38	–	4.69
N Killeen (Durham)	128.2	30	458	24	19.08	4-24	1	3.56
MM Betts (Middx)	43	5	211	11	19.18	3-23	–	4.90
OD Gibson (Leics)	94	12	425	22	19.31	3-36	–	4.52
SCG MacGill (Notts)	99.2	7	493	25	19.72	4-18	2	4.96
RSC M-Jenkins (Sussex)	135.4	20	553	28	19.75	4-39	1	4.07
RKJ Dawson (Yorks)	100.5	5	436	22	19.81	4-20	1	4.32
S Sriram (Scotland)	58	4	238	12	19.83	3-17	–	4.10
CM Wright (Scotland)	78	8	340	17	20.00	5-44	1	4.35
MN Malik (Worcs)	77.5	10	363	18	20.16	4-42	1	4.66
DS Lehmann (Yorks)	45	1	213	10	21.30	3-34	–	4.73
CEW Silverwood (Yorks)	43.3	4	219	10	21.90	2-14	–	5.03
DL Maddy (Leics)	57.5	4	293	13	22.53	2-25	–	5.06
PJ Franks (Notts)	42.1	2	229	10	22.90	3-37	–	5.43
AG Botha (Derbys)	67	3	285	12	23.75	3-24	–	4.25
KA Parsons (Somerset)	76.5	2	386	16	24.12	5-39	1	5.02
Mohammad Ali (Derbys)	86.1	6	416	17	24.47	3-22	–	4.82
AJ Bichel (Worcs)	83.3	6	369	15	24.60	4-60	1	4.41
M Hayward (Middx)	62.1	3	308	12	25.66	4-21	1	4.95
NAM McLean (Somerset)	75	5	418	16	26.12	4-35	1	5.57
Yasir Arafat (Scotland)	119.4	10	577	22	26.22	4-22	1	4.82
CB Keegan (Middx)	69	5	346	13	26.61	3-28	–	5.01
AR Caddick (Somerset)	73	5	364	13	28.00	3-32	–	4.98
G Onions (Durham)	64.2	3	300	10	30.00	2-24	–	4.66
MA Sheikh (Derbys)	72	4	372	12	31.00	3-25	–	5.16
G Welch (Derbys)	142	18	562	18	31.22	4-26	1	3.95
DA Leatherdale (Worcs)	74.3	5	406	13	31.23	3-28	–	5.44
GM Andrew (Somerset)	49.1	2	314	10	31.40	4-48	1	6.38
Asim Butt (Scotland)	76.2	7	349	11	31.72	3-47	–	4.57
AW Laraman (Somerset)	59	3	321	10	32.10	2-39	–	5.44
MS Mason (Worcs)	76	4	354	11	32.18	3-32	–	4.65
M Akram (Sussex)	69	5	324	10	32.40	2-35	–	4.69
MF Cleary (Leics)	88	2	456	14	32.57	3-17	–	5.18
MJG Davis (Sussex)	101.4	3	494	15	32.93	4-40	1	4.85

Qualification: average of 34 or less (minimum of ten wickets)

LEADING WICKET-TAKERS – TOP 20

	W	O
SJ Cook (Middx)	39	133.4
CW Henderson (Leics)	28	109.1
RSC Martin-Jenkins (Sussex)	28	135.4
SCG MacGill (Notts)	25	99.2
N Killeen (Durham)	24	128.2
OD Gibson (Leics)	22	94
RKJ Dawson (Yorks)	22	100.5
MA Ealham (Notts)	22	112.5
Yasir Arafat (Scotland)	22	119.4
AJ Hall (Worcs)	21	88
GJ Smith (Notts)	19	79.1
MN Malik (Worcs)	18	77.5
G Welch (Derbys)	18	142
CM Wright (Scotland)	17	78
Mohammad Ali (Derbys)	17	86.1
TT Bresnan (Yorks)	17	118
IJ Harvey (Yorks)	16	61.3
NAM McLean (Somerset)	16	75
KA Parsons (Somerset)	16	76.5
SRG Francis (Somerset)	16	100.1

FIELDING: LEADING DISMISSALS – TOP 20

BJM Scott (Middx) – 32 (24 ct, 8 st); PA Nixon (Leics) – 31 (24 ct, 7 st); LD Sutton (Derbys) – 20 (19 ct, 1 st); SJ Rhodes (Worcs) – 20 (16 ct, 4 st); A Pratt (Durham) – 19 (17 ct, 2 st); CMW Read (Notts) – 18 (10 ct, 8 st); CJO Smith (Scotland) – 15 (13 ct, 2 st); M Burns (Somerset) – 13 (12 ct, 1 st); MJ Prior (Sussex) – 13 (11 ct, 2 st); PN Weekes (Middx) – 12 (12 ct); JER Gallian (Notts) – 11 (11 ct); KA Parsons (Somerset) – 11 (11 ct); DI Stevens (Leics) – 11 (11 ct); DR Lockhart (Scotland) – 11 (7 ct, 4 st); GJ Pratt (Durham) – 10 (10 ct); RJ Turner (Somerset) – 10 (9 ct, 1 st); TR Ambrose (Sussex) – 10 (8 ct, 2 st); I Dawood (Yorks) – 10 (7 ct, 3 st); MH Yardy (Sussex) – 8 (8 ct); SM Guy (Yorks) – 8 (5 ct, 3 st)

TOTESPORT LEAGUE COUNTY COLOURS: DIVISION ONE

ESSEX CCC
League nickname:
ESSEX EAGLES

GLAMORGAN CCC
League nickname:
GLAMORGAN DRAGONS

GLOUCESTERSHIRE CCC
League nickname:
GLOUCESTERSHIRE GLADIATORS

HAMPSHIRE CCC
League nickname:
HAMPSHIRE HAWKS

LANCASHIRE CCC
League nickname:
LANCASHIRE LIGHTNING

KENT CCC
League nickname:
KENT SPITFIRES

NORTHAMPTONSHIRE CCC
League nickname:
STEELBACKS

SURREY CCC
League nickname:
SURREY LIONS

WARWICKSHIRE CCC
League nickname:
THE BEARS

For full county details, please refer to the form charts at the back of the book.

TOTESPORT LEAGUE COUNTY COLOURS: DIVISION TWO

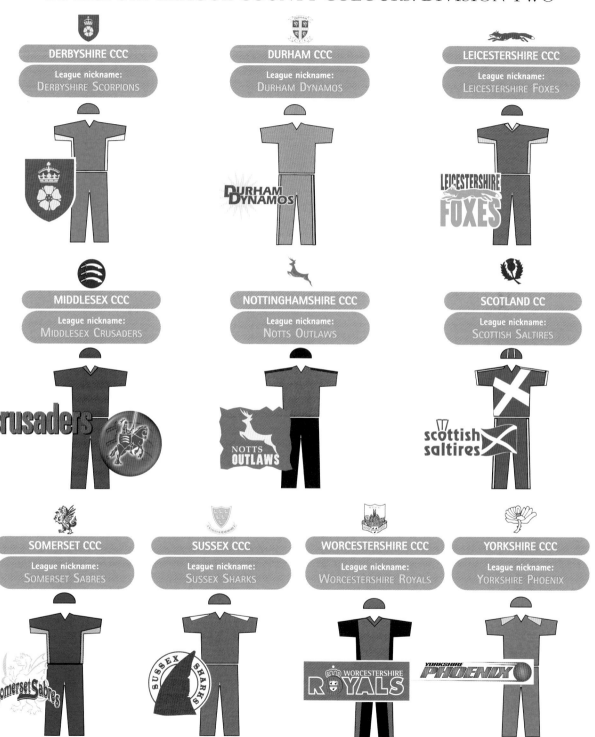

DERBYSHIRE CCC
League nickname:
DERBYSHIRE SCORPIONS

DURHAM CCC
League nickname:
DURHAM DYNAMOS

LEICESTERSHIRE CCC
League nickname:
LEICESTERSHIRE FOXES

MIDDLESEX CCC
League nickname:
MIDDLESEX CRUSADERS

NOTTINGHAMSHIRE CCC
League nickname:
NOTTS OUTLAWS

SCOTLAND CC
League nickname:
SCOTTISH SALTIRES

SOMERSET CCC
League nickname:
SOMERSET SABRES

SUSSEX CCC
League nickname:
SUSSEX SHARKS

WORCESTERSHIRE CCC
League nickname:
WORCESTERSHIRE ROYALS

YORKSHIRE CCC
League nickname:
YORKSHIRE PHOENIX

For full county details, please refer to the form charts at the back of the book.

TWENTY20 CUP
By Mark Baldwin

And still the people came. In its second year, and despite the dampening effect of generally poor weather, the Twenty20 Cup underlined its new status as the biggest seller in English domestic cricket.

Around 250,000 spectators had revelled in the 2003 launch, and the long hot days and evenings of that golden summer. This time, with rain around and temperatures down, would the enthusiasm remain?

The answer was, emphatically, yes. No match in the competition better summed up its popularity than the London derby between Middlesex and Surrey at Lord's on 15 July. It was the first time that Lord's had opened the Grace Gates to this new phenomenon, and how the people came … all 26,500 of them.

Overall, the Twenty20 Cup was watched by 286,000 fans, an increase of 12 per cent on 2003. And, although the introduction of a quarter-final stage technically resulted in four more games, three complete washouts due to the bad weather meant that, in effect, just one more match had been played compared to the inaugural year.

The question now for the authorities is what to do next. Finals Day at Edgbaston was just as well supported as it had been at Trent Bridge first time around, while capacity crowds also greeted the arrival of the additional quarter-final stage. It just happened that these four games were played at The Oval, the Rose Bowl, Sophia Gardens in Cardiff and Leicester's Grace Road. Any of the 18 counties would have seen similar interest.

There is a school of thought, however, which believes that the Finals Day is too long, with ten-and-a-half hours being required to accommodate the three matches and all the attendant razzmatazz of pop acts and mascot racing. Certainly, by the time Leicestershire triumphed over holders Surrey under the Edgbaston lights, many of the children brought along for the short-form game's longest day had either been taken home or were far too weary to appreciate fully the dramatic action on show before them.

It would be tempting to split up the semi-finals and final, into two or three separate occasions. Perhaps, on Finals Day itself, the two beaten semi-finalists could play for third-place prize-money (and a Bronze Medal?) as a precursor to the Gold Medal event. And does the Finals Day need a pop music interlude? Neither Atomic Kitten in 2003 nor Liberty X and Natasha Bedingfield in 2004 added much to the occasion, apart from the chance for some laddish leering.

The mascots' race, however, was a splendid addition to the entertainment this time, especially with former England coach David Lloyd attempting to run the course himself with the likes of Roary the Lion and Lanky the Giraffe while commentating for Sky Sports. Breathless is certainly the word for Twenty20 fun and games.

For 2005, though, please can we have a longer and tougher course for the 18 county mascots to negotiate (ie, more Becher's Brook pile-up moments!), and can we also draft in Stuart Hall to provide the live commentary for spectators, with the equally irrepressible Lloyd helping out with his roving role? It would be a knockout.

Anyway, back to the serious stuff, because that, in truth, is what the Twenty20 Cup became in 2004. Commercially, it needs extremely serious thought – as a precious commodity it must be nurtured carefully and not flogged to death. Playing-wise, it is also becoming more serious because teams are beginning to work out little strategies and tactics in order to deal more efficiently and effectively with the 120-ball innings that lies before them.

What is certain, too, is that counties need to have more than three (or two in alternate years) home matches in the group stage. As I have argued in the introduction to the domestic section of this book, the culling of the out-of-date totesport League – coupled with the expansion of the Cheltenham & Gloucester Trophy – would easily create enough new space in the calendar for an increase to eight, or ten, group matches.

Ten group games would be provided if you kept the existing three-group format but gave each county five home and away games. My own preference, however, would be for two groups of nine teams, giving each county four home and four away matches. Don't overdo it – the novelty factor remains a big part of Twenty20's attraction, along with the excitement of the cricket itself.

The top four in each group would then qualify for the quarter-finals, with the top two being guaranteed the added financial benefit of an extra home tie. Semi-finals would be staged at one venue (like Edgbaston or Trent Bridge), and Finals Day should be played out at Lord's during afternoon hours. The larger capacity of Lord's would also enable ticket prices to be kept far more family-friendly than is the case for other major events.

Darren Maddy, meanwhile, was the unlikely star of the 2004 Cup, perhaps in keeping with both unfancied Leicestershire's victory and the manner in which the competition thrives on its unpredictability.

Maddy hit 72 from 48 balls as Glamorgan were blown away in the second semi-final, and he then helped Brad Hodge to add a crucial 62 runs for the first wicket as Leicestershire set out to overhaul Surrey's 168 for 6 in the final.

However, while Maddy confirmed his status as the 2004 competition's leading run scorer, with 356, it was Hodge and Jeremy Snape who were mainly responsible for upstaging Adam Hollioake in the former Surrey captain's last Twenty20 appearance.

The man who lifted the inaugural trophy did take two wickets to give his side late hope, but Hodge strode on to 77 not out from 53 balls, with ten fours and a six, while Snape marched in at 122 for 3 to swipe an unbeaten 34 off just 16 balls, with two sixes and three fours.

Earlier in the day, it was Hollioake who seemed fated to go through his Twenty20 career unbeaten. The leading wicket-taker had been inspirational with the ball again as Surrey won a thrilling contest against Lancashire by one run by successfully defending an inadequate total of 133.

Andrew Flintoff and James Anderson, given permission by the England management to take part in proceedings, were left to go off and sign hundreds of autographs instead of experiencing a final that had been widely expected to be Lancashire v. Glamorgan. As they say, that's showbusiness!

2 July 2004

North Division

at Trent Bridge
Durham 120 (19.4 overs) (P Mustard 64)
Nottinghamshire 122 for 7 (19.1 overs) (KP Pietersen 67)
Nottinghamshire (2pts) won by 3 wickets

at Old Trafford
Leicestershire 139 for 9 (19 overs) (DL Maddy 51)
Lancashire 131 for 6 (19 overs)
Leicestershire (2pts) won by 8 runs

at Derby
Derbyshire 133 for 8 (20 overs)
Yorkshire 108 for 9 (15 overs)
Yorkshire (2pts) won by 1 wicket – DL Method: target 108 from 15 overs

7 July 2004

at Leicester
Durham 138 for 4 (20 overs)

Leicestershire 97 for 9 (20 overs)
(N Killeen 4 for 7, GR Breese 4 for 14)
Durham (2pts) won by 41 runs

at Trent Bridge
Yorkshire 207 for 7 (20 overs) (MJ Wood 96*)
Nottinghamshire 210 for 7 (19.5 overs)
(MA Ealham 91)
Nottinghamshire (2pts) won by 3 wickets

8 July 2004

at Headingley
Leicestershire 221 for 3 (20 overs) (DL Maddy 111, BJ Hodge 78)
Yorkshire 211 for 6 (20 overs) (PA Jaques 92)
Leicestershire (2pts) won by 10 runs

at Derby
Derbyshire 142 for 4 (20 overs)
Lancashire 144 for 5 (17.1 overs) (D Mongia 50)
Lancashire (2pts) won by 5 wickets

9 July 2004

at Trent Bridge
Derbyshire 163 for 7 (20 overs) (J Moss 68)
Nottinghamshire 154 for 8 (20 overs)
Derbyshire (2pts) won by 9 runs

at The Riverside
Durham 111 for 8 (20 overs)
Lancashire 112 for 5 (18.2 overs)
Lancashire (2pts) won by 5 wickets

13 July 2004

at Leicester
Leicestershire 150 for 7 (20 overs)
Nottinghamshire 110 (19.2 overs) (CE Dagnall 4 for 22)
Leicestershire (2pts) won by 40 runs

at The Riverside
Durham 117 for 9 (20 overs)
Derbyshire 118 for 6 (18.3 overs)
Derbyshire (2pts) won by 4 wickets

14 July 2004

at Headingley
Lancashire 168 (19.1 overs) (A Flintoff 85)
Yorkshire 170 for 2 (17.5 overs) (IJ Harvey 108*)
Yorkshire (2pts) won by 8 wickets

Leicestershire's Darren Maddy was the star turn of the tournament. He scored 356 runs in the competition, including match-winning knocks in both the quarter- and semi-finals. He scored 22 in the final before being bowled by Surrey's Phil Sampson.

15 July 2004

at Derby
Derbyshire v. Leicestershire
Match abandoned – 1pt each

at Old Trafford
Nottinghamshire 79 for 5 (8 overs)
Lancashire 82 for 3 (6.5 overs)
Lancashire (2pts) won by 7 wickets

at The Riverside
Yorkshire 126 for 7 (20 overs)
Durham 129 for 3 (18.2 overs)
Durham (2pts) won by 7 wickets

Midlands/West/Wales Division

2 July 2004

at Edgbaston
Somerset 120 (19.5 overs) (GB Hogg 4 for 9)
Warwickshire 101 for 3 (9.3 overs)
Warwickshire (2pts) won by 7 wickets – DL Method: target 101 from 16 overs

at Northampton
Northamptonshire 162 for 5 (20 overs)
(M van Jaarsveld 61*)
Glamorgan 166 for 5 (19.1 overs)
Glamorgan (2pts) won by 5 wickets

at Worcester
Worcestershire 184 for 9 (20 overs) (GA Hick 73, AJ Bichel 58*)
Gloucestershire 183 for 5 (20 overs) (SJ Adshead 81)
Worcestershire (2pts) won by 1 run

5 July 2004

at Taunton
Somerset 193 for 8 (20 overs) (JC Hildreth 66)
Glamorgan 194 for 2 (19.3 overs) (IJ Thomas 116*)
Glamorgan (2pts) won by 8 wickets

at Luton
Worcestershire 173 for 5 (20 overs) (GA Hick 116*)
Northamptonshire 80 for 8 (11 overs)
*Worcestershire (2pts) won by 21 runs – DL Method:
target 102 from 11 overs*

8 July 2004

at Cardiff
Warwickshire 152 for 9 (20 overs)
Glamorgan 126 (19 overs) (MP Maynard 53,
GB Hogg 4 for 30)
Warwickshire (2pts) won by 26 runs

at Northampton
Northamptonshire 42 for 5 (5 overs)
Gloucestershire 44 for 2 (4.1 overs)
Gloucestershire (2pts) won by 8 wickets

9 July 2004

at Bristol
Somerset 151 (19.1 overs) (MJ Wood 50,
ID Fisher 4 for 22)
Gloucestershire
Match abandoned – 1pt each

at Edgbaston
Warwickshire 146 (19.5 overs)
Worcestershire 150 for 7 (19.3 overs) (VS Solanki 50)
Worcestershire (2pts) won by 3 wickets

12 July 2004

at Edgbaston
Warwickshire 123 for 7 (20 overs)
Northamptonshire 125 for 6 (19 overs)
Northamptonshire (2pts) won by 4 wickets

13 July 2004

at Taunton
Somerset 178 for 6 (20 overs) (JC Hildreth 51)
Worcestershire 144 for 4 (20 overs)
(DA Leatherdale 52*, AW Laraman 4 for 15)
Somerset (2pts) won by 34 runs

14 July 2004

at Cardiff
Glamorgan 162 for 7 (20 overs)
Gloucestershire 130 (19.1 overs) (THC Hancock 56)
Glamorgan (2pts) won by 32 runs

15 July 2004

at Bristol
Gloucestershire 135 for 7 (20 overs)
Warwickshire 135 for 5 (20 overs) (NV Knight 63)
Warwickshire (2pts) won by losing fewer wickets

at Taunton
Somerset 211 for 5 (20 overs) (ME Trescothick 56)
Northamptonshire 207 for 5 (20 overs)
(M van Jaarsveld 61, DJG Sales 60*)
Somerset (2pts) won by 4 runs

at Worcester
Glamorgan 140 for 6 (16 overs)
Worcestershire 120 (14.1 overs)
Glamorgan (2pts) won by 20 runs

South Division

2 July 2004

at Maidstone
Middlesex 155 for 7 (18 overs)
Kent 157 for 3 (13.1 overs) (A Symonds 112)
Kent (2pts) won by 7 wickets

at Chelmsford
Essex 135 for 9 (18 overs)
Hampshire 95 (15 overs)
Essex (2pts) won by 40 runs

at Hove
Surrey 221 for 8 (20 overs)
Sussex 121 (17.2 overs) (AJ Hollioake 4 for 14)
Surrey (2pts) won by 100 runs

3 July 2004

at The Oval
Surrey 198 for 5 (20 overs)
(MR Ramprakash 76*,
MA Butcher 53)
Hampshire 167 for 9 (20 overs)
(AJ Hollioake 5 for 34)
Surrey (2pts) won by 31 runs

5 July 2004

at Maidstone
Kent 125 (19.2 overs) (SA Brant 4 for 20)
Essex 128 for 2 (15.3 overs) (RC Irani 64*)
Essex (2pts) won by 8 wickets

7 July 2004

at Richmond
Middlesex v. Sussex
Match abandoned – 1pt each

at Chelmsford
Essex v. Surrey
Match abandoned – 1pt each

9 July 2004

at The Oval
Surrey 185 for 7 (20 overs) (MA Butcher 60)
Kent 182 for 9 (20 overs) (RWT Key 66*)
Surrey (2pts) won by 3 runs

at Hove
Sussex 67 (14.5 overs) (AD Mascarenhas 5 for 14)
Hampshire 69 for 7 (19 overs)
Hampshire (2pts) won by 3 wickets

12 July 2004

at Southgate
Essex 120 for 8 (20 overs)
Middlesex 121 for 1 (18.2 overs) (PN Weekes 55*)
Middlesex (2pts) won by 9 wickets

13 July 2004

at Canterbury
Kent 163 for 6 (20 overs)
Sussex 116 (19.5 overs)
Kent (2pts) won by 47 runs

at The Rose Bowl
Hampshire 170 for 7 (20 overs)
(AD Mascarenhas 52)
Middlesex 140 for 8 (20 overs)
Hampshire (2pts) won by 30 runs

15 July 2004

at The Rose Bowl
Hampshire 177 for 3 (20 overs) (SR Watson 97*)

Kent 113 for 9 (20 overs)
Hampshire (2pts) won by 64 runs

at Lord's
Surrey 183 for 5 (20 overs) (AJ Hollioake 65*)
Middlesex 146 for 7 (20 overs) (L Klusener 53)
Surrey (2pts) won by 37 runs

at Chelmsford
Essex 134 for 8 (20 overs)
Sussex 136 for 1 (17 overs) (MJ Prior 68*)
Sussex (2pts) won by 9 wickets

FINAL GROUP TABLES

NORTH

	P	W	L	T	NR	Pts	RR
Leicestershire	5	3	1	0	1	7	0.22
Lancashire	5	3	2	0	0	6	0.28
Derbyshire	5	2	2	0	1	5	-0.04
Durham	5	2	3	0	0	4	0.26
Yorkshire	5	2	3	0	0	4	-0.11
Nottinghamshire	5	2	3	0	0	4	-0.56

MIDLANDS/WEST/WALES

	P	W	L	T	NR	Pts	RR
Glamorgan	5	4	1	0	0	8	0.44
Worcestershire	5	3	2	0	0	6	-0.28
Warwickshire	5	3	2	0	0	6	0.61
Somerset	5	2	2	0	1	5	-0.39
Gloucestershire	5	1	2	1	1	3	-0.38
Northamptonshire	5	1	4	0	0	2	-0.46

SOUTH

	P	W	L	T	NR	Pts	RR
Surrey	5	4	0	0	1	9	2.14
Hampshire	5	3	2	0	0	6	0.33
Essex	5	2	2	0	1	5	0.53
Kent	5	2	3	0	0	4	-0.21
Middlesex	5	1	3	0	1	3	-1.24
Sussex	5	1	3	0	1	3	-1.72

Quarter-finals

19 July 2004

at Sophia Gardens
Warwickshire 158 for 7 (20 overs) (GB Hogg 54)
Glamorgan 161 for 5 (19 overs) (DL Hemp 74)
Glamorgan won by 5 wickets

at The Rose Bowl
Hampshire 120 for 9 (20 overs)
Lancashire 121 for 1 (16.3 overs) (M Loye 64*)
Lancashire won by 9 wickets

at Grace Road
Leicestershire 180 for 6 (20 overs) (DL Maddy 84)
Essex 166 for 7 (20 overs) (A Flower 58,
AP Grayson 55)
Leicestershire won by 14 runs

at The Oval
Surrey 145 for 7 (20 overs)
Worcestershire 131 for 8 (20 overs)
Surrey won by 14 runs

It wasn't to be for Adam Hollioake, who had hoped to end his
Twenty20 career unbeaten.

SEMI-FINAL - LANCASHIRE v. SURREY
7 August 2004 at Edgbaston

SURREY

AD Brown	b Flintoff	32
JGE Benning	b Anderson	16
SA Newman	c Mongia b Flintoff	12
MR Ramprakash	b Keedy	24
R Clarke	lbw b Keedy	18
AJ Hollioake	c Hegg b Mongia	1
Azhar Mahmood	c Chilton b Keedy	13
*JN Batty (capt)	c Chapple b Mongia	3
J Ormond	not out	5
PJ Sampson	run out	0
ND Doshi	b Anderson	1
Extras	lb 5, w 3	8
	(20 overs)	**133**

	O	M	R	W
Anderson	4	0	28	2
Chapple	2	0	28	0
Flintoff	3	0	15	2
Hooper	4	0	26	0
Keedy	4	0	25	3
Mongia	3	0	6	2

Fall of Wickets: 1-24, 2-61, 3-66, 4-109, 5-111, 6-111, 7-121, 8-127, 9-128

LANCASHIRE

A Flintoff	c Brown b Azhar Mahmood	15
SP Crook	c sub b Clarke	12
MJ Chilton	c & b Azhar Mahmood	11
D Mongia	c Batty b Sampson	15
CL Hooper	b Doshi	26
G Chapple	lbw b Doshi	11
CP Schofield	run out	8
DG Cork	c Clarke b Hollioake	25
*WK Hegg (capt)	not out	3
G Keedy		
JM Anderson		
Extras	lb 6	6
	(20 overs) (8 wkts)	**132**

	O	M	R	W
Azhar Mahmood	4	0	22	2
Clarke	4	0	31	1
Ormond	3	0	12	0
Sampson	1	0	5	1
Doshi	4	0	27	2
Hollioake	4	0	29	1

Fall of Wickets: 1-22, 2-37, 3-47, 4-63, 5-94, 6-95, 7-124, 8-132

Umpires: IJ Gould & JH Hampshire
Toss: Surrey
Man of the Match: Azhar Mahmood

Surrey won by 1 run

SEMI-FINAL – LEICESTERSHIRE v. GLAMORGAN
7 August 2004 at Edgbaston

LEICESTERSHIRE

BJ Hodge (capt)	c Hemp b Croft	22
DL Maddy	c Hemp b Dale	72
DI Stevens	c Dale b Croft	27
JN Snape	b Wharf	5
*PA Nixon	not out	14
OD Gibson	c Elliott b Kasprowicz	17
JL Sadler	not out	1
JM Dakin		
CW Henderson		
MF Cleary		
CE Dagnall		
Extras	lb 4, w 1, nb 2	7
	(20 overs) (5 wkts)	**165**

	O	M	R	W
Kasprowicz	3	0	16	1
Thomas SD	3	0	35	0
Wharf	4	0	29	1
Dale	3	0	30	1
Croft	4	0	27	2
Thomas IJ	3	0	24	0

Fall of Wickets: 1-82, 2-106, 3-129, 4-135, 5-161

GLAMORGAN

MP Maynard	c Sadler b Cleary	9
IJ Thomas	b Cleary	3
MTG Elliott	run out	15
DL Hemp	c Hodge b Henderson	44
*MA Wallace	c Snape b Maddy	22
RDB Croft (capt)	b Henderson	6
MJ Powell	c Sadler b Henderson	5
SD Thomas	not out	20
A Dale	run out	2
AG Wharf	c Hodge b Cleary	2
MS Kasprowicz	c sub b Gibson	2
Extras	lb 9, w 3, nb 2	14
	(18.5 overs)	**144**

	O	M	R	W
Cleary	3	0	20	3
Gibson	2.5	0	14	1
Dagnall	4	0	27	0
Dakin	1	0	7	0
Snape	2	0	19	0
Maddy	3	0	22	1
Henderson	4	0	26	3

Fall of Wickets: 1-13, 2-18, 3-30, 4-79, 5-108, 6-111, 7-120, 8-131, 9-133

Umpires: JH Hampshire & NJ Llong
Toss: Leicestershire
Man of the Match: DL Maddy

Leicestershire won by 21 runs

FINAL – LEICESTERSHIRE v. SURREY
7 August 2004 at Edgbaston

SURREY

AD Brown	c Sadler b Henderson	64
JGE Benning	c Henderson b Gibson	5
SA Newman	c Cleary b Dagnall	21
MR Ramprakash	not out	23
R Clarke	c Cleary b Henderson	13
AJ Hollioake	c Hodge b Cleary	4
Azhar Mahmood	b Cleary	13
*JN Batty (capt)	not out	1
J Ormond		
PJ Sampson		
ND Doshi		
Extras	b 6, lb 6, w 10, nb 2	24
	(20 overs) (6 wkts)	**168**

	O	M	R	W
Cleary	4	0	38	2
Gibson	3	0	21	1
Dagnall	4	0	36	1
Maddy	2	0	16	0
Snape	4	0	30	0
Henderson	3	0	15	2

Fall of Wickets: 1-11, 2-91, 3-109, 4-135, 5-141, 6-160

LEICESTERSHIRE

BJ Hodge (capt)	not out	77
DL Maddy	b Sampson	22
DI Stevens	c Azhar Mahmood b Hollioake	20
JL Sadler	c Clarke b Hollioake	6
JN Snape	not out	34
*PA Nixon		
OD Gibson		
DG Brandy		
CW Henderson		
MF Cleary		
CE Dagnall		
Extras	lb 3, w 7	10
	(19.1 overs) (3 wkts)	**169**

	O	M	R	W
Azhar Mahmood	3.1	0	33	0
Clarke	2	0	27	0
Sampson	2	0	14	1
Ormond	4	0	30	0
Doshi	4	0	26	0
Hollioake	4	0	36	2

Fall of Wickets: 1-62, 2-114, 3-122

Umpires: IJ Gould & NJ Llong
Toss: Surrey
Man of the Match: BJ Hodge

Leicestershire won by 7 wickets

Above: A jubilant Jeremy Snape and Brad Hodge leave the field following their surprise victory over Surrey in the final.

Left: Leicestershire may not have been anybody's favourites for the title, but they emerged as the 20-over kings of 2004.

CHELTENHAM & GLOUCESTER TROPHY

By Mark Baldwin

First Round: 28 August 2003

at Luton
Cheshire 241 for 8 (50 overs) (NA Din 75, SA Twigg 68,
AR Roberts 4 for 38)
Bedfordshire 202 (47.3 overs)
Cheshire won by 39 runs

at Exmouth
Devon 333 for 6 (50 overs) (DF Lye 121, MP Hunt 74,
RI Dawson 55, P Joubert 4 for 82)
Suffolk 245 for 9 (50 overs)
Devon won by 88 runs

at Manor Park
Lincolnshire 228 for 9 (50 overs) (MC Dobson 52,
MA Higgs 50)
Norfolk 176 (44 overs) (MP Dowman 4 for 30)
Lincolnshire won by 52 runs

at Amstelveen
Holland 237 for 5 (50 overs)
Cornwall 225 (49.3 overs) (SC Pope 74)
Holland won by 12 runs

at Abergavenny
Denmark 189 for 8 (50 overs) (B Singh 58)
Wales 190 for 3 (48.2 overs) (AJ Jones 93,
AW Evans 60)
Wales won by 7 wickets

at Bishop's Stortford
Ireland 387 for 4 (50 overs) (AC Botha 139,
G Dros 124, JAM Molins 84)
Hertfordshire 312 (43.2 overs) (GP Butcher 126,
SG Cordingley 58, AC Botha 4 for 37)
Ireland won by 75 runs

at Dean Park
Buckinghamshire 272 for 6 (48 overs) (RP Lane 95,
HJH Marshall 66*, DJ Barr 51)
Dorset Did not bat
Match abandoned. Dorset won bowl-out 4–1

31 August 2003

at Banbury
Herefordshire 267 for 9 (50 overs) (MJ Rawnsley 61,
I Dawood 53)

Oxfordshire 141 (31.4 overs) (AP Cook 66,
FA Rose 5 for 19)
Herefordshire won by 126 runs

at Edinburgh
Cumberland 237 for 9 (50 overs)
(GD Lloyd 123)
Scotland 239 for 6 (46.4 overs)
(JG Williamson 77, CJO Smith 56)
Scotland won by 4 wickets

Second Round: 5–6 May 2004

at Amstelveen
Gloucestershire 264 for 6 (50 overs) (WPC Weston 106,
MGN Windows 62)
Holland 192 (47.2 overs) (MW Alleyne 4 for 33)
Gloucestershire won by 72 runs

at Alderley Edge
Hampshire 273 for 8 (50 overs) (WS Kendall 53,
AD Mascarenhas 53, JP Whittaker 4 for 45)
Cheshire 184 (47.5 overs)
Hampshire won by 89 runs

at Derby
Somerset 290 for 6 (50 overs) (J Cox 131, M Burns 59,
AW Laraman 50*)
Derbyshire 276 (48.5 overs) (CJL Rogers 93,
Hassan Adnan 78, SRG Francis 8 for 66)
Somerset won by 14 runs

at The Grange
Essex 272 for 3 (50 overs) (WI Jefferson 97,
N Hussain 85)
Scotland 227 for 9 (48 overs) (RR Watson 76,
S Sriram 56)
Essex won by 45 runs

at Lincoln Lindum
Glamorgan 340 for 4 (50 overs) (RDB Croft 143,
MTG Elliott 87)
Lincolnshire 230 for 6 (50 overs) (GE Welton 60,
SA Deitz 56)
Glamorgan won by 110 runs

at Stone
Lancashire 232 (47 overs)
Staffordshire 212 for 8 (50 overs)
Lancashire won by 20 runs

at Dublin
Surrey 261 (49.5 overs) (AD Brown 67, AJ Hollioake 52)

Simon Francis appeals during his remarkable eight-wicket haul for Somerset against Derbyshire.

Ireland 262 for 5 (48.2 overs) (JAM Molins 58, JP Bray 52)
Ireland won by 5 wickets

at Lamphey
Middlesex 277 for 6 (50 overs) (JWM Dalrymple 104*, PN Weekes 66)
Wales 103 (41.1 overs) (MM Betts 4 for 15)
Middlesex won by 174 runs

at Dean Park
Dorset 97 (38.2 overs) (CEW Silverwood 4 for 18)
Yorkshire 101 for 2 (16.5 overs) (MJ Wood 71*)
Yorkshire won by 8 wickets

at Canterbury
Berkshire 143 (44.4 overs) (MJ Saggers 4 for 6)
Kent 144 for 1 (16.3 overs) (RWT Key 61*, MA Carberry 51)
Kent won by 9 wickets

at Northampton
Northamptonshire 273 (49.1 overs) (M van Jaarsveld 85, DJG Sales 67, GP Swann 50)
Cambridgeshire 110 (40.1 overs) (JF Brown 5 for 19)
Northamptonshire won by 163 runs

at The Riverside
Sussex 245 (49.4 overs) (CJ Adams 68, IJ Ward 54)
Durham 223 (48.4 overs) (M Akram 4 for 61)
Sussex won by 22 runs

at Worcester
Worcestershire 279 for 8 (47 overs) (BF Smith 91)
Herefordshire 146 for 4 (29 overs) (RJ Hall 54*)
Worcestershire won by 18 runs – DL Method: target 164 from 29 overs

at Edgbaston
Shropshire 119 (42.5 overs) (DR Brown 4 for 30)
Warwickshire 121 for 2 (21 overs) (IR Bell 58*)
Warwickshire won by 8 wickets

at Exmouth
Leicestershire 156 (47.2 overs)
Devon 156 for 9 (50 overs)
Devon won by losing fewer wickets

at Trent Bridge
Wiltshire 186 for 7 (50 overs)
Nottinghamshire 189 for 4 (38.2 overs) (CMW Read 77*)
Nottinghamshire won by 6 wickets

Ireland and Devon proved that the romance of the cup is still very much alive in domestic cricket with thrilling and dramatic second-round victories against Surrey and Leicestershire respectively.

Devon's triumph at Exmouth will long be savoured. Needing four runs off the final over of the match, bowled by Jon Dakin, the minor county saw skipper Bobby Dawson – their top scorer with 42 – caught at mid-on from the third ball, after two runs had been garnered.

Last man Aqeel Ahmed now joined Andy Procter, the No. 10, and two more runs were squeezed out. Now Dakin knew that, with the scores level, he had to take a wicket with the last ball or Leicestershire would be out because they themselves had lost all ten wickets in being bowled out for 156.

Dakin fired in a yorker at Procter, but it missed the leg stump and Devon began to celebrate after a chase that had looked to be dead in the water after they had slid to 75 for 6 but which was revitalised by a stand of 51 between Dawson, the former

Gloucestershire batsman, and David Court, who hit two sixes in his vital innings of 36.

The historic Irish win was achieved, quite properly for an Irish one-day team, over two days at Clontarf. Surrey, with eight internationals in their line-up, were outplayed as they failed to defend a total of 261 when the match resumed on the reserve day.

Jason Molins, the captain, thumped an aggressive 58 during a 103-run opening stand with Jeremy Bray and, after the powerful Gerald Dros and Peter Gillespie had kept the momentum going, off-spinning all-rounder Andrew White followed up his 3 for 43 of the day before by striking an unbeaten 20 and winning himself the Man of the Match award.

In the end victory came by five wickets with ten balls to spare and Molins said it was an achievement to rank alongside Ireland's 1997 win over Middlesex in the Benson and Hedges Cup, and the successes against the touring South Africans in 1904 and 1947, the West Indies of 1928 and 1969, and the 2003 Zimbabweans.

More importantly, added 29-year-old investment manager Molins, it further raised the profile of cricket in Ireland and boosted their confidence ahead of their attempt to qualify for the 2007 World Cup.

Bad weather affected most of the ties in this round, with the game between Wiltshire and Nottinghamshire at Westbury proving impossible to get under way at all on either of the two days set aside for it. After a meeting between officials and players from both sides, it was agreed to play the match ten days later at Trent Bridge – a match that Notts won comfortably.

Worcestershire scraped through by just 18 runs in a Duckworth-Lewis situation against a Herefordshire side boasting Franklyn Rose, Martin McCague, Ismail

Bobby Dawson, the captain of giant-killers Devon.

Upsets in the C&G Trophy, or its forerunners:	
1973:	Durham* (v. Yorkshire)
1974:	Lincolnshire (v. Glamorgan)
1976:	Hertfordshire (v. Essex)
1984:	Shropshire (v. Yorkshire)
1985:	Durham* (v. Derbyshire)
1987:	Buckinghamshire (v. Somerset)
1988:	Cheshire (v. Northamptonshire)
1991:	Hertfordshire (v. Derbyshire)
1998:	Scotland (v. Worcestershire)
1999:	Holland (v. Durham)
2001:	Herefordshire (v. Middlesex)
2004:	Ireland (v. Surrey)
	Devon (v. Leicestershire)

* denotes that they were then a minor county

Dawood and former Worcestershire slow left-armer Matthew Rawnsley. The match was switched from Hereford's Luctonians ground to New Road, and computer engineer Richard Hall was on 54 not out when rain interrupted the game for the final time.

Berkshire were another minor county team to switch their match in an effort to get some play. With Reading unplayable, Kent's offer to use Canterbury the following day was accepted, and half-centuries from Rob Key and Michael Carberry saw the first-class county romp home by nine wickets after Berkshire had struggled against Martin Saggers and the rest of the Kent attack. Shropshire and Cambridgeshire also agreed to switch their ties from Wellington and March to Edgbaston and Northampton respectively.

A century from Phil Weston, and good support from Craig Spearman and Matt Windows, underpinned a highly professional victory for Gloucestershire in Amstelveen against Holland, who would have fancied their chances of an upset on home soil.

Scotland got to 172 for 3 in reply to Essex's Will Jefferson-inspired 272 for 3 before slipping away, while Staffordshire fought hard against Lancashire at Stone before going down to a 20-run defeat.

Derbyshire and Durham were the two losers in the all first-class county ties, with Simon Francis taking 8 for 66 but losing out in the Man of the Match stakes to Jamie Cox, whose 131 was the basis of Somerset's 14-run win at Derby.

At the Riverside, there was a comic, and almost heroic, last-wicket stand of 48 between Durham's Neil Killeen and Alan Walker, the 41-year-old bowling coach recalled to action but who failed to bowl a ball in Sussex's 245 due to a torn calf muscle. At 175 for 9, Walker hobbled out with a runner to join Killeen, and the pair heaved and thrashed their way to within sight of an improbable victory before, with nine balls remaining and the odds lengthening, Killeen ran himself out.

Third Round: 26–30 May 2004

at Exmouth
Yorkshire 411 for 6 (50 overs) (MJ Wood 160, MJ Lumb 77, A McGrath 64*, PA Jaques 55)
Devon 279 for 8 (50 overs) (RI Dawson 52, A McGrath 4 for 56)
Yorkshire won by 132 runs

at Worcester
Somerset 95 (27.3 overs) (AJ Bichel 4 for 17)
Worcestershire 100 for 2 (14.3 overs)
Worcestershire won by 8 wickets

at Trent Bridge
Essex 309 for 4 (50 overs) (WI Jefferson 126, A Flower 106)
Nottinghamshire 125 (21.2 overs) (SA Brant 4 for 54)
Essex won by 184 runs

at Bristol
Hampshire 154 (46.1 overs) (AD Mascarenhas 52, J Lewis 4 for 39)
Gloucestershire 157 for 7 (37.5 overs) (CM Spearman 50, SK Warne 4 for 23)
Gloucestershire won by 3 wickets

at Edgbaston
Kent 211 (49.4 overs) (DP Fulton 78)
Warwickshire 215 for 1 (42.1 overs) (MA Wagh 102*, NV Knight 74*)
Warwickshire won by 9 wickets

at Lord's
Glamorgan 256 for 8 (50 overs) (MTG Elliott 85)
Middlesex 260 for 4 (46.1 overs) (JWM Dalrymple 107, EC Joyce 100*)
Middlesex won by 6 wickets

at Hove
Lancashire 242 for 7 (50 overs) (MJ Chilton 62, MB Loye 54)

Matthew Wood, whose 160 at Exmouth helped Yorkshire to burst the Devon bubble.

Sussex 230 for 9 (50 overs) (RSC Martin-Jenkins 61*, CJ Adams 51)
Lancashire won by 12 runs

at Dublin
Ireland 263 for 8 (50 overs) (JP Bray 76, PG Gillespie 66, PS Jones 6 for 56)
Northamptonshire 267 for 4 (41.5 overs)
(M van Jaarsveld 93*)
Northamptonshire won by 6 wickets

Devon's cup adventure came to an end amid a flurry of sixes and fours on an idyllic sunshine-filled day at Exmouth. The scene of their second-round triumph over Leicestershire was this time dominated by the first-class cricketers of Yorkshire, and opener Matthew Wood in particular. Wood entertained the 2,000 crowd royally, hitting 160 from just 124 balls and looking extremely disappointed when he was out with ten overs still to be bowled. Wood, however, had made the highest individual score for Yorkshire in the competition, beating Geoff Boycott's 146 against Surrey at Lord's in the 1965 final. Michael Lumb, Phil Jaques, Anthony McGrath and then a clutch of Devon batsmen also joined in the merriment on Dave Fouracre's belter of a pitch. There was no cup upset, but there were 690 runs, 24 sixes and a refreshing sea breeze to fan those sunning themselves on the boundary's edge.

Shane Warne was part of an ugly top-order Hampshire collapse at Bristol, but the Australian still managed to put the jitters into Gloucestershire before the holders squeezed through by three wickets. At 4 for 3, with Warne coming in at No. 3 and going to Jon Lewis for a duck that was noisily celebrated by the home fieldsmen, Hampshire were in danger of being humiliated after their captain, Warne, had won the toss. At 49 for 6, and then 91 for 8, things were not looking much better, but at least Dimitri Mascarenhas and Chris Tremlett put on 60 for the ninth wicket to give Hampshire some sort of a total to defend. Gloucestershire, however, cruised to 76 without loss by the 14th over, with James Hamblin seeing 27 plundered from his second over, before Craig Spearman was bowled by Alan Mullally for 50. When Mullally then dismissed Alex Gidman in his next over, Warne saw the chance he needed. He bowled Spearman's fellow opener, Phil Weston, in a mesmerising spell which brought him 4 for 23. At 137 for 7, Gloucestershire were by no means home, and it

took some calm batting from Shoaib Malik – who finished unbeaten on 32 – and Lewis to take them past Hampshire's 154.

Hundreds from Ed Joyce and Jamie Dalrymple, in a third-wicket partnership of 220, swept Middlesex past Glamorgan at Lord's, while Somerset collapsed to 95 all out and defeat by eight wickets to Worcestershire in seam-friendly conditions at New Road. Andy Bichel followed up his 4 for 17 by finishing on 38 not out.

Will Jefferson and Andy Flower hit 126 and 106 respectively to set up Essex's thumping 184-run victory over Nottinghamshire at Trent Bridge with a magnificent opening stand of 248, and Lancashire's full-strength seam attack proved too hot for Sussex to handle on a sporty Hove pitch. Andrew Flintoff, playing his first county match of the season, also smashed a car window with his first scoring shot – a six off Robin Martin-Jenkins – and there was so much glass embedded in the ball that it had to be changed.

Mark Wagh, meanwhile, finished the game and completed his maiden one-day century with a six off Alamgir Sheriyar as Warwickshire overwhelmed Kent at Edgbaston by nine wickets. David Fulton, the Kent captain, made 78, but, after an initial blast by Neil Carter, it was left to Wagh and Nick Knight to cruise past Kent's 211 with an unbroken stand of 183.

The round's final match took place on 30 May, at Clontarf, where Ireland were planning on adding the scalp of Northamptonshire to that of Surrey. Despite a courageous performance, however, they could never shake off their first-class opponents and an unbeaten 93 by the classy Martin van Jaarsveld was, in the end, the difference between the two sides. Ireland can take a lot of credit, nevertheless, for the way they built a total of 263 for 8 after being put in and then slipping to 37 for 3. Opener Jeremy Bray made 76 and added 115 for the fourth wicket with Peter Gillespie (66). Andrew White then struck a well-made 44 and, at 124 for 3 in reply, Northants still had a lot of work to do. It was done largely through the strokeplay of van Jaarsfeld and David Sales, who hit 49, and – after four stoppages for rain – the match finally ended at 8.47 pm.

Quarter-finals: 15–16 June 2004

at Worcester
Worcestershire 204 (50 overs)
(BF Smith 54)

Essex 183 (48.1 overs) (A Flower 58)
Worcestershire won by 21 runs

at Bristol
Gloucestershire 239 for 8 (50 overs)
(CM Spearman 62, WPC Weston 54)
Middlesex 223 for 8 (50 overs) (EC Joyce 53)
Gloucestershire won by 16 runs

at Old Trafford
Lancashire 286 for 5 (50 overs) (CL Hooper 66,
DG Cork 54*, MB Loye 50)
Yorkshire 287 for 7 (47.4 overs) (MP Vaughan 116*,
DS Lehmann 62)
Yorkshire won by 3 wickets

at Edgbaston
Warwickshire 343 for 4 (50 overs) (GB Hogg 94*,
IR Bell 68, IJL Trott 65*)
Northamptonshire 270 (43.5 overs) (DJG Sales 52,
DR Brown 5 for 43)
Warwickshire won by 73 runs

On a greenish New Road pitch of sometimes-
variable bounce, Worcestershire put in a solid all-
round display to see off Essex's challenge by 21
runs. Vikram Solanki, Ben Smith and David
Leatherdale all made valuable contributions to
Worcestershire's 204, but three run outs almost
certainly cost Essex the match during the visitors'
reply. The first, that of Ravi Bopara, was bad

Michael Vaughan cuts Carl Hooper for four during his match-winning hundred for Yorkshire in the Roses quarter-final tie
at Old Trafford.

enough – but the dismissals of Andy Flower and James Middlebrook really hurt. Flower, who had played so well for his 98-ball 58, was run out at the non-striker's end as he tried to push a single off Gareth Batty but then saw the bowler anticipate superbly to swoop on the ball and throw down the stumps. Finally, with the game still in the balance at 176 for 7 in the 46th over, Kabir Ali's excellent diving stop at short fine leg and accurate throw to the wicketkeeper ended Middlebrook's dashing 47 off 57 balls.

Another team came to fortress Bristol and had their hopes crushed by Gloucestershire's all-too-familiar ploy of getting a decent score up on the board and then strangling the life out of their opponents' reply on a pitch that lost pace and bounce as the day wore on. Craig Spearman and Phil Weston opened up with a stand of 118 in the first 20 overs, and Gloucestershire would have been disappointed in the end to have totalled only 239 for 8. Their defence of that total was, though, masterly – with Mark Alleyne, the captain, once again providing the deciding spell of 3 for 31 just when the match looked as though it was hanging in the balance.

Yorkshire won the Roses clash with Lancashire at Old Trafford, with Michael Vaughan's sublime 116 not out from 109 balls sweeping them to victory with 14 balls to spare. Even reaching a target as stiff as 287, set thanks to half-centuries from Mal Loye, Carl Hooper and Dominic Cork – who blasted an unbeaten 54 from a mere 20 balls – was made to look comfortable as Vaughan batted with class and style. A pair of sixes towards the end, the second pulled with Vaughan's familiar pirouette, put the seal on his performance.

Neil Carter pillaged a record 28 runs from a six-ball over by Steffan Jones, and Brad Hogg then thrashed an unbeaten 94 off 61 balls, as Warwickshire buried Northamptonshire at Edgbaston. There were also free-flowing contributions from Nick Knight, Ian Bell and Jonathan Trott as Warwickshire amassed 343 for 4 from their 50 overs. Poor Jones ended up with 0 for 75 while Johann Louw's ten overs cost 83. Carter's assault on Jones went four, four, four, top-edged six over the wicketkeeper's head, four, six over midwicket. In reply, only David Sales

threatened to do something spectacular and Dougie Brown capped the home side's 73-run win by taking the last three wickets in five balls.

Semi-finals: 17 July 2004

at Bristol
Yorkshire 243 for 6 (50 overs)
(DS Lehmann 80*)
Gloucestershire 247 for 5 (46.1 overs)
(CM Spearman 143*)
Gloucestershire won by 5 wickets

at Edgbaston
Worcestershire 257 for 4 (50 overs)
(VS Solanki 126, SC Moore 57)
Warwickshire 216 (47.4 overs)
Worcestershire won by 41 runs

Gloucestershire and Worcestershire set up a repeat of their 2003 Cheltenham & Gloucester Trophy final meeting with semi-final wins of comfortable margins that were due to outstanding innings from Craig Spearman and Vikram Solanki.

Spearman's superb unbeaten 143 against Yorkshire at Bristol was described by Michael Atherton, commentating on television, as 'the perfect one-day innings'. Michael Vaughan, by contrast, laboured for 21 balls over his first run and it took a fine 80 not out from Darren Lehmann to hoist Yorkshire's total to 243 for 6. It was not nearly enough as Spearman set about an attack containing six international bowlers and an England Under 19 prospect in Tim Bresnan. The speed of his scoring was astonishing. He faced only 122 balls in all, hitting 14 fours and four sixes. His first half-century took just 30 balls, and he warmed up by flicking Bresnan for two sixes over midwicket before pulling another one off Matthew Hoggard. In the end, Spearman swept Gloucestershire past the winning post with 23 balls in hand.

At Edgbaston the talent of Solanki, who hit 126 and then took three catches and ran out the dangerous Jonathan Trott, lit up the West Midlands derby match between Worcestershire and Warwickshire. There were eight fours and three sixes in Solanki's elegant innings, but it was also a perfectly judged anchor role in an eventual total of 257 for 4. Warwickshire, in reply, could find no one to match Solanki's skill or dedication to the cause of crease occupation and the miserly off-spin bowling of Gareth Batty was also a significant factor in an excellent all-round Worcestershire performance in the field.

Semi-final hero: Vikram Solanki's responsible hundred was the main difference between the two sides in the West Midlands derby at Edgbaston.

FINAL – GLOUCESTERSHIRE v. WORCESTERSHIRE
28 August 2004 at Lord's

WORCESTERSHIRE

VS Solanki	st Adshead b Ball	115
SC Moore	c Adshead b Lewis	0
GA Hick	c Adshead b Lewis	0
BF Smith	c Hussey b Lewis	1
DA Leatherdale	c Hancock b Averis	66
AJ Bichel	st Adshead b Ball	19
AJ Hall	c Hussey b Averis	1
GJ Batty	c Weston b Averis	1
*SJ Rhodes (capt)	not out	1
MS Mason	b Averis	1
RW Price	not out	2
Extras	b 2, lb 4, w 17, nb 6	29
	(9 wkts 50 overs)	**236**

	O	M	R	W
Lewis	10	2	32	3
Averis	10	3	23	4
Alleyne	8	0	32	0
Gidman	7	1	40	0
Ball	9	0	65	2
Hussey	6	0	38	0

Fall of Wickets
1-4, 2-4, 3-8, 4-202, 5-218, 6-231, 7-232, 8-232, 9-234

GLOUCESTERSHIRE

WPC Weston	not out	110
CM Spearman	c Rhodes b Batty	70
MEK Hussey	b Price	20
CG Taylor	not out	22
APR Gidman		
MW Alleyne (capt)		
*SJ Adshead		
MCJ Ball		
THC Hancock		
J Lewis		
JMM Averis		
Extras	b 3, lb 2, w 6, nb 4	15
	(2 wkts 48.5 overs)	**237**

	O	M	R	W
Mason	10	0	40	0
Bichel	7	0	46	0
Hall	5	0	28	0
Leatherdale	2.5	0	25	0
Price	9	0	51	1
Batty	10	0	42	1

Fall of Wickets
1-141, 2-171

Umpires: NA Mallender & P Willey
Toss: Gloucestershire
Man of the Match: VS Solanki

Gloucestershire won by 8 wickets

Final: 28 August 2004 at Lord's

It was billed, like so many rematches, as a revenge mission. Worcestershire, who had been so completely humbled in the 2003 Cheltenham & Gloucester Trophy final that the game was all over by 4.30 pm, had sworn to take the fight to Gloucestershire this time. They were determined to win.

The reality, in the dazzling light of a lovely late-summer afternoon, was that they had come up well short once again. Gloucestershire, in their fourth C&G final in six years, won by eight wickets and – even if century-maker and Man of the Match Vikram Solanki and David Leatherdale did make them scrap a little harder for the prize – victory in the end came with ease.

There were 6.1 overs still to be bowled when Phil Weston, formerly of Worcestershire and unbeaten on 110, and Chris Taylor, the man being groomed to be Mark Alleyne's full-time captaincy successor, breasted the tape. Worcestershire's 236 for 9, which itself had represented a determined recovery from the depths of 8 for 3, was exposed as being totally inadequate.

Again, though, Gloucestershire had the advantage of winning the toss and taking first use of a pitch that was always going to have a little bit more juice in it early on a late August morning. Yet, it was swing and a highly disciplined line – rather than excessive seam movement – that enabled Jon Lewis to wreck the start of the Worcestershire innings.

Stephen Moore and Graeme Hick were both taken at the wicket for ducks, and Ben Smith had made just a single when he steered a low catch to Mike Hussey in the gully. Gloucestershire's travelling supporters – perhaps because of familiarity and finance not as large a band as they were at the outset of their county's golden run of six one-day final trophies since 1999, but still vocal and enthusiastic enough – were dancing in anticipation of a rerun of 12 months earlier.

Solanki, with skill and maturity, and Leatherdale, with grit and experience, rode out the storm. The scoring rate, however, dipped as a result of the need to regroup and, at the 15-over mark, Worcestershire had still only made 34 for 3 and had taken no advantage at all of the fielding restrictions. Later, tellingly, Gloucestershire reached the same staging post on 83 without loss.

With Ian Harvey gone, and Mike Smith injured, Gloucestershire's bowling resources were not as strong as they had been in previous triumphs. Lewis, however, led the line magnificently and James Averis, willing as ever, followed up a tight new-ball

Jon Lewis celebrates his third wicket with the new ball ... Ben Smith is caught in the gully and Worcestershire are in deep trouble at 8 for 3.

spell by returning at the end of the Worcestershire innings and having great fun at the lower-middle-order's expense. Averis, indeed, even took a hat-trick with the last ball of the 48th over and the first two deliveries of the 50th.

In the hurly-burly of the last overs, it escaped the notice of many in the 22,000 crowd. It even seemed to bypass the attentions of the Gloucestershire players, but slowly the realisation of Averis' feat dawned on them. Leatherdale, holing out at deep mid-on for a brave 66, Gareth Batty, swinging to deep midwicket, and Andrew Hall, driving to cover, were the three victims in what was only the second hat-trick achieved in a Lord's final. The first was by Ken Higgs, for Leicestershire, in the 1974 Benson and Hedges Cup final.

Solanki had fallen in the 45th over, stumped as he attempted to hit Martyn Ball's off spin into the Nursery Ground, and with him went Worcestershire's hopes of totalling the 250 or 260 that they realised was a minimum requirement in the conditions.

His 115, though, was testimony both to his technical improvement and to his growing awareness of what makes an international-class batsman. He had made hundreds in both the C&G semi-final and final; it was no surprise to those who saw them that, a few days later, Solanki had been recalled to the England one-day team after an absence of nine months.

Worcestershire, however, desperately needed early wickets. Unfortunately for them, Kabir Ali was absent with injury and none of their remaining

seamers could make the breakthrough as Spearman and Weston continued an alliance that had been central to Gloucestershire's 2004 success. Their eventual opening partnership here of 141 was added to stands of 76, 118 and 73 in earlier rounds and the game was all but up for Worcestershire when Spearman was caught at the wicket off Batty.

Weston's fourth one-day century, from 125 balls and containing 11 fours and six, was particularly sweet for a player who had spent 12 largely frustrating seasons at New Road before moving a little way south down the M5 for the start of the 2003 summer. With the successful introduction of Weston, Spearman, Hussey and Steve Adshead into the club's winning formula, the 2004 C&G Trophy represented a major entry into Alleyne's growing CV of achievement.

Left: Vikram Solanki acknowledges the crowd after his brave Lord's hundred.

Below: Philip Weston builds his match-winning century as Worcestershire skipper Steve Rhodes looks on.

It's ours – again! Gloucestershire's victorious players pose with the C&G Trophy after beating Worcestershire in a second successive Lord's final.

Alleyne, who had taken over from John Bracewell as the county's coach when the New Zealander left to take charge of his national team at the end of the 2003 season, decided to stay on as one-day captain but hand the championship reins to Taylor.

Being a player-coach, however part-time, is not easy, but the way Alleyne managed to keep Gloucestershire's remarkable run of success going in 2004, despite the loss of Harvey, Jonty Rhodes and Jack Russell – the last two through retirement – must surely make him a candidate for involvement in England's one-day management structure at some stage in the near future.

BANGLADESH

ENGLAND IN BANGLADESH

ENGLAND IN BANGLADESH
By Jonathan Agnew

FIRST TEST
21–25 October 2003 at Dhaka

England's inaugural Test tour of Bangladesh represented a leap into the unknown for Michael Vaughan's men, as well as an early start to what was a busy winter.

Still without a Test victory in 24 attempts, the odds were stacked against the home team, which elected to bat first under threatening skies. Only 15 overs were possible on the opening day, and there was little in that time to suggest that Bangladesh's batsmen would offer any more than token resistance to England's bowlers, Steve Harmison in particular. The tall fast bowler claimed three of the first wickets to fall as Bangladesh slipped to 72 for 5 on the second morning. A stand of 60 for the sixth wicket between Mushfiqur Rahman and the former captain, Khaled Mashud, denied England's bowlers the rout they might have been expecting, but after Mashud became Rikki Clarke's first Test victim for a hard-fought 51, only Mohammad Rafique – who hit three sixes in his 32 – stood in Harmison's way for long. The Durham paceman claimed his first five-wicket haul for England as Bangladesh were bundled out for 203, but Matthew Hoggard, with 3 for 55, had bowled well with little luck.

By the close of the second day, England had raced to 111 for no wicket, and the stage was set for them to build an imposing first-innings lead.

Nine wickets fell to Steve Harmison in England's inaugural Test match against Bangladesh.

However, the script had to be torn up after Michael Vaughan had added 17 to his overnight 31. Mark Butcher perished lbw for a third-ball duck, and Nasser Hussain edged his seventh delivery to the wicketkeeper, also for nought. Graham Thorpe added 37 with Marcus Trescothick, who completed his second consecutive century before – having been dropped twice – he swept Haque to square leg. Clarke made 14, Gareth Batty 19 – both of them making their Test debut – and Ashley Giles also made 19, but England's total of 295 was the lowest recorded by a touring side in Bangladesh and, having been 137 for no wicket, represented a wonderful fightback by the hosts, for whom Mashrafe Mortaza and Mohammad Rafique both took three wickets.

Facing a deficit of 92, Bangladesh lost Saleh to Harmison before another premature close, but then knuckled down on the fourth morning to produce some of the most inspired batting in their brief Test history. Half-centuries by Hannan Sarkar and Habibul Bashar, and an undefeated 43 from Rahman, pushed them into a lead of 153 at the end of the day, and England's players would not be entirely telling the truth if they denied feeling some concern. England took four wickets either side of lunch, but on a slow pitch with increasingly low bounce, it was a day for determined, if rather strokeless, batting against an attack that, Harmison and Hoggard apart, offered little.

Much would depend on the Bangladesh lower order on the final morning, and when the last four wickets were blown away in nine overs for the addition of only ten runs, the realisation dawned on the home fans that the chances of their watching a first Test win had been snuffed out.

England's victory target was only 164 and, typically, Vaughan and Trescothick set off in a positive vein. Trescothick was stumped as he charged and attempted to slog Rafique out of the ground and Butcher was lbw for the second time in the game, this time for eight. Hussain was put down at slip, but reached only 17 before Mortaza trapped him lbw. England were only 36 runs from home, however, and Thorpe joined Vaughan – whose 81 was his highest score since becoming captain – to complete the task. England's success was achieved in some comfort in the end, but Bangladesh had shown welcome signs of improvement to both their technique and their approach.

FIRST TEST – BANGLADESH v. ENGLAND
21–25 October 2003 at Dhaka

BANGLADESH

	First Innings			Second Innings	
Hannan Sarkar	b Hoggard	20		c Trescothick b Hoggard	59
Javed Omar	c Clarke b Harmison	3		(7) lbw b Hoggard	27
Habibul Bashar	c Trescothick b Harmison	2		c Trescothick b Batty	58
Rajin Saleh	c Read b Harmison	11		(2) c Read b Harmison	8
Alok Kapali	b Batty	28		(4) c Butcher b Harmison	12
Mushfiqur Rahman	lbw b Hoggard	34		(5) not out	46
*Khaled Mashud	lbw b Clarke	51		(6) c Hussain b Giles	7
Khaled Mahmud (capt)	lbw b Hoggard	4		lbw b Harmison	18
Mohammad Rafique	b Harmison	32		c Read b Harmison	1
Mashrafe Mortaza	b Harmison	11		c Trescothick b Hoggard	1
Enamul Haque jnr	not out	0		lbw b Hoggard	0
Extras	b 2, lb 3, nb 2	7		lb 10, nb 3, p 5	18
	(83.5 overs)	203		(107 overs)	255

	First Innings				Second Innings			
	O	M	R	W	O	M	R	W
Hoggard	23	6	55	3	27	11	48	4
Harmison	21.5	6	35	5	25	8	44	4
Clarke	6	1	18	1	15	6	31	0
Batty	21	6	43	1	20	2	65	1
Giles	12	1	47	0	20	4	52	1

Fall of Wickets
1-12, 2-24, 3-38, 4-40, 5-72, 6-132, 7-148, 8-182, 9-198
1-12, 2-120, 3-140, 4-148, 5-176, 6-219, 7-248, 8-254, 9-255

ENGLAND

	First Innings			Second Innings	
ME Trescothick	c K Mahmud b E Haque jnr	113		st K Mashud b M Rafique	32
MP Vaughan (capt)	b Mohammad Rafique	48		not out	81
MA Butcher	lbw b Mushfiqur Rahman	0		lbw b Mohammad Rafique	8
N Hussain	c K Mashud b M Rahman	0		lbw b Mashrafe Mortaza	17
GP Thorpe	c Rajin Saleh b Mashrafe Mortaza	64		not out	18
R Clarke	b Mohammad Rafique	14			
*CMW Read	c K Mashud b E Haque jnr	1			
GJ Batty	c K Mashud b M Mortaza	19			
AF Giles	c sub b Mohammad Rafique	19			
SJ Harmison	lbw b Mashrafe Mortaza	0			
MJ Hoggard	not out	6			
Extras	lb 4, w 2, nb 5	11		b 1, lb 1, w 1, nb 5	8
	(120.3 overs)	295		(3 wkts 39.2 overs)	164

	First Innings				Second Innings			
	O	M	R	W	O	M	R	W
Mashrafe Mortaza	23	6	41	3	11	2	46	1
Mushfiqur Rahman	17	6	55	2	3	1	16	0
Khaled Mahmud	17	7	45	0	3	1	14	0
Mohammad Rafique	35.3	9	84	3	13.2	0	57	2
Enamul Haque jnr	23	8	53	2	7	0	27	0
Rajin Saleh	2	0	9	0	2	0	2	0
Alok Kapali	3	1	4	0	-	-	-	-

Fall of Wickets
1-137, 2-140, 3-140, 4-175, 5-224, 6-225, 7-266, 8-267, 9-267
1-64, 2-86, 3-128

Umpires: Aleem Dar and EAR de Silva
Toss: Bangladesh
Test debuts: Enamul Haque jnr, GJ Batty, R Clarke
Man of the Match: SJ Harmison

England won by 7 wickets

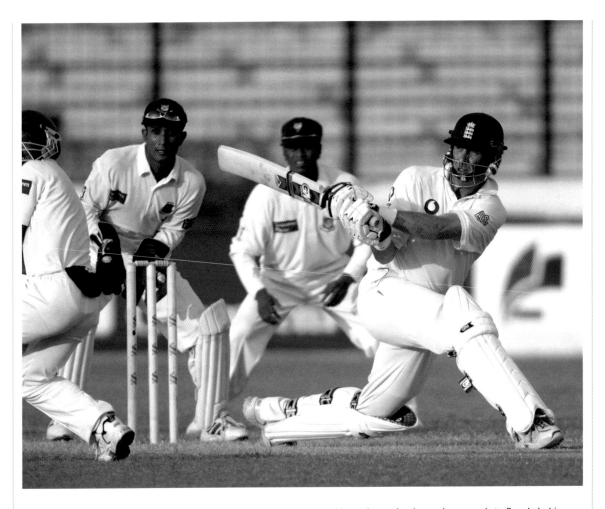

Marcus Trescothick sweeps during his first-innings 113 in Dhaka. He had been dropped twice early on much to Bangladeshi disappointment.

SECOND TEST
29 October–1 November 2003 at Chittagong

As had been the case in Dhaka, Bangladesh competed rather more honourably than the heavy defeat suggested. England, put in to bat, suffered another of their customary collapses to find themselves on 134 for 4, having been 120 for no wicket. Once again, the young seamer Mortaza was the architect of the tourists' problems, whipping out Vaughan and Thorpe in the space of three balls, after Trescothick had been caught at point for 60 and Butcher – whose trip to Bangladesh was developing into a nightmare – was bowled for six. It required some disciplined rebuilding of the innings, and Hussain teamed up

with Clarke to move the score on to 237 for 4 at the close.

Hussain, one feels, is hanging on grimly these days. Strokes are few and far between – a sliced drive here or a hook shot there. Often a desperate-looking slog over the top is his only means of scoring off the spinners. Here he grafted away for the best part of six hours, facing 266 balls in his 76. He hit only five of them to the boundary.

Clarke – in his second Test – was rather more entertaining, in that he scored eight fours in his 55 before he became Mortaza's fourth victim. Chris Read – who always has something to prove with the bat – added 63 with Hussain before their dismissals, both on 313, sparked a second collapse as the last five wickets fell chaotically for only 13 runs.

At least that moved the game on speedily, and as

Nasser Hussain hit 76 and 95 in the second Test at Chittagong but he had to work hard for his runs.

the second day came towards its end, the writing was already on the wall as Bangladesh slipped to 63 for 4. With Harmison nursing a sore back, Richard Johnson took the new ball and claimed his second five-wicket haul in only two matches. True, one might argue that he could not have chosen his opponents (Zimbabwe and Bangladesh) any more prudently, but he was rewarded for bowling accurately and, as Bangladesh's first innings crumbled to 152 all out, there was some inept lower-order batting.

In contrast to Dhaka, England now took the opportunity to bat the hosts out of the game, and they did so to such an extent that they led by 467 by the end of only the third day. Hussain played with greater fluency this time as he and Thorpe came together after Butcher (42) had fallen to Rafique and Vaughan (25) had been run out. Together the old campaigners added 132 for the third wicket with Hussain falling caught and bowled just five runs short of what would have been his 14th Test century and Thorpe lbw for 54.

Richard Johnson, with nine wickets, picks up the Man of the Match award in the second Test.

Read and Clarke both enjoyed themselves briefly before Vaughan declared on the overnight score of 293 for 5, and Bangladesh's batsmen knew that they would be hard pushed to survive the fourth day.

In fact they collapsed rather feebly within 38 overs, with Johnson nabbing another four wickets to give him match figures of 9 for 93, and the Man of the Match award. In two Tests, the popular Somerset swing bowler had taken 15 wickets at only 12 runs each! Mahmud, the Bangladesh captain, top scored with 33 before falling to a catch by his opposite number, Vaughan, who knew that his next opponents – Sri Lanka – would not be so generous.

ONE-DAY INTERNATIONALS

Match One
7 November 2003 at Chittagong
Bangladesh 143 (44.4 overs) (A Flintoff 4 for 14)
England 144 for 3 (25.3 overs) (A Flintoff 55*)
England won by 7 wickets

Match Two
10 November 2003 at Dhaka
Bangladesh 134 for 9 (50 overs)
England 137 for 3 (27.4 overs) (A Flintoff 70*)
England won by 7 wickets

Match Three
12 November 2003 at Dhaka
Bangladesh 182 (49.1 overs)
England 185 for 3 (39.3 overs) (A Flintoff 52*,
ME Trescothick 50)
England won by 7 wickets

England won a grotesquely one-sided series of three one-day internationals by exactly the same margin – seven wickets. To sum up the gulf between the two teams, one only needs to add up the overs that Bangladesh required to amass their aggregate total of 459 runs (143.5) compared to the 92 needed by England to win all three games. Only in the final match did Bangladesh manage to set a target of more than 150.

In Chittagong, Bangladesh suffered a quite bewildering collapse of five wickets for one run. At the end of this remarkable sequence, the home team were 66 for 7 and the contest was already over. Giles and Flintoff were the men responsible, with Flintoff ending up with 4 for 14 from 9.4 overs.

England's target was only 144, and although they were 55 for 3, having lost Solanki for ten, Vaughan for nine and Trescothick for 28, Flintoff weighed in with the bat, scoring 55 not out from 52 balls as, with Collingwood, he bludgeoned England to victory in only the 26th over.

Three days later, in Dhaka, the match was effectively over even earlier than had been the case with its predecessor. At 7 for 4, Bangladesh were pitifully placed, and although Saleh scored 37, and Rafique hit 27 at the end, this was another yawn-maker. England needed 13 more balls this time to overhaul their target of 135, and once again it was Flintoff – who bullied his way to 70 from only 47 balls – who did the damage.

The burly Lancastrian hit his third half-century of the series in the third and final game, this time

SECOND TEST – BANGLADESH v. ENGLAND
29 October–1 November 2003 at Chittagong

ENGLAND

	First Innings		Second Innings	
ME Trescothick	c M Rahman b K Mahmud	60	(7) not out	1
MP Vaughan (capt)	c K Mashud b M Mortaza	54	run out	25
MA Butcher	b Mohammad Rafique	6	(1) c K Mashud b M Rafique	42
N Hussain	c K Mashud b M Mortaza	76	(3) c & b M Rafique	95
GP Thorpe	b Mashrafe Mortaza	0	(4) lbw b M Rafique	54
R Clarke	c H Sarkar b M Mortaza	55	lbw b Enamul Haque jnr	27
*CMW Read	c Rajin Saleh b E Haque jnr	37	(5) not out	38
AF Giles	lbw b Mushfiqur Rahman	6		
RL Johnson	c K Mashud b M Rahman	6		
MJ Saggers	lbw b Mohammad Rafique	1		
MJ Hoggard	not out	0		
Extras	b 8, lb 5, w 7, nb 5	25	b 4, w 1, nb 6	11
	(135.3 overs)	326	(5 wkts dec 67 overs)	293

	First Innings				Second Innings			
	O	M	R	W	O	M	R	W
Mashrafe Mortaza	28	11	60	4	4	0	23	0
Mushfiqur Rahman	18.3	6	50	2	5	0	41	0
Khaled Mahmud	23	8	46	1	14	3	64	0
Mohammad Rafique	37	15	63	2	29	3	106	3
Enamul Haque jnr	23	4	81	1	14	5	40	1
Alok Kapali	4	0	12	0	-	-	-	-
Rajin Saleh	2	1	1	0	1	0	15	0

Fall of Wickets
1-126, 2-133, 3-134, 4-134, 5-250, 6-313, 7-313, 8-321, 9-326
1-66, 2-70, 3-208, 4-231, 5-290

BANGLADESH

	First Innings		Second Innings	
Hannan Sarkar	lbw b Clarke	28	c Read b Johnson	4
Javed Omar	c Vaughan b Johnson	2	c Read b Saggers	18
Habibul Bashar	c Butcher b Hoggard	18	run out	21
Rajin Saleh	c Read b Johnson	32	c Read b Clarke	9
Alok Kapali	c Butcher b Clarke	0	(6) c Saggers b Johnson	19
Mushfiqur Rahman	c Read b Saggers	28	(5) run out	6
*Khaled Mashud	c sub b Johnson	0	c Read b Johnson	15
Khaled Mahmud (capt)	c sub b Johnson	15	c Vaughan b Johnson	33
Mohammad Rafique	not out	12	c Read b Hoggard	0
Mashrafe Mortaza	b Johnson	1	absent hurt	
Enamul Haque jnr	c Hoggard b Saggers	9	(10) not out	1
Extras	lb 1, nb 6	7	b 4, lb 5, w 1, nb 2	12
	(62.1 overs)	152	(37.1 overs)	138

	First Innings				Second Innings			
	O	M	R	W	O	M	R	W
Hoggard	20	3	64	1	12	3	37	1
Johnson	21	6	49	5	12.1	1	44	4
Clarke	7	4	7	2	1	0	4	1
Saggers	12.1	3	29	2	7	1	33	1
Giles	2	1	2	0	5	1	11	0

Fall of Wickets
1-6, 2-44, 3-61, 4-63, 5-107, 6-110, 7-126, 8-138, 9-139
1-5, 2-33, 3-51, 4-58, 5-70, 6-91, 7-108, 8-126, 9-138

Umpires: Aleem Dar and EAR de Silva
Toss: Bangladesh
Test debut: MJ Saggers
Man of the Match: RL Johnson
Man of the Series: MJ Hoggard

England won by 329 runs

SERIES AVERAGES
Bangladesh v. England

BANGLADESH

Batting	M	Inns	NO	Runs	HS	Av	100	50	c/st
Mushfiqur Rahman	2	4	1	114	46*	38.00	-	-	1/-
Hannan Sarkar	2	4	0	111	59	27.75	-	1	1/-
Habibul Bashar	2	4	0	99	58	24.75	-	1	-/-
Khaled Mashud	2	4	0	73	51	18.25	-	1	7/1
Khaled Mahmud	2	4	0	70	33	17.50	-	-	1/-
Mohammad Rafique	2	4	1	45	32	15.00	-	-	1/-
Rajin Saleh	2	4	0	60	32	15.00	-	-	2/-
Alok Kapali	2	4	0	59	28	14.75	-	-	-/-
Javed Omar	2	4	0	50	27	12.50	-	-	-/-
Enamul Haque jnr	2	4	2	10	9	5.00	-	-	-/-
Mashrafe Mortaza	2	3	0	13	11	4.33	-	-	-/-

Bowling	Overs	Mds	Runs	Wkts	Av	Best	5/inn	10m
Mashrafe Mortaza	66	19	170	8	21.25	4-60	-	-
Mohammad Rafique	114.5	27	310	10	31.00	3-84	-	-
Mushfiqur Rahman	43.3	13	162	4	40.50	2-50	-	-
Enamul Haque jnr	67	17	201	4	50.25	2-53	-	-
Khaled Mahmud	57	19	169	1	169.00	1-46	-	-

Also bowled: Alok Kapali 7-1-16-0, Rajin Saleh 7-1-27-0.

ENGLAND

Batting	M	Inns	NO	Runs	HS	Av	100	50	c/st
MP Vaughan	2	4	1	208	81*	69.33	-	2	2/-
ME Trescothick	2	4	1	206	113	68.66	1	1	4/-
N Hussain	2	4	0	188	95	47.00	-	2	1/-
GP Thorpe	2	4	1	136	64	45.33	-	2	-/-
CMW Read	2	3	1	76	38*	38.00	-	-	10/-
R Clarke	2	3	0	96	55	32.00	-	1	1/-
GJ Batty	1	1	0	19	19	19.00	-	-	-/-
MA Butcher	2	4	0	56	42	14.00	-	-	3/-
AF Giles	2	2	0	25	19	12.50	-	-	-/-
RL Johnson	1	1	0	6	6	6.00	-	-	-/-
MJ Saggers	1	1	0	1	1	1.00	-	-	1/-
SJ Harmison	1	1	0	0	0	0.00	-	-	-/-
MJ Hoggard	2	2	2	6	6*	-	-	-	1/-

Bowling	Overs	Mds	Runs	Wkts	Av	Best	5/inn	10m
SJ Harmison	46.5	17	79	9	8.77	5-35	1	-
RL Johnson	33.1	7	93	9	10.33	5-49	1	-
R Clarke	29	11	60	4	15.00	2-7	-	-
MJ Saggers	19.1	4	62	3	20.66	2-29	-	-
MJ Hoggard	82	23	204	9	22.66	4-48	-	-
GJ Batty	41	8	108	2	54.00	1-43	-	-
AF Giles	39	7	112	1	112.00	1-52	-	-

Andrew Flintoff blasted half-centuries in each of England's one-day internationals in Bangladesh.

making 52 from only 39 balls. When Bangladesh had slipped to 103 for 6, another low total seemed inevitable, but the tail all contributed to set England 183 to win. Trescothick scored 50 from 70 balls, but it was Flintoff's powerful hitting that provided the only entertainment of the day. For him, at least, the series was a triumph – best emphasised by his amazing batting statistics: 177 runs from only 138 balls. In striking ten sixes and 22 fours, all but 29 of those runs came in boundaries.

BANGLADESH REPORT
By Qamar Ahmed

If Bangladesh's victory by 83 runs in a one-day international at Harare and their drawn Test against the West Indies on their first tour of the Caribbean is taken into consideration, then surely Bangladesh, though still bottom of the ICC

rankings table, did show some kind of progress in both forms of the world game.

On an individual level, there were also a number of encouraging performances by both batsmen and bowlers. Again, this has done a lot to boost morale, and that they were able to take up the challenge against some formidable opposition during the last year was itself an example of the benefit of added experience.

At home in their first series against England, they lost both the Test matches and the three-match one-day series, but they did put up a brave fight, despite circumstances beyond their own control. In particular, a general lack of depth in experience saw them disintegrate in pressure situations.

In the first Test at Dhaka, for instance, Bangladesh hung on until the fifth and final day before conceding the match by seven wickets. Skipper Khaled Mahmud impressed with 51 in the first innings and, second time around, the Bangladeshis reached a comfortable 248 for 6 at one point before losing their last four wickets in quick succession to leave England requiring just 164 to win.

Captain Khaled Mahmud was sacked after their disappointing performances against England.

Hannan Sarkar and Habibul Bashar both hit excellent half-centuries in this second innings, and the way they resisted against both Matthew Hoggard and Steve Harmison demonstrated both their technical ability and their fighting qualities.

The first Test defeat was Bangladesh's 24th in 25 Tests, and their effort fell away with a further loss in the second Test at Chittagong. Following defeats in each of the three one-day internationals against England, Khaled Mahmud was sacked from the captaincy and was even dropped from the team to tour Zimbabwe and the West Indies. Disgusted, he announced his retirement before, 48 hours later, reversing his decision.

In Zimbabwe, Bangladesh lost the first Test in Harare by 183 runs after being on the wrong end of a hat-trick by pace bowler Andy Blignaut. His victims were Hannan Sarkar, Mohammad Ashraful and Mushfiqur Rahman, and Bangladesh – left to make 353 runs to win – slumped from an already-perilous 14 for 2 to 14 for 5. They eventually managed to reach 169, with Khaled Mashud and Rajin Saleh scoring 61 and 47 respectively.

Mohammad Ashraful was one of Andy Blignaut's hat-trick victims in Harare after scoring 98 in the first innings.

This Test was also notable for Heath Streak reaching the 200-wicket milestone and, for Bangladesh, Ashraful batting beautifully to reach 98 in a first-innings total of 331. It would have been his second Test century.

The first, second and fourth days were washed out in Bulawayo, consigning the second Test to a watery draw. Only three hours of play were possible on the third day, too, and Zimbabwe's first innings of 210 was held together by an unbeaten 103 from Stuart Carlisle, who hit nine fours and a six.

In the one-day series against Zimbabwe, the first two matches were abandoned due to rain before Bangladesh won the third. Zimbabwe then won the last two matches without much fuss to take the series 2–1.

On their first tour to the West Indies, the Bangladeshis failed to impress in the one-day matches but did spring a surprise by holding the West Indians to a draw in the first Test at St Lucia.

They punished the West Indian bowling to post 416 in their first innings, their highest total in Tests, and then earned a lead of 64 by bowling the hosts out for 352 in reply. A century each by Habibul Bashar (113) and Mohammad Rafique (111), who hit 11 fours and three sixes, and a fine 81 by Ashraful were the features of their big score. The bowling of Mushfiqur Rahman (4 for 65) and left-arm spinner Rafique also impressed.

Bangladesh even managed to declare their second innings at 271 for 9 after having been, at one stage, 79 for 6. Khaled Mashud made his maiden Test hundred and the West Indies, left to make 336, could only accumulate 113 without loss in the time available.

The tourists, however, failed to carry on from where they had left off in St Lucia and lost the second Test at Sabina Park in Jamaica by an innings and 99 runs. Bashar's 77 was the only Bangladeshi performance of note as the West Indies batsmen ran riot against the visiting bowlers.

In the Asia Cup, in Sri Lanka, they enjoyed success against Hong Kong, by 116 runs, but lost to Pakistan by 76 runs.

In the domestic first-class tournament, Dhaka Division won the National Cricket League by defeating Sylhat Division in the final. In the one-day League, Chittagong emerged as champions by defeating Rajshahi in the final. During the first-class matches, Nuruzzaman of Rajshahi made 633 runs at an average of 48.69 and Faisal Hussain of Chittagong 611 at 40.73. Saifullah Khan of Rajshahi was the most successful bowler, taking 63 wickets at 16.33.

SRI LANKA

ENGLAND IN SRI LANKA

ENGLAND IN SRI LANKA
By Jonathan Agnew

ONE-DAY INTERNATIONALS

Match One
18 November 2003 at Dambulla
England 88 (46.1 overs)
Sri Lanka 89 for 0 (13.5 overs)
Sri Lanka won by 10 wickets

Match Two
21 November 2003 at Colombo (RPS)
Sri Lanka v. England
Match abandoned – no result

Match Three
23 November 2003 at Colombo (RPS)
Sri Lanka v. England
Match abandoned – no result

The three-match series of one-day internationals which preceded the Tests was all but destroyed by rain. Only one game survived and, played in Dambulla, it was one of the most one-sided games ever played at this level.

Having decided to bat first, England were bowled out for a miserable 88. To make matters worse for spectators, viewers and commentators alike, those precious few runs were eked out over 46.1 overs! It really was a dreadful spectacle.

Only two batsmen reached double figures as Vaas and Dinusha Fernando took the early wickets and condemned England to 45 for 7: Collingwood – who faced 96 balls for his 31 and Giles, who scored an obdurate 21 batting at No. 9. Just four boundaries were hit in the entire innings – England's lowest-ever total in one-day internationals.

If it were possible for it to get any worse, Sri Lanka's openers, Jayasuriya and Kaluwitharana then knocked off their target in less than 14 overs! It was a ghastly experience for England, who were probably grateful for the fact that monsoon-like

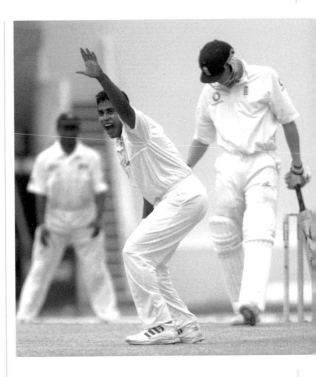

Chaminda Vaas appeals as Sri Lanka steamroller England at Dambulla.

rain then battered Colombo for the following week, to spare them even the remotest possibility of it happening again.

FIRST TEST
2–6 December 2003 at Galle

Three years after recording their memorable 2–1 victory on Sri Lankan soil, England returned knowing that the hosts were determined for revenge. At least Michael Vaughan's team arrived having enjoyed a build-up in Bangladesh that, while hardly being taxing, had, at least, prepared them for the slow pitches and some of the heat they might expect in Sri Lanka.

Hashan Tillekeratne had deposed Sanath Jayasuriya as captain since England's previous visit and, after four matches in his second stint at the helm, his team was still looking for a win. It would seem that, in Muttiah Muralitharan, Tillekeratne held the trump card, and although Murali had developed an extraordinary delivery, which, in spinning away from the bat with an apparently orthodox off-spinner's action, was a real threat, there were already murmurs about the legality of the delivery called the 'doosra'. In fact the ICC referee, Chris Broad, reported Murali's action during the series against Australia, which followed England's tour.

Galle – the venue for the first Test – has long been one of Murali's happier hunting grounds. In his eight Tests there, the spinner had already taken 60 wickets at an average of only 15 runs apiece. Only in Kandy had he taken more – 64 – but these were taken in two more matches.

Galle is a pretty cricket field, and the pitch would take spin – no doubt about it. When Tillekeratne won the toss and elected to bat first, Vaughan's heart must have sunk. What followed, however, was such uncharacteristically lacklustre batting that one had to check that Sri Lanka really were at the crease.

Is it the 'doosra'? Muttiah Muralitharan spins his latest web.

FIRST TEST – SRI LANKA v. ENGLAND
2–6 December 2003 at Galle

SRI LANKA

	First Innings		Second Innings	
MS Atapattu	c Read b Flintoff	29	st Read b Batty	35
ST Jayasuriya	c Collingwood b Giles	48	c Trescothick b Giles	17
*KC Sangakkara	lbw b Johnson	71	run out	19
DPMD Jayawardene	c Collingwood b Giles	17	not out	86
HP Tillekeratne (capt)	c Read b Giles	0	lbw b Batty	1
TT Samaraweera	c Read b Flintoff	45	c Trescothick b Giles	1
UDU Chandana	lbw b Giles	21	(8) lbw b Giles	19
HDPK Dharmasena	lbw b Batty	27	(9) lbw b Hoggard	2
WPUJC Vaas	not out	22	(7) c Collingwood b Giles	19
KADM Fernando	c Collingwood b Batty	4	c Trescothick b Flintoff	1
M Muralitharan	c Read b Giles	38	c Collingwood b Batty	13
Extras	b 5, lb 2, w 1, nb 1	9	b 4, lb 9	13
	(127.5 overs)	331	(99 overs)	226

	First Innings				Second Innings			
	O	M	R	W	O	M	R	W
Hoggard	20	4	49	0	9	2	33	1
Johnson	17	5	54	1	7	2	28	0
Flintoff	23	7	42	3	17	5	32	1
Collingwood	4	0	12	0	-	-	-	-
Batty	31	5	98	2	23.2	7	55	3
Giles	32.5	9	69	4	40	14	63	4
Vaughan	-	-	-	-	1	0	2	0

Fall of Wickets
1-76, 2-88, 3-132, 4-132, 5-202, 6-238, 7-239, 8-279, 9-291
1-26, 2-72, 3-72, 4-78, 5-85, 6-123, 7-163, 8-179, 9-180

ENGLAND

	First Innings		Second Innings	
ME Trescothick	c Sangakkara b Muralitharan	23	b Jayasuriya	24
MP Vaughan (capt)	b Muralitharan	24	c Tillekeratne b Fernando	8
MA Butcher	c Sangakkara b Jayasuriya	51	c Sangakkara b Vaas	54
GP Thorpe	lbw b Vaas	43	c Vaas b Muralitharan	10
PD Collingwood	c Jayasuriya b Muralitharan	1	c Tillekeratne b Dharmasena	36
A Flintoff	lbw b Muralitharan	1	c Tillekeratne b Vaas	0
*CMW Read	c Tillekeratne b Muralitharan	0	c Jayawardene b Muralitharan	14
GJ Batty	c Jayasuriya b Dharmasena	14	b Muralitharan	26
AF Giles	c Atapattu b Muralitharan	18	not out	17
RL Johnson	c Atapattu b Muralitharan	26	b Muralitharan	3
MJ Hoggard	not out	6	not out	0
Extras	b 12, lb 8, nb 8	28	b 10, lb 1, nb 7	18
	(100.4 overs)	235	(9 wkts 108 overs)	210

	First Innings				Second Innings			
	O	M	R	W	O	M	R	W
Vaas	12	2	25	1	14	4	23	2
Fernando	3	1	21	0	4	0	29	1
Dharmasena	24	6	55	1	18	8	36	1
Muralitharan	31.4	15	46	7	37	18	47	4
Chandana	13	2	24	0	11	2	24	0
Jayasuriya	17	2	44	1	21	5	31	1
Samaraweera	-	-	-	-	3	1	9	0

Fall of Wickets
1-56, 2-67, 3-142, 4-143, 5-151, 6-155, 7-177, 8-183, 9-208
1-16, 2-62, 3-73, 4-125, 5-125, 6-148, 7-170, 8-204, 9-208

Umpires: DJ Harper and S Venkataraghavan
Toss: Sri Lanka
Test debuts: PD Collingwood, KADM Fernando
Man of the Match: M Muralitharan

<u>Match drawn</u>

Ashley Giles: five-wicket haul in Kandy.

Jayasuriya, in particular, looked completely out of sorts and the only possible explanation was that the arrival of John Dyson as Sri Lanka's new and completely unknown coach had put the players on the defensive. After 57 overs, Sri Lanka had crawled to 132 for 4, with Giles claiming three wickets. Jayasuriya's 48 came from 110 balls, while Atapattu was even more subdued – 29 from 99 – before aiming to pull Flintoff and gloving a catch to Read.

The first delivery with the second new ball accounted for Sangakkara, whose 71 was the highest score of the innings, and at the end of the first day, Sri Lanka were 240 for 7, and extremely disappointed.

Sri Lanka were always capable of posting a decent score while Vaas remained at the crease, but he joined the others in batting with remarkable

restraint for more than two hours. He finished on 22 not out but, not for the first time, Murali's wild, but effective, slogging at No. 11 frustrated the bowlers and produced the most entertaining batting of the innings. He thrashed 38 from only 37 balls to take his team from 291 for 9 to 331 all out, while Giles' figures of 4 for 69 were his best for a year. By the end of the day, the game was well poised with Muralitharan having removed both openers, Vaughan and Trescothick, for 24 and 23 respectively. Butcher and Thorpe battled away in poor light to take England to within 228, and although they extended their partnership to 75 the next morning, Murali ripped his way through the lower order as England lost their last seven wickets for just 83 runs. Muralitharan finished with figures of 7 for 46 and, in this form, and with a lead of 96, a Sri Lankan victory seemed all but inevitable.

Again, however, Sri Lanka's batsmen seemed all at sea. Needing to do no more than consolidate their position, they gifted England three needless wickets while Trescothick took two excellent catches at slip off Giles. The last of these – Samaraweera – left Sri Lanka floundering on 85 for 5 but, after a barren spell, it was now time for Jayawardene to come good. He completed only his third half-century in 18 months and, in all, batted for more than five hours for his 86 not out. Chandana weighed in with 19 and Murali 13, which enabled Sri Lanka to hobble to 226 all out at tea on the fourth afternoon, setting England an unlikely 323 to win. It did mean, though, that Tillekeratne would not be able to be particularly attacking with his field placings in England's final innings.

Meanwhile, the rain that had so blighted the one-day series returned to the south-west and England faced only one over, leaving them with a fighting chance of saving the game.

By lunch on the final day, England had lost three wickets – Vaughan for eight, Trescothick 24 and Thorpe for ten. Butcher remained on 30, but with Collingwood already at the crease, the odds still strongly favoured Sri Lanka. Four more wickets fell in the following session, including Butcher for 54, his second half-century of the match. The weather was closing in, however, and one could sense Sri Lanka's nervousness.

As the light deteriorated, Giles' defence became increasingly determined. He lost Batty 45 minutes after tea playing a dreadful slog-sweep at Muralitharan having resisted for 70 balls. Johnson defended a further 35 deliveries before Murali bowled him for three, but as dark clouds hung around the ground, the umpires finally offered the light to a grateful Giles who, having blocked heroically for 111 balls, sped to the pavilion where, having survived for 108 overs in extremely difficult conditions, England celebrated their moral victory.

SECOND TEST
10–14 December 2003 at Kandy

A valiant rearguard action was the order of the day in the following Test in Kandy. This time, England even managed to surpass their last-innings defence in Galle: once again Sri Lanka could not bowl them out for a second time, on this occasion in 140 overs.

The game followed a familiar pattern to the first Test. Sri Lanka won the toss again and, not surprisingly, chose to bat. Again, the top order seemed surprisingly tentative against an England team that had replaced a bowler with a batsman – Nasser Hussain, who had missed the opening match through illness. This gave England an attack comprising Kirtley (who had replaced Hoggard), Flintoff and Collingwood, with Giles and Batty providing the spin. At 84 for 3, Sri Lanka had already lost Atapattu for 11, Sangakkara for 34 and Jayasuriya for a patient 32. However, Jayawardene's confidence had clearly received a welcome boost at Galle, and he now teamed up with the promising youngster, Tillekeratne Dilshan, to add 103 for the fourth wicket.

When three wickets fell for 19 runs – including Jayawardene for 45 and Dilshan for 63, it seemed as though England's depleted attack might dismiss Sri Lanka cheaply after all, but Tillekeratne played a typically obdurate, largely strokeless innings of 45 from 115 balls and the tail rallied around him. Vaas' 32 contained six fours, and was far more in character than his innings in the first Test had been, Dharmasena's 29 ended when he became Giles' fifth victim and while Murali again made hay with 19 from 22 balls, Dinusha Fernando completed a patient and highly valuable half-century. Muralitharan later complained to the match referee that Hussain had verbally abused him as he walked out to bat. Lloyd took no action, and the fact that Sri Lanka's last four wickets had added 176 runs made their total of 382 respectable indeed.

At 89 for no wicket, however, England had made the perfect reply. Batting was not easy, and Murali – on his home ground – seemed to expect a wicket with every ball. Finally, Trescothick was caught at bat and pad on the stroke of tea for 36, and that sparked a collapse of four wickets for 30.

SECOND TEST – SRI LANKA v. ENGLAND
10–14 December 2003 at Kandy

SRI LANKA

	First Innings		Second Innings	
MS Atapattu	lbw b Kirtley	11	lbw b Giles	8
ST Jayasuriya	c Read b Giles	32	b Kirtley	27
*KC Sangakkara	run out	34	c Collingwood b Giles	10
DPMD Jayawardene	c Kirtley b Giles	45	b Flintoff	52
TM Dilshan	c Trescothick b Flintoff	63	st Read b Batty	100
HP Tillekeratne (capt)	c Butcher b Flintoff	45	c Thorpe b Giles	20
TT Samaraweera	lbw b Giles	3	not out	23
WPUJC Vaas	lbw b Kirtley	32	c Vaughan b Kirtley	20
HDPK Dharmasena	lbw b Giles	29	not out	7
KADM Fernando	not out	51		
M Muralitharan	b Giles	19		
Extras	b 1, lb 15, nb 2	18	lb 6, w 1, nb 5	12
	(126.4 overs)	382	(7 wkts dec 71 overs)	279

	First Innings				Second Innings			
	O	M	R	W	O	M	R	W
Kirtley	33	10	109	2	17	4	62	2
Flintoff	24	5	60	2	15	3	40	1
Giles	37.4	7	116	5	22	3	101	3
Collingwood	9	3	13	0	3	0	12	0
Batty	18	3	59	0	11	1	47	1
Vaughan	5	0	9	0	3	0	11	0

Fall of Wickets
1-20, 2-76, 3-84, 4-187, 5-201, 6-206, 7-270, 8-278, 9-354
1-33, 2-41, 3-53, 4-206, 5-212, 6-243, 7-272

ENGLAND

	First Innings		Second Innings	
ME Trescothick	c Dilshan b Muralitharan	36	c Jayawardene b Vaas	14
MP Vaughan (capt)	c Jayawardene b Muralitharan	52	c Dilshan b Muralitharan	105
MA Butcher	st Sangakkara b Dharmasena	4	st Sangakkara b Muralitharan	6
N Hussain	lbw b Vaas	10	c Sangakkara b Vaas	17
GP Thorpe	lbw b Muralitharan	57	c Sangakkara b Muralitharan	41
PD Collingwood	c Sangakkara b Vaas	28	c Jayawardene b Dharmasena	24
A Flintoff	b Muralitharan	16	lbw b Muralitharan	19
*CMW Read	lbw b Jayasuriya	0	not out	18
GJ Batty	c Dilshan b Vaas	38	not out	25
AF Giles	c Jayawardene b Vaas	16		
RJ Kirtley	not out	3		
Extras	b 16, lb 10, nb 8	34	b 5, lb 6, nb 5	16
	(114.2 overs)	294	(7 wkts 140 overs)	285

	First Innings				Second Innings			
	O	M	R	W	O	M	R	W
Vaas	24.2	4	77	4	29	7	59	2
Fernando	7	0	36	0	7	1	21	0
Dharmasena	19	3	63	1	26	2	74	1
Muralitharan	40	18	60	4	56	28	64	4
Jayasuriya	24	6	32	1	17	2	45	0
Tillekeratne	-	-	-	-	1	0	1	0
Samaraweera	-	-	-	-	1	1	0	0
Dilshan	-	-	-	-	3	1	10	0

Fall of Wickets
1-89, 2-100, 3-119, 4-119, 5-177, 6-202, 7-205, 8-256, 9-279
1-24, 2-50, 3-90, 4-167, 5-208, 6-233, 7-239

Umpires: Aleem Dar and DJ Harper
Toss: Sri Lanka
Man of the Match: MP Vaughan

Match drawn

The promising Tillekeratne Dilshan sweeps on his way to a second Test century. It helped to set up a second-innings Sri Lankan declaration.

Collingwood had batted with great character in Galle, and the main reason for England fielding such a weak attack was based on the desire to accommodate both the Durham all-rounder and the fit-again Hussain. The northerner gritted his teeth once again to lift the score to 177 for 5 – he edged Vaas behind for 28 – and, as Thorpe continued the fightback, Batty, with 38, and Giles (16) all weighed in. Thorpe's determined 57 came from 198 balls, and when Batty eventually succumbed to Vaas, England were all out for 294, giving Sri Lanka an 88-run advantage – only eight fewer than at Galle.

Bad light brought a premature close to the third day, but Tillekeratne's men consolidated their position on the fourth. Dilshan reached his second Test century after Kirtley had bowled Jayasuriya in the third over of the morning for 27, and Sri Lanka were 53 for 3 when Sangakkara was caught at short leg by Collingwood for ten. Any hopes England had of dismissing the home team cheaply, however, were snuffed out by Jayawardene and Dilshan, who took the score to 206, and after Dilshan's dismissal – stumped off Batty for 100,

Tillekeratne and Vaas both scored quick 20s to set up the declaration at tea.

The target of 368 to win was never remotely achievable but, galvanised by their fighting draw at Kandy, England knew they had an outside chance of saving the game if good fortune was with them. By the time bad light again descended to end play early, the tourists had already lost two key wickets – Trescothick loosely carved a catch to point for 14, and Butcher was stumped off Murali for six.

So the final day dawned with England needing to bat through to the close to save the game, and this was the moment Michael Vaughan chose to bury speculation that the captaincy had adversely affected his batting. Showing immense power of concentration, Vaughan batted for six-and-a-half hours for his 105 – his first century since becoming England captain – and although he fell to Murali, Batty and Read hung on for the last hour and a half to save the game.

Despite the friendly conditions, Muralitharan was again unable to dismiss England, taking just four wickets in 56 overs, although part of the

Michael Vaughan drives during his valiant hundred in Kandy.

blame for this must be heaped on Tillekeratne's shoulders for setting bewilderingly defensive fields when it was clear that England could not possibly win the game. The fact is that Sri Lanka had 140 overs in which to bowl England out, and they failed to do so for the second time. The locals were becoming increasingly restless.

THIRD TEST
18–21 December 2003 at Colombo

Although England had battled magnificently against the odds to save the Tests at Galle and Kandy, there was still the feeling of inevitability about the fate of the series. It was, however, in the hands of the Sri Lankans because the odd – and certainly rudderless – attitude of the team had contributed greatly to their failure to capitalise on their strong positions in both matches.

Tillekeratne's confidence as a leader seemed to be ebbing away in every session of play, and since he was hardly the most robust of captains at the start of

THIRD TEST – SRI LANKA v. ENGLAND
18–21 December 2003 at Colombo (SSC)

ENGLAND

	First Innings		Second Innings	
ME Trescothick	c Jayawardene b Muralitharan	70	c sub b Vaas	0
MP Vaughan (capt)	c Jayawardene b Chandana	18	c Jayasuriya b Fernando	14
MA Butcher	c Sangakkara b Fernando	23	b Jayasuriya	37
N Hussain	lbw b Vaas	8	c Sangakkara b Muralitharan	11
GP Thorpe	lbw b Muralitharan	13	st Sangakkara b Muralitharan	19
A Flintoff	c & b Muralitharan	77	(7) c Sangakkara b Fernando	30
GJ Batty	c Atapattu b Chandana	14	(6) st Sangakkara b Muralitharan	0
*CMW Read	not out	17	lbw b Jayasuriya	0
AF Giles	run out	10	b Fernando	13
RJ Kirtley	lbw b Vaas	1	b Muralitharan	12
JM Anderson	lbw b Vaas	1	not out	1
Extras	b 4, lb 8, nb 1	13	b 2, lb 8, nb 1	11
	(101 overs)	265	(68 overs)	148

	First Innings				Second Innings			
	O	M	R	W	O	M	R	W
Vaas	17	5	64	3	7	2	25	1
Fernando	12	3	55	1	12	4	27	3
Samaraweera	4	1	11	0	-	-	-	-
Chandana	26	7	82	2	13	7	18	0
Muralitharan	40	21	40	3	27	9	63	4
Jayasuriya	2	1	1	0	9	6	5	2

Fall of Wickets
1-78, 2-108, 3-114, 4-135, 5-139, 6-226, 7-236, 8-258, 9-259
1-0, 2-22, 3-44, 4-82, 5-82, 6-84, 7-84, 8-124, 9-137

SRI LANKA

	First Innings	
*KC Sangakkara	c Trescothick b Kirtley	31
ST Jayasuriya	c Trescothick b Flintoff	85
TT Samaraweera	run out	142
DPMD Jayawardene	c sub b Flintoff	134
TM Dilshan	b Giles	83
HP Tillekeratne (capt)	b Giles	12
UDU Chandana	c Vaughan b Kirtley	76
WPUJC Vaas	run out	9
M Muralitharan	not out	21
CRD Fernando	not out	1
MS Atapattu		
Extras	b 7, lb 16, w 5, nb 6	34
	(8 wkts dec 182 overs)	628

	First Innings			
	O	M	R	W
Kirtley	31	4	131	2
Anderson	24	5	85	0
Flintoff	18	0	47	2
Giles	65	16	190	2
Batty	41	4	137	0
Vaughan	1	0	5	0
Trescothick	2	0	10	0

Fall of Wickets
1-71, 2-138, 3-400, 4-428, 5-456, 6-582, 7-605, 8-606

Umpires: Aleem Dar and SA Bucknor
Toss: England
Man of the Match: TT Samaraweera
Man of the Series: M Muralitharan

Sri Lanka won by an innings and 215 runs

A forceful 142 by Thilan Samaraweera led the way for
Sri Lanka in the third Test ...

the series, he was now utterly devoid of any spirit of
adventure. He needed a victory – and the country as
a whole felt very much the same way.

It was at Colombo on England's last tour here
three years previously that Hussain's team won a
famous – and highly improbable – victory that
secured the series. By the end of the first day,
however, it was clear that Vaughan's men would be
up against it. After a good start – in which England
were 108 for 1 shortly before lunch – the Sri
Lankans struck back in the afternoon, removing
Butcher for 23, Hussain for eight and Thorpe for 13.
Much depended on Flintoff, and he responded not
only typically, but also responsibly, by scoring 77
from 109 balls. Four sixes had the spectators taking
cover, but after a stand of 87 with Gareth Batty, who
made only 14 from 101 balls, Flintoff succumbed to
Muralitharan and, next morning, Vaas polished off
the tail for a total of 265: it was not enough.

Sri Lanka were without the injured Atapattu, who
had damaged a finger in the field, but he was not

... and Mahela Jayawardene joined Samaraweera in a third-
wicket stand of 262.

missed. Samaraweera led the way, and although he
was dropped three times by Trescothick in the slips
– twice off the unlucky Flintoff – his 142 was
precisely the cornerstone his team required to build
a huge total. The resurgent Jayawardene made a
fluent 134, Dilshan 83 and Chandana 76 as they
piled on the runs, while the ineffectiveness of
England's spin attack was highlighted once again. In
a combined total of 106 overs, Giles and Batty took
just 2 for 327 between them, and when the
declaration finally came at 628 for 8, Sri Lanka's
lead was a mighty 363 and England would be
required to survive for a minimum of 168 overs.

In fact, they lasted only 68, slumping at one stage
to 84 for 7 from which there was no return. Murali
led the way with four wickets, to give him a series
tally of 26 at an average of 12.3, but the openers –
Vaughan and Trescothick – both fell to unnecessarily
cavalier strokes to the pace bowlers, and were both
dismissed by the eighth over of the innings.

Butcher scored 37 in dogged fashion, and Flintoff
weighed in with 30 in what had become a hopeless
cause. Having fought so hard for their draws in
Galle and Kandy, this was a sorrowful effort, but the
heat and humidity of this part of the world tends to
make three back-to-back matches as much of a test
of endurance as of skill.

SERIES AVERAGES
Sri Lanka v. England

SRI LANKA

Batting	M	Inns	NO	Runs	HS	Av	100	50	c/st
DPMD Jayawardene	3	5	1	334	134	83.50	1	2	7/-
TM Dilshan	2	3	0	246	100	82.00	1	2	3/-
TT Samaraweera	3	5	1	214	142	53.50	1	-	-/-
ST Jayasuriya	3	5	0	209	85	41.80	-	1	3/-
UDU Chandana	2	3	0	116	76	38.66	-	1	-/-
KC Sangakkara	3	5	0	165	71	33.00	-	1	9/4
M Muralitharan	3	4	1	91	38	30.33	-	-	1/-
KADM Fernando	2	3	1	56	51*	28.00	-	1	-/-
WPUJC Vaas	3	5	1	102	32	25.50	-	-	1/-
HDPK Dharmasena	2	4	1	65	29	21.66	-	-	-/-
MS Atapattu	3	4	0	83	35	20.75	-	-	3/-
HP Tillekeratne	3	5	0	78	45	15.60	-	-	4/-
CRD Fernando	1	1	1	1	1*	-	-	-	-/-

Bowling	Overs	Mds	Runs	Wkts	Av	Best	5/inn	10m
M Muralitharan	231.4	109	320	26	12.30	7-46	1	1
CRD Fernando	24	7	82	4	20.50	3-27	-	-
WPUJC Vaas	103.2	24	273	13	21.00	4-77	-	-
ST Jayasuriya	90	22	158	5	31.60	2-5	-	-
HDPK Dharmasena	87	19	228	4	57.00	1-36	-	-
UDU Chandana	63	18	148	2	74.00	2-82	-	-
KADM Fernando	21	2	107	1	107.00	1-29	-	-

Also bowled: HP Tillekeratne 1-0-1-0, TM Dilshan 3-1-10-0, TT Samaraweera 8-3-20-0

ENGLAND

Batting	M	Inns	NO	Runs	HS	Av	100	50	c/st
MP Vaughan	3	6	0	221	105	36.83	1	1	2/-
GP Thorpe	3	6	0	183	57	30.50	-	1	1/-
MA Butcher	3	6	0	175	54	29.16	-	2	1/-
ME Trescothick	3	6	0	167	70	27.83	-	1	6/-
A Flintoff	3	6	0	143	77	23.83	-	1	-/-
GJ Batty	3	6	1	117	38	23.40	-	-	-/-
PD Collingwood	2	4	0	89	36	22.25	-	-	6/-
AF Giles	3	5	1	74	18	18.50	-	-	-/-
RL Johnson	1	2	0	29	26	14.50	-	-	-/-
CMW Read	3	6	2	49	18*	12.25	-	-	5/2
N Hussain	2	4	0	46	17	11.50	-	-	-/-
RJ Kirtley	2	3	1	16	12	8.00	-	-	1/-
JM Anderson	1	2	1	2	1*	2.00	-	-	-/-
MJ Hoggard	1	2	2	6	6*	-	-	-	-/-

Bowling	Overs	Mds	Runs	Wkts	Av	Best	5/inn	10m
A Flintoff	97	20	221	9	24.55	3-42	-	-
AF Giles	197.3	49	539	18	29.94	5-116	1	-
RJ Kirtley	81	18	302	6	50.33	2-62	-	-
GJ Batty	124.2	20	396	6	66.00	3-55	-	-
MJ Hoggard	29	6	82	1	82.00	1-33	-	-
RL Johnson	24	7	82	1	82.00	1-54	-	-

Also bowled: ME Trescothick 2-0-10-0, MP Vaughan 10-0-27-0, PD Collingwood 16-3-37-0, JM Anderson 24-5-85-0

After a difficult year Sri Lanka are hoping for a more disciplined approach under the strong leadership of new captain Marvan Atapattu.

SRI LANKA REPORT
By Charlie Austin

Sri Lanka started the year afresh, with a new Cricket Board, a new coach, Australia's John Dyson, a new physiotherapist and a new fitness trainer. It was a difficult but progressive year, both on and especially off the field, as the Cricket Board lost credibility after its president, Thilanga Sumathipala, was remanded in police custody for several months having become embroiled in an immigration scandal.

By the end of the year, however, despite failure in the ICC Champions Trophy, Sri Lankan cricket emerged stronger and with renewed optimism, as the team were unified and confident under the strong leadership of Marvan Atapattu, and the Board were financially secure with a record broadcasting and sponsorship deal in the pipeline.

Dyson, a surprise choice having had no top-flight coaching experience, started his 18-month contract

in September 2003 as Sri Lanka's cricketers enjoyed a much-needed three-month break.

His first assignment was England's tour in November and December. Hashan Tillekeratne, another eyebrow-raising selection, was retained as Test captain and Sri Lanka started the year well, dominating a rain-marred one-day series and attritional Test series 1–0. England, missing Steve Harmison and handicapped by other injuries, fought hard but were unable to replicate their success against Muttiah Muralitharan in 2001, leaving him to finish the series with 26 wickets at 12.30.

England's batsmen were initially confident of repelling Muralitharan, but the off spinner had been revitalised after the short break. The time off had also given him the chance to polish up his doosra, a wicked (and later controversial) wrong'un that he flipped out of the back of his hand to devastating effect.

England's batsmen, even Graham Thorpe who had frustrated him in 2001, were unable to predict

Newly appointed Aravinda de Silva brought in radical changes to strengthen Sri Lankan cricket.

consistently which way the ball would spin and they faced a constant struggle for survival. However, when Muralitharan grew fatigued, they mounted some resistance and, helped by some bizarrely negative captaincy throughout the series from Tillekeratne, were able to escape with draws in both Galle and Kandy.

Sri Lanka's next tour was Australia in February and the focus switched to matters off the field. The Board had appointed Aravinda de Silva to look over cricket affairs and he introduced several radical changes.

His first success was the announcement of an intensive schedule for the A team, with 13 tours pencilled in over the coming three years. With domestic cricket still weak and unprofessional, the A team was identified as a crucial finishing school for bright new talent before their elevation to the senior team.

This was followed by the announcement of a new centrally organised provincial tournament, which was also designed to raise standards with the best 75 players in the country spilt into five squads. The tournament suffered some teething problems, but was generally considered to be a resounding success, exposing the cream of the island's domestic cricketers to a stiffer level of competition.

The Board was having less success in other areas, however. A renaming of it, from the unwieldy 'Board of Control for Cricket in Sri Lanka' to 'Sri Lanka Cricket', progressed smoothly enough, but the new brand was dealt a massive blow when Sumathipala was arrested and charged with helping an accused contract murderer to travel to England to watch the 1999 World Cup on a false passport.

Police raids and a constant stream of negative media publicity ensued and the Board's image was shattered. When television rights were offered up for sale in February 2004 for a three-year period, broadcasters steered clear and the rights were eventually sold off on a cut-price tour-by-tour basis. Also facing a potentially crippling court action in Singapore after the cancellation of an earlier television contract with WSG Nimbus in 2001, the administration was facing a financial crisis.

When Australia's cricketers arrived in February, the spotlight turned back to the cricket, much to the relief of the administrators. The tour kicked off with a five-match one-day series that set the tone for the Tests that followed, with Australia's greater self-confidence and mental resilience being the key difference between the two sides during crucial high-pressure phases.

Australia won 3–2 and, worryingly for Sri Lanka, appeared comfortable against Muralitharan, who they claimed they could read like a book. Muralitharan was still a handful in the three Tests, picking up 28 wickets at 23.17, but he was forced to toil for 70 overs per game and could not stop Australia's batsmen from piling up match-winning totals.

Sri Lanka fought hard and in each of the three games they had their noses ahead at the midway stage, but were unable to ram home the advantage of first-innings leads, despite the deteriorating nature of the pitches.

They came agonisingly close to a memorable win in Kandy, as Sanath Jayasuriya clicked into hurricane mode and smashed a glorious 131, but their nerve evaporated on the final morning and they collapsed dramatically.

It summed up the series, and when Australia won again in Colombo to seal a whitewash – the first ever against Sri Lanka at home – it prompted a serious bout of soul-searching and hard-nosed self-assessment from within the team. Ironically, the defeat proved a turning point as the bitter truth sank in: they had been the masters of their own downfall.

The defeat also signalled the end of Tillekeratne's tenure. An intolerably defensive leader, he had been unable to capture the full respect of his players or to inspire confidence within them. When he announced his resignation minutes after the final defeat, it was neither unexpected nor unwanted in either the dressing room or the media box.

But Tillekeratne's exit, eventually into obscurity after being overlooked for the next tour, was overshadowed by the almost-simultaneous announcement by Chris Broad, the ICC's match referee, that he believed Muralitharan's action when bowling the doosra to be suspect.

Broad's decision was greeted with predictable anger and outrage at home, but biomechanical tests at the University of Western Australia revealed that his arm did straighten when bowling the delivery, by 15 degrees at the outset and by ten degrees after remedial action, which was double the permissible level of bending allowed under the ICC's recently introduced 'levels of tolerance'.

Although the scientists argued that the tolerance levels for spinners needed to be reviewed and that the doosra should be permitted until the completion of further research, Muralitharan was advised not to bowl the delivery by the Sri Lanka Board when it became clear that he could face a possible ICC ban. The saga threw a cloud over a year in which he finally broke Courtney Walsh's 519-wicket world Test record.

Sri Lanka's next assignment was against a third-rate Zimbabwe side ravaged by the rebel player dispute with the Zimbabwe Cricket Union. Despite the political and racially-tinged turmoil, there was never any doubt about the tour going ahead.

The Cricket Board ruled out cancellation for any reason other than security and the only discussion on morality revolved around the rights and wrongs of the ICC's treatment of Muralitharan's doosra. As Sri Lanka coasted to a predictable one-day and Test whitewash, however, important changes were taking place behind the scenes.

Marvan Atapattu had been appointed captain and he soon marked out a new direction and approach with Dyson. Their main priority was the fostering of greater team unity and a stronger team spirit. That was followed by the adoption of a new mental approach.

Instead of being focused on results, which during the Tillekeratne tenure had contributed to dangerous anxiety and timidity at key stages, Atapattu urged his players to back their natural talent and to play a bolder brand of cricket. He encouraged his players to place greater trust in their ability and judgement.

To this end, a new training regime was introduced. Practices were short and snappy and players were handed greater responsibility over their own preparation. The mood of the squad lifted as they set off to Australia.

Muralitharan, fed up with being barracked by boisterous Australian crowds and upset by the comments of Prime Minister John Howard who had labelled him a 'chucker', pulled out of the two-Test tour in Darwin and Cairns.

His absence tested the newfound spirit within the side to the limit and, although the first Test was lost on a Darwin greentop and the series 1–0, the fight showed in the drawn second Test provided a vital confidence fillip ahead of the Asia Cup and a series against South Africa.

A new zest to Sri Lanka's cricket became obvious to all during the six-nation Asia Cup. India had started as favourites following their fine form against Pakistan early in the year, but, after a long break, key players slipped out of form and Sri Lanka, now battle-hardened after their scrapes with Australia, pounced on their early-season rustiness. From the time they snatched a 12-run victory against India in the first round, they dominated the tournament.

They were riding a wave of confidence when the South Africa tour started. All departments of their game had clicked and, without exception, all the players were making telling contributions.

South Africa battled hard for a surprise draw in

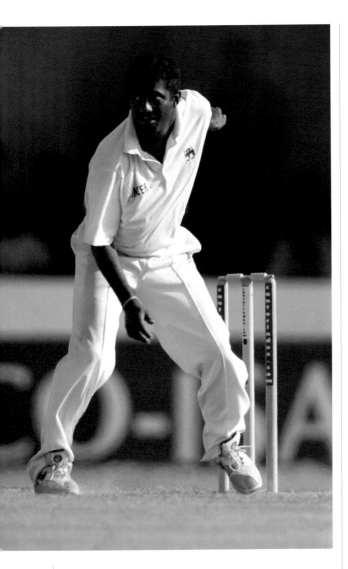

More controversy stalked Muttiah Muralitharan in 2004.

Galle, defying the pre-Test predictions of a three-day rout on the crazy-paved pitch, but then folded in catastrophic fashion in Colombo. Sri Lanka mopped up the one-day series 5–0 without any fuss, too, despite resting key senior players in the final two matches.

The revival was halted during the ICC Champions Trophy, where the cold of an English autumn threw their fielding into disarray, but after a period of stagnation, and even decline, after the 2003 World Cup, the team was back, climbing the ICC's Test and one-day international ratings once again.

Atapattu had claimed full control and total respect from his players for his strong and straight-talking

brand of leadership. Moreover, tomorrow's senior players – the likes of Kumar Sangakkara, Mahela Jayawardene, Tillekeratne Dilshan, Nuwan Zoysa, Kaushal Lokuarachchi, Farveez Maharoof and Lasith Malinga – were blossoming under him.

Even the Cricket Board was regaining credibility, with the most transparent television and sponsorship rights bid processes in its history, which was to yield a record $50 million over the next four years. The future for Sri Lankan cricket suddenly looked bright again.

ONE-DAY INTERNATIONALS
v. Australia

Match One
20 February 2004 at Dambulla
Australia 262 for 6 (50 overs) (AC Gilchrist 66, RT Ponting 58)
Sri Lanka 178 (43.3 overs) (DPMD Jayawardene 61, KC Sangakkara 58, GB Hogg 5 for 41)
Australia won by 84 runs

Match Two
22 February 2004 at Dambulla
Sri Lanka 245 (49.5 overs) (ST Jayasuriya 55, MJ Clarke 5 for 35)
Australia 244 for 5 (50 overs) (ML Hayden 93, RT Ponting 69)
Sri Lanka won by 1 run

Match Three
25 February 2004 at Colombo (RPS)
Sri Lanka 226 for 8 (50 overs)
(DPMD Jayawardene 80)
Australia 227 for 5 (48.3 overs) (RT Ponting 63, DR Martyn 62)
Australia won by 5 wickets

Match Four
27 February 2004 at Colombo (RPS)
Australia 233 (47.4 overs) (RT Ponting 67, A Symonds 53)
Sri Lanka 193 (43.4 overs) (KC Sangakkara 101, MS Kasprowicz 5 for 45)
Australia won by 40 runs

Match Five
29 February 2004 at Colombo (SSC)
Australia 198 for 7 (50 overs)
Sri Lanka 202 for 7 (47.5 overs)
Sri Lanka won by 3 wickets

FIRST TEST – SRI LANKA v. AUSTRALIA
8–12 March 2004 at Galle

AUSTRALIA

	First Innings		Second Innings	
JL Langer	c Sangakkara b Dharmasena	12	lbw b Jayasuriya	32
ML Hayden	c Chandana b Muralitharan	41	c Jayawardene b Muralitharan	130
RT Ponting (capt)	st Sangakkara b Chandana	21	run out	28
DR Martyn	c Jayawardene b Dharmasena	42	c sub b Muralitharan	110
DS Lehmann	b Muralitharan	63	c & b Muralitharan	129
A Symonds	c Jayawardene b Muralitharan	0	st Sangakkara b Muralitharan	24
*AC Gilchrist	c Dharmasena b Muralitharan	4	lbw b Chandana	0
SK Warne	c Sangakkara b Vaas	23	st Sangakkara b Muralitharan	0
JN Gillespie	not out	4	not out	11
MS Kasprowicz	b Muralitharan	1	not out	3
SCG MacGill	lbw b Muralitharan	0		
Extras	b 3, lb 6	9	b 15, lb 28, nb 2	45
	(67.4 overs)	220	(8 wkts dec 152 overs)	512

	First Innings				Second Innings			
	O	M	R	W	O	M	R	W
Vaas	12	2	39	1	27	3	67	0
Dharmasena	20	4	52	2	24	1	100	0
Muralitharan	21.3	5	59	6	56	9	153	5
Chandana	14	1	59	1	24.3	2	102	1
Jayasuriya	1	0	2	0	14.3	2	38	1
Dilshan	-	-	-	-	6	3	9	0

Fall of Wickets
1-31, 2-62, 3-76, 4-148, 5-153, 6-163, 7-215, 8-219, 9-220
1-91, 2-175, 3-245, 4-451, 5-480, 6-498, 7-498, 8-498

SRI LANKA

	First Innings		Second Innings	
MS Atapattu	b Gillespie	47	c Hayden b Warne	16
ST Jayasuriya	lbw b Warne	35	(5) c Hayden b MacGill	5
*KC Sangakkara	c & b Kasprowicz	22	(2) lbw b Kasprowicz	7
DPMD Jayawardene	c Hayden b Symonds	68	(3) c Hayden b Warne	21
TM Dilshan	c Langer b Kasprowicz	104	(4) lbw b Warne	6
HP Tillekeratne (capt)	lbw b Warne	33	c Symonds b Warne	25
TT Samaraweera	not out	36	b MacGill	15
UDU Chandana	c Gilchrist b Warne	27	c Langer b MacGill	43
WPUJC Vaas	c Hayden b MacGill	0	not out	10
HDPK Dharmasena	c Hayden b Warne	6	c Hayden b Warne	0
M Muralitharan	c & b Warne	0	st Gilchrist b MacGill	0
Extras	b 2, nb 1	3	b 4, w 1, nb 1	6
	(136.4 overs)	381	(45.2 overs)	154

	First Innings				Second Innings			
	O	M	R	W	O	M	R	W
Gillespie	28	9	61	1	9	2	20	0
Kasprowicz	23	3	56	2	5	1	13	1
Warne	42.4	9	116	5	15	5	43	5
Symonds	19	3	68	1	-	-	-	-
MacGill	22	4	69	1	16.2	2	74	4
Lehmann	2	0	9	0	-	-	-	-

Fall of Wickets
1-53, 2-92, 3-123, 4-198, 5-298, 6-323, 7-369, 8-372, 9-381
1-14, 2-41, 3-49, 4-56, 5-56, 6-89, 7-119, 8-153, 9-153

Umpires: RE Koertzen and DR Shepherd
Toss: Australia
Test debut: A Symonds
Man of the Match: ML Hayden

Australia won by 197 runs

SECOND TEST – SRI LANKA v. AUSTRALIA
16–20 March 2004 at Kandy

AUSTRALIA

	First Innings		Second Innings	
JL Langer	lbw b Zoysa	3	c Sangakkara b Zoysa	9
ML Hayden	lbw b Muralitharan	54	c & b Vaas	5
RT Ponting (capt)	lbw b Vaas	10	(6) c Sangakkara b Vaas	27
DR Martyn	lbw b Muralitharan	1	st Sangakkara b Muralitharan	161
DS Lehmann	b Zoysa	8	lbw b Vaas	21
A Symonds	c Tillekeratne b Zoysa	6	(7) lbw b Muralitharan	23
*AC Gilchrist	c Sangakkara b Zoysa	0	(3) lbw b Muralitharan	144
SK Warne	c Muralitharan b Vaas	18	c Zoysa b Muralitharan	6
JN Gillespie	c Jayawardene b Muralitharan	4	c Atapattu b Muralitharan	11
MS Kasprowicz	b Muralitharan	0	c Jayawardene b Zoysa	8
SCG MacGill	not out	8	not out	17
Extras	b 1, lb 3	4	b 2, lb 7, nb 1	10
	(42.2 overs)	120	(134.3 overs)	442

	First Innings				Second Innings			
	O	M	R	W	O	M	R	W
Vaas	11.2	5	14	2	33	6	103	3
Zoysa	16	3	54	4	33	11	102	2
Muralitharan	15	4	48	4	50.3	8	173	5
Lokuarachchi	-	-	-	-	12	2	33	0
Jayasuriya	-	-	-	-	5	0	16	0
Dilshan	-	-	-	-	1	0	6	0

Fall of Wickets
1-25, 2-47, 3-50, 4-60, 5-84, 6-84, 7-86, 8-100, 9-106
1-11, 2-26, 3-226, 4-255, 5-304, 6-360, 7-376, 8-393, 9-408

SRI LANKA

	First Innings		Second Innings	
MS Atapattu	lbw b Kasprowicz	9	lbw b Gillespie	8
ST Jayasuriya	lbw b Kasprowicz	1	c Gilchrist b Gillespie	131
DA Gunawardene	lbw b Kasprowicz	13	lbw b Kasprowicz	9
*KC Sangakkara	c Symonds b Gillespie	5	c & b Warne	29
DPMD Jayawardene	c Symonds b Warne	17	c Gilchrist b Gillespie	13
HP Tillekeratne (capt)	c Gilchrist b Warne	16	(7) c Ponting b Warne	7
TM Dilshan	lbw b Warne	0	(6) b Warne	43
WPUJC Vaas	not out	68	c Langer b Warne	45
DNT Zoysa	c Gilchrist b Kasprowicz	4	(10) c Gilchrist b Gillespie	0
KS Lokuarachchi	c Kasprowicz b Warne	15	(9) b Warne	16
M Muralitharan	c Symonds b Warne	43	not out	4
Extras	b 8, lb 9, nb 3	20	b 4, lb 14, nb 1	19
	(63.1 overs)	211	(73.1 overs)	324

	First Innings				Second Innings			
	O	M	R	W	O	M	R	W
Gillespie	12	4	25	1	20	1	76	4
Kasprowicz	24	5	83	4	17	1	55	1
Warne	20.1	3	65	5	21.1	2	90	5
Symonds	2	1	1	0	3	0	16	0
MacGill	5	1	20	0	12	0	69	0

Fall of Wickets
1-6, 2-34, 3-39, 4-49, 5-67, 6-67, 7-88, 8-111, 9-132
1-17, 2-36, 3-98, 4-174, 5-218, 6-239, 7-272, 8-319, 9-320

Umpires: SA Bucknor and DL Orchard
Toss: Australia
Man of the Match: SK Warne

Australia won by 27 runs

THIRD TEST – SRI LANKA v. AUSTRALIA
24–28 March 2004 at Colombo (SSC)

AUSTRALIA

	First Innings					Second Innings	
JL Langer	c Dilshan b Vaas				19	b Vaas	166
ML Hayden	c sub b Samaraweera				25	lbw b Vaas	28
RT Ponting (capt)	c Muralitharan b Vaas				92	c Samaraweera b Herath	20
DR Martyn	c Sangakkara b Vaas				14	(5) lbw b Herath	5
DS Lehmann	c Jayasuriya b Muralitharan				153	(6) c Sangakkara b Muralitharan	1
SM Katich	c and b Muralitharan				14	(7) lbw b Muralitharan	86
*AC Gilchrist	c Jayasuriya b Muralitharan				22	(8) not out	31
SK Warne	lbw b Muralitharan				32	(9) c Samaraweera b Herath	0
JN Gillespie	c Tillekeratne b Muralitharan				0	(4) c Jayawardene b Muralitharan	1
MS Kasprowicz	b Jayasuriya				4	run out	3
BA Williams	not out				0	c & b Herath	2
Extras	b 13, lb 9, nb 4				26	b 11, lb 11, w 4, nb 6	32
	(115.1 overs)				**401**	(106.2 overs)	**375**

	First Innings				Second Innings			
	O	M	R	W	O	M	R	W
Vaas	26	3	93	3	21	3	61	2
Zoysa	3.3	1	23	0	12	0	54	0
Samaraweera	14.3	1	38	1	15	4	40	0
Muralitharan	37.1	6	123	5	29	5	93	3
Herath	23	5	75	0	24.2	1	92	4
Jayasuriya	11	1	27	1	4	0	13	0
Dilshan	–	–	–	–	1	1	0	0

Fall of Wickets
1-43, 2-60, 3-96, 4-217, 5-244, 6-299, 7-376, 8-380, 9-387
1-40, 2-79, 3-80, 4-89, 5-98, 6-316, 7-341, 8-346, 9-368

SRI LANKA

	First Innings					Second Innings	
MS Atapattu	b Kasprowicz				118	b Kasprowicz	14
ST Jayasuriya	c Gillespie b Lehmann				71	c Katich b Lehmann	51
*KC Sangakkara	c Gillespie b Lehmann				22	(5) b Warne	27
DPMD Jayawardene	c Gilchrist b Gillespie				29	c Gilchrist b Lehmann	37
TM Dilshan	b Gillespie				0	(6) c Martyn b Warne	31
HP Tillekeratne (capt)	not out				74	(4) lbw b Gillespie	17
TT Samaraweera	c Gilchrist b Gillespie				41	(3) st Gilchrist b Lehmann	53
WPUJC Vaas	b Warne				24	lbw b Warne	9
DNT Zoysa	st Gilchrist b Lehmann				3	lbw b Warne	1
HMRKB Herath	c Martyn b Warne				3	lbw b Kasprowicz	0
M Muralitharan	c Warne b Kasprowicz				8	not out	0
Extras	b 4, lb 7, w 1, nb 2				14	b 4, lb 1, w 1, nb 2	8
	(127.1 overs)				**407**	(93.4 overs)	**248**

	First Innings				Second Innings			
	O	M	R	W	O	M	R	W
Gillespie	23	3	96	3	18	6	38	1
Kasprowicz	22.1	5	58	2	16.4	5	37	2
Williams	19	5	48	0	5	0	19	0
Warne	36	7	115	2	33	11	92	4
Lehmann	19	2	50	3	17	2	42	3
Katich	8	0	29	0	4	1	15	0

Fall of Wickets
1-134, 2-175, 3-240, 4-240, 5-256, 6-327, 7-378, 8-381, 9-390
1-45, 2-92, 3-156, 4-181, 5-191, 6-232, 7-245, 8-247, 9-248

Umpires: SA Bucknor and DL Orchard
Toss: Australia
Man of the Match: DS Lehmann
Man of the Series: SK Warne

Australia won by 121 runs

SERIES AVERAGES
Sri Lanka v. Australia

SRI LANKA

Batting	M	Inns	NO	Runs	HS	Av	100	50	c/st
ST Jayasuriya	3	6	0	294	131	49.00	1	2	2/-
TT Samaraweera	2	4	1	145	53	48.33	-	1	2/-
WPUJC Vaas	3	6	2	156	68*	39.00	-	1	1/-
MS Atapattu	3	6	0	212	118	35.33	1	-	1/-
UDU Chandana	1	2	0	70	43	35.00	-	-	1/-
HP Tillekeratne	3	6	1	172	74*	34.40	-	1	2/-
DPMD Jayawardene	3	6	0	185	68	30.83	-	1	6/-
TM Dilshan	3	6	0	184	104	30.66	1	-	1/-
KC Sangakkara	3	6	0	112	29	18.66	-	-	7/4
KS Lokuarachchi	1	2	0	31	16	15.50	-	-	-/-
M Muralitharan	3	6	2	55	43	13.75	-	-	4/-
DA Gunawardene	1	2	0	22	13	11.00	-	-	-/-
HDPK Dharmasena	1	2	0	6	6	3.00	-	-	1/-
DNT Zoysa	2	4	0	8	4	2.00	-	-	1/-
HMRKB Herath	1	2	0	3	3	1.50	-	-	1/-

Bowling	Overs	Mds	Runs	Wkts	Av	Best	5/inn	10m
M Muralitharan	209.1	37	649	28	23.17	6-59	4	1
WPUJC Vaas	130.2	22	377	11	34.27	3-93	-	-
DNT Zoysa	64.3	15	233	6	38.83	4-54	-	-
HMRKB Herath	47.2	6	167	4	41.75	4-92	-	-
ST Jayasuriya	35.3	3	96	2	48.00	1-27	-	-
HDPK Dharmasena	44	5	152	2	76.00	2-52	-	-
TT Samaraweera	29.3	5	78	1	78.00	1-38	-	-
UDU Chandana	38.3	3	161	2	80.50	1-59	-	-

Also bowled: TM Dilshan 8-4-15-0, KS Lokuarachchi 12-2-33-0.

AUSTRALIA

Batting	M	Inns	NO	Runs	HS	Av	100	50	c/st
DS Lehmann	3	6	0	375	153	62.50	2	1	-/-
DR Martyn	3	6	0	333	161	55.50	2	-	2/-
SM Katich	1	2	0	100	86	50.00	-	1	1/-
ML Hayden	3	6	0	283	130	47.16	1	1	7/-
AC Gilchrist	3	6	1	201	144	40.20	1	-	11/3
JL Langer	3	6	0	241	166	40.16	1	-	3/-
RT Ponting	3	6	0	198	92	33.00	-	1	1/-
SCG MacGill	2	3	2	25	17*	25.00	-	-	-/-
A Symonds	2	4	0	53	24	13.25	-	-	4/-
SK Warne	3	6	0	79	32	13.16	-	-	3/-
JN Gillespie	3	6	2	35	11*	8.75	-	-	1/-
MS Kasprowicz	3	6	1	19	8	3.80	-	-	2/-
BA Williams	1	2	0	2	2	2.00	-	-	-/-

Bowling	Overs	Mds	Runs	Wkts	Av	Best	5/inn	10m
DS Lehmann	38	4	101	6	16.83	3-42	-	-
SK Warne	168	37	521	26	20.03	5-43	4	2
MS Kasprowicz	107.5	20	302	12	25.16	4-83	-	-
JN Gillespie	110	25	316	10	31.60	4-76	-	-
SCG MacGill	55.2	7	232	5	46.40	4-74	-	-
A Symonds	24	4	85	1	85.00	1-68	-	-

Also bowled: SM Katich 12-1-44-0, BA Williams 24-5-67-0.

FIRST TEST – SRI LANKA v. SOUTH AFRICA
4–8 August 2004 at Galle

SRI LANKA

	First Innings		Second Innings	
MS Atapattu (capt)	c Boucher b Pollock	9	lbw b Klusener	25
ST Jayasuriya	c Klusener b Pollock	12	c Boucher b Pollock	74
KC Sangakkara	c Boucher b Boje	58	c Hayward b Boje	13
DPMD Jayawardene	lbw b Hayward	237	c Rudolph b Boje	5
TT Samaraweera	lbw b Pollock	13	b Klusener	19
TM Dilshan	b Hayward	25	lbw b Pollock	1
*RS Kaluwitharana	b Pollock	33	c Pollock b Boje	19
UDU Chandana	b Ntini	5	c Dippenaar b Boje	29
WPUJC Vaas	c Hayward b Boje	69	not out	13
MF Maharoof	not out	6	(11) not out	3
M Muralitharan	b Hayward	0	(10) c Dippenaar b Boje	2
Extras	b 8, lb 3, w 2, nb 6	19	b 4, lb 1, w 2, nb 4	11
	(145.4 overs)	486	(9 wkts dec 67 overs)	214

	First Innings				Second Innings			
	O	M	R	W	O	M	R	W
Pollock	23	5	48	4	12	2	19	2
Ntini	20	1	61	1	5	0	19	0
Hayward	16.4	0	81	3	6	1	21	0
Kallis	16	3	52	0	8	1	22	0
Klusener	19	0	69	0	14	2	40	2
Boje	42	3	148	2	22	0	88	5
Rudolph	9	2	16	0	–	–	–	–

Fall of Wickets
1-13, 2-22, 3-108, 4-145, 5-189, 6-274, 7-279, 8-449, 9-486
1-62, 2-89, 3-103, 4-140, 5-142, 6-166, 7-172, 8-199, 9-209

SOUTH AFRICA

	First Innings		Second Innings	
HH Dippenaar	run out	46	(2) c Jayawardene b Muralitharan	11
M van Jaarsveld	c Samaraweera b Muralitharan	37	(3) lbw b Dilshan	29
JA Rudolph	c Kaluwitharana b Muralitharan	102	(5) not out	27
JH Kallis	c Samaraweera b Muralitharan	59	not out	52
GC Smith (capt)	lbw b Jayasuriya	23	(1) b Chandana	74
*MV Boucher	c Kaluwitharana b Jayasuriya	6		
SM Pollock	c Sangakkara b Vaas	25		
L Klusener	c Jayawardene b Dilshan	2		
N Boje	c Kaluwitharana b Vaas	31		
M Ntini	c Chandana b Muralitharan	10		
M Hayward	not out	2		
Extras	b 14, lb 8, w 1, nb 10	33	b 1, lb 4, w 2, nb 3	10
	(139.4 overs)	376	(3 wkts 90 overs)	203

	First Innings				Second Innings			
	O	M	R	W	O	M	R	W
Vaas	25	10	50	2	10	3	20	0
Maharoof	19	9	42	0	5	2	4	0
Muralitharan	46.4	9	130	4	20	5	37	1
Chandana	18	0	68	0	18	1	60	1
Jayasuriya	25	9	40	2	17	7	30	0
Dilshan	6	0	24	1	16	5	30	1
Samaraweera	–	–	–	–	3	0	13	0
Sangakkara	–	–	–	–	1	0	4	0

Fall of Wickets
1-84, 2-96, 3-168, 4-213, 5-225, 6-287, 7-295, 8-348, 9-363
1-34, 2-98, 3-135

Umpires: DJ Harper and DR Shepherd
Toss: Sri Lanka
Man of the Match: DPMD Jayawardene

Match drawn

SECOND TEST – SRI LANKA v. SOUTH AFRICA
11–15 August 2004 at Colombo (SSC)

SRI LANKA

	First Innings		Second Innings	
MS Atapattu (capt)	c Boucher b Pollock	4	b Rudolph	72
ST Jayasuriya	lbw b Boje	43	st Boucher b Boje	19
KC Sangakkara	c Kallis b Pollock	232	c Ntini b Kallis	64
DPMD Jayawardene	b Ntini	82	c Boucher b Kallis	3
WPUJC Vaas	c van Jaarsveld b Pollock	10		
TT Samaraweera	c Ntini b Kallis	21	(5) not out	21
TM Dilshan	b Ntini	3	(6) not out	23
*RS Kaluwitharana	c Boucher b Hayward	7		
UDU Chandana	st Boucher b Boje	40		
HMRKB Herath	b Ntini	7		
SL Malinga	not out	6		
Extras	lb 6, w 1, nb 8	15	b 6, lb 1, w 2	9
	(142.3 overs)	470	(4 wkts dec 55 overs)	211

	First Innings				Second Innings			
	O	M	R	W	O	M	R	W
Pollock	30	8	81	4	8	0	46	0
Ntini	33	6	108	2	4	0	19	0
Hayward	17	4	75	1	3	1	15	0
Kallis	17	6	54	1	6	4	6	2
Boje	34.3	5	102	2	23	6	81	1
Rudolph	4	0	16	0	7	2	22	1
van Jaarsveld	7	0	28	0	–	–	–	–
Smith	–	–	–	–	4	0	15	0

Fall of Wickets
1-4, 2-99, 3-291, 4-316, 5-392, 6-399, 7-416, 8-418, 9-437
1-46, 2-142, 3-149, 4-179

SOUTH AFRICA

	First Innings		Second Innings	
GC Smith (capt)	c & b Jayasuriya	65	c Samaraweera b Malinga	17
HH Gibbs	lbw b Vaas	0	c Samaraweera b Malinga	4
M van Jaarsveld	c Sangakkara b Jayasuriya	51	b Vaas	2
N Boje	b Jayasuriya	0	(9) lbw b Vaas	16
JH Kallis	b Jayasuriya	13	(4) c Dilshan b Vaas	3
JA Rudolph	c Kaluwitharana b Malinga	6	(5) c Malinga b Vaas	1
HH Dippenaar	c Dilshan b Herath	25	(6) not out	59
*MV Boucher	not out	10	(7) c Kaluwitharana b Vaas	51
SM Pollock	lbw b Herath	1	(8) c Atapattu b Dilshan	3
M Ntini	b Herath	0	(3) c Kaluwitharana b Vaas	0
M Hayward	b Jayasuriya	1	c & b Malinga	1
Extras	b 1, lb 8, nb 8	17	b 6, lb 3, w 1, nb 12	22
	(69.1 overs)	189	(67 overs)	179

	First Innings				Second Innings			
	O	M	R	W	O	M	R	W
Vaas	7	3	10	1	18	8	29	6
Malinga	13	1	51	1	13	1	54	3
Herath	25	6	60	3	8	5	13	0
Chandana	6	0	21	0	7	1	26	0
Dilshan	4	1	4	0	12	6	26	1
Jayasuriya	14.1	4	34	5	9	3	22	0

Fall of Wickets
1-1, 2-109, 3-109, 4-140, 5-141, 6-166, 7-186, 8-188, 9-188
1-4, 2-18, 3-24, 4-36, 5-36, 6-137, 7-140, 8-163, 9-163

Umpires: SA Bucknor and BF Bowden
Toss: Sri Lanka
Man of the Match: KC Sangakkara
Man of the Series: WPUJC Vaas

Sri Lanka won by 313 runs

SERIES AVERAGES
Sri Lanka v. South Africa

SRI LANKA

Batting	M	Inns	NO	Runs	HS	Av	100	50	c/st
KC Sangakkara	2	4	0	367	232	91.75	1	2	3/-
DPMD Jayawardene	2	4	0	327	237	81.75	1	1	2/-
WPUJC Vaas	2	3	1	92	69	46.00	-	1	-/-
ST Jayasuriya	2	4	0	148	74	37.00	-	1	1/-
MS Atapattu	2	4	0	110	72	27.50	-	1	1/-
UDU Chandana	2	3	0	74	40	24.66	-	-	1/-
TT Samaraweera	2	4	1	74	21*	24.66	-	-	3/-
RS Kaluwitharana	2	3	0	59	33	19.66	-	-	6/-
TM Dilshan	2	4	1	52	25	17.33	-	-	2/-
HMRKB Herath	1	1	0	7	7	7.00	-	-	-/-
M Muralitharan	1	2	0	2	2	1.00	-	-	-/-
MF Maharoof	1	2	2	9	6*	-	-	-	-/-
SL Malinga	1	1	1	6	6*	-	-	-	2/-

Bowling	Overs	Mds	Runs	Wkts	Av	Best	5/inn	10m
WPUJC Vaas	60	24	109	9	12.11	6-29	1	-
ST Jayasuriya	65.1	23	126	7	18.00	5-34	1	-
HMRKB Herath	33	11	73	3	24.33	3-60	-	-
SL Malinga	26	2	105	4	26.25	3-54	-	-
TM Dilshan	38	12	84	3	28.00	1-24	-	-
M Muralitharan	66.4	14	167	5	33.40	4-130	-	-
UDU Chandana	49	2	175	1	175.00	1-60	-	-
KC Sangakkara	1	0	4	0	-	-	-	-
TT Samaraweera	3	0	13	0	-	-	-	-
MF Maharoof	24	11	46	0	-	-	-	-

SOUTH AFRICA

Batting	M	Inns	NO	Runs	HS	Av	100	50	c/st
HH Dippenaar	2	4	1	141	59*	47.00	-	1	2/-
JA Rudolph	2	4	1	136	102	45.33	1	-	1/-
GC Smith	2	4	0	179	74	44.75	-	2	-/-
JH Kallis	2	4	1	127	59	42.33	-	2	-/-
MV Boucher	2	3	1	67	51	33.50	-	1	6/2
M van Jaarsveld	2	4	0	119	51	29.75	-	1	1/-
N Boje	2	3	0	47	31	15.66	-	-	1/-
SM Pollock	2	3	0	29	25	9.66	-	-	1/-
M Ntini	2	3	0	10	10	3.33	-	-	2/-
HH Gibbs	1	2	0	4	4	2.00	-	-	-/-
L Klusener	1	1	0	2	2	2.00	-	-	1/-
M Hayward	2	3	1	4	2*	2.00	-	-	2/-

Bowling	Overs	Mds	Runs	Wkts	Av	Best	5/inn	10m
SM Pollock	73	15	194	10	19.40	4-48	-	-
N Boje	121.3	14	419	10	41.90	5-88	1	-
JH Kallis	47	14	134	3	44.66	2-6	-	-
M Hayward	42.4	6	192	4	48.00	3-81	-	-
JA Rudolph	20	4	54	1	54.00	1-22	-	-
L Klusener	33	2	109	2	54.50	2-40	-	-
M Ntini	62	7	207	3	69.00	2-108	-	-
GC Smith	4	0	15	0	-	-	-	-
M van Jaarsveld	7	0	28	0	-	-	-	-

ONE-DAY INTERNATIONALS
v. South Africa

Match One
20 August 2004 at Colombo (RPS)
South Africa 263 for 9 (50 overs) (JH Kallis 74, MV Boucher 58, WPUJC Vaas 4 for 33)
Sri Lanka 265 for 7 (49 overs) (MS Atapattu 64, DA Gunawardene 51)
Sri Lanka won by 3 wickets

Match Two
22 August 2004 at Colombo (RPS)
Sri Lanka 213 for 9 (50 overs) (KC Sangakkara 63, UDU Chandana 61*)
South Africa 176 (48.5 overs) (SM Pollock 54, DNT Zoysa 5 for 26, TM Dilshan 4 for 52)
Sri Lanka won by 37 runs

Match Three
25 August 2004 at Dambulla
South Africa 191 (50 overs) (JH Kallis 52)
Sri Lanka 192 for 6 (47.4 overs) (MS Atapattu 97*)
Sri Lanka won by 4 wickets

Match Four
28 August 2004 at Dambulla
South Africa 235 for 7 (50 overs) (SM Pollock 52*)
Sri Lanka 236 for 3 (46.1 overs) (KC Sangakkara 74*, DA Gunawardene 52)
Sri Lanka won by 7 wickets

Match Five
31 August 2004 at Colombo (SSC)
Sri Lanka 308 for 8 (50 overs) (ST Jayasuriya 79, KC Sangakkara 72, WS Jayantha 51)
South Africa 259 (48.1 overs) (JH Kallis 101, UDU Chandana 5 for 61)
Sri Lanka won by 49 runs

WEST INDIES

ENGLAND IN THE WEST INDIES

ENGLAND IN THE WEST INDIES
By Jonathan Agnew

FIRST TEST
11–14 March 2004 at Sabina Park, Kingston

This match will always be remembered for an astonishing burst of fast bowling by England's Steve Harmison. On the fourth and final morning, he ran amok, taking 7 for 12, as he condemned the West Indies to their lowest-ever total in Test cricket: 47 all out.

With the home team already under fire for their recent poor record, this performance sparked a furious outburst from their supporters, and this was hardly helped by the fact that three West Indian players were reported to have been seen in what became known as the 'party stand' shortly after the match ended.

This was the first Test to be played at Sabina Park by England since the now-infamous match which was abandoned there five years ago. A warm-up game was staged on the ground a week or so before this opening Test of the four-match series, and, as it did for the Test itself, the pitch behaved more or less blamelessly.

It was pressure that undid the West Indian batsmen. On that fateful fourth morning, they continued their second innings with the match virtually all square. However, lurking in the back of their minds was the knowledge that Fidel Edwards, their best fast bowler, was out of the rest of the game through a side strain.

They needed to bat all day, at least, to prevent England from knocking off a target against their reduced attack on the last day. It seems, with so much uncertainty hanging over their heads, that the situation was simply too much for them.

Of course, Harmison bowled quite brilliantly, and in a manner we had not seen

from him at this level before. Having left Bangladesh before Christmas under an injury cloud, Harmison was not best pleased to read comments questioning his commitment which were quite deliberately leaked to the press from the England camp.

This is not a new tactic – Duncan Fletcher gave Andrew Flintoff the same treatment, with the result that Flintoff realised he had to double his workload if he was to succeed.

Harmison, too, appears to have been stung into action, and spent some time training with his beloved Newcastle United and, in particular, listening to their manager, Sir Bobby Robson. Even

Mark Butcher hit an invaluable half-century for England in the opening Test.

Fletcher cannot have anticipated quite such a dramatic turnaround in Harmison's attitude and desire, however, but the extraordinary events of that fourth day – and the rest of the series – spoke for themselves.

The West Indies chose to bat first and, at tea on the first day, were reasonably placed on 185 for 4. Chris Gayle had played on to Harmison for five, Ramnaresh Sarwan played across his pads and fell lbw to Matthew Hoggard, Brian Lara was taken by Andrew Flintoff at second slip for 23 and Shivnarine Chanderpaul played on to Hoggard for seven.

Holding the innings together was Devon Smith, who reached his first Test century in his fifth Test, and who put on a valuable 122 with Ryan Hinds, but England fought back in the final session, taking five wickets for 126 runs, and when Hoggard dismissed Edwards with the 12th ball of the second morning, the West Indies were all out for 311.

England managed to secure a small lead of 28 during a rain-affected first innings, largely due to a battling third-wicket partnership of 119 between Mark Butcher and Nasser Hussain. Both made 58, and neither innings was pretty, but with Edwards and the aggressive Tino Best bowling with plenty of fire, batting was not easy.

Flintoff played a typically forceful knock, scoring 46 from 50 balls, but Edwards had, by this stage, already left the field with the injury that was to rule him out of the next Test and, crucially, the rest of this encounter.

Ashley Giles added 35 with Hoggard as England got their noses in front after tea on the third day. When Harmison was run out for 13, the West Indies had 13 overs in which to bat and, when bad light stopped play, they were 8 for no wicket, with no inkling of what was to come.

In bright and sunny conditions, Gayle and Smith duly returned to continue their innings. Almost immediately, the left-handed Gayle was superbly caught for nine by Graham Thorpe, two-handed above his head at third slip off Harmison and, in five overs of mayhem, the West Indies lost Sarwan, Chanderpaul and Lara – all for ducks – as they crashed to 16 for 4.

Harmison was extracting steepling bounce, but Hoggard took his second wicket when Smith was caught and bowled for 12: that was 21 for 5, and already the home team was doomed. Ridley Jacobs and Hinds put on the biggest partnership of the innings – 20 – before another rearing Harmison delivery accounted for Jacobs, who fended to short leg.

There was no stopping Harmison now, and he demolished a reluctant lower order to finish with the best bowling figures ever recorded in a Test match at Sabina Park.

Trescothick and Vaughan needed just 2.3 overs to knock off the 20 required for England to take an early lead in the series, but the sudden emergence of a high-quality opening bowler would prove to be of far greater importance.

Storm force hits the Windies: Hurricane Harmison in Jamaica.

FIRST TEST – WEST INDIES v. ENGLAND
11–14 March 2004 at Kingston

WEST INDIES

	First Innings		Second Innings	
CH Gayle	b Harmison	5	c Thorpe b Harmison	9
DS Smith	st Read b Giles	108	c & b Hoggard	12
RR Sarwan	lbw b Hoggard	0	lbw b Harmison	0
BC Lara (capt)	c Flintoff b Jones	23	(5) c Flintoff b Hoggard	0
S Chanderpaul	b Hoggard	7	(4) b Harmison	0
RO Hinds	c Butcher b Giles	84	c Read b Jones	3
*RD Jacobs	c Vaughan b Jones	38	c Hussain b Harmison	15
TL Best	lbw b Harmison	20	c Read b Harmison	0
A Sanford	c Trescothick b Flintoff	1	c Trescothick b Harmison	1
CD Collymore	not out	3	not out	2
FH Edwards	c Flintoff b Hoggard	1	c Trescothick b Harmison	0
Extras	lb 6, w 1, nb 14	21	lb 4, nb 1	5
	(86.4 overs)	311	(25.3 overs)	47

	First Innings				Second Innings			
	O	M	R	W	O	M	R	W
Hoggard	18.4	3	68	3	9	2	21	2
Harmison	21	6	61	2	12.3	8	12	7
Flintoff	16	3	45	1	–	–	–	–
Jones	18	2	62	2	4	1	10	1
Giles	12	0	67	2	–	–	–	–
Vaughan	1	0	2	0	–	–	–	–

Fall of Wickets
1-17, 2-22, 3-73, 4-101, 5-223, 6-281, 7-289, 8-300, 9-307
1-13, 2-13, 3-15, 4-16, 5-21, 6-41, 7-41, 8-43, 9-43

ENGLAND

	First Innings		Second Innings	
ME Trescothick	b Edwards	7	not out	6
MP Vaughan (capt)	c Lara b Edwards	15	not out	11
MA Butcher	c Jacobs b Edwards	58		
N Hussain	c sub b Best	58		
GP Thorpe	c Sanford b Best	19		
A Flintoff	c Hinds b Sarwan	46		
*CMW Read	c Hinds b Best	20		
AF Giles	b Sanford	27		
MJ Hoggard	not out	9		
SP Jones	c Sanford b Hinds	7		
SJ Harmison	run out	13		
Extras	b 7, lb 28, w 7, nb 18	60	b 1, nb 2	3
	(103.2 overs)	339	(0 wkts 2.3 overs)	20

	First Innings				Second Innings			
	O	M	R	W	O	M	R	W
Collymore	26	7	55	0	–	–	–	–
Edwards	19.3	3	72	3	–	–	–	–
Best	19	1	57	3	1.3	0	8	0
Sanford	22	1	90	1	–	–	–	–
Hinds	11.5	2	18	1	1	0	11	0
Gayle	1	0	6	0	–	–	–	–
Sarwan	4	1	6	1	–	–	–	–

Fall of Wickets
1-28, 2-33, 3-152, 4-194, 5-209, 6-268, 7-278, 8-313, 9-325

Umpires: BF Bowden and DJ Harper
Toss: West Indies
Man of the Match: SJ Harmison

England won by 10 wickets

SECOND TEST
19–23 March 2004 at Port-of-Spain, Trinidad

The vibrant, music-loving island of Trinidad is the most independent country in the Caribbean. It is home to some of the most passionate and outspoken cricket supporters in the region, and had the captain of the West Indies been from any island other than Trinidad, he would have expected a dreadful reception when he walked out to toss the coin with Michael Vaughan.

However, since it was Brian Lara, the majority of the home supporters were prepared to forget the disastrous effort in Jamaica and hope for better here. There were still some dissenters, however, and they would grow in number by the end of the game.

Vaughan duly lost his ninth toss out of 11 and England found themselves in the field once again. In some ways this was no bad thing, since the West Indies batsmen were sure to be reeling from their defeat of only a few days before. After 25 overs, however, they were 100 for no wicket, with Gayle, in particular, going like a train and Harmison appearing innocuous.

But the tall fast bowler changed to the pavilion end and, in his first over, Gayle edged to Chris Read for 62 from only 81 balls. In his next over, Harmison trapped Smith lbw for 35, bringing Lara out to bat in the last over before lunch. This was the ideal opportunity for England and, fourth ball, Harmison hurled in a short delivery aimed at Lara's throat. It was a brute, which flicked the glove, cannoned off his helmet and Giles, in the gully, took the catch.

Immediately after the break, Chanderpaul flashed unwisely at Simon Jones, and West Indies had suddenly lost four key men for 13.

Dwayne Smith is an extremely talented and promising batsman, but I am not sure he is yet the man for a crisis. He flogged Harmison for a mighty six amongst the conch-blowers at deep midwicket and then, unbelievably, tried to do the same to the very next ball. The result was a straightforward catch to Hussain and, in the same over, Flintoff caught Sarwan at second slip for 21.

A rout seemed possible again as the West Indies slumped to 148 for 7, and then 165 for 8, but Jacobs was doing his best to halt the slide. Not especially renowned for his judgement of a run, Jacobs was first involved in the run out of Adam Sanford and then, after he and Pedro Collins had put on 37, he ran himself out for 40. 208 all out was a feeble effort from 100 for no wicket, and England were well in control of the match.

Graham Thorpe sweeps during his fine innings of 90 in Port-of-Spain which helped England to a lead of 111.

For the second time, the openers, Vaughan and Trescothick, failed to make an impression and it was left to Butcher and Hussain to undertake their second rescue act of the series. From 8 for 2, they added 120 – one more run than at Sabina Park – before Butcher was taken at slip off Best for 61. Hussain then put on 58 with his old friend, Thorpe, before Best bowled him for 58 with England only 20 runs behind.

Flintoff thumped 23 and Read fell for only three and, once again, it was Giles adding crucial runs at No. 8 that made all the difference. With Thorpe, he took England's innings into the third morning, putting on 85 for the seventh wicket before Giles

edged Collins to slip for 37. Thorpe fell ten runs short of his century – again caught in the slips – and England managed to lose four wickets for 19 as the innings was wrapped up for 319 – a lead of 111.

With shades of Jamaica, the West Indies found themselves batting under great pressure, and could not cope. They lost three wickets before erasing the arrears and, worst of all, Lara opted to bat down the order.

It was this decision that cost him a great deal of support in his home town and, from a distance, it did seem to be a remarkable one. He appeared at No. 6, possibly feeling justified because Jacobs responded to his promotion by scoring 70, but one wonders what the

SECOND TEST – WEST INDIES v. ENGLAND
19–23 March 2004 at Port-of-Spain

WEST INDIES

	First Innings			Second Innings	
CH Gayle	c Read b Harmison	62		b Jones	16
DS Smith	lbw b Harmison	35		c Hoggard b Jones	17
RR Sarwan	c Flintoff b Harmison	21		lbw b Jones	13
BC Lara (capt)	c Giles b Harmison	0		(6) lbw b Harmison	8
S Chanderpaul	c Read b Jones	2		c Hussain b Flintoff	42
DR Smith	c Hussain b Harmison	16		(7) c sub b Flintoff	14
*RD Jacobs	run out	40		(4) c Flintoff b Jones	70
TL Best	c Read b Hoggard	1		lbw b Hoggard	2
A Sanford	run out	1		c Trescothick b Hoggard	1
PT Collins	b Harmison	10		b Jones	7
CD Collymore	not out	3		not out	0
Extras	lb 7, w 6, nb 4	17		b 1, lb 3, w 5, nb 10	19
	(60.1 overs)	208		(67 overs)	209

	First Innings				Second Innings			
	O	M	R	W	O	M	R	W
Hoggard	15	3	38	1	16	5	48	2
Harmison	20.1	5	61	6	16	5	40	1
Flintoff	10	3	38	0	12	1	27	2
Giles	3	0	20	0	7	1	29	0
Jones	12	2	44	1	15	2	57	5
Trescothick	-	-	-	-	1	0	4	0

Fall of Wickets
1-100, 2-110, 3-110, 4-113, 5-142, 6-143, 7-148, 8-165, 9-202
1-34, 2-45, 3-56, 4-158, 5-171, 6-194, 7-195, 8-200, 9-205

ENGLAND

	First Innings			Second Innings	
ME Trescothick	c Sanford b Best	1		b Best	4
MP Vaughan (capt)	lbw b Best	0		lbw b Sanford	23
MA Butcher	c Jacobs b Best	61		not out	46
N Hussain	b Best	58		c Jacobs b Sanford	5
GP Thorpe	c Gayle b Collins	90		not out	13
A Flintoff	c & b Smith DR	23			
*CMW Read	lbw b Collins	3			
AF Giles	c Smith DS b Collins	37			
MJ Hoggard	not out	0			
SP Jones	b Gayle	1			
SJ Harmison	b Gayle	0			
Extras	b 5, lb 20, w 3, nb 17	45		b 4, lb 3, nb 1	8
	(139.5 overs)	319		(3 wkts 15 overs)	99

	First Innings				Second Innings			
	O	M	R	W	O	M	R	W
Collins	29	8	71	4	4	0	25	0
Best	28	5	71	3	4	0	27	1
Sanford	26	6	60	0	4	1	32	2
Collymore	24	7	39	0	3	1	8	0
Smith DR	9	0	30	1	-	-	-	-
Gayle	16.5	6	20	2	-	-	-	-
Sarwan	1	0	3	0	-	-	-	-

Fall of Wickets
1-2, 2-8, 3-128, 4-186, 5-218, 6-230, 7-315, 8-318, 9-319
1-8, 2-59, 3-71

Umpires: BF Bowden and DJ Harper
Toss: West Indies
Man of the Match: SJ Harmison

England won by 7 wickets

There was a first five-wicket Test haul for Andrew Flintoff in the Third Test in Barbados.

effect of the captain – and best batsman – dropping down the order had on an already jittery dressing room.

In the event, Vaughan brought back Harmison and, first ball, he had Lara lbw for eight and, from 171 for 5, the West Indies lost their last five wickets for 38 to leave England 99 to win.

Trescothick failed again – he was bowled by Best for four – and Vaughan was lbw to Sanford for 23, but all that remained on the final morning was for England to score a further 28, and although Hussain was caught behind to the second ball of the day, Butcher steered England to victory with 46 not out.

THIRD TEST
1–5 April 2004 at Bridgetown, Barbados

Thirty-six years of history was buried when, on only the third day and in front of a crowd that was a remarkable 90 per cent English, Mark Butcher hit the winning run that sealed the series for Michael Vaughan's jubilant team.

Immediately Barbados, which was overwhelmed by cricket supporters, witnessed celebrations of a kind that can never have been seen on the island before.

'Fortress Kensington' is the nickname for the famous ground in the middle of Bridgetown: so-called for the many years of West Indian domination. Those glory days are now a distant memory and, in being hustled out for a feeble 94, the West Indies recorded their lowest-ever total in Barbados. It is also worth noting that it was the seventh time in only six years they had been bowled out for less than 100.

Before the match, Brian Lara had expressed his hope that the split in the crowd would be 50:50. Clearly, he feared the worst. However, despite the outrageous surcharge that had been applied to the tickets of all England supporters, they still flocked to Bridgetown. Many of them had clearly bought their tickets from locals, thereby defying the action of the West Indian Cricket Board, for which it will surely pay in the future.

For the third Test in a row, Michael Vaughan was able to name an unchanged team and, for once, he won the toss. His decision to put the West Indies into bat was based more on their recent batting collapses than anything the weather or conditions had to offer and, within 12 overs, both openers were back in the pavilion.

Lara and Sarwan added 68 before Lara was caught in the gully off Hoggard for 36, and Sarwan then teamed up with Chanderpaul to put on 79 before it all went horribly

Matthew Hoggard's hat-trick at 'Fortress Kensington' included the wickets of Sarwan, Chanderpaul and Ryan Hinds and sent the largely English crowd into paroxysms of delight.

wrong for the West Indies once again. At 167 for 3, Sarwan was caught in the slips off Harmison for 63, and the West Indies lost seven wickets for 57 – with their last five wickets falling for 27 runs. Flintoff ran through the lower order to claim his first five-wicket haul in Test cricket, while Harmison finished with 3 for 42.

England were left with 12 overs in which to survive on the first evening, losing Trescothick for two, and the following day was comfortably the West Indies' most productive of the series to date.

Had it not been for a wonderfully determined century by Thorpe, the outcome of the match might have been very different. As wickets tumbled all around him, the left-hander battled away, facing 217 balls for his unbeaten 119. The true value of the innings is best illustrated by the fact that the next top score was only 17, and the highest partnership was the 39 runs added by Thorpe and Harmison for the last wicket, of which Harmison's contribution was just three!

At the start of the third day, the West Indies led by only 19 with nine wickets in hand, and you could cut the tension with a knife. It felt like Sabina Park revisited, with the West Indies having to bat under pressure once again – only this time they were doing so in order to save the series. The crowd urged England's bowlers on – but not even the most optimistic follower could have anticipated the rout they were about to see.

Daren Ganga edged Hoggard to Thorpe for 11, and when Sarwan was taken in the gully off the same bowler, the West Indies were 45 for 3, only 41 runs ahead. Next ball, Chanderpaul was lbw to Hoggard and, to complete the hat-trick, Hinds was nonchalantly taken by the ever-dependable Flintoff at second slip. Kensington erupted, and although Lara was still at the crease, the game was up. Flintoff ripped out Jacobs and Best, and when Lara finally mistimed a pull at Harmison, the West Indies were 85 for 9. Harmison applied the *coup de grâce* when Edwards fended to short leg, and as Hoggard led his team from the field, it was nip and tuck as to whether England could score the 93 runs they needed before the end of the day.

This was not helped by the fact that rain had already disrupted play, and it was always a threat, but Vaughan and Trescothick wanted to finish it, and the score rattled up to 57 before Vaughan was caught behind for 32. Trescothick batted fluently to make 42 and, with rain clouds scudding over the ground, Butcher made the winning hit to wrap up a thoroughly one-sided series.

THIRD TEST – WEST INDIES v. ENGLAND
1–5 April 2004 at Bridgetown

WEST INDIES

	First Innings		Second Innings	
CH Gayle	lbw b Hoggard	6	b Harmison	15
D Ganga	lbw b Harmison	11	c Thorpe b Hoggard	11
BC Lara (capt)	c Butcher b Flintoff	36	c Vaughan b Harmison	33
RR Sarwan	c Flintoff b Harmison	63	c Giles b Hoggard	5
S Chanderpaul	c Thorpe b Flintoff	50	lbw b Hoggard	0
RO Hinds	c Jones b Harmison	5	c Flintoff b Hoggard	0
*RD Jacobs	c sub b Flintoff	6	c Butcher b Flintoff	1
TL Best	c Butcher b Flintoff	17	c Trescothick b Flintoff	12
PT Collins	c Trescothick b Jones	7	run out	1
CD Collymore	not out	1	not out	6
FH Edwards	c Read b Flintoff	0	c Hussain b Harmison	2
Extras	lb 14, w 1, nb 7	22	lb 5, nb 3	8
	(75.2 overs)	224	(42.1 overs)	94

	First Innings				Second Innings			
	O	M	R	W	O	M	R	W
Hoggard	16	5	34	1	14	4	35	4
Harmison	18	6	42	3	15.1	5	34	3
Flintoff	16.2	2	58	5	13	4	20	2
Jones	16	1	55	1	-	-	-	-
Giles	9	1	21	0	-	-	-	-

Fall of Wickets
1-6, 2-20, 3-88, 4-167, 5-179, 6-197, 7-198, 8-208, 9-224
1-19, 2-34, 3-45, 4-45, 5-45, 6-48, 7-80, 8-81, 9-85

ENGLAND

	First Innings		Second Innings	
ME Trescothick	b Edwards	2	c Jacobs b Collymore	42
MP Vaughan (capt)	c Jacobs b Edwards	17	c Jacobs b Collymore	32
MA Butcher	c Gayle b Edwards	5	not out	13
N Hussain	b Collymore	17	not out	0
GP Thorpe	not out	119		
A Flintoff	c Collymore b Best	15		
*CMW Read	lbw b Edwards	13		
AF Giles	c sub b Collins	11		
MJ Hoggard	lbw b Collins	0		
SP Jones	c Sarwan b Best	4		
SJ Harmison	b Collins	3		
Extras	lb 5, w 3, nb 12	20	lb 3, w 1, nb 2	6
	(90 overs)	226	(2 wkts 20 overs)	93

	First Innings				Second Innings			
	O	M	R	W	O	M	R	W
Edwards	20	4	70	4	6	0	32	0
Collins	23	6	60	3	4	0	16	0
Collymore	16	3	26	1	7	2	24	2
Hinds	4	1	7	0	-	-	-	-
Best	14	4	26	2	3	0	18	0
Gayle	13	3	32	0	-	-	-	-

Fall of Wickets
1-8, 2-24, 3-33, 4-65, 5-90, 6-119, 7-147, 8-155, 9-187
1-57, 2-91

Umpires: DB Hair and RE Koertzen
Toss: England
Man of the Match: GP Thorpe

England won by 8 wickets

Brian Lara bagged a world record for the second time in St John's in Antigua becoming the first man ever to score 400 in a Test innings.

– and this one looked dreadfully flat. Hardly the sort of thing he would have liked to bowl on?

'Something always happens in an Antigua Test', he assured me, with a cheerful slap on my back. And sure enough it did. Indeed, it is difficult to think that anything more remarkable can ever have happened in international cricket.

On the very same ground where, almost exactly ten years earlier, he broke the record for the highest score in Test cricket, Brian Lara did it again and, in so doing, became the first man ever to score 400 in a Test innings.

Since losing his crown to Australia's Matthew Hayden in October 2003, this was only Lara's tenth opportunity to reclaim it. There are those who claim that it was an entirely selfish innings, in which he put his personal ambition before the needs of his team, which was facing the prospect of its first-ever whitewash. However, Lara's defence is that the pitch was so desperately slow and unforgiving that only a massive weight of runs could possibly have put pressure on England.

As was the case with Lara's 375 in 1994, much of the innings was unremarkable. It was methodical, and owed much to his ruthless

FOURTH TEST
10–14 April 2004 at St John's, Antigua

The day before the final match of the series, I was inspecting the pitch at St John's with my old friend Andy Roberts. Once one of the most feared fast bowlers in the world, Andy is now the man who prepares the Test pitches on the Recreation Ground

powers of concentration. By tea on the second day, Lara was 224 not out and, suddenly, the possibility of reclaiming the record from Hayden seemed a realistic aim. The West Indies were by then 449 for 4, so there was enough batting to support him, and also enough time.

His triple-century came up before the close of play, and in the course of that second day, his personal contribution to the West Indies' 387 runs was 227. Ridley Jacobs had by now joined his captain and, the following morning, they broke the record for the highest sixth-wicket stand against England.

Lara had already broken Hayden's record, by sweeping Batty for four and, at lunch, he was 384 not out. This is the moment many people thought he should have declared, but out he came again to reach exactly 400 not out from 582 balls, including 43 fours, four sixes and a five. Jacobs completed his century as the West Indies settled for 751 for 5 declared, the highest Test score ever conceded by England.

England needed the small matter of 552 to avoid the follow-on, and when they were dismissed for 285 – still 466 runs behind – it seemed that Lara's extended time at the crease was justified. England were 98 for 5 at one stage, as Edwards, Best and Collins preyed on the weary batsmen, but Flintoff then played one of his most responsible innings for England.

Dropped three times, the Lancastrian went on to score an unbeaten 102 from 224 balls, and he shared a stand of 84 with Geraint Jones, the wicketkeeper who was brought in at the expense of Chris Read in order to bolster England's lower order. Jones scored a promising 38 in his first innings, but it was not enough to prevent England from following on, with a minimum of 141 overs in which to survive.

Many teams would have folded in this situation. The series was won and almost over, and a number of the players were going home, but as if to prove that there is some new-found fight in the England dressing room, Vaughan led from the front. Trescothick was fortunate to survive an appeal for a catch behind before he had scored, and I wonder what difference that made as the openers posted 182 for the first wicket? Trescothick made 88, but Vaughan went on to complete a fine hundred as, with Butcher (61) and then Hussain (56), England made the game safe. With five overs

Michael Vaughan scored 140 to ensure that England drew the Antigua Test.

FOURTH TEST – WEST INDIES v. ENGLAND
10–14 April 2004 at St John's

WEST INDIES

	First Innings	
CH Gayle	c & b Batty	69
D Ganga	lbw b Flintoff	10
BC Lara (capt)	not out	400
RR Sarwan	c Trescothick b Harmison	90
RL Powell	c Hussain b Jones SP	23
RO Hinds	c & b Batty	36
*RD Jacobs	not out	107
TL Best		
PT Collins		
CD Collymore		
FH Edwards		
Extras	b 4, lb 5, w 2, nb 5	16
	(5 wkts dec 202 overs)	751

	First Innings			
	O	M	R	W
Hoggard	18	2	82	0
Harmison	37	6	92	1
Flintoff	35	8	109	1
Jones SP	29	0	146	1
Batty	52	4	185	2
Vaughan	13	0	60	0
Trescothick	18	3	68	0

Fall of Wickets
1-33, 2-98, 3-330, 4-380, 5-469

ENGLAND

	First Innings		Second Innings	
ME Trescothick	c Jacobs b Best	16	c Sarwan b Edwards	88
MP Vaughan (capt)	c Jacobs b Collins	7	c Jacobs b Sarwan	140
MA Butcher	b Collins	52	c Gayle b Hinds	61
N Hussain	b Best	3	b Hinds	56
GP Thorpe	c Collins b Edwards	10	not out	23
A Flintoff	not out	102	c Lara b Sarwan	14
*GO Jones	b Edwards	38	not out	10
GJ Batty	c Gayle b Collins	8		
MJ Hoggard	c Jacobs b Collins	1		
SP Jones	lbw b Hinds	11		
SJ Harmison	b Best	5		
Extras	b 1, lb 5, w 4, nb 22	32	b 4, lb 7, w 3, nb 16	30
	(99 overs)	285	(5 wkts 137 overs)	422

	First Innings				Second Innings			
	O	M	R	W	O	M	R	W
Collins	26	4	76	4	8	2	34	0
Edwards	18	3	70	2	20	2	81	1
Collymore	19	5	45	0	18	3	58	0
Best	10.3	3	37	3	16	1	57	0
Hinds	17.3	7	29	1	38	8	83	2
Sarwan	7	0	18	0	12	2	26	2
Gayle	1	0	4	0	17	6	36	0
Powell	–	–	–	–	8	0	36	0

Fall of Wickets
1-8, 2-45, 3-54, 4-98, 5-98, 6-182, 7-205, 8-229, 9-283
1-182, 2-274, 3-366, 4-387, 5-408

Umpires: Aleem Dar and DB Hair
Toss: West Indies
Man of the Match: BC Lara
Man of the Series: SJ Harmison

Match drawn

SERIES AVERAGES
West Indies v. England

WEST INDIES

Batting	M	Inns	NO	Runs	HS	Av	100	50	c/st
BC Lara	4	7	1	500	400*	83.33	1	–	2/-
RD Jacobs	4	7	1	277	107*	46.16	1	1	10/-
DS Smith	2	4	0	172	108	43.00	1	–	1/-
RR Sarwan	4	7	0	192	90	27.42	–	2	2/-
CH Gayle	4	7	0	182	69	26.00	–	2	4/-
RO Hinds	3	5	0	128	84	25.60	–	1	2/-
RL Powell	1	1	0	23	23	23.00	–	–	-/-
S Chanderpaul	3	6	0	101	50	16.83	–	1	-/-
DR Smith	1	2	0	30	16	15.00	–	–	1/-
D Ganga	2	3	0	32	11	10.66	–	–	-/-
TL Best	4	6	0	52	20	8.66	–	–	-/-
PT Collins	3	4	0	25	10	6.25	–	–	1/-
A Sanford	2	4	0	4	1	1.00	–	–	3/-
FH Edwards	3	4	0	3	2	0.75	–	–	-/-
CD Collymore	4	6	6	15	6*	–	–	–	1/-

Bowling	Overs	Mds	Runs	Wkts	Av	Best	5/inn	10m
RR Sarwan	24	3	53	3	17.66	2-26	–	–
TL Best	96	14	301	12	25.08	3-37	–	–
PT Collins	94	20	282	11	25.63	4-71	–	–
DR Smith	9	0	30	1	30.00	1-30	–	–
FH Edwards	83.3	12	325	10	32.50	4-70	–	–
RO Hinds	72.2	18	148	4	37.00	2-83	–	–
CH Gayle	48.5	15	98	2	49.00	2-20	–	–
A Sanford	52	8	182	3	60.66	2-32	–	–
CD Collymore	113	28	255	3	85.00	2-24	–	–
RL Powell	8	0	36	0	–	–	–	–

ENGLAND

Batting	M	Inns	NO	Runs	HS	Av	100	50	c/st
GP Thorpe	4	6	3	274	119*	91.33	1	1	3/-
MA Butcher	4	7	2	296	61	59.20	–	4	4/-
A Flintoff	4	5	1	200	102*	50.00	1	–	7/-
GO Jones	1	2	1	48	38	48.00	–	–	-/-
MP Vaughan	4	8	1	245	140	35.00	1	–	2/-
N Hussain	4	7	0	197	58	32.83	–	3	5/-
AF Giles	3	3	0	75	37	25.00	–	–	2/-
ME Trescothick	4	8	1	166	88	23.71	–	1	7/-
CMW Read	3	3	0	36	20	12.00	–	–	6/1
GJ Batty	1	1	0	8	8	8.00	–	–	2/-
SP Jones	4	4	0	23	11	5.75	–	–	1/-
SJ Harmison	4	4	0	21	13	5.25	–	–	-/-
MJ Hoggard	4	4	2	10	9*	5.00	–	–	2/-

Bowling	Overs	Mds	Runs	Wkts	Av	Best	5/inn	10m
SJ Harmison	139.5	41	342	23	14.86	7-12	2	–
MJ Hoggard	106.4	24	326	13	25.07	4-35	–	–
A Flintoff	102.2	21	297	11	27.00	5-58	1	–
SP Jones	94	8	374	11	34.00	5-57	1	–
AF Giles	31	2	137	2	68.50	2-67	–	–
GJ Batty	52	4	185	2	92.50	2-185	–	–
MP Vaughan	14	0	62	0	–	–	–	–
ME Trescothick	19	3	72	0	–	–	–	–

remaining, Lara called it off with a great deal of personal satisfaction to show from a game in which the winner was Andy Roberts' pitch.

ONE–DAY INTERNATIONALS
v. England

Match One
18 April 2004 at Georgetown
West Indies 156 for 5 (30 overs) (S Chanderpaul 84)
England 157 for 8 (29.3 overs)
England won by 2 wickets

Match Two
24 April 2004 at Port-of-Spain
West Indies 57 for 2 (16 overs)
England Did not bat
Match abandoned due to rain

Match Three
25 April 2004 at Port-of-Spain
West Indies v. England
Match abandoned due to rain

Match Four
28 April 2004 at St George's
West Indies v. England
Match abandoned due to rain

Match Five
1 May 2004 at Boursejour
England 281 for 8 (50 overs) (ME Trescothick 130, A Flintoff 59)
West Indies 284 for 5 (48 overs) (RR Sarwan 73*)
West Indies won by 5 wickets

Match Six
2 May 2004 at Boursejour
England 280 for 8 (50 overs) (MP Vaughan 67, AJ Strauss 67)
West Indies 282 for 6 (47.1 overs) (S Chanderpaul 63, BC Lara 57)
West Indies won by 4 wickets

Match Seven
5 May 2004 at Bridgetown
West Indies 261 for 6 (50 overs) (RR Sarwan 104*)
England 262 for 5 (47.2 overs) (ME Trescothick 82, AJ Strauss 66)
England won by 5 wickets

After two of their three one-day internationals in Sri Lanka were obliterated by the weather, the last thing England expected was for the torrential rain to follow them to the Caribbean. But follow them it did, to such an extent that three consecutive games were washed out, meaning that Michael Vaughan's team had, at that stage, lost five out of nine one-day internationals to the elements.

It was a miracle that the first match in Guyana was played at all, and this was almost entirely due to the efforts of a helicopter, which hovered just above the ground and dried the soggy outfield. Only 30 overs per side were possible, and the West Indies reached 156 for 5, thanks to Shivnarine Chanderpaul's 84 from 96 balls.

England made rather a mess of their reply, and slipped to 131 for 7, but their unlikely hero was Chris Read, who had only just been dropped from the Test team because of his lack of success with the bat.

Read thrashed three sixes when England needed 35 from four overs and, with Darren Gough, reduced the requirement to just three from the last, which was achieved with three balls to spare.

The next three games, scheduled for Trinidad and Grenada, were all abandoned – although 16 overs

Chris Read was the hero of England's dramatic one–day victory in Georgetown.

were possible in the first game at Queens Park before the rain returned – and the frustration finally eased when the teams arrived in St Lucia and, finally, found blue skies.

The West Indies drew level in the series, easing to their target of 282 with two overs and five wickets in hand. Dwayne Smith served a timely reminder of his awesome hitting with 44 from 28 balls as he and Sarwan, who made 73 not out, put on 80 in just nine overs. This steered the home side to an exciting victory after Trescothick showed his first glimpse of form on the tour by hitting 130.

The following day, the West Indies took the lead with a four-wicket win. Their target was just one run less than in the previous match, although they needed a solid contribution from Dwayne Bravo in the lower order to achieve it. Lara scored 57 and Chanderpaul 63, after England failed to capitalise on their position of 199 for 2.

So, England needed to win the final game in Barbados to level the series, and this they achieved after restricting the West Indies to 261 for 6 from their 50 overs – an innings entirely dominated by Sarwan's unbeaten 104.

Jacobs also weighed in with 32 at the end, but it had been a struggle, and once England had progressed to 123 for 1, with Trescothick scoring 82 from 57 balls, they were well on course. Clarke and Flintoff both fell cheaply, but Paul Collingwood steered his team home with 22 balls to spare by scoring 46 not out.

ONE-DAY INTERNATIONALS
v. Bangladesh

Match One
15 May at Arnos Vale
Bangladesh 144 for 8 (50 overs) (TL Best 4 for 35)
West Indies 145 for 9 (46.4 overs) (RL Powell 52)
West Indies won by 1 wicket

Match Two
16 May at Arnos Vale
West Indies 124 for 7 (25 overs) (DR Smith 62*, Tapash Baisya 4 for 16)
Bangladesh 101 for 8 (25 overs)
West Indies won by 23 runs

Match Three
19 May at St George's
Bangladesh 118 for 7 (25 overs)
West Indies 119 for 3 (24.1 overs)
West Indies won by 7 wickets

FIRST TEST – WEST INDIES v. BANGLADESH
28 May–1 June 2004 at Gros Islet

BANGLADESH

	First Innings		Second Innings	
Hannan Sarkar	lbw b Collins	0	b Edwards	9
Javed Omar	c Smith DS b Collins	32	c Jacobs b Collins	7
Habibul Bashar (capt)	c Smith DR b Lawson	113	b Best	25
Rajin Saleh	c Jacobs b Sarwan	26	lbw b Edwards	51
Mohammad Ashraful	lbw b Lawson	81	c and b Sarwan	1
Faisal Hossain	c Best b Collins	5	c Gayle b Sarwan	2
Mushfiqur Rahman	c Jacobs b Sarwan	1	lbw b Sarwan	0
*Khaled Mashud	st Jacobs b Gayle	2	not out	103
Mohammad Rafique	b Collins	111	c Jacobs b Sarwan	29
Tapash Baisya	c & b Sarwan	9	c & b Gayle	26
Tareq Aziz	not out	6	not out	1
Extras	lb 10, w 1, nb 19	30	lb 5, nb 12	17
	(135.3 overs)	416	(9 wkts dec 105.2 overs)	271

	First Innings				Second Innings			
	O	M	R	W	O	M	R	W
Collins	27.3	8	83	4	17	5	42	1
Edwards	21	2	78	0	19	1	61	2
Lawson	16	2	66	2	16	0	60	0
Best	20	4	64	0	13	1	33	1
Smith DR	4	1	5	0	-	-	-	-
Gayle	24	3	51	1	19.2	7	33	1
Sarwan	23	7	59	3	20	9	37	4
Chanderpaul					1	1	0	0

Fall of Wickets: 1-0, 2-121, 3-171, 4-227, 5-238, 6-241, 7-250, 8-337, 9-370
1-17, 2-21, 3-70, 4-73, 5-79, 6-79, 7-123, 8-179, 9-253

WEST INDIES

	First Innings		Second Innings	
DS Smith	run out	0	(2) not out	40
CH Gayle	c Habibul Bashar b Tapash Baisya	141	(1) not out	66
RR Sarwan	c M Rafique b Tapash Baisya	40		
BC Lara (capt)	c K Mashud b Mushfiqur Rahman	53		
S Chanderpaul	c K Mashud b Mohammad Rafique	7		
DR Smith	c T Aziz b Mohammad Rafique	42		
*RD Jacobs	not out	46		
TL Best	b Mohammad Rafique	3		
PT Collins	c H Bashar b Mushfiqur Rahman	4		
JJC Lawson	c H Sarkar b Mushfiqur Rahman	0		
FH Edwards	lbw b Mushfiqur Rahman	5		
Extras	lb 3, nb 8	11	b 4, lb 1, nb 2	7
	(116.4 overs)	352	(23 overs)	113

	First Innings				Second Innings			
	O	M	R	W	O	M	R	W
Tapash Baisya	26	5	87	2	3	0	26	0
Tareq Aziz	23	3	95	0	6	1	31	0
Mushfiqur Rahman	25.4	8	65	4	6	0	25	0
Mohammad Rafique	36	12	90	3	5	1	7	0
Rajin Saleh	6	0	12	0	-	-	-	-
Mohammad Ashraful	-	-	-	-	3	0	19	0

Fall of Wickets: 1-2, 2-89, 3-162, 4-183, 5-253, 6-312, 7-321, 8-336, 9-342

Umpires: DJ Harper and JW Lloyds
Toss: Bangladesh
Man of the Match: CH Gayle

Match drawn

SECOND TEST – WEST INDIES v. BANGLADESH
4–7 June 2004 at Kingston

BANGLADESH

	First Innings		Second Innings	
Hannan Sarkar	lbw b Collins	0	(2) lbw b Collins	10
Javed Omar	c Jacobs b Edwards	20	(1) c Smith DR b Best	5
Habibul Bashar (capt)	c Banks b Collins	20	lbw b Collins	77
Rajin Saleh	c & b Banks	47	c Smith DR b Collins	0
Mohammad Ashraful	c Sarwan b Banks	16	(6) c Lara b Sarwan	9
Manjural Islam Rana	c Jacobs b Best	7	(5) c Lara b Banks	35
Mushfiqur Rahman	st Jacobs b Banks	22	c Smith DR b Collins	0
*Khaled Mashud	c Banks b Edwards	39	c Sarwan b Banks	0
Mohammad Rafique	c Collins b Banks	30	b Collins	2
Tapash Baisya	c Smith DS b Collins	48	c Sarwan b Collins	3
Tareq Aziz	not out	10	not out	5
Extras	b 4, lb 7, w 2, nb 12	25	b 8, lb 6, w 8, nb 8	30
	(95 overs)	284	(51 overs)	176

	First Innings				Second Innings			
	O	M	R	W	O	M	R	W
Collins	19	2	64	3	18	3	53	6
Edwards	20	5	66	2	–	–	–	–
Best	20	4	53	1	10	0	32	1
Banks	31	5	87	4	13	2	40	2
Sarwan	2	2	0	0	3	1	9	1
Smith DR	3	1	3	0	5	1	19	0
Gayle	–	–	–	–	2	0	9	0

Fall of Wickets: 1-0, 2-37, 3-54, 4-88, 5-97, 6-145, 7-152, 8-192, 9-238
1-16, 2-24, 3-34, 4-154, 5-154, 6-154, 7-155, 8-160, 9-164

WEST INDIES

	First Innings	
CH Gayle	c Khaled Mashud b Tareq Aziz	14
DS Smith	run out	44
RR Sarwan	not out	261
BC Lara (capt)	c K Mashud b Mohammad Rafique	120
TL Best	c Khaled Mashud b Tapash Baisya	4
S Chanderpaul	not out	101
DR Smith		
*RD Jacobs		
OAC Banks		
PT Collins		
FH Edwards		
Extras	b 4, lb 5, w 1, nb 5	15
	(4 wkts dec 151 overs)	559

	First Innings			
	O	M	R	W
Tapash Baisya	25	5	99	1
Tareq Aziz	19	2	76	1
Mushfiqur Rahman	33	3	127	0
Mohammad Rafique	38	2	124	1
Manjural Islam Rana	28	2	100	0
Mohammad Ashraful	1	1	0	0
Rajin Saleh	7	1	24	0

Fall of Wickets: 1-26, 2-109, 3-288, 4-297

Umpires: RE Koertzen and JW Lloyds
Toss: Bangladesh
Man of the Match: RR Sarwan
Man of the Series: RR Sarwan

West Indies won by an innings and 99 runs

SERIES AVERAGES
West Indies v. Bangladesh

WEST INDIES

Batting	M	Inns	NO	Runs	HS	Av	100	50	c/st
RR Sarwan	2	2	1	301	261*	301.00	1	–	5/-
CH Gayle	2	3	1	221	141	110.50	1	1	2/-
S Chanderpaul	2	2	1	108	101*	108.00	1	–	-/-
BC Lara	2	2	0	173	120	86.50	1	1	2/-
DS Smith	2	3	1	84	44	42.00	–	–	2/-
DR Smith	2	1	0	42	42	42.00	–	–	4/-
FH Edwards	2	1	0	5	5	5.00	–	–	-/-
PT Collins	2	1	0	4	4	4.00	–	–	1/-
TL Best	2	2	0	7	4	3.50	–	–	1/-
JJC Lawson	1	1	0	0	0	0.00	–	–	-/-
RD Jacobs	2	1	1	46	46*	–	–	–	6/2
OAC Banks	1	0	0	0	0	–	–	–	3/-

Bowling	Overs	Mds	Runs	Wkts	Av	Best	5/inn	10m
RR Sarwan	48	19	105	8	13.12	4-37	–	–
PT Collins	81.3	18	242	14	17.28	6-53	–	1
OAC Banks	44	7	127	6	21.16	4-87	–	–
CH Gayle	45.2	10	93	2	46.50	1-33	–	–
FH Edwards	60	8	205	4	51.25	2-61	–	–
TL Best	63	9	182	3	60.66	1-32	–	–
JJC Lawson	32	2	126	2	63.00	2-66	–	–

Also bowled: S Chanderpaul 1-1-0-0, DR Smith 12-3-27-0.

BANGLADESH

Batting	M	Inns	NO	Runs	HS	Av	100	50	c/st
Habibul Bashar	2	4	0	235	113	58.75	1	1	2/-
Khaled Mashud	2	4	1	144	103*	48.00	1	–	5/-
Mohammad Rafique	2	4	0	172	111	43.00	1	–	-/-
Rajin Saleh	2	4	0	124	51	31.00	–	1	-/-
Mohammad Ashraful	2	4	0	107	81	26.75	–	1	-/-
Tapash Baisya	2	4	0	86	48	21.50	–	–	-/-
Manjural Islam Rana	1	2	0	42	35	21.00	–	–	-/-
Javed Omar	2	4	0	64	32	16.00	–	–	-/-
Mushfiqur Rahman	2	4	0	23	22	5.75	–	–	-/-
Hannan Sarkar	2	4	0	19	10	4.75	–	–	1/-
Faisal Hossain	1	2	0	7	5	3.50	–	–	-/-
Tareq Aziz	2	4	4	22	10*	–	–	–	1/-

Bowling	Overs	Mds	Runs	Wkts	Av	Best	5/inn	10m
Mushfiqur Rahman	64.4	11	217	4	54.25	4-65	–	–
Mohammad Rafique	79	15	221	4	55.25	3-90	–	–
Tapash Baisya	54	10	212	3	70.66	2-87	–	–
Tareq Aziz	48	6	202	1	202.00	1-76	–	–

Also bowled: Mohammad Ashraful 4-1-19-0, Rajin Saleh 13-1-36-0,
Manjural Islam Rana 28-2-100-0.

LARA'S 400 NOT OUT

By Tony Cozier

As he had done five years earlier, Brian Lara once again transformed a situation of deep personal, and team, crisis into one of critical revival and triumph at the scene of his most celebrated innings.

The sheer statistical weight of his unbeaten 400 speaks for itself, as did the unforgettable 375 at the same Antigua Recreation Ground ten years earlier which eclipsed the Test cricket record of another phenomenal West Indian left-hander, Sir Gary Sobers.

That feat linked him with the finest all-round cricketer the game has known. Now he joined the greatest of all batsmen, the great Sir Don Bradman, as the only players to pass 300 twice in Tests.

Indeed, it surpassed anything even The Don had achieved, as Lara reclaimed the record that had been snatched from him by the Australian left-handed opener Matthew Hayden when he scored 380 against Zimbabwe in Perth the previous October and in the process became the first player to reach the unimaginable figure of 400.

What such bland facts and figures do not reveal is the immense pressure that had to be borne to fashion them.

When Lara walked to the middle at the early fall of the first wicket on the first morning, his own fortunes, and those of West Indies cricket, were at a lower ebb than they have ever been.

England, an old enemy for reasons beyond cricket alone, had heaped humiliation on Lara and his team with crushing victories in the first three Tests. They had routed them for 47 in the first Test, a tiny tots total, and the lowest they had ever recorded in 76 years of Test cricket. They had blown them away for 94 in the third Test at Kensington Oval, a ground that had once been regarded as their impenetrable fortress.

England were on the verge of the unthinkable: the first clean sweep of a series in the Caribbean by any visiting team. As a result, hordes of English fans had flown across the Atlantic and shelled out plenty of money to enjoy the experience that would compensate for decades of similar defeats in reverse.

As for his captaincy, Lara's tactics, always unconventional, were now widely seen as simply illogical. His second tenure as captain was proving even more disastrous than his first had been, prompting calls, from the great and the humble, for his replacement.

He himself, the team's only batsman fit to be ranked among the best of the day, had been dismissed cheaply in his six previous innings. He had jumped around uncertainly at the crease in a vain effort to counter England's fast, bouncing bowling on fast, bouncing pitches.

In the second innings at his home ground, the Queen's Park Oval, he had slipped himself down to as low as No. 6, describing it as a 'tactical' decision but transmitting to England the idea of a leader abrogating his responsibility.

It was an error he duly recognised, for he was back at No. 3 in the following Test, his natural place but one that he had not filled for three years.

The burden he carried into the match was, therefore, greater than any West Indies captain could ever have known – except Lara himself. As he acknowleged, he was once more drinking in the last-chance saloon.

'The next five days are very important in terms of my future as captain', he said prior to the match. 'No captain, no team, wants to go down for the first time in their history as losing all their Test matches at home.'

But he had travelled the same rocky path before and he knew the way out.

In 1999, in his first term as captain, a 5–0 walloping in the Test series in South Africa was followed two months later by defeat by 312 runs in the first Test on his home ground at the Queen's Park Oval where the West Indies were routed for 51 in the second innings by Australia. Placed on probation prior to that series by a Board that criticised his leadership in South Africa, Lara was the boy on the burning deck.

What followed was the stuff of dreams. All but single-handedly, he revived the West Indies' fortunes with innings of 213 at Sabina Park and 153 not out at Kensington Oval that secured incredible victories and a 2–2 share of the series.

This time, the contest may have already been decided but just as much was at stake, perhaps even more. His latest act of revival, like the first, could not mask the serious problems confronting West Indies cricket or the reasons why his team should be relying on him to save them from the indignity of a clean sweep. However, at least it rekindled the confidence and assuaged the anguish of a depressed people, if only temporarily.

A torrid year ended in triumph for Lara as he led the West Indies to victory in the ICC Champions Trophy in England.

Under Pressure: Facing a series whitewash for the first time in the Caribbean, Brian Lara responded by beating Matthew Hayden's record to become the first player to score 400 in Test cricket.

Though the West Indies had a poor Test Series in England, Lara's captaincy was firm and consistent as was his dependable slip catching.

WEST INDIES REPORT
By Tony Cozier

The gloom and doom that has settled over West Indies cricket for several years intensified during a period of uninterrupted international campaigns between November 2002 and August 2004.

There were heavy defeats in three of the four Tests in South Africa and, more humiliating for reasons far beyond cricket alone, in seven out of eight at home and away against England.

The shame was complete with a 4–0 whitewash in England, inflicted through victory by ten wickets, in three days, at The Oval in late August.

Suddenly, however, and just over a month later at the same venue, a bright shaft of light emerged from a sky as dark and dismal as the mood that has enveloped West Indies cricket for so long.

The stirring triumph on a shivering early autumn day in the ICC Champions Trophy final, over the same opponents who had so mastered them in the preceding six months, was the first success in a global tournament since Clive Lloyd lifted the 1979 World Cup.

It instantly lifted spirits in a part of the world where the game is followed with religious fervour, even more so as it coincided with the devastation and loss of life caused throughout the region by a couple of hurricanes.

Until then, Brian Lara's phenomenal unbeaten 400 in the final Test in Antigua in April, which reclaimed for him Test cricket's highest score and prevented England from achieving their clean sweep four months earlier, was the only crumb of comfort for the public of the cricketing Caribbean.

The departure of Sir Viv Richards as chief selector, following the home series against England, was further troubling evidence of internal divisions.

After five years of similar reversals, the West Indies Cricket Board (WICB) decided that profound changes were needed to try to put things right.

The most significant were the new powers accorded to the head coach, similar to those of English football managers and coaches in American sport. Ironically, the incumbent Gus Logie had his contract terminated immediately following the Champions Trophy triumph with the assumption that his successor would come from outside the West Indies.

The hope was that the changes would lead to a turnaround in the team's fortune – a turnaround similar to Barbados' at domestic level.

Barbados had won the regional championship more than all the other teams combined but had failed to make the top four and qualify for the semi-finals in 2002.

In the succeeding seasons, they comfortably won both the renamed Carib Beer Cup and Carib Beer International Challenge, extending their unbeaten run to 21 matches.

They just failed to retain the limited-overs Red Stripe Bowl they won in 2002, losing to Guyana in the 2003 final, but their Under 15s and Under 19s were champions in their tournaments.

Victory in all seven first-round Carib Beer Cup matches was a record. No other team won more than three. They had a gap of 32 points over second-placed Jamaica.

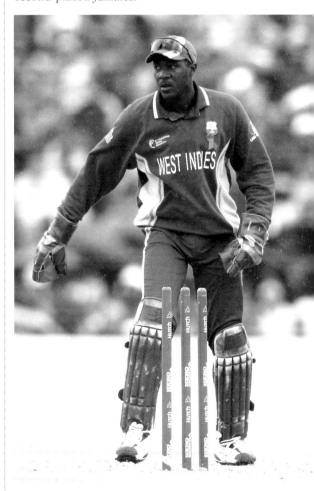

Courtney Browne: a successful season at the helm of Barbados climaxed with him leading the West Indies to victory in the ICC Champions Trophy final.

Their captain was Courtney Browne who, along with another Barbadian, the left-handed all-rounder Ian Bradshaw, was one of the heroes of the victory in the Champions Trophy final. His leadership, the team's self-belief and their combination of proven experience and enthusiastic youth were at the heart of their success.

Barbados had the two leading wicket-takers in Pedro Collins, the left-arm swing bowler, whose 43 were taken at 18.13 runs each, six more than the lively, enthusiastic Tino Best who had 37 at a cost of 13.75 in two fewer matches.

The Windwards, who gained a semi-final berth for the first time since the format was changed in 2001, had the batsman of the season. The left-handed opener Devon Smith's 842-run tally (at an average of 76.54) was 283 more than the next highest, the veteran Sherwin Campbell's 559 for Barbados, and was based on four hundreds.

The top all-rounder was Dwayne Bravo, the 20-year-old Trinidadian, with 481 runs (average 37) and 28 wickets (at 13.66 each). It was this form that brought him into the West Indies team for the first time.

Kenya was the invited foreign team, following the A teams of England, India and Bangladesh in previous years, but their players were daunted by the unusual experience of seven four-day matches in less than seven weeks. It proved too demanding for them and they did not win a match. The WICB later announced that it was the last year an overseas team would be invited to the tournament.

As preparations for the 2007 ICC World Cup were intensified, Guyana, Antigua and Jamaica announced that they would construct new stadiums. Kensington Oval in Barbados would be almost totally rebuilt to hold 30,000 spectators. Others chosen to host matches would be upgraded.

Preliminary groups, of six matches each, were assigned to Jamaica, St Lucia, Trinidad and

Dwayne Bravo was the leading all-rounder in West Indies domestic cricket – form he took into the Test series in England.

St Kitts. Antigua, Barbados, Grenada and Guyana gained the quarter-finals, the so-called Super Eights, and Jamaica and St Lucia a semi-final each. The final went to Barbados.

The WICB expects some US$100 million to be generated by the event, but acknowledges that its success depends on its organisational ability and on a strong showing by the West Indies team.

AUSTRALIA

AUSTRALIA REPORT
By Jim Maxwell

India's challenging performance threatened to derail Steve Waugh's farewell season, with Australia scrambling a win out of the deciding Test for a draw that left the series tied at 1–1.

Like a departing film star, however, Waugh had the last word with a valedictory innings that frustrated opponents who were thwarted by his defiance.

The season had begun spectacularly when Matt Hayden eclipsed Brian Lara's Test record against Zimbabwe in October. He pummelled underwhelming bowling to set the tone for high scoring throughout the Test matches.

Australia's 735 for 6 was followed by innings totals of 556 (by Australia) and 523 (by India) in the Adelaide Test, Australia's 558 in Melbourne and India's imposing 705 for 7 in Sydney.

Australia defeated Zimbabwe convincingly in two Tests, as Hayden followed his massive 380 with another century in Sydney from just 84 deliveries. Small crowds cheered Hayden's powerful, applied batting, as a schedule with an enforced early start in October, and the competing excitement of the Rugby World Cup, affected attendances.

While Australia were winning a one-day series in India, Steve Waugh, given no security of tenure by the selectors and tiring of the constant speculation about his future, announced his retirement.

Glenn McGrath's ankle surgery and Shane Warne's continued absence while he carried out his suspension for drug abuse, placed expectations on Lee, Gillespie and MacGill to deliver a resounding home win.

Warne talked up the 'chin music' from the commentary box, and several Australian players swaggered that the combination of higher bounce, and India's inability to cope with it, would be overwhelming.

At 62 for 3, with Gillespie having removed Tendulkar for a duck, India seemed to be heading for that anticipated demise on the second morning at the Gabba, but, rivalling the celebrated deeds of

Matthew Hayden, who began the year as the holder of the Test record score following his 380 against Zimbabwe in October 2003.

Rahul Dravid underlined his high class with a string of fine performances against Australia.

his adversary, Steve Waugh, Ganguly counter-punched with the most satisfying century of his Test career. With Laxman's support, he carried India to a healthy position and, in the process, built the visitors' confidence in a drawn game.

Hayden's second-innings 99 took him past a thousand Test runs for a third successive year, the first player in the history of the game to achieve the feat.

In Adelaide, India were again on the precipice at 85 for 4, chasing 556. The heroes of Calcutta in 2001, Dravid and Laxman, mounted a wonderful recovery with a triple-century partnership. The underrated Agarkar then cut through Australia's top order in the second innings, with Waugh and Martyn both falling to loose shots, leaving India 230 to win.

Gilchrist dropped Dravid on nine and, following his majestic first-innings 233, India's No. 3 steered his side to an unlikely six-wicket win with 72 not out. It had been ten years since Australia had been one down in a home series, and India's star batsman Tendulkar had made only 38 runs in three innings.

Virender Sehwag celebrated Christmas on Boxing Day, lambasting the bowling all over the MCG. Aiming for his seventh six and a double-hundred, he holed out to deep midwicket – it was a disappointing stroke that cued a rapid turn of fortune for a ragged Australian attack.

India nosedived from 311 for 3 to 366 all out. Ponting played straight and ruthlessly, forging out his second double-century of the series, and was helped by Hayden's chanceless 136. India, guided by Dravid and Ganguly, worked hard to set a target, but Australia won by nine wickets before lunch on the final day.

Three days later, Ganguly sat back after winning the toss and watched Tendulkar and Laxman create a memorable, massive partnership on an SCG road. Tendulkar avoided any off-stump invitations, confining his attack to precise onside placements, while the wristy Laxman found gaps with the efficiency of a dart thrower hitting bull's-eyes.

Langer and Hayden set off at a rate of four-plus runs an over in reply, attacking Kumble's bouncing top spin. Langer raised his 17th Test hundred with a cheeky reverse sweep, before becoming one of eight victims for the persevering Kumble.

Ganguly did not enforce the follow-on, hoping that the pitch would deteriorate. His declaration, offering the home side 443 from 94 overs, had a hint of 'we could still lose', and with Kumble carrying the attack on a pitch that remained unblemished, India seemed unable to press harder for victory.

Waugh's innings sustained the crowd's fascination, and prolonged their applause when he was caught on the boundary attempting to score a valedictory hundred in the final overs.

A draw gave India their best result in Australia since 1980–81 – a series that also ended with a 1–1 scoreline – and completed Steve Waugh's remarkable reign as captain, in which he won 41 out of 57 Tests.

Jubilant Indian supporters could reason a points victory for their team, but it was presumptuous to predict the start of an Australian slide.

India maintained their excellent form in the one-day series, eclipsing Zimbabwe for the finals, where, alas, they were overwhelmed, with Australia equalling their record World Cup final total of 359. At the end of an arduous tour, India's energies were spent and they were enveloped by Ponting's powerful and versatile team.

In January, meanwhile, cricket fans were numbed by the sudden death of David Hookes, the victim of a nightclub bouncer's assault after an evening out with members of the team he was coaching, Victoria.

Hookes' popularity as a dashing batsman flowed into his media career, and the Victorian team were understandably devastated by such a senseless act. They recovered to record an impressive win over Queensland in the Pura Cup final, an emotional victory encapsulated by a banner that read: 'Hookesy and the Vics – We Salute You.'

Australia's leadership moved seamlessly from Waugh to Ponting, who followed a clean-sweep win over Sri Lanka with a victory in the out-of-season 'top-end' tour.

Warne made a dramatic return from suspension, taking 26 wickets in Sri Lanka, and with Muralitharan avoiding a visit Down Under, saying that he needed a rest, Warne dramatically took his 527th Test wicket to equal his rival's distinguished record.

Steve Waugh hits out during the final months of his great Test career.

VB SERIES
(Australia, India and Zimbabwe)

Match One
9 January 2004 at Melbourne (MCG)
Australia 288 (48.3 overs) (A Symonds 88,
MJ Clarke 63, AB Agarkar 6 for 42)
India 270 (49 overs) (SC Ganguly 82,
SR Tendulkar 63)
Australia won by 18 runs

Match Two
11 January 2004 at Sydney
Australia 225 for 8 (50 overs) (SM Ervine 3 for 53)
Zimbabwe 126 (37.3 overs) (BA Williams 5 for 22)
Australia won by 99 runs

Match Three
14 January 2004 at Hobart
Zimbabwe 208 for 6 (50 overs) (HH Streak 59*)
India 211 for 3 (37.4 overs) (V Sehwag 90)
India won by 7 wickets

Match Four
16 January 2004 at Hobart
Australia 344 for 7 (50 overs) (AC Gilchrist 172,
ML Hayden 63)
Zimbabwe 196 for 6 (50 overs) (HH Streak 64*)
Australia won by 148 runs

Match Five
18 January 2004 at Brisbane
India 303 for 4 (50 overs) (VVS Laxman 103*,
SR Tendulkar 86, R Dravid 74)
Australia 284 (49.4 overs) (ML Hayden 109,
L Balaji 4 for 48)
India won by 19 runs

Match Six
20 January 2004 at Brisbane
India 255 for 6 (50 overs) (R Dravid 84,
Yuvraj Singh 69)
Zimbabwe 231 for 9 (47.1 overs)
India won by 24 runs

Match Seven
22 January 2004 at Sydney
India 296 for 4 (50 overs) (Yuvraj Singh 139,
VVS Laxman 106*)
Australia 225 for 8 (33.5 overs)
(AC Gilchrist 95)
*Australia won by 2 wickets – DL Method: target 225
from 34 overs*

Match Eight
24 January 2004 at Adelaide
India 280 for 7 (50 overs) (VVS Laxman 131,
R Dravid 56, RS Gavaskar 54)
Zimbabwe 277 for 6 (50 overs) (SV Carlisle 109,
SM Ervine 100)
India won by 3 runs

Match Nine
26 January 2004 at Adelaide
Australia 279 for 7 (50 overs) (MG Bevan 75,
RT Ponting 63)
Zimbabwe 266 for 8 (50 overs) (GW Flower 94)
Australia won by 13 runs

Andrew Symonds: consistent form in the one-day arena saw a
Test call-up for this talented all-rounder.

Match Ten
29 January 2004 at Melbourne (MCG)
Australia 263 for 9 (50 overs) (MG Bevan 56)
Zimbabwe
Match abandoned

Match Eleven
1 February 2004 at Perth
India 203 (49 overs)
Australia 204 for 5 (32 overs) (AC Gilchrist 75,
A Symonds 73)
Australia won by 5 wickets

Match Twelve
3 February 2004 at Perth
Zimbabwe 135 (34.4 overs) (IK Pathan 4 for 24)
India 136 for 6 (30.3 overs)
India won by 4 wickets

Match Thirteen (First Final)
6 February 2004 at Melbourne (MCG)
India 222 (49 overs) (HK Badani 60*, AB Agarkar 53)
Australia 224 for 3 (40.1 overs) (RT Ponting 88,
ML Hayden 50)
Australia won by 7 wickets

Match Fourteen (Second Final)
8 February 2004 at Sydney
Australia 359 for 5 (50 overs) (ML Hayden 126,
DR Martyn 67, A Symonds 66)
India 151 (33.2 overs)
Australia won by 208 runs

STOP PRESS:
In many of the world's newspapers, as we went
to press in mid-October 2004, the obituary of
Keith Miller, Australia's finest and most charismatic
all-round cricketer, appeared alongside that
of Christopher Reeve, the actor otherwise
known as Superman.
Miller, who died on 11 October, aged 84, was perhaps
the nearest thing to a cricketing superhuman in
terms of his personality, physique, good looks and
effortless glamour as well as his rare talent.
A fighter pilot during the Second World War, he
survived combat to play the game with a verve and a
cavalier approach which endeared him to spectators.
He scored 2958 runs at 36.97 and took 170 wickets
at 22.97 in 55 Tests – then a record. You can read
the next instalment of the enduring Ashes story,
which heroes like Keith Miller helped to create, in
the *Cheltenham & Gloucester Cricket Year 2005*.

FIRST TEST – AUSTRALIA v. ZIMBABWE
9–13 October 2003 at Perth

AUSTRALIA

	First Innings		
JL Langer	b Ervine		26
ML Hayden	c Carlisle b Gripper		380
RT Ponting	lbw b Ervine		37
DR Martyn	c Wishart b Gripper		53
SR Waugh (capt)	c & b Ervine		78
DS Lehmann	c & b Ervine		30
*AC Gilchrist	not out		113
AJ Bichel			
B Lee			
JN Gillespie			
SCG MacGill			
Extras	b 4, lb 10, w 1, nb 3		18
	(6 wkts dec 146.3 overs)		**735**

	First Innings			
	O	M	R	W
Streak	26	6	131	0
Blignaut	28	4	115	0
Ervine	31	4	146	4
Price	36	5	187	0
Gripper	25.3	0	142	2

Fall of Wickets
1-43, 2-102, 3-199, 4-406, 5-502, 6-735

ZIMBABWE

	First Innings		Second Innings	
DD Ebrahim	b Gillespie	29	b Gillespie	4
TR Gripper	c Lehmann b Lee	53	c Gilchrist b Gillespie	0
MA Vermeulen	c Hayden b MacGill	38	c Gilchrist b Lee	63
SV Carlisle	c Hayden b MacGill	2	c Hayden b Lehmann	35
CB Wishart	c Gilchrist b Bichel	46	lbw b Bichel	8
CN Evans	b Bichel	22	b Lehmann	5
*T Taibu	lbw b Gillespie	15	c Gilchrist b Bichel	3
HH Streak (capt)	b Lee	9	(9) not out	71
SM Ervine	c Waugh b Gillespie	6	(8) b Bichel	53
AM Blignaut	lbw b Lee	0	st Gilchrist b Lehmann	22
RW Price	not out	2	c Waugh b Bichel	36
Extras	lb 10, w 2, nb 5	17	b 4, lb 6, w 5, nb 6	21
	(89.3 overs)	**239**	(127.2 overs)	**321**

	First Innings				Second Innings			
	O	M	R	W	O	M	R	W
Lee	15	4	48	3	35	8	96	1
Gillespie	25.3	9	52	3	3	0	6	2
Bichel	21	2	62	2	28.2	15	63	4
MacGill	21	4	54	2	3.4	1	10	0
Lehmann	2	1	3	0	31.2	15	61	3
Waugh	5	1	10	0	8	2	26	0
Martyn	-	-	-	-	13	5	34	0
Ponting	-	-	-	-	5	1	15	0

Fall of Wickets
1-61, 2-105, 3-120, 4-131, 5-199, 6-200, 7-231, 8-231, 9-231
1-2, 2-11, 3-110, 4-112, 5-118, 6-126, 7-126, 8-209, 9-247

Umpires: S Venkataraghavan and P Willey
Toss: Zimbabwe
Man of the Match: ML Hayden

Australia won by an innings and 175 runs

SECOND TEST – AUSTRALIA v. ZIMBABWE
17–20 October 2003 at Sydney

SERIES AVERAGES
Australia v. Zimbabwe

ZIMBABWE

	First Innings		Second Innings	
DD Ebrahim	b Lee	9	c Katich b Williams	0
TR Gripper	c Gilchrist b Bichel	15	c Hayden b Katich	47
MA Vermeulen	lbw b Williams	17	c Waugh b Williams	48
SV Carlisle	c Ponting b Bichel	118	c Williams b Katich	5
CB Wishart	c Gilchrist b Williams	14	st Gilchrist b Katich	45
*T Taibu	c Gilchrist b Hogg	27	c Ponting b Katich	35
HH Streak (capt)	lbw b Hogg	14	run out	25
GM Ewing	c Martyn b Lee	2	c Gilchrist b Hogg	0
AM Blignaut	not out	38	c Williams b Katich	44
RW Price	c Williams b Bichel	20	lbw b Katich	0
NB Mahwire	c Gilchrist b Bichel	6	not out	1
Extras	b 4, lb 12, w 3, nb 9	28	b 6, lb 5, w 1, nb 4	16
	(107.2 overs)	308	(91.5 overs)	266

	First Innings				Second Innings			
	O	M	R	W	O	M	R	W
Lee	23	5	78	2	–	–	–	–
Williams	23	6	58	2	16	8	56	2
Bichel	24.2	7	66	4	19	5	64	0
Hogg	23	8	49	2	31	9	70	1
Waugh	4	0	7	0	–	–	–	–
Katich	7	0	25	0	25.5	3	65	6
Martyn	3	1	9	0	–	–	–	–

Fall of Wickets
1-15, 2-45, 3-47, 4-95, 5-151, 6-218, 7-222, 8-243, 9-296
1-0, 2-93, 3-103, 4-114, 5-176, 6-212, 7-216, 8-230, 9-244

AUSTRALIA

	First Innings		Second Innings	
JL Langer	c Streak b Blignaut	2	c Taibu b Streak	8
ML Hayden	c Carlisle b Blignaut	20	not out	101
RT Ponting	b Price	169	not out	53
DR Martyn	lbw b Price	32		
SR Waugh (capt)	c Carlisle b Price	61		
SM Katich	b Price	52		
*AC Gilchrist	b Streak	20		
GB Hogg	c Ebrahim b Price	13		
AJ Bichel	c Wishart b Blignaut	5		
B Lee	not out	6		
BA Williams	c & b Price	7		
Extras	lb 2, w 1, nb 13	16	b 3, lb 3, nb 4	10
	(103.3 overs)	403	(1 wkt 29.1 overs)	172

	First Innings				Second Innings			
	O	M	R	W	O	M	R	W
Streak	21	3	83	1	9	1	46	1
Blignaut	20	4	83	3	4	0	35	0
Mahwire	10	1	61	0	–	–	–	–
Price	41.3	6	121	6	12.1	0	63	0
Ewing	11	1	53	0	3	0	20	0
Gripper	–	–	–	–	1	0	2	0

Fall of Wickets
1-7, 2-51, 3-148, 4-283, 5-306, 6-347, 7-375, 8-384, 9-394
1-21

Umpires: BF Bowden and S Venkataraghavan
Toss: Zimbabwe
Test debuts: BA Williams, GM Ewing
Man of the Match: RT Ponting
Man of the Series: ML Hayden

Australia won by 9 wickets

AUSTRALIA

Batting	M	Inns	NO	Runs	HS	Av	100	50	c/st
ML Hayden	2	3	1	501	380	250.50	2	–	4/-
AC Gilchrist	2	2	1	133	113*	133.00	1	–	9/2
RT Ponting	2	3	1	259	169	129.50	1	1	2/-
SR Waugh	2	2	0	139	78	69.50	–	2	3/-
SM Katich	1	1	0	52	52	52.00	–	1	1/-
DR Martyn	2	2	0	85	53	42.50	–	1	1/-
DS Lehmann	1	1	0	30	30	30.00	–	–	1/-
GB Hogg	1	1	0	13	13	13.00	–	–	-/-
JL Langer	2	3	0	36	26	12.00	–	–	-/-
BA Williams	1	1	0	7	7	7.00	–	–	3/-
AJ Bichel	2	1	0	5	5	5.00	–	–	-/-
B Lee	2	1	1	6	6*	–	–	–	-/-
JN Gillespie	1	0	0	0	0	–	–	–	-/-
SCG MacGill	1	0	0	0	0	–	–	–	-/-

Bowling	Overs	Mds	Runs	Wkts	Av	Best	5/inn	10m
JN Gillespie	28.3	9	58	5	11.60	3-52	–	–
SM Katich	32.5	3	90	6	15.00	6-65	1	–
DS Lehmann	33.2	16	64	3	21.33	3-61	–	–
AJ Bichel	92.4	29	255	10	25.50	4-63	–	–
BA Williams	39	14	114	4	28.50	2-56	–	–
SCG MacGill	24.4	5	64	2	32.00	2-54	–	–
B Lee	73	17	222	6	37.00	3-48	–	–
GB Hogg	54	17	119	3	39.66	2-49	–	–

Also bowled: RT Ponting 5-1-15-0, SR Waugh 17-3-43-0, DR Martyn 16-6-43-0.

ZIMBABWE

Batting	M	Inns	NO	Runs	HS	Av	100	50	c/st
MA Vermeulen	2	4	0	166	63	41.50	–	1	-/-
SV Carlisle	2	4	0	160	118	40.00	1	–	3/-
HH Streak	2	4	1	119	71*	39.66	–	1	1/-
AM Blignaut	2	4	1	104	44	34.66	–	–	-/-
SM Ervine	1	2	0	59	53	29.50	–	1	2/-
TR Gripper	2	4	0	115	53	28.75	–	1	-/-
CB Wishart	2	4	0	113	46	28.25	–	–	2/-
T Taibu	2	4	0	80	35	20.00	–	–	1/-
RW Price	2	4	1	58	36	19.33	–	–	1/-
CN Evans	1	2	0	27	22	13.50	–	–	-/-
DD Ebrahim	2	4	0	42	29	10.50	–	–	1/-
NB Mahwire	1	2	1	7	6	7.00	–	–	-/-
GM Ewing	1	2	0	2	2	1.00	–	–	-/-

Bowling	Overs	Mds	Runs	Wkts	Av	Best	5/inn	10m
SM Ervine	31	4	146	4	36.50	4-146	–	–
RW Price	89.4	11	371	6	61.83	6-121	1	–
TR Gripper	26.3	0	144	2	72.00	2-142	–	–
AM Blignaut	52	6	233	3	77.66	3-83	–	–
HH Streak	56	10	260	2	130.00	1-46	–	–

Also bowled: NB Nahwire 10-1-61-0, GM Ewing 14-1-73-0.

FIRST TEST – AUSTRALIA v. INDIA
4–8 December 2003 at Brisbane

AUSTRALIA

	First Innings		Second Innings	
JL Langer	lbw b Agarkar	121	(2) c Patel b Agarkar	0
ML Hayden	c Laxman b Khan	37	(1) c Sehwag b Harbhajan Singh	99
RT Ponting	c Patel b Khan	54	c Sehwag b Nehra	50
DR Martyn	run out	42	not out	66
SR Waugh (capt)	hit wkt b Khan	0	not out	56
SM Katich	c Patel b Khan	16		
*AC Gilchrist	c Laxman b Khan	0		
AJ Bichel	c Laxman b Agarkar	11		
JN Gillespie	run out	8		
NW Bracken	not out	6		
SCG MacGill	c Chopra b Agarkar	1		
Extras	b 4, lb 7, w 2, nb 14	27	b 4, nb 9	13
	(78.1 overs)	323	(3 wkts dec 62 overs)	284

	First Innings				Second Innings			
	O	M	R	W	O	M	R	W
Khan	23	2	95	5	3	0	15	0
Nehra	15	4	51	0	19	1	89	1
Agarkar	25.1	5	90	3	12	3	45	1
Harbhajan Singh	14	1	68	0	21	1	101	1
Ganguly	1	0	8	0	-	-	-	-
Tendulkar	-	-	-	-	2	0	9	0
Sehwag	-	-	-	-	5	1	21	0

Fall of Wickets
1-73, 2-162, 3-268, 4-275, 5-275, 6-276, 7-302, 8-310, 9-317
1-6, 2-146, 3-156

INDIA

	First Innings		Second Innings	
A Chopra	c Hayden b Gillespie	36	c Langer b Bracken	4
V Sehwag	c Hayden b Bracken	45	c Martyn b Bracken	0
R Dravid	c Hayden b Gillespie	1	not out	43
SR Tendulkar	lbw b Gillespie	0		
SC Ganguly (capt)	c Gillespie b MacGill	144		
VVS Laxman	c Katich b MacGill	75	(4) not out	24
*PA Patel	c Bichel b Gillespie	37		
AB Agarkar	c Hayden b Bichel	12		
Harbhajan Singh	not out	19		
Z Khan	b MacGill	27		
A Nehra	lbw b MacGill	0		
Extras	lb 6, w 1, nb 6	13	nb 2	2
	(120.1 overs)	409	(2 wkts 16 overs)	73

	First Innings				Second Innings			
	O	M	R	W	O	M	R	W
Gillespie	31	12	65	4	5	1	17	0
Bracken	26	5	90	1	4	1	12	2
Bichel	28	6	130	1	3	0	12	0
MacGill	26.1	4	86	4	4	0	32	0
Waugh	7	3	16	0	-	-	-	-
Katich	2	0	16	0	-	-	-	-

Fall of Wickets
1-61, 2-62, 3-62, 4-127, 5-273, 6-329, 7-362, 8-362, 9-403
1-4, 2-4

Umpires: SA Bucknor and RE Koertzen
Toss: India
Test debut: NW Bracken
Man of the Match: SC Ganguly

Match drawn

SECOND TEST – AUSTRALIA v. INDIA
12–16 December 2003 at Adelaide

AUSTRALIA

	First Innings		Second Innings	
JL Langer	c Sehwag b Kumble	58	lbw b Agarkar	10
ML Hayden	c Patel b Pathan	12	c Sehwag b Nehra	17
RT Ponting	c Dravid b Kumble	242	c Chopra b Agarkar	0
DR Martyn	c Laxman b Nehra	30	c Dravid b Tendulkar	38
SR Waugh (capt)	b Nehra	30	c Dravid b Tendulkar	42
SM Katich	c Sehwag b Agarkar	75	c Nehra b Agarkar	31
*AC Gilchrist	c Sehwag b Agarkar	29	b Kumble	43
AJ Bichel	c Chopra b Kumble	19	b Agarkar	1
JN Gillespie	not out	48	c Patel b Agarkar	3
BA Williams	b Kumble	0	not out	4
SCG MacGill	lbw b Kumble	0	b Agarkar	1
Extras	b 1, lb 7, w 1, nb 4	13	b 2, lb 2, w 1, nb 1	6
	(127 overs)	556	(56.2 overs)	196

	First Innings				Second Innings			
	O	M	R	W	O	M	R	W
Agarkar	26	1	119	2	16.2	2	41	6
Pathan	27	3	136	1	7	0	24	0
Nehra	25	3	115	2	7	2	21	1
Kumble	43	3	154	5	17	2	58	1
Sehwag	5	0	21	0	3	0	12	0
Tendulkar	1	0	3	0	6	0	36	2

Fall of Wickets
1-22, 2-135, 3-200, 4-252, 5-390, 6-426, 7-473, 8-556, 9-556
1-10, 2-18, 3-44, 4-109, 5-112, 6-183, 7-184, 8-188, 9-192

INDIA

	First Innings		Second Innings	
A Chopra	c & b Bichel	27	lbw b Gillespie	20
V Sehwag	c Hayden b Bichel	47	st Gilchrist b MacGill	47
R Dravid	c Bichel b Gillespie	233	not out	72
SR Tendulkar	c Gilchrist b Bichel	1	lbw b MacGill	37
SC Ganguly (capt)	run out	2	c Katich b Bichel	12
VVS Laxman	c Gilchrist b Bichel	148	c Bichel b Katich	32
*PA Patel	c Ponting b Katich	31	b Katich	3
AB Agarkar	c MacGill b Katich	11	not out	0
A Kumble	lbw b MacGill	12		
IK Pathan	c & b MacGill	1		
A Nehra	not out	0		
Extras	b 4, lb 2, w 2, nb 2	10	b 3, lb 6, w 1	10
	(161.5 overs)	523	(6 wkts 72.4 overs)	233

	First Innings				Second Innings			
	O	M	R	W	O	M	R	W
Gillespie	40.5	13	106	1	10.2	2	22	1
Williams	23	7	72	0	14	6	34	0
Bichel	28	3	118	4	11.4	1	35	1
MacGill	44	8	143	2	24.4	3	101	2
Katich	16	3	59	2	8	1	22	2
Waugh	9	2	15	0	4	0	10	0
Ponting	1	0	4	0	-	-	-	-

Fall of Wickets
1-66, 2-81, 3-83, 4-85, 5-388, 6-447, 7-469, 8-510, 9-518
1-48, 2-79, 3-149, 4-170, 5-221, 6-229

Umpires: RE Koertzen and DR Shepherd
Toss: Australia
Test debut: IK Pathan
Man of the Match: R Dravid

India won by 4 wickets

THIRD TEST – AUSTRALIA v. INDIA
26–30 December 2003 at Melbourne

INDIA

	First Innings		Second Innings	
A Chopra	c Katich b MacGill	48	c Gilchrist b Bracken	4
V Sehwag	c Bracken b Katich	195	c Williams b Lee	11
R Dravid	c Martyn b Waugh	49	c Gilchrist b Lee	92
SR Tendulkar	c Gilchrist b Lee	0	(5) c Gilchrist b Williams	44
SC Ganguly (capt)	c Langer b Lee	37	(4) b Bracken	73
VVS Laxman	c Hayden b MacGill	19	c Hayden b MacGill	18
*PA Patel	c Gilchrist b Bracken	0	not out	27
AB Agarkar	run out	0	b Williams	1
A Kumble	c Langer b Williams	3	lbw b Williams	0
Z Khan	not out	0	c Hayden b Williams	1
A Nehra	c Gilchrist b MacGill	0	c Hayden b MacGill	0
Extras	lb 3, w 1, nb 11	15	b 4, lb 3, w 1, nb 7	15
	(103 overs)	366	(99.5 overs)	286

	First Innings				Second Innings			
	O	M	R	W	O	M	R	W
Lee	27	7	103	2	22	3	97	2
Bracken	28	6	71	1	25	13	45	2
Williams	20	6	66	1	22	5	53	4
MacGill	15	3	70	3	26.5	5	68	2
Katich	4	0	18	1	4	0	16	0
Waugh	9	0	35	1	-	-	-	-

Fall of Wickets
1-141, 2-278, 3-286, 4-311, 5-350, 6-353, 7-353, 8-366, 9-366
1-5, 2-19, 3-126, 4-160, 5-253, 6-258, 7-271, 8-271, 9-277

AUSTRALIA

	First Innings		Second Innings	
JL Langer	c Tendulkar b Agarkar	14	lbw b Agarkar	2
ML Hayden	lbw b Kumble	136	not out	53
RT Ponting	st Patel b Kumble	257	not out	31
*AC Gilchrist	c Nehra b Kumble	14		
DR Martyn	c Patel b Agarkar	31		
SR Waugh (capt)	lbw b Kumble	19		
SM Katich	c Chopra b Kumble	29		
B Lee	c Laxman b Kumble	8		
NW Bracken	c & b Tendulkar	1		
BA Williams	not out	10		
SCG MacGill	lbw b Agarkar	0		
Extras	b 4, lb 8, w 5, nb 17, p 5	39	b 4, lb 2, w 1, nb 4	11
	(151.2 overs)	558	(1 wkt 22.2 overs)	97

	First Innings				Second Innings			
	O	M	R	W	O	M	R	W
Agarkar	33.2	5	115	3	7	2	25	1
Khan	25	4	103	0	-	-	-	-
Nehra	29	3	90	0	6	3	16	0
Kumble	51	8	176	6	6.2	0	43	0
Tendulkar	13	0	57	1	-	-	-	-
Sehwag	-	-	-	-	3	0	7	0

Fall of Wickets
1-30, 2-264, 3-295, 4-373, 5-437, 6-502, 7-535, 8-542, 9-555
1-9

Umpires: BF Bowden and DR Shepherd
Toss: India
Man of the Match: RT Ponting

Australia won by 9 wickets

FOURTH TEST – AUSTRALIA v. INDIA
2–6 January 2004 at Sydney

INDIA

	First Innings		Second Innings	
A Chopra	b Lee	45	c Martyn b Gillespie	2
V Sehwag	c Gilchrist b Gillespie	72	c Gillespie b MacGill	47
R Dravid	lbw b Gillespie	38	not out	91
SR Tendulkar	not out	241	not out	60
VVS Laxman	b Gillespie	178		
SC Ganguly (capt)	b Lee	16		
*PA Patel	c Gilchrist b Lee	62		
AB Agarkar	b Lee	2		
IK Pathan	not out	13		
A Kumble				
M Kartik				
Extras	b 4, lb 5, w 4, nb 25	38	lb 3, w 1, nb 7	11
	(7 wkts dec 187.3 overs)	705	(2 wkts dec 99.5 overs)	211

	First Innings				Second Innings			
	O	M	R	W	O	M	R	W
Lee	39.3	5	201	4	12.2	2	75	0
Gillespie	45	11	135	3	7	2	32	1
Bracken	37	13	97	0	8	0	36	0
MacGill	38	5	146	0	16	1	65	1
Waugh	2	0	6	0	-	-	-	-
Katich	17	1	84	0	-	-	-	-
Martyn	9	1	27	0	-	-	-	-

Fall of Wickets
1-123, 2-128, 3-194, 4-547, 5-570, 6-671, 7-678
1-11, 2-73

AUSTRALIA

	First Innings		Second Innings	
JL Langer	c Patel b Kumble	117	c Sehwag b Kartik	47
ML Hayden	c Ganguly b Kumble	67	c Dravid b Kumble	30
RT Ponting	lbw b Kumble	25	c & b Pathan	47
DR Martyn	c & b Kumble	7	c sub b Kumble	40
SR Waugh (capt)	c Patel b Pathan	40	c Tendulkar b Kumble	80
SM Katich	c Sehwag b Kumble	125	not out	77
*AC Gilchrist	b Pathan	6	st Patel b Kumble	4
B Lee	c Chopra b Kumble	0		
JN Gillespie	st Patel b Kumble	47	(8) not out	4
NW Bracken	c Agarkar b Kumble	2		
SCG MacGill	not out	0		
Extras	b 6, lb 9, w 3, nb 20	38	b 6, lb 7, w 2, nb 13	28
	(117.5 overs)	474	(6 wkts 94 overs)	357

	First Innings				Second Innings			
	O	M	R	W	O	M	R	W
Agarkar	25	3	116	0	10	2	45	0
Pathan	26	3	80	2	8	1	26	1
Kumble	46.5	7	141	8	42	8	138	4
Kartik	19	1	122	0	26	5	89	1
Ganguly	1	1	0	0	-	-	-	-
Tendulkar	-	-	-	-	6	0	36	0
Sehwag	-	-	-	-	2	0	10	0

Fall of Wickets
1-147, 2-214, 3-229, 4-261, 5-311, 6-341, 7-350, 8-467, 9-473
1-75, 2-92, 3-170, 4-196, 5-338, 6-342

Umpires: BF Bowden and SA Bucknor
Toss: India
Man of the Match: SR Tendulkar
Man of the Series: R Dravid

Match drawn

SERIES AVERAGES
Australia v. India

AUSTRALIA

Batting	M	Inns	NO	Runs	HS	Av	100	50	c/st
RT Ponting	4	8	1	706	257	100.85	2	2	1/-
SM Katich	4	6	1	353	125	70.60	1	2	3/-
ML Hayden	4	8	1	451	136	64.42	1	3	9/-
JL Langer	4	8	0	369	121	46.12	2	1	3/-
SR Waugh	4	7	1	267	80	44.50	-	2	-/-
DR Martyn	4	7	1	254	66*	42.33	-	1	3/-
JN Gillespie	3	5	2	110	48*	36.66	-	-	2/-
AC Gilchrist	4	6	0	96	43	16.00	-	-	10/1
BA Williams	2	3	2	14	10*	14.00	-	-	1/-
AJ Bichel	2	3	0	31	19	10.33	-	-	4/-
NW Bracken	3	3	1	9	6*	4.50	-	-	1/-
B Lee	2	2	0	8	8	4.00	-	-	-/-
SCG MacGill	4	5	1	2	1	0.50	-	-	2/-

Bowling	Overs	Mds	Runs	Wkts	Av	Best	5/inn	10m
JN Gillespie	139.1	41	377	10	37.70	4-65	-	-
SM Katich	51	5	215	5	43.00	2-22	-	-
BA Williams	79	24	225	5	45.00	4-53	-	-
AJ Bichel	70.4	10	295	6	49.16	4-118	-	-
SCG MacGill	194.4	29	711	14	50.78	4-86	-	-
NW Bracken	128	38	351	6	58.50	2-12	-	-
B Lee	100.5	17	476	8	59.50	4-201	-	-
SR Waugh	31	5	82	1	82.00	1-35	-	-

Also bowled: RT Ponting 1-0-4-0, DR Martyn 9-1-27-0.

INDIA

Batting	M	Inns	NO	Runs	HS	Av	100	50	c/st
R Dravid	4	8	3	619	233	123.80	1	3	4/-
VVS Laxman	4	7	1	494	178	82.33	2	1	5/-
SR Tendulkar	4	7	2	383	241*	76.60	1	1	3/-
V Sehwag	4	8	0	464	195	58.00	1	1	8/-
SC Ganguly	4	6	0	284	144	47.33	1	1	1/-
PA Patel	4	6	1	160	62	32.00	-	1	8/3
A Chopra	4	8	0	186	48	23.25	-	-	5/-
Z Khan	2	3	1	28	27	14.00	-	-	-/-
IK Pathan	2	2	1	14	13*	14.00	-	-	1/-
AB Agarkar	4	6	1	26	12	5.20	-	-	1/-
A Kumble	3	3	0	15	12	5.00	-	-	1/-
A Nehra	3	4	1	0	0*	0.00	-	-	2/-
Harbhajan Singh	1	1	1	19	19*	-	-	-	1/-
M Kartik	1	0	0	0	0	-	-	-	-/-

Bowling	Overs	Mds	Runs	Wkts	Av	Best	5/inn	10m
A Kumble	206.1	28	710	24	29.58	8-141	3	1
AB Agarkar	154.5	23	596	16	37.25	6-41	1	-
Z Khan	51	6	213	5	42.60	5-95	1	-
SR Tendulkar	28	0	141	3	47.00	2-36	-	-
IK Pathan	68	7	266	4	66.50	2-80	-	-
A Nehra	101	16	382	4	95.50	2-115	-	-
Harbhajan Singh	35	2	169	1	169.00	1-101	-	-
M Kartik	45	6	211	1	211.00	1-89	-	-

Also bowled: SC Ganguly 2-1-8-0, V Sehwag 18-1-71-0.

FIRST TEST – AUSTRALIA v. SRI LANKA
1–3 July 2004 at Darwin

AUSTRALIA

	First Innings		Second Innings	
JL Langer	c Chandana b Samaraweera	30	c Sangakkara b Vaas	10
ML Hayden	c Jayasuriya b Vaas	37	c Sangakkara b Zoysa	2
MTG Elliott	c Arnold b Vaas	1	c Dilshan b Vaas	0
DR Martyn	c Arnold b Jayasuriya	47	c Sangakkara b Malinga	7
DS Lehmann	lbw b Malinga	57	c Sangakkara b Malinga	51
SM Katich	c Sangakkara b Vaas	9	c Dilshan b Chandana	15
*AC Gilchrist (capt)	c Sangakkara b Malinga	0	run out	80
SK Warne	run out	2	lbw b Malinga	1
JN Gillespie	lbw b Vaas	4	c Samaraweera b Chandana	16
MS Kasprowicz	not out	2	c & b Malinga	15
GD McGrath	c Samaraweera b Vaas	0	not out	0
Extras	b 2, lb 6, w 2, nb 8	18	lb 3, nb 1	4
	(71.3 overs)	207	(61.3 overs)	201

	First Innings				Second Innings			
	O	M	R	W	O	M	R	W
Vaas	18.3	6	31	5	14	4	51	2
Malinga	14	3	50	2	15.1	3	42	4
Zoysa	13	4	24	0	16	3	57	1
Samaraweera	9	1	43	1	-	-	-	-
Chandana	6	0	30	0	11	1	30	2
Jayasuriya	11	4	21	1	6	3	9	0
Arnold	-	-	-	-	1	0	9	0

Fall of Wickets: 1-72, 2-73, 3-80, 4-177, 5-189, 6-189, 7-201, 8-202, 9-207
1-12, 2-12, 3-14, 4-64, 5-77, 6-114, 7-127, 8-154, 9-201

SRI LANKA

	First Innings		Second Innings	
MS Atapattu (capt)	b McGrath	4	c Warne b Kasprowicz	10
ST Jayasuriya	lbw b McGrath	8	lbw b McGrath	16
*KC Sangakkara	lbw b Gillespie	2	run out	0
DPMD Jayawardene	c Langer b Gillespie	14	b McGrath	44
DNT Zoysa	c Gilchrist b McGrath	12	(5) c Gilchrist b Kasprowicz	32
TT Samaraweera	c Gilchrist b McGrath	1	(6) c Gilchrist b Kasprowicz	14
TM Dilshan	not out	17	(7) c Gilchrist b Kasprowicz	11
RP Arnold	c Elliott b McGrath	6	(8) b Kasprowicz	17
UDU Chandana	c Gilchrist b Warne	14	(9) not out	10
WPUJC Vaas	c Hayden b Warne	5	(3) c Gilchrist b Kasprowicz	0
LS Malinga	c Gillespie b Warne	0	lbw b Warne	7
Extras	lb 7, nb 7	14	lb 1, w 1, nb 5	7
	(41.5 overs)	97	(65.4 overs)	162

	First Innings				Second Innings			
	O	M	R	W	O	M	R	W
McGrath	15	4	37	5	16	9	24	2
Gillespie	13	4	18	2	13	2	37	0
Kasprowicz	7	1	15	0	17.4	3	39	7
Warne	6.5	1	20	3	19	2	61	0

Fall of Wickets: 1-10, 2-20, 3-33, 4-47, 5-50, 6-51, 7-59, 8-85, 9-91
1-23, 2-23, 3-30, 4-109, 5-113, 6-132, 7-141, 8-152, 9-162

Umpires: BF Bowden and Aleem Dar
Toss: Sri Lanka
Test debut: LS Malinga
Man of the Match: GD McGrath

Australia won by 149 runs

SECOND TEST – AUSTRALIA v. SRI LANKA
9–13 July 2004 at Cairns

AUSTRALIA

	First Innings		Second Innings	
JL Langer	c Jayawardene b Malinga	162	c Kaluwitharana b Zoysa	8
ML Hayden	c Jayasuriya b Samaraweera	117	b Chandana	132
RT Ponting (capt)	c Atapattu b Malinga	22	c Jayasuriya b Zoysa	45
DR Martyn	lbw b Chandana	97	st Kaluwitharana b Chandana	52
DS Lehmann	c Sangakkara b Chandana	50	c Jayawardene b Chandana	21
SM Katich	b Chandana	1	st Kaluwitharana b Dilshan	1
*AC Gilchrist	c Kaluwitharana b Malinga	35	b Dilshan	0
SK Warne	c Samaraweera b Chandana	2	c Samaraweera b Chandana	4
JN Gillespie	c Kaluwitharana b Malinga	1	st Kaluwitharana b Chandana	1
MS Kasprowicz	c Atapattu b Chandana	9	not out	3
GD McGrath	not out	0		
Extras	b 7, lb 3, w 4, nb 7	21	lb 20, w 1, nb 4	25
	(124.2 overs)	517	(9 wkts dec 66.4 overs)	292

	First Innings				Second Innings			
	O	M	R	W	O	M	R	W
Vaas	27	2	102	0	13	3	52	0
Zoysa	19	5	72	0	14	6	34	2
Samaraweera	17	2	55	1	11	0	50	0
Malinga	29.2	2	149	4	5	0	23	0
Chandana	26	2	109	5	18.4	1	101	5
Jayasuriya	6	0	20	0	3	0	8	0
Dilshan	–	–	–	–	2	0	4	2

Fall of Wickets: 1-255, 2-291, 3-392, 4-454, 5-462, 6-469, 7-474, 8-476, 9-485
1-10, 2-105, 3-195, 4-261, 5-284, 6-284, 7-288, 8-288, 9-292

SRI LANKA

	First Innings		Second Innings	
MS Atapattu (capt)	c Hayden b McGrath	133	c Warne b Gillespie	9
ST Jayasuriya	c Gilchrist b Gillespie	13	c Gilchrist b Warne	22
KC Sangakkara	c Gillespie b Warne	74	b Warne	66
DPMD Jayawardene	c & b Kasprowicz	43	c Gilchrist b McGrath	6
TT Samaraweera	c Ponting b Gillespie	70	run out	0
TM Dilshan	c Kasprowicz b Warne	35	c Warne b Gillespie	21
*RS Kaluwitharana	c Warne b McGrath	34	c Lehmann b Warne	14
UDU Chandana	st Gilchrist b Warne	19	st Gilchrist b Warne	14
WPUJC Vaas	c Ponting b Gillespie	2	not out	11
DNT Zoysa	not out	0	not out	3
LS Malinga	run out	0		
Extras	b 3, lb 10, w 2, nb 17	32	b 5, lb 3, nb 9	17
	(144.4 overs)	455	(8 wkts 85 overs)	183

	First Innings				Second Innings			
	O	M	R	W	O	M	R	W
McGrath	34	10	79	2	16	7	31	1
Gillespie	37.4	6	116	3	18	6	39	2
Kasprowicz	32	5	113	1	11	4	34	0
Warne	38	7	129	3	37	14	70	4
Lehmann	3	0	5	0	3	2	1	0

Fall of Wickets: 1-18, 2-156, 3-280, 4-280, 5-345, 6-420, 7-445, 8-455, 9-455
1-15, 2-49, 3-58, 4-64, 5-107, 6-136, 7-159, 8-174

Umpires: BF Bowden and Aleem Dar
Toss: Sri Lanka
Man of the Match: ML Hayden
Man of the Series: ML Hayden

Match drawn

SERIES AVERAGES
Australia v. Sri Lanka

AUSTRALIA

Batting	M	Inns	NO	Runs	HS	Av	100	50	c/st
ML Hayden	2	4	0	288	132	72.00	2	–	2/-
JL Langer	2	4	0	210	162	52.50	1	–	1/-
DR Martyn	2	4	0	203	97	50.75	–	2	-/-
DS Lehmann	2	4	0	179	57	44.75	–	3	1/-
RT Ponting	1	2	0	67	45	33.50	–	–	2/-
AC Gilchrist	2	4	0	115	80	28.75	–	1	11/2
MS Kasprowicz	2	4	2	29	15	14.50	–	–	2/-
SM Katich	2	4	0	26	15	6.50	–	–	-/-
JN Gillespie	2	4	0	22	16	5.50	–	–	2/-
SK Warne	2	4	0	9	4	2.25	–	–	4/-
MTG Elliott	1	2	0	1	1	0.50	–	–	1/-
GD McGrath	2	3	2	0	0*	0.00	–	–	-/-

Bowling	Overs	Mds	Runs	Wkts	Av	Best	5/inn	10m
GD McGrath	81	30	171	10	17.10	5-37	1	–
MS Kasprowicz	67.4	13	201	8	25.12	7-39	1	–
SK Warne	100.5	24	280	10	28.00	4-70	–	–
JN Gillespie	81.4	18	210	7	30.00	3-116	–	–

Also bowled: DS Lehmann 6-2-6-0.

SRI LANKA

Batting	M	Inns	NO	Runs	HS	Av	100	50	c/st
MS Atapattu	2	4	0	156	133	39.00	1	–	2/-
KC Sangakkara	2	4	0	142	74	35.50	–	2	7/-
TM Dilshan	2	4	1	87	35	29.00	–	–	2/-
DPMD Jayawardene	2	4	0	107	44	26.75	–	–	2/-
TT Samaraweera	2	4	0	103	70	25.75	–	1	4/-
RS Kaluwitharana	1	2	0	48	34	24.00	–	–	3/3
UDU Chandana	2	4	0	64	19	16.00	–	–	1/-
ST Jayasuriya	2	4	0	59	22	14.75	–	–	3/-
WPUJC Vaas	2	4	2	28	11*	14.00	–	–	-/-
RP Arnold	1	2	0	17	11	8.50	–	–	2/-
DNT Zoysa	2	4	2	16	12	8.00	–	–	-/-
LS Malinga	2	3	0	0	0	0.00	–	–	1/-

Bowling	Overs	Mds	Runs	Wkts	Av	Best	5/inn	10m
TM Dilshan	2	0	4	2	2.00	2-4	–	–
UDU Chandana	61.4	4	270	12	22.50	5-101	2	1
LS Malinga	63.3	8	264	10	26.40	4-42	–	–
WPUJC Vaas	72.3	15	236	7	33.71	5-31	1	–
ST Jayasuriya	26	7	58	1	58.00	1-21	–	–
DNT Zoysa	62	18	187	3	62.33	2-34	–	–
TT Samaraweera	37	3	148	2	74.00	1-43	–	–

Also bowled: RP Arnold 1-0-9-0.

STEVE WAUGH

By Jim Maxwell

Steve Waugh chose his moment. Few sportsmen are able to nominate their time of goodbye, and none of Waugh's celebrated predecessors had been able to enjoy such a well-planned farewell.

'The SCG has the best atmosphere of any ground in the world. It's intimate, you can hear the crowd, you can feel them. I couldn't think of a better place to have played my last match', he said. A record crowd sent him off in style, with a lap of honour, after a final, gritty innings.

Waugh had wanted to play on, seeking the chance to win in Sri Lanka and India, but he realised that it was better to go out on a high, on his own terms, rather than risk a tap on the shoulder.

He could have taken a bow following a brilliant hundred against England the previous summer. Instead he was reinvigorated, and led Australia to the win in the Caribbean that had eluded him in 1999. And he kept making runs, enjoying the chance to add Bangladesh to his hundred hit list.

Waugh's toughness and survival instincts are the stuff of legend. Who, for instance, could forget his injury-defying hundred at The Oval in 2001?

A calf muscle tear at Trent Bridge was so severe that he was advised to rest and return home, as the series had already been won. Wary of deep vein thrombosis, he stayed on and decided to try to repair the injury. Guided by team physiotherapist Errol Alcott, Waugh made enough progress to satisfy himself that he could play.

Remember the scramble for the single – diving for the crease – when he reached his century? And then he supervised Australia's win in the field, proving again that the mind can overcome injury.

Waugh's bloody-minded determination grew from failures that cast him briefly out of the team when he was replaced by his twin brother Mark. Curbing offside recklessness and making application a priority over a desire to dominate, he became a disciplined occupier, taking his cue from the relentless approach of Allan Border.

It was, of course, his all-round skills that shone spectacularly in the 1987 World Cup, as he became the 'death' bowler of the tournament with his canny medium pacers. Until an assortment of hamstring twinges took their toll, you could guarantee a Waugh

Lifting the World Cup as Australia's captain in the 1999 tournament represented one of the peaks of Waugh's career.

wicket whenever he intervened – bowling's version of batting's pinch-hitter.

Carl Hooper became Waugh's bunny – just like McGrath's hold over Michael Atherton – and a unique Test double of 10,000 runs and 100 wickets eluded him by just nine victims.

Waugh's determined character needed the responsibility of leadership to challenge him. I recall discussing Border's successor with him in 1994, and he was anxious to know if I had any inside information. I didn't, and Waugh's ambition had to wait another five years for fulfilment.

From a cautious beginning in the Caribbean in 1999, where he did not always back his instincts, Waugh produced a miraculous resurrection performance at the World Cup, inspired by his batting and South Africa's nervous semi-final complicity.

One of Waugh's leadership strengths was to encourage players whom others underestimated, showing faith in bowlers when they seemed overdone and developing a self-belief that became crucial to the victorious team culture.

Like all great generals he ruthlessly crushed opposition, quickly turning evenly-balanced matches into routs when he sensed any mental drift.

He rated the victory by an innings and 360 runs over South Africa at the Wanderers as 'almost the perfect Test. That was the best I had ever seen a side play.'

Leading from the Front: Steve Waugh's Test record, both as captain and batsman, was impeccable.

Waugh felt that enjoying the success of those around him was important in shaping a team. In ceding to Ricky Ponting the job regarded by many Australians as more important than that of the prime minister, the baggy-green warrior reflected on the role of the captain.

'It's about taking care of your own game and thinking about your team-mates around you and making sure that you are playing as a side. You see quite a lot of talented sides that don't quite make it. That's because they are playing as individuals rather than as a team'.

Popular adulation for Waugh also earned official recognition when he was named Australian of the Year, an honour that had previously been bestowed on his predecessors Mark Taylor and Allan Border.

Right: With the Ashes trophy at The Oval in 2001.

Below: It's goodbye from him – Steve Waugh bows out as one of cricket's toughest leaders, and toughest competitors.

INDIA

INDIA REPORT
By Gulu Ezekiel

The year started disappointingly for the Indian cricket team with two drawn Tests at home to New Zealand and also ended with a whimper, with another loss in the final of a one-day tournament, this time to Sri Lanka at the Asia Cup in Colombo.

In between those two lows, however, the 2003–04 season was perhaps the national side's finest since the golden summer of 1971, when India won away Test series for the first time in both the West Indies and in England.

India had not won a series abroad since 1993 in Sri Lanka. Now, not only did they win both a one-day series and a Test series in Pakistan, but, under the dynamic captaincy of Saurav Ganguly, they did so in a totally dominant fashion.

Ganguly and coach John Wright, the former New Zealand captain, built on the momentum of the 2003 World Cup to such an extent that, by the end of the season, this Indian team was being talked about as perhaps the greatest of all time.

Ganguly's captaincy record, notably on foreign soil where the Indians have been notoriously weak, merited his ranking as India's best-ever captain.

On a January evening as the shadows began to fall across the Sydney Cricket Ground on Steve Waugh's final day in international cricket, Ganguly's men came as close as any side has done before them to pulling off the impossible – defeating the mighty Australians in their own backyard. Indeed it was only another obdurate display by the retiring captain himself that staved off humiliation for the hosts.

India have never won a Test series Down Under and this was only the third occasion that they have managed a draw. The four-Test series ended 1–1, but there was little doubt that it was the Indians who came home smelling of roses.

Even a trouncing in the finals of the VB triangular one-day series at the hands of the world champions did little to dim their achievements in the Test matches and the Indian batting line-up was now acknowledged as the best in the world.

It was all a far cry from India's last visit in 1999–2000, under Tendulkar's captaincy, when the visitors were whitewashed 3–0.

Ironically, it was the master batsman, on his third tour of Australia, who appeared as the weakest link … until his unbeaten 241 in the final Test at Sydney.

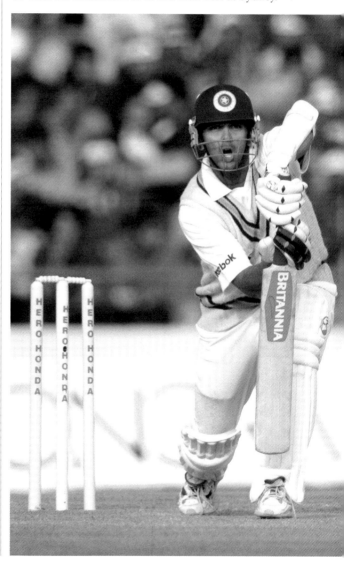

Rahul Dravid, one of the stars of a golden year for India.

By the end of the season, middle-order batsman Rahul Dravid had emerged as India's best batsman and the wonderfully artistic VVS Laxman gave the batting line-up a solidity the Indian side had not witnessed since the early to mid-1980s. Dravid's scores of 233 and 72 not out in the second Test at Adelaide was the major factor in giving India their first win in Australia for 22 years.

Laxman had saved India's blushes in the home series against New Zealand and had a sublime run in the VB series following the four Test matches in Australia.

The discovery of an obdurate opening batsman in Aakash Chopra did much to blunt the Aussie bowling attack, weakened by the absence through injury of Glenn McGrath and Shane Warne, who was serving out his one-year doping ban.

Chopra offset the dynamic batting style of fellow-opener and Delhi state-mate Virender Sehwag – who smashed a rollicking 194 in the third Test at Melbourne that India lost – wonderfully.

Down the order, Ganguly's century in the opening Test at Brisbane was arguably the most vital innings by an Indian captain since Mohammed Azharuddin's 182 in the first Test at Calcutta against England in 1993.

There had been much talk of Ganguly being targeted for a high dosage of 'chin music' in the series. The Indian captain's dislike of the short stuff was, by now, common knowledge.

His defiant 144 had the rival bowlers dancing to his tune, however, and the Aussie media – whose antagonism towards Ganguly is matched only by that of the British media – were suddenly singing his praises.

Virender Sehwag, the scorer of India's first Test triple-hundred ... and against Pakistan, too.

To add to this, the Indian bowlers had the Australian batsmen in all sorts of trouble on a truncated second day in which seven wickets fell in a heap for just 62 runs. Left-arm pace bowler Zaheer Khan picked up 5 for 95 as India gained a useful first-innings lead of 86 runs.

Khan would limp off with an injury in the second innings and he faded out for the rest of the tour. This proved to be a blessing in disguise, however, as by the end of the one-day tri-series, India had made the twin discoveries in the quick bowling department of Irfan Pathan and Laxmipathy Balaji. The pair would emerge as two of the stars of the Pakistan tour.

Even as the one-day tournament was going on in Australia, the Indian government gave the Board the green light to send an Indian team to Pakistan for the first fully-fledged tour there since 1989, Tendulkar's maiden series.

For weeks, speculation was rife about the feasibility of visiting Pakistan, given the country's fragile security scenario. Indeed, the Indian players themselves were initially extremely wary of playing there, despite all of the assurances from the Pakistani authorities.

In the event, the tour proved to be an extraordinary success, with the Indians winning in style and also proving to be a great hit with the Pakistan public, who opened their arms to welcome the players. The hordes of Indian fans who had crossed the border witnessed some magnificent cricket.

After Pakistan lost by just five runs in the opening one-day international at Karachi, they drew level following another thriller at Rawalpindi. Tendulkar's 141 made him the first Indian to score a one-day international century in Pakistan, but it was not enough – just as Pakistan captain Inzamam-ul-Haq's 122 had not been enough at Karachi.

Pakistan took the lead by winning the third match at Peshawar, only for India to come back strongly and clinch the next two at Lahore for a 3–2 series victory.

Inevitably, and as is so often the case with subcontinental cricket, rumours of match-fixing immediately began to swirl in Pakistan. It did nothing to lighten the dour Inzamam's grim mood, nor did it take off any of the gloss from India's achievement.

For 72 years, one of the biggest gaps in India's cricket record was the lack of a Test-match triple-century. The odds would have favoured Tendulkar, Dravid or Laxman – the previous record holder with 281 against Australia in 2001 – to achieve the feat.

Instead it was left to Sehwag, who perhaps surprised himself as much as his team-mates and Indian cricket fans, with an explosive 309 in the first Test at Multan.

Sehwag had fallen short of his double-century against the Australians at Melbourne when attempting to hit a six. Now he reached his 300 from 353 balls with a huge six off Saqlain Mushtaq as the stuffing was knocked out of the clueless Pakistan bowlers.

The bowling hero was leg spinner Anil Kumble with eight wickets in the match. This followed his haul of 24 wickets from three Tests in Australia, and he finally dispelled any doubts about his effectiveness on foreign wickets.

The only false note crept in when Tendulkar admitted he was disappointed at Dravid's declaration (he was captaining in place of the injured Ganguly) as he was left on 194 not out.

Pakistan came back strongly to level the series at Lahore, despite a maiden Test century by Yuvraj Singh.

The Indian batting was back to its best at Rawalpindi, though, as the tourists amassed their third total of 600 or more in four Tests. Dravid followed up his match-winning double-century at Adelaide with 270 this time around and Pakistan were beaten by an innings for the second time in the series.

The reaction back home was one of national ecstasy. The adulation and euphoria that the team received on its return could only have been matched by the celebrations following the World Cup triumph of 1983.

On the domestic scene, Mumbai regained the Ranji Trophy by beating Tamil Nadu in the final for the second year running and they also claimed the Ranji Trophy one-day tournament. The Duleep Trophy saw North Zone coast to victory on the back of twin centuries in the final by Yuvraj Singh, while losing finalists East Zone lifted the one-day Deodhar Trophy.

For the first time, a foreign team was invited to compete in the domestic tournament with England A (actually the English Academy team) losing both of their matches in the Duleep Trophy. They also had the mortification, in their opening match at Gurgaon, of allowing South Zone to become the first side on Indian soil to score 500-plus for victory.

The other big story of the year was the 'Abhijit Kale affair' with two of the national selectors alleging that the Maharashtra middle-order batsman – who played one match for India in a triangular tournament in Dhaka in 2003 – had offered them bribes to choose him in the national squad. The lack of evidence meant that the whole thing died a quiet death with Kale let off with a slap on the wrist.

FIRST TEST – INDIA v. NEW ZEALAND
8–12 October 2003 at Ahmedabad

INDIA

	First Innings		Second Innings	
A Chopra	c & b Vettori	42	c Styris b Vettori	31
V Sehwag	lbw b Tuffey	29	c Hart b Oram	17
R Dravid	c Hart b Oram	222	c Vincent b Wiseman	73
SR Tendulkar	c Astle b Styris	8	c Vettori b Wiseman	7
VVS Laxman	c Wiseman b Vettori	64	c Vettori b Wiseman	44
SC Ganguly (capt)	not out	100	b Wiseman	25
*PA Patel	not out	29	not out	5
A Kumble				
Harbhajan Singh				
Z Khan				
L Balaji				
Extras	b 2, lb 3, nb 1	6	b 3, lb 4	7
	(5 wkts dec 159 overs)	500	(6 wkts dec 44.5 overs)	209

	First Innings				Second Innings			
	O	M	R	W	O	M	R	W
Tuffey	31	6	103	1	9	2	18	0
Oram	33	8	95	1	8	0	39	1
Styris	26	5	83	1	-	-	-	-
Vettori	44	9	128	2	16	0	81	1
McMillan	4	1	6	0	-	-	-	-
Wiseman	21	0	80	0	11.5	0	64	4

Fall of Wickets
1-35, 2-107, 3-134, 4-264, 5-446
1-20, 2-97, 3-118, 4-166, 5-177, 6-209

NEW ZEALAND

	First Innings		Second Innings	
MH Richardson	b Khan	6	c Chopra b Kumble	21
L Vincent	c Patel b Khan	7	b Kumble	67
SP Fleming (capt)	b Khan	0	(4) c Laxman b Harbhajan Singh	8
SB Styris	c Chopra b Harbhajan Singh	34	(5) lbw b Kumble	0
NJ Astle	st Patel b Harbhajan Singh	103	(8) not out	51
CD McMillan	c Chopra b Sehwag	54	not out	83
JDP Oram	c Dravid b Kumble	5	c Dravid b Harbhajan Singh	7
*RG Hart	lbw b Balaji	15		
DL Vettori	c Dravid b Kumble	60		
PJ Wiseman	c Laxman b Khan	27		
DR Tuffey	not out	2	(3) b Kumble	8
Extras	b 4, lb 18, nb 4	26	b 4, lb 11, nb 12	27
	(131.1 overs)	340	(6 wkts 107 overs)	272

	First Innings				Second Innings			
	O	M	R	W	O	M	R	W
Khan	23	3	68	4	10	1	36	0
Balaji	26	7	84	1	11	4	21	0
Kumble	35.1	11	58	2	39	12	95	4
Harbhajan Singh	36	8	86	2	38	9	65	2
Sehwag	8	2	17	1	2	2	0	0
Tendulkar	3	2	5	0	7	0	40	0

Fall of Wickets
1-11, 2-16, 3-17, 4-108, 5-199, 6-223, 7-227, 8-265, 9-332
1-44, 2-68, 3-85, 4-86, 5-150, 6-169

Umpires: RE Koertzen and DR Shepherd
Toss: India
Test debuts: A Chopra, L Balaji
Man of the Match: R Dravid

Match drawn

SECOND TEST – INDIA v. NEW ZEALAND
16–20 October 2003 at Mohali

NEW ZEALAND

	First Innings	
MH Richardson	c Kumble b Harbhajan Singh	145
L Vincent	lbw b Kumble	106
SB Styris	lbw b Kumble	119
SP Fleming (capt)	b Tendulkar	30
NJ Astle	c Patel b Harbhajan Singh	18
CD McMillan	not out	100
*RG Hart	b Kumble	11
DL Vettori	not out	48
IG Butler		
DR Tuffey		
PJ Wiseman		
Extras	b 21, lb 28, w 1, nb 3	53
	(6 wkts dec 198.3 overs)	630

	First Innings			
	O	M	R	W
Khan	26	8	95	0
Balaji	30	10	78	0
Tendulkar	22	3	55	1
Kumble	66	17	181	3
Harbhajan Singh	48	7	149	2
Sehwag	5.3	1	22	0
Yuvraj Singh	1	0	1	0

Fall of Wickets
1-231, 2-382, 3-433, 4-447, 5-507, 6-540

INDIA

	First Innings		Second Innings	
A Chopra	c Astle b Tuffey	60	c Richardson b Wiseman	52
V Sehwag	b Styris	130	c Fleming b Tuffey	1
R Dravid (capt)	c Hart b Butler	13	c Fleming b Tuffey	5
SR Tendulkar	c Richardson b Vettori	55	b Tuffey	1
VVS Laxman	not out	104	not out	67
Yuvraj Singh	c Hart b Tuffey	20	not out	5
*PA Patel	c Richardson b Vettori	18		
A Kumble	run out	5		
Harbhajan Singh	run out	8		
L Balaji	c Hart b Tuffey	4		
Z Khan	c Hart b Tuffey	0		
Extras	b 2, lb 1, w 2, nb 2	7	lb 4, w 1	5
	(172 overs)	424	(4 wkts 69 overs)	136

	First Innings				Second Innings			
	O	M	R	W	O	M	R	W
Tuffey	29	5	80	4	14	4	30	3
Butler	35	7	116	1	5	1	12	0
Styris	19	7	40	1	4	2	4	0
Vettori	56	24	84	2	23	8	40	0
Wiseman	32	7	95	0	17	6	37	1
McMillan	1	0	6	0	6	3	9	0

Fall of Wickets
1-164, 2-208, 3-218, 4-330, 5-364, 6-388, 7-397, 8-408, 9-424
1-6, 2-12, 3-18, 4-128

Umpires: RE Koertzen and DR Shepherd
Toss: New Zealand
Test debut: Yuvraj Singh
Man of the Match: DR Tuffey
Man of the Series: VVS Laxman

Match drawn

SERIES AVERAGES
India v. New Zealand

INDIA

Batting	M	Inns	NO	Runs	HS	Av	100	50	c/st
VVS Laxman	2	4	2	279	104*	139.50	1	2	2/-
SC Ganguly	1	2	1	125	100*	125.00	1	-	-/-
R Dravid	2	4	0	313	222	78.25	1	1	3/-
PA Patel	2	3	2	52	29*	52.00	-	-	2/1
A Chopra	2	4	0	185	60	46.25	-	2	3/-
V Sehwag	2	4	0	177	130	44.25	1	-	-/-
Yuvraj Singh	1	2	1	25	20	25.00	-	-	-/-
SR Tendulkar	2	4	0	71	55	17.75	-	1	-/-
Harbhajan Singh	2	1	0	8	8	8.00	-	-	-/-
A Kumble	2	1	0	5	5	5.00	-	-	1/-
L Balaji	2	1	0	4	4	4.00	-	-	-/-
Z Khan	2	1	0	0	0	0.00	-	-	-/-

Bowling	Overs	Mds	Runs	Wkts	Av	Best	5/inn	10m
A Kumble	140.1	40	334	9	37.11	4-95	-	-
V Sehwag	15.3	5	39	1	39.00	1-17	-	-
Z Khan	59	12	199	4	49.75	4-68	-	-
Harbhajan Singh	122	24	300	6	50.00	2-65	-	-
SR Tendulkar	32	5	100	1	100.00	1-55	-	-
L Balaji	67	21	183	1	183.00	1-84	-	-

Also bowled: Yuvraj Singh 1-0-1-0.

NEW ZEALAND

Batting	M	Inns	NO	Runs	HS	Av	100	50	c/st
CD McMillan	2	3	2	237	100*	237.00	1	2	-/-
DL Vettori	2	2	1	108	60	108.00	-	1	3/-
NJ Astle	2	3	1	172	103	86.00	1	1	2/-
L Vincent	2	3	0	180	106	60.00	1	1	1/-
MH Richardson	2	3	0	172	145	57.33	1	-	3/-
SB Styris	2	3	0	153	119	51.00	1	-	1/-
PJ Wiseman	2	1	0	27	27	27.00	-	-	1/-
SP Fleming	2	3	0	39	30	13.00	-	-	2/-
RG Hart	2	2	0	26	15	13.00	-	-	6/-
DR Tuffey	2	2	1	10	8	10.00	-	-	-/-
JDP Oram	1	2	0	12	7	6.00	-	-	-/-
IG Butler	1	0	0	0	0	-	-	-	-/-

Bowling	Overs	Mds	Runs	Wkts	Av	Best	5/inn	10m
DR Tuffey	83	17	231	8	28.87	4-80	-	-
PJ Wiseman	81.5	13	276	5	55.20	4-64	-	-
SB Styris	49	14	127	2	63.50	1-40	-	-
DL Vettori	139	41	333	5	66.60	2-84	-	-
JDP Oram	41	8	134	2	67.00	1-39	-	-
IG Butler	40	8	128	1	128.00	1-116	-	-

Also bowled: CD McMillan 11-4-21-0.

TRIANGULAR TOURNAMENT
(India, Australia and New Zealand)

Match One
23 October 2003 at Chennai
India 141 for 3 (26.5 overs)
New Zealand Did not bat
Match abandoned

Match Two
26 October 2003 at Gwalior
India 283 for 5 (50 overs) (VVS Laxman 102,
SR Tendulkar 100)
Australia 246 for 9 (50 overs) (AC Gilchrist 83)
India won by 37 runs

Match Three
29 October 2003 at Faridabad
New Zealand 97 (33.4 overs) (BA Williams 4 for 22)
Australia 101 for 2 (16.4 overs) (ML Hayden 51*)
Australia won by 8 wickets

Match Four
1 November 2003 at Mumbai
Australia 286 for 8 (50 overs) (DR Martyn 100,
AB Agarkar 4 for 37)
India 209 (46.2 overs)
(SR Tendulkar 68, R Dravid 59, NW Bracken 4 for 29,
MJ Clarke 4 for 42)
Australia won by 77 runs

Match Five
3 November 2003 at Pune
New Zealand 258 for 9 (50 overs) (JDP Oram 81,
BB McCullum 51*, BA Williams 5 for 53)
Australia 259 for 8 (49.5 overs)
(MJ Clarke 70, MG Bevan 50, DR Tuffey 4 for 30)
Australia won by 2 wickets

Match Six
6 November 2003 at Cuttack
India 246 for 9 (50 overs) (M Kaif 64)
New Zealand 249 for 6 (47.3 overs) (CD McMillan 82*,
SB Styris 68)
New Zealand won by 4 wickets

Match Seven
9 November 2003 at Guwahati
Australia 225 for 7 (50 overs) (MG Bevan 84*,
RT Ponting 52)
New Zealand 181 (45.3 overs)
(SB Styris 54)
Australia won by 44 runs

Match Eight

12 November 2003 at Bangalore
Australia 347 for 2 (50 overs) (AC Gilchrist 111, RT Ponting 108*, DR Martyn 61*)
India 286 for 8 (50 overs) (SR Tendulkar 89)
Australia won by 61 runs

Match Nine

15 November 2003 at Hyderabad
India 353 for 5 (50 overs) (V Sehwag 130, SR Tendulkar 102, R Dravid 50*)
New Zealand 208 (47 overs) (SB Styris 54)
India won by 145 runs

Match Ten (Final)

18 November 2003 at Calcutta
Australia 235 for 5 (50 overs) (DR Martyn 61)
India 198 (41.5 overs) (IJ Harvey 4 for 21)
Australia won by 37 runs

ENGLAND A IN INDIA
By Kate Laven

Whether they were stationed at Chinnaswamy or Chidambaram, the mixed bag of ECB National Academy recruits who toured India in February 2004 as the England A side found the stench of defeat as hard to take as the dust.

During six weeks of intense heat and testing conditions, the squad, featuring both old and young heads, from England international Ed Smith to Worcestershire rookie Shaftab Khalid, struggled to acclimatise to the conditions, recording seven defeats in eight matches and generously offering up a chance for India to rewrite its first-class record books.

The poor results were incidental, as far as coach Rod Marsh was concerned. The Academy is a training ground for quality English cricketers with international prospects, so being pitted against some quality Indian cricketers, many with international reputations, was, in his book, a key learning opportunity.

What angered him, however, to the point of moustache-twitching incandescence, was the immature way many of them managed responsibility. Lack of concentration in all departments at important times proved to be his biggest bugbear and the invectives which blasted out from the dressing room became a feature of the tour as well as a source of amusement among the locals.

It was during the Duleep Trophy match against South Zone in the lush, eco-friendly setting at Gurgaon near Delhi that things reached a low point. On another slow, flat track, Kevin Pietersen scored two excellent centuries in two innings to put England in a winning position – his trademark sweep shots proving to be too powerful for his opponents.

South Zone were one man down after their captain, the former India opener Sadagopan Ramesh, split the webbing in his hand in the opening overs of the match. Without him, the 503 target for victory looked

Kevin Pietersen was one of the few England A players to shine on the development tour to India.

impossible and England set their sights on a place in the finals, more so when Somerset's Simon Francis and Sajid Mahmood of Lancashire removed both openers with just one run on the board.

However, an ugly complacency then set in and Venugopal Rao and Subramaniam Badrinath plundered the woeful offerings of eight England bowlers to share an unbroken stand of 212 which, on top of Sridharan Sriram's 117, was enough to secure an astonishingly easy six-wicket win.

It was the highest total ever recorded by a side in India to secure victory, and the humiliation worsened the morale of an England side already fragmented by the departure of captain Alex Gidman, just one week into the tour, when his hand, broken during training at Loughborough before Christmas, showed no signs of healing.

A natural leader, the Gloucestershire all-rounder left a gaping hole both in the order and the dressing room, and his successor James Tredwell, while conscientious and shrewd on the field, proved too inconspicuous an influence off it. He could not harness the disparate elements that emerged early on in the tour when England lost their first two practice matches and three one-day games against an India A team that featured a wealth of internationals. Many of the younger players were also intimidated by Marsh, who is not only head honcho at the Academy but also an England selector, with the power to make or break a career.

'He is such a legend, just awesome, and everyone really wants to do well for him, but all we have done is let him down', Yorkshire batsman Michael Lumb commented.

Marsh was well aware of their anxieties. 'They got mixed up emotionally with trying to impress me rather than do what they do best, which is to bat or bowl well. That disappoints me because it's not what I think of someone, it's how well he does', he said.

There were some who did very well, however, and, despite the results, the tour could yet prove a rich spawning ground for England's next generation of players. Pietersen refused to be distracted by his contractual difficulties with Nottinghamshire and finished as the top batsman with four hundreds, all of them high-class, while Mahmood, a cousin of Olympic silver medal-winning boxer Amir Khan, confirmed his pedigree with an impressive show of pace, movement, control and versatility, and emerged as England's most effective young bowler.

Matt Prior, the 21-year-old Sussex wicketkeeper, made his mark with the bat, but appeared to lose confidence behind the stumps until the final Duleep

Sajid Mahmood did enough in Indian conditions to show Rod Marsh, the ECB Academy director, that he is one for England's future.

Trophy game against East Zone, when he made up lost ground.

Fifteen months earlier, Simon Jones had been stretchered off the field in Brisbane during England's first Ashes Test match after rupturing his cruciate ligament. Now, returning to first-class cricket in order to prove his fitness for the full England tour to the West Indies, he produced an intoxicating mix of accuracy and aggression to earn ten wickets in the friendly against Tamil Nadu in Chennai, but then put in an indifferent display in his finale at Gurgaon.

Essex all-rounder Graham Napier made useful contributions with bat and ball, but the squad's stylish left-handers, Lumb and Surrey's Scott Newman, failed to capitalise on good starts – Newman's confidence seemed to be particularly affected by a fractious relationship with his censorious coach.

The tour ended with a disappointing 93-run defeat against East Zone in Amritsar and the despondent team left for London a few hours later, most of them aware that a precious career opportunity had been squandered.

Kate Laven covered the England A tour of India for the Daily Telegraph.

NEW ZEALAND

NEW ZEALAND REPORT
By Bryan Waddle

There can be no greater compliment than to be rated highly by your peers. New Zealand captain Stephen Fleming has often been called 'the best in the world', but the tag has placed an undue burden on the Kiwi skipper.

Fleming is a commanding figure, tall and imposing, but he has not always been able to live up to such an exalted station in a year in which New Zealand's performances fluctuated.

There is no doubt that Fleming is New Zealand's most successful captain in both Test and one-day cricket, but recent team performances have not reached his own high standards.

By losing 3–0 to a professional and focussed England side, New Zealand did not live up to the expectations of a nation that considered them as 'probably the best team to tour England'.

This Test series loss, however, was offset by a commanding win in the NatWest Series; a victory that lifted New Zealand to second in the ICC world rankings.

Fleming displayed greater maturity both as a player and as a leader. His personal record was boosted by an improved conversion rate of half-centuries into centuries and by a successful transition to Test-match opener. While he may have had an excellent year with the bat, however, those he relied on for a general improvement in the New Zealand game were erratic and inconsistent.

The 5–0 loss in a one-day series in Pakistan was not a fair reflection of New Zealand's effort either. Given the option

to bypass the 'payback' tour on security grounds, a number of key players, including Fleming, opted out, leaving the team seriously depleted.

That tour did, however, reveal an emerging talent in Hamish Marshall, a young player who has yet to register a first-class hundred but who has carved out a regular place in the one-day team.

Stephen Fleming ... a commanding figure in New Zealand cricket.

With an average of 46 and a strike rate of 76, Marshall has provided both substance and discipline to a batting order that badly needed it. His introduction to the team has also coincided with the best record New Zealand has achieved in the one-day arena for some time.

Following the disastrous Pakistan venture, New Zealand played 16 one-day internationals under Fleming, losing just two, with one no result. It was no coincidence either that this run came at the beginning of John Bracewell's reign as coach. His success with Gloucestershire, particularly in the one-day game, was quickly conveyed to New Zealand.

However, while New Zealand's one-day record has improved, there has been a corresponding decline at Test level. Encouraging signs in a drawn two-Test series in India did not materialise on the home front as first Pakistan took the honours in a two-Test programme and then South Africa denied New Zealand a series win.

December in New Zealand invariably provides changeable weather that has not always been satisfactory for staging Test cricket. Hamilton and Wellington are the only true Test-match venues in a country of multi-purpose grounds, but they have not always offered the best conditions.

Rain and some sublime individual skills dominated the first Test. Pakistan quickly regretted bowling first on a flat, dry-looking pitch in Hamilton.

Fleming, his batteries recharged after a short break from the game, ensured that New Zealand had the best possible start with an outstanding innings of 192. An elegant striker of the ball when in top form, Fleming seemed determined to stamp his authority on the series, but it proved to be his only innings of substance. His eight subsequent innings produced just 125 runs.

Daniel Vettori may not have been a force with the ball in the home series, his seven wickets in five Tests coming at a cost of 96 runs apiece, but his batting was a revelation. There had been signs of greater maturity with the bat before, but his maiden Test hundred, on his home ground, lifted him into the genuine all-rounder class.

A massive first innings of 563 should have been enough to guarantee safety, but New Zealand ultimately had to rely on the conditions to snatch a draw.

The exquisite skills of Yasir Hameed, the belligerent and unorthodox hitting of Moin Khan and a strangely out-of-sorts Inzamam, ensured that New Zealand only had a lead of 100.

The irresistible pace of Shoaib Akhtar humbled New Zealand in Wellington.

Any thoughts of another home victory to add to New Zealand's proud record in home Tests were quickly dispelled in a lively burst of pace bowling from Mohammad Sami. With Shoaib Ahktar injured, Sami was left to lead an inexperienced attack. He struggled for rhythm in New Zealand's first innings – his 0 for 126 from 27 overs included 15 no-balls – but he was lethal in the second innings, with only Jacob Oram and Vettori standing firm as the Test was quickly brought to a close.

When Shoaib returned for the second Test, he was irresistible. New Zealand struggled to 366 with the lower order adding 221 for the last five wickets after the top order had faltered.

New Zealand pace bowler Ian Butler might not be able to match the Pakistan speedster for out-and-out pace, but his aggression and hostility can never be denied. Butler's career-best 6 for 46 gave New Zealand a lead of 170.

That is just the kind of challenge that Shoaib thrives on, however, and New Zealand were humbled for just 103 in 53 overs, with Shoaib adding six wickets to his first-innings haul of five, and leaving Pakistan to coast to victory.

Desperate for their first series win over South Africa in 73 years of contests between the two, New Zealand were at their combative best from the outset. The new breed of 'Black Cap' has developed a confidence fortified by the side's recent successes.

This series was not only between two talented teams, hugely charged, it turned into a battle of captains – one astute and experienced, the other a novice anxious to succeed. Graeme Smith knew he was in for a sterner test than just fronting up in the middle from the early stages of the series.

Smith and Fleming exchanged verbal jousts during the one-day series, with Fleming acknowledging the fact that he purposely targeted his lesser-experienced opponent.

Hamilton's Westpac Park provided the initial drama in the three-Test series; the pitch area had been attacked by a grass-eating virus that left the strip scruffy and worn.

The wear and tear soon created a large hole outside the left-handers' off stump at one end, and with a total of seven 'lefties' in the batting line-ups it was expected to be a batsman's nightmare. The

Graeme Smith ... targeted by the Black Caps in their fiercely-fought Test series against South Africa.

reality was less than the imagined, however, and, while it had a slight impact, three centuries and 870 runs for 25 wickets suggested that it had no real effect on the match.

The spotlight fell on Gary Kirsten in the lead-up to the second Test on Auckland's drop-in pitch. Kirsten had announced that he would retire from Test cricket following the end of the series and he promptly fell for one and one in what turned out to be New Zealand's most confident and controlled performance for some time.

Pace bowler Chris Martin had been out of the Test scene for three years, but he made a triumphant return. Eleven wickets in the Test were enough to earn him the Man of the Match award, but he was challenged for that by some exhilarating cricket from both Chris Cairns and Scott Styris.

Cairns is not often overshadowed in the big-hitting battle, but Styris shaded him momentarily with a blazing innings of 170 from 220 balls. Craig McMillan and Oram both played important roles, while Cairns crisply smashed 158 from 171 balls. Despite a cultured century from another elegant left-hander, Jacques Rudolph, the Test was New Zealand's to celebrate.

One up and, with a series to secure, New Zealand faced the expected backlash of a team disappointed and seemingly down on spirit. Graeme Smith was more resilient than New Zealand gave him credit for, however. The South Africa captain demanded accuracy and control from the bowlers who had been so wayward in Auckland and his appeal to their pride was effective.

New Zealand's batsmen, so confident and assertive in Auckland, played like millionaires on a pauper's budget, and failed to recapture their Auckland dominance. Even Nicky Boje overshadowed his much-celebrated New Zealand counterpart. His eight wickets in the match gave him nine in the series compared to Vettori's four.

The blowtorch had been applied to the South African skipper from the start of the tour, but Smith extinguished the flame with a match-winning century. It was enough to square the series.

FIRST TEST – NEW ZEALAND v. PAKISTAN
19–23 December 2003 at Hamilton

NEW ZEALAND

	First Innings		Second Innings	
MH Richardson	run out	44	c Moin Khan b Umar Gul	15
L Vincent	c Inzamam-ul-Haq b Shabbir	8	c Imran Farhat b Mohammad Sami	4
SP Fleming (capt)	lbw b Umar Gul	192	c Moin Khan b Mohammad Sami	0
SB Styris	c Taufeeq Umar b Danish Kaneria	33	c Taufeeq Umar b Mohammad Sami	20
CD McMillan	c Taufeeq Umar b Danish Kaneria	22	run out	2
CL Cairns	c Moin Khan b Shabbir	11	b Umar Gul	0
JDP Oram	b Shabbir Ahmed	6	not out	23
*RG Hart	c Yousuf Youhana b Shabbir	10	b Mohammad Sami	0
DL Vettori	not out	137	c Taufeeq Umar b Mohammad Sami	20
DR Tuffey	b Umar Gul	35	not out	1
IG Butler	c Imran Farhat b Shabbir	7		
Extras	b 4, lb 12, w 9, nb 33	58	lb 4, w 1, nb 6	11
	(151.2 overs)	563	(8 wkts 41.1 overs)	96

	First Innings				Second Innings			
	O	M	R	W	O	M	R	W
Mohammad Sami	27	2	126	0	16	4	44	5
Shabbir	43.2	9	117	5	10	7	10	0
Umar Gul	31	5	118	2	8.1	2	25	2
Abdul Razzaq	18	2	74	0	3	1	7	0
Danish Kaneria	32	6	112	2	4	2	6	0

Fall of Wickets
1-16, 2-117, 3-217, 4-249, 5-266, 6-274, 7-314, 8-439, 9-538
1-13, 2-13, 3-42, 4-42, 5-42, 6-47, 7-52, 8-95

PAKISTAN

	First Innings	
Imran Farhat	c Hart b Oram	20
Taufeeq Umar	c Butler b Tuffey	27
Yasir Hameed	lbw b Tuffey	80
Yousuf Youhana	c Vincent b Tuffey	28
Inzamam-ul-Haq (capt)	lbw b Tuffey	51
Abdul Razzaq	c Hart b Tuffey	48
*Moin Khan	lbw b Oram	137
Mohammad Sami	c Hart b Vettori	25
Shabbir Ahmed	c Hart b Butler	8
Umar Gul	c Vettori b Butler	3
Danish Kaneria	not out	0
Extras	lb 4, w 11, nb 21	36
	(144.4 overs)	463

	First Innings			
	O	M	R	W
Tuffey	33	8	87	5
Butler	23.4	6	113	2
Oram	23	7	55	2
Cairns	17	0	60	0
Vettori	36	4	117	1
Styris	12	4	27	0

Fall of Wickets
1-47, 2-55, 3-134, 4-209, 5-256, 6-285, 7-437, 8-453, 9-462

Umpires: SJ Davis and DL Orchard
Toss: Pakistan
Man of the Match: SP Fleming

Match drawn

SECOND TEST – NEW ZEALAND v. PAKISTAN
26-30 December 2003 at Wellington

NEW ZEALAND

	First Innings		Second Innings	
MH Richardson	c Yousuf Youhana b Shabbir	82	c Moin Khan b Shoaib Akhtar	41
L Vincent	b Shoaib Akhtar	0	lbw b Shoaib Akhtar	4
SP Fleming (capt)	lbw b Shoaib Akhtar	0	lbw b Danish Kaneria	24
RA Jones	b Abdul Razzaq	16	c Moin Khan b Shoaib Akhtar	7
SB Styris	c Moin Khan b Shoaib Akhtar	36	(6) b Shoaib Akhtar	0
CD McMillan	lbw b Shabbir	26	(7) not out	3
*RG Hart	c Imran Farhat b Shoaib Akhtar	19	(10) b Shoaib Akhtar	0
JDP Oram	c Moin Khan b Shabbir	97	lbw b Shabbir	3
DL Vettori	c Yasir Hameed b Mohammad Sami	44	lbw b Shabbir	0
DR Tuffey	not out	9	(5) run out	13
IG Butler	c Moin Khan b Shoaib Akhtar	4	b Shoaib Akhtar	0
Extras	b 5, lb 14, w 3, nb 11	33	lb 4, w 1, nb 3	8
	(142.3 overs)	366	(53 overs)	103

	First Innings				Second Innings			
	O	M	R	W	O	M	R	W
Shoaib Akhtar	20.3	5	48	5	18	3	30	6
Mohammad Sami	30	12	64	1	4	1	12	0
Shabbir	37	8	87	3	17	5	20	2
Danish Kaneria	32	5	86	0	9	2	18	1
Abdul Razzaq	23	6	62	1	5	1	19	0

Fall of Wickets
1-1, 2-1, 3-41, 4-94, 5-145, 6-171, 7-247, 8-327, 9-361
1-8, 2-43, 3-73, 4-95, 5-95, 6-96, 7-101, 8-102, 9-103

PAKISTAN

	First Innings		Second Innings	
Imran Farhat	c Hart b Oram	20	c Hart b Oram	14
Taufeeq Umar	c Oram b Tuffey	16	lbw b Vettori	34
Yasir Hameed	b Butler	3	c Hart b Butler	59
Yousuf Youhana	c Fleming b Vettori	60	not out	88
Inzamam-ul-Haq (capt)	lbw b Oram	34	not out	72
Abdul Razzaq	b Butler	26		
*Moin Khan	c Vettori b Butler	19		
Mohammad Sami	c Hart b Butler	4		
Shoaib Akhtar	b Butler	0		
Shabbir Ahmed	not out	0		
Danish Kaneria	lbw b Butler	0		
Extras	b 4, lb 3, w 1, nb 6	14	b 4, lb 2, nb 4	10
	(90 overs)	196	(3 wkts 74.5 overs)	277

	First Innings				Second Innings			
	O	M	R	W	O	M	R	W
Tuffey	24	9	46	1	14	5	41	0
Butler	20	6	46	6	18.5	1	100	1
Oram	22	5	49	2	9	1	34	1
Vettori	22	6	47	1	23	5	59	1
Styris	2	1	1	0	6	1	26	0
McMillan	-	-	-	-	4	0	11	0

Fall of Wickets
1-27, 2-30, 3-60, 4-112, 5-168, 6-171, 7-194, 8-195, 9-196
1-37, 2-75, 3-156

Umpires: SJ Davis and EAR de Silva
Toss: New Zealand
Test debut: RA Jones
Man of the Match: Shoaib Akhtar

Pakistan won by 7 wickets

SERIES AVERAGES
New Zealand v. Pakistan

NEW ZEALAND

Batting	M	Inns	NO	Runs	HS	Av	100	50	c/st
DL Vettori	2	4	1	201	137*	67.00	1	-	2/-
SP Fleming	2	4	0	216	192	54.00	1	-	1/-
MH Richardson	2	4	0	182	82	45.50	-	1	-/-
JDP Oram	2	4	1	129	97	43.00	-	1	1/-
DR Tuffey	2	4	2	58	35	29.00	-	-	-/-
SB Styris	2	4	0	89	36	22.25	-	-	-/-
CD McMillan	2	4	1	53	26	17.66	-	-	-/-
RA Jones	1	2	0	23	16	11.50	-	-	-/-
RG Hart	2	4	0	29	19	7.25	-	-	8/-
CL Cairns	1	2	0	11	11	5.50	-	-	-/-
L Vincent	2	4	0	16	8	4.00	-	-	1/-
IG Butler	2	3	0	11	7	3.66	-	-	1/-

Bowling	Overs	Mds	Runs	Wkts	Av	Best	5/inn	10m
JDP Oram	54	13	138	5	27.60	2-49	-	-
IG Butler	62.3	13	259	9	28.77	6-46	1	-
DR Tuffey	71	22	174	6	29.00	5-87	1	-
DL Vettori	81	14	223	3	74.33	1-47	-	-

Also bowled: CD McMillan 4-0-11-0, SB Styris 20-6-54-0, CL Cairns 17-0-60-0

PAKISTAN

Batting	M	Inns	NO	Runs	HS	Av	100	50	c/st
Yousuf Youhana	2	3	1	176	88*	88.00	-	2	2/-
Inzamam-ul-Haq	2	3	1	157	72*	78.50	-	2	1/-
Moin Khan	2	2	0	156	137	78.00	1	-	8/-
Yasir Hameed	2	3	0	142	80	47.33	-	2	1/-
Abdul Razzaq	2	2	0	74	48	37.00	-	-	-/-
Taufeeq Umar	2	3	0	77	34	25.66	-	-	4/-
Imran Farhat	2	3	0	54	20	18.00	-	-	3/-
Mohammad Sami	2	2	0	29	25	14.50	-	-	-/-
Shabbir Ahmed	2	2	1	8	8	8.00	-	-	-/-
Umar Gul	1	1	0	3	3	3.00	-	-	-/-
Shoaib Akhtar	1	1	0	0	0	0.00	-	-	-/-
Danish Kaneria	2	2	1	0	0*	0.00	-	-	-/-

Bowling	Overs	Mds	Runs	Wkts	Av	Best	5/inn	10m
Shoaib Akhtar	38.3	8	78	11	7.09	6-30	2	1
Shabbir Ahmed	107.2	29	234	10	23.40	5-117	1	-
Umar Gul	39.1	7	143	4	35.75	2-25	-	-
Mohammad Sami	77	19	246	6	41.00	5-44	1	-
Danish Kaneria	77	15	222	3	74.00	2-112	-	-
Abdul Razzaq	49	10	162	1	162.00	1-62	-	-

ONE-DAY INTERNATIONALS
v. Pakistan

Match One
3 January 2004 at Auckland
Pakistan 229 for 7 (50 overs) (Moin Khan 72*)
New Zealand 230 for 6 (49.1 overs) (SB Styris 101*)
New Zealand won by 4 wickets

Match Two
7 January 2004 at Queenstown
New Zealand 235 for 8 (50 overs) (BB McCullum 56*,
JDP Oram 54)
Pakistan 236 for 4 (47 overs) (Yousuf Youhana 88*,
Imran Farhat 87)
Pakistan won by 6 wickets

Match Three
10 January 2004 at Christchurch
Pakistan 255 for 9 (50 overs) (Saleem Elahi 80,
Abdul Razzaq 50*)
New Zealand 259 for 3 (46.2 overs) (SP Fleming 115*,
HJH Marshall 64)
New Zealand won by 7 wickets

Match Four
14 January 2004 at Napier
Pakistan 126 (36.3 overs)
New Zealand 127 for 2 (22.5 overs)
New Zealand won by 8 wickets

Match Five
17 January 2004 at Wellington
New Zealand 307 for 8 (50 overs) (HJH Marshall 84,
CD McMillan 81)
Pakistan 303 (49.3 overs) (Abdul Razzaq 89,
Inzamam-ul-Haq 67, Moin Khan 52)
New Zealand won by 4 runs

ONE-DAY INTERNATIONALS
v. South Africa

Match One
13 February 2004 at Auckland
New Zealand 225 for 8 (50 overs) (SB Styris 60,
CL Cairns 58)
South Africa 226 for 5 (49.4 overs) (GC Smith 72)
South Africa won by 5 wickets

Match Two
17 February 2004 at Christchurch
South Africa 253 for 8 (50 overs) (GC Smith 80)
New Zealand 255 for 5 (45.1 overs) (SP Fleming 108,
CD McMillan 70*)
New Zealand won by 5 wickets

Match Three
20 February 2004 at Wellington
New Zealand 254 for 5 (38 overs) (MHW Papps 67)
South Africa 249 for 7 (38 overs) (HH Gibbs 69)
New Zealand won by 5 runs

Match Four
25 February 2004 at Dunedin
South Africa 259 for 7 (50 overs) (JA Rudolph 70*,
N Boje 50)
New Zealand 264 for 4 (49 overs) (HJH Marshall 74,
SB Styris 69, SP Fleming 51)
New Zealand won by 6 wickets

Match Five
29 February 2004 at Auckland
New Zealand 193 for 8 (33 overs) (CZ Harris 55)
South Africa 175 for 5 (29 overs) (JH Kallis 58*)
*New Zealand won by 2 runs – DL Method: target 178
from 29 overs*

Match Six
2 March 2004 at Napier
South Africa 186 for 9 (50 overs)
New Zealand 190 for 5 (46 overs) (MHW Papps 92*)
New Zealand won by 5 wickets

FIRST TEST – NEW ZEALAND v. SOUTH AFRICA
10-14 March 2004 at Hamilton

SOUTH AFRICA

	First Innings		Second Innings	
GC Smith (capt)	c Oram b Vettori	25	c McCullum b Tuffey	5
HH Gibbs	c Styris b Vettori	40	c McCullum b Wiseman	47
JA Rudolph	c McCullum b Styris	72	b Cairns	0
JH Kallis	c Tuffey b Oram	92	not out	150
G Kirsten	c Papps b Vettori	137	(6) not out	34
PR Adams	b Oram	7		
ND McKenzie	lbw b Vettori	10	(5) c Richardson b Wiseman	52
*MV Boucher	lbw b Styris	22		
SM Pollock	run out	10		
M Ntini	run out	21		
A Nel	not out	4		
Extras	b 1, lb 5, w 1, nb 12	19	b 12, lb 5, nb 8	25
	(139.2 overs)	459	(4 wkts dec 116.1 overs)	313

	First Innings				Second Innings			
	O	M	R	W	O	M	R	W
Tuffey	26	11	62	0	15	3	28	1
Oram	27	7	76	2	15	4	29	0
Cairns	18	2	52	0	15	3	48	1
Vettori	39.2	2	158	4	34	11	79	0
Wiseman	12	1	54	0	19	4	68	2
Styris	16	4	46	2	13	4	29	0
McMillan	1	0	5	0	5.1	0	15	0

Fall of Wickets
1-51, 2-79, 3-211, 4-271, 5-281, 6-305, 7-364, 8-379, 9-415
1-15, 2-16, 3-108, 4-215

NEW ZEALAND

	First Innings		Second Innings	
MH Richardson	lbw b Pollock	4		
MHW Papps	lbw b Kallis	59	(1) c Boucher b Nel	12
SP Fleming (capt)	lbw b Adams	27		
SB Styris	b Pollock	74	(3) not out	3
CD McMillan	lbw b Kallis	19		
CL Cairns	c Boucher b Ntini	28		
JDP Oram	not out	119		
*BB McCullum	c Boucher b Kallis	57	(2) not out	19
DL Vettori	b Adams	53		
PJ Wiseman	b Pollock	36		
DR Tuffey	c Boucher b Pollock	0		
Extras	b 12, lb 11, nb 10	33	lb 1, w 1, nb 3	5
	(164.4 overs)	509	(1 wkt 16 overs)	39

	First Innings				Second Innings			
	O	M	R	W	O	M	R	W
Pollock	30.4	4	98	4	4	2	5	0
Ntini	29	9	74	1	4	0	15	0
Kallis	26	7	71	3	-	-	-	-
Nel	27	8	91	0	4	0	15	1
Adams	45	11	118	2	3	1	2	0
Rudolph	5	0	52	0	-	-	-	-
Smith	2	0	14	0	-	-	-	-
McKenzie	-	-	-	-	1	0	1	0

Fall of Wickets
1-20, 2-75, 3-127, 4-172, 5-223, 6-225, 7-309, 8-422, 9-509
1-34

Umpires: SJ Davis and RB Tiffin
Toss: South Africa
Test debuts: BB McCullum, MHW Papps
Man of the Match: JH Kallis

Match drawn

SECOND TEST – NEW ZEALAND v. SOUTH AFRICA
18-22 March 2004 at Auckland

SOUTH AFRICA

	First Innings		Second Innings	
GC Smith (capt)	lbw b Martin	88	b Martin	0
HH Gibbs	b Cairns	80	lbw b Oram	61
JA Rudolph	c Papps b Martin	17	not out	154
JH Kallis	c McCullum b Martin	40	lbw b McMillan	71
G Kirsten	b Oram	1	lbw b Martin	1
ND McKenzie	c Papps b Martin	27	c Papps b Martin	0
*MV Boucher	c McMillan b Martin	4	c Fleming b Martin	10
SM Pollock	b Tuffey	10	c Fleming b Martin	10
N Boje	not out	12	c McCullum b Cairns	24
M Ntini	c McCullum b Martin	0	c McMillan b Cairns	6
DJ Terbrugge	lbw b Oram	0	c sub b Cairns	2
Extras	lb 13, w 1, nb 3	17	b 6, lb 1, nb 3	10
	(123.3 overs)	296	(108.3 overs)	349

	First Innings				Second Innings			
	O	M	R	W	O	M	R	W
Tuffey	24	7	41	1	4	1	13	0
Martin	31	7	76	6	23	5	104	5
Oram	28.3	6	60	2	27	13	47	1
Cairns	21	6	54	1	13.3	1	63	3
Styris	14	5	37	0	13	5	39	0
Vettori	5	1	15	0	24	4	73	0
McMillan	-	-	-	-	4	1	3	1

Fall of Wickets
1-177, 2-177, 3-235, 4-236, 5-240, 6-246, 7-273, 8-289, 9-289
1-0, 2-103, 3-249, 4-250, 5-250, 6-272, 7-290, 8-327, 9-337

NEW ZEALAND

	First Innings		Second Innings	
MH Richardson	c Gibbs b Kallis	45	(2) c Boje b Ntini	10
MHW Papps	c Boje b Pollock	0	(1) not out	8
SP Fleming (capt)	c Kallis b Ntini	4	not out	31
SB Styris	c Pollock b Boje	170		
CD McMillan	b Pollock	82		
*BB McCullum	b Ntini	13		
CL Cairns	c Kallis b Smith	158		
JDP Oram	b Ntini	90		
DL Vettori	not out	4		
DR Tuffey	b Pollock	13		
CS Martin	b Pollock	0		
Extras	lb 10, nb 6	16	nb 4	4
	(148.5 overs)	595	(1 wkt 10.2 overs)	53

	First Innings				Second Innings			
	O	M	R	W	O	M	R	W
Pollock	32.5	6	113	4	5	1	16	0
Ntini	36	7	110	3	5	0	31	1
Terbrugge	22	4	93	0	-	-	-	-
Kallis	23	1	108	1	-	-	-	-
Boje	22	2	108	1	0.2	0	6	0
McKenzie	2	0	8	0	-	-	-	-
Rudolph	6	0	26	0	-	-	-	-
Smith	5	0	19	1	-	-	-	-

Fall of Wickets
1-5, 2-12, 3-137, 4-285, 5-314, 6-349, 7-574, 8-578, 9-595
1-20

Umpires: EAR de Silva and Aleem Dar
Toss: New Zealand
Man of the Match: CS Martin

New Zealand won by 9 wickets

THIRD TEST – NEW ZEALAND v. SOUTH AFRICA
26-30 March 2004 at Wellington

NEW ZEALAND

	First Innings		Second Innings	
MH Richardson	c Boucher b Kallis	14	(2) c Smith b Boje	37
MHW Papps	lbw b Ntini	7	(1) lbw b Pollock	0
SP Fleming (capt)	c Pollock b Boje	30	c Boucher b Nel	9
MS Sinclair	lbw b Boje	74	lbw b Pollock	21
SB Styris	b Boje	1	c & b Nel	73
*BB McCullum	lbw b Pollock	55	b Boje	3
CL Cairns	b Pollock	69	c van Jaarsveld b Boje	41
JDP Oram	st Boucher b Boje	34	lbw b Boje	40
DL Vettori	c Boucher b Pollock	0	c van Jaarsveld b Ntini	9
MJ Mason	c van Jaarsveld b Nel	3	run out	0
CS Martin	not out	1	not out	1
Extras	b 2, lb 1, w 1, nb 5	9	b 1, lb 9, w 3, nb 5	18
	(104 overs)	297	(96.2 overs)	252

	First Innings				Second Innings			
	O	M	R	W	O	M	R	W
Pollock	29	2	85	3	22	10	65	2
Ntini	21	6	63	1	20	6	50	1
Kallis	7	5	4	1	-	-	-	-
Nel	27	9	77	1	21	5	58	2
Boje	20	2	65	4	33.2	7	69	4

Fall of Wickets
1-23, 2-23, 3-90, 4-97, 5-163, 6-248, 7-257, 8-257, 9-264
1-1, 2-42, 3-73, 4-107, 5-111, 6-198, 7-201, 8-220, 9-224

SOUTH AFRICA

	First Innings		Second Innings	
GC Smith (capt)	b Cairns	47	not out	125
HH Gibbs	c sub b Martin	77	c Fleming b Martin	16
JA Rudolph	not out	93	b Martin	0
G Kirsten	c McCullum b Martin	1	(5) lbw b Styris	76
M van Jaarsveld	c Oram b Martin	59	(6) not out	13
JH Kallis	c McCullum b Martin	0	(4) lbw b Oram	1
*MV Boucher	c Papps b Martin	0		
SM Pollock	c Fleming b Oram	5		
N Boje	b Cairns	25		
M Ntini	c McCullum b Cairns	4		
A Nel	c Oram b Cairns	0		
Extras	lb 1, nb 4	5	lb 2, nb 1	3
	(99.5 overs)	316	(4 wkts 72.2 overs)	234

	First Innings				Second Innings			
	O	M	R	W	O	M	R	W
Martin	20	6	55	5	18.2	2	65	2
Mason	16	4	73	0	6	1	32	0
Oram	11	3	21	1	11	3	23	1
Vettori	26	6	76	0	18	2	53	0
Cairns	16.5	2	60	4	10	2	19	0
Styris	10	4	30	1	9	1	40	1

Fall of Wickets
1-103, 2-130, 3-136, 4-251, 5-265, 6-265, 7-270, 8-304, 9-308
1-29, 2-31, 3-36, 4-207

Umpires: Aleem Dar and EAR de Silva
Toss: South Africa
Test debut: MJ Mason
Man of the Match: GC Smith

South Africa won by 6 wickets

SERIES AVERAGES
New Zealand v. South Africa

NEW ZEALAND

Batting	M	Inns	NO	Runs	HS	Av	100	50	c/st
JDP Oram	3	4	1	283	119*	94.33	1	1	3/-
SB Styris	3	5	1	321	170	80.25	1	2	1/-
CL Cairns	3	4	0	296	158	74.00	1	1	-/-
CD McMillan	2	2	0	101	82	50.50	-	1	2/-
MS Sinclair	1	2	0	95	74	47.50	-	1	-/-
BB McCullum	3	5	1	147	57	36.75	-	2	9/-
PJ Wiseman	1	1	0	36	36	36.00	-	-	-/-
SP Fleming	3	5	1	101	31*	25.25	-	-	4/-
DL Vettori	3	4	1	66	53	22.00	-	1	-/-
MH Richardson	3	5	0	110	45	22.00	-	-	1/-
MHW Papps	3	6	1	86	59	17.20	-	1	5/-
DR Tuffey	2	2	0	13	13	6.50	-	-	1/-
CS Martin	2	3	2	2	1*	2.00	-	-	-/-
MJ Mason	1	2	0	3	3	1.50	-	-	-/-

Bowling	Overs	Mds	Runs	Wkts	Av	Best	5/inn	10m
CS Martin	92.2	20	300	18	16.66	6-76	3	1
CD McMillan	10.1	1	23	1	23.00	1-3	-	-
CL Cairns	94.2	16	296	9	32.88	4-60	-	-
JDP Oram	119.3	36	256	7	36.57	2-60	-	-
PJ Wiseman	31	5	122	2	61.00	2-68	-	-
DR Tuffey	69	22	144	2	72.00	1-28	-	-
SB Styris	75	23	221	3	73.66	2-46	-	-
DL Vettori	146.2	26	454	4	113.50	4-158	-	-

Also bowled: MJ Mason 22-5-105-0

SOUTH AFRICA

Batting	M	Inns	NO	Runs	HS	Av	100	50	c/st
JA Rudolph	3	6	2	336	154*	84.00	1	2	-/-
M van Jaarsveld	1	2	1	72	59	72.00	-	1	3/-
JH Kallis	3	6	1	354	150*	70.80	1	2	2/-
GC Smith	3	6	1	290	125*	58.00	1	1	1/-
HH Gibbs	3	6	0	321	80	53.50	-	3	1/-
G Kirsten	3	6	1	250	137	50.00	1	-	-/-
N Boje	2	3	1	61	25	30.50	-	-	2/-
ND McKenzie	2	4	0	89	52	22.25	-	1	-/-
MV Boucher	3	4	0	36	22	9.00	-	-	7/1
SM Pollock	3	4	0	35	10	8.75	-	-	2/-
M Ntini	3	4	0	31	21	7.75	-	-	-/-
PR Adams	1	1	0	7	7	7.00	-	-	-/-
A Nel	2	2	1	4	4*	4.00	-	-	1/-
DJ Terbrugge	1	2	0	2	2	1.00	-	-	-/-

Bowling	Overs	Mds	Runs	Wkts	Av	Best	5/inn	10m
N Boje	75.4	11	248	9	27.55	4-65	-	-
SM Pollock	123.3	25	382	13	29.38	4-98	-	-
GC Smith	7	0	33	1	33.00	1-19	-	-
JH Kallis	56	13	183	5	36.60	3-71	-	-
M Ntini	115	28	343	7	49.00	3-110	-	-
PR Adams	48	12	120	2	60.00	2-118	-	-
A Nel	79	22	241	4	60.25	2-58	-	-

Also bowled: ND McKenzie 3-0-9-0, JA Rudolph 11-0-46-0, DJ Terbrugge 22-4-93-0

PAKISTAN

PAKISTAN REPORT
By Qamar Ahmed

In a season that lasted nearly ten months, Pakistan, as always, had their full share of triumphs and tribulations. However, they can take solace from the fact that, generally, there was more gain than pain in the 2003–04 season.

A first home Test series victory against South Africa, a clean sweep in the five-match one-day international series at home against New Zealand, and, later, their domination over the Kiwis to win the two-match Test series in New Zealand, were all very comforting.

Despite their success against both South Africa and New Zealand, the icing on the cake was unquestionably the visit of their arch-rivals India for the first time in 14 years. The reasons for such a big gap between visits had more to do with antics at political level and the never-ending Kashmir dispute than anything to do with cricket.

Although the two neighbouring countries have played against each other in outside events such as the World Cup, India had not toured Pakistan since 1989, whilst the last time that Pakistan had crossed the border was in early 1999 for three Tests, which also included the first-ever Asian Test Championship match at Calcutta.

The long-awaited tour was announced after the Indian government lifted a three-year ban on bilateral cricket ties with Pakistan following a thaw in diplomatic relations.

Inzamam-ul-Haq was appointed as Pakistan's new captain at the end of 2003.

The visit in March and April of 2004 was preceded by a three-member Indian government team visiting Pakistan to gauge the security arrangements. Karachi and Peshawar were rejected as Test venues, although India agreed to play a one-day game at each.

That the tour took place at all and that it ended without any incident was itself a miracle of sorts. It certainly generated a lot of goodwill on either side, as thousands of cricket fans crossed the border to enjoy the tussle between the two countries.

India, the better of the two outfits, clinched the five-match one-day series 3–2. They also managed to take the three-match Test series by winning the first and final Test after Pakistan had emphatically won the second Test at Lahore to level the series.

India's victories over Pakistan in both the one-day

and Test series were their first on Pakistan soil for six tours. Reasons enough to celebrate.

Following the end of the home Test series against Bangladesh last year the captaincy had changed hands, with Inzamam-ul-Haq taking over from Rashid Latif who was banned for five matches by referee Mike Procter for claiming a catch which he dropped in the final Test at a crucial juncture of the match.

Inzamam, both as a captain and batsman, did well to fulfil his commitments under difficult circumstances.

At Multan, in the first Test, Pakistan were totally outplayed by the Indians, who inflicted an innings-and-52-run defeat on the final morning of the match as both Pakistan's batsmen and bowlers struggled. This was India's first-ever win in a Test in Pakistan.

India, having made a massive 675 for 5 with the help of Virender Sehwag's 309, a century by Sachin Tendulkar (194*) and an unbeaten 59 by Yuvraj Singh, had enforced the follow-on after Pakistan trailed by 268 runs. Yasir Hameed's 91 and Inzamam's 77 were not enough to save humiliation as young left-arm paceman, Irfan Pathan, bagged 4 for 100 in the first innings.

Pakistan, despite Yousuf Youhana's 112 in the second innings, failed to avoid the inevitable. Sehwag's triple-century was studded with 39 fours and six sixes and was the first by an Indian in Tests. Moreover, India's first-innings score was their highest in 48 Tests against Pakistan.

In the second Test at Lahore, Pakistan lifted themselves up to level the series with a victory by nine wickets and a day to spare.

The Indian batsmen faltered to 287 all out in the first innings on a seaming pitch. Only Yuvraj Singh with his maiden Test century (112) offered resistance as medium pacer Umar Gul picked up a career-best haul of 5 for 31.

Pakistan, having replied with 489 – with Imran Farhat making 101, Inzamam 118 and other useful contributions coming from Youhana (72) and left-hander Asim Kamal (73) – led India by 202 runs. India failed in the second innings as well, with Shoaib Akhtar and leg spinner Danish Kaneria doing the damage as the visitors fell for 241. Left to make only 40 runs, Pakistan reached the target in only seven overs on the fourth day.

In an exciting finale at Rawalpindi, Pakistan were found wanting as India beat them by an innings and 131 runs, their biggest-ever margin of victory over Pakistan.

After being inserted, Pakistan were reduced to 137 for 8, but were salvaged by a 70-run, ninth-wicket stand between Mohammad Sami and Fazle Akbar to reach 224.

India's 600 in reply owed much to Rahul Dravid, who made a brilliant 270 – containing 34 fours and a six – and there were valuable contributions from VVS Laxman (71) and Saurav Ganguly (77), who came back into the team to replace Dravid as captain after being injured during the one-day series.

Pakistan, 376 behind, were bowled out for 245 in their second innings despite a knock of 48 by Youhana and an unbeaten 60 by Asim Kamal. Anil Kumble and Lakshmipathy Balaji had dented Pakistan's batting and with it their pride.

The one-day matches were played in front of packed grounds, but the Tests failed to attract similar crowds. Ganguly summed up the tour perfectly when he said: 'I do not think we have ever been treated so well, even at home in India. The whole experience has been very overwhelming. The hospitality we have received is astonishing.'

Just as had been the case with India, the South Africans who toured earlier in the season did not play in Karachi and Peshawar citing security fears. Their visit, however, dispelled any doubts about the security situation as it progressed without any incident.

The Proteas, after initial hiccups, were at least brave enough to come to Pakistan. The Australians and West Indians had both pulled out a year before – calling off their tours and instead playing Pakistan in Sri Lanka and Sharjah.

Pakistan, having won the first two one-day internationals against South Africa, lost the series 3–2 but won the two-match Test series 1–0, their first-ever series win against the South Africans.

In the first Test, at Lahore, Pakistan won by eight wickets. Having taken a lead of 81 runs on the first innings, Pakistan bowled out the visitors second time round for 241, leaving them to chase 161 in the last innings. On the final day, Pakistan required only 24 runs, which were duly knocked off in 7.1 overs.

The highlights of the Test were 111 and a second-innings half-century by opener Taufeeq Umar, off spinner Shoaib Malik's first-innings 4 for 42 and Danish Kaneria's match haul of 7 for 111.

Asim Kamal's well-made 99 in Pakistan's first-innings total of 401 was a valuable contribution, as was left-arm spinner Paul Adams' career-best 7 for 128 for South Africa.

In the second Test, Pakistan clung on to earn a draw and win the series. Imran Farhat made 128 in the first innings, sharing a third-successive century opening stand with Taufeeq Umar (68).

Shaun Pollock's 6 for 78 was a fine effort and so was Gary Kirsten's 19th Test century in South Africa's second-innings total of 371 for 8. Pakistan, chasing 302 to win with a day to spare, hung on to make 242 for 6 and drew the game.

The series was not without occasional flare-ups between the players. Shoaib Akhtar was banned for one Test and two one-day games by referee Clive Lloyd for using abusive and offensive language at Adams in the first Test.

Graeme Smith was banned for one limited-overs international after the fourth one-dayer at Rawalpindi and was fined 50 per cent of his match fee. Andrew Hall was slapped with a two-Test ban for an altercation with Yousuf Youhana – who was also fined 50 per cent of his match fee for his part in the incident.

Pakistan continued to show progress as they whitewashed the visiting Kiwis under Chris Cairns in a five-match one-day series and then went to New Zealand to win a two-match Test series 1–0. A return one-day series was lost 4–1, however.

In the Asia Cup, in Sri Lanka, Pakistan beat India, Bangladesh and Hong Kong, but failed to make it to the final against Sri Lanka because of a nonsensical bonus-points system. They beat India again in Holland in a tri-nation series, but failed by just 17 runs to topple Australia.

At junior level, Pakistan's Under 19 team won the Youth World Cup in Bangladesh, whilst at home, Lt Gen Tauqir Zia, the chairman of the Pakistan Cricket Board, resigned after four years in office following criticism of his leadership style.

He was replaced by the former Foreign Secretary, Shaharyar Khan. A couple of months later, the chief executive of the Board – former Test batsman Ramiz Raja – also tendered his resignation. Chief selector Aamir Sohail was replaced by Wasim Bari and the coach Javed Miandad also made way for Bob Woolmer.

At domestic level, Faisalabad achieved a rare double by winning both the Quaid-e-Azam Trophy

The Rawalpindi Express ... Shoaib Akhtar.

first-class tournament and the Quaid-e-Azam Cup national one-day competition for the first time.

Three batsmen – Shoaib Khan of Peshawar, Naved Yousuf of Rawalpindi and Aamer Bashir of Multan – passed 1,000 runs in the season. The best innings of the domestic season came from Shoaib Khan who made an unbeaten 300 against Quetta in the Quaid-e-Azam Trophy.

ONE-DAY INTERNATIONALS
v. South Africa

Match One
3 October 2003 at Lahore
Pakistan 277 for 6 (50 overs) (Shoaib Malik 82*,
Yousuf Youhana 68, Yasir Hameed 56)
South Africa 269 for 6 (50 overs) (HH Dippenaar 110*,
GC Smith 71, ND McKenzie 62,
Shoaib Akhtar 4 for 49)
Pakistan won by 8 runs

Match Two
5 October 2003 at Lahore
Pakistan 267 for 7 (50 overs) (Yousuf Youhana 65,
M Ntini 4 for 46)
South Africa 225 for 9 (50 overs)
(HH Dippenaar 58)
Pakistan won by 42 runs

Match Three
7 October 2003 at Faisalabad
Pakistan 243 for 8 (50 overs) (Yasir Hameed 72)
South Africa 221 for 6 (45 overs) (JH Kallis 62,
GC Smith 51)
South Africa won by 13 runs – DL Method

Match Four
10 October 2003 at Rawalpindi
Pakistan 157 (47.4 overs) (Yousuf Youhana 60,
A Nel 4 for 39)
South Africa 158 for 4 (38.5 overs) (JH Kallis 58*)
South Africa won by 6 wickets

Match Five
12 October 2003 at Rawalpindi
Pakistan 192 (49.3 overs)
South Africa 193 for 3 (45.5 overs)
(HH Dippenaar 74)
South Africa won by 7 wickets

FIRST TEST – PAKISTAN v. SOUTH AFRICA
17–21 October 2003 at Lahore

SOUTH AFRICA

	First Innings		Second Innings	
GC Smith (capt)	c Asim Kamal b Mohammad Sami	33	c Taufeeq Umar b Shoaib Akhtar	12
HH Gibbs	c Taufeeq Umar b Danish Kaneria	27	c Taufeeq Umar b Shoaib Akhtar	59
G Kirsten	retired hurt	53	(6) c Yousuf Youhana b Danish Kaneria	46
JH Kallis	c Moin Khan b Danish Kaneria	29	c Moin Khan b Shoaib Akhtar	18
HH Dippenaar	c Imran Farhat b Shoaib Malik	24	(3) c Yousuf Youhana b Shoaib Akhtar	27
ND McKenzie	lbw b Shoaib Akhtar	0	(5) b Danish Kaneria	14
*MV Boucher	c Imran Farhat b Shoaib Malik	72	c Imran Farhat b Danish Kaneria	15
SM Pollock	b Shoaib Malik	28	b Danish Kaneria	18
PR Adams	not out	18	lbw b Danish Kaneria	0
A Nel	lbw b Shoaib Akhtar	0	b Mushtaq Ahmed	0
M Ntini	c Asim Kamal b Shoaib Malik	8	not out	0
Extras	lb 5, nb 23	28	b 1, lb 11, nb 20	32
	(83 overs)	320	(84.3 overs)	241

	First Innings				Second Innings			
	O	M	R	W	O	M	R	W
Shoaib Akhtar	14	1	62	2	14.3	2	36	4
Mohammad Sami	13	2	66	1	19.3	0	77	0
Mushtaq Ahmed	18	1	80	0	8	1	18	1
Danish Kaneria	21	2	65	2	28.3	8	46	5
Shoaib Malik	17	4	42	4	14	0	52	0

Fall of Wickets
1-52, 2-84, 3-154, 4-159, 5-229, 6-282, 7-302, 8-307, 9-320
1-43, 2-104, 3-108, 4-149, 5-149, 6-192, 7-237, 8-238, 9-241

PAKISTAN

	First Innings		Second Innings	
Taufeeq Umar	c & b Adams	111	b Adams	63
Imran Farhat	b Adams	41	c Gibbs b Smith	58
Yasir Hameed	c Boucher b Pollock	16	not out	20
Yousuf Youhana (capt)	c Boucher b Nel	8		
Asim Kamal	b Nel	99		
Shoaib Malik	b Adams	47	(4) not out	8
*Moin Khan	lbw b Adams	37		
Shoaib Akhtar	st Boucher b Adams	1		
Mohammad Sami	b Adams	0		
Mushtaq Ahmed	not out	14		
Danish Kaneria	c Smith b Adams	0		
Extras	b 2, lb 17, w 2, nb 6	27	lb 6, w 5, nb 4	15
	(148 overs)	401	(2 wkts 40.1 overs)	164

	First Innings				Second Innings			
	O	M	R	W	O	M	R	W
Pollock	22	7	48	1	7	2	21	0
Ntini	28	4	88	0	6	0	24	0
Adams	45	11	128	7	11	1	57	1
Nel	27	5	67	2	5	1	13	0
Kallis	18	3	37	0	6	1	30	0
Smith	8	1	14	0	5.1	2	13	1

Fall of Wickets
1-109, 2-151, 3-160, 4-223, 5-322, 6-363, 7-366, 8-366, 9-401
1-134, 2-141

Umpires: DB Hair and NA Mallender
Toss: South Africa
Test debut: Asim Kamal
Men of the Match: Taufeeq Umar and Danish Kaneria

Pakistan won by 8 wickets

SECOND TEST – PAKISTAN v. SOUTH AFRICA
24–28 October 2003 at Faisalabad

SERIES AVERAGES
Pakistan v. South Africa

SOUTH AFRICA

	First Innings		Second Innings	
GC Smith (capt)	c Inzamam-ul-Haq b Shabbir	2	lbw b Shabbir	65
HH Gibbs	lbw b Mushtaq Ahmed	98	lbw b Danish Kaneria	20
HH Dippenaar	c Taufeeq Umar b Shabbir	4	lbw b Shoaib Malik	21
JH Kallis	c Taufeeq Umar b Danish Kaneria	10	(6) lbw b Abdul Razzaq	43
G Kirsten	c Taufeeq Umar b Abdul Razzaq	54	(4) c Taufeeq Umar b Abdul Razzaq	118
ND McKenzie	c Mushtaq Ahmed b Shabbir	27	(5) c Taufeeq Umar b Danish Kaneria	35
*MV Boucher	b Abdul Razzaq	27	b Abdul Razzaq	0
SM Pollock	run out	16	not out	30
RJ Peterson	c sub b Shabbir	4	c Inzamam-ul-Haq b Shabbir	17
PR Adams	c Taufeeq Umar b Danish Kaneria	14	not out	9
M Ntini	not out	16		
Extras	lb 1, w 1, nb 4	6	b 1, lb 7, w 2, nb 3	13
	(99.1 overs)	278	(8 wkts dec 127.3 overs)	371

	First Innings				Second Innings			
	O	M	R	W	O	M	R	W
Shabbir	26	8	74	4	34.3	10	70	2
Abdul Razzaq	22	4	68	2	18	3	70	3
Danish Kaneria	33.1	10	68	2	37	6	100	2
Shoaib Malik	5	0	19	0	26	5	70	1
Mushtaq Ahmed	13	1	48	1	12	3	53	0

Fall of Wickets
1-6, 2-20, 3-40, 4-148, 5-195, 6-212, 7-236, 8-247, 9-250
1-42, 2-93, 3-128, 4-213, 5-303, 6-303, 7-325, 8-358

PAKISTAN

	First Innings		Second Innings	
Taufeeq Umar	c Gibbs b Adams	68	c Smith b Peterson	71
Imran Farhat	c Peterson b Pollock	128	lbw b Kallis	8
Yasir Hameed	c Gibbs b Pollock	21	c Dippenaar b Ntini	17
Inzamam-ul-Haq (capt)	lbw b Pollock	23	lbw b Ntini	60
Asim Kamal	c Pollock b Ntini	1	c Boucher b Adams	38
Shoaib Malik	c Smith b Pollock	9	(7) not out	23
Abdul Razzaq	c sub b Ntini	37	(6) b Pollock	10
*Moin Khan	c Gibbs b Kallis	18	not out	9
Mushtaq Ahmed	lbw b Pollock	6		
Shabbir Ahmed	not out	24		
Danish Kaneria	c Smith b Pollock	0		
Extras	b 3, lb 8, w 1, nb 1	13	b 1, lb 1, nb 4	6
	(116.2 overs)	348	(6 wkts 98 overs)	242

	First Innings				Second Innings			
	O	M	R	W	O	M	R	W
Pollock	29.2	9	78	6	22	12	27	1
Ntini	29	9	64	2	20	7	45	2
Kallis	22	4	57	1	19	6	51	1
Peterson	8	1	40	0	15	6	21	1
Adams	25	5	82	1	20	2	75	1
Smith	3	0	16	0	2	0	21	0

Fall of Wickets
1-137, 2-178, 3-248, 4-251, 5-257, 6-261, 7-293, 8-309, 9-339
1-18, 2-46, 3-125, 4-187, 5-209, 6-209

Umpires: DJ Harper and SJA Taufel
Toss: South Africa
Men of the Match: Taufeeq Umar and G Kirsten
Man of the Series: Taufeeq Umar

Match drawn

PAKISTAN

Batting	M	Inns	NO	Runs	HS	Av	100	50	c/st
Taufeeq Umar	2	4	0	313	111	78.25	1	3	9/-
Imran Farhat	2	4	0	235	128	58.75	1	1	3/-
Asim Kamal	2	3	0	138	99	46.00	-	1	2/-
Shoaib Malik	2	4	2	87	47	43.50	-	-	-/-
Inzamam-ul-Haq	1	2	0	83	60	41.50	-	1	2/-
Moin Khan	2	3	1	64	37	32.00	-	-	2/-
Yasir Hameed	2	4	1	74	21	24.66	-	-	-/-
Abdul Razzaq	1	2	0	47	37	23.50	-	-	-/-
Mushtaq Ahmed	2	2	1	20	14*	20.00	-	-	1/-
Yousuf Youhana	1	1	0	8	8	8.00	-	-	2/-
Shoaib Akhtar	1	1	0	1	1	1.00	-	-	-/-
Danish Kaneria	2	2	0	0	0	0.00	-	-	-/-
Mohammad Sami	1	1	0	0	0	0.00	-	-	-/-
Shabbir Ahmed	1	1	1	24	24*	-	-	-	-/-

Bowling	Overs	Mds	Runs	Wkts	Av	Best	5/inn	10m
Shoaib Akhtar	28.3	3	98	6	16.33	4-36	-	-
Shabbir Ahmed	60.3	18	144	6	24.00	4-74	-	-
Danish Kaneria	119.4	26	279	11	25.36	5-46	1	-
Abdul Razzaq	40	7	138	5	27.60	3-70	-	-
Shoaib Malik	62	9	183	5	36.60	4-42	-	-
Mushtaq Ahmed	51	6	199	2	99.50	1-18	-	-
Mohammad Sami	32.3	2	143	1	143.00	1-66	-	-

SOUTH AFRICA

Batting	M	Inns	NO	Runs	HS	Av	100	50	c/st
G Kirsten	2	4	1	271	118	90.33	1	2	5/-
HH Gibbs	2	4	0	204	98	51.00	-	2	4/-
SM Pollock	2	4	1	92	30*	30.66	-	-	1/-
MV Boucher	2	4	0	114	72	28.50	-	1	3/1
GC Smith	2	4	0	112	65	28.00	-	1	4/-
JH Kallis	2	4	0	100	43	25.00	-	-	-/-
M Ntini	2	3	2	24	16*	24.00	-	-	-/-
PR Adams	2	4	2	41	18*	20.50	-	-	1/-
HH Dippenaar	2	4	0	76	27	19.00	-	-	1/-
ND McKenzie	2	4	0	76	35	19.00	-	-	-/-
RJ Peterson	1	2	0	21	17	10.50	-	-	1/-
A Nel	1	2	0	0	0	0.00	-	-	-/-

Bowling	Overs	Mds	Runs	Wkts	Av	Best	5/inn	10m
SM Pollock	80.2	30	174	8	21.75	6-78	1	-
PR Adams	101	19	342	10	34.20	7-128	1	-
A Nel	32	6	80	2	40.00	2-67	-	-
M Ntini	83	20	221	4	55.25	2-45	-	-
RJ Peterson	23	7	61	1	61.00	1-21	-	-
GC Smith	18.1	3	64	1	64.00	1-13	-	-
JH Kallis	65	14	175	2	87.50	1-51	-	-

ONE–DAY INTERNATIONALS
v. New Zealand

Match One
29 November 2003 at Lahore
New Zealand 291 for 5 (50 overs) (CL Cairns 84*,
MS Sinclair 55, HJH Marshall 55)
Pakistan 292 for 7 (48 overs) (Yasir Hameed 52)
Pakistan won by 3 wickets

Match Two
1 December 2003 at Lahore
Pakistan 281 for 6 (50 overs) (Saleem Elahi 70,
Imran Farhat 68, Yasir Hameed 53)
New Zealand 157 (38.5 overs) (RA Jones 63,
Mohammad Sami 5 for 10)
Pakistan won by 124 runs

Match Three
3 December 2003 at Faisalabad
Pakistan 314 for 7 (50 overs) (Imran Farhat 91,
Yousuf Youhana 64, Yasir Hameed 63,
MDJ Walker 4 for 49)
New Zealand 263 for 7 (50 overs)
(HJH Marshall 101*)
Pakistan won by 51 runs

Match Four
5 December 2003 at Rawalpindi
New Zealand 183 (47.5 overs)
Pakistan 184 for 3 (41.2 overs) (Imran Farhat 82,
Yasir Hameed 61)
Pakistan won by 7 wickets

Match Five
7 December 2003 at Rawalpindi
Pakistan 277 for 4 (50 overs) (Yasir Hameed 127*,
Imran Farhat 107)
New Zealand 228 for 6 (50 overs)
(HJH Marshall 62*)
Pakistan won by 49 runs

ONE–DAY INTERNATIONALS
v. India

Match One
13 March 2004 at Karachi
India 349 for 7 (50 overs) (R Dravid 99,
V Sehwag 79)
Pakistan 344 for 8 (50 overs) (Inzamam-ul-Haq 122,
Yousuf Youhana 73)
India won by 5 runs

Match Two
16 March 2004 at Rawalpindi
Pakistan 329 for 6 (50 overs) (Yasir Hameed 86,
Shahid Afridi 80)
India 317 (48.4 overs) (SR Tendulkar 141)
Pakistan won by 12 runs

Match Three
19 March 2004 at Peshawar
India 244 for 9 (50 overs) (Yuvraj Singh 65)
Pakistan 247 for 6 (47.2 overs) (Yasir Hameed 98,
Abdul Razzaq 53*)
Pakistan won by 4 wickets

Match Four
21 March 2004 at Lahore
Pakistan 293 for 9 (50 overs)
(Inzamam-ul-Haq 123)
India 294 for 5 (45 overs)
(R Dravid 76*, M Kaif 71*)
India won by 5 wickets

Match Five
24 March 2004 at Lahore
India 293 for 7 (50 overs) (VVS Laxman 107)
Pakistan 253 (47.5 overs) (Moin Khan 72,
Shoaib Malik 65)
India won by 40 runs

FIRST TEST – PAKISTAN v. INDIA
28 March–1 April 2004 at Multan

INDIA

	First Innings	
A Chopra	c Imran Farhat b Saqlain Mushtaq	42
V Sehwag	c Taufeeq Umar b Mohammad Sami	309
R Dravid (capt)	c Yasir Hameed b Mohammad Sami	6
SR Tendulkar	not out	194
VVS Laxman	run out	29
Yuvraj Singh	c & b Imran Farhat	59
*PA Patel		
A Kumble		
Z Khan		
IK Pathan		
L Balaji		
Extras	b 8, lb 20, w 1, nb 7	36
	(5 wkts dec 161.5 overs)	**675**

	First Innings			
	O	M	R	W
Shoaib Akhtar	32	4	119	0
Mohammad Sami	34	4	110	2
Shabbir	31	6	122	0
Saqlain Mushtaq	43	4	204	1
Abdul Razzaq	15	3	61	0
Imran Farhat	6.5	0	31	1

Fall of Wickets
1-160, 2-173, 3-509, 4-565, 5-675

PAKISTAN

	First Innings		Second Innings	
Imran Farhat	lbw b Balaji	38	c Patel b Kumble	24
Taufeeq Umar	c Dravid b Pathan	23	lbw b Kumble	9
Yasir Hameed	c Patel b Pathan	91	c Sehwag b Yuvraj Singh	23
Inzamam-ul-Haq (capt)	c Chopra b Kumble	77	run out	0
Yousuf Youhana	c Patel b Khan	35	c Dravid b Pathan	112
Abdul Razzaq	c Patel b Pathan	47	c Chopra b Kumble	22
*Moin Khan	b Tendulkar	17	lbw b Pathan	5
Saqlain Mushtaq	c Khan b Pathan	5	(9) lbw b Kumble	0
Mohammad Sami	b Kumble	15	(8) lbw b Kumble	0
Shoaib Akhtar	c & b Tendulkar	0	c Laxman b Kumble	4
Shabbir Ahmed	not out	19	not out	0
Extras	b 4, lb 26, nb 10	40	b 4, lb 5, w 1, nb 2	12
	(126.3 overs)	**407**	(77 overs)	**211**

	First Innings				Second Innings			
	O	M	R	W	O	M	R	W
Khan	23	6	76	1	-	-	-	-
Pathan	28	5	100	4	21	12	26	2
Kumble	39.3	12	100	2	30	10	72	6
Balaji	20	4	54	1	11	3	48	0
Sehwag	2	0	11	0	3	0	8	0
Tendulkar	14	1	36	2	6	2	23	0
Yuvraj Singh	-	-	-	-	6	1	25	1

Fall of Wickets
1-58, 2-73, 3-233, 4-243, 5-321, 6-364, 7-364, 8-371, 9-371
1-33, 2-44, 3-44, 4-75, 5-106, 6-113, 7-124, 8-136, 9-206

Umpires: DR Shepherd and SJA Taufel
Toss: India
Man of the Match: V Sehwag

India won by an innings and 52 runs

SECOND TEST – PAKISTAN v. INDIA
5–8 April 2004 at Lahore

INDIA

	First Innings		Second Innings	
A Chopra	lbw b Mohammad Sami	4	lbw b Shoaib Akhtar	5
V Sehwag	c Kamran Akmal b Umar Gul	39	c Kamran Akmal b Shoaib Akhtar	90
R Dravid (capt)	c Inzamam-ul-Haq b Umar Gul	33	run out	0
SR Tendulkar	lbw b Umar Gul	2	lbw b Mohammad Sami	8
VVS Laxman	c Taufeeq Umar b Umar Gul	11	b Umar Gul	13
Yuvraj Singh	c Imran Farhat b Danish Kaneria	112	c Kamran Akmal b Mohammad Sami	12
*PA Patel	lbw b Umar Gul	0	not out	62
AB Agarkar	c Kamran Akmal b Shoaib Akhtar	2	(9) c Taufeeq Umar b Danish Kaneria	36
IK Pathan	c & b Danish Kaneria	49	(8) c Taufeeq Umar b Shoaib Akhtar	0
L Balaji	c Kamran Akmal b Mohammad Sami	0	(11) lbw b Danish Kaneria	0
A Kumble	not out	6	(10) st Kamran Akmal b Danish Kaneria	0
Extras	b 6, lb 8, w 6, nb 9	29	lb 8, w 1, nb 6	15
	(64.1 overs)	**287**	(62.4 overs)	**241**

	First Innings				Second Innings			
	O	M	R	W	O	M	R	W
Shoaib Akhtar	16	1	69	1	17	4	62	3
Mohammad Sami	23	1	117	2	26	6	92	2
Umar Gul	12	2	31	5	13	1	65	1
Danish Kaneria	13.1	1	56	2	6.4	2	14	3

Fall of Wickets
1-5, 2-69, 3-75, 4-94, 5-125, 6-127, 7-147, 8-264, 9-265
1-15, 2-15, 3-43, 4-88, 5-105, 6-160, 7-160, 8-235, 9-241

PAKISTAN

	First Innings		Second Innings	
Imran Farhat	c Patel b Balaji	101	c Yuvraj Singh b Balaji	9
Taufeeq Umar	b Balaji	24	not out	14
Yasir Hameed	c Dravid b Agarkar	19	not out	16
Inzamam-ul-Haq (capt)	lbw b Pathan	118		
Yousuf Youhana	c Patel b Balaji	72		
Asim Kamal	c Patel b Kumble	73		
*Kamran Akmal	lbw b Pathan	5		
Mohammad Sami	b Pathan	2		
Shoaib Akhtar	c Yuvraj Singh b Kumble	19		
Umar Gul	hit wkt b Tendulkar	14		
Danish Kaneria	not out	0		
Extras	b 4, lb 18, w 4, nb 16	42	nb 1	1
	(160.1 overs)	**489**	(1 wkt 7 overs)	**40**

	First Innings				Second Innings			
	O	M	R	W	O	M	R	W
Pathan	44	14	107	3	4	0	25	0
Balaji	33	11	81	3	3	0	15	1
Agarkar	23	5	80	1	-	-	-	-
Kumble	44.1	5	146	2	-	-	-	-
Tendulkar	12	1	38	1	-	-	-	-
Yuvraj Singh	3	0	7	0	-	-	-	-
Sehwag	1	0	8	0	-	-	-	-

Fall of Wickets
1-47, 2-95, 3-205, 4-356, 5-366, 6-379, 7-386, 8-432, 9-470
1-15

Umpires: SA Bucknor and SJA Taufel
Toss: India
Man of the Match: Umar Gul

Pakistan won by 9 wickets

THIRD TEST – PAKISTAN v. INDIA
13–16 April 2004 at Rawalpindi

PAKISTAN

	First Innings		Second Innings	
Imran Farhat	lbw b Nehra	16	c Sehwag b Balaji	3
Taufeeq Umar	lbw b Balaji	9	lbw b Pathan	13
Yasir Hameed	c Laxman b Pathan	26	c Patel b Nehra	20
Inzamam-ul-Haq (capt)	c Patel b Nehra	15	(5) c Patel b Balaji	9
Yousuf Youhana	b Pathan	13	(6) c & b Kumble	48
Asim Kamal	lbw b Balaji	21	(7) not out	60
*Kamran Akmal	c Laxman b Balaji	17	(4) b Balaji	23
Mohammad Sami	run out	49	c Dravid b Kumble	0
Shoaib Akhtar	b Balaji	0	c Nehra b Kumble	28
Fazl-e-Akbar	lbw b Kumble	25	c Pathan b Kumble	12
Danish Kaneria	not out	4	c Ganguly b Tendulkar	0
Extras	b 14, lb 5, w 7, nb 3	29	b 5, lb 11, w 2, nb 11	29
	(72.5 overs)	224	(54 overs)	241

	First Innings				Second Innings			
	O	M	R	W	O	M	R	W
Pathan	22	7	49	2	15	6	35	1
Balaji	19	4	63	4	20	2	108	3
Nehra	21	4	60	2	6	2	20	1
Ganguly	2	0	9	0	4	0	18	0
Kumble	8.5	2	24	1	8	2	47	4
Tendulkar	–	–	–	–	1	0	1	1

Fall of Wickets
1-34, 2-34, 3-77, 4-77, 5-110, 6-120, 7-137, 8-137, 9-207
1-30, 2-34, 3-64, 4-90, 5-94, 6-175, 7-179, 8-221, 9-244

INDIA

	First Innings	
V Sehwag	c Yasir Hameed b Shoaib Akhtar	0
*PA Pater	c Kamran Akmal b Fazl-e-Akbar	69
R Dravid	b Imran Farhat	270
SR Tendulkar	c Kamran Akmar b Shoaib Akhtar	1
VVS Laxman	b Shoaib Akhtar	71
SC Ganguly (capt)	run out	77
Yuvraj Singh	lbw b Mohammad Sami	47
IK Pathan	c Fazl-e-Akbar b Danish Kaneria	15
A Kumble	st Kamran Akmar b Danish Kaneria	9
L Balaji	c sub b Imran Farhat	11
A Nehra	not out	1
Extras	b 11, lb 12, w 6	29
	(177.2 overs)	600

	First Innings			
	O	M	R	W
Shoaib Akhtar	21.2	7	47	3
Fazl-e-Akbar	40.4	3	162	1
Danish Kaneria	62	4	178	2
Mohammad Sami	40	11	116	1
Imran Farhat	12.2	1	69	2
Yasir Hameed	1	0	5	0

Fall of Wickets
1-47, 2-95, 3-205, 4-356, 5-366, 6-379, 7-386, 8-432, 9-470

Umpires: RE Koertzen and DR Shepherd
Toss: India
Man of the Match: R Dravid
Man of the Series: V Sehwag

India won by an innings and 131 runs

SERIES AVERAGES
Pakistan v. India

PAKISTAN

Batting	M	Inns	NO	Runs	HS	Av	100	50	c/st
Asim Kamal	2	3	1	154	73	77.00	–	2	-/-
Yousuf Youhana	3	5	0	280	112	56.00	1	1	-/-
Inzamam-ul-Haq	3	5	0	219	118	43.80	1	1	1/-
Yasir Hameed	3	6	1	195	91	39.00	–	1	2/-
Abdul Razzaq	1	2	0	69	47	34.50	–	–	-/-
Imran Farhat	3	6	0	191	101	31.83	1	–	3/-
Fazl-e-Akbar	1	2	0	37	25	18.50	–	–	1/-
Taufeeq Umar	3	6	1	92	24	18.40	–	–	4/-
Kamran Akmal	2	3	0	45	23	15.00	–	–	7/2
Umar Gul	1	1	0	14	14	14.00	–	–	-/-
Mohammad Sami	3	5	0	66	49	13.20	–	–	-/-
Moin Khan	1	2	0	22	17	11.00	–	–	-/-
Shoaib Akhtar	3	5	0	51	28	10.20	–	–	-/-
Danish Kaneria	2	3	2	4	4*	4.00	–	–	1/-
Saqlain Mushtaq	1	2	0	5	5	2.50	–	–	-/-
Shabbir Ahmed	1	2	2	19	19*	–	–	–	-/-

Bowling	Overs	Mds	Runs	Wkts	Av	Best	5/inn	10m
Umar Gul	25	3	96	6	16.00	5-31	1	–
Imran Farhat	19.1	1	100	3	33.33	2-69	–	–
Danish Kaneria	81.5	7	248	7	35.42	3-14	–	–
Shoaib Akhtar	86.2	16	297	7	42.42	3-47	–	–
Mohammad Sami	123	22	435	7	62.14	2-92	–	–
Fazl-e-Akbar	40.4	3	162	1	162.00	1-162	–	–
Saqlain Mushtaq	43	4	204	1	204.00	1-204	–	–
Yasir Hameed	1	0	5	0	–	–	–	–
Abdul Razzaq	15	3	61	0	–	–	–	–
Shabbir Ahmed	31	6	122	0	–	–	–	–

INDIA

Batting	M	Inns	NO	Runs	HS	Av	100	50	c/st
V Sehwag	3	4	0	438	309	109.50	1	1	2/-
R Dravid	3	4	0	309	270	77.25	1	–	4/-
SC Ganguly	1	1	0	77	77	77.00	–	1	1/-
SR Tendulkar	3	4	1	205	194*	68.33	1	–	1/-
PA Patel	3	3	1	131	69	65.50	–	2	10/-
Yuvraj Singh	3	4	0	230	112	57.50	1	1	2/-
VVS Laxman	3	4	0	124	71	31.00	–	1	3/-
IK Pathan	3	3	0	64	49	21.33	–	–	1/-
AB Agarkar	1	2	0	38	36	19.00	–	–	-/-
A Chopra	2	3	0	51	42	17.00	–	–	2/-
A Kumble	3	3	1	15	9	7.50	–	–	1/-
L Balaji	3	3	0	11	11	3.66	–	–	-/-
A Nehra	1	1	1	1	1*	–	–	–	1/-
Z Khan	1	0	0	0	0	–	–	–	1/-

Bowling	Overs	Mds	Runs	Wkts	Av	Best	5/inn	10m
SR Tendulkar	33	4	98	4	24.50	2-36	–	–
A Kumble	130.3	31	389	15	25.93	6-72	1	–
A Nehra	27	6	80	3	26.66	2-60	–	–
IK Pathan	134	44	342	12	28.50	4-100	–	–
L Balaji	106	24	369	12	30.75	4-63	–	–
Yuvraj Singh	9	1	32	1	32.00	1-25	–	–
Z Khan	23	6	76	1	76.00	1-76	–	–
AB Agarkar	23	5	80	1	80.00	1-80	–	–
SC Ganguly	6	0	27	0	–	–	–	–
V Sehwag	6	0	27	0	–	–	–	–

SOUTH AFRICA

SOUTH AFRICA REPORT
By Telford Vice

Had they paused to consider matters beyond the boundary, the South African team might have winced in empathy at the news of Saddam Hussein's rude removal from a hole in Iraq's smouldering earth.

South Africa spent much of that day, 14 December 2003 – less momentously the third day of the first Test against the West Indies – leaking runs to Brian Lara.

Lara delivered a shimmering century that he would convert into a double-hundred the next day. He unleashed his full fury amid the shadows that shrouded the penultimate over of the third day's play when he despatched Robin Peterson to far-

flung parts of the Wanderers for a world-record 28 runs. Lara drove for four, six, six, four and four, and then cut the last ball for four.

George W Bush probably knows less about cricket than he does about hurrying to war, but he would doubtless have cracked a skew and knowing grin had he witnessed Lara's inhumanity to his fellow man as the runs rained down.

Then Bush would have made a phone call: 'Tony? Doggone it! WMD – I've found me some of the darn critters at last!'

Peterson took his hiding with the good grace all spinners need if they are to survive more than their first net practice. 'When he hit the first ball for four, me and Graeme [Smith] both thought, "He won't try it again,"' the stripling off spinner said.

'After the second ball, we looked at each other and thought, "He won't try it again." After the third ball we thought, "He definitely won't try it now." Unfortunately, we thought that all through the over.'

Just as Saddam must have thought, 'They'll never look here.' But they did, and the Saddam moments kept coming for Smith's team as one set of opponents after the other discovered their hideaways and dragged them into the ever-harsher light.

South Africa, however, held their nerve to win the four-match series 3–0, and there was light relief for everybody but Andre Nel after the second day's play in the fourth Test at Centurion, when the paceman bowled his maiden over by galumphing to the church on time for his wedding.

Both teams, meanwhile, passed 300 in a rousing decider in a pyrotechnic one-day series, which South Africa won 3–1.

The match was gilded by a century of rare quality from Jacques Kallis, who crowned a remarkable run in which he scored a century in each Test and another two in the one-dayers. All told, he made 1,073 runs at an average of 178.83 in 11 innings.

Lara himself was impressed enough to tell the South African that his performance over the summer was 'the greatest batting in a series I have ever experienced, for or against' as Kallis departed a

Brian Lara launched a stunning assault on South African spinner Robin Peterson.

Jacques Kallis was denied a 'Bradman moment' in Auckland.

nursed Pakistan both to safety and a series victory.

No matter. The winter tour to New Zealand would surely allow for the resumption of normal service. Instead, it brought South Africa's first Test defeat in the land of the long, flat vowel.

They recovered to draw the three-match series, but that was after they had crashed to a 1 for 5 disaster in the limited-overs matches.

Kallis provided a compelling sub-plot to all that by scoring an undefeated 150 in the drawn first Test at Hamilton. Another in the second Test and he would match Don Bradman's record of scoring centuries in six consecutive Test matches.

Auckland waited, and not just for Kallis. The match would make Gary Kirsten the first South African to play 100 Tests, and Shaun Pollock needed one wicket to pass the retired Allan Donald as the country's most prolific wicket-taker.

quaking Wanderers arena to the accompaniment of the kind of roar that would have raised the hairs on the back of even Ben Hur's neck.

Hopes soared, as they seem to do with every win for this nation fuelled by noisy naivety, that the forgettable 2003 World Cup could at last be forgotten. South Africans thought that they could finally return their attention to the national obsession of trying to shake off the inferiority they feel whenever Australians enter the equation.

An exploding wastepaper basket on the 12th floor of an empty Karachi office building threatened to derail the tour to Pakistan, but sanity prevailed and the venture went ahead, albeit with a revised itinerary.

The South Africans were no doubt happy they decided to make the trip when they won the last three games of the one-day series after having lost the first two.

However, faces lengthened when they lost the first of the two Test matches, with Shoaib Akhtar and Danish Kaneria sharing nine wickets in the second innings.

There were 14 overs left in the second Test when Inzamam-ul-Haq and Abdul Razzaq were dismissed with consecutive deliveries to leave four wickets standing. However, Shoaib Malik and Moin Khan

Kallis was denied his Bradman moment, but Kirsten and Pollock duly reached their milestones. The trouble was, from a South African perspective at least, that the more meaningful achievements of the match belonged to the New Zealanders.

The home side took the most important step towards their nine-wicket win when they claimed five wickets for 46 runs on the second morning. Chris Martin allied swing with accuracy and took 6 for 76 as South Africa collapsed from 235 for 2 to a total of 296.

Then Scott Styris and Chris Cairns bettered their highest scores with innings of 170 and 158 respectively in putting on 225 – a New Zealand seventh-wicket record – to forge a lead of 299.

Martin proved equally effective in the second innings, taking another five wickets as South Africa shuddered to a halt just 50 runs to the good.

The Wellington Test would be Kirsten's last, and he underlined his worth to the team with a superb 76 in his final innings.

South Africa, in search of 234 to win, dwindled to 36 for 3 before Kirsten took guard. The experience of 176 innings lubricated what would otherwise have been a precarious passage, and – with the help of Smith's 125 not out – the series was saved.

Shaun Pollock ... not the pace of old, but still a rock-steady influence at the centre of South Africa's bowling attack.

The tour to Sri Lanka began promisingly with a drawn first Test at Galle. Mahela Jayawardene's double-century was ominous, but South Africa were comfortably, if not competitively, placed on 203 for 3, chasing 325, when the match ended.

Another double-century, a masterful 232 by Kumar Sangakkara, made light of Sri Lanka's plight of losing Muttiah Muralitharan to injury for the second Test at the SSC in Colombo. That innings also set up Sri Lanka's emphatic win, by 313 runs.

A 5–0 Sri Lankan triumph in the one-day series meant that South Africa had equalled their most barren run in limited-overs matches – ten consecutive losses.

They ended that drought by beating, gulp, Bangladesh in their ICC Champions Trophy match at Edgbaston, but even Herschelle Gibbs' 101 – halting a wretched run of 34 innings between centuries for the opener – could not stop the West Indies from winning at The Oval to put South Africa on the plane home.

They returned to a certain coldness of shoulder not often visited on sports stars by this public, which no longer seems to care that the troubles stem in large part from the triple whammy of the retirements of Jonty Rhodes, Donald and Kirsten, and, of course, Smith's inexperience.

Coach Eric Simons is under increasing pressure, not least for his proclamation of 'positives' amid the rubble.

Smith's passionate prattle is wearing thin, and the number of people who think selection convenor Omar Henry has no idea about how to put together a winning team seems to grow daily.

The United Cricket Board has lurched from lawsuits to corruption scandals and back to lawsuits, while there is widespread alarm about replacing the 11 provinces with six franchises in the senior domestic competitions.

When you consider all of that, a hole in the ground does not seem like such a bad place to take refuge in.

FIRST TEST – SOUTH AFRICA v. WEST INDIES
12–16 December 2003 at Johannesburg

SOUTH AFRICA

	First Innings		Second Innings	
GC Smith (capt)	c Lara b Edwards	132	c sub b Drakes	44
HH Gibbs	b Collymore	60	retired hurt	6
JA Rudolph	c Lara b Drakes	2	c Sarwan b Hinds	44
JH Kallis	b Dillon	158	lbw b Hinds	44
M van Jaarsveld	lbw b Dillon	73	(6) run out	15
ND McKenzie	c Jacobs b Edwards	8	(8) not out	9
*MV Boucher	c Ganga b Collymore	27	(5) st Jacobs b Sarwan	18
SM Pollock	c Jacobs b Hinds	30	(7) b Collymore	10
RJ Peterson	c Jacobs b Hinds	25	not out	18
A Nel	b Hinds	0		
M Ntini	not out	22		
Extras	b 4, lb 7, w 4, nb 9	24	b 2, lb 3, w 6, nb 7	18
	(148.4 overs)	561	(6 wkts dec 63 overs)	226

	First Innings				Second Innings			
	O	M	R	W	O	M	R	W
Edwards	27	3	102	2	13	0	60	0
Dillon	36	7	96	2	10	0	26	0
Collymore	26	2	118	2	9	3	19	1
Drakes	29	5	92	1	10	2	21	1
Ganga	4	0	26	0	–	–	–	–
Sarwan	9	0	37	0	10	0	40	1
Hinds	17.4	3	79	3	11	0	55	2

Fall of Wickets
1-149, 2-160, 3-240, 4-372, 5-398, 6-456, 7-510, 8-520, 9-520
1-72, 2-145, 3-158, 4-180, 5-188, 6-206

WEST INDIES

	First Innings		Second Innings	
WW Hinds	c Peterson b Nel	10	b Ntini	0
D Ganga	c Peterson b Ntini	60	lbw b Ntini	10
RR Sarwan	c Boucher b Pollock	21	(4) lbw b Pollock	8
BC Lara (capt)	c van Jaarsveld b Nel	202	(5) b Pollock	5
S Chanderpaul	b Ntini	34	(6) c Nel b Pollock	74
*RD Jacobs	c Boucher b Ntini	4	(7) b Nel	25
VC Drakes	lbw b Kallis	21	(3) b Ntini	6
M Dillon	b Ntini	13	(9) b Ntini	7
CH Gayle	c Kallis b Ntini	8	(8) c Boucher b Nel	26
FH Edwards	c McKenzie b Nel	0	(11) not out	0
CD Collymore	not out	1	(10) lbw b Pollock	0
Extras	b 12, lb 15, w 4, nb 5	36	b 10, lb 6, nb 11	27
	(133.5 overs)	410	(51 overs)	188

	First Innings				Second Innings			
	O	M	R	W	O	M	R	W
Pollock	30	7	65	1	17	6	31	4
Ntini	32	9	94	5	14	4	53	4
Nel	32.5	11	78	3	13	3	49	2
Kallis	22	6	53	1	4	0	21	0
Peterson	13	2	76	0	3	0	18	0
Smith	4	0	17	0	–	–	–	–

Fall of Wickets
1-43, 2-94, 3-141, 4-266, 5-278, 6-314, 7-380, 8-405, 9-409
1-5, 2-18, 3-25, 4-41, 5-43, 6-141, 7-168, 8-176, 9-188

Umpires: DB Hair and SJA Taufel
Toss: South Africa
Man of the Match: M Ntini

South Africa won by 189 runs

SECOND TEST – SOUTH AFRICA v. WEST INDIES
26–29 December 2003 at Durban

WEST INDIES

	First Innings		Second Innings	
WW Hinds	c Boucher b Pollock	0	b Nel	11
D Ganga	c Pollock b Ntini	6	lbw b Pollock	12
RR Sarwan	c Kallis b Pollock	4	b Ntini	114
BC Lara (capt)	c Pollock b Ntini	72	c McKenzie b Hall	11
S Chanderpaul	c Hall b Ntini	0	(7) c McKenzie b Ntini	109
CS Baugh	c Kallis b Nel	21	(5) c Ntini b Kallis	2
*RD Jacobs	lbw b Nel	58	(6) c Kirsten b Rudolph	15
VC Drakes	c Boucher b Nel	67	c Rudolph b Nel	4
M Dillon	b Ntini	6	c Gibbs b Nel	0
A Sanford	c Hall b Ntini	15	not out	18
FH Edwards	not out	1	c Boucher b Ntini	5
Extras	lb 6, nb 8	14	lb 16, w 1, nb 11	28
	(77.5 overs)	264	(113 overs)	329

	First Innings				Second Innings			
	O	M	R	W	O	M	R	W
Pollock	23	3	59	2	22	9	42	1
Ntini	25.5	8	66	5	26	8	72	3
Hall	10	2	51	0	13	3	20	1
Nel	13	4	43	3	18	3	68	3
Kallis	4	0	30	0	11	3	20	1
Rudolph	2	0	9	0	23	3	91	1

Fall of Wickets
1-0, 2-4, 3-15, 4-17, 5-50, 6-148, 7-172, 8-191, 9-261
1-31, 2-32, 3-78, 4-95, 5-130, 6-243, 7-271, 8-271, 9-317

SOUTH AFRICA

	First Innings	
GC Smith (capt)	c Sarwan b Edwards	14
HH Gibbs	b Sanford	142
JA Rudolph	c Ganga b Sanford	36
JH Kallis	c Sarwan b Dillon	177
G Kirsten	c Drakes b Sarwan	137
ND McKenzie	c Jacobs b Drakes	32
*MV Boucher	lbw b Drakes	12
SM Pollock	not out	38
AJ Hall	c sub b Sarwan	32
M Ntini	c Lara b Sanford	0
A Nel		
Extras	lb 9, w 6, nb 23	38
	(9 wkts dec 166.2 overs)	658

	First Innings			
	O	M	R	W
Dillon	33	5	111	1
Edwards	25	1	115	1
Sanford	38.2	4	170	3
Sarwan	21	2	65	2
Drakes	30	3	113	2
Hinds	13	2	50	0
Ganga	6	1	25	0

Fall of Wickets
1-38, 2-99, 3-267, 4-516, 5-562, 6-572, 7-599, 8-649, 9-658

Umpires: DB Hair and SJA Taufel
Toss: South Africa
Man of the Match: JH Kallis

South Africa won by an innings and 65 runs

THIRD TEST – SOUTH AFRICA v. WEST INDIES
2–6 January 2004 at Cape Town

SOUTH AFRICA

	First Innings		Second Innings	
GC Smith (capt)	c Lara b Sanford	42	b Edwards	24
HH Gibbs	c Jacobs b Sanford	33	c Gayle b Sarwan	142
JA Rudolph	lbw b Mohammed	101	c Jacobs b Drakes	0
JH Kallis	lbw b Sanford	73	not out	130
G Kirsten	c Sanford b Edwards	16	not out	10
ND McKenzie	b Mohammed	76		
PR Adams	b Edwards	0		
*MV Boucher	not out	122		
SM Pollock	c Jacobs b Edwards	9		
M Ntini	c Jacobs b Mohammed	18		
A Nel	c Jacobs b Sanford	4		
Extras	b 6, lb 12, w 2, nb 18	38	b 3, lb 7, w 8, nb 11	29
	(145 overs)	532	(3 wkts dec 76 overs)	335

	First Innings				Second Innings			
	O	M	R	W	O	M	R	W
Drakes	26	7	64	0	20	0	68	1
Edwards	30	3	132	3	14	0	86	1
Sanford	37	4	132	4	8	1	38	0
Smith	2	0	4	0	-	-	-	-
Mohammed	33	5	112	3	6	0	30	0
Gayle	10	0	39	0	9	3	34	0
Hinds	7	2	31	0	-	-	-	-
Sarwan	-	-	-	-	19	1	69	1

Fall of Wickets
1-70, 2-90, 3-162, 4-304, 5-305, 6-305, 7-315, 8-461, 9-513
1-48, 2-50, 3-301

WEST INDIES

	First Innings		Second Innings	
CH Gayle	lbw b Pollock	116	c Gibbs b Ntini	32
D Ganga	b Nel	17	c Boucher b Ntini	10
RR Sarwan	c McKenzie b Nel	44	c Gibbs b Ntini	69
BC Lara (capt)	b Nel	115	c Boucher b Nel	86
WW Hinds	c Boucher b Kallis	13	b Pollock	25
DR Smith	c Kallis b Nel	20	not out	105
*RD Jacobs	c Pollock b Ntini	23	not out	9
VC Drakes	c Boucher b Nel	20		
D Mohammed	c Kallis b Pollock	36		
A Sanford	run out	0		
FH Edwards	not out	0		
Extras	b 6, lb 7, nb 10	23	b 2, lb 7, w 2, nb 7	18
	(112.1 overs)	427	(5 wkts 100 overs)	354

	First Innings				Second Innings			
	O	M	R	W	O	M	R	W
Pollock	24	6	88	2	17	3	64	1
Ntini	20	1	105	1	21	4	82	3
Nel	28.1	8	87	5	21	5	57	1
Kallis	21	8	64	1	16	3	38	0
Adams	19	1	70	0	22	3	103	0
Rudolph	-	-	-	-	1	1	0	0
Kirsten	-	-	-	-	2	1	1	0

Fall of Wickets
1-126, 2-183, 3-187, 4-224, 5-252, 6-306, 7-361, 8-409, 9-426
1-28, 2-47, 3-203, 4-224, 5-296

Umpires: DJ Harper and S Venkataraghavan
Toss: South Africa
Test debuts: D Mohammed, DR Smith
Man of the Match: JH Kallis

Match drawn

FOURTH TEST – SOUTH AFRICA v. WEST INDIES
16–20 January 2004 at Centurion

SOUTH AFRICA

	First Innings		Second Innings	
GC Smith (capt)	c Jacobs b Collymore	139	not out	23
HH Gibbs	c Ganga b Sarwan	192	not out	8
JA Rudolph	b Edwards	37		
JH Kallis	not out	130		
G Kirsten	c & b Sarwan	10		
ND McKenzie	c Lara b Dillon	40		
*MV Boucher	c Edwards b Smith	13		
SM Pollock	not out	1		
AJ Hall				
M Ntini				
A Nel				
Extras	b 1, lb 17, w 12, nb 12	42	b 4, w 10, nb 1	15
	(6 wkts dec 158 overs)	604	(0 wkts 3.4 overs)	46

	First Innings				Second Innings			
	O	M	R	W	O	M	R	W
Dillon	31	5	109	1	2	0	17	0
Edwards	24	2	128	1	1.4	0	25	0
Drakes	33	5	101	0	-	-	-	-
Collymore	26	5	91	1	-	-	-	-
Gayle	7	0	39	0	-	-	-	-
Sarwan	14	0	55	2	-	-	-	-
Smith	13	1	42	1	-	-	-	-
Ganga	10	0	21	0	-	-	-	-

Fall of Wickets
1-301, 2-373, 3-422, 4-446, 5-532, 6-567

WEST INDIES

	First Innings		Second Innings	
CH Gayle	c McKenzie b Ntini	77	c McKenzie b Ntini	107
D Ganga	c Kallis b Ntini	7	b Ntini	0
RR Sarwan	b Ntini	13	lbw b Pollock	119
BC Lara (capt)	c Boucher b Nel	34	lbw b Nel	6
S Chanderpaul	c Pollock b Nel	42	c Gibbs b Kallis	27
DR Smith	c Boucher b Kallis	39	b Ntini	0
*RD Jacobs	c Boucher b Nel	8	lbw b Pollock	3
VC Drakes	b Ntini	35	c Gibbs b Pollock	4
M Dillon	b Ntini	30	c Smith b Pollock	29
CD Collymore	b Pollock	4	not out	13
FH Edwards	not out	0	b Nel	10
Extras	lb 7, nb 5	12	b 4, lb 11, w 7, nb 8	30
	(82.2 overs)	301	(106.4 overs)	348

	First Innings				Second Innings			
	O	M	R	W	O	M	R	W
Pollock	16.2	6	46	1	32	10	69	4
Ntini	20	7	49	5	28	4	99	3
Nel	18	6	64	3	15.4	2	64	2
Hall	11	0	65	0	0.2	0	4	0
Kallis	12	4	46	1	16	4	49	1
Smith	3	1	7	0	8.4	1	24	0
Rudolph	2	0	17	0	6	0	24	0

Fall of Wickets
1-22, 2-37, 3-139, 4-142, 5-195, 6-224, 7-241, 8-280, 9-301
1-18, 2-32, 3-99, 4-273, 5-277, 6-278, 7-284, 8-309, 9-322

Umpires: DR Shepherd and S Venkataraghavan
Toss: West Indies
Man of the Match: M Ntini
Man of the Series: HH Gibbs

South Africa won by 10 wickets

SERIES AVERAGES
South Africa v. West Indies

SOUTH AFRICA

Batting	M	Inns	NO	Runs	HS	Av	100	50	c/st
JH Kallis	4	6	2	712	177	178.00	4	1	6/-
HH Gibbs	4	7	2	583	192	116.60	3	1	5/-
GC Smith	4	7	1	418	139	69.66	2	-	1/-
G Kirsten	3	4	1	173	137	57.66	1	-	1/-
MV Boucher	4	5	1	192	122*	48.00	1	-	13/-
M van Jaarsveld	1	2	0	88	73	44.00	-	1	1/-
RJ Peterson	1	2	1	43	25	43.00	-	-	2/-
ND McKenzie	4	5	1	165	76	41.25	-	1	6/-
JA Rudolph	4	6	0	220	101	36.66	1	-	1/-
AJ Hall	2	1	0	32	32	32.00	-	-	1/-
SM Pollock	4	5	2	88	38*	29.33	-	-	4/-
M Ntini	4	3	1	40	22*	20.00	-	-	1/-
A Nel	4	2	0	4	4	2.00	-	-	1/-
PR Adams	1	1	0	0	0	0.00	-	-	-/-

Bowling	Overs	Mds	Runs	Wkts	Av	Best	5/inn	10m
M Ntini	186.5	45	620	29	21.37	5-49	3	-
A Nel	159.4	42	510	22	23.18	5-87	1	-
SM Pollock	181.2	50	464	16	29.00	4-31	-	-
JH Kallis	106	28	321	5	64.20	1-20	-	-
AJ Hall	34.2	5	140	1	140.00	1-20	-	-
JA Rudolph	34	4	141	1	141.00	1-91	-	-

Also bowled: G Kirsten 2-1-1-0, GC Smith 15.4-2-48-0, RJ Peterson 16-2-94-0, PR Adams 41-4-173-0.

WEST INDIES

Batting	M	Inns	NO	Runs	HS	Av	100	50	c/st
BC Lara	4	8	0	531	202	66.37	2	2	5/-
CH Gayle	3	6	0	366	116	61.00	2	1	1/-
DR Smith	2	4	1	164	105*	54.66	1	-	-/-
RR Sarwan	4	8	0	392	119	49.00	2	1	4/-
S Chanderpaul	3	6	0	286	109	47.66	1	1	-/-
D Mohammed	1	1	0	36	36	36.00	-	-	-/-
VC Drakes	4	7	0	157	67	22.42	-	-	1/-
RD Jacobs	4	8	1	145	58	20.71	-	1	10/1
A Sanford	2	3	1	33	18*	16.50	-	-	1/-
D Ganga	4	8	0	122	60	15.25	-	1	3/-
M Dillon	3	6	0	85	30	14.16	-	-	-/-
CS Baugh	1	2	0	23	21	11.50	-	-	-/-
WW Hinds	3	6	0	59	25	9.83	-	-	-/-
CD Collymore	2	4	2	18	13*	9.00	-	-	-/-
FH Edwards	4	7	4	16	10	5.33	-	-	1/-

Bowling	Overs	Mds	Runs	Wkts	Av	Best	5/inn	10m
WW Hinds	48.4	7	215	5	43.00	3-79	-	-
RR Sarwan	73	3	266	6	44.33	2-55	-	-
DR Smith	15	1	46	1	46.00	1-42	-	-
D Mohammed	39	5	142	3	47.33	3-112	-	-
A Sanford	83.2	8	340	7	48.57	4-132	-	-
CD Collymore	61	10	228	4	57.00	2-118	-	-
FH Edwards	134.4	9	648	8	81.00	3-132	-	-
M Dillon	112	17	359	4	89.75	2-96	-	-
VC Drakes	148	22	459	5	91.80	2-113	-	-

Also bowled: D Ganga 20-1-72-0, CH Gayle 26-3-112-0.

ONE-DAY INTERNATIONALS
v. West Indies

Match One
25 January 2004 at Cape Town
South Africa 263 for 4 (50 overs) (JH Kallis 109*, JA Rudolph 61*, GC Smith 53)
West Indies 54 (23.2 overs)
South Africa won by 209 runs

Match Two
28 January 2004 at Port Elizabeth
South Africa 179 for 7 (50 overs) (HH Dippenaar 83)
West Indies 163 (42.4 overs) (SM Pollock 4 for 26)
South Africa won by 16 runs

Match Three
30 January 2004 at Durban
West Indies 147 for 8 (40 overs) (RL Powell 50)
South Africa 15 for 1 (5 overs)
Match abandoned

Match Four
1 February 2004 at Centurion
South Africa 297 for 4 (50 overs) (JH Kallis 95*)
West Indies 300 for 3 (45 overs) (S Chanderpaul 92, RR Sarwan 77*, BC Lara 59*)
West Indies won by 7 wickets

Match Five
4 February 2004 at Johannesburg
West Indies 304 for 2 (50 overs) (CH Gayle 152*, S Chanderpaul 85)
South Africa 310 for 6 (49.4 overs) (JH Kallis 139, GC Smith 58)
South Africa won by 4 wickets

ZIMBABWE

ZIMBABWE REPORT
By Telford Vice

Zimbabwean cricket's crash to Ground Zero proves that sport and politics should never separate. Those who question that statement should know that tyranny hurries to swamp the void when politics is unable to meet its responsibilities to any sector of society.

We learnt that truth in reverse in South Africa, where politics put sport on the path to the real world after centuries of racial injustice. More broadly, we are re-learning the difference between politics and tyranny in places as apparently diverse as Iraq, Britain and the United States. And, of course, in Zimbabwe, where politics as a platform for differing opinion and change has only ever flourished for a handful of years after the country gained independence in 1980.

Heath Streak – treated shamefully by the Zimbabwe Cricket Union.

Except for the window briefly opened by that hopeful event, Zimbabwe's history is a tale of tyranny.

Cricket was a useful cog in the brutal machine that enforced white rule, and, for Robert Mugabe's regime, it has become both a weapon and a target.

Zimbabwe is polarised and dysfunctional enough for the game to be forced to endure these competing extremes simultaneously. Blacks of varying militancy – most of them sincerely committed to progress – regard cricket as an instrument for change; whites, on the other hand, used to see it as an island of neo-colonial splendour in a sea of deterioration. The colour of the game was darkening, but at a pace and in a fashion that whites could tolerate. However, whites who thought Zimbabwean cricket belonged to them were arrogant and naive enough to believe that they were in control of their changing world.

The crisis that erupted on 2 April, when Heath Streak was relieved of the Zimbabwe captaincy in circumstances that became murkier by the minute, marked the bursting of the whites' bubble. It also served notice that a new breed of black cricket administrator had taken control. He does not know a googly from a thighpad, and he doesn't care to know. What he does understand is that Mugabe's jackboot state is a virus in a dying host. He knows that he can delay that death by infiltrating the less-stricken areas of what will be a corpse once starvation, AIDS and the government have done their worst.

Against this grim background, is it any wonder that Tatenda Taibu leads a miserable excuse for an international team?

Instead, the wonder is that the ICC saw fit to involve itself effectively in this mess only after its chief executive, Malcolm Speed, was locked out of a Board meeting by the same Zimbabwe Cricket Union that had invited him to Harare. By then, the 15 white players who had shown gob-smacking naivety in their rebellion against the ZCU's recklessly wielded authority had been fired, taking almost all of Zimbabwe's international experience with them.

By then hearts and minds on all sides of the conflict had hardened. By then it was too late for politics – tyranny had clamped its jaws shut.

On the field, Taibu's side lurched from one disaster to the next. They are not simply an inexperienced

Tatenda Taibu was appointed captain of the national team after Streak's sacking.

team struggling bravely to make their way in the game, a picture the ZCU tries to paint all too gauchely. They are an unfortunate collection of promising cricketers destined to be robbed of the future they should have had. They know that they dare not differ with the menacing suits that control their every move, one of whom reportedly demands that they address him as 'Sir'. They know that the ZCU could, in a more ideal world, call on players who are vastly more experienced and talented. They know that genuine international teams are loath to play them, not because they are hopeless, but because they regard them as illegitimate opponents. They know that even the ICC realises they have no business playing Test matches.

Who will win in this desperate struggle? Most of the rebels' careers are over, and we can only wonder what heights class performers like Ray Price, Andy Blignaut and Sean Ervine might have reached.

Streak, who was the acceptable white face of cricket to moderate black Zimbabweans, has been treated shamefully. No one could disapprove if he should spit on the ZCU chairman, Peter Chingoka.

The ZCU will be bankrupted when the sponsors and television broadcasters who keep it afloat cut off funds, while the ICC has proved again that it is no more than a splodge of amoeba worthy only of a flush of the nearest toilet.

Where are the few good men? Where are the politicians?

FIRST TEST – ZIMBABWE v. WEST INDIES
4–8 November 2003 at Harare

ZIMBABWE

	First Innings		Second Innings	
V Sibanda	c Jacobs b Edwards	18	c Ganga b Collymore	16
TR Gripper	c Lara b Taylor	41	lbw b Drakes	26
MA Vermeulen	c Hinds b Edwards	8	c Chanderpaul b Edwards	2
SV Carlisle	c Lara b Collymore	8	lbw b Drakes	10
CB Wishart	c Jacobs b Hinds	47	b Drakes	34
S Matsikenyeri	c Jacobs b Edwards	57	not out	46
*T Taibu	b Edwards	83	b Drakes	21
HH Streak (capt)	not out	127	(9) not out	7
AM Blignaut	c Gayle b Drakes	91	(8) c Jacobs b Collymore	13
RW Price	lbw b Edwards	2		
NB Mahwire	not out	1		
Extras	b 1, lb 5, w 3, nb 15	24	b 8, lb 2, w 2, nb 13	25
	(9 wkts dec 152.3 overs)	507	(7 wkts dec 52 overs)	200

	First Innings				Second Innings			
	O	M	R	W	O	M	R	W
Collymore	29	6	131	1	15	2	59	2
Edwards	34.3	3	133	5	16	5	52	1
Hinds	15	6	40	1	-	-	-	-
Drakes	34	4	85	1	20	2	67	4
Taylor	9.4	4	32	1	-	-	-	-
Gayle	19.2	6	38	0	-	-	-	-
Sarwan	9	0	35	0	1	0	12	0
Chanderpaul	1	0	7	0	-	-	-	-
Ganga	1	1	0	0	-	-	-	-

Fall of Wickets
1-26, 2-35, 3-58, 4-112, 5-154, 6-233, 7-314, 8-482, 9-495
1-21, 2-27, 3-60, 4-90, 5-107, 6-152, 7-175

WEST INDIES

	First Innings		Second Innings	
CH Gayle	lbw b Streak	14	c Taibu b Price	13
WW Hinds	c Blignaut b Mahwire	79	c Carlisle b Streak	24
D Ganga	b Mahwire	73	b Price	16
BC Lara (capt)	c Mahwire b Price	29	lbw b Streak	1
RR Sarwan	lbw b Price	9	st Taibu b Gripper	39
S Chanderpaul	lbw b Streak	36	c Sibanda b Price	39
*RD Jacobs	c Vermeulen b Price	5	not out	60
VC Drakes	c Streak b Price	31	c Taibu b Blignaut	4
JE Taylor	c Wishart b Price	9	c Matsikenyeri b Blignaut	3
CD Collymore	not out	11	c Vermeulen b Price	1
FH Edwards	c Matsikenyeri b Price	18	not out	1
Extras	b 7, lb 7, w 3, nb 4	21	b 1, lb 1, w 1, nb 3	6
	(114.2 overs)	335	(9 wkts 83 overs)	207

	First Innings				Second Innings			
	O	M	R	W	O	M	R	W
Blignaut	14	3	68	0	14	2	50	2
Streak	28	9	74	2	15	7	28	2
Mahwire	25	7	75	2	2	0	10	0
Price	37.2	13	73	6	38	11	88	4
Matsikenyeri	2	0	10	0	2	0	6	0
Gripper	8	1	21	0	12	5	23	1

Fall of Wickets
1-50, 2-127, 3-179, 4-211, 5-215, 6-240, 7-290, 8-294, 9-309
1-37, 2-37, 3-38, 4-73, 5-103, 6-171, 7-184, 8-194, 9-204

Umpires: BF Bowden and SJA Taufel
Toss: Zimbabwe
Test debuts: S Matsikenyeri, V Sibanda
Man of the Match: HH Streak

Match drawn

SECOND TEST – ZIMBABWE v. WEST INDIES
12-16 November 2003 at Bulawayo

WEST INDIES

	First Innings		Second Innings	
CH Gayle	c Taibu b Blignaut	47	lbw b Streak	0
WW Hinds	st Taibu b Price	81	c Carlisle b Price	28
D Ganga	c Matsikenyeri b Price	23	c Carlisle b Blignaut	8
BC Lara (capt)	c Wishart b Blignaut	191	b Streak	1
RR Sarwan	c Vermeulen b Price	65	c Wishart b Blignaut	9
S Chanderpaul	c Wishart b Price	15	lbw b Streak	15
*RD Jacobs	c Gripper b Streak	1	c Blignaut b Price	10
OAC Banks	lbw b Blignaut	3	c Vermeulen b Price	16
M Dillon	c Matsikenyeri b Price	19	not out	27
CD Collymore	not out	16	b Price	0
FH Edwards	c Taibu b Blignaut	0	b Blignaut	0
Extras	b 1, lb 12, w 2, nb 5	20	b 5, lb 3, w 4, nb 2	14
	(107 overs)	481	(52.4 overs)	128

	First Innings				Second Innings			
	O	M	R	W	O	M	R	W
Streak	24	4	87	1	15	2	39	3
Blignaut	20	4	86	4	14.4	6	29	3
Mahwire	15	3	79	0	2	0	16	0
Price	43	1	199	5	21	7	36	4
Gripper	5	1	17	0	–	–	–	–

Fall of Wickets
1-73, 2-146, 3-161, 4-351, 5-389, 6-394, 7-422, 8-449, 9-475
1-0, 2-17, 3-21, 4-51, 5-51, 6-82, 7-82, 8-127, 9-127

ZIMBABWE

	First Innings		Second Innings	
V Sibanda	c & b Edwards	2	c Lara b Dillon	0
TR Gripper	b Dillon	1	c Ganga b Banks	8
MA Vermeulen	b Banks	118	b Hinds	24
SV Carlisle	b Edwards	11	c Jacobs b Banks	9
CB Wishart	lbw b Collymore	96	c Jacobs b Hinds	13
S Matsikenyeri	b Collymore	8	(7) run out	5
*T Taibu	c Gayle b Collymore	27	(8) lbw b Collymore	1
HH Streak (capt)	lbw b Dillon	3	(9) not out	33
AM Blignaut	lbw b Collymore	31	(6) lbw b Banks	3
RW Price	c Ganga b Banks	35	b Collymore	4
NB Mahwire	not out	8	b Dillon	4
Extras	b 17, lb 4, w 1, nb 15	37		0
	(133.1 overs)	377	(49 overs)	104

	First Innings				Second Innings			
	O	M	R	W	O	M	R	W
Hinds	6	2	18	0	9	2	20	2
Edwards	15	3	48	2	–	–	–	–
Dillon	34	13	57	2	8	2	17	2
Collymore	24	5	70	4	15	7	29	2
Banks	41.1	13	106	2	15	2	35	3
Gayle	6	1	23	0	–	–	–	–
Sarwan	7	0	34	0	2	1	3	0

Fall of Wickets
1-5, 2-10, 3-31, 4-185, 5-201, 6-279, 7-289, 8-302, 9-336
1-0, 2-32, 3-33, 4-54, 5-56, 6-62, 7-63, 8-67, 9-75

Umpires: RE Koertzen and SJA Taufel
Toss: West Indies
Man of the Match: BC Lara

West Indies won by 128 runs

SERIES AVERAGES
Zimbabwe v. West Indies

ZIMBABWE

Batting	M	Inns	NO	Runs	HS	Av	100	50	c/st
HH Streak	2	4	3	170	127*	170.00	1	–	1/-
CB Wishart	2	4	0	190	96	47.50	–	1	4/-
S Matsikenyeri	2	4	1	116	57	38.66	–	1	4/-
MA Vermeulen	2	4	0	152	118	38.00	1	–	4/-
AM Blignaut	2	4	0	138	91	34.50	–	1	2/-
T Taibu	2	4	0	132	83	33.00	–	1	4/2
TR Gripper	2	4	0	76	41	19.00	–	–	1/-
RW Price	2	3	0	41	35	13.66	–	–	-/-
NB Mahwire	2	3	2	13	8*	13.00	–	–	1/-
SV Carlisle	2	4	0	38	11	9.50	–	–	3/-
V Sibanda	2	4	0	36	18	9.00	–	–	1/-

Bowling	Overs	Mds	Runs	Wkts	Av	Best	5/inn	10m
RW Price	139.2	32	396	19	20.84	6-73	2	1
AM Blignaut	62.4	15	233	9	25.88	4-86	–	–
HH Streak	82	22	228	8	28.50	3-39	–	–
TR Gripper	25	7	61	1	61.00	1-23	–	–
NB Mahwire	44	10	180	2	90.00	2-75	–	–

Also bowled: S Matsikenyeri 4-0-16-0.

WEST INDIES

Batting	M	Inns	NO	Runs	HS	Av	100	50	c/st
BC Lara	2	4	0	222	191	55.50	1	–	3/-
WW Hinds	2	4	0	212	81	53.00	–	2	1/-
M Dillon	1	2	1	46	27*	46.00	–	–	-/-
RR Sarwan	2	4	0	122	65	30.50	–	1	-/-
D Ganga	2	4	0	120	73	30.00	–	1	3/-
S Chanderpaul	2	4	0	105	39	26.25	–	–	1/-
RD Jacobs	2	4	1	76	60*	25.33	–	1	6/-
CH Gayle	2	4	0	74	47	18.50	–	–	2/-
VC Drakes	1	2	0	35	31	17.50	–	–	-/-
CD Collymore	2	4	2	28	16*	14.00	–	–	-/-
OAC Banks	1	2	0	19	16	9.50	–	–	-/-
FH Edwards	2	4	1	19	18	6.33	–	–	1/-
JE Taylor	1	2	0	12	9	6.00	–	–	-/-

Bowling	Overs	Mds	Runs	Wkts	Av	Best	5/inn	10m
M Dillon	42	15	74	4	18.50	2-17	–	–
WW Hinds	30	10	78	3	26.00	2-20	–	–
OAC Banks	56.1	15	141	5	28.20	3-35	–	–
FH Edwards	65.3	11	233	8	29.12	5-133	1	–
VC Drakes	54	6	152	5	30.40	4-67	–	–
JE Taylor	9.4	4	32	1	32.00	1-32	–	–
CD Collymore	83	20	289	9	32.11	4-70	–	–

Also bowled: D Ganga 1-1-0-0, S Chanderpaul 1-0-7-0, CH Gayle 25.2-7-61-0, RR Sarwan 19-1-84-0.

ONE-DAY INTERNATIONALS
v. West Indies

Match One
22 November 2003 at Bulawayo
West Indies 347 for 6 (50 overs) (CH Gayle 153*, BC Lara 113)
Zimbabwe 173 for 3 (34.5 overs) (CB Wishart 72*, V Sibanda 58)
West Indies won by 51 runs – DL Method

Match Two
23 November 2003 at Bulawayo
West Indies 125 (42.3 overs)
Zimbabwe 128 for 4 (29.4 overs) (MA Vermeulen 66*)
Zimbabwe won by 6 wickets

Match Three
26 November 2003 at Harare
Zimbabwe 229 for 5 (50 overs) (MA Vermeulen 66, HH Streak 65*)
West Indies 208 (47.2 overs) (CH Gayle 61, AM Blignaut 4 for 43)
Zimbabwe won by 21 runs

Match Four
29 November 2003 at Harare
West Indies 256 for 3 (45 overs) (WW Hinds 127*, CH Gayle 51)
Zimbabwe 150 for 7 (32 overs) (T Taibu 66, FH Edwards 6 for 22)
West Indies won by 72 runs – DL Method

Match Five
30 November 2003 at Harare
Zimbabwe 196 (47.5 overs) (CH Gayle 4 for 24)
West Indies 197 for 2 (25.4 overs) (CH Gayle 112*)
West Indies won by 8 wickets

FIRST TEST – ZIMBABWE v. BANGLADESH
19–23 February 2004 at Harare

ZIMBABWE

	First Innings		Second Innings	
DD Ebrahim	st Khaled Mashud b M Rafique	65	c Hannan Sarkar b Tapash Baisya	31
TR Gripper	c Habibul Bashar b Tapash Baisya	0	c Khaled Mashud b Manjural Islam	5
SV Carlisle	c and b Tapash Baisya	58	run out	33
GW Flower	c Hannan Sarkar b Mohammad Rafique	5	c Khaled Mashud b Tapash Baisya	3
*T Taibu	lbw b Mohammad Rafique	59	c Habibul Bashar b Mohammad Rafique	58
SM Ervine	c Hannan Sarkar b Tapash Baisya	86	c Tapash Baisya b Manjural Islam Rana	74
HH Streak (capt)	c Khaled Mashud b Mushfiqur Rahman	68		
AM Blignaut	st Khaled Mashud b M Rafique	7	(7) b Manjural Islam Rana	32
GM Ewing	c Khaled Mashud b Mushfiqur Rahman	71	(8) c Khaled Mashud b M Rafique	1
RW Price	c Rajin Saleh b Mushfiqur Rahman	9	(9) not out	1
DT Hondo	not out	0		
Extras	b 1, lb 7, w 3, nb 2	13	lb 2, w 2	4
	(160.2 overs)	**441**	(8 wkts dec 64.2 overs)	**242**

	First Innings				Second Innings			
	O	M	R	W	O	M	R	W
Manjural Islam	28	8	69	0	12	4	24	1
Tapash Baisya	36	6	133	3	16	1	65	2
Mushfiqur Rahman	24.2	8	75	3	9	0	49	0
Mohammad Rafique	57	11	121	4	20	3	62	2
Manjural Islam Rana	13	4	26	0	7.2	0	40	2
Mohammad Ashraful	2	1	9	0	-	-	-	-

Fall of Wickets
1-0, 2-107, 3-130, 4-133, 5-258, 6-299, 7-306, 8-412, 9-433
1-12, 2-50, 3-54, 4-90, 5-180, 6-232, 7-234, 8-242

BANGLADESH

	First Innings		Second Innings	
Hannan Sarkar	lbw b Streak	4	lbw b Blignaut	10
Shahriar Hossain	lbw b Hondo	48	lbw b Hondo	1
Tapash Baisya	c Taibu b Streak	4	(9) lbw b Price	2
Habibul Bashar (capt)	c Taibu b Blignaut	0	(3) lbw b Hondo	0
Rajin Saleh	b Price	49	(4) st Taibu b Price	47
Mohammad Ashraful	b Streak	98	(5) c sub b Blignaut	0
Mushfiqur Rahman	b Streak	44	(6) c Taibu b Blignaut	0
Manjural Islam Rana	not out	35	(7) c Gripper b Price	31
*Khaled Mashud	c Taibu b Hondo	6	(8) st Taibu b Price	61
Mohammad Rafique	c Ervine b Hondo	3	c & b Ewing	5
Manjural Islam	c Taibu b Blignaut	5	not out	1
Extras	b 1, lb 11, w 8, nb 15	35	b 5, lb 1, nb 5	11
	(115.4 overs)	**331**	(57.5 overs)	**169**

	First Innings				Second Innings			
	O	M	R	W	O	M	R	W
Streak	26.2	11	44	4	-	-	-	-
Blignaut	22.4	6	73	2	4	1	12	3
Ervine	12	2	52	0	12	3	34	0
Hondo	19.4	5	49	3	12	3	24	2
Price	25	4	79	1	20.5	3	61	4
Ewing	7	2	19	0	8	3	27	1
Gripper	3	2	3	0	1	0	5	0

Fall of Wickets
1-13, 2-34, 3-35, 4-77, 5-162, 6-259, 7-265, 8-278, 9-288
1-12, 2-14, 3-14, 4-14, 5-14, 6-81, 7-110, 8-112, 9-123

Umpires: NA Mallender and DL Orchard
Toss: Zimbabwe
Test debut: Manjural Islam Rana
Man of the Match: SM Ervine

Zimbabwe won by 183 runs

SECOND TEST – ZIMBABWE v. BANGLADESH
26 February–1 March 2004 at Bulawayo

SERIES AVERAGES
Zimbabwe v. Bangladesh

BANGLADESH

	First Innings	
Hannan Sarkar	b Ervine	25
Shahriar Hossain	c Taibu b Ervine	31
Habibul Bashar (capt)	c Friend b Streak	4
Rajin Saleh	c Ervine b Hondo	6
Mohammad Ashraful	c Carlisle b Friend	1
Manjural Islam Rana	c Taibu b Price	39
Mushfiqur Rahman	lbw b Hondo	0
*Khaled Mashud	lbw b Ervine	9
Tapash Baisya	c Flower b Price	2
Mohammad Rafique	not out	26
Alamgir Kabir	c Ebrahim b Price	3
Extras	lb 4, w 6, nb 12	22
	(75.5 overs)	**168**

	First Innings			
	O	M	R	W
Streak	15	9	19	1
Hondo	18	5	25	2
Ervine	15	4	44	3
Mahwire	10	2	36	0
Friend	9	2	20	1
Price	8.5	2	20	3

Fall of Wickets
1-64, 2-73, 3-73, 4-81, 5-87, 6-89, 7-126, 8-137, 9-144

ZIMBABWE

	First Innings	
DD Ebrahim	c Hannan Sarkar b Tapash Baisya	2
TR Gripper	c Khaled Mashud b Tapash Baisya	65
SV Carlisle	not out	103
GW Flower	not out	37
SM Ervine		
*T Taibu		
HH Streak (capt)		
TJ Friend		
NB Mahwire		
RW Price		
DT Hondo		
Extras	nb 3	3
	(2 wkts 60.2 overs)	**210**

	First Innings			
	O	M	R	W
Tapash Baisya	15	3	43	2
Alamgir Kabir	8	1	39	0
Mushfiqur Rahman	10	1	36	0
Mohammad Rafique	20	7	53	0
Manjural Islam Rana	6	0	33	0
Mohammad Ashraful	1.2	0	6	0

Fall of Wickets
1-5, 2-134

Umpires: NA Mallender and DL Orchard
Toss: Zimbabwe

Match drawn

ZIMBABWE

Batting	M	Inns	NO	Runs	HS	Av	100	50	c/st
SV Carlisle	2	3	1	194	103*	97.00	1	1	1/-
SM Ervine	2	2	0	160	86	80.00	-	2	2/-
HH Streak	2	1	0	68	68	68.00	-	1	-/-
T Taibu	2	2	0	117	59	58.50	-	2	7/2
GM Ewing	1	2	0	72	71	36.00	-	1	1/-
DD Ebrahim	2	3	0	98	65	32.66	-	1	1/-
TR Gripper	2	3	0	70	65	23.33	-	1	1/-
GW Flower	2	3	1	45	37*	22.50	-	-	1/-
AM Blignaut	1	2	0	39	32	19.50	-	-	-/-
RW Price	2	2	1	10	9	10.00	-	-	-/-
TJ Friend	1	0	0	0	0	-	-	-	1/-
DT Hondo	2	1	1	0	0*	-	-	-	-/-
NB Mahwire	1	0	0	0	0	-	-	-	-/-

Bowling	Overs	Mds	Runs	Wkts	Av	Best	5/inn	10m
HH Streak	41.2	20	63	5	12.60	4-44	-	-
DT Hondo	49.4	13	98	7	14.00	3-49	-	-
AM Blignaut	26.4	7	85	5	17.00	3-12	-	-
RW Price	54.4	9	160	8	20.00	4-61	-	-
TJ Friend	9	2	20	1	20.00	1-20	-	-
SM Ervine	39	9	130	3	43.33	3-44	-	-
GM Ewing	15	5	46	1	46.00	1-27	-	-

Also bowled: TR Gripper 4-2-8-0, NB Mahwire 10-2-36-0.

BANGLADESH

Batting	M	Inns	NO	Runs	HS	Av	100	50	c/st
Manjural Islam Rana	2	3	1	105	39	52.50	-	-	-/-
Rajin Saleh	2	3	0	102	49	34.00	-	-	1/-
Mohammad Ashraful	2	3	0	99	98	33.00	-	1	-/-
Shahriar Hossain	2	3	0	80	48	26.66	-	-	-/-
Khaled Mashud	2	3	0	76	61	25.33	-	1	6/2
Mohammad Rafique	2	3	1	34	26*	17.00	-	-	-/-
Mushfiqur Rahman	2	3	0	44	44	14.66	-	-	-/-
Hannan Sarkar	2	3	0	39	25	13.00	-	-	4/-
Manjural Islam	1	2	1	6	5	6.00	-	-	-/-
Alamgir Kabir	1	1	0	3	3	3.00	-	-	-/-
Tapash Baisya	2	3	0	8	4	2.66	-	-	2/-
Habibul Bashar	2	3	0	4	4	1.33	-	-	2/-

Bowling	Overs	Mds	Runs	Wkts	Av	Best	5/inn	10m
Tapash Baisya	67	10	241	7	34.42	3-133	-	-
Mohammad Rafique	97	21	236	6	39.33	4-121	-	-
Manjural Islam Rana	26.2	4	99	2	49.50	2-40	-	-
Mushfiqur Rahman	43.2	9	160	3	53.33	3-75	-	-
Manjural Islam	40	12	93	1	93.00	1-24	-	-

Also bowled: Mohammad Ashraful 3.2-1-15-0, Alamgir Kabir 8-1-39-0.

ONE-DAY INTERNATIONALS
v. Bangladesh

Match One
6 March 2004 at Bulawayo
Zimbabwe v. **Bangladesh**
Match abandoned – no result

Match Two
7 March 2004 at Bulawayo
Zimbabwe v. **Bangladesh**
Match abandoned – no result

Match Three
10 March 2004 at Harare
Bangladesh 238 for 7 (50 overs) (Habibul Bashar 61, Rajin Saleh 57, Mohammad Ashraful 51*)
Zimbabwe 230 for 9 (50 overs) (SV Carlisle 71, BG Rogers 51)
Bangladesh won by 8 runs

Match Four
12 March 2004 at Harare
Zimbabwe 242 for 8 (50 overs) (SM Ervine 50)
Bangladesh 228 (49.2 overs) (HH Streak 4 for 30)
Zimbabwe won by 14 runs

Match Five
14 March 2004 at Harare
Bangladesh 183 (48.5 overs) (Manjural Islam Rana 63, Hannan Sarkar 59)
Zimbabwe 185 for 7 (42.3 overs) (GW Flower 59, BG Rogers 54, Khaled Mahmud 4 for 19)
Zimbabwe won by 3 wickets

FIRST TEST – ZIMBABWE v. SRI LANKA
6–8 May 2004 at Harare

ZIMBABWE

	First Innings		Second Innings	
S Matsikenyeri	c Jayawardene DPMD b Zoysa	10	c Jayawardene DPMD b Zoysa	11
BRM Taylor	c & b Maharoof	19	c Muralitharan b Vaas	4
DD Ebrahim	lbw b Zoysa	1	c Jayawardene HAPW b Zoysa	2
T Taibu (capt)	c Jayawardene DPMD b Muralitharan	40	lbw b Zoysa	0
E Chigumbura	c Muralitharan b Zoysa	14	c Jayawardene HAPW b Zoysa	0
*A Maregwede	lbw b Muralitharan	0	c & b Muralitharan	22
ML Nkala	lbw b Muralitharan	2	c Jayawardene DPMD b Muralitharan	24
P Utseya	b Muralitharan	45	b Maharoof	0
NB Mahwire	b Muralitharan	0	c Jayawardene DPMD b Zoysa	2
DT Hondo	b Muralitharan	19	not out	15
T Panyangara	not out	32	c Jayawardene DPMD b Jayasuriya	18
Extras	b 4, lb 6, nb 7	17	lb 2, nb 2	4
	(71.2 overs)	**199**	(32 overs)	**102**

	First Innings				Second Innings			
	O	M	R	W	O	M	R	W
Vaas	19	6	39	0	8	2	24	1
Zoysa	17	6	53	3	9.5	2	20	5
Maharoof	10	3	45	1	4	0	18	1
Muralitharan	24.2	10	45	6	9.1	1	37	2
Jayasuriya	1	0	7	0	1	0	1	1

Fall of Wickets
1-30, 2-32, 3-35, 4-57, 5-69, 6-85, 7-118, 8-118, 9-149
1-13, 2-15, 3-17, 4-17, 5-18, 6-63, 7-64, 8-64, 9-72

SRI LANKA

	First Innings	
MS Atapattu (capt)	b Hondo	170
ST Jayasuriya	c Hondo b Taibu	157
KC Sangakkara	c Taibu b Matsikenyeri	11
DPMD Jayawardene	c Utseya b Chigumbura	37
TM Dilshan	c Utseya b Mahwire	10
TT Samaraweera	c Taibu b Panyangara	6
*HAPW Jayawardene	b Panyangara	4
WPUJC Vaas	c Matsikenyeri b Mahwire	28
MF Maharoof	lbw b Mahwire	40
DNT Zoysa	not out	28
M Muralitharan	c Maregwede b Panyangara	26
Extras	b 2, lb 13, w 3, nb 6	24
	(125.1 overs)	**541**

	First Innings			
	O	M	R	W
Hondo	27	6	103	1
Panyangara	26.1	2	101	3
Mahwire	18	1	97	3
Nkala	7	1	41	0
Utseya	12	2	55	0
Matsikenyeri	15	.2	58	1
Taibu	8	1	27	1
Chigumbura	12	2	44	1

Fall of Wickets
1-281, 2-312, 3-369, 4-387, 5-399, 6-403, 7-414, 8-457, 9-496

Umpires: BF Bowden and RE Koertzen
Toss: Sri Lanka
Test debuts: E Chigumbura, A Maregwede, T Panyangara, BRM Taylor, P Utseya, MF Maharoof
Man of the Match: M Muralitharan

Sri Lanka won by an innings and 240 runs

SECOND TEST – ZIMBABWE v. SRI LANKA
14–17 May 2004 at Bulawayo

ZIMBABWE

	First Innings		Second Innings	
S Matsikenyeri	run out	45	c Jayawardene HAPW b Zoysa	14
BRM Taylor	c Jayawardene HAPW b Vaas	5	c Jayawardene DPMD b Muralitharan	61
MA Vermeulen	c Muralitharan b Vaas	0	c Muralitharan b Zoysa	6
DD Ebrahim	c Dilshan b Maharoof	70	c Atapattu b Jayasuriya	42
*T Taibu (capt)	c Samaraweera b Maharoof	27	c Dilshan b Muralitharan	0
A Maregwede	run out	24	lbw b Vaas	28
E Chigumbura	c Jayawardene DPMD b Vaas	0	lbw b Muralitharan	12
ML Nkala	c Sangakkara b Muralitharan	19	c Dilshan b Vaas	0
T Panyangara	c Vaas b Zoysa	11	not out	40
T Mupariwa	not out	1	c Vaas b Jayasuriya	14
DT Hondo	b Muralitharan	11	c Atapattu b Muralitharan	3
Extras	lb 2, w 3, nb 10	15	lb 7, w 1, nb 3	11
	(75 overs)	228	(75.1 overs)	231

	First Innings				Second Innings			
	O	M	R	W	O	M	R	W
Vaas	19	8	41	3	18	6	53	2
Zoysa	14	0	50	1	13	4	27	2
Maharoof	16	2	62	2	6	0	32	0
Muralitharan	22	3	58	2	28.1	6	79	4
Jayasuriya	4	0	15	0	10	0	33	2

Fall of Wickets
1-24, 2-31, 3-82, 4-134, 5-176, 6-176, 7-193, 8-211, 9-216
1-22, 2-40, 3-125, 4-127, 5-143, 6-173, 7-173, 8-173, 9-204

SRI LANKA

	First Innings	
MS Atapattu (capt)	c Taibu b Chigumbura	249
ST Jayasuriya	c Taibu b Nkala	48
KC Sangakkara	c Taibu b Panyangara	270
DPMD Jayawardene	not out	100
TT Samaraweera	not out	32
TM Dilshan		
*HAPW Jayawardene		
WPUJC Vaas		
MF Maharoof		
DNT Zoysa		
M Muralitharan		
Extras	lb 5, w 4, nb 5	14
	(3 wkts dec 165.3 overs)	713

	First Innings			
	O	M	R	W
Hondo	29	5	116	0
Panyangara	25	4	120	1
Mupariwa	34	1	136	0
Nkala	32	3	111	1
Chigumbura	21	2	108	1
Matsikenyeri	23.3	1	112	0
Vermeulen	1	0	5	0

Fall of Wickets
1-100, 2-538, 3-627

Umpires: BF Bowden and RE Koertzen
Toss: Sri Lanka
Test debut: T Mupariwa
Man of the Match: KC Sangakkara
Man of the Series: MS Atapattu

Sri Lanka won by an innings and 254 runs

SERIES AVERAGES
Zimbabwe v. Sri Lanka

ZIMBABWE

Batting	M	Inns	NO	Runs	HS	Av	100	50	c/st
T Jayangara	2	4	2	101	40*	50.50	-	-	-/-
DD Ebrahim	2	4	0	115	70	28.75	-	1	-/-
P Utseya	1	2	0	45	45	22.50	-	-	2/-
BRM Taylor	2	4	0	89	61	22.25	-	1	-/-
S Matsikenyeri	2	4	0	80	45	20.00	-	-	1/-
A Maregwede	2	4	0	74	28	18.50	-	-	1/-
T Taibu	2	4	0	67	40	16.75	-	-	5/-
DT Hondo	2	4	1	48	19	16.00	-	-	-/-
T Mupariwa	1	2	1	15	14	15.00	-	-	-/-
ML Nkala	2	4	0	45	24	11.25	-	-	-/-
E Chigumbura	2	4	0	26	14	6.50	-	-	-/-
MA Vermeulen	1	2	0	6	6	3.00	-	-	-/-
NB Mahwire	1	2	0	2	2	1.00	-	-	-/-

Bowling	Overs	Mds	Runs	Wkts	Av	Best	5/inn	10m
T Taibu	8	1	27	1	27.00	1-27	-	-
NB Mahwire	18	1	97	3	32.33	3-97	-	-
T Panyangara	51.1	6	221	4	55.25	3-101	-	-
E Chigumbura	33	4	152	2	76.00	1-44	-	-
ML Nkala	39	4	152	1	152.00	1-111	-	-
S Matsikenyeri	38.3	3	170	1	170.00	1-58	-	-
DT Hondo	56	11	219	1	219.00	1-103	-	-
MA Vermeulen	1	0	5	0	-	-	-	-
P Utseya	12	2	55	0	-	-	-	-
T Mupariwa	34	1	136	0	-	-	-	-

SRI LANKA

Batting	M	Inns	NO	Runs	HS	Av	100	50	c/st
MS Atapattu	2	2	0	419	249	209.50	2	-	2/-
KC Sangakkara	2	2	0	281	270	140.50	1	-	1/-
DPMD Jayawardene	2	2	1	137	100*	137.00	1	-	8/-
ST Jayasuriya	2	2	0	205	157	102.50	1	-	-/-
MF Maharoof	2	1	0	40	40	40.00	-	-	1/-
TT Samaraweera	2	2	1	38	32*	38.00	-	-	1/-
WPUJC Vaas	2	1	0	28	28	28.00	-	-	2/-
M Muralitharan	2	1	0	26	26	26.00	-	-	5/-
TM Dilshan	2	1	0	10	10	10.00	-	-	3/-
HAPW Jayawardene	2	1	0	4	4	4.00	-	-	4/-
DNT Zoysa	2	1	1	28	28*	-	-	-	-/-

Bowling	Overs	Mds	Runs	Wkts	Av	Best	5/inn	10m
DNT Zoysa	53.5	12	150	11	13.63	5-20	1	-
M Muralitharan	83.4	20	219	14	15.64	6-45	1	-
ST Jayasuriya	16	0	56	3	18.66	2-33	-	-
WPUJC Vaas	64	22	157	6	26.16	3-41	-	-
MF Maharoof	36	5	157	4	39.25	2-62	-	-

ONE-DAY INTERNATIONALS
v. Sri Lanka

Match One
20 April 2004 at Bulawayo
Zimbabwe 211 for 6 (50 overs) (T Taibu 96*)
Sri Lanka 144 for 4 (27 overs) (KC Sangakkara 73*)
Sri Lanka won by 12 runs – DL Method

Match Two
22 April 2004 at Bulawayo
Zimbabwe 136 (36.4 overs) (M Muralitharan 4 for 32, WPUJC Vaas 4 for 38)
Sri Lanka 139 for 1 (20.5 overs) (WS Jayantha 74*)
Sri Lanka won by 9 wickets

Match Three
25 April 2004 at Harare
Zimbabwe 35 (18 overs) (WPUJC Vaas 4 for 11)
Sri Lanka 40 for 1 (9.2 overs)
Sri Lanka won by 9 wickets

Match Four
27 April 2004 at Harare
Sri Lanka 223 for 9 (50 overs) (KC Sangakkara 63, UDU Chandana 51)
Zimbabwe 151 (43.4 overs) (DD Ebrahim 50*)
Sri Lanka won by 72 runs

Match Five
29 April 2004 at Harare
Sri Lanka 246 for 7 (50 overs) (RP Arnold 51*)
Zimbabwe 221 for 9 (50 overs) (BRM Taylor 74, M Muralitharan 5 for 23)
Sri Lanka won by 25 runs

ONE-DAY INTERNATIONALS
v. Australia

Match One
25 May 2004 at Harare
Zimbabwe 205 for 9 (50 overs) (BRM Taylor 59, T Taibu 57)
Australia 207 for 3 (39.4 overs) (RT Ponting 91, DR Martyn 74*)
Australia won by 7 wickets

Match Two
27 May 2004 at Harare
Australia 323 for 8 (50 overs) (ML Hayden 87, DS Lehmann 67)
Zimbabwe 184 (44.3 overs) (BRM Taylor 65, DS Lehmann 4 for 7)
Australia won by 139 runs

Match Three
29 May 2004 at Harare
Zimbabwe 196 (48.5 overs) (E Chigumbura 77, JN Gillespie 5 for 32)
Australia 199 for 2 (30.4 overs) (MJ Clarke 105*)
Australia won by 8 wickets

OTHER ONE-DAY INTERNATIONAL TOURNAMENTS

ASIA CUP

Group A

16 July 2004 at Colombo (SSC)
Bangladesh 221 for 9 (50 overs) (Javed Omar 68)
Hong Kong 105 (45.2 overs)
Bangladesh (6pts) won by 116 runs

17 July 2004 at Colombo (SSC)
Pakistan 257 for 6 (50 overs) (Yasir Hameed 102, Inzamam-ul-Haq 58)
Bangladesh 181 (45.2 overs) (Javed Omar 62)
Pakistan (6pts) won by 76 runs

18 July 2004 at Colombo (SSC)
Pakistan 343 for 5 (50 overs) (Younis Khan 144, Shoaib Malik 118)
Hong Kong 165 (44.1 overs) (Shoaib Malik 4 for 19)
Pakistan (6pts) won by 173 runs – DL Method

Group B

16 July 2004 at Dambulla
India 260 for 6 (50 overs) (R Dravid 104, SC Ganguly 56)
United Arab Emirates 144 (35 overs) (Mohammad Tauqir 55)
India (6pts) won by 116 runs

17 July 2004 at Dambulla
Sri Lanka 239 (50 overs) (DA Gunawardene 73, Khuram Khan 4 for 32)
United Arab Emirates 123 (47.5 overs) (UDU Chandana 4 for 22)
Sri Lanka (6pts) won by 116 runs

18 July 2004 at Dambulla
Sri Lanka 282 for 4 (50 overs) (DPMD Jayawardene 58*, KC Sangakkara 57, MS Atapattu 50)
India 270 for 8 (50 overs) (R Dravid 82)
Sri Lanka (5pts) won by 12 runs – India (1pt)

Phase Two

21 July 2004 at Colombo (SSC)
Bangladesh 177 (49.1 overs)
India 178 for 2 (38.3 overs) (SR Tendulkar 82*, SC Ganguly 60)
India (6pts) won by 8 wickets

21 July 2004 at Colombo (RPS)
Pakistan 122 (39.5 overs)
Sri Lanka 123 for 3 (32 overs)
Sri Lanka (6pts) won by 7 wickets

23 July 2004 at Colombo (RPS)
Bangladesh 190 for 9 (50 overs) (Mohammad Ashraful 66)
Sri Lanka 191 for 0 (33.3 overs) (ST Jayasuriya 107*,
DA Gunawardene 64*)
Sri Lanka (6pts) won by 10 wickets

25 July 2004 at Colombo (RPS)
Pakistan 300 for 9 (50 overs) (Shoaib Malik 143)
India 241 for 8 (50 overs) (SR Tendulkar 78)
Pakistan (5pts) won by 59 runs – India (1pt)

27 July 2004 at Colombo (RPS)
India 271 for 6 (50 overs) (V Sehwag 81, SC Ganguly 79, Yuvraj Singh 50)
Sri Lanka 267 for 9 (50 overs) (ST Jayasuriya 130)
India (5pts) won by 4 runs – Sri Lanka (1pt)

29 July 2004 at Colombo (RPS)
Bangladesh 166 (45.2 overs) (Khaled Mashud 54)
Pakistan 167 for 4 (41 overs)
Pakistan (5pts) won by 6 wickets – Bangladesh (1pt)

Final

1 August 2004 at Colombo (RPS)
Sri Lanka 228 for 9 (50 overs) (MS Atapattu 65, KC Sangakkara 53)
India 203 for 9 (50 overs) (SR Tendulkar 74)
Sri Lanka won by 25 runs

VIDEOCON CUP (Australia, India and Pakistan)

Match One

21 August 2004 at Amstelveen
Pakistan 192 for 6 (33 overs) (Shoaib Malik 68)
India 127 (27 overs) (Shahid Afridi 4 for 20)
Pakistan (6pts) won by 66 runs – DL Method

Match Two

23 August 2004 at Amstelveen
Australia 175 for 7 (31.4 overs)
India Did not bat
Match abandoned – 3pts each

Match Three

25 August 2004 at Amstelveen
Australia v. **Pakistan**
Match abandoned – 3pts each

Videocon Cup Table

	P	W	L	T	NR	RR	Pts
Pakistan	2	1	0	0	1	2.00	9
Australia	2	0	0	0	2	0.00	6
India	2	0	1	0	1	-2.00	3

Final

28 August 2004 at Amstelveen
Australia 192 for 7 (50 overs) (ML Hayden 59)
Pakistan 175 (47.1 overs)
Australia won by 17 runs

ENGLAND: FIRST-CLASS COUNTIES FORM CHARTS

DERBYSHIRE

DURHAM

ESSEX

GLAMORGAN

GLOUCESTERSHIRE

HAMPSHIRE

KENT

LANCASHIRE

LEICESTERSHIRE

MIDDLESEX

NORTHAMPTONSHIRE

NOTTINGHAMSHIRE

SOMERSET

SURREY

SUSSEX

WARWICKSHIRE

WORCESTERSHIRE

YORKSHIRE

DERBYSHIRE CCC

FIRST-CLASS MATCHES
BATTING

Match	Hassan Adnan	LD Sutton	G Welch	SD Stubbings	CWG Bassano	AI Gait	MA Sheikh	J Moss	AG Botha	JDC Bryant	NGE Walker	PMR Havell	KJ Dean	CJL Rogers	Mohammad Ali	BJ France	SA Selwood	NRC Dumelow	CD Paget	NEL Gunter	DB Powell	L Goddard	DR Hewson	JR Chapman	ID Hunter	Extras	Total	Wickets	Result	Poi
v. Glamorgan (Cardiff) 16-19 April	36	0	1		31	15*		0	6			0		47	21	2										15	174	10		
	42	61*	48		4			12*	15*					43		1										12	238	5	D	7
v. Somerset (Taunton) 21-24 April	107*	6	9	8	43						8*		8				38	18			0					30	275	8		
					36*									58*		3										15	112	1	D	9
v. Durham (Derby) 28 April-1 May	72	27	37*	9	22	37			2				17*	156									9			12	400	8		
																										—	—	—	D	12
v. Hampshire (The Rose Bowl) 7-10 May	0	8	40	24	53	9		9	31	31*				87	12											20	324	10		
	0	5	12	20	21	20		12	0	0*				0	3*											9	102	9	D	10
v. Somerset (Derby) 19-22 May	45	17	28	37	83	12	22*	0	20		80			8												15	367	10		
	60	41	45*	17	16	81		9	12*					91												15	387	7	D	11
v. Glamorgan (Derby) 25-28 May	95	24	22	96	64	2	17		0	1	25*						17									29	392	10		
	55	4	45	9	6	13	9*		7	16	8						13									28	213	10	L	7
v. Leicestershire (Oakham School) 2-5 June	5	14	1	6	32	5			63*	35				0												18	291	10		
	0	58	115*	66	7	24			2	10			7	0*												28	323	10	L	4
v. Durham UCCE (Derby) 9-11 June	96		39		69		0	0	103	8								15*	3					7		39	379	8	W	
																										—	—	—		
v. Nottinghamshire (Trent Bridge) 18-21 June	43	36*	29	0	3	0	1	69	9				1	14												15	220	10		
	129*	8	9	0	52	5	1	20	40				8	50												33	355	10	L	7
v. Essex (Derby) 23-26 June	1	131	26	12	0	33	10	79	52				8*	10												27	389	10	D	9
																										—	—	—		
v. Durham (The Riverside) 21-23 July	4	2	59	8		30	1	0	42	3	1*							8								37	195	10		
	29	45	23*	18		21		147*	30									11								16	340	6	W	17
v. Yorkshire (Derby) 28-31 July	86	25	6	51	100	1	42	10	19	5		13*														48	406	10		
	41	6	24	1	25	12	36*	56	49	20		4*														31	305	9	D	12
v. West Indies (Derby) 5-7 August	31	36	56		13			10	7	1					5	2	0*	2								25	188	10		
	6	27	5		2			2	13	1					0	12	0*	10								10	88	10	L	0
v. Yorkshire (Headingley) 12-15 August	86	35	1	37	35	0	0	7		1	1*								7							30	240	10		
	6	33*	58	29*	5			87	10																	17	245	5	D	7
v. Nottinghamshire (Derby) 19-22 August	140	6	12	31	123*		5*	30	8					9												36	400	7		
	28	0	0	23	7		17*	1	2	1				12						0						5	96	10	L	8
v. Leicestershire (Derby) 24-27 August	30*		0				13*		25							56										14	138	3	D	9
																										—	—	—		
v. Essex (Chelmsford) 9-10 September	58	48	5	0	0		23	28			5*				2			6							0	17	192	10		
	3	44	0	7	34		8	11			2*				33			0							6	18	166	10	L	3
v. Hampshire (Derby) 16-19 September	41*		35*								1				2											16	95	2		
	5		12	34	64*	14	20				23		3		12					12		8				22	229	10	L	3

	Hassan Adnan	LD Sutton	G Welch	SD Stubbings	CWG Bassano	AI Gait	MA Sheikh	J Moss	AG Botha	JDC Bryant	NGE Walker	PMR Havell	KJ Dean	CJL Rogers	Mohammad Ali	BJ France	SA Selwood	NRC Dumelow	CD Paget	NEL Gunter	DB Powell	L Goddard	DR Hewson	JR Chapman	ID Hunter
Matches	18	16	16	16	14	14	13	12	11	9	8	8	7	6	4	4	4	4	2	2	2	2	2	1	1
Innings	31	27	25	28	22	25	18	20	18	16	9	10	10	11	6	7	8	6	4	3	3	1	2	1	2
Not Out	4	3	4	1	3	1	6	2	2	1	3	6	4	2	1	0	0	0	2	1	0	0	0	0	0
Highest Score	140	131	115*	96	123*	81	42	147*	103	30	80	13*	35	156	50	56	38	18	7	15*	17	8	9	7	6
Runs	1380	747	609	743	814	509	259	608	405	169	221	32	117	498	110	126	68	50	7	27	33	8	9	7	6
Average	51.11	31.12	29.00	27.51	42.84	21.20	21.58	33.77	25.31	11.26	36.83	8.00	19.50	55.33	22.00	18.00	8.50	8.33	3.50	13.50	11.00	8.00	4.50	7.00	3.00
100s	3	1	1	0	2	0	0	1	1	0	0	0	0	1	0	0	0	0	0	0	0	0	0	0	0
50s	8	2	1	6	6	2	0	4	1	0	2	0	0	3	1	1	0	0	0	0	0	0	0	0	0
Catches/Stumpings	11/0	34/3	12/0	8/0	4/0	12/0	1/0	5/0	5/0	3/0	3/0	2/0	3/0	6/0	1/0	2/0	1/0	0/0	0/0	2/0	1/0	7/0	0/0	0/0	0/0

Home Ground: Derby
Address: County Ground, Nottingham Road, Derby, DE21 6DA
Tel: 01332 383211
Fax: 01332 290251
Email: derby@ecb.co.uk
Directions: By road: From the South & East, exit M1 junction 25, follow the A52 into Derby, take the fourth exit off the Pentagon Island. From the North, exit M1 junction 28, join the A38 into Derby and follow directional signs; the cricket ground is seen on the left approaching the city. From the West, on A50 follow signs for A52 Nottingham and on leaving the city centre inner ring road take the second exit off the Pentagon Island into the ground.

Capacity: 4,000
Other grounds used: Chesterfield
Year formed: 1870

Chief Executive: John Smedley
General Manager: Keith Stevenson
Director of Cricket: Dave Houghton
Academy Director & 2nd XI Coach: Karl Krikken
Captain: Luke Sutton
County colours: Blue, brown and gold

Honours
County Championship
1936
Sunday League/NCL
1990
Benson & Hedges Cup
1993
Gillette Cup/NatWest/C&G Trophy
1981

Website:
www.dccc.org.uk

DERBYSHIRE CCC

FIRST-CLASS MATCHES
BOWLING

Match	G Welch	AG Botha	MA Sheikh	PMR Havell	KJ Dean	NGE Walker	J Moss	DB Powell	Mohammad Ali	NRC Dumelow	NEL Gunter	DR Hewson	ID Hunter	CD Paget	Hassan Adnan	BJ France	Overs	Total	Byes/Leg-byes	Wickets	Run outs
v. Glamorgan (Cardiff) 16-19 April	12-6-24-1		10-0-40-0		10.3-2-41-4				16-2-75-4								48.3	185	5	10	1
	21-4-64-2	16.3-0-95-1	3-0-12-0		14-1-46-1				20-2-84-0						1-0-4-0		75.3	323	18	4	
v. Somerset (Taunton) 21-24 April	16-5-33-0			26-6-86-5	23-0-111-4					22-2-92-0		21-8-48-1			2-0-11-0		110	388	7	10	
				6-2-10-0	19-3-49-2					25-5-60-1		18-8-39-3			3-0-7-0		71	170	5	6	
v. Durham (Derby) 28 April-1 May	18-2-64-3	17.5-6-66-4			3.3-1-13-1	11.3-3-55-2						7-2-25-0					57.5	232	9	10	
																	–	–	–	–	
v. Hampshire (The Rose Bowl) 7-10 May	33-8-100-1	23-2-59-1				10-1-40-1	26-5-91-1		32.2-8-121-4								124.2	419	8	9	
	8-0-51-2					5-0-27-1	5-0-33-2		14-3-61-1								32	178	6	6	
v. Somerset (Derby) 19-22 May	28-12-79-3	22-6-76-1	22-5-68-1			19.5-7-68-5									2-0-4-0		93.5	307	12	10	
	23-4-70-1	25-6-58-1	15-4-43-1			11-0-45-1									4-1-26-0		78	252	10	4	
v. Glamorgan (Derby) 25-28 May	26-5-96-1	20-5-64-1	19-6-53-2		19-2-77-3	17-0-83-1	20.1-2-85-2										121.1	474	16	10	
	23-4-3-100-5	18-4-48-1	9-3-21-1		5-0-21-1	3-0-14-0	9-0-47-0										67.4	259	8	8	
v. Leicestershire (Oakham School) 2-5 June	35-8-141-2	24.4-3-92-3	35-11-97-1		29-3-111-3		21-2-82-0								2-0-4-0		143.4	534	7	10	1
		4-0-28-2	6-0-30-2		3-0-24-0												13	83	1	4	
v. Durham UCCE (Derby) 9-11 June		10-6-9-0		12-5-24-1			19.5-7-49-6				13-3-52-3						54.5	148	14	10	
		29-13-55-5		18-5-47-2		1-0-3-1	21.3-5-72-2				11-1-37-0						80.3	226	12	10	
v. Nottinghamshire (Trent Bridge) 18-21 June	28-1-101-0	14-1-71-2	27-8-78-2		21-1-138-2	24-4-65-0			19.2-3-83-1								133.2	551	15	7	
	2-0-14-0								1-0-14-0								3	28	0	0	
v. Essex (Derby) 23-26 June	14-3-40-3		11-0-31-0	4-2-16-0		7-0-30-0	12-2-39-0		14-0-48-0						3-1-11-0		65	222	7	3	1
v. Durham (The Riverside) 21-23 July	12-6-12-0		11-7-9-4			6-0-36-2	17-7-30-3										46	91	4	10	
	21-4-56-3	12-2-47-1	18-2-68-2	16.1-3-75-4			9-1-27-0										76.1	279	6	10	
v. Yorkshire (Derby) 28-31 July	23-7-54-1	20-6-51-2	20-4-68-3		14-0-85-1		30-7-73-2								2-0-4-1		109	354	19	10	
	22-2-101-2	24-2-88-1	9-1-33-1		7-0-33-1		18.5-2-66-2								2-0-12-0		82.5	341	8	8	1
v. West Indies (Derby) 5-7 August				10-1-47-2		6-0-44-1				12-3-51-5	9-1-0-68-2			3-1-6-0			40.1	223	7	10	1
				16-2-56-0		8-1-49-0				28-5-131-2	12-1-58-0			17-1-63-3			81	368	11	6	1
v. Yorkshire (Headingley) 12-15 August	31-6-118-3		23-3-85-2	16-0-100-1			20-4-60-1							19-3-69-0			109	442	10	8	1
																	–	–	–	–	
v. Nottinghamshire (Derby) 19-22 August	29-7-101-5		31-7-99-1		24-1-137-2		13-0-65-0							17-1-68-0	13-0-58-0		127	552	24	9	1
																	–	–	–	–	
v. Leicestershire (Derby) 24-27 August																	–	–	–	–	
																	–	–	–	–	
v. Essex (Chelmsford) 9-10 September	8-2-28-2		4-1-24-1	8-1-23-2						12-2-52-1			8.3-1-32-3				40.3	167	8	10	1
	7-1-21-0		3.3-0-24-0	7-0-38-0		6-2-19-2				10-1-58-0			6-0-20-0				39.3	194	14	2	
v. Hampshire (Derby) 16-19 September	31.1-7-57-5		28-5-76-2	24-2-113-3			26-5-75-0			13-2-39-0						4-0-20-0	126.1	396	16	10	
			1-0-1-0							4-0-5-0					3.3-0-13-0		8.3	19	0	0	

	G Welch	AG Botha	MA Sheikh	PMR Havell	KJ Dean	NGE Walker	J Moss	DB Powell	Mohammad Ali	NRC Dumelow	NEL Gunter	DR Hewson	ID Hunter	CD Paget	Hassan Adnan	BJ France
Overs	471.5	291	298.3	178.1	144	151.2	207.5	70.3	116.4	126	45.1	46	14.3	56	37.3	4
Maidens	103	62	69	20	18	17	39	14	18	20	5	18	1	6	2	0
Runs	1525	938	945	814	597	667	646	253	486	488	215	112	52	206	154	20
Wickets	45	26	26	21	20	18	14	10	10	9	5	4	3	3	1	0
Average	33.88	36.07	36.34	38.76	29.85	37.05	46.14	25.30	48.60	54.22	43.00	28.00	17.33	68.66	154.00	–

FIELDING

37	LD Sutton (34 ct, 3 st)
12	G Welch
12	AI Gait
11	Hassan Adnan
8	SD Stubbings
7	L Goddard
6	CJL Rogers
5	J Moss
5	AG Botha
4	CWG Bassano
3	KJ Dean
3	NGE Walker
3	JDC Bryant
2	PMR Havell
2	NEL Gunter
2	BJ France
1	MA Sheikh
1	SA Selwood
1	Mohammad Ali
1	DB Powell
0	CD Paget
0	DR Hewson
0	NRC Dumelow
0	ID Hunter
0	JR Chapman

DURHAM CCC

FIRST-CLASS MATCHES
BATTING

Match / Innings	MJ North	JJB Lewis	GJ Muchall	GR Breese	A Pratt	N Killeen	GD Bridge	LE Plunkett	N Peng	M Davies	GJ Pratt	GM Hamilton	G Onions	PD Collingwood	KJ Coetzer	P Mustard	I Pattison	Shoaib Akhtar	JA Lowe	AM Blignaut	P Kumar	SW Tait	RD King	Tahir Mughal	Extras	Total	Wickets	Result	Points
v. Durham UCCE (The Riverside) 10-12 April	30	9	5		67	22	30	33*	30		45	8	1												31	311	10		
	60	19	0		68	29*	0	27	0		6	42	15*												25	291	9	D	0
v. Hampshire (The Rose Bowl) 16-19 April	29	3	0	0	3	15*		49	0		13	6						0							10	128	10		
	4	50	1	20	6	21			66	6*	4	15						0							8	201	10	L	3
v. Nottinghamshire (The Riverside) 21-24 April	27	15	14	53	48			54	51	0*	50	4											1		33	350	10		
	0	0	16	6	17			12	0	9*	8	7											3		15	93	10	L	6
v. Derbyshire (Derby) 28 April-1 May	119	2		15	44		0	7	0	0	7			0*	23										15	232	10		
	-	-																							-	-	-	D	7
v. Essex (The Riverside) 7-10 May	15	8	94	42	20	26	6	14*	43						26						0				45	339	10		
	0	9	40	4	19	9*	1		1						10									17*	11	121	8	D	10
v. Somerset (Taunton) 12-15 May	20	65	0	41	46*	3	0	10	1			9			25										15	235	10		
	33	2	19	165*	25	35			88	4*	12	4			46										20	453	9	W	18
v. Glamorgan (The Riverside) 19-21 May	13	0	93	11	4	0	3			29	12						33	13*							9	220	10		
	9	51	27	4	59	14	7			21*	15	14						0							16	237	10	L	4
v. Nottinghamshire (Trent Bridge) 25-28 May	17	77	60	0	39*	16		32	0		14			31	2										12	300	10		
	44	16	18	27	5	3*		19	6		71			68	21										17	315	10	L	6
v. Yorkshire (The Riverside) 8-10 June	1	6	20	6	7	2		37	2*		17			26					7						19	150	10		
	59	14	1	7	24	3		0	4		5			65					16*						16	214	10	L	3
v. Glamorgan (Cardiff) 23-26 June	219	27	23	76	9	4	4	28	2					0*	67										7	466	10		
	-	-																							-	-	-	D	11
v. Derbyshire (The Riverside) 21-23 July	3	35*	7	6	1	8		1				0		9	0		3								18	91	10		
	68	25	49	4	42	9		2*				11		22	5		19								23	279	10	L	3
v. Leicestershire (Leicester) 27-30 July	48	9	60	0	9	0	19*		0					17	33					12					12	219	10		
	5	21	95	43	1	6	26		2*					57	58					56					39	389	10	L	3
v. Somerset (The Riverside) 13-16 August	4	8	40	10	16	35*	8					41			16							0			15	231	10		
	7	25	4	5	24*	0*						12			6										2	85	6	D	7
v. Essex (Colchester) 18-21 August	7	127	0	34	10	6*	26	7				9			29						4				9	268	10		
	-	-																							-	-	-	D	7
v. Hampshire (The Riverside) 24-27 August	0	29	47	6	0		51*	14				25		11	6		7								21	217	10		
	23*	37	4	6								9*			12										18	109	4	D	8
v. Yorkshire (Scarborough) 1-3 September	24	12	142*	35	6	8	5					2			16	15	31								29	325	10		
	62	15	18	68	20		46*	0				58			26				41						21	375	9	W	20
v. Leicestershire (The Riverside) 9-12 September	8	27	35	5	30		52	7			29		20*			60	9								16	298	10		
	11	14	43	65	0		5	17*			53		0			40	10								22	280	10	L	5

	MJ North	JJB Lewis	GJ Muchall	GR Breese	A Pratt	N Killeen	GD Bridge	LE Plunkett	N Peng	M Davies	GJ Pratt	GM Hamilton	G Onions	PD Collingwood	KJ Coetzer	P Mustard	I Pattison	Shoaib Akhtar	JA Lowe	AM Blignaut	P Kumar	SW Tait	RD King	Tahir Mughal
Matches	17	17	16	14	14	13	11	10	10	10	9	8	8	6	6	3	3	2	2	2	2	2	2	1
Innings	31	31	30	25	25	22	18	16	18	17	17	15	12	11	10	5	4	4	4	4	4	2	4	2
Not Out	1	1	1	1	3	5	3	4	0	8	0	1	5	0	0	0	0	1	0	0	1	0	0	1
Highest Score	219	127	142*	165*	68	35*	52	54	88	29	71	58	20*	68	67	60	33	46	41	56	21	4	3	17*
Runs	969	757	975	685	618	269	321	302	417	110	324	320	76	322	212	148	92	94	91	90	36	4	4	17
Average	32.30	25.23	33.62	28.54	28.09	15.82	21.40	25.16	23.16	12.22	19.05	22.85	10.85	29.27	21.20	29.60	23.00	31.33	22.75	22.50	12.00	2.00	1.00	17.00
100s	2	1	1	1	0	0	0	0	0	0	0	0	0	0	0	0	0	0	0	0	0	0	0	0
50s	4	4	5	3	4	0	2	1	3	0	2	2	0	3	1	1	0	0	1	0	0	0	0	0
Catches/Stumpings	8/0	7/0	14/0	12/0	33/2	1/0	1/0	2/0	6/0	2/0	7/0	3/0	2/0	4/0	0/0	9/0	3/0	2/0	2/0	0/0	0/0	0/0	1/0	0/0

Home Ground: Chester-le-Street
Address: County Ground, The Riverside, Chester-le-Street, County Durham, DH3 3QR
Tel: 0191 3871717
Fax: 0191 3889210
Email: reception.durham@ecb.co.uk
Directions: *By rail:* Chester-le-Street (approx 5 minutes by taxi or a 10-minute walk). *By road:* Easily accessible from junction 63 of the A1(M).

Capacity: 10,000
Other grounds used: Darlington CC, Hartlepool CC, Stockton CC
Year formed: 1882

Chief Executive: David Harker
Director of Cricket: Geoff Cook
First XI Coach: Martyn Moxon
Captain: Jonathan Lewis
County colours: Yellow, blue and burgundy

Honours
None yet

Website:
www.durhamccc.co.uk

DURHAM CCC

FIRST-CLASS MATCHES
BOWLING

	M Davies	LE Plunkett	GR Breese	GD Bridge	N Killeen	PD Collingwood	G Onions	Shoaib Akhtar	GM Hamilton	MJ North	GJ Muchall	P Kumar	RD King	AM Blignaut	Tahir Mughal	I Pattison	GJ Pratt	KJ Coetzer	SW Tait	Overs	Total	Byes/Leg-byes	Wickets	Run outs
v. Durham UCCE The Riverside) 10-12 April		10-1-26-2	19-8-25-2 12-9-7-2	9-0-21-0 11-2-23-0		10-1-26-1 9-6-7-0			3-0-9-0 12-2-30-3	12-4-16-4	1-0-3-0 8-2-22-1						2-0-2-0			64 65	133 132	7 5	9 8	
v. Hampshire The Rose Bowl) 16-19 April	17.2-7-53-6 15-7-34-3	17-4-66-2 18-5-48-4		5-1-12-0					6-1-19-0 1-0-2-0			11-1-65-2 32-0-21-0								56.2 37.2	221 112	6 7	10 7	
v. Nottinghamshire (The Riverside) 21-24 April	26-9-78-2	26-3-119-1		35-14-73-1					22-5-99-1	1-0-2-0	3-0-14-1		243-5-120-3							137.3	523	18	10	1
v. Derbyshire Derby) 28 April-1 May	23-3-67-2	26.3-4-71-2	17-2-69-1	14-3-40-0		27-7-99-2										13-2-42-1				120.3	400	12	8	
v. Essex The Riverside) 7-10 May	20-11-30-5		13-1-64-1		21.4-7-68-1										19-4-54-2	12-4-30-1				85.4	265	19	10	
v. Somerset Taunton) 12-15 May	22-6-55-3 20-3-69-2		18-3-85-0 21-1-79-1	19-5-52-2 20-3-59-1	14-4-50-1 12-3-37-0		14-3-63-3 13-3-45-0				7-0-30-0 14-0-6-1	5-0-33-1								99 87.4	375 310	7 15	10 5	
v. Glamorgan The Riverside) 19-21 May	21-4-95-3 17-2-71-2		26-6-85-2 8.3-1-28-2	22-6-62-2 22-4-53-1	11-1-49-3							1-0-4-0	15-1-78-3 9-1-60-0		14-1-57-0					99 56.3	393 265	12 4	10 9	
v. Nottinghamshire Trent Bridge) 25-28 May	22.5-2-78-6 19-4-78-2		7-0-51-0 16.2-1-51-2	23-8-81-1 18-0-74-1	14-3-42-1 15-4-57-1							11-1-56-2 7-2-25-1								77.5 75.2	325 294	17 9	10 7	
v. Yorkshire The Riverside) 8-10 June	16-3-66-1 19-3-51-3		23-3-74-1 14-1-78-0		21-9-69-2 17-5-40-0	17-8-41-2 16-3-53-2	16.2-3-64-4 14-3-46-1		4-2-7-0 8-0-46-2	5-0-17-1										97.2 93	331 353	10 23	10 9	
v. Glamorgan Cardiff) 23-26 June	13-3-31-2		18-6-42-1	23-2-88-1	15-2-50-1		11-2-34-2													80	258	13	7	
v. Derbyshire The Riverside) 21-23 July	18.5-6-44-6 14.2-2-38-2			14-4-32-1 22-1-73-1	14-2-40-0	12-3-27-2 12-4-47-0	15-4-35-0 20.4-4-80-1				3-2-4-0 1-0-5-0		11-2-43-1 15-1-48-1							73.5 99	195 340	10 9	10 6	1
v. Leicestershire Leicester) 27-30 July		25.4-1-132-1 27-4-114-2			24-4-81-1	14-4-52-0	23-4-110-3				5-1-22-0				16-0-109-2		1-0-2-0			135.4	634	12	9	
v. Somerset The Riverside) 13-16 August		16-0-100-2	6-1-42-0	4-0-26-1	18-4-62-2				12-2-28-2	0.3-0-3-0	3-1-15-1								12-0-113-2	71.3	400	11	8	
v. Essex Colchester) 18-21 August		11-1-49-0	6-2-17-1	9-2-49-2	11-4-31-0				9-0-57-1									6-0-63-0		52	274	8	4	
v. Hampshire The Riverside) 24-27 August			20-1-74-6		20-5-58-2	14-3-64-1	5-0-46-0		7-0-26-1											66	280	12	10	
v. Yorkshire Scarborough) 1-3 September		15-3-55-2 10.5-3-57-1	13.3-1-41-5 35-3-110-5	17-1-41-1 21-7-64-4	16-6-39-2 7-2-34-0	2-0-22-0														63.3 80.5	200 290	2 7	10 10	
v. Leicestershire The Riverside) 9-12 September		33-8-104-3 6.5-1-27-3	24.2-6-93-4	20-3-82-1	35-9-93-1		20-3-93-0 5-1-41-0				7-1-21-0 1-0-1-1									139.2 12.5	508 71	12 2	10 4	1

	M Davies	LE Plunkett	GR Breese	GD Bridge	N Killeen	PD Collingwood	G Onions	Shoaib Akhtar	GM Hamilton	MJ North	GJ Muchall	P Kumar	RD King	AM Blignaut	Tahir Mughal	I Pattison	GJ Pratt	KJ Coetzer	SW Tait
Overs	304.2	247.5	307.4	235	343.4	137	146.4	57.2	79	34.1	43	42	38.5	42	19	39	2	1	18
Maidens	75	37	44	60	83	37	32	12	11	6	7	5	6	3	4	7	0	0	0
Runs	938	964	1163	680	1056	455	593	218	288	109	161	219	206	200	54	129	2	2	176
Wickets	50	31	28	19	19	12	9	8	8	7	6	6	5	4	2	2	0	0	0
Average	18.76	31.09	41.53	35.78	55.57	37.91	65.88	27.25	36.00	15.57	26.83	36.50	41.20	50.00	27.00	64.50	-	-	-

FIELDING

35 A Pratt (33 ct, 2 st)
14 GJ Muchall
12 GR Breese
P Mustard
MJ North
JJB Lewis
GJ Pratt
N Peng
PD Collingwood
GM Hamilton
I Pattison
Shoaib Akhtar
M Davies
LE Plunkett
G Onions
JA Lowe
N Killeen
GD Bridge
RD King
AM Blignaut
KJ Coetzer
P Kumar
Tahir Mughal
SW Tait

ESSEX CCC

FIRST–CLASS MATCHES

BATTING

Match	WJ Jefferson	JS Foster	A Flower	JD Middlebrook	A Habib	GR Napier	AN Cook	Danish Kaneria	RC Irani	AR Adams	D Gough	SA Brant	AP Grayson	AGAM McCoubrey	RS Bopara	AP Cowan	AJ Clarke	JP Stephenson	ML Pettini	N Hussain	AP Palladino	RN ten Doeschate	Extras	Total	Wickets	Result	Points
v. Cambridge UCCE	144*			39	54			1							40*			0					14	292	5		
(Fenner's) 10-12 April			101*												13			71*	27				10	222	2	W	0
v. Yorkshire	74	0	7	25	29	13	5				6		1					10*	67				25	262	10		
(Headingley) 21-24 April	20	0	29	6	62	30	52				2		2*					34	0				36	273	10	L	5
v. Somerset	85	75*	1	8	25	0	20	0					1			6	10						0	231	10		
(Chelmsford) 28 April-1 May	0	13*					20*																3	36	1	D	6
v. Durham	31	15	15		8	25	20	3					0*					40		70			31	265	10		
(The Riverside) 7-10 May																							–	–	–	D	9
v. Glamorgan	4	17	38	80	157	82	10	13*		16			0				0						20	437	10		
(Cardiff) 12-15 May	5	26	66	28	2	13*	51	0		3			0*							102			29	325	9	D	12
v. Leicestershire	128	212	22	3	97		126	5*			50	5	7										53	708	9		
(Chelmsford) 19-22 May																							–	–	–	D	12
v. Somerset	95	37	42	115	0	79	8				6*	4	1*				2						11	400	9		
(Taunton) 25-28 May	14	104*	172	1	28	9	10				0		30				28						17	413	10	D	12
v. Yorkshire	45	20	43	2	80	13	0	7*	107	13							12						17	359	10		
(Chelmsford) 2-5 June	8	5	37	4	17	5	2	0*	8	15							0						15	116	10	L	7
v. Hampshire	15	6	1	30*	42	7	25	1	4				17				0						10	158	10		
(Chelmsford) 9-11 June	26	39	0	0	13	51*	22	13	20				19				8						24	235	10	L	3
v. Derbyshire	39		88*	3			34		51*														21	322	10		
(Derby) 23-26 June																							–	–	–	D	8
v. Leicestershire	29	0	14	92	13	7	0		6	124	11					5*							21	322	10		
(Leicester) 21-24 July	11	0	12	0	55	29	55		49	16	12*					6							27	272	10	W	20
v. Nottinghamshire	75	2	18	30	7	8			122*	1		19	119			6							24	431	10		
(Southend-on-Sea) 28-31 July	12	44*	1	8	48	13			60	14		0	35			0							13	248	10	L	8
v. Hampshire	222	40	32	0	19	8			17	22	0		7					21*					28	416	10		
(The Rose Bowl) 3-5 August	4	7	33	93	0	31*			41				75										10	294	7	W	22
v. Durham	134	0*	72		17				7*				26										18	274	4		
(Colchester) 18-21 August																							–	–	–	D	9
v. Glamorgan	0	188	119	3			50	2*	164	3			57		4	25							27	642	10		
(Chelmsford) 2-5 September	8	45	48	34			2	2*	3	6			5		0	0							12	165	10	L	8
v. Derbyshire	0	22	5	7		52	22	1*	0	10			29								0		19	167	10		
(Chelmsford) 9-10 September	60		0				68*		43*									34					23	194	2	W	12
v. Nottinghamshire	167	23	56	14		106*	7	0	16									34			41		36	500	10		
(Trent Bridge) 16-19 September	100*		61*						11														7	179	1	L	7
Matches	17	16	16	16	14	14	12	11	10	7	7	7	6	6	5	5	5	4	3	2	2	2					
Innings	29	24	28	24	22	22	21	13	16	8	10	8	10	7	8	7	6	5	5	3	2	1					
Not Out	1	4	3	2	0	4	2	7	4	0	1	1	0	4	1	2	0	2	0	0	0	0					
Highest Score	222	212	172	115	157	106*	126	13*	164	124	50	19	119	2*	40*	25	28	71*	67	102	41	7					
Runs	1555	927	1045	723	776	633	568	47	695	196	144	39	365	4	156	63	50	161	104	172	41	7					
Average	55.53	46.35	41.80	32.86	35.27	35.16	29.89	7.83	57.91	24.50	16.00	5.57	36.50	1.33	22.28	12.60	8.33	53.66	20.80	57.33	20.50	7.00					
100s	6	3	2	2	1	1	1	0	3	1	0	0	1	0	0	0	0	0	0	1	0	0					
50s	5	1	5	3	5	5	4	0	2	0	1	0	2	0	0	0	0	1	1	1	0	0					
Catches/Stumpings	15/0	39/5	18/0	4/0	3/0	6/0	18/0	7/0	1/0	4/0	0/0	0/0	0/0	3/0	5/0	3/0	2/0	0/0	1/0	2/0	0/0	1/0					

Home Ground: Chelmsford
Address: County Ground, New Writtle Street, Chelmsford, Essex, CM2 0PG
Tel: 01245 252420
Fax: 01245 254030
Email: administration.essex@ecb.co.uk
Directions: By rail: Chelmsford Station (8 minutes' walk away). By road: M25 then A12 to Chelmsford. Exit Chelmsford and follow AA signs to Essex Cricket Club.
Capacity: 6,000

Other grounds used: Colchester, Ilford, Southend-on-Sea
Year formed: 1876

Chief Executive: David East
Cricket Operations Manager: Alan Lilley
Club Coach: Graham Gooch
Captain: Ronnie Irani
County colours: Blue, gold and red

Honours
County Championship
1979, 1983, 1984, 1986, 1991, 1992
Sunday League/NCL
1981, 1984, 1985
Refuge Assurance Cup
1989
Benson & Hedges Cup
1979, 1998
Gillette Cup/NatWest/C&G Trophy
1985, 1997

Website:
www.essexcricket.org.uk

ESSEX CCC

FIRST-CLASS MATCHES

BOWLING

Match	Danish Kaneria	GR Napier	JD Middlebrook	D Gough	AR Adams	AGAM McCoubrey	AP Cowan	AJ Clarke	SA Brant	JP Stephenson	RN ten Doeschate	AP Palladino	AP Grayson	A Habib	RS Bopara	Overs	Total	Byes/Leg-byes	Wickets	Run outs
v. Cambridge UCCE (Fenner's) 10–12 April			11-1-36-2			7-2-16-4 / 16-3-56-3	8-0-32-3 / 10-1-55-0	8-1-35-1 / 13-5-34-2	9-2-24-0	7-2-20-2 / 11.5-3-29-3						30 / 70.5	116 / 245	13 / 11	10 / 10	
v. Yorkshire (Headingley) 21–24 April		28.2-5-119-4 / 10-1-52-1	14-1-47-1 / 3-0-18-1			18.4-3-76-1			25.2-6-86-2 / 11.3-4-30-1	15-1-76-2 / 7-2-29-0				1-0-1-0		102.2 / 31.3	408 / 129	3 / 0	10 / 3	
v. Somerset (Chelmsford) 28 April–1 May	34.3-8-92-1	31-5-99-0	11-0-63-0						32-7-85-1	13-0-43-1				2-0-6-0		124.3 / –	400 / –	12 / –	3 / –	
v. Durham (The Riverside) 7–10 May	23-5-83-3 / 3-1-8-1	23-6-62-2 / 11-4-25-1				18-2-87-1 / 11-2-40-3				11-2-47-2 / 9-2-28-3	15-2-52-2 / 13-0-16-0					90 / 37	339 / 121	8 / 4	10 / 8	
v. Glamorgan (Cardiff) 12–15 May	42-9-111-3 / 45-13-91-2	26-5-91-4 / 7-1-31-2	24.2-4-70-2 / 27-5-92-4	23-6-77-1 / 16-2-61-1		13-4-59-0 / 3-0-27-0							3-1-11-0			131.2 / 98	435 / 335	16 / 33	10 / 10	1
v. Leicestershire (Chelmsford) 19–22 May	41.5-7-139-3 / 31-14-42-3		35-3-117-3 / 12-4-38-0	18-4-61-2 / 17-3-38-2		14-1-89-1 / 10-2-26-0				20-3-96-1 / 11-3-49-1				1-0-6-0		128.5 / 82	510 / 212	8 / 13	10 / 6	
v. Somerset (Taunton) 25–28 May		16-7-52-2 / 22-1-84-1	10-1-59-1 / 17-2-52-1			10-1-52-2 / 6-2-35-0	21-2-61-3 / 19-5-50-2	17.3-1-87-2 / 11-4-24-1				4-0-21-0 / 8-1-24-0				78.3 / 83	339 / 271	7 / 2	10 / 6	1
v. Yorkshire (Chelmsford) 2–5 June	33.5-5-121-6 / 23.1-5-65-7	7-0-36-0 / 8-0-54-0	27-1-122-2 / 12-0-40-0	11-1-27-2 / 21-7-54-2				9-2-42-0 / 11-4-29-1								87.5 / 75.1	363 / 249	15 / 7	10 / 10	
v. Hampshire (Chelmsford) 9–11 June	35-4-108-4 / 19.2-4-68-5	19-3-68-1 / 6-1-26-0	11-1-58-0	23.5-6-57-5 / 13-2-36-2					15-3-58-0 / 11-6-12-2					1-0-3-0		108.5 / 49.2	363 / 154	1 / 12	10 / 10	1
v. Derbyshire (Derby) 23–26 June	40-10-88-2	23-8-56-5	20.1-4-58-1				27-2-105-1		18-3-65-0							128.1 / –	389 / –	17 / –	10 / –	1
v. Leicestershire (Leicester) 21–24 July		10-2-33-3 / 26-6-85-1	22-7-55-4 / 27-7-50-1	12-3-41-2 / 10-2-30-1	15-4-54-1 / 28-9-75-1											59 / 116.5	197 / 349	14 / 20	10 / 10	2
v. Nottinghamshire (Southend-on-Sea) 28–31 July		14-1-65-1 / 4-0-24-0	16-1-102-0 / 15-3-62-1		22.4-1-93-5 / 13-1-42-1	24-5-70-3 / 8-0-39-0			14-3-48-0 / 7-2-27-0			11-0-48-0 / 8.1-0-50-0				103.4 / 55.1	435 / 246	9 / 2	9 / 2	1
v. Hampshire (The Rose Bowl) 3–5 August		14-2-40-2 / 5-1-26-2	3-0-13-0		15-3-44-2 / 8-2-39-2	14-1-46-4 / 9-2-23-3	17-3-45-2 / 8-2-44-3									60 / 33	177 / 149	2 / 4	10 / 10	
v. Durham (Colchester) 18–21 August	33-11-70-4			9.5-2-38-2	13-3-34-1	25-5-77-1	21-8-42-2									101.5 / –	268 / –	7 / –	10 / –	
v. Glamorgan (Chelmsford) 2–5 September	47.2-6-193-5 / 26.2-5-80-3	12-0-82-1 / 7-0-26-1	18-5-81-2 / 18-3-60-1			22-1-107-1 / 5-1-19-0	21-5-79-1 / 6-3-15-0						5-1-5-0 / 3-0-13-0		2-0-13-0	127.2 / 65.2	587 / 223	22 / 10	10 / 6	1
v. Derbyshire (Chelmsford) 9–10 September	12-4-20-0 / 22.4-9-36-4	5-0-46-1 / 5-1-14-1	14.3-5-26-5 / 14-3-47-3		14-5-44-3 / 11-1-39-2							7-1-28-1 / 3-0-17-0			6-0-20-0	58.3 / 55.4	192 / 166	8 / 13	10 / 10	
v. Nottinghamshire (Trent Bridge) 16–19 September	26-2-102-4 / 24-1-92-2	10-1-43-0 / 17-0-105-3	12.4-1-73-1 / 6-0-37-0									9-2-38-1 / 15-2-75-1			6-1-24-0 / 9-0-48-0	63.4 / 71	301 / 379	21 / 22	6 / 7	

	Danish Kaneria	GR Napier	JD Middlebrook	D Gough	AR Adams	AGAM McCoubrey	AP Cowan	AJ Clarke	SA Brant	JP Stephenson	RN ten Doeschate	AP Palladino	AP Grayson	A Habib	RS Bopara
Overs	563	366.2	394.3	226.4	157.4	126.4	148	131	188.2	64	36.5	34	40.1	7	24
Maidens	123	61	57	52	23	22	39	25	42	9	7	5	2	1	1
Runs	1609	1444	1459	672	561	563	463	444	666	247	117	158	167	18	108
Wickets	63	39	34	30	23	15	13	12	12	8	7	3	0	0	0
Average	25.53	37.02	42.91	22.40	24.39	37.53	35.61	37.00	55.50	30.87	16.71	52.66	–	–	–

FIELDING

44	JS Foster (39 ct, 5 st)
18	A Flower
18	AN Cook
15	WI Jefferson
7	Danish Kaneria
6	GR Napier
5	RS Bopara
4	JD Middlebrook
4	AR Adams
3	A Habib
3	AP Cowan
3	AGAM McCoubrey
2	N Hussain
2	AJ Clarke
1	RC Irani
1	ML Pettini
1	RN ten Doeschate
0	D Gough
0	JP Stephenson
0	AP Grayson
0	AP Palladino
0	SA Brant

GLAMORGAN CCC

FIRST–CLASS MATCHES
BATTING

	DL Hemp	ROB Croft	MA Wallace	DS Harrison	MJ Powell	MTG Elliott	MP Maynard	SD Thomas	J Hughes	AG Wharf	SP Jones	A Dale	DA Cosker	MS Kasprowicz	DD Cherry	ML Lewis	IJ Thomas	AP Davies	Extras	Total	Wickets	Result	Points
v. Derbyshire	0	0	20	37*	29	4	26	0		17		41	0						11	185	10		
(Cardiff) 16-19 April	20		105		94	3	59*					5*							37	323	4	D	7
v. Leicestershire	82	21*	20		55	37	163	5				41							31	455	7		
(Leicester) 21-24 April	9	6	15	0*	3	33	11	9*		12		6	10						11	125	9	D	12
v. Nottinghamshire	82	2	13	32*	53	41	11	13	0	11	2								14	274	10		
(Trent Bridge) 7-10 May	23*		24		2*	12													12	73	2	D	9
v. Essex	55	14	0	0	21	114	64	23		78	0*	44							22	435	10		
(Cardiff) 12-15 May	21	27	14	2	61	11	63	39		35	0	28*							34	335	10	D	12
v. Durham	45	81	26	2	124	37	10	30*		2		15	1						20	393	10		
(The Riverside) 19-21 May	25	6	36	32	38	35	54*	5		20		0							14	265	9	W	21
v. Derbyshire	26	43	87	22	56	77	10	16		29		40	21*						47	474	10		
(Derby) 25-28 May	102*	16	46	24	6	15	17	4*		10		0							19	259	8	W	22
v. Somerset	66	6	22	22	36	157	25		35	0			4*	0					15	388	10		
(Swansea) 2-5 June	57		5	21*	87	31*													11	212	3	W	
v. Leicestershire	26	20	5	42	9	31	114		21	0			1*	42					22	333	10		
(Cardiff) 9-12 June	10	138	19	21	5	42	13		110	51			11*	14*					34	468	9	W	20
v. Durham	37	19	0				17	52*	7	53*						29	29		15	258	7		
(Cardiff) 23-26 June																			-	-	-	D	9
v. Sri Lanka A	10	4	11	3	3	48		16	44				6*				9	1	14	169	10		
(Swansea) 21-24 July	73	37	91	22*	2	53		13	50				8				68	3	31	451	10	L	
v. Hampshire	77	16	23	7	72	54	7		23	0			3*	0					19	301	10		
(Cardiff) 29-31 July	7	1	2	15	10	77*	9		7	0			13	8					20	169	10	L	6
v. Somerset	5	23	0	4	39	103	4	54	5		0*		0						25	262	10		
(Taunton) 3-5 August	3	16	70	5	0	85	25	52	1		2*		14						21	294	10	L	5
v. Hampshire	17	14*	27	0	89	8	5	105*	3			15		18					41	342	10		
(The Rose Bowl) 11-14 August	32	18	9	0	26	34	0		0			4*		20*					7	150	8	D	10
v. Yorkshire																			-	-	-	D	5
(Colwyn Bay) 24-27 August																							
v. Essex	67	125	42	88	31		136	22	11		0*				22	0			43	587	10		
(Chelmsford) 2-5 September	83*	28*	19		10		32	0	24						17				10	223	6	W	21
v. Nottinghamshire																			-	-	-	D	6
(Cardiff) 10-13 September																							
v. Yorkshire	60	31*	25	15	5	125	41	20		20					21			6	41	410	10		
(Headingley) 16-19 September	0*				125		23								18*				14	55	1	D	1
Matches	17	17	17	17	16	15	15	14	11	10	8	7	7	7	3	3	2	2					
Innings	29	25	28	22	27	26	24	19	15	15	7	13	9	11	5	1	3	3					
Not Out	4	4	0	4	2	1	3	5	0	1	4	3	6	2	1	0	0	0					
Highest Score	102*	138	105	88	124	157	163	105*	110	78	20	44	21*	42	29	0	68	6					
Runs	1120	712	776	395	900	1346	906	499	361	307	33	241	68	126	107	0	106	10					
Average	44.80	33.90	27.71	21.94	36.00	53.84	43.14	35.64	24.06	21.92	11.00	24.10	22.66	14.00	26.75	0.00	35.33	3.33					
100s	1	2	1	0	1	4	3	1	1	0	0	0	0	0	0	0	0	0					
50s	10	1	3	1	7	6	4	3	1	3	0	0	0	0	0	0	1	0					
Catches/Stumpings	15/0	2/0	40/3	8/0	14/0	15/0	14/0	8/0	5/0	4/0	2/0	3/0	8/0	2/0	0/0	1/0	2/0	0/0					

Home Ground: Cardiff
Address: Sophia Gardens, Cardiff, CF11 9XR
Tel: 0871 2823401
Fax: 02920 409390
Email: info@glamorgancricket.co.uk
Directions: *By rail:* Cardiff central train station. *By road:* From North, A470 and follow signs to Cardiff until junction with Cardiff bypass then A48 Port Talbot and City Centre. Cathedral Road is situated off A48 for Sophia Gardens.

Capacity: 4,000
Other grounds used: Swansea, Colwyn Bay
Year formed: 1888

Chief Executive: Mike Fatkin
Chairman: Paul Russell
First XI Coach: John Derrick
Captain: Robert Croft
County colours: Navy blue and yellow/gold

Honours
County Championship
1948, 1969, 1997
Sunday League/NCL
1993, 2002, 2004

Website:
www.glamorgancricket.com

GLAMORGAN CCC

FIRST-CLASS MATCHES
BOWLING

	DS Harrison	RDB Croft	SD Thomas	AG Wharf	SP Jones	MS Kasprowicz	DA Cosker	ML Lewis	AP Davies	A Dale	MP Maynard	MTG Elliott	IJ Thomas	Overs	Total	Byes/Leg-byes	Wickets	Run outs
v. Derbyshire (Cardiff) 16–19 April	13-5-31-2		11.4-1-48-3	14-2-43-2		17-6-48-2								55.4	174	4	10	1
	13.4-5-27-1	14-3-40-1	13-2-46-0	19-5-54-2		19-6-62-1				3-1-7-0				83.4	238	2	5	
v. Leicestershire (Leicester) 21–24 April	7-1-24-0	16-4-42-2	15-1-73-2	10-0-63-0		16.5-2-54-5								64.5	264	8	10	1
	23-6-61-2	16.4-4-56-1	20-5-56-2	20-4-77-2		27-5-86-2								106.4	353	15	10	1
v. Nottinghamshire (Trent Bridge) 7–10 May	17-0-64-1	26.1-9-56-2	19-2-82-2	25-7-76-1	25-5-98-4									112.1	384	8	10	
	–													–	–	–	–	
v. Essex (Cardiff) 12–15 May	28-11-99-5	21-1-95-1	19.3-1-85-3	14-0-77-1	22-3-75-0									104.3	437	6	10	
	11-1-63-0	20-2-78-0	11-0-47-4		12-0-44-3									69	325	22	9	
v. Durham (The Riverside) 19–21 May	16-2-75-5	15-3-61-1	8-0-42-1	13-4-31-2			15-0-3-1							53.5	220	8	10	
	10-0-51-1	13-2-48-3	9-0-41-1	17-1-93-5			2-1-1-0							51	237	3	9	
v. Derbyshire (Derby) 25–28 May	25-9-58-3	39.4-12-79-2	23-3-87-1	14-2-57-1			27-3-93-3			1-0-2-0				129.4	392	16	10	
	10-4-23-2	23-10-35-3	9-1-33-0	15.5-3-66-2			26-13-40-3							83.5	213	14	10	
v. Somerset (Swansea) 2–5 June	17-5-48-5	11-2-44-3		10-2-41-0		16.5-1-87-2								54.5	229	9	10	
	20-4-57-1	38.4-12-78-3		16-3-58-3		30-7-101-1	33-13-62-2							137.4	370	14	10	
v. Leicestershire (Cardiff) 9–12 June	18-9-49-3	20-4-70-3			7-0-30-0	22-5-60-1	12.1-3-40-3							79.1	255	6	10	
	11-6-17-3	11-5-20-2			9-1-37-3	16.3-5-43-2	3-0-18-0							50.3	137	2	2	
v. Durham (Cardiff) 23–26 June	27-5-116-3	42-8-128-3	19-4-62-2	18-3-79-0			23.1-1-74-2							129.1	466	7	10	
	–													–	–	–	–	
v. Sri Lanka A (Swansea) 21–24 July	20-3-76-3	21-4-67-1	18.3-0-80-3			22-3-93-2		15-2-48-0						96.3	367	3	10	1
	12-2-43-1	12-2-45-2				14-2-48-0		9-1-25-1				0.3-0-10-0	1-0-6-0	72.3	256	6	6	
v. Hampshire (Cardiff) 29–31 July	20-8-52-2	28-5-68-3		13-1-56-1		24-5-71-2	10-3-41-1							95	298	10	10	
	10-3-37-0	18.1-5-59-0				13-2-49-1					3-0-8-0	1-0-16-0		45.1	173	2	4	
v. Somerset (Taunton) 3–5 August	18-2-62-2	30-8-87-1	18-1-62-1		19.5-1-94-5	21-3-81-1								104.5	394	8	10	
	5-1-27-1	17.4-3-71-1	4-0-25-0		7-2-27-0	4-0-12-0								37.4	164	2	2	
v. Hampshire (The Rose Bowl) 11–14 August	20-4-51-1	25-3-73-3	26.3-1-103-4			31-5-100-1				9-1-33-0				111.3	369	9	10	1
	18-8-58-0	9-0-81-1				14-2-37-0								40	241	14	14	1
v. Yorkshire (Colwyn Bay) 24–27 August	12-5-36-2	10-5-11-0	10-2-34-1		9-1-49-1				7-0-25-1			3-0-8-0		51	158	5	5	
	–													–	–	–	–	
v. Essex (Chelmsford) 2–5 September	25-3-101-2	58-9-203-3	21-3-86-0		25.2-3-100-4				24-3-128-1		1-0-11-0			154.2	642	15	10	
	2-0-7-0	19-1-52-4	4-0-16-0		16-2-50-2				9.1-0-39-4					50.1	165	1	10	
v. Nottinghamshire (Cardiff) 10–13 September	14-7-23-2	23-2-77-2	5-0-23-0		19-3-83-1				13-2-63-0					74	273	4	6	1
	–													–	–	–	–	
v. Yorkshire (Headingley) 16–19 September	17-3-75-0	31-8-93-3	10-0-42-0		24-5-77-5				24-3-95-2					106	401	19	10	
	20.5-2-73-4	34-9-61-3	14.2-3-44-2		26-5-60-1				7.4-1-35-0					102.5	286	13	10	

	DS Harrison	RDB Croft	SD Thomas	AG Wharf	SP Jones	MS Kasprowicz	DA Cosker	ML Lewis	AP Davies	A Dale	MP Maynard	MTG Elliott	IJ Thomas
Overs	480.3	674	320.3	249.5	215.1	272.1	174.1	53.1	55.4	13	7	1.3	1
Maidens	123	146	32	38	31	54	42	5	7	2	0	0	0
Runs	1584	2006	1252	1011	808	893	513	253	203	42	27	26	6
Wickets	57	57	34	27	26	21	17	6	3	0	0	0	0
Average	27.78	35.19	36.82	37.44	31.07	42.52	30.17	42.16	67.66	–	–	–	–

FIELDING

43	MA Wallace (40 ct, 3 st)
15	DL Hemp
15	MTG Elliott
14	MP Maynard
14	MJ Powell
8	SD Thomas
8	DA Cosker
8	DS Harrison
5	J Hughes
4	AG Wharf
3	A Dale
2	RDB Croft
2	MS Kasprowicz
2	SP Jones
2	IJ Thomas
1	ML Lewis
0	AP Davies
0	DD Cherry

GLOUCESTERSHIRE CCC

FIRST-CLASS MATCHES
BATTING

	CM Spearman	WPC Weston	CG Taylor	APR Gidman	J Lewis	SJ Adshead	JMM Averis	ID Fisher	THC Hancock	MGN Windows	MCJ Ball	MEK Hussey	Shabbir Ahmed	Shoaib Malik	MW Alleyne	JEC Franklin	AM Smith	AN Bressington	RJ Sillence	RC Russell	NW Bracken	MA Hardinges	Extras	Total	Wickets	Result	Pots
v. Kent (Bristol) 16-19 April	27	0	96	10					13	11	28*							58*		2			56	301	7		
																							–	–	–	L	3
v. Loughborough UCCE (Bristol) 21-23 April	38	39	33						40	9					22			6*	28*				13	228	6		
																										D	0
v. Warwickshire (Edgbaston) 28 April-1 May	77	122	22	1		56*			44	48					0			19*					11	400	7		
																										D	11
v. Kent (Canterbury) 7-10 May	42	6	32*	4		15*			0					18									10	127	5		
																										D	7
v. Northamptonshire (Bristol) 12-15 May	139	36	18	68	7	14	1		65	31			2*	63									30	474	10		
																										D	12
v. Worcestershire (Worcester) 18-21 May	62	26	7	54	0*	10	2	20	4	1				33									13	232	10		
	0	12	28	77	24*	61	10	11	68	0				3									7	301	10	L	2
v. Surrey (Bristol) 2-4 June	4	135	24	8	30	14			43	58		0*		1	51								38	406	10		
	28	10	0						21	23*					12*								12	106	4	W	22
v. Middlesex (Gloucester) 9-12 June	341	85	100	51	12	35*		6		6				5	0	3*							51	695	9		
	29*	3*																					15	47	0	W	22
v. Surrey (The Oval) 18-21 June	0	19	177	62	0	13	48*	5		6		0		4									34	368	10		
	30	31	9	25	34*	28	0	38		20		10*		0									30	255	9	D	11
v. Sussex (Arundel Castle) 23-25 June	36	81	12	26	8	5		21	33				34*		10		9						25	300	10		
	21*	0							3*														1	25	1	W	20
v. Lancashire (Cheltenham) 21-24 July	9	44	33	1	14	40	10*	1			8	5			34								35	234	10		
	8	65	74	21		57*		31		29*	44						0						37	366	7	D	8
v. Worcestershire (Cheltenham) 28-31 July	8	14	103	70	1	48		45		38		0			77*	9							32	445	10		
	5	30	7	25	0	11		0		5		68			11	8*							19	189	10	L	8
v. Middlesex (Lord's) 3-6 August	16	98	8	1	21	19	28*	28		7		43			44								34	347	10		
	100	7	91	56		37		28		2*		0			39*								40	400	7	D	9
v. Warwickshire (Bristol) 19-22 August	237	30	30	47		32	0*	13				26							92			68*	17	592	8		
																										D	12
v. Northamptonshire (Northampton) 24-27 August	20	2	20	1	29	6	23	17			31*	78							4				9	240	10		
	69	6	2	13		13*						49*											8	160	4	D	8
v. Sussex (Bristol) 9-12 September	12	1	0	22	27*	19	14	17	44			1									8		13	178	10		
	65	13	15	82	0*				77*			37											15	304	5	D	7
v. Lancashire (Old Trafford) 16-19 September	34	19	60	0	52*		5	61	6			46											28	311	8		
	5	27	109	28	8	8		34	1			45									13*		10	289	10	D	10
Matches	17	17	16	16	16	15	13	11	9	9	8	7	6	6	5	3	3	3	2	2	2	1					
Innings	28	28	25	24	15	23	11	17	13	13	10	13	6	9	6	6	2	3	2	2	2	1					
Not Out	2	1	1	0	4	7	4	0	1	2	4	1	4	1	1	2	1	3	0	1	1	1					
Highest Score	341	135	177	82	34*	61	48*	45	77*	58	38	78	34*	63	77*	44	9	58*	92	28*	13*	68*					
Runs	1462	961	1077	778	193	609	150	320	481	249	155	442	51	134	171	134	12	83	96	30	21	68					
Average	56.23	35.59	44.87	32.41	17.54	38.06	21.42	18.82	40.08	22.63	25.83	36.83	25.50	16.75	34.20	33.50	12.00	–	48.00	30.00	21.00	–					
100s	4	2	4	0	0	0	0	0	0	0	0	0	0	0	0	0	0	0	0	0	0	0					
50s	4	4	4	8	0	4	0	0	4	1	0	2	0	1	0	0	1	1	0	0	1						
Catches/Stumpings	15/0	18/0	6/0	13/0	1/0	39/2	2/0	4/0	4/0	4/0	5/0	10/0	1/0	2/0	5/0	1/0	1/0	1/0	0/0	1/0	0/0	3/0					

Home Ground: Bristol
Address: County Ground, Nevil Road, Bristol, BS7 9EJ
Tel: 01179 108000
Fax: 01179 241193
Directions: *By road:* M5, M4, M32 into Bristol, exit at second exit (Fishponds/Horfield), then third exit – Muller Road. Almost at end of Muller Road (bus station on right), turn left at Ralph Road. Go to the top, turn left and then right almost immediately into Kennington Avenue. Follow the signs for County Cricket.

Capacity: 8,000
Other grounds used: Gloucester, Cheltenham College
Year formed: 1870

Chief Executive: Tom Richardson
Chairman: Alan Haines
Director of Cricket: Andy Stovold
First XI Player/Coach: Mark Alleyne
Captains: Chris Taylor (championship), Mark Alleyne (one-day)
County colours: Blue, brown, gold, green and red

Honours
Sunday League/NCL
2000
Benson & Hedges Cup
1977, 1999, 2000
Gillette Cup/NatWest/C&G Trophy
1973, 1999, 2000, 2003, 2004

Website:
www.gloscricket.co.uk

GLOUCESTERSHIRE CCC

FIRST-CLASS MATCHES
BOWLING

Match	J Lewis	JMM Averis	ID Fisher	Shabbir Ahmed	APR Gidman	JEC Franklin	MW Alleyne	MCJ Ball	Shoaib Malik	AM Smith	NW Bracken	RJ Sillence	THC Hancock	WPC Weston	MA Hardinges	AN Bressington	MEK Hussey	CG Taylor	Overs	Total	Byes/Leg-byes	Wickets	Run outs
v. Kent (Bristol) 16–19 April	16.4-4-62-2	19-2-97-0		16-1-62-1			3-0-22-0									6-0-55-0			60.4	302	4	3	
																			–	–	–	–	
v. Loughborough UCCE (Bristol) 21–23 April		14-4-24-2		8-1-28-1		10-3-21-2	14-2-45-1			11.5-10-7-2		6-2-7-2				9-2-45-0			72.5	202	25	10	
																			–	–	–	–	
v. Warwickshire (Edgbaston) 28 April–1 May	12-5-21-3	7-0-40-2			5-0-31-0		3-2-6-0									6-0-38-1			33	139	3	6	
																			–	–	–	–	
v. Kent (Canterbury) 7–10 May	12.3-1-46-5	12-1-39-7		11-2-34-3			1-0-9-0												36.3	129	1	10	
																			–	–	–	–	
v. Northamptonshire (Bristol) 12–15 May	17-7-31-1	19-7-32-6		16.2-3-78-0	8.4-1-35-1				11-3-30-2										72	218	12	10	
	35-13-60-1	28-5-86-0		5-1-27-0	30-10-78-1				45-14-109-3			19-5-41-0	3-1-8-1						165	427	18	7	1
v. Worcestershire (Worcester) 18–21 May	32-10-73-2	33-6-139-0	23.3-0-105-1		24-3-129-1				39-8-118-2			10-1-41-0							161.3	619	14	6	
																			–	–	–	–	
v. Surrey (Bristol) 2–4 June	14-6-43-1	12-2-41-2			18-2-91-2		17.3-4-71-5		10-0-34-0										71.3	298	18	10	
	21-3-72-7	6-0-24-1			15.2-3-48-1		6-2-24-0		10-0-36-1										58.2	213	9	10	
v. Middlesex (Gloucester) 9–12 June	30-10-88-2		19-4-49-0	26.1-7-96-4	6-0-30-1				20-2-49-1	16-3-55-1									117.1	383	16	10	1
	12-3-36-3		32-7-110-4	17.1-4-69-2					30-3-104-1	3-0-11-0									94.1	358	28	10	
v. Surrey (The Oval) 18–21 June	26.4-3-120-2	22-1-124-1		31-2-132-2	30-9-90-3	13-0-75-1			10-0-41-0										132.4	598	16	10	1
																			–	–	–	–	
v. Sussex (Arundel Castle) 23–25 June	13-4-33-5				14-3-33-1		7-2-11-2			9.4-3-20-2									43.4	106	9	10	
	18.5-3-67-3			2-0-23-0	16.4-3-92-1	1-0-8-0	11-3-45-2			14-6-34-3									62.5	218	2	10	
v. Lancashire (Cheltenham) 21–24 July	24-4-66-0	14-1-62-0	19-1-78-1		7-1-27-0	22.1-7-60-7	25-3-70-1												111.1	375	12	10	1
	14-3-71-0	9-3-51-1	15-0-68-0			10-4-39-0	18-1-109-1												66	354	16	2	
v. Worcestershire (Cheltenham) 28–31 July	18.5-6-38-5		9-0-32-0		8-1-50-2	17-5-58-1	8-3-23-0	19-3-62-2											79.5	274	11	10	
	19-3-72-0		19.1-1-100-2		2-0-14-0	16-4-53-1	4-0-26-0	32-2-83-2											92.1	363	5	5	
v. Middlesex (Lord's) 3–6 August	21.5-9-48-3	16-3-40-1	14-2-32-0		7-1-33-0	18-7-42-3		17-1-43-0									1-0-2-0		94.5	253	13	8	1
																			–	–	–	–	
v. Warwickshire (Bristol) 19–22 August	23-7-59-3	18-3-89-1	20-5-42-3		5-1-21-0							14-4-50-2			17-2-78-1		1-0-1-0	1-0-2-0	97	350	11	10	
	27-6-89-3	15-4-57-1	36-20-50-2		12-4-26-1							17-8-33-1			13-2-42-0				122	308	8	8	
v. Northamptonshire (Northampton) 24–27 August	23.2-6-84-3	13-7-25-3	31-11-63-3		22-1-5-0		10-3-15-0					14-4-33-1					2-1-6-0		95.4	222	11	10	
	12-0-62-1	18-1-84-0	16-2-55-0		11-3-33-0		12-2-40-1					7-3-19-1							76	307	14	3	
v. Sussex (Bristol) 9–12 September	18-4-81-1	10.2-1-45-5			7-2-12-2						17-6-58-2								52.1	199	3	10	
																			–	–	–	–	
v. Lancashire (Old Trafford) 16–19 September	11-1-38-1			29-6-114-5	3-2-10-0			28-8-96-3			15-4-36-1								86	311	17	10	
				5-0-20-0	5-1-16-1			5-0-14-0			7-2-12-2	2-0-16-0	1-1-0-0				4-1-13-0		29	99	8	3	

	J Lewis	JMM Averis	ID Fisher	Shabbir Ahmed	APR Gidman	JEC Franklin	MW Alleyne	MCJ Ball	Shoaib Malik	AM Smith	NW Bracken	RJ Sillence	THC Hancock	WPC Weston	MA Hardinges	AN Bressington	MEK Hussey	CG Taylor
Overs	472.4	285.2	320.4	169	181	83.1	66.3	183	176	54.3	39	52	37	4	30	21	8	1
Maidens	121	51	61	38	33	27	19	25	30	22	12	19	8	2	4	2	2	0
Runs	1440	1099	1073	605	723	252	227	609	530	127	106	135	105	8	120	138	22	2
Wickets	57	28	23	18	13	12	11	11	10	8	5	5	2	1	1	1	0	0
Average	25.26	39.25	46.65	33.61	55.61	21.00	20.63	55.36	53.00	15.87	21.20	27.00	52.50	8.00	120.00	138.00	–	–

FIELDING

41	SJ Adshead (39 ct, 2 st)
18	WPC Weston
15	CM Spearman
13	APR Gidman
10	MEK Hussey
6	CG Taylor
5	MW Alleyne
5	MCJ Ball
4	THC Hancock
4	MGN Windows
4	ID Fisher
3	MA Hardinges
2	JMM Averis
2	Shoaib Malik
1	RC Russell
1	AM Smith
1	J Lewis
1	AN Bressington
1	Shabbir Ahmed
1	JEC Franklin
0	RJ Sillence
0	NW Bracken

HAMPSHIRE CCC

FIRST–CLASS MATCHES
BATTING

	N Pothas	MJ Brown	AD Mascarenhas	DA Kenway	JP Crawley	SD Udal	MJ Clarke	SK Warne	BV Taylor	CT Tremlett	AD Mullally	JHK Adams	WS Kendall	LR Prittipaul	SM Katich	JTA Bruce	SR Watson	GA Lamb	CC Benham	JA Tomlinson	Extras	Total	Wickets	Result	Points
v. Durham (The Rose Bowl) 16-19 April	10	28	3	35	35		75	3	5	8*	5	0									14	221	10		
	11	0	33*	9	0		0	9	10			31*									9	112	7	W	18
v. Leicestershire (The Rose Bowl) 28 April-1 May	21	102*	2	23			0	29*				38	31								22	268	6		
																					-	-		W	19
v. Derbyshire (The Rose Bowl) 7-10 May	131*	1	46	101	27		21	4		12		25	40								11	419	9		
	22*	1	15	33			45	10*				19	25								8	178	6	D	12
v. Yorkshire (Headingley) 12-14 May	100	13	49	4	21		11		12	13	1*	50	12								36	322	10		
	77	20	25	20		52	6		7	35	22*	0	17								32	313	10	W	20
v. Nottinghamshire (The Rose Bowl) 2-3 June	26	20	9	21	25	36	28	14	11	5*		0									4	199	10		
	3	10	18	23	7	8*	7	8	3	0		21									5	113	10	L	3
v. Essex (Chelmsford) 9-11 June	57	0	32	25	97	43*	69	0	2	0		19									9	353	10		
	12	29	0	27	0	8	8	34	22	0*		2									12	154	10	W	21
v. Somerset (The Rose Bowl) 18-21 June	16	81	6	7	3	50	18		4*	57		13					24				11	290	10		
	6	23	9	31	40	74	1		0	0*		5					112*				33	334	9	W	21
v. Yorkshire (The Rose Bowl) 23-26 June	45	1	22	12	53	41	27			0*		15									43	259	8		
																					-	-		D	9
v. Nottinghamshire (Trent Bridge) 23-26 July	56*	74	0		301*		140					36									34	641	4		
		30	41*	28	23*		103	27			0	16									27	295	6	D	11
v. Glamorgan (Cardiff) 29-31 July	18	6	2	5	18	3	109	29			0*	75		9							24	298	10		
		57			45*							65*									6	173	1	W	19
v. Essex (The Rose Bowl) 3-5 August	0	13	0	21	55		18	21	4*	15		21				1					8	177	10		
	12	0	0	5	24		18	0	40	19*		23				0					8	149	10	L	3
v. Glamorgan (The Rose Bowl) 11-14 August	26	90	34	64	47	40	5	42	2*		0	6									13	369	10		
		109*			70*							42									20	241	1	D	11
v. Somerset (Taunton) 18-21 August	5	17	1	37	34			47	14			31		44	38	0*					33	301	10		
		5										21*		21*	49						3	99	2	W	17
v. Durham (The Riverside) 24-27 August	54	0	104	0	1	0		41	17*			16		27	0						20	280	10		
																					-	-		D	9
v. Leicestershire (Leicester) 1-4 September	107	0	0	4	22		57	8*	48			16		9	30						20	321	10		
	7	51	4	61	39		42	4*	16			20		4	66						15	329	10	W	20
v. Derbyshire (Derby) 16-19 September	12	57	22	18	1				0			27		22				94	74	12*	57	396	10		
												10*						7*			2	19	0	W	18

	N Pothas	MJ Brown	AD Mascarenhas	DA Kenway	JP Crawley	SD Udal	MJ Clarke	SK Warne	BV Taylor	CT Tremlett	AD Mullally	JHK Adams	WS Kendall	LR Prittipaul	SM Katich	JTA Bruce	SR Watson	GA Lamb	CC Benham	JA Tomlinson
Matches	16	16	16	14	13	13	12	12	11	10	10	8	8	5	4	4	1	1	1	1
Innings	24	28	24	23	21	17	20	16	16	15	10	15	14	9	5	5	2	2	1	1
Not Out	3	2	2	1	3	3	0	2	6	4	5	3	1	0	0	1	1	1	0	1
High Score	131*	109*	104	101	301*	74	140	57	40	57	22*	75	50	49	66	9	112*	94	74	12*
Runs	834	838	477	552	938	488	709	381	177	213	67	425	238	231	183	10	136	101	74	12
Average	39.71	32.23	21.68	25.09	52.11	34.85	35.45	27.21	17.70	19.36	13.40	35.41	18.30	25.66	36.60	2.50	136.00	101.00	74.00	-
100s	3	2	1	1	1	0	3	0	0	0	0	0	0	0	0	0	1	0	0	0
50s	4	6	0	1	5	3	2	1	0	1	0	2	1	0	1	0	0	1	1	0
Catches/Stumpings	45/5	12/0	8/0	9/0	4/0	8/0	20/0	9/0	3/0	2/0	1/0	1/0	7/0	3/0	3/0	1/0	0/0	0/0	0/0	1/0

Home Ground: Southampton
Address: The Rose Bowl, Botley Road, West End, Southampton, SO30 3XH
Tel: 02380 472002
Fax: 02380 472122
Email: enquiries@rosebowlplc.com
Directions: From the North: M3 Southbound to junction 14, follow signs for M27 Eastbound (Fareham and Portsmouth). At junction 7 of M27, filter left onto Charles Watts Way (A334) and from there follow the brown road signs to The Rose Bowl. From the South: M27 to junction 7 and follow the brown road signs to The Rose Bowl.

Capacity: 9,950
Year formed: 1863

Chief Executive: Roger Bransgrove
Director of Cricket: Tim Tremlett
Captain: Shane Warne
County colours: Navy blue, old gold

Honours
County Championship
1961, 1973
Sunday League/NCL
1975, 1978, 1986
Benson & Hedges Cup
1988, 1992
Gillette Cup/NatWest/C&G Trophy
1991

Website:
www.hampshirecricket.com

HAMPSHIRE CCC

FIRST-CLASS MATCHES

BOWLING

	AD Mascarenhas	SK Warne	CT Tremlett	SD Udal	BV Taylor	AD Mullally	JTA Bruce	WS Kendall	JHK Adams	JA Tomlinson	LR Prittipaul	MJ Clarke	JP Crawley	DA Kenway	SM Katich	SR Watson	GA Lamb	Overs	Total	Byes/Leg-byes	Wickets	Run outs
Durham (The Rose Bowl) 16-19 April	12-5-28-3 / 17-10-13-1	8.3-1-27-2 / 29-8-68-5	11-6-10-2 / 16-3-42-2	10-5-23-2 / 7-2-14-0	12-3-26-1 / 10-4-32-2							1-0-6-0 / 6-1-24-0						54.3 / 85	128 / 201	8 / 7	10 / 10	
Leicestershire (The Rose Bowl) 28 April-1 May	15-9-22-3 / 10-5-22-5	12-6-17-2 / 11-4-26-2	14-5-33-2 / 9-1-35-1	12-3-39-1 / 2.4-2-4-2		11-4-22-2 / 11-4-18-0												64 / 43.4	139 / 111	6 / 6	10 / 10	
Derbyshire (The Rose Bowl) 7-10 May	10-4-25-1 / 17-9-25-6	26-8-75-1 / 14-7-18-1	16-4-49-3 / 11-3-23-2	23-2-78-3 / 3-0-6-0		20-4-58-1 / 6-2-14-0					5-0-14-1 / 2-0-11-0	7-2-11-0						107 / 53	324 / 102	14 / 5	10 / 9	
Yorkshire (Headingley) 12-14 May	19-3-85-1 / 13.5-2-44-5		21-3-77-3 / 15-3-56-2	4.4-1-8-3	14-4-46-2 / 13-2-50-3	19-4-71-1 / 14-3-47-0					2-0-7-0	1-0-5-0						80.4 / 55.5	316 / 200	17 / 3	10 / 10	
Nottinghamshire (The Rose Bowl) 2-3 June	20-8-55-1	21-3-85-2	22.2-3-102-4	14-3-57-2		15-7-29-0	2-0-12-1				1-0-6-0							95.2	356	10	10	
Essex (Chelmsford) 9-11 June	6-3-12-2 / 8-3-17-1	14-6-40-2 / 4-0-20-0	16.5-6-29-4 / 11-1-54-0	10-2-32-1 / 13.4-1-55-4	16-3-39-1 / 19-4-73-5													62.5 / 55.4	158 / 235	6 / 16	10 / 10	
Somerset (The Rose Bowl) 18-21 June	10.3-1-45-3		18-6-44-2 / 11.1-1-43-3	6.5-1-17-2 / 6-0-37-1	15.2-3-62-1 / 15-2-38-3				8-2-20-1			1-0-1-0				8.4-2-28-0		60.2 / 40.1	203 / 146	6 / 8	8 / 8	
Yorkshire (The Rose Bowl) 23-26 June	22-6-71-0		23-5-93-1	21-2-78-2	25-8-56-1	31.4-13-68-6		2-0-12-0				2-0-7-0						126.4	395	10	10	
Nottinghamshire (Trent Bridge) 23-26 July	28-7-81-1	39-5-133-2		22.2-1-93-1	33-4-159-3	24-3-83-2						9-2-24-0	4-1-24-0					159.2	612	15	10	1
Glamorgan (Cardiff) 29-31 July	18-5-69-2 / 25-8-53-3	27-5-77-3 / 27.5-6-65-6		13.5-2-46-2 / 2-0-7-0					13-3-45-1	15-2-62-2 / 9-1-27-1		2-2-0-0						88.5 / 69.5	301 / 169	2 / 3	10 / 10	
Essex (The Rose Bowl) 3-5 August	3-1-5-0 / 17-5-33-1	32-1-118-4 / 17-2-53-1			23-3-111-2 / 12-0-56-1	20-6-72-1 / 14-4-36-1	19-3-74-3 / 13-1-62-2					6-1-24-0 / 8.1-0-52-1						103 / 79.1	416 / 294	12 / 2	10 / 7	
Glamorgan (The Rose Bowl) 11-14 August	24-6-64-5 / 14-4-44-1	22-1-87-0 / 18.5-12-26-4		8.5-1-48-1 / 16-6-39-3	21-5-64-3 / 7-0-24-0	16-3-64-0 / 3-0-16-0												91.5 / 58.5	342 / 150	15 / 1	9 / 8	
Somerset (Taunton) 18-21 August	17-4-46-1	30.4-1-127-6			4-2-7-1 / 15-2-55-0	5-0-13-0 / 16-3-77-0		5-2-6-0			4-2-13-0 / 2-1-9-0			2-2-0-0	6-0-11-0 / 3-0-21-0			26 / 83.4	50 / 340	0 / 5	1 / 10	3
Durham (The Riverside) 24-27 August	21-5-48-3 / 9-4-21-2	21-9-53-3 / 7-1-23-1	8.1-0-27-2	6-1-26-0	8-4-16-2 / 2-0-10-0	6-1-13-0 / 5-0-27-1												76.1 / 29	217 / 109	12 / 2	10 / 4	
Leicestershire (Leicester) 1-4 September	19-7-40-2 / 14-5-38-1	12-0-31-1 / 18-3-62-3	14-3-49-0 / 14-1-44-2	13.5-3-44-2 / 12-0-51-1	15-2-55-2 / 13.5-2-53-3				2-0-15-0			6-1-17-0			9-1-29-0			88.5 / 75.5	282 / 282	17 / 19	10 / 10	
Derbyshire (Derby) 16-19 September	6-1-18-0 / 9-2-22-2		9-1-24-1 / 16-1-60-2	7-2-14-0 / 26.5-8-79-6			2-0-14-0			8-4-9-1 / 12-3-34-0							3-2-1-0 / 2-0-14-0	35 / 65.5	95 / 229	5 / 20	2 / 10	

	AD Mascarenhas	SK Warne	CT Tremlett	SD Udal	BV Taylor	AD Mullally	JTA Bruce	WS Kendall	JHK Adams	JA Tomlinson	LR Prittipaul	MJ Clarke	JP Crawley	DA Kenway	SM Katich	SR Watson	GA Lamb
Overs	404.2	411.5	268.2	247.4	298.1	245.4	88	12	19	20	21	42.1	4	2	18	8.4	5
Maidens	132	88	56	40	59	69	11	2	6	7	4	8	1	2	1	2	2
Runs	1046	1231	867	869	1039	711	375	44	61	43	71	160	24	0	61	28	15
Wickets	56	51	39	39	33	18	9	2	2	1	1	1	0	0	0	0	0
Average	18.67	24.13	22.23	22.28	31.48	39.50	41.66	22.00	30.50	43.00	71.00	160.00	-	-	-	-	-

FIELDING

- 50 N Pothas (45 ct, 5 st)
- 20 MJ Clarke
- 12 MJ Brown
- 9 SK Warne
- 8 DA Kenway
- 8 SD Udal
- 8 AD Mascarenhas
- 7 WS Kendall
- 4 JP Crawley
- 3 LR Prittipaul
- 3 BV Taylor
- 3 SM Katich
- 2 CT Tremlett
- 1 AD Mullally
- 1 JHK Adams
- 1 JA Tomlinson
- 1 JTA Bruce
- 0 CC Benham
- 0 SR Watson
- 0 GA Lamb

KENT CCC

FIRST–CLASS MATCHES
BATTING

Match	ET Smith	MJ Walker	DP Fulton	NJ O'Brien	MA Carberry	MM Patel	RWT Key	AGR Loudon	A Khan	A Sheriyar	JC Tredwell	MJ Dennington	RH Joseph	MJ Saggers	DA Stiff	A Symonds	IG Butler	Mohammad Sami	BJ Trott	GO Jones	MG Bevan	SMJ Cusden	RS Ferley	JL Denly	Extras	Total	Wickets	Result	Points
v. Gloucestershire (Bristol) 16-19 April	36	30	10		104*	118*																			4	302	3	W	16
v. Worcestershire (Canterbury) 21-24 April	0	70	107	10	13	1	5				51*			1	4	0									27	289	10	W	
	6	151*	16		112		46							64				20*							14	429	5	W	19
v. Oxford UCCE (The Parks) 28-30 April	0*			9*																				0	0	9	1	D	0
v. Gloucestershire (Canterbury) 7-10 May	9	21	18	4	11				0*		14			3		33	0	1							15	129	10	D	
																									–	–	–	D	5
v. New Zealand (Canterbury) 13-16 May	7	32	9		75	44	114	16	4*					3*						101	1				26	432	9		
	1*		67			117*																			4	189	1	W	0
v. Northamptonshire (Northampton) 19-22 May	35	8	6	32*	22	10	16		11					5		107	0	0							2	254	10		
	1	21	109	8*	11		173							61											21	405	6	W	19
v. Surrey (The Oval) 25-28 May	25	20	30	15	17		86	9*			11		1	5											20	239	10		
	23	0	13	21	61		199	22*			12		0				29	4							29	413	10	L	4
v. Lancashire (Tunbridge Wells) 2-5 June	116	72	42	0	85	25	180				5*				18	33	0								39	615	10		
	21*	4*	14				44									4									4	91	3	W	22
v. Worcestershire (Worcester) 9-12 June	1	62		67	8	29	59	5	47							103	0					2*			37	420	10		
	35	14		20*	64	10	12	0*	45							9	12					0			23	244	9	D	12
v. Warwickshire (Beckenham) 23-26 June	2	21	15	13	13	24	9		0							156*	18	0							26	297	10		
			5*		14*																				4	23	0	D	7
v. Sussex (Hove) 23-26 July	79	17	122	6	29	2	14	0	12	17						16*									16	330	10		
	4	62	47	11	3	2	34	27	5*	12						17									19	243	10	L	5
v. Middlesex (Southgate) 28-31 July	63	50*	8	12	0	28	4				0					1	8			9					9	192	10		
	9	28	121	67*	1	14	44				10					14	0				66				36	410	10	L	4
v. Sussex (Canterbury) 3-6 August	166	157	4	30		26	55	29			0		7					0				12*			41	527	10		
	93	100*	13	20			50				0		6							8		3*			26	319	7	W	22
v. Warwickshire (Edgbaston) 11-14 August	95	1	100	69	0			92	16				19*							2	4		0		22	420	10	D	12
v. Surrey (Canterbury) 18-21 August	0	2	57	20	10		18	3			2*						68			7			29		10	226	10		
	0	57	42	5	2		18	50*									48*			0			0		12	234	8	D	7
v. Lancashire (Old Trafford) 24-27 August	0	61	18	19	17	52	45	0			15		7*				19								13	266	10		
	35*	0		18	34																				5	92	3	D	9
v. Northamptonshire (Canterbury) 3-6 September	70	63	57	10*	1		131	60	3		1*	0						5*							13	414	10		
	156	34	39	9*	17		51																		12	318	5	W	21
v. Middlesex (Canterbury) 16-18 September	189	108	17	2	5		131	8					26	5				0		4*					40	535	10	W	22

	ET Smith	MJ Walker	DP Fulton	NJ O'Brien	MA Carberry	MM Patel	RWT Key	AGR Loudon	A Khan	A Sheriyar	JC Tredwell	MJ Dennington	RH Joseph	MJ Saggers	DA Stiff	A Symonds	IG Butler	Mohammad Sami	BJ Trott	GO Jones	MG Bevan	SMJ Cusden	RS Ferley	JL Denly
Matches	18	17	16	14	12	12	11	11	9	8	7	7	7	6	6	5	5	5	5	4	4	4	4	1
Innings	30	27	28	19	19	17	19	17	9	8	7	9	9	7	4	8	8	6	7	4	7	6	5	1
Not Out	4	4	1	4	4	1	2	0	2	0	2	5	1	2	3	0	1	1	2	0	1	1	0	4
Highest Score	189	157	122	69	112	44	199	92	29	12	51*	50*	26	64	18	156*	68	29	12	101	66	12*	29	0
Runs	1277	1266	1106	439	639	230	1505	597	107	36	197	108	77	74	30	506	185	52	28	122	90	22	34	0
Average	49.11	55.04	40.96	29.26	42.60	14.37	88.52	35.11	15.28	12.00	32.83	15.42	12.83	10.57	10.00	72.28	30.83	8.66	4.66	40.66	12.85	11.00	6.80	0.00
100s	4	4	5	0	2	0	8	0	0	0	0	0	0	0	0	3	0	0	0	1	0	0	0	0
50s	5	8	3	3	4	0	2	6	0	0	1	1	0	1	0	1	1	0	0	1	0	0	0	0
Catches/Stumpings	6/0	17/0	21/0	33/5	5/0	1/0	4/0	6/0	0/0	0/0	7/0	2/0	3/0	4/0	1/0	6/0	2/0	1/0	1/0	7/1	2/0	2/0	1/0	0/0

Home Ground: Canterbury
Address: St Lawrence Ground, Old Dover Road, Canterbury, CT1 3NZ
Tel: 01227 456886
Fax: 01227 762168
Email: jon.fordham.kent@ecb.co.uk
Directions: From the North, from M20 junction 7 turn left onto A249. At M2 junction 5 (Sittingbourne) bear right onto M2. At junction 7 (Boughton Street) turn right on to A2. Follow this to junction with A2050, turn left. Follow yellow signs to cricket ground. From the South, from M20 junction 13 bear right onto A20. Follow this road to junction with A260. Bear left and continue to junction with A2 (north). Continue to junction with A2050 and then proceed as north.
Capacity: 10,000
Other grounds used: Beckenham, Maidstone, Tunbridge Wells
Year formed: 1870

Chief Executive: Paul Millman
First XI Coach: Simon Willis
Captain: David Fulton
County colours: Red, yellow and black

Honours
County Championship
1906, 1909, 1910, 1913, 1970, 1978
Joint Champions 1977
Sunday League/NCL
1972, 1973, 1976, 1995, 2001
Benson & Hedges Cup
1973, 1978
Gillette Cup/NatWest/C&G Trophy
1967, 1974

Website:
www.kentccc.com

KENT CCC

FIRST-CLASS MATCHES
BOWLING

Match	MM Patel	AGR Loudon	A Khan	RH Joseph	A Sheriyar	MJ Saggers	A Symonds	Mohammad Sami	SMJ Cusden	IG Butler	BJ Trott	MJ Dennington	DA Stiff	MJ Walker	RS Ferley	JC Tredwell	MA Carberry	MG Bevan	Overs	Total	Byes/Leg-byes	Wickets	Run outs
Gloucestershire (Bristol) 16–19 April			12-0-63-2	13-2-60-0	17.5-7-43-4								8-1-24-0	5-0-36-1		10-1-34-0	3-0-21-0		68.5	301	20	7	
																			–	–	–	–	
Worcestershire (Canterbury) 21–24 April		20-2-100-2			22.3-1-94-5	26-9-70-1							17-3-68-1			16-2-51-1			101.3	401	18	10	
		8-1-42-0			10-1-49-1	10-3-32-0							9-2-46-0			15-1-83-0	8-0-56-1		60	316	8	2	
Oxford UCCE (The Parks) 28–30 April																			–	–	–	–	
																			–	–	–	–	
Gloucestershire (Canterbury) 7–10 May					8-0-41-1	10.5-2-30-3	6-1-24-1	9-1-22-0								1-0-2-0			34.5	127	8	5	
																			–	–	–	–	
New Zealand (Canterbury) 13–16 May	22.3-3-56-5	28-7-106-2			28-8-94-0								20-2-88-3	16-3-48-0					114.3	409	17	10	
	13-1-55-1	11-2-50-4			15-2-45-2								6-1-32-1	7.4-1-23-2					52.4	211	6	10	
Northamptonshire (Northampton) 19–22 May	28-6-81-3					15-4-34-1	13.5-3-44-2	22-6-39-4								14-1-44-0			92.5	250	8	10	
	26-8-50-3					14-6-18-1	9-3-20-0	31-11-99-6								20-6-55-0			100	264	22	10	
Surrey (The Oval) 25–28 May		27-3-102-2				31.1-6-111-3			24-6-75-2		21-5-71-0					24-2-107-3			127.1	479	13	10	
		23-0-20-0				4-1-9-1			3-0-24-0		6-0-21-0					7-0-24-1	12-0-67-1		34.3	174	9	3	
Lancashire (Tunbridge Wells) 2–5 June				15-4-57-2					23-8-51-3	18-3-117-2			9-1-58-2	2-0-11-0					67	307	13	10	
	32-8-77-2			20-3-72-3					54.2-13-140-5	8-2-39-0			8-0-54-0						120.4	395	13	10	
Worcestershire (Worcester) 9–12 June		1-0-1-0			31-7-106-3		27-8-114-3				26-5-91-2	29-4-78-1				13.2-3-54-1			127.2	453	9	10	
		4-0-26-0			10-2-34-0						15-2-63-0	24-1-109-4			15-5-57-1	16.5-2-84-1	4-0-13-0		88.5	405	19	6	
Warwickshire (Beckenham) 23–26 June	33-8-103-3	17-1-88-0					24-5-63-1	8-3-26-0	25-3-111-0			32-7-102-2							139	502	9	6	
																			–	–	–	–	
Sussex (Hove) 23–26 July	39.4-6-138-5	17-4-48-1	20-3-94-1		27-3-120-1						24-2-100-1			3-0-5-0		18-0-88-0			148.4	618	25	10	1
																			–	–	–	–	
Middlesex (Southgate) 28–31 July	32-8-106-2	17.3-3-53-5		20-3-55-1						15-1-62-1	15-2-67-1								99.3	351	8	10	
	33.2-3-94-4	24-4-88-0		11-1-50-2						14-1-68-1	10-1-34-0							3-0-16-0	95.2	370	20	8	1
Sussex (Canterbury) 3–6 August	11-1-44-2	12-2-56-1	9-0-47-1	13.2-1-70-3						10-1-61-0			14-3-48-3						69.2	332	6	10	
	35-9-75-4	20-5-60-3		13-6-38-1						9-1-45-1			12-2-41-1						89	278	19	10	
Warwickshire (Edgbaston) 11–14 August	23.2-5-57-2	9-2-31-1		18-4-83-1							24-3-114-4	13-0-67-1	15-1-60-1		7-0-21-0			3-0-9-0	112.2	457	15	10	
		12-2-30-2		6-0-24-0							4-0-21-0	6-3-13-0	5-0-29-0		3-1-5-0				36	123	1	2	
Surrey (Canterbury) 18–21 August	30-2-96-3	16-1-47-0		16-2-76-1							14-2-71-1		18-2-88-3			4-0-14-0			98	402	10	8	
																			–	–	–	–	
Lancashire (Old Trafford) 24–27 August	20-4-51-3	3-3-0-0	6-1-32-0	15-1-70-3							6.3-2-10-3		2-0-10-1						52.3	184	11	10	
																			–	–	–	–	
Northamptonshire (Canterbury) 3–6 September	5.1-1-21-1		11-3-47-4	13-6-38-2					8-3-18-2					7-2-24-1					44.1	151	3	10	
	33-8-102-1	18-3-47-1	16-2-53-2	22-4-71-2					15.3-3-68-4					7-0-24-0					111.3	387	22	10	
Middlesex (Canterbury) 16–18 September	9-3-22-0	7-1-31-1		11-2-47-3						12-1-37-3			14-4-37-1		9-2-31-0	10-2-21-2			72	235	9	10	
	31-5-89-3	14.5-1-47-6		7-1-26-0						5-1-21-1			10-1-31-0		2-1-18-0				69.5	251	19	10	
Overs	457	192.2	170.3	165.2	199.3	152.5	139.3	140	100.3	101.3	153	93	88	66	51.4	124.1	27	6					
Maidens	89	32	24	31	33	43	39	32	17	11	23	13	13	10	6	16	0	0					
Runs	1317	653	756	648	772	410	419	526	404	446	538	368	419	228	192	495	157	25					
Wickets	47	21	20	19	18	15	14	14	13	11	10	9	7	6	5	3	2	0					
Average	28.02	31.09	37.80	34.10	42.88	27.33	29.92	37.57	31.07	40.54	53.80	40.88	59.85	38.00	38.40	165.00	78.50	–					

FIELDING

NJ O'Brien (33 ct, 5 st)
DP Fulton
MJ Walker
GO Jones (7 ct, 1 st)
JC Tredwell
A Symonds
ET Smith
AGR Loudon
MA Carberry
MJ Saggers
RWT Key
RH Joseph
MG Bevan
MJ Dennington
IG Butler
SMJ Cusden
MM Patel
BJ Trott
RS Ferley
Mohammad Sami
DA Stiff
A Sheriyar
A Khan
JL Denly

LANCASHIRE CCC

FIRST-CLASS MATCHES
BATTING

	MJ Chilton	G Keedy	MB Love	G Chapple	IJ Sutcliffe	DG Cork	CL Hooper	SG Law	WK Hegg	SI Mahmood	D Mongia	PJ Martin	AJ Swann	SP Crook	KW Hogg	JJ Haynes	JM Anderson	CP Schofield	J Wood	AR Crook	PJ Horton	OJ Newby	Extras	Total	Wickets	Result	Points
v. Northamptonshire (Northampton) 16-19 April	46		55		104	19	115	108	45			2*	0		0								10	504	9	D	12
v. Sussex (Hove) 21-23 April	5	0	15	10	45	0	34	171*	0	9		0											46	335	10		
	10*				14*																		0	24	0	W	20
v. Middlesex (Lord's) 7-10 May	2	1*	101	32	21	0	0	33	36	5													4	236	10		
	103	60	17	38	4	33*	91	12*					12										31	401	7	D	8
v. Worcestershire (Old Trafford) 12-14 May	28	7	59*	21	9	15	1	8	15			0						0					24	187	10		
	12	1	20	38	95	1	100	0	21*			2						3					12	305	10	W	12
v. Middlesex (Old Trafford) 25-28 May	93	3*	98	1	59		4	49	34	0			34					1					41	417	10	D	10
v. Kent (Tunbridge Wells) 2-5 June	37	4	1	28	50	35*		17	24				19	37	4								51	307	10		
	25	3*	34	102	10	1		48	44				6	68	20								34	395	10	L	4
v. Sussex (Old Trafford) 9-11 June	9	14*	0	21	7	9		25	3	94				6	9								17	214	10		
	21	5	24	27	31	55		42	11	24				27			2*						28	297	10	L	4
v. Warwickshire (Stratford) 18-21 June	13	0	184					44	54		89	2	20		23				13*		22		44	508	10	D	12
v. Northamptonshire (Liverpool) 26-29 June	35	5	10	48	74			3	30		18		20						35			0*	6	284	10	D	12
v. Gloucestershire (Cheltenham) 21-24 July	69	1*	90	0	10	0	19		0		111	20				24							31	375	10		
	124*		69		61						76*												24	354	2	D	11
v. Warwickshire (Old Trafford) 28-31 July	19	0	44*	112	72	23	16			3*	15						0	99					9	412	10		
	20		5*	5			11				108*						0	40					5	194	4	D	12
v. Surrey (Whitgift School) 11-13 August	2	0*		36	0	2	32			15	12			23		2		69					17	210	10		
	0	4*		5	17	109	51			31	0			12		22		2					7	260	10	L	4
v. Kent (Old Trafford) 24-27 August	26	2	4	18	5	28	0			10	41	33*					0						17	184	10	D	7
v. Surrey (Old Trafford) 2-4 September	6	4	54	67	6	0	0	34	18	11*								65					13	278	10		
	21	17	1	8	11	3	10	24	17*	4								4					9	129	10	L	5
v. Worcestershire (Worcester) 9-12 September	3	10*	17	50	51	8	8	159	43	24*										27			3	403	9		
	30		63		29		75*	0												24			21	242	6	D	12
v. Gloucestershire (Old Trafford) 16-19 September	47	9	4	10	28	77*	77	11	5	3										17			23	311	10		
	3		45*	0		43*														0			8	99	3	D	9

	MJ Chilton	G Keedy	MB Love	G Chapple	IJ Sutcliffe	DG Cork	CL Hooper	SG Law	WK Hegg	SI Mahmood	D Mongia	PJ Martin	AJ Swann	SP Crook	KW Hogg	JJ Haynes	JM Anderson	CP Schofield	J Wood	AR Crook	PJ Horton	OJ Newby
Matches	16	16	14	14	14	14	13	12	12	11	6	6	5	4	4	4	4	3	2	2	1	1
Innings	27	20	22	22	24	20	21	18	17	14	9	7	7	5	7	5	4	6	2	4	1	1
Not Out	2	8	3	1	1	2	3	1	3	3	2	2	0	0	0	0	1	0	1	0	0	1
Highest Score	124*	17	184	112	104	109	115	171*	54	94	111	33*	34	68	23	24	3	99	35	27	22	0*
Runs	809	90	934	726	788	437	693	867	412	233	470	59	112	157	72	48	6	279	48	68	22	0
Average	32.36	7.50	49.15	34.57	34.26	24.27	38.50	51.00	29.42	21.18	67.14	11.80	16.00	31.40	10.28	9.60	2.00	46.50	48.00	17.00	22.00	–
100s	2	0	2	2	1	1	2	3	0	0	2	0	0	0	0	0	0	0	0	0	0	0
50s	2	0	6	4	6	2	4	1	1	1	2	0	0	1	0	0	0	3	0	0	0	0
Catches/Stumpings	9/0	7/0	8/0	3/0	5/0	17/0	19/0	17/0	23/5	2/0	2/0	2/0	2/0	1/0	0/0	12/2	1/0	0/0	1/0	0/0	0/0	0/0

Home Ground: Old Trafford
Address: Old Trafford, Manchester, M16 0PX
Tel: 0870 0625000
Fax: 0161 2824100
Email: enquiries@lccc.co.uk
Directions: *By rail,* Manchester Piccadilly or Victoria then Metro link to Old Trafford. *By road:* M63, Stretford slip-road (junction 7) on to A56; follow signs.
Capacity: 21,500
Other grounds used: Blackpool, Liverpool
Year formed: 1864

Chairman: Jack Simmons
Chief Executive: Jim Cumbes
First XI Coach: Mike Watkinson
Captain: Warren Hegg
County colours: Red and white

Website:
www.lccc.co.uk

Honours
County Championship
1881, 1897, 1904, 1926, 1927, 1928, 1930, 1934. Joint champions 1879, 1882, 1889, 1950
Sunday League/NCL
1970, 1989, 1998, 1999
Benson & Hedges Cup
1984, 1990, 1995, 1996
Gillette Cup/NatWest/C&GTrophy
1970, 1971, 1972, 1975, 1990, 1996, 1998

LANCASHIRE CCC

FIRST-CLASS MATCHES
BOWLING

	G Keedy	DG Cork	G Chapple	SI Mahmood	JM Anderson	CL Hooper	PJ Martin	SP Crook	D Mongia	KW Hogg	J Wood	OJ Newby	AR Crook	AJ Swann	MJ Chilton	CP Schofield	MB Loye	SG Law	Overs	Total	Byes/Leg-byes	Wickets	Run outs
v. Northamptonshire (Northampton) 16-19 April	26.1-7-55-3	16-3-51-0	17-5-50-1			22-10-50-2	19-10-25-2			13-1-62-1									112.1	298	5	10	1
	15-6-29-0	2-0-13-0	7-2-13-0			12-2-19-0	5-1-12-0			5-0-14-1				1-0-3-0					47	113	10	1	
v. Sussex (Hove) 21-23 April	1-0-1-0	13-0-61-3	15-4-52-2	13-1-41-3			14-4-37-2												56	195	3	10	
	2-2-0-0	13.5-2-58-5	15-2-37-1	9-1-35-2			13-4-25-1												52.5	163	8	10	1
v. Middlesex (Lord's) 7-10 May	10-3-35-0		31.3-6-120-7	27-7-93-3	11-2-48-0	9-2-15-0				7-2-25-0									95.3	338	12	10	
	1-0-2-0			5-2-17-0		2-0-4-0				5-2-16-0									13	41	2	0	
v. Worcestershire (Old Trafford) 12-14 May	8.2-3-20-4		4-1-6-0	14-4-32-0	17-2-49-6	16-4-36-0													59.2	146	3	10	
	19-4-62-5			9-2-18-1	10.3-1-32-4	2-1-7-0	3-1-8-0												42.3	127	0	10	
v. Middlesex (Old Trafford) 25-28 May	34.2-6-99-3		34-9-60-1	17-3-58-2	33-7-95-3	15-3-43-1													133.2	382	27	10	
	10-1-23-0		9-3-17-0	3-1-8-0	12-2-45-2	9-1-32-0													43	129	4	2	
v. Kent (Tunbridge Wells) 2-5 June	28-2-114-1		28-3-116-0	36.1-7-136-5				25-1-117-2		17-2-52-1				4-2-14-1	7-0-23-0			5-1-16-0	150.1	615	27	10	
	7-2-23-0		5-0-26-0	4-0-26-1						4-1-16-2									20	91	0	3	
v. Sussex (Old Trafford) 9-11 June	19-2-67-1	27.3-4-85-3	23-2-110-2	19-1-102-3		14-2-39-1		7-0-50-0											109.3	470	17	10	
		4-2-11-1		2-0-11-1	6.3-1-18-0														6	44	4	2	
v. Warwickshire (Stratford) 18-21 June	26-5-98-2						18.5-2-81-4	18-2-78-2	17-1-82-1	20-2-122-1					5-1-22-0			104.5	499	16	10	
	12-1-31-1						6-1-30-0	6.1-0-31-0		10-1-31-1				1-0-1-0					35.1	124	0	2	
v. Northamptonshire (Liverpool) 26-29 June	25-3-73-5		25-5-69-0						12-2-33-2	18-2-70-2	26-6-75-0								114.4	357	12	10	
	23-7-58-1		6-1-19-0						11-6-14-1	3-0-20-0	9-0-32-2					1-0-1-0			53	146	2	4	
v. Gloucestershire (Cheltenham) 21-24 July	12-3-31-1	16-4-54-5	11.1-2-23-2	7-0-46-0	19-5-40-1		6-1-24-1												52.1	234	16	10	
	48.4-14-95-1	15-4-50-0	13-3-15-0	8-4-24-0	28.9-9-95-3	29-9-55-3			4-1-9-0										115.4	366	23	7	
v. Warwickshire (Old Trafford) 28-31 July	40-7-109-5	27-6-53-2	26-5-73-0	25-4-100-1		7-1-15-0									12-2-39-1	6.3-1-13-1			143.3	410	8	10	
	38-7-109-4	9-2-24-1	17-1-68-1	12-0-76-0					8-1-19-0							11-0-43-0			95	353	14	7	1
v. Surrey (Whitgift School) 11-13 August	27-3-96-2	24-2-110-3	26-8-72-1	29-3-131-2		3-0-27-1				0.3-0-7-1	20-2-74-0								129.3	525	8	10	
	–																		–	–	–	–	
v. Kent (Old Trafford) 24-27 August	21-4-62-4	11-3-18-2	16-3-79-2	8-0-45-1		4-1-13-1	15-6-41-0												75	266	8	10	
	11-1-30-1	2-0-4-0	5-0-18-1	6-0-20-0		8-0-16-0				1.1-0-1-1									33.1	92	3	3	
v. Surrey (Old Trafford) 2-4 September	44.4-7-112-3	16-4-37-1	16-3-46-1	20-4-59-4		25-3-66-1										9-2-78-0			130.4	369	20	10	
	31.2-7-95-6			5-0-22-0		27-8-56-4													63.2	185	12	10	
v. Worcestershire (Worcester) 9-12 September	17-1-74-3	17-5-61-4	14-6-30-1	12-0-78-1		16-4-39-0										1-1-45-0			87	352	25	9	
	11-3-19-2	11-2-62-1	10-1-35-2	8-0-41-2		3-0-21-0										4-1-8-1			47	199	13	8	
v. Gloucestershire (Old Trafford) 16-19 September	42-9-95-7	8-0-29-0	13.2-1-35-1	6-0-34-0		17-4-40-0										14-1-67-0			100.2	311	11	8	
	35-2-132-7	2-0-7-0				10-0-38-1										21-3-92-1			73	289	6	10	

	G Keedy	DG Cork	G Chapple	SI Mahmood	JM Anderson	CL Hooper	PJ Martin	SP Crook	D Mongia	KW Hogg	J Wood	OJ Newby	AR Crook	AJ Swann	MJ Chilton	CP Schofield	MB Loye	SG Law
Overs	645.3	332.5	374.4	230	126	234	115.5	68.1	50.2	71	51	35	50	6	24	26.3	1	5
Maidens	122	59	80	26	27	51	34	5	9	10	5	6	6	2	3	3	0	1
Runs	1849	1144	1128	1010	374	595	319	309	157	259	243	107	212	18	84	85	1	16
Wickets	72	38	29	23	19	15	10	6	5	5	4	2	2	1	1	1	0	0
Average	25.68	30.10	38.89	43.91	19.68	39.66	31.90	51.50	31.40	51.80	60.75	53.50	106.00	18.00	84.00	85.00	–	–

FIELDING

28	WK Hegg (23 ct, 5 st)
19	CL Hooper
17	DG Cork
17	SG Law
14	JJ Haynes (12 ct, 2 st)
9	MJ Chilton
8	MB Loye
7	G Keedy
5	IJ Sutcliffe
3	G Chapple
2	PJ Martin
2	AJ Swann
2	SI Mahmood
2	D Mongia
1	J Wood
1	JM Anderson
1	SP Crook
0	CP Schofield
0	KW Hogg
0	PJ Horton
0	OJ Newby
0	AR Crook

LEICESTERSHIRE CCC

FIRST-CLASS MATCHES
BATTING

	DL Maddy	DDJ Robinson	CW Henderson	BJ Hodge	OD Gibson	JL Sadler	DI Stevens	PAJ DeFreitas	PA Nixon	MF Cleary	JK Maunders	CE Dagnall	DD Masters	JM Dakin	TJ New	JN Snape	DG Brandy	DS Brignull	Extras	Total	Wickets	Result	Points
v. Glamorgan	26	0	6	105	22		27	20	19	0	0			23*					16	264	10		
(Leicester) 21-24 April	28	36	63	158	20*		0	0	2	3	5			15					23	353	10	D	8
v. Hampshire	7	11	31	1		1	11	24	0	8*	34	5							6	139	10		
(The Rose Bowl) 28 April-1 May	0	8	13*	29		7	3	0	3	4	23	9							12	111	10	L	2
v. Nottinghamshire	3	4	4	30	57*	62		10	11		0			32		0			10	223	10		
(Leicester) 12-15 May	53	98	8*	36	30	72		10	0		0			34		66			23	430	10	W	18
v. Essex	5	56	10*	240	13	46		47	41	2	22				15				13	510	10		
(Chelmsford) 19-22 May	23	53		5		43		15*	10		7				39*				17	212	6	D	10
v. New Zealand	23	13				15	14				85	2	9	10	18			0*	21	210	10		
(Leicester) 28-31 May	87	2				18	9				54	17	9	0	2	5		0*	29	232	10	L	0
v. Derbyshire	1	64	35	221	0	41		46	40	11*	28	15							32	534	10		
(Oakham School) 2-5 June	12*	29		29	0*				10		2								1	83	4	W	22
v. Glamorgan	145	5	15	5	15	33		6	4	17*	3	1							6	255	10		
(Cardiff) 9-12 June	3	18	1	61	0	1		0	14	8*	8	5							18	137	10	L	5
v. Yorkshire	9	22	1	37	13	6		67	78	23	2*		0						31	289	10		
(Headingley) 18-21 June																						D	9
v. Somerset	84	72	52	2	16	10		37	13	63*	31*								22	402	8		
(Taunton) 23-26 June	59*	21		1				12*											2	95	2	D	12
v. Essex	1	33	0	7	14	8		50	38	11	14*		0						21	197	10		
(Leicester) 21-24 July	25	38	0	4	39	95		20	39	30	27*		0						32	349	10	L	5
v. Durham	11	62	9	262	21	21		84		22	38		4*	71*					29	634	9		
(Leicester) 27-30 July																						W	22
v. Nottinghamshire	51	4	37	9	26	4		13	4	18	14			9*					23	212	10		
(Trent Bridge) 11-14 August	31	88		76		7		5	8*	17*									31	263	5	D	8
v. Yorkshire	27	154	1	24	60*			48	11	1	20	6				0			30	382	10		
(Leicester) 19-22 August	1	14		60				2	19*	22*		3				15			30	166	6	D	11
v. Derbyshire																						D	5
(Derby) 24-27 August																							
v. Hampshire	21		3	26	50	5	105			13		1	21*	0			7		30	282	10		
(Leicester) 1-4 September	30		1	74	27	15	70			0		0	4	22*			4		35	282	10	L	5
v. Durham	70	65	4	46	0	28	92				116	16	1		51*				19	508	10		
(The Riverside) 9-12 September	10	38			0		19*			0				0*					4	71	4	W	22
v. Somerset	52	59			1*	0*	1	6		9									2	123	3		
(Leicester) 16-19 September	2	20	1		57	27	1	6		29	9*		31		1				15	199	10	L	3
Matches	17	16	16	15	15	14	13	13	12	11	11	11	6	5	5	5	1	1					
Innings	30	28	21	25	19	25	22	20	21	14	22	12	9	9	7	8	2	2					
Not Out	2	0	3	0	3	2	3	3	3	8	0	2	1	3	3	1	0	2					
Highest Score	145	154	63	262	60*	95	105	78	63*	38	116	17	31	71*	51*	66	7	0*					
Runs	900	1087	295	1548	480	566	689	394	361	179	461	75	74	210	94	140	11	0					
Average	32.14	38.82	16.38	61.92	30.00	24.60	36.26	23.17	20.05	29.83	20.95	7.50	9.25	35.00	23.50	20.00	5.50	-					
100s	1	1	0	5	0	0	1	0	0	0	1	0	0	0	0	0	0	0					
50s	7	9	2	4	4	3	5	1	1	0	2	0	0	1	1	1	0	0					
Catches/Stumpings	24/0	18/0	6/0	6/0	5/0	7/0	13/0	1/0	34/6	3/0	6/0	4/0	3/0	1/0	11/1	1/0	0/0	0/0					

Home Ground: Grace Road, Leicester
Address: County Ground, Grace Road, Leicester, LE2 8AD
Tel: 0871 2821879
Fax: 0871 2821873
Email: enquiries@leicestershireccc.co.uk
Directions: *By road:* Follow signs from city centre, or from southern ring road from M1 or A6.
Capacity: 5,500
Other grounds used: Oakham School
Year formed: 1879

Chief Executive: Kevin Hill
Director of Cricket: James Whitaker
Operations Manager: Gus Mackay
Head Coach: Phil Whitticase
Club Captain: Brad Hodge
County colours: Dark green and scarlet

Website:
www.leicestershireccc.com

Honours
County Championship
1975, 1996, 1998
Sunday League/NCL
1974, 1977
Benson & Hedges Cup
1972, 1975, 1985
Twenty20 Cup
2004

LEICESTERSHIRE CCC

FIRST-CLASS MATCHES
BOWLING

	OD Gibson	CW Henderson	PAJ DeFreitas	CE Dagnall	MF Cleary	DL Maddy	DD Masters	BJ Hodge	JM Dakin	DI Stevens	JK Maunders	DS Brignull	JL Sadler	JN Snape	DDJ Robinson	Overs	Total	Byes/Leg-byes	Wickets	Run outs
v. Glamorgan	23-4-97-3	16-3-52-0	27-5-109-1		18-3-80-0	2-0-7-0		4.5-0-27-2	21-3-79-1							111.5	455	4	7	
(Leicester) 21–24 April	11-2-38-2	15-9-28-5			5-0-31-0				7-2-20-1							38	125	8	9	1
v. Hampshire		12-1-65-1	22-2-62-1		17-4-57-3	5-1-23-0	11-3-24-0	5-0-19-0								72	268	18	6	1
(The Rose Bowl) 28 April–1 May																–	–	–	–	
v. Nottinghamshire	24-8-98-5	17-6-33-0	26-8-81-2			13.4-1-56-2		6-2-12-0	24-9-76-1							110.4	366	10	10	
(Leicester) 12–15 May	17-7-43-6	16-7-31-0	17-3-53-3			11.2-2-35-1		4-1-9-0	5-1-17-0							70.2	195	7	10	
v. Essex	28-4-97-1	29-4-111-0	45-11-145-3		27.4-2-130-4	12-1-67-0		16-2-52-0						20-2-78-1	1-0-5-0	178.4	708	23	9	
(Chelmsford) 19–22 May																–	–	–	–	
v. New Zealand			26-4-92-3		14-1-61-1	23-4-92-3		23-5-61-1		4-0-30-1	19-0-78-2			6-1-23-0		111	413	6	10	
(Leicester) 28–31 May			21-0-90-2		6-1-36-1	12-2-43-0		12-1-57-0			10-3-43-0	1.4-0-22-1			3-0-26-0	69.4	369	10	5	
v. Derbyshire	9.4-1-36-0	13-3-41-0	17.2-7-37-3	14-5-37-4	15-2-47-0	11.4-1-59-1		6-1-30-1								86.4	291	4	10	1
(Oakham School) 2–5 June		36-16-71-1	27-6-64-1	20-7-39-0	23.3-5-80-7	8-3-19-0		6-0-29-0		1-0-7-0						121.3	323	14	9	
v. Glamorgan	19-3-80-5	3-0-22-0	13-4-44-3	18-2-60-0	19-1-74-0	9-1-41-2										81	333	12	10	
(Cardiff) 9–12 June	14-1-66-0	45-9-146-4	14.1-1-51-2	15-0-64-1	11.5-2-53-1	5-0-18-0		14-2-46-1								119	468	24	9	
v. Yorkshire	12-2-58-1	3-0-14-0	13-3-42-3	12.4-4-46-3	12-0-95-2	6-0-22-1										58.4	283	6	10	
(Headingley) 18–21 June																–	–	–	–	
v. Somerset	28-8-83-1	2-0-13-0	23-8-46-1	18-5-49-2	16-2-50-5	3-2-2-1										90	262	19	10	
(Taunton) 23–26 June																–	–	–	–	
v. Essex	20.2-10-73-4	7-2-49-0	4.2-1-11-0	19-1-71-4	14-0-76-1	6.4-1-37-0										71.2	322	5	10	1
(Leicester) 21–24 July	22-5-74-6	7.1-3-21-1	15-6-33-0	14-2-65-2	5-0-20-0	10-2-34-1		1-0-5-0								74.1	272	20	10	
v. Durham	19-4-62-2	25.4-7-74-7		8-1-42-1	9-3-20-0				2-0-9-0							63.4	219	12	10	
(Leicester) 27–30 July	16.3-2-67-3	36-11-104-2		14-1-64-2	13-2-50-2	3-0-16-0		5-0-35-0	9-2-33-0						1-0-3-0	97.3	389	17	10	1
v. Nottinghamshire	30-5-106-4	12-1-54-0	29-5-107-0		22-3-66-2	6-0-30-1	22-3-97-1	4-0-17-1								125	490	13	10	1
(Trent Bridge) 11–14 August																–	–	–	–	
v. Yorkshire	20-5-55-0	32-16-41-4	17.1-3-49-4	5-0-23-0		6-3-19-0		8-3-18-2						6-1-18-0		94.1	239	16	10	
(Leicester) 19–22 August	16-5-39-2	23.5-10-26-2	16-5-48-2	7-3-11-1		3-1-2-1		3-0-7-0								68.5	147	14	8	
v. Derbyshire	6-3-10-1	9-3-25-1	7.4-2-19-0	7-2-19-0	2-0-17-0	2-0-16-0		5-2-13-1						4.2-1-14-0		43	138	5	3	
(Derby) 24–27 August																–	–	–	–	
v. Hampshire	18-4-42-1	25.4-4-103-4				12-3-28-1	16-2-59-1	4-1-14-1	17-2-66-2							92.4	321	9	10	
(Leicester) 1–4 September	20-8-38-2	37-9-88-2				5-0-23-0	20-3-74-4	2-0-14-0	17-3-72-2		2-0-9-0		1-0-2-0			104	329	9	10	
v. Durham	14.2-1-69-3	18-5-62-0		14-5-42-2		7-0-26-1	16-5-62-2	2-0-18-1			9-6-11-1					80.2	298	8	10	
(The Riverside) 9–12 September	19-1-70-3	13.4-2-44-4		18-3-73-2		2-0-9-0	19-5-54-1				2-0-12-0					73.4	280	18	10	
v. Somerset	18-4-44-5	15-2-55-1	7-1-44-2	6-1-36-0			10-2-28-2									56	213	6	10	
(Leicester) 16–19 September		3-0-19-0								13.2-1-50-2	8-0-45-1			4-0-34-0	2-0-30-0	30.2	184	6	3	

	OD Gibson	CW Henderson	PAJ DeFreitas	CE Dagnall	MF Cleary	DL Maddy	DD Masters	BJ Hodge	JM Dakin	DI Stevens	JK Maunders	DS Brignull	JL Sadler	JN Snape	DDJ Robinson
Overs	424.5	469	343.4	256.4	230	169.2	149	95.5	137	17.2	22	29	6.4	36.2	7
Maidens	97	132	81	46	29	24	29	14	28	1	6	3	0	5	0
Runs	1445	1373	1064	923	946	686	533	365	490	80	84	121	58	133	64
Wickets	60	39	31	29	27	15	14	10	8	3	2	2	1	1	0
Average	24.08	35.20	34.32	31.82	35.03	45.73	38.07	36.50	61.25	26.66	42.00	60.50	58.00	133.00	–

FIELDING

40	PA Nixon (34 ct, 6 st)
24	DL Maddy
18	DDJ Robinson
13	DI Stevens
12	TJ New (11 ct, 1 st)
7	JL Sadler
6	JK Maunders
6	CW Henderson
6	BJ Hodge
5	OD Gibson
4	CE Dagnall
3	DD Masters
3	MF Cleary
1	PAJ DeFreitas
1	JN Snape
1	JM Dakin
0	DS Brignull
0	DG Brandy

MIDDLESEX CCC

FIRST-CLASS MATCHES
BATTING

	OA Shah	SG Koenig	PN Weekes	JWM Dalrymple	BL Hutton	EC Joyce	DC Nash	SJ Cook	M Hayward	CT Peploe	PM Hutchison	BJM Scott	MM Betts	L Klusener	CB Keegan	NRD Compton	SR Clark	AB Agarkar	GD McGrath	AJ Strauss	TF Bloomfield	CJC Wright	Extras	Total	Wickets	Result	Points
v. Warwickshire (Edgbaston) 16-19 April	17	10	118	77	30	39	55	22				31*											33	432	8		
	20*	2			20	10*																	2	54	2	D	12
v. Surrey (Lord's) 21-24 April	93	1	7	0	78	45	26	21	8*	2			5										39	325	10		
	65	62	9*		88	47	3*																26	300	4	W	20
v. Lancashire (Lord's) 7-10 May	34	3	50		4	44	19		7	7*			19	26						95			30	338	10		
		14*																		19*			8	41	0	D	10
v. Cambridge UCCE (Fenner's) 12-14 May	56	3		81	15	113						38*				25*							28	359	5		
		64			134		8		5	0*	8	12				6*							26	263	6	D	0
v. Surrey (The Oval) 19-22 May	0	9	7	244	15	123	12	0*		1*			4		44								28	487	9		
																							-	-	-	D	12
v. Lancashire (Old Trafford) 25-28 May	35	171	8	17	27	0	81*	1	3	4			2										33	382	10		
	67*	7			41	7*																	7	129	2	D	10
v. Warwickshire (Lord's) 2-5 June	0	1	70	19	17	5	29	0*	3	0			0										19	163	10		
	3	57	62	17	126	66	32	7	19*	0			12										36	437	10	L	5
v. Gloucestershire (Gloucester) 9-12 June	34	45	50	49	14	28	12	7		28*	8			63									45	383	10		
	72	3	53	0	6	71	16	1		28	0			68*									40	358	10	L	5
v. Worcestershire (Lord's) 18-21 June	12	104*	102	41	90	82	24					11	2	0							8		32	508	10		
	5*				3*							0											0	8	1	D	11
v. Worcestershire (Worcester) 22-25 July	140*	37	42	84	108		12	0					5			40		22				0	35	525	10		
	10	11	11*	0*	43											20							10	105	4	W	22
v. Kent (Southgate) 28-31 July	60	31	45	31	100		26*	0					7			2		0	24				25	351	10		
	3	86	54	27	107		23	29								16		1*					24	370	8	W	21
v. Gloucestershire (Lord's) 3-6 August	103	36	4	2	1		59*	8		3						2		4*					31	253	8		
																							-	-	-	D	9
v. Sussex (Lord's) 10-13 August	25	9	11	8	14	69	11	17				13	22*					4					9	212	10		
	60*	23	1	10	10	2	0	19				7	5					0					18	155	10	L	4
v. Northamptonshire (Northampton) 18-21 August	62	28	44	2	100	23	13	0*	4			31					34						4	345	10		
	100	22	51	11	1	0						22*											9	216	6	D	10
v. Sussex (Hove) 4-6 September	4	26	19	39*	0	3		5	9	16		0						11					3	135	10		
	108	49	50*	14*	0	18				7													39	285	5	W	17
v. Northamptonshire (Lord's) 9-12 September	85	6	54	1	7	71	40	0	21			101*					24						15	425	10		
	24	51	38	2	31	59						1*											6	212	6	D	11
v. Kent (Canterbury) 16-18 September	25	39	12	52*	16	20	30	0	0			4	0										37	235	10		
	14	28	29	20	32	74	15	0*	6			0	5										28	251	10	L	4

	OA Shah	SG Koenig	PN Weekes	JWM Dalrymple	BL Hutton	EC Joyce	DC Nash	SJ Cook	M Hayward	CT Peploe	PM Hutchison	BJM Scott	MM Betts	L Klusener	CB Keegan	NRD Compton	SR Clark	AB Agarkar	GD McGrath	AJ Strauss	TF Bloomfield	CJC Wright
Matches	17	17	16	16	16	14	12	12	11	8	8	7	7	6	5	4	3	3	2	1	1	1
Innings	30	31	26	25	29	25	17	15	13	12	10	13	8	8	4	7	3	4	3	2	1	1
Not Out	5	2	3	4	1	2	4	0	5	2	3	4	2	1	0	2	0	2	0	1	0	0
Highest Score	140*	171	118	244	126	134	113	40	9	28*	8	101*	31*	68*	44	40	34	22	24	95	8	0
Runs	1336	1038	1001	848	1129	1055	529	251	40	140	25	236	87	170	75	111	69	27	28	114	8	0
Average	53.44	35.79	43.52	40.38	40.32	45.86	40.69	16.73	5.00	14.00	3.57	26.22	14.50	24.28	18.75	22.20	23.00	13.50	9.33	114.00	8.00	0.00
100s	4	2	2	1	5	2	1	0	0	0	0	1	0	0	0	0	0	0	0	0	0	0
50s	9	5	9	4	3	7	3	0	0	0	0	0	2	0	0	0	0	0	1	0	0	
Catches/Stumpings	19/0	5/0	14/0	9/0	23/0	12/0	26/2	6/0	4/0	3/0	3/0	8/3	3/0	2/0	2/0	3/0	0/0	2/0	0/0	0/0	0/0	0/0

Home Ground: Lord's
Address: Lord's Cricket Ground, London, NW8 8QN
Tel: 0207 289 1300
Fax: 0207 289 5831
Email: enquiries@middlesexccc.com
Directions: *By underground:* St John's Wood on Jubilee Line. *By bus:* 13, 82, 113 stop along east side of ground; 139 at south-west corner; 274 at top of Regent's Park.
Capacity: 28,000

Other grounds used: Southgate, Shenley, Richmond
Year formed: 1864

Chairman: Phil Edmonds
First XI Coach: John Emburey
Captain: Andrew Strauss/Owais Shah/Ed Joyce
County colours: Navy blue

Website:
www.middlesexccc.co.uk

Honours
County Championship
1903, 1920, 1921, 1947, 1976, 1980, 1982, 1985, 1990, 1993. Joint champions 1949, 1977
Sunday League/NCL
1992
Benson & Hedges Cup
1983, 1986
Gillette Cup/NatWest/C&G Trophy
1977, 1980, 1984, 1988, 1989

MIDDLESEX CCC

FIRST-CLASS MATCHES
BOWLING

	SJ Cook	M Hayward	JWM Dalrymple	PN Weekes	CB Keegan	CT Peploe	MM Betts	L Klusener	PM Hutchison	SR Clark	AB Agarkar	GD McGrath	BL Hutton	EC Joyce	TF Bloomfield	OA Shah	DC Nash	SG Koenig	CJC Wright	Overs	Total	Byes/Leg-byes	Wickets	Run outs
v. Warwickshire (Edgbaston) 16-19 April	14-2-56-0	14-3-41-2		20.4-1-76-5 1-0-5-0	14-1-63-3		8-0-74-0							1-0-4-0		1-0-7-0	2-0-8-0			70.4 5	317 24	7 0	10 0	
v. Surrey (Lord's) 21-24 April	20-5-57-0 9-2-44-0	21-2-100-2 11-1-41-4		5-0-27-0 10-0-49-1	22-0-138-5 18-4-47-3				21-4-72-3 6-1-11-1				2-0-5-0							91 54	418 203	19 11	10 10	1
v. Lancashire (Lord's) 7-10 May		17-1-75-2 18-5-36-1		4-1-21-0 21-4-77-2	20-3-36-5 23-6-70-0			13.5-1-60-1 23.4-1-89-4	14-2-40-2 15-2-52-0				9-0-26-0	9-2-26-0						68.5 118.4	236 401	4 25	10 7	
v. Cambridge UCCE (Fenner's) 12-14 May	19-4-49-1 6-1-15-0		24-9-66-2 5-1-16-0			28-8-62-0 2-0-11-0	8-3-51-0 4-0-17-0		16.4-2-76-2 6-1-18-0					9-1-34-2		4-1-13-0				108.4 23	357 81	4 4	10 0	
v. Surrey (The Oval) 19-22 May		20-2-72-2 16-3-53-0	0.5-0-9-1 8.4-0-33-0	13-2-57-0 20-3-53-1	20-2-72-1 20-6-46-2			17-2-86-3 14-2-59-0	16-3-50-3 10-2-32-0							4-2-3-0				86.5 92.4	359 300	13 21	10 4	1
v. Lancashire (Old Trafford) 25-28 May		21-5-39-3	37-4-117-3	4-0-22-0		50.1-16-80-3		25-3-39-1	9-2-35-0				1-0-2-0							147.1 —	417 —	23 —	10 —	
v. Warwickshire (Lord's) 2-5 June		26-4-82-3	21-4-2-99-2	28-1-120-1		10-2-33-0		28-3-104-1	3.5-2-92-0				12-1-45-0	4-0-17-0		1-0-3-0				162.4 —	608 —	13 —	7 —	
v. Gloucestershire (Gloucester) 9-12 June		9-1-37-0	11-2-38-0	13-0-62-2 2-0-10-0		43-3-199-4 3-0-12-0		23-1-116-0	22-4-91-0				13-1-64-2 4-1-16-0	14-0-62-1		1-1-0-0 0-0-4-0	2-1-1-0			149 11	695 47	26 4	9 0	
v. Worcestershire (Lord's) 18-21 June	25-6-69-2		17-5-64-1	14.2-3-47-1	24-7-78-1			26-5-60-3					3-2-3-0		20-3-55-1					129.2	399	23	10	1
v. Worcestershire (Worcester) 22-25 July	23-4-61-1 32-6-89-6		2-0-20-0 14-1-43-2	2-0-8-0 10-1-25-0			18-3-89-5 23.1-5-78-2			20.3-4-72-3 14-2-62-0	6-1-22-0								7-0-31-0 13-3-19-0	78.3 106.1	305 323	2 7	10 10	1
v. Kent (Southgate) 28-31 July	14-3-33-3 11-3-46-2		15-2-52-2 24-5-51-1	2-0-6-0 44.3-7-128-3		4.3-0-14-1 8-1-37-0			4-0-27-0 17-6-53-0	22-7-59-4 30-10-71-1					3-0-9-1					61.3 137.3	192 410	1 21	10 10	
v. Gloucestershire (Lord's) 3-6 August	30-7-63-3 8-0-31-0		10-2-35-1 25-0-141-3	18.2-1-50-1 28-2-31-2		13-3-49-0 7-2-20-0		9-0-39-0 6-0-37-0	29-7-81-5 9-1-28-2	11-2-21-0					3-0-20-0					120.2 92	347 400	9 24	10 7	
v. Sussex (Lord's) 10-13 August	19-5-69-2 19-4-51-5		12-1-43-0 7-1-27-1	16-2-58-1		19-6-29-3 14-5-41-1						28.2-15-44-3 20.2-9-41-1	8-2-31-1 10-2-24-1	4-0-26-0					106.2 70.2	314 196	4 12	10 10	1
v. Northamptonshire (Northampton) 18-21 August	23-6-53-1 9-2-16-1	19.3-4-62-4 13-5-36-2	18-6-48-1 8-0-35-1	2-0-13-0		28-10-66-2 10.4-2-43-2			19-5-47-2 7-1-21-0										109.3 47.4	295 155	6 4	10 7	1
v. Sussex (Hove) 4-6 September	16-4-46-0 14-3-38-2	17-5-59-2 12-3-20-1		10-3-29-2 6.4-1-14-2		18.3-4-65-4 15-6-41-2			21-5-46-2 10-1-28-3				4-0-16-0							86.3 57.4	277 141	11 0	10 10	
v. Northamptonshire (Lord's) 9-12 September	20-4-68-1 12-8-11-2	21.3-5-54-2 14-5-30-1	17-5-35-1 10-0-45-0	7-1-27-0		14-5-46-0 7-3-14-0			22-6-51-3 10-5-24-0				9-6-14-3 13-3-47-1		2-1-1-0		1-0-6-0			105.3 74	282 224	13 20	10 4	
v. Kent (Canterbury) 16-18 September	28-3-107-3	19-0-81-0	19.4-1-66-4	23-1-91-2		12-0-73-0	21-2-72-1						2-0-9-0		3-0-7-0					128.4 —	535 —	29 —	10 —	

	SJ Cook	M Hayward	JWM Dalrymple	PN Weekes	CB Keegan	CT Peploe	MM Betts	L Klusener	PM Hutchison	SR Clark	AB Agarkar	GD McGrath	BL Hutton	EC Joyce	TF Bloomfield	OA Shah	DC Nash	SG Koenig	CJC Wright
Overs	371	289	306.5	325.3	161	242.2	147.4	170.3	182.4	89	93.3	100.4	113	41	20	22	2	3	20
Maidens	82	54	47	34	29	59	30	18	28	23	20	41	23	3	3	5	0	1	3
Runs	1072	918	1083	1166	550	745	577	673	645	217	323	215	353	169	55	67	8	7	50
Wickets	35	31	28	26	20	17	13	13	11	10	10	9	8	3	1	1	0	0	0
Average	30.62	29.61	38.67	44.84	27.50	43.82	44.38	51.76	58.63	21.70	32.30	23.88	44.12	56.33	55.00	67.00	–	–	–

FIELDING

28	DC Nash (26 ct, 2 st)
23	BL Hutton
19	OA Shah
14	PN Weekes
12	EC Joyce
11	BJM Scott (8 ct, 3 st)
9	JWM Dalrymple
6	SJ Cook
5	SG Koenig
4	M Hayward
3	MM Betts
3	PM Hutchison
3	NRD Compton
3	CT Peploe
2	L Klusener
2	AB Agarkar
2	CB Keegan
0	SR Clark
0	GD McGrath
0	AJ Strauss
0	TF Bloomfield
0	CJC Wright

NORTHAMPTONSHIRE CCC

FIRST-CLASS MATCHES
BATTING

	TW Roberts	DJG Sales	U Afzaal	GL Brophy	J Louw	BJ Phillips	GP Swann	JF Brown	TB Huggins	PS Jones	M van Jaarsveld	MJ Powell	JW Cook	RA White	PC Rofe	CG Greenidge	TMB Bailey	ML Love	AR White	AJ Shantry	CJR Jennings	MJ Cawdron	RSG Anderson	CM Goode	Extras	Total	Wickets	Result	Points
v. Lancashire	89	84	51	17	5	0	1	0	5	15*	26														5	298	10		
(Northampton) 16-19 April	15*								38*		48														12	113	1	D	8
v. Durham UCCE			0		50		13			49	18	19		52*					33*						10	244	6		
(Northampton) 21-23 April																									-	-	-	D	0
v. Surrey	22*		15*				14			11															2	64	2		
(The Oval) 28 April-1 May																									-	-	-	D	6
v. Sussex	1	27	167*	4	0	73	54	1*		12	37	4													20	400	9		
(Northampton) 7-10 May	10	72*	25	0*		40				27	15														3	192	5	D	12
v. Gloucestershire	16	11	63	0	26*	6	14	0		11	7	21													43	218	10		
(Bristol) 12-15 May	68	43	64	58	34*	0*	8				84	33													35	427	7	D	6
v. Kent	69	70	7	4	8	4	5	11			46	5					8*								13	250	10		
(Northampton) 19-22 May	0	12	11	6	19	2	42	4*			114	13					5								36	264	10	L	5
v. Sussex	10	171	69	181	9	58		1*	7	7	27		2												28	570	10		
(Hove) 25-28 May																									-	-	-	D	12
v. Worcestershire	30	0	32	0	11	1	2	21	51		13									2*					14	177	10		
(Northampton) 2-5 June	22	22	57	25	28	4	6	3	17		28									0*					52	264	10	L	3
v. Warwickshire	18	8	21	25	38	90	35	0*		18	46			18											12	329	10		
(Edgbaston) 9-12 June	0	76	37	41	10	0	29	7*		0	48			8											24	280	10	L	5
v. Lancashire	14	59	133*	36	2	5	47			35	7						2		5						12	357	10		
(Liverpool) 26-29 June	20		20	67		26*					0						11*								2	146	4	D	11
v. Surrey	57	61*	29		11	1	37	34					9		0	4	51								38	332	10		
(Northampton) 29 July-1 August	64		16*				1						52			20	49*								18	220	4	W	20
v. Worcestershire	53	0	45	1	1		16						49	0			133*		6			0			7	311	10		
(Worcester) 11-14 August	10	13	22	94	18*		10						0				161*								31	359	6	D	10
v. Middlesex	1	57	111	1	63	10	32	0			14		0	0*											6	295	10		
(Northampton) 18-21 August	46	73*	6	11	8	0*	2				0		3												6	155	7	D	9
v. Gloucestershire	7	10	96	34	13	1	29	0	0				2	0*											30	222	10		
(Northampton) 24-27 August	33	82*	100*						45				23												24	307	3	D	8
v. Kent	16	3	34	10	1	12	16		1	37			4	0*											17	151	10		
(Canterbury) 3-6 September	0	92	41	20	0	4	9		44	4			114	15*											44	387	10	L	2
v. Middlesex	0	22	62	81	32	30		0*	4				8	1					22						20	282	10		
(Lord's) 9-12 September	11	90	12	5*					82*				0												24	224	4	D	8
v. Warwickshire	46	72*	19	23	5	0		0	34				51	4					0						11	265	10		
(Northampton) 16-19 September																									-	-	-	D	9
Matches	17	16	16	16	16	15	14	13	9	8	7	7	6	5	5	4	3	2	2	2	1	1	1	1					
Innings	29	25	28	25	22	21	22	15	14	9	13	12	9	9	6	4	5	4	2	3	1	0	1	1					
Not Out	2	5	5	2	3	3	0	6	2	1	0	0	0	0	4	1	2	3	0	2	0	0	1	0					
Highest Score	89	171	167*	181	63	90	54	34	82*	37	114	49	114	52	15*	8*	52*	161*	22	5	6	0	33*	0					
Runs	748	1230	1365	744	342	327	485	82	355	139	484	239	222	158	20	13	89	394	22	7	6	0	33	0					
Average	27.70	61.50	59.34	32.34	18.00	18.16	22.04	9.11	29.58	17.37	37.23	19.91	24.66	17.55	10.00	4.33	29.66	394.00	11.00	7.00	6.00	-	-	0.00					
100s	0	1	4	1	0	0	0	0	0	0	1	0	1	0	0	0	0	2	0	0	0	0	0	0					
50s	6	12	7	4	1	3	2	0	2	0	1	0	1	1	0	0	1	1	0	0	0	0	0	0					
Catches/Stumpings	12/0	18/0	9/0	27/2	8/0	2/0	13/0	4/0	3/0	1/0	7/0	2/0	4/0	3/0	1/0	0/0	3/4	3/0	0/0	1/0	0/0	1/0	0/0	0/0					

Home Ground: Northampton
Address: Wantage Road, Northampton, NN1 4TJ
Tel: 01604 514455
Fax: 01604 514488
Email: commercial@nccc.co.uk
Directions: Junction 15 from M1 onto A508 (A45) towards Northampton. Follow the dual carriageway for approx 3 miles. Keeping in left-hand lane, take next exit from dual carriageway marked A428 Bedford and Town Centre. Move into middle lane approaching the roundabout at bottom of slip road. Take second exit following signs for Abington/Kingsthorpe onto Rushmere Road. Follow Rushmere Road (A5095) across the junction with Billing Road and continue straight on through Abington Park to traffic lights at main junction with Wellingborough Road.
Capacity: 4,250
Other grounds used: Campbell Park, Milton Keynes
Year formed: 1878

Chief Executive: Stephen Coverdale
Chairman: Lynn Wilson
First XI Coach: Kepler Wessels
Captain: David Sales
County colours: Claret and gold

Honours
Benson & Hedges Cup
1980
Gillette Cup/NatWest/C&G Trophy
1976, 1992

Website:
www.nccc.co.uk

NORTHAMPTONSHIRE CCC

FIRST-CLASS MATCHES
BOWLING

FIRST-CLASS MATCHES	J Louw	JF Brown	BJ Phillips	GP Swann	PC Rofe	CG Greenidge	PS Jones	JW Cook	U Afzaal	RA White	AJ Shantry	RSG Anderson	AR White	TW Roberts	MJ Cawdron	CJR Jennings	CM Goode	DJG Sales	GL Brophy	M van Jaarsveld	Overs	Total	Byes/Leg-byes	Wickets	Run outs
v. Lancashire (Northampton) 16-19 April	28-7-71-4	37-7-110-0	31-6-112-1	26.2-4-95-3			25-2-94-1		2-0-12-0												149.2	504	10	9	
																					-	-	-	-	
v. Durham UCCE (Northampton) 21-23 April							22-6-58-1	15-5-22-2	20-5-46-2		16-3-43-1		12-6-10-1	20-7-46-1							105	229	4	8	
							5-2-11-0				5-0-11-1										10	22	0	1	
v. Surrey (The Oval) 28 April-1 May	26.3-3-87-3	7-1-48-0		21-2-100-0	9-0-44-1		28-5-114-3														91.3	403	10	7	
																					-	-	-	-	
v. Sussex (Northampton) 7-10 May	5.2-1-24-0	39-6-93-4	12-6-24-0	34-6-94-4			13-1-51-1														103.2	294	8	10	1
	6-0-19-1	16.4-6-20-3	7-1-9-2	9-5-10-0			5-3-11-1														43.4	69	0	7	
v. Gloucestershire (Bristol) 12-15 May	35-12-81-2	30-4-83-2	34.1-4-106-5	16-1-68-1			39-7-115-0														154.1	474	20	10	
																					-	-	-	-	
v. Kent (Northampton) 19-22 May	11-4-33-4	24.3-4-75-1	6-2-15-0	24-4-81-2		7-0-48-0															72.3	254	2	10	2
	20-3-82-0	21-2-69-0	10-1-36-0	27-6-63-1		12-0-79-2			15.1-1-65-3												105.1	405	11	6	
v. Sussex (Hove) 25-28 May	18.2-4-85-2	35-12-71-0	29-8-103-4				27-4-75-3	16-3-33-0	8-0-29-1											4-2-8-0	133.2	406	10	10	
	16-0-70-1	27-9-70-2	14-2-34-2				11-4-20-0	10-2-29-0	10-3-36-0												92	271	4	5	
v. Worcestershire (Northampton) 2-5 June	8.3-2-18-1			20-7-41-1	41-9-111-4					12-4-34-1											103.3	292	5	10	1
		19-5-38-0		5-1-14-1	22-1-51-0			6.5-1-31-0		2-0-9-0											54.5	152	9	1	
v. Warwickshire (Edgbaston) 9-12 June	27-6-83-1	41-9-128-0		34-7-110-4	26.3-5-69-3		31-5-115-1			3-0-12-1											162.3	524	7	10	
	7-0-27-2	1.4-0-15-0		5-1-14-0			4-0-32-0														17.4	88	0	2	
v. Lancashire (Liverpool) 26-29 June	19.1-6-57-3			13-0-52-1	32-9-69-3		8-1-32-0			4-1-4-0			21-6-67-2								97.1	284	3	10	1
v. Surrey (Northampton) 29 July-1 August	17.1-1-68-2	47-10-113-5		20-6-46-0	20-3-76-0	12-1-66-2				4-0-25-0											120.1	402	8	10	1
	6-1-28-1	23-5-51-4			22.3-2-50-3	5-1-13-2															56.3	147	5	10	
v. Worcestershire (Worcester) 11-14 August	27-6-63-5				17-4-66-0		20.2-4-71-3			3-0-13-0					14-3-64-1	16-3-70-1					97.2	361	14	10	
v. Middlesex (Northampton) 18-21 August	31.3-7-110-4	24-5-76-1	23-7-38-2	20-5-49-2	24-6-66-1				2-1-2-0												124.3	345	4	10	
	12.5-2-44-5	17-3-50-0	9-2-27-0	12-0-50-0	12-3-38-1																62.5	216	7	6	
v. Gloucestershire (Northampton) 24-27 August	27-4-90-3	14-8-14-2	21.2-11-32-2	1-0-1-0	17-4-58-0				12-4-42-3												92.2	240	3	10	1
	11-1-35-1	14-3-40-2	7-1-37-0	9-2-14-1	11-6-20-0				1-1-0-0												62	160	4	4	
v. Kent (Canterbury) 3-6 September	22.5-4-92-4		21-9-58-2	21-2-65-1	19-2-78-1		15-1-67-0	7-0-45-0													105.5	414	9	8	
	9.4-0-66-2		9-1-21-1	14-3-41-0	11-1-48-1		14-0-66-0	18-1-66-1													75.4	318	10	5	
v. Middlesex (Lord's) 9-12 September	34-8-112-4	36.4-8-87-2	23-7-78-0		35-7-109-4		8-2-19-0	5-0-28-0	3-0-12-0				3-0-10-0								139.4	425	10	10	
	9-3-35-0	18-2-65-3	7-1-22-0		7.5-2-23-3		5-0-28-0						5-0-23-0								54.5	212	4	6	
v. Warwickshire (Northampton) 16-19 September	20.4-2-93-5	35-11-67-2	19-11-36-1		28-9-63-1		7-1-23-1						3-0-10-0					2-1-2-0	1-0-1-0		112.4	295	3	10	
	7-2-18-0	26-8-47-1	8-3-10-2		3-2-2-0		2.3-1-7-0						15.3-1-19-2				1-1-0-0				65.3	109	3	5	

	J Louw	JF Brown	BJ Phillips	GP Swann	PC Rofe	CG Greenidge	PS Jones	JW Cook	U Afzaal	RA White	AJ Shantry	RSG Anderson	AR White	TW Roberts	MJ Cawdron	CJR Jennings	CM Goode	DJG Sales	GL Brophy	M van Jaarsveld
Overs	463.3	584.3	408.3	403.2	167.5	83.2	220	99	51.3	32	35	21	26	13	20	14	16	2	1	4
Maidens	89	133	107	71	42	14	33	19	7	6	10	3	7	3	3	1			0	2
Runs	1591	1523	1175	1168	505	346	792	307	196	98	110	54	62	10	46	64	70	2	1	8
Wickets	60	36	31	30	12	10	10	7	4	3	3	2	2	1	1	1	1	0	0	0
Average	26.51	42.30	37.90	38.93	42.08	34.60	79.20	43.85	49.00	32.66	36.66	27.00	31.00	10.00	46.00	64.00	70.00	-	-	-

FIELDING

29	GL Brophy (27 ct, 2 st)
18	DJG Sales
13	GP Swann
12	TW Roberts
9	U Afzaal
8	J Louw
7	TMB Bailey (3 ct, 4 st)
7	M van Jaarsveld
4	JF Brown
4	JW Cook
3	ML Love
3	RA White
3	TB Huggins
2	BJ Phillips
2	MJ Powell
1	PC Rofe
1	PS Jones
1	MJ Cawdron
1	AJ Shantry
0	CJR Jennings
0	CG Greenidge
0	RSG Anderson
0	CM Goode
0	AR White

NOTTINGHAMSHIRE CCC

FIRST–CLASS MATCHES

BATTING

	DJ Hussey	JER Gallian	DJ Bicknell	PJ Franks	MA Ealham	KP Pietersen	SCG MacGill	CMW Read	RJ Warren	GJ Smith	RJ Sidebottom	CE Shreck	A Singh	D Alleyne	RJ Logan	AJ Harris	BM Shafayat	PJ McMahon	Extras	Total	Wickets	Result	Points
v. Oxford UCCE (The Parks) 16-18 April	107*	89	1		52*	62			67										18	396	4		
			13	24					20*					43*					6	106	2	D	0
v. Durham (The Riverside) 21-24 April	76	58	41	41	36	52	5*		120	34		0		27					33	523	10		
																			–	–	–	W	22
v. Yorkshire (Trent Bridge) 28 April-1 May	18	133	41	44	54	21			9		3			14*					16	353	8		
																			–	–	–	D	11
v. Glamorgan (Trent Bridge) 7-10 May	55	0	20	45	10	70	0		97	30	15*			28					14	384	10		
																			–	–	–	D	11
v. Leicestershire (Leicester) 12-15 May	5	1	17	45	139	32	1	31	72		0	13*							10	366	10		
	0	24	0	51	85	2	10	6	7		1	0*							9	195	10	L	7
v. Yorkshire (Headingley) 19-21 May	15	0	48	17	6	167	21	59	8		4	1*							47	393	10		
	125	13	19	0	34	0		11	55		0*								12	269	8	W	21
v. Durham (Trent Bridge) 25-28 May	166*	36	0	12		0	24	10	31	2	13				7				24	325	10		
	35	50	23	14		19		108*	0	28*					4				13	294	7	W	20
v. Hampshire (The Rose Bowl) 2-3 June	48	9	54	32	96	49	4	5	0	21					9*				29	356	10		
																			–	–	–	W	21
v. Somerset (Bath) 9-12 June	21	10	150	54	24			4*	66	32	5	5	55						34	460	10		
	35*	10	26						48*				33						8	160	3	W	22
v. Derbyshire (Trent Bridge) 18-21 June	0	190	24	27*	14	107		130	13						25*				21	551	7		
		1*	25*																2	28	0	D	10
v. Hampshire (Trent Bridge) 23-26 July	170	26	103	30	113*	0	28	75	21		8	1							37	612	10		
																			–	–	–	D	10
v. Essex (Southend-on-Sea) 28-31 July	116	74	0	0	17	167	18	0	14	8		1*							20	435	10		
		120*	13			69*			36										8	246	2	W	22
v. Leicestershire (Trent Bridge) 11-14 August	140	66	2	57*	1	0	2	62	134	1	0								25	490	10		
																			–	–	–	D	12
v. Derbyshire (Derby) 19-22 August	15	8	175	0	1	153	9	90*		35			14			1*			51	552	9		
																			–	–	–	W	21
v. Somerset (Trent Bridge) 3-6 September	25	68	6	11	104			59	8				7			13	13	0*	23	337	10		
	7	55	142	6	44			24	13*				1			10	3	0	12	317	10	L	4
v. Glamorgan (Cardiff) 10-13 September	11	10	3	52*	30	20			15				112*						20	273	6		
																			–	–	–	D	6
v. Essex (Trent Bridge) 16-19 September	124*	13	24	50*	1	37			7				21						24	301	6		
	1	57	110	22*	10	0			49		16*		89						25	379	7	W	20

	DJ Hussey	JER Gallian	DJ Bicknell	PJ Franks	MA Ealham	KP Pietersen	SCG MacGill	CMW Read	RJ Warren	GJ Smith	RJ Sidebottom	CE Shreck	A Singh	D Alleyne	RJ Logan	AJ Harris	BM Shafayat	PJ McMahon
Matches	17	17	17	17	16	15	15	13	13	13	10	8	5	4	3	2	1	1
Innings	23	25	26	22	20	20	12	18	19	12	10	6	8	4	4	3	2	2
Not Out	4	2	1	5	2	1	2	2	2	3	2	4	1	2	2	1	0	1
Highest Score	170	190	175	57*	139	167	28	130	134	35	15*	13*	112*	43*	25*	13	13	0*
Runs	1315	1121	1080	634	871	1027	126	807	784	201	49	16	332	112	45	24	16	0
Average	69.21	48.73	43.20	37.29	48.38	54.05	12.60	50.43	46.11	22.33	6.12	8.00	47.42	56.00	22.50	12.00	8.00	0.00
100s	7	3	5	0	3	4	0	2	2	0	0	0	1	0	0	0	0	0
50s	2	8	1	5	4	4	0	6	4	0	0	0	2	0	0	0	0	0
Catches/Stumpings	24/0	16/0	4/0	2/0	13/0	17/0	3/0	35/3	4/0	2/0	3/0	2/0	3/0	11/0	3/0	0/0	0/0	1/0

Home Ground: Trent Bridge
Address: Trent Bridge, Nottingham, NG2 6AG
Tel: 01159 823000
Fax: 01159 455730
Email: administration.notts@ecb.co.uk
Directions: *By road:* Follow signs from ring road towards city centre.
Capacity: 14,500 (16,000 during international matches)
Other grounds used: Cleethorpes
Year formed: 1841

Chief Executive: David Collier
Director of Cricket: Mike Newell
Captain: Jason Gallian
County colours: Green and gold

Website:
www.nottsccc.co.uk

Honours
County Championship
1883, 1884, 1885, 1886, 1907, 1929, 1981, 1987
Sunday League/NCL
1991
Benson & Hedges Cup
1976, 1989
Gillette Cup/NatWest/C&G Trophy
1987

NOTTINGHAMSHIRE CCC

FIRST–CLASS MATCHES
BOWLING

	PJ Franks	SCG MacGill	GJ Smith	CE Shreck	RJ Sidebottom	MA Ealham	RJ Logan	AJ Harris	KP Pietersen	DJ Bicknell	PJ McMahon	DJ Hussey	BM Shafayat	Overs	Total	Byes/Leg-byes	Wickets	Run outs
v. Oxford UCCE (The Parks) 16-18 April	10.5-1-36-1	10-6-13-1	21-6-52-5	19-9-30-2		13-5-42-0						8-5-6-1		81.5	190	11	10	
														–	–	–	–	
v. Durham (The Riverside) 21-24 April	15-4-37-2	12-3-59-1	29-6-80-2	31-6-92-3		19.4-7-51-2					1-0-4-0			107.4	350	27	10	
	2-1-3-0		11-4-28-3	16-4-46-6		3.4-2-5-1								32.4	93	11	10	
v. Yorkshire (Trent Bridge) 28 April-1 May	7-0-38-1		16-2-75-3	16-2-55-2	17-2-48-2	12-3-38-1			4-1-6-1					72	264	4	10	
v. Glamorgan (Trent Bridge) 7-10 May	13-0-45-1	8-3-27-0	18-5-56-1		25.1-6-88-5	20-8-55-3								84.1	274	5	10	
		10-2-32-2							8-0-33-0			2-0-6-0		20	73	2	2	
v. Leicestershire (Leicester) 12-15 May	9-3-19-0	10-1-41-0		19-5-73-4	19-7-52-4	13-3-30-2								70	223	8	10	
	22-5-92-1	23-3-74-1		31-7-87-3	28.2-4-98-3	15-5-34-2			6-1-23-0					125.2	430	22	10	
v. Yorkshire (Headingley) 19-21 May	16-1-54-2	14-6-54-4		4-0-9-0	14-7-19-3	8.3-3-18-1								56.3	164	10	10	
	13-3-62-3	14-1-55-3			16-3-52-2	19-3-74-2								62	254	11	10	
v. Durham (Trent Bridge) 25-28 May	15-5-53-2	24-4-81-6	19.1-4-44-0			17-6-40-1	18-3-72-0							93.1	300	10	10	1
	21-9-41-5	17.2-3-54-3	15-2-64-0			14-3-64-0	18-1-79-2							85.2	315	13	10	
v. Hampshire (The Rose Bowl) 2-3 June	14-5-43-3		17-6-52-2			13-5-46-1		10.1-2-56-4						54.1	199	2	10	
	10-0-35-3		10.4-0-34-3			4-2-5-0		11-2-34-4						35.4	113	5	10	
v. Somerset (Bath) 9-12 June	24.2-6-72-7	22-4-85-0	25-4-105-1			13-3-56-0						2-1-2-0		107.2	399	19	10	
	8-1-45-1	7-0-28-0	17-4-49-5			15-3-46-1								54.5	220	14	9	
v. Derbyshire (Trent Bridge) 18-21 June	14-5-43-3	8.1-2-16-2		14-4-47-2		12-3-35-2		10-1-69-0	1-1-0-0					59.1	220	10	10	1
	7-0-28-0	25.5-5-89-3		25-5-103-6		11-1-46-1		8-0-43-0	6-1-26-1					82.5	355	20	10	
v. Hampshire (Trent Bridge) 23-26 July	20-3-102-0	27-0-114-1		30-6-106-2	25-4-108-1	24-8-68-0			7-0-56-0			19.2-2-74-0		152.2	641	13	4	
	4-1-21-0	14-4-35-1		5-0-53-0	10-3-32-1				13-1-72-3	13-2-32-1		5-0-33-0		64	295	17	6	
v. Essex (Southend-on-Sea) 28-31 July	16-3-52-0	35-9-124-3	24-6-80-2	16-1-84-0		17.1-5-57-2			11-1-23-2					119.1	431	11	10	1
	7-1-29-0	28-5-109-7		9-2-34-1		9-2-39-1			7.5-1-28-0					65.5	248	5	10	1
v. Leicestershire (Trent Bridge) 11-14 August	9-1-40-2	10.2-1-48-0	12.1-3-27-2			16.4-4-37-2	17-3-43-4		1-0-5-0					66.1	212	13	10	
	13-1-68-2	28-10-66-2	11-1-48-0				14-5-40-0		3-0-24-0			5-1-7-1		74	263	10	5	
v. Derbyshire (Derby) 19-22 August	16.5-3-67-2	26-4-82-0	20-2-95-1			17-5-44-0		24-4-61-4				4-0-21-0		108.5	400	25	7	
	4-1-8-0	11-1-26-1	11.1-2-35-5					13-6-22-4	1-0-5-0					39.1	96	5	10	
v. Somerset (Trent Bridge) 3-6 September	22-2-80-0		22-4-99-1			18-4-64-0		30-5-113-1		11.1-0-32-2	43-4-169-3	14-1-62-0	2-0-16-0	162.1	654	18	8	1
										0.4-0-1-0				0.4	1	0	0	
v. Glamorgan (Cardiff) 10-13 September														–	–	–	–	
v. Essex (Trent Bridge) 16-19 September	19-4-77-2	20-3-72-0	25-6-97-2	21-3-103-1		13-4-37-1			11-0-58-0	6.5-0-33-3		2-0-5-0		117.5	500	18	9	
		5.2-0-24-0		3-0-17-0	6-0-22-1				2-0-7-0	8-0-37-0		10-0-69-0		34.2	179	3	1	

	PJ Franks	SCG MacGill	GJ Smith	CE Shreck	RJ Sidebottom	MA Ealham	RJ Logan	AJ Harris	KP Pietersen	DJ Bicknell	PJ McMahon	DJ Hussey	BM Shafayat
Overs	352	410	336.1	235	258	317	75.1	67	81.5	39.4	43	72.2	2
Maidens	68	80	69	51	59	90	9	15	7	2	4	10	0
Runs	1287	1408	1161	823	859	952	353	196	365	135	169	290	16
Wickets	43	40	39	31	30	26	10	9	7	6	3	2	0
Average	29.93	35.20	29.76	26.54	28.63	36.61	35.30	21.77	52.14	22.50	56.33	145.00	-

FIELDING

38	CMW Read (35 ct, 3 st)
24	DJ Hussey
17	KP Pietersen
16	JER Gallian
13	MA Ealham
11	D Alleyne
4	DJ Bicknell
4	RJ Warren
3	A Singh
3	RJ Sidebottom
3	SCG MacGill
3	RJ Logan
2	GJ Smith
2	PJ Franks
2	CE Shreck
1	PJ McMahon
0	AJ Harris
0	BM Shafayat

SOMERSET CCC

FIRST-CLASS MATCHES
BATTING

	PD Bowler	M Burns	RJ Turner	RL Johnson	AR Caddick	J Cox	JC Hildreth	ID Blackwell	MJ Wood	AW Laraman	SRG Francis	JD Francis	NJ Edwards	NAM McLean	KP Dutch	RT Ponting	KA Parsons	CM Gazzard	WJ Durston	GM Andrew	AV Suppiah	TA Hunt	Extras	Total	Wickets	Result	Points
v. Loughborough UCCE	7	1	27	29	12	172			57	13		12	40									1*	8	379	10		
(Taunton) 10-12 April																								-	-	D	0
v. Derbyshire	127	68	10	1	1	35			66	20		17	14	1*									28	388	10		
(Taunton) 21-24 April	28	5	22*		6				26	29*		36	13										5	170	6	D	10
v. Essex	187*	124*				22			34			18											15	400	3		
(Chelmsford) 28 April-1 May																								-	-	D	12
v. Durham	12		0	1	8	66	101		5				23	14*	72		55						18	375	10		
(Taunton) 12-15 May	25					124	72		7				30		36*								16	310	5	L	7
v. Derbyshire		4	45	9	9	36	31	111			2*	1	30	4									25	307	10		
(Derby) 19-22 May		33*				16	31	64*				68	13										27	252	4	D	10
v. Essex	0	32	25	58	54	86	9	3					26	22*			12						12	339	10		
(Taunton) 25-28 May	138*	6	20*		3		41	30					19				11						3	271	6	D	10
v. Glamorgan	4	11	2	17	9*	2	61	64					4	1	31								23	229	10		
(Swansea) 2-5 June	2	54	18	27	22*	50	0	131					15	7	27								17	370	10	L	4
v. Nottinghamshire	39	35			27	1	60	78			7*		87	1	5			18					41	399	10		
(Bath) 9-12 June	25	24			3	63	29	9			5*		15	0	22								25	220	10	L	7
v. Hampshire	15	36	4	28*	24	61					8	13			2								12	203	10		
(The Rose Bowl) 18-21 June	6	30	0		5	23	14				0*	0			60								8	146	10	L	4
v. Leicestershire	46	27	37	7	2	4			33*	4	6	52		11									33	262	10		
(Taunton) 23-26 June																								-	-	D	8
v. Yorkshire	6	74	1				14	73		9	1	109		0	29*	112							23	451	10		
(Scarborough) 21-23 July	1*											5*											0	6	0	W	22
v. Sri Lanka A	22						38		128*	28		35	24			35	5	0			33		24	372	10		
(Taunton) 27-30 July	48						81	17	1			7	93					44*	34	44	11		22	424	9	W	0
v. Glamorgan	86	10	36	9		0	98			1	1*	12				117							24	394	10		
(Taunton) 3-5 August	55						32*					54				18*							5	164	2	W	21
v. Durham	30	8	46	101*		0	0			66*		14			50					15			70	400	8		
(The Riverside) 13-16 August																								-	-	D	12
v. Hampshire	22*					12*					4												12	50	2		
(Taunton) 18-21 August	25	79	11	4	0	20	40		18	3	1*	110											29	340	10	L	3
v. Nottinghamshire	2	34	41*	8		250	108	0	113										47				51	654	8		
(Trent Bridge) 3-6 September	1*								0*														0	1	0	W	22
v. Yorkshire	75*								62*														4	141	0		
(Taunton) 10-13 September																								-	-	D	7
v. Leicestershire		12	1	11	19*	0	38	35	12	15			45								0		25	213	10		
(Leicester) 16-19 September		26					52*	46*	3				33										24	184	3	W	16
Matches	16	16	16	15	14	13	13	11	11	11	11	10	10	10	10	6	3	3	2	2	2	1					
Innings	27	22	18	14	14	20	20	16	16	11	10	16	19	11	8	4	4	3	3	3	3	1					
Not Out	6	2	3	2	4	1	2	2	4	2	6	1	0	3	1	1	1	1	0	0	0	1					
Highest Score	187*	124*	46	101*	54	250	108	131	128*	66*	15	110	93	22*	72	117	55	44*	47	44	33	1*					
Runs	1034	733	346	297	204	1013	760	864	604	186	46	554	537	61	248	297	114	97	86	59	44	1					
Average	49.23	36.65	23.06	24.75	20.40	53.31	42.22	61.71	50.33	20.66	11.50	36.93	28.26	7.62	35.42	99.00	38.00	48.50	28.66	19.66	14.66	-					
100s	3	1	0	1	0	3	2	2	0	0	0	2	0	0	0	2	0	0	0	0	0	0					
50s	3	4	0	1	1	4	5	6	3	1	0	3	2	0	2	1	1	0	0	0	0	0					
Catches/Stumpings	11/0	17/0	61/4	3/0	5/0	7/0	12/0	5/0	5/0	5/0	6/0	6/0	11/0	1/0	2/0	7/0	2/0	3/0	8/0	2/0	1/0	0/0					

Home Ground: Taunton
Address: County Ground, St James Street, Taunton, Somerset, TA1 1JT
Tel: 01823 272946
Fax: 01823 332395
Email: somerset@ecb.co.uk
Directions: *By road:* M5 junction 25, follow A358 to town centre. Signposted from there.

Other grounds used: Bath
Year formed: 1875

Chief Executive: Peter Anderson
First XI Coach: Kevin Shine
Captain: Mike Burns
County colours: Black, white and maroon

Honours
Sunday League/NCL
1979
Benson & Hedges Cup
1981, 1982
Gillette Cup/NatWest/C&G Trophy
1979, 1983, 2001

Website:
www.somersetcountycc.com

SOMERSET CCC

FIRST-CLASS MATCHES
BOWLING

Match	AR Caddick	RL Johnson	NAM McLean	SRG Francis	ID Blackwell	AW Laraman	KP Dutch	GM Andrew	AV Suppiah	WJ Durston	M Burns	JC Hildreth	NJ Edwards	JD Francis	TA Hunt	PD Bowler	KA Parsons	RT Ponting	J Cox	MJ Wood	Overs	Total	Byes/Leg-byes	Wickets	Run outs
v. Loughborough UCCE (Taunton) 10-12 April	29.2-7-80-2	24-6-69-2			13-4-42-1						3-0-6-0		6-2-11-1		17-2-85-2						92.2	304	11	8	
	15-5-24-0	8-4-15-1			9-8-4-1						1-1-0-0		15-4-54-0		11-2-39-0				1-0-8-0		60	154	10	2	
v. Derbyshire (Taunton) 21-24 April	19-6-61-1	20-7-58-0	21-5-62-1		16-4-58-5						3-0-9-0		3-0-16-1	4-0-11-0							82	275	11	8	
	8-1-27-1	4-1-16-0	5-1-15-0		4-0-13-0								6-1-24-0								31	112	6	1	
v. Essex (Chelmsford) 28 April-1 May	28-1-114-2	6-5-2-0	11-3-31-1		6-2-19-0	22-3-65-5															73	231	0	10	2
	0.1-0-0-0		5-1-18-1		2-0-14-0	3-1-4-0															10.1	36	0	1	
v. Durham (Taunton) 12-15 May	22-5-59-1	23-4-69-7	18-3-52-2				6-0-37-2										9-2-48-0				72	235	7	10	
	42-8-149-5	31.5-4-141-0	31-4-93-2									1-0-4-0					2-0-13-0				113.5	453	16	9	
v. Derbyshire (Derby) 19-22 May	30-9-92-6	17-2-60-0	24.2-5-80-2	18-3-66-2	21-8-58-0							3-0-7-0									113.2	367	4	10	
	34-4-119-3	13-2-45-1	10-2-30-0	6.5-0-53-1	30-4-105-2							3-0-26-0									96.5	387	9	7	
v. Essex (Taunton) 25-28 May	24-5-80-6		21-2-90-0	20.3-3-75-2	13-3-44-0						3-0-18-0						17-2-86-0				98.3	400	7	9	
	29-5-84-2		26-7-79-0	26.1-4-87-5	39-4-146-3							3-0-8-0									123.1	413	9	10	1
v. Glamorgan (Swansea) 2-5 June	25-1-93-0	26.1-8-83-4	19-5-91-4		7-2-23-1		25-8-85-1														102.1	388	13	10	
	13-4-49-0	1-0-10-0	12-1-62-1		13.5-1-52-1		9-1-34-1														48.5	212	5	3	
v. Nottinghamshire (Bath) 9-12 June	36-4-156-2		24-6-78-3	25.1-1-106-4	22-5-79-1						6-2-28-0										113.1	460	13	10	
	19-3-64-2		8-3-26-1	8.3-0-41-0	4-1-11-0		3-1-15-0														42.3	160	3	3	
v. Hampshire (The Rose Bowl) 18-21 June	29-9-75-4	13-2-38-0		20.1-5-57-4			20-2-75-2				16-4-46-3						9-3-36-0				91.1	290	9	10	
	30-8-119-2			24.2-7-113-4			4-1-20-0				3-0-20-0										77	334	16	9	
v. Leicestershire (Taunton) 23-26 June	28.5-7-103-1		22-0-100-4	19-2-118-2		18-2-74-1								3-1-14-0							87.5	402	7	8	
	10-1-31-1		6-2-18-1	7-1-32-0																	26	95	0	2	
v. Yorkshire (Scarborough) 21-23 July			22.5-6-79-6	10-2-50-0	13-2-30-0	13-3-43-1	21-2-87-3											5-2-6-0			84.5	296	1	10	
			15-5-45-5	5-0-16-0	1-0-10-0	1-0-13-0	11.1-2-26-5														42	160	2	10	
v. Sri Lanka A (Taunton) 27-30 July		16-2-73-3		3-0-16-0	12-0-72-2			15-2-63-4		2-0-19-0			7-0-31-1								55	280	6	10	
		12-2-32-2			12.3-5-34-3			9-0-53-0	18-1-69-2	9-0-23-3			3-0-14-0								63.3	227	5	10	
v. Glamorgan (Taunton) 3-5 August		16-4-82-2		19.3-3-73-2	15-6-42-5	8-2-20-1	9-0-39-0														67.3	262	6	10	
		23-2-102-2		1.5-0-12-0	14.1-1-67-1	35.5-12-90-7	4-0-9-0														78.5	294	14	10	
v. Durham (The Riverside) 13-16 August		20.5-2-71-2		23-6-75-5	19-7-35-2			10-1-29-1					3-0-12-0								75.5	231	4	10	
		7-3-11-1		16-5-34-1	4-2-8-1			6-2-24-2					2.3-1-4-1			2-1-2-0					37.3	85	2	6	
v. Hampshire (Taunton) 18-21 August	29-4-97-5	26-9-61-3		20-5-62-0	17-3-67-2					10.4-0-40-0		10-1-39-2	3-1-14-0								92	301	14	10	
	25.4																			2-0-6-0	25.4	99	0	2	
v. Nottinghamshire (Trent Bridge) 3-6 September	25.4-8-97-2	25-9-69-5		19-3-66-1	38-16-64-2					5-1-23-0	2-0-8-0										114.4	337	10	10	
	8-1-55-0	21-5-64-2		17-2-50-0	43.3-17-90-7					19-5-50-1											108.3	317	8	10	
v. Yorkshire (Taunton) 10-13 September	19.3-1-94-4	22-4-78-2		8-1-22-0	31-4-75-2	13-3-43-2															93.3	324	12	10	1
	3-0-23-0	3-0-30-0		5-0-35-2	5-0-33-1																16	125	4	4	
v. Leicestershire (Leicester) 16-19 September	6-2-12-0	14-4-33-3		5-1-24-0	10-2-28-0	3-0-26-0															38	123	0	3	
	16.2-1-69-4	10-4-31-2		5-2-27-1	8-2-25-0				7-0-36-2												46.2	199	11	10	

	AR Caddick	RL Johnson	NAM McLean	SRG Francis	ID Blackwell	AW Laraman	KP Dutch	GM Andrew	AV Suppiah	WJ Durston	M Burns	JC Hildreth	NJ Edwards	JD Francis	TA Hunt	PD Bowler	KA Parsons	RT Ponting	J Cox	MJ Wood
Overs	578.5	449.5	322.1	295.5	345.1	180.3	124	40	25	35	44.4	17	25	36.3	28	2	37	5	1	2
Maidens	110	104	62	51	85	43	21	5	1	6	7	1	1	9	4	1	7	2	0	0
Runs	2026	1512	1127	1201	972	638	448	179	105	115	155	76	110	120	124	2	183	6	8	6
Wickets	56	44	43	33	27	22	19	7	4	4	3	2	2	2	2	0	0	0	0	0
Average	36.17	34.36	26.20	36.39	36.00	29.00	23.57	25.57	26.25	28.75	51.66	38.00	55.00	60.00	62.00	-	-	-	-	-

FIELDING

65	RJ Turner (61 ct, 4 st)
17	M Burns
12	JC Hildreth
11	PD Bowler
11	NJ Edwards
8	WJ Durston
7	RT Ponting
7	J Cox
6	SRG Francis
6	JD Francis
5	AR Caddick
5	ID Blackwell
5	AW Laraman
5	MJ Wood
3	RL Johnson
3	CM Gazzard
2	KA Parsons
2	KP Dutch
2	GM Andrew
1	NAM McLean
1	AV Suppiah
0	TA Hunt

SURREY CCC

FIRST–CLASS MATCHES
BATTING

Match	MR Ramprakash	SA Newman	JN Batty	J Ormond	AD Brown	MP Bicknell	Azhar Mahmood	TJ Murtagh	AJ Hollioake	R Clarke	IDK Salisbury	ND Doshi	JGE Benning	RS Clinton	MA Butcher	GP Thorpe	N Shahid	Saqlain Mushtaq	AJ Tudor	PJ Sampson	Z Khan	Extras	Total	Wickets	Result	Points
v. Oxford UCCE	113*	100	10		61*				12				128			11						17	452	5		
(The Parks) 10-12 April		15	24		32				23				0			44*			18*			8	164	5	D	0
v. Sussex	25	14	10	27	27	45	84	0*	4	40	24											4	304	10		
(The Oval) 16-19 April	21	86*	22	19	13	37	0	9*	4	18	1											24	254	9	D	10
v. Middlesex	29	86	35	1	18		14	8*	106	77	20								2			22	418	10		
(Lord's) 21-24 April	68	18	0	1*	4		70	0	4	13	12								1			12	203	10	L	8
v. Northamptonshire	34	131	28		28	9*	65		73	4*						13						18	403	7		
(The Oval) 28 April-1 May																						–			D	9
v. Warwickshire	11	28	92*	4	37	27	0		34						0	42	14					13	302	10		
(Edgbaston) 12-15 May	35	55	8	3*	21	7	0		0						184	89	0					12	414	10	L	5
v. Middlesex	89	56	0	40	0	19		74*	8	2	25	4										42	359	10		
(The Oval) 19-22 May	66	87	3		64*			41*	12													27	300	4	D	11
v. Kent	157	0	129	6	79	6	27		2	44						1					2*	26	479	10		
(The Oval) 25-28 May	91*	31	18*							15						0						19	174	3	W	22
v. Gloucestershire	6	18	5	11	5	47*	14	25	62	0							53					52	298	10		
(Bristol) 2-4 June	64*	10	11	57	0	26	11	0	12	11	0											11	213	10	L	5
v. Gloucestershire	5	73	106	39	170	36		33*	0	43	23	15										55	598	10		
(The Oval) 18-21 June																						–			D	12
v. Worcestershire	0	23	53	0	0	3		2*	16	8				4	41							5	155	10		
(Worcester) 23-26 June	13	65	10	1*	31	9		0	2					17	26*							13	187	8	D	5
v. Warwickshire	145*	9	1	30	25		25	0	33	21	22							1				19	331	10		
(Guildford) 21-24 July	1	13	145	12*	103	14	57	9	6	18								1				33	412	10	L	6
v. Northamptonshire	161	28	61	15	21		76	11	17	0	2									0*		10	402	10		
(Northampton) 29 July-1 August	0	4	4	19	21	1	5	24	20	33										11*		5	147	10	L	8
v. Worcestershire	130	46	8	0	22		25	36	0*				6	73					0			29	375	10		
(The Oval) 3-6 August	100*	59		25	22				47				35*	27					0			14	329	5	W	21
v. Lancashire	134	61	15	10	50	41	30	56	64			29*			1							34	525	10		
(Whitgift School) 11-13 August																						–			W	22
v. Kent	9	111	46	8	85	14*	24	1*	33					58								13	402	8		
(Canterbury) 18-21 August																						–			D	12
v. Lancashire	3	17	36	4*	154	14	18	65	6					2	30							20	369	10		
(Old Trafford) 2-4 September	0	8	3	1	14	2	58*	17	2					35	33							12	185	10	W	21
v. Sussex	3	0	8	22	54	40	13			112	11*	4	6									10	283	10		
(Hove) 16-19 September	51	25	42		123	9	14*			5	0	5	24									13	311	10	W	19
Matches	17	17	17	17	15	13	12	11	11	10	9	9	6	5	4	3	3	3	2	2	1					
Innings	29	30	29	24	24	19	20	17	19	17	13	13	11	8	8	5	6	4	2	4	1					
Not Out	5	1	2	5	2	3	1	8	1	0	1	3	1	0	0	1	1	0	1	2	1					
Highest Score	161	131	145	57	170	47*	84	74*	106	112	77	29*	128	73	184	89	53	14	18*	11*	2*					
Runs	1564	1277	933	330	1155	447	577	374	412	530	285	134	265	205	298	211	109	17	18	13	2					
Average	65.16	44.03	34.55	17.36	52.50	27.93	30.36	41.55	22.88	31.17	23.75	13.40	26.50	25.62	37.25	52.75	21.80	4.25	18.00	6.50	–					
100s	7	3	3	0	4	0	0	0	1	1	0	0	1	0	1	0	0	0	0	0	0					
50s	6	9	3	1	6	0	4	4	2	2	1	0	0	0	2	0	1	1	0	0	0					
Catches/Stumpings	7/0	11/0	50/6	4/0	15/0	4/0	8/0	8/0	6/0	15/0	3/0	2/0	3/0	8/0	1/0	0/0	2/0	1/0	3/0	0/0	0/0					

Home Ground: The Brit Oval
Address: The Brit Oval,
Kennington, London, SE11 5SS
Tel: 0207 582 6660
Fax: 0207 735 7769
Email: enquiries@surreycricket.com
Directions: *By road:* The Brit Oval is located south of the Thames in Kennington on the A202, near the junction with the A3 and A24, just south of Vauxhall Bridge and 10 minutes from Victoria and Waterloo (Eurostar). *By rail:* Take South West Trains to Vauxhall which is a short walk from the ground. The station is well served by trains from throughout Surrey and Hampshire as well as from the Greater London area. Connections include Clapham Junction and Waterloo.

Capacity: 16,500
Other grounds used: Guildford, Whitgift School
Year formed: 1845

Chief Executive: Paul Sheldon
Chairman: Richard Thompson
First XI Coach: Steve Rixon
Captain: Jonathan Batty
County colours: Blue, white and yellow

Website:
www.surreycricket.com

Honours
County Championship
1890, 1891, 1892, 1894, 1895, 1899, 1914,
1952, 1953, 1954, 1955, 1956, 1957, 1958,
1971, 1999, 2000, 2002
Joint Champions 1950
Sunday League/NCL
1996, 2003
Benson & Hedges Cup
1974, 1997, 2001
Gillette Cup/NatWest/C&G Trophy
1982, 1992
Twenty20 Cup
2003

SURREY CCC

FIRST-CLASS MATCHES
BOWLING

	J Ormond	MP Bicknell	Azhar Mahmood	ND Doshi	TJ Murtagh	IDK Salisbury	Saqlain Mushtaq	R Clarke	AJ Hollioake	PJ Sampson	AJ Tudor	MR Ramprakash	JGE Benning	Z Khan	N Shahid	AD Brown	RS Clinton	Overs	Total	Byes/Leg-byes	Wickets	Run outs
v. Oxford UCCE (The Parks) 10-12 April	16-2-75-1 / 13-3-34-3	16-7-43-2 / 8-0-25-1				19-4-43-3 / 21-9-30-3			12-1-36-1 / 6-0-17-0		11-3-39-2	/ 2-0-16-0	7-3-27-0 / 11-2-28-1		3-3-0-0			81 / 64	267 / 154	4 / 4	10 / 8	1
v. Sussex (The Oval) 16-19 April	28-6-85-1	24-4-87-2	23-2-83-1		23-8-65-3	23.4-2-86-1		6-0-35-1					2-0-15-0			6-0-24-0		135.4	493	13	10	1
v. Middlesex (Lord's) 21-24 April	18-5-52-1 / 17-3-39-0		19-4-96-4 / 15-2-43-0	10-0-55-0 / 5-0-22-0		17-6-32-2 / 21.4-2-77-0	18.4-2-71-3 / 24-1-107-4											82.4 / 82.4	325 / 300	14 / 12	10 / 4	
v. Northamptonshire (The Oval) 28 April-1 May	6-2-28-1	9.3-3-29-1	3-1-7-0															18.3 / -	64 / -	0 / -	2 / -	
v. Warwickshire (Edgbaston) 12-15 May	29-2-103-1 / 4-0-30-0	27.3-5-130-4 / 8-0-37-0	20-4-94-0 / 1-0-6-0			32-8-97-2 / 7.5-0-44-0	32-5-77-3 / 12-1-49-2		4-0-21-0									144.3 / 32.5	546 / 171	24 / 5	10 / 3	1
v. Middlesex (The Oval) 19-22 May	34-9-117-3	35-8-109-3			23-5-84-3	20-0-76-0		12-1-65-0	4.3-0-18-0				1-0-5-0					130 / -	487 / -	13 / -	9 / -	
v. Kent (The Oval) 25-28 May	15-5-25-0 / 44-14-97-2	21.4-6-51-3 / 34-8-128-5	15-5-56-4 / 22-5-63-1					11-2-47-3 / 14-2-49-1				2-0-7-0		11-2-53-0 / 15.4-0-48-1	2-1-6-0			73.4 / 133.4	239 / 413	7 / 15	10 / 10	
v. Gloucestershire (Bristol) 2-4 June	26-5-75-0 / 4-1-21-0	34.2-11-107-4 / 10-2-46-2	16-4-45-2 / 5-2-14-0	19-7-26-0 / 3-1-10-2	21-5-78-3 / 3.4-0-13-0			9-0-58-1										125.2 / 25.4	406 / 106	17 / 2	10 / 4	
v. Gloucestershire (The Oval) 18-21 June	16.3-2-78-3 / 25-11-53-3	31-10-84-2 / 13-4-39-1		11-1-34-0 / 2-0-3-0	16.5-1-74-5 / 15-3-49-1	9-0-23-0 / 11-6-10-0		7.3-0-47-0 / 18.6-3-62-2	6-2-12-0 / 10-1-38-2									97.5 / 94	368 / 255	16 / 25	10 / 9	
v. Worcestershire (Worcester) 23-26 June	31-5-109-0	11-4-27-0			22-1-107-0	18-0-79-1		21-3-69-3										103	400	9	4	
v. Warwickshire (Guildford) 21-24 July	31-7-90-2 / 13-4-37-1		20-3-78-0 / 11-1-40-0	25-0-101-3 / 10-1-37-0	26-4-105-0 / 6-2-22-0			2-0-22-1	4-0-21-0 / 2-0-12-0	24.3-1-121-5 / 8-3-19-1						3.3-0-13-0		130.3 / 55.3	537 / 207	21 / 5	10 / 3	
v. Northamptonshire (Northampton) 29 July-1 August	28-6-90-2 / 13.5-3-56-0		22.4-5-46-3 / 8-2-27-1	31-6-103-4 / 27-7-58-1		15-2-42-1 / 7-0-21-0		1-0-5-0		3-0-11-0	2-0-14-0		16-3-35-2					99.4 / 74.5	332 / 220	32 / 12	10 / 4	
v. Worcestershire (The Oval) 3-6 August	23.2-4-63-2 / 25-7-62-6		19-4-83-3 / 22.2-6-69-4	9-2-15-0 / 14-2-60-0				12-3-62-1 / 10-2-45-0			13-2-61-4 / 9-2-57-0	2-0-9-0	3-0-17-0				1-0-9-0	77.2 / 85.2	295 / 341	2 / 22	10 / 10	
v. Lancashire (Whitgift School) 11-13 August	15-2-72-2 / 18-4-60-3	15-3-41-3 / 14-3-61-2	13.2-3-40-4 / 16-5-61-2	14-5-42-1 / 6.4-0-50-2	12-4-25-0													57.2 / 66.4	210 / 260	15 / 3	10 / 10	1
v. Kent (Canterbury) 18-21 August	20-6-57-1 / 22-6-65-3	22-1-72-3 / 18-2-67-1	20.1-7-54-5 / 20-8-55-3	4-1-13-0	12-4-35-1 / 12-6-25-1											2-2-0-0		74.1 / 78	226 / 234	8 / 9	10 / 8	
v. Lancashire (Old Trafford) 2-4 September	15-4-47-1 / 6.5-1-22-4	15-4-38-1 / 7-1-19-0	18-4-56-1 / 7-0-22-0		31-6-125-5 / 20-3-57-6									2-1-1-0				81 / 40.5	278 / 129	11 / 9	10 / 10	
v. Sussex (Hove) 16-19 September	23.5-8-69-4 / 28-6-98-2	13-7-26-1			25-5-73-3 / 27.4-3-110-7	10-1-37-1 / 12-1-35-1		8-0-49-0 / 5-0-31-0										79.5 / 72.4	271 / 286	12 / 12	10 / 10	1

	J Ormond	MP Bicknell	Azhar Mahmood	ND Doshi	TJ Murtagh	IDK Salisbury	Saqlain Mushtaq	R Clarke	AJ Hollioake	PJ Sampson	AJ Tudor	MR Ramprakash	JGE Benning	Z Khan	N Shahid	AD Brown	RS Clinton
Overs	609.2	387	336.3	265.2	243.3	222.1	86.4	109.3	78.3	34.3	33	24	24.3	26.4	3	13.3	1
Maidens	143	95	77	45	50	39	9	16	7	4	7	4	5	2	3	3	0
Runs	1909	1266	1138	875	873	660	304	518	290	154	157	68	92	101	0	43	9
Wickets	52	43	38	33	20	13	12	9	7	6	6	2	1	1	0	0	0
Average	36.71	29.44	29.94	26.51	43.65	50.76	25.33	57.55	41.42	25.66	26.16	34.00	92.00	101.00	-	-	-

FIELDING

56	JN Batty (50 ct, 6 st)
15	AD Brown
15	R Clarke
11	SA Newman
8	Azhar Mahmood
8	RS Clinton
8	TJ Murtagh
7	MR Ramprakash
6	AJ Hollioake
4	MP Bicknell
4	J Ormond
3	IDK Salisbury
3	AJ Tudor
3	JGE Benning
2	N Shahid
2	ND Doshi
1	MA Butcher
1	Saqlain Mushtaq
0	GP Thorpe
0	PJ Sampson
0	Z Khan

SUSSEX CCC

FIRST–CLASS MATCHES
BATTING

Match	MJ Prior	RR Montgomerie	MW Goodwin	Mushtaq Ahmed	CJ Adams	IJ Ward	RSC Martin-Jenkins	M Akram	RJ Kirtley	PA Cottey	JD Lewry	TR Ambrose	MJG Davis	MH Yardy	KJ Innes	LJ Wright	CD Hopkinson	JA Voros	Extras	Total	Wickets	Result	Points
v. MCC (Lord's) 9-12 April	13	61	17	6		19	12	1*		20	9	35	4						3	200	10		
	92	50	102	2*		28	0			19		60	37*						9	399	7	D	0
v. Surrey (The Oval) 16-19 April	36	25	2	17	101	82	31	31*		72	56		22						18	493	10		
																			-	-	-	D	12
v. Lancashire (Hove) 21-23 April	11	60*	33	21	3	0	29	4		11	0		5						18	195	10		
	33	27	14	2	0	37	0	1*		0	28		3						18	163	10	L	3
v. Worcestershire (Worcester) 28 April-1 May																			-	-	-	D	4
v. Northamptonshire (Northampton) 7-10 May	32	9	3	27	11	115	51	19			1*	12	6						8	294	10		
	6	13	21	1*	15	0	1			1	11*								0	69	7	D	9
v. Loughborough UCCE (Hove) 12-14 May	201*	5								10	0*	13	38	100	0				22	391	7		
		85						3*	3	4	15	31				13	3*		15	172	6	D	10
v. Warwickshire (Horsham) 19-22 May	17	61	9	62	144	160	0	34	8*		1		39						27	562	10		
																			-	-	-	D	11
v. Northamptonshire (Hove) 25-28 May	0	82	1	8*	200	33	25		1	13	28	0							15	406	10		
	70	30	11		26*	107*	13				0								14	271	5	D	10
v. Lancashire (Old Trafford) 9-11 June	61	5	83	6	150*	84	9	11	14	7	8								32	470	10		
		0	11*		3*	26													4	44	2	W	22
v. Gloucestershire (Arundel Castle) 23-25 June	5	6	28	1	6	0	2	5*	17		7	14							15	106	10		
	0	15		54	12	69	43	0	0	5*									15	218	10	L	3
v. Kent (Hove) 23-26 July	123	20	55	22	57	6	25	1	19	185			17*						88	618	10		
																			-	-	-	W	22
v. Kent (Canterbury) 3-6 August	112	70	28	45	5	20	22	6*	3	0				0					21	332	10		
	53	80	12	2*	2	14	23	4	0	49				18					21	278	10	L	5
v. Middlesex (Lord's) 10-13 August	4	4	105	1	14	148		2*	0	25	1		5						5	314	10		
	0	34	6	0	54	28		2	9	42	0*		6						15	196	10	W	20
v. Worcestershire (Hove) 19-22 August	93	69	85	0	34	2	7	18*	36	34			43						11	432	10		
		37	8*		18*	1				45									2	111	3	W	22
v. Warwickshire (Edgbaston) 24-27 August	95	78	75	21	7	34	26	35*	53*	30			8						20	482	9		
																			-	-	-	D	12
v. Middlesex (Hove) 4-6 September	11	40	5	48	26	3	64*	18	3	23				11					25	277	10		
	12	12	16	49*	25	0	0	7	15	0				3					2	141	10	L	5
v. Gloucestershire (Bristol) 9-12 September	27	7	5	13	9	16	6	20*	21	32			11						32	199	10		
																			-	-	-	D	7
v. Surrey (Hove) 16-19 September	12	25	16	0	40		23	0*		8	0		9	115					23	271	10		
	39	0	119	16	41		12		11	4	1*		1	25					17	286	10	L	5

	MJ Prior	RR Montgomerie	MW Goodwin	Mushtaq Ahmed	CJ Adams	IJ Ward	RSC Martin-Jenkins	M Akram	RJ Kirtley	PA Cottey	JD Lewry	TR Ambrose	MJG Davis	MH Yardy	KJ Innes	LJ Wright	CD Hopkinson	JA Voros
Matches	18	18	17	17	16	16	16	14	13	11	11	10	10	4	3	2	1	1
Innings	26	29	27	24	25	25	23	18	18	17	14	15	14	8	4	3	2	1
Not Out	1	1	2	5	4	1	1	8	5	0	4	0	3	1	0	0	0	1
Highest Score	201*	85	119	62	200	160	64*	35*	53*	185	72	60	43	115	38	100	13	3*
Runs	1158	1010	875	424	1003	1032	424	199	212	510	159	257	171	239	68	118	13	3
Average	46.32	36.07	35.00	22.31	47.76	43.00	19.27	19.90	16.30	30.00	15.90	17.13	15.54	34.14	17.00	39.33	6.50	–
100s	3	0	3	0	4	4	0	0	0	1	0	0	0	1	0	1	0	0
50s	6	10	4	2	2	3	2	0	1	0	1	2	0	0	0	0	0	0
Catches/Stumpings	25/2	12/0	9/0	6/0	14/0	5/0	6/0	2/0	3/0	7/0	2/0	21/1	6/0	3/0	1/0	1/0	0/0	0/0

Home Ground: Hove
Address: County Ground, Eaton Road, Hove, BN3 3AN
Tel: 0871 2822000
Fax: 01273 771549
Email: simon.dyke@sussexcricket.co.uk
Directions: *By rail:* Hove station is a 10-minute walk. *By road:* Follow AA signs. Street parking at no cost.
Capacity: 5,500

Other grounds used: Horsham, Arundel Castle
Year formed: 1839

Chief Executive: Hugh Griffiths
Director of Cricket: Peter Moores
Captain: Chris Adams
County colours: Red, black and white

Honours
County Championship
2003
Sunday League/NCL
1982
Gillette Cup/NatWest/C&G Trophy
1963, 1964, 1978, 1986

Website:
www.sussexcricket.co.uk

SUSSEX CCC

FIRST-CLASS MATCHES
BOWLING

	Mushtaq Ahmed	M Akram	RJ Kirtley	RSC Martin-Jenkins	JD Lewry	MJG Davis	JA Voros	KJ Innes	CD Hopkinson	LJ Wright	MH Yardy	CJ Adams	RR Montgomerie	Overs	Total	Byes/Leg-byes	Wickets	Run outs
v. MCC (Lord's) 9-12 April	40-11-92-2	31-7-130-3		30-10-84-1	28-2-117-2					15-1-71-0		4-0-17-0		148	539	28	8	
v. Surrey (The Oval) 16-19 April	13-1-72-1	19-6-74-1		20.5-4-59-4	18-4-60-3			11-3-35-1						81.5	304	4	10	
	14-2-54-1	19.3-6-85-4		20-7-47-3	16-5-46-1			4-0-12-0						73.3	254	10	9	
v. Lancashire (Hove) 21-23 April	28-3-88-4	25-3-79-3		13-2-37-1	19-5-60-0			13-2-50-2						98	335	21	10	
					4.5-0-12-0			4-0-12-0						8.5	24	0	0	
v. Worcestershire (Worcester) 28 April-1 May		9-1-37-1			8-3-8-1									17	46	1	2	
v. Northamptonshire (Northampton) 7-10 May	32-6-119-3	33.5-4-105-0		19-8-44-0	25-8-78-3	19-5-34-3						1-0-10-0		128.5	400	20	9	
	17-4-49-2	9-3-32-1		12-6-22-1	9-4-23-0	12-0-55-1								60	192	1	5	
v. Loughborough UCCE (Hove) 12-14 May			15-2-44-1			16-3-25-2	14.5-5-40-4	11-1-37-0	7-2-20-1	6-2-8-0	5-1-18-1			74.5	201	9	10	
			7-6-1-3				6-1-22-1	3.3-1-10-0	3-3-14-0					19.3	51	4	4	
v. Warwickshire (Horsham) 19-22 May	50-6-194-4	29-2-94-2	28-3-130-0	23.4-6-62-0		31-3-96-0					4-1-13-0			165.4	600	6	6	
		6-1-33-0	10-4-23-1	10-2-36-0		19-1-68-1					5-1-12-0		4-0-9-0	54	188	7	2	
v. Northamptonshire (Hove) 25-28 May	49-12-143-3			32-4-106-1	26.1-5-96-5	32-4-123-0	27-8-80-1							166.1	570	22	10	
v. Lancashire (Old Trafford) 9-11 June	14-0-64-2	10-1-48-3	8-1-23-1	7-3-30-1		16-8-32-3								55	214	16	10	
	22.2-2-105-5	15.3-2-60-2	16-5-53-1	4-1-14-0		13.3-3-45-2								71.2	297	20	10	
v. Gloucestershire (Arundel Castle) 23-25 June	30-10-58-5	20-3-86-2	15-5-34-1	18-4-38-0	11-0-61-2									94	300	23	10	
			2-0-20-0	3-1-14-0										3.3	25	1	1	1
v. Kent (Hove) 23-26 July	39-13-59-3	19-0-98-2	18.3-4-64-2	12-4-41-0		27-10-54-3								115.3	330	14	10	
	42-12-94-4	14-4-38-1	13-1-38-0	9.2-1-11-1		19.1-3-57-4								97.1	243	5	10	
v. Kent (Canterbury) 3-6 August	41.5-6-126-4	28-5-100-2	30-6-99-2	17-1-95-0						20-1-74-1				136.5	527	33	10	1
	35-3-119-2	19-3-85-2	16-1-52-3	5-0-22-0						7.5-1-22-0				82.5	319	19	7	
v. Middlesex (Lord's) 10-13 August	24.5-3-66-5	15-5-55-3	22-5-56-2			4-0-26-0								65.5	212	9	10	
	27-6-83-5	15-4-30-2	19.2-6-37-3											61.2	155	5	10	
v. Worcestershire (Hove) 19-22 August	23-8-67-6	14.2-2-52-3	10-3-29-0	12-4-41-1		10-1-31-0								59.2	202	13	10	
	38.2-12-73-7	24.2-8-83-2	23-3-98-0	14-1-37-1										109.2	340	18	10	
v. Warwickshire (Edgbaston) 24-27 August	27-3-74-1	27-5-94-3	22-7-75-2	21-5-62-4		13-0-33-0								120	346	8	10	
	31-13-52-2	20-6-45-3	21-5-68-1	14-6-20-1		3-2-2-0								89	205	13	7	
v. Middlesex (Hove) 4-6 September	21-3-66-4	1-0-4-1	18.3-7-32-4	11-3-30-1							9-2-23-0			51.3	135	3	10	
	37-5-137-3	9-1-33-0	20-7-34-1	15.3-6-29-1										90.3	285	29	5	
v. Gloucestershire (Bristol) 9-12 September	23-5-64-2		18.3-4-52-3	12-6-24-2	13-6-27-3	3-1-2-0								69.3	178	9	10	
	34-10-68-1		17-4-46-1	17-3-74-0	10-2-35-0	17.2-0-67-2								95.2	304	9	5	1
v. Surrey (Hove) 16-19 September	21-3-87-2		15-2-80-3	5-0-40-0	16-7-30-2	9-2-26-3						4-0-23-0		70	283	3	10	
	17-2-51-1		20-2-87-1	19-4-67-2	16-3-66-5	10-1-32-1								82	311	8	10	

	Mushtaq Ahmed	M Akram	RJ Kirtley	RSC Martin-Jenkins	JD Lewry	MJG Davis	JA Voros	KJ Innes	CD Hopkinson	LJ Wright	MH Yardy	CJ Adams	RR Montgomerie
Overs	791.2	432.1	446.5	388.4	259.2	235.3	20.5	46.3	10	33.5	33	10	8
Maidens	164	76	97	101	64	40	6	7	2	4	4	2	0
Runs	2318	1581	1381	1166	849	662	62	156	34	104	135	35	26
Wickets	84	46	37	30	27	21	5	3	1	1	1	0	0
Average	27.59	34.36	37.32	38.86	31.44	31.52	12.40	52.00	34.00	104.00	135.00	-	-

FIELDING

27	MJ Prior (25 ct, 2 st)
22	TR Ambrose (21 ct, 1 st)
14	CJ Adams
12	RR Montgomerie
9	MW Goodwin
7	PA Cottey
6	Mushtaq Ahmed
6	RSC Martin-Jenkins
6	MJG Davis
5	IJ Ward
3	RJ Kirtley
3	MH Yardy
2	JD Lewry
2	M Akram
1	KJ Innes
1	LJ Wright
0	CD Hopkinson
0	JA Voros

WARWICKSHIRE CCC

FIRST-CLASS MATCHES

BATTING

	IJL Trott	DR Brown	T Frost	MA Wagh	IR Bell	NV Knight	JD Troughton	NM Carter	GB Hogg	N Tahir	MJ Powell	D Pretorius	A Richardson	HH Streak	AF Giles	IJ Westwood	NA Warren	GG Wagg	Extras	Total	Wickets	Result	Points
v. Middlesex (Edgbaston) 16-19 April	67	42	4	78	12	4	4	18	51		1		8*						28	317	10		
			19*			5*													0	24	0	D	9
v. Cambridge UCCE (Fenner's) 21-23 April	44	46	80*	105	54	21	2												9	361	6		
					4	47	57*		44*										9	161	2	W	0
v. Gloucestershire (Edgbaston) 28 April-1 May	76	0	0*	0	0	34	14		8*										7	139	6		
																			-	-	-	D	6
v. Surrey (Edgbaston) 12-15 May	61	44	10	0	34	28	77	29	158			2*			70				33	546	10		
	35*			12	31	62*		24											7	171	3	W	22
v. Sussex (Horsham) 19-22 May	26	21	135*	20	262*	26	10		68										32	600	6		
	40*				14	62*	59												13	188	2	D	11
v. Worcestershire (Edgbaston) 25-27 May	3	82	27	22	8	16	67	95		16	49		0*						20	405	10		
					63*	5*	83												10	161	1	W	22
v. Middlesex (Lord's) 2-5 June	3	13	11*	43	129	303*	0	13	71										22	608	7	W	22
v. Northamptonshire (Edgbaston) 9-12 June	44	45	85*	92	2	100	54	9	20	1				61					11	524	10		
	22*			10	0	56*													0	88	2	W	22
v. Lancashire (Stratford) 18-21 June	54	16	0	167	49	53	8	32	56	26			1*						37	499	10		
	36*			18	1	67*													2	124	2	D	11
v. Kent (Beckenham) 23-26 June	115	27*		86	49		21	1*	28		134								41	502	6	D	12
v. Surrey (Guildford) 21-24 July	25	106	0	0	155	36			67	4	110	4*	1						29	537	10		
	61			4	96*	21					12*								13	207	3	W	22
v. Lancashire (Old Trafford) 28-31 July	9	162	6	41	112	25	7	0	12*	0			17						19	410	10		
	41	0		24	181	3	3*	72*	7	0									22	353	7	D	11
v. Kent (Edgbaston) 11-14 August	50	49	25	5	121	18		0	63	3*	96	2							25	457	10		
	1*			33		63*						11							15	123	2	D	12
v. Gloucestershire (Bristol) 19-22 August	21	91	2	17	7	120	0		18*	10	9			29					26	350	10		
	79	49	28	73	0	21	0*		11*	9				4					34	308	8	D	10
v. Sussex (Edgbaston) 24-27 August	90	12	48	6	87	65	2		3*	5	14			2					12	346	10		
	0	14	45*	6	23	33				39				27*					18	205	7	D	11
v. Worcestershire (Worcester) 31 August-3 September	63	3	19	15	54	37	64	13		49	69			30*					44	460	10		
	51	27*	20	40	17	39	6	1*		0	43								10	254	8	D	11
v. Northamptonshire (Northampton) 16-19 September	15	108*	23	7	24	20	27				49			14		3	0		5	295	10		
	38*	0		19	1	3					5*			14		38			5	109	5	D	9
Matches	17	17	17	17	16	16	14	14	12	12	9	9	7	6	1	1	1	1					
Innings	28	22	19	30	27	30	18	15	13	12	15	6	4	9	1	2	1	0					
Not Out	6	3	6	2	4	6	1	4	3	5	2	3	2	2	0	0	0	0					
Highest Score	115	162	135*	167	262*	303*	120	95	158	49	134	14	17	61	70	38	0	0					
Runs	1170	957	568	1033	1556	1324	587	245	706	150	630	31	26	180	70	41	0	0					
Average	53.18	50.36	43.69	36.89	67.65	55.16	34.52	22.27	70.60	21.42	48.46	10.33	13.00	25.71	70.00	20.50	0.00	-					
100s	1	3	1	2	6	2	1	0	1	0	2	0	0	0	0	0	0	0					
50s	10	2	2	5	5	8	5	1	7	0	2	0	0	1	1	0	0	0					
Catches/Stumpings	12/0	7/0	47/6	16/0	7/0	9/0	4/0	3/0	6/0	1/0	4/0	1/0	2/0	0/0	0/0	0/0	0/0	0/0					

Home Ground: Edgbaston
Address: County Ground, Edgbaston, Birmingham, B5 7QU
Tel: 0121 4464422
Fax: 0121 4467516
Email: info@thebears.co.uk
Directions: *By rail:* New Street station, Birmingham.
By road: M6 to A38(M) to city centre, then follow signs
to county ground.
Capacity: 20,000

Other grounds used: Stratford upon Avon
Year formed: 1882

Chief Executive: Dennis Amiss MBE
Chairman: MJK Smith OBE
First XI Coach: John Inverarity
Captain: Nick Knight
County colours: Blue and white

Honours
County Championship
1911, 1951, 1972, 1994, 1995, 2004
Sunday League/NCL
1980, 1994, 1997
Benson & Hedges Cup
1994, 2002
Gillette Cup/NatWest/C&G Trophy
1989, 1993, 1995

Website:
www.thebears.co.uk

WARWICKSHIRE CCC

FIRST-CLASS MATCHES
BOWLING

	DR Brown	N Tahir	NM Carter	HH Streak	D Pretorius	MA Wagh	GB Hogg	IR Bell	JO Troughton	A Richardson	GG Wagg	AF Giles	NA Warren	IJL Trott	MJ Powell	Overs	Total	Byes/Leg-byes	Wickets	Run outs
v. Middlesex (Edgbaston) 16-19 April	25-7-65-3		20-5-59-1 8-3-21-1		20-5-95-1	8.2-0-31-1 1-0-4-0	22-5-45-1 6-2-15-0	2-0-10-0 5-2-8-0		24-4-92-1				3-0-22-0 3-1-6-1		124.2 23	432 54	13 0	8 2	
v. Cambridge UCCE (Fenner's) 21-23 April	6-4-2-1 7-2-18-1	13-7-29-2	10-5-13-0 8-3-7-0			2-4-1-1-1 22-11-42-1	20-7-37-2 21-9-38-2	5-1-15-1 4-1-7-1	2.2-1-1-3			12-4-21-3 6-3-12-1		1-0-4-0 7-5-6-0		69.4 77.2	131 144	8 13	10 10	1
v. Gloucestershire (Edgbaston) 28 April-1 May	26-12-75-4		13-2-57-1		18-4-69-2	8.2-0-35-0	20-5-61-0	4-1-34-0	3-2-5-0	14-1-62-0						106.2 -	400 -	2 -	7 -	
v. Surrey (Edgbaston) 12-15 May	4-0-14-0 15.3-3-40-2		9-5-22-2 14-2-39-3		11-2-47-1 18-2-88-3	26-9-60-2 18-2-69-1	24-0-87-2 16-2-65-0	3-1-10-0	13-5-9-0 6-0-18-0		35-13-55-3 27-4-73-1					122 119.3	302 414	8 12	10 10	
v. Sussex (Horsham) 19-22 May	29.3-5-74-2		29-6-104-0		33-7-119-4	18-4-81-2	17-4-68-0		6-0-17-0	25-7-82-2						157.3 -	562 -	17 -	10 -	
v. Worcestershire (Edgbaston) 25-27 May	24-6-83-2 7-0-40-1	17-1-47-4 10-0-43-4	18-2-70-0 12-1-44-2			2-0-10-0		26-4-55-2 7-3-12-3		17-2-87-1 5-0-31-0			2-0-13-0			106 45	379 185	14 15	10 10	1
v. Middlesex (Lord's) 2-5 June	11-3-33-1 18-4-46-2	9-1-29-0 12-3-38-1	16.3-2-50-4 29-9-64-0		11-2-29-1 27.3-6-86-3		30-3-85-3	4-1-4-4 9-3-14-1	6-1-18-0							51.3 153.3	163 437	18 35	10 10	
v. Northamptonshire (Edgbaston) 9-12 June	15-4-46-1 23.1-5-73-1	16-4-38-0 4-0-17-0	20-8-60-2 25.1-5-67-2	21.5-4-80-7 21.5-2-76-6		3-2-48-0 3-0-14-0	6-1-19-0	7-2-24-0 11-8-10-0	2-1-4-0 2-0-8-0							96.5 90.1	329 280	8 13	10 10	1
v. Lancashire (Stratford) 18-21 June	9-1-34-0	20-5-47-2	16-1-93-2		27.3-6-76-2	19-1-77-1	21-2-66-1	18-1-66-2	4-0-30-0							134.3 -	508 -	19 -	10 -	
v. Kent (Beckenham) 23-26 June	10-2-31-0 5-3-6-0	9-2-50-3 3-0-7-0	19-7-44-2			2-0-4-0	22.2-3-90-4	2-0-15-0		11-3-55-0 6-4-4-0			3-2-6-0			75.2 17	297 23	8 0	10 0	1
v. Surrey (Guildford) 21-24 July	16-4-57-2 25-3-80-3	11.1-2-62-4 18.3-1-84-3			19-2-73-1 18-4-71-3	3-0-9-0 15-1-41-0	8-0-46-1 13-2-48-1	2-0-11-0 5-0-22-0		19-4-62-2 12-3-38-0				1-0-8-0		78.1 107.3	331 412	10 19	10 10	
v. Lancashire (Old Trafford) 28-31 July	18-3-81-0 7-2-26-2	8-1-29-0 3-1-14-0	20-2-71-2 16-4-40-1			30-7-86-3 15-4-56-1	25-2-107-4 11-2-53-0	2-0-12-0		7-0-18-0						110 52	412 194	8 5	9 4	
v. Kent (Edgbaston) 11-14 August	11-1-52-0	15-1-71-1	19-4-85-2	23-4-85-4		18-4-55-2	20-1-58-0	0.4-0-1-1								106.4 -	420 -	13 -	10 -	
v. Gloucestershire (Bristol) 19-22 August	31-9-84-2	5-0-43-1	23-1-93-0	8-1-24-0	20-2-84-1	28-3-107-1			37-9-106-2				2-1-1-1	7-0-36-0		161 -	592 -	14 -	8 -	
v. Sussex (Edgbaston) 24-27 August	26-8-71-0	24-4-81-3		31-8-92-2	22-1-99-2	5-0-23-0		24-4-57-1	10-3-24-0				1-0-15-0			143 -	482 -	20 -	9 -	1
v. Worcestershire (Worcester) 31 August-3 September	32-3-89-5 4-0-20-0	8-0-48-0 2-0-16-0	20-2-71-0 3-0-35-0	29.2-8-81-4 7-0-20-1		7-2-11-0 6-1-33-0		2-0-18-0	25-6-76-1 6-0-21-0					1-0-10-0		123.2 29	416 156	22 1	10 1	1
v. Northamptonshire (Northampton) 16-19 September	20.3-3-53-5		17-2-62-0		10-2-37-1		5-2-17-0	3-0-10-0					17-3-60-3	8-1-20-1		80.3 -	265 -	6 -	10 -	

	DR Brown	N Tahir	NM Carter	HH Streak	D Pretorius	MA Wagh	GB Hogg	IR Bell	JO Troughton	A Richardson	GG Wagg	AF Giles	NA Warren	IJL Trott	MJ Powell
Overs	425.4	207.4	367.4	159	245	306.2	297.2	146.4	125.2	144	18	62	17	31	8
Maidens	97	33	79	29	43	56	54	34	28	28	7	17	3	10	0
Runs	1293	791	1209	522	936	1020	956	422	345	532	33	128	60	96	51
Wickets	40	28	27	24	24	20	18	16	6	6	4	4	3	3	0
Average	32.32	28.25	44.77	21.75	39.00	51.00	53.11	26.37	57.50	88.66	8.25	32.00	20.00	32.00	–

FIELDING

53	T Frost (47 ct, 6 st)
16	MA Wagh
12	IJL Trott
9	NV Knight
7	DR Brown
7	IR Bell
6	GB Hogg
4	MJ Powell
4	JO Troughton
3	NM Carter
2	A Richardson
1	N Tahir
1	D Pretorius
0	AF Giles
0	HH Streak
0	NA Warren
0	GG Wagg
0	IJ Westwood

WORCESTERSHIRE CCC

FIRST–CLASS MATCHES
BATTING

	GA Hick	SC Moore	SJ Rhodes	SD Peters	MS Mason	BF Smith	AJ Bichel	VS Solanki	AJ Hall	GJ Batty	Kabir Ali	MN Malik	Kadeer Ali	MA Harrity	RW Price	SA Khalid	DJ Pipe	Extras	Total	Wickets	Result	Points
v. Kent	38	5	42*	76	16	8	50	84				7				0	12	63	401	10		
(Canterbury) 21-24 April	89	108*		29		78*												12	316	2	L	8
v. Sussex	7*	12		16		8*												3	46	2		
(Worcester) 28 April-1 May																		-	-	-	D	4
v. New Zealand	36	18	14	9	12	92			7			39*	27	3*			0	13	270	9		
(Worcester) 7-10 May	204*	29	7*			14			32				8				8	16	318	6	D	0
v. Lancashire	3	8	19*	41	10	23	3		34	0		2	0					3	146	10		
(Old Trafford) 12-14 May	4	45	6	10	4	10	4		7	31*		0	6					0	127	10	L	3
v. Gloucestershire	262	10		20		187		74	7*				35					24	619	6		
(Worcester) 18-21 May																		-	-	-	W	22
v. Warwickshire	158	5	3	31	14*	67	35	12		22	0		0					32	379	10		
(Edgbaston) 25-27 May	29	30	7	2		7	41	28	21	1	0*		0					19	185	10	L	7
v. Northamptonshire	34	18	7	63	1	46	21	32		36	24				1*			9	292	10		
(Northampton) 2-5 June	63*	66*		8														15	152	1	W	19
v. Kent	2	15	8	123	35*	65	0	107	12	36	31							19	453	10		
(Worcester) 9-12 June	27	4		117		127		86	9*	14								21	405	6	D	12
v. Middlesex	86	111	12	6	0*	12	53	8	28	52	4							27	399	10		
(Lord's) 18-21 June																		-	-	-	D	9
v. Surrey	0	146		108		80*		0	53*									13	400	4		
(Worcester) 23-26 June																		-	-	-	D	12
v. Middlesex	10	33	5*	24	6		28	92	71	8	3		0					25	305	10		
(Worcester) 22-25 July	2	20	20	13	5*		108	9	81	0	7		36					22	323	10	L	4
v. Gloucestershire	26	35	16	19	4	56	36	7	0	30	11*							34	274	10		
(Cheltenham) 28-31 July	178	53		5		4	103*	3		3*								14	363	5	W	19
v. Surrey	39	76	46*	74	13	4		0	5	12	11	0						15	295	10		
(The Oval) 3-6 August	5	5	59*	4	13	8		86	1	133	0	0						27	341	10	L	5
v. Northamptonshire	66	0	4*	9	1	13	142	26	12	51	2							35	361	10		
(Worcester) 11-14 August																		-	-	-	D	11
v. Sussex	47	4	7	28	0*	1	29	26	11	28					6			15	202	10		
(Hove) 19-22 August	12	32	35	14	1	40	0	84	60	6					31*			25	340	10	L	4
v. Warwickshire	93	0	44*	19	63	2	36		26			0	66		32			35	416	10		
(Worcester) 31 August-3 September	56*	83*		9														8	156	1	D	11
v. Lancashire	6	14	53	27	0	0	31		70				11		76*	6*		58	352	9		
(Worcester) 9-12 September	7	19	19*	3	0*	50			39				27		1			24	199	8	D	11
Matches	17	17	17	17	17	16	14	13	12	12	8	8	6	4	3	3	3					
Innings	29	29	21	29	20	25	18	18	19	18	9	9	10	3	5	3	3					
Not Out	4	3	9	0	6	3	1	0	2	3	1	2	0	1	2	2	0					
Highest Score	262	146	59*	123	63	187	142	107	81	133	31	39*	66	3*	76*	6*	12					
Runs	1589	1004	433	907	205	1036	717	757	558	470	93	48	216	3	146	7	20					
Average	63.56	38.61	36.08	31.27	14.64	47.09	42.17	42.05	32.82	31.33	11.62	6.85	21.60	1.50	48.66	7.00	6.66					
100s	4	3	0	3	0	2	3	1	0	1	0	0	0	0	0	0	0					
50s	6	4	2	3	1	7	2	6	5	2	0	0	1	0	1	0	0					
Catches/Stumpings	25/0	7/0	44/4	13/0	5/0	17/0	3/0	10/0	16/0	7/0	2/0	2/0	4/0	0/0	1/0	1/0	0/0					

Home Ground: New Road, Worcester
Address: County Ground, New Road, Worcester, WR2 4QQ
Tel: 01905 748474
Fax: 01905 748005
Email: info@wccc.co.uk
Directions: From the M5 Junction 7, follow the brown 'broken stumps' logos to WCCC.
Capacity: 4,500

Other grounds used: None
Year formed: 1865

Chief Executive: Mark Newton
Chairman: John Elliott
First XI Coach: Tom Moody
Captains: Ben Smith, Steve Rhodes
County colours: Green, black and white

Honours
County Championship
1964, 1965, 1974, 1988, 1989
Sunday League/NCL
1971, 1987, 1988
Benson & Hedges Cup
1991
Gillette Cup/NatWest/C&G Trophy
1994

Website:
www.wccc.co.uk

WORCESTERSHIRE CCC

FIRST-CLASS MATCHES
BOWLING

	MS Mason	GJ Batty	AJ Bichel	AJ Hall	Kabir Ali	MN Malik	RW Price	MA Harrity	VS Solanki	SA Khalid	SC Moore	GA Hick	Kadeer Ali	SD Peters	Overs	Total	Byes/Leg-byes	Wickets	Run outs
v. Kent (Canterbury) 21-24 April	20.3-8-55-4		24-5-74-1			20-3-88-5				14-4-42-0		3-0-15-0			84.3	289	15	10	
	24-6-86-3		21-2-101-0			19-3-93-2		16-1-51-0		29.3-7-88-0					109.3	429	10	5	
v. Sussex (Worcester) 28 April-1 May	-	-	-	-	-	-	-	-	-	-	-	-	-	-	-	-	-	-	-
	-	-	-	-	-	-	-	-	-	-	-	-	-	-	-	-	-	-	-
v. New Zealand (Worcester) 7-10 May	17-5-46-1		12.3-2-52-1			19-3-57-1		22-3-111-3			4-0-28-1	4-0-24-0	7-0-55-0		85.3	379	6	7	
	6-2-19-0		4-0-17-0			6-1-10-0		7-1-31-1							23	77	0	1	
v. Lancashire (Old Trafford) 12-14 May	20-7-52-2	7-4-9-2	20-3-51-2	8-0-37-2		14-5-26-2									69	187	12	10	
	25-8-60-2	37-8-111-3	20.2-6-64-3	15-5-34-1		13-3-24-1									110.2	305	12	10	
v. Gloucestershire (Worcester) 18-21 May	21.2-9-46-2	29-10-63-3				19-4-58-3		24-6-60-2	5-1-20-0						93.2	232	5	10	
	24-9-62-5	24.4-11-48-2				15-4-52-1		28-7-106-2				4-1-10-0			100.4	301	3	10	
v. Warwickshire (Edgbaston) 25-27 May	22-6-80-4	13-3-48-0	20.1-3-126-5			11-0-83-1			8-2-48-0						74.1	405	20	10	
	6-2-10-0	7-0-21-0	8-0-51-0			8-1-21-0			5-0-26-0			6.3-1-30-1			40.3	161	2	1	
v. Northamptonshire (Northampton) 2-5 June	14-5-28-1	27-10-52-7	13-4-54-0		4-0-21-0						9-2-20-2				67	177	2	10	
	16-4-34-1	34.4-11-61-3	16-4-42-2		6-0-26-2					6-0-15-1	20-4-53-1				98.4	264	33	10	
v. Kent (Worcester) 9-12 June	20.2-4-83-2	22-6-57-1	24-6-121-1	11-2-53-3	18-2-93-2					5-1-5-0					100.2	420	8	10	1
	14-8-19-1	29-14-60-3	14-3-55-1	15-5-63-2	12-1-39-2										84	244	8	9	
v. Middlesex (Lord's) 18-21 June	35-8-87-1	33-6-107-1	27-7-69-0		32-7-92-1	32-9-84-2			13.4-3-40-5			3-0-11-0			175.4	508	18	10	
			3-0-6-1			2-1-2-0									5	8	0	1	
v. Surrey (Worcester) 23-26 June	17.1-5-46-4		4-0-28-0		7-2-16-0	19-6-60-5									47.1	155	5	10	1
	22-7-47-2	4-3-6-1	10-3-46-1		8-3-10-3	16-2-65-1									60	187	13	8	
v. Middlesex (Worcester) 22-25 July	30-10-77-1	41.5-5-141-6	21-5-76-0	3-0-71-0	24-1-95-1				12-1-36-0					5-1-15-1	153.5	525	14	10	1
	6-1-21-0	5.4-2-12-2	6-0-27-0	2-0-10-0	6-0-29-1										25.4	105	6	4	1
v. Gloucestershire (Cheltenham) 28-31 July	29-8-82-2	30.2-8-82-4	19-2-73-0	22-0-101-1	22-4-86-2										122.2	445	21	10	1
	11-3-18-0	34-10-68-2	11.1-4-26-1	10-3-31-2	13-5-33-4										79.1	189	13	10	1
v. Surrey (The Oval) 3-6 August	25.2-10-89-3	13-2-44-0		21-6-55-1	25-5-93-3	19-4-71-2									103.2	375	23	10	1
	11-4-38-1	19-2-85-1		12-3-33-0	12-1-73-0	12-0-76-2			15-0-15-0						67.5	329	9	5	1
v. Northamptonshire (Worcester) 11-14 August	20-9-37-3	16-0-49-0	19-0-87-5		22-6-57-1	15-3-52-1				6-0-22-0					98	311	7	10	
	23-4-55-1	20-6-76-1	12-1-55-0		17-4-38-2	22-5-48-2				4-0-21-0	8-1-35-0			2-0-12-0	108	359	19	6	
v. Sussex (Hove) 19-22 August	32.3-8-57-3	32-6-126-1	6.3-1-29-1		32.3-7-105-3		28-5-91-2			5-0-15-0					136.3	432	9	10	
	4-0-18-0	13-2-55-2			6-1-18-1		10.1-2-18-0								33.1	111	2	3	
v. Warwickshire (Worcester) 31 August-3 September	33-10-84-1		29-5-108-4	24-7-74-1		16-3-68-2	56-24-95-2					1-0-2-0			159	460	29	10	
	12-4-36-0		11-1-47-0	10-1-24-1		13-1-54-2	35-9-83-4						2-1-1-1		83	254	9	8	
v. Lancashire (Worcester) 9-12 September	29-5-102-1		36.4-8-91-4	23-1-92-1			31-10-79-2				6-0-28-1			4-0-8-0	119.4	403	3	9	
	4-2-8-1		13-2-42-1	13-4-41-3			9-0-54-0				8-0-46-0	1.3-0-13-1		4-0-26-0	52.3	242	12	6	

	MS Mason	GJ Batty	AJ Bichel	AJ Hall	Kabir Ali	MN Malik	RW Price	MA Harrity	VS Solanki	SA Khalid	SC Moore	GA Hick	Kadeer Ali	SD Peters
Overs	597.1	492.1	398.5	347	248	204	169.1	94	74.3	86.3	27	9	21	2
Maidens	181	129	75	72	45	35	50	19	7	17	3	1	1	0
Runs	1582	1381	1549	1124	899	781	420	382	240	277	127	40	106	12
Wickets	52	45	33	30	28	24	10	8	6	4	3	1	1	0
Average	30.42	30.68	46.93	37.46	32.10	32.54	42.00	47.75	40.00	69.25	42.33	40.00	106.00	-

FIELDING

- 48 SJ Rhodes (44 ct, 4 st)
- 15 GA Hick
- 7 BF Smith
- 6 AJ Hall
- 3 SD Peters
- 0 VS Solanki
- GJ Batty
- SC Moore
- MS Mason
- Kadeer Ali
- AJ Bichel
- Kabir Ali
- MN Malik
- SA Khalid
- RW Price
- MA Harrity
- DJ Pipe

YORKSHIRE CCC

FIRST–CLASS MATCHES
BATTING

	MJ Wood	RKJ Dawson	MJ Lumb	SP Kirby	PA Jaques	TT Bresnan	A McGrath	JAR Blain	I Dawood	SM Guy	DS Lehmann	IJ Harvey	C White	CEW Silverwood	VJ Craven	JJ Sayers	MJ Hoggard	RM Pyrah	CR Taylor	AW Gale	MAK Lawson	ND Thornicroft	AKD Gray	DJ Wainwright	Extras	Total	Wickets	Result	Pts
v. Essex (Headingley) 21-24 April	16	76	0*				0			7	53	95	60	37	5			32							27	408	10		
	9		0*								26		39					43*							12	129	3	W	22
v. Nottinghamshire (Trent Bridge) 28 April-1 May	15	81	16		0		28*			0	62	35	4	14					0						9	264	10		
																									–	–	–	D	8
v. Hampshire (Headingley) 12-14 May	16	35	83	31		37	6			7		22	17	30			2*								30	316	10		
	45	8	0	78		18	1			8		4	10	10			1*								17	200	10	L	6
v. Nottinghamshire (Headingley) 19-21 May	4	0	4		20	21*	1	6		9	28	28										30			13	164	10		
	9	40	4		43	21	25	7*		26	18	44										4			13	254	10	L	3
v. Essex (Chelmsford) 2-5 June	0	49	45	0	115	10*	93			3	27	1	3												17	363	10		
	81	5	36	1	13	0	5			6	86	4	4*												8	249	10	W	22
v. Durham (The Riverside) 8-10 June	55	23	28	1*	36	2	126			0	9		27								6				18	331	10		
	71	15	0	0	53	4*	8			21	120		31												30	353	9	W	20
v. Leicestershire (Headingley) 18-21 June	63	17	77	0	30	9				24	17	0*	12		8										26	283	10		
																									–	–	–	D	9
v. Hampshire (The Rose Bowl) 23-26 June	1	7	18	0	243					13				11*	41	1	22				10				28	395	10		
																									–	–	–	D	10
v. Somerset (Scarborough) 21-23 July	59	23	10	0		48	8				90*	14	26						0	11					7	296	10		
	66*	0	11	7		12					36	10	3						9	1					4	160	10	L	5
v. Derbyshire (Derby) 28-31 July	89	25	27	0		18	0	36			19				81*				10				27		22	354	10		
	25	26	18			174	1*	46*			12				19				3				0		17	341	8	D	11
v. Derbyshire (Headingley) 12-15 August	123	22				109	28*	5			66	16			11				29	6*					27	442	8		
																									–	–	–	D	12
v. Leicestershire (Leicester) 19-22 August	20	76		0	11	35	2	3*	2						24	35			13						18	239	10		
	14	19		1	4	6	0*	42*							11	18			14						18	147	8	D	8
v. Glamorgan (Colwyn Bay) 24-27 August	5				21		46	11*							10	18			25*						22	158	5	D	4
																									–	–	–		
v. Durham (Scarborough) 1-3 September	22	6	17	0	66	0	21*										54	6	4		1				3	200	10		
	42	13	4	14*	53	6			75								17	0	34			14			18	290	10	L	4
v. Somerset (Taunton) 10-13 September	46	0	4	0*	95	13	31									62	7	39						5	22	324	10		
	26*	0			27		6*									46	8								12	125	4	D	7
v. Glamorgan (Headingley) 16-19 September	3	16	55	9*	173	17	4	24								56	1	12							31	401	10		
	30	58	13	7	9	1	10	2								5	89*	36							26	286	10	D	12

	MJ Wood	RKJ Dawson	MJ Lumb	SP Kirby	PA Jaques	TT Bresnan	A McGrath	JAR Blain	I Dawood	SM Guy	DS Lehmann	IJ Harvey	C White	CEW Silverwood	VJ Craven	JJ Sayers	MJ Hoggard	RM Pyrah	CR Taylor	AW Gale	MAK Lawson	ND Thornicroft	AKD Gray	DJ Wainwright
Matches	16	15	13	13	11	10	9	9	8	8	7	7	7	7	7	6	5	5	4	4	4	3	2	2
Innings	27	23	23	16	19	15	16	13	14	12	11	11	12	10	8	9	8	7	5	7	5	3	3	1
Not Out	2	0	1	5	0	3	0	6	5	0	1	0	1	2	1	0	3	1	1	0	1	0	0	0
Highest Score	123	81	83	14*	243	35	174	28*	75	26	120	95	60	37	81*	62	89*	39	43*	29	14	30	27	5
Runs	955	564	546	39	1118	143	728	94	310	124	592	273	265	150	202	311	107	158	105	78	33	40	37	5
Average	38.20	24.52	24.81	3.54	58.84	11.91	45.50	13.42	34.44	10.33	59.20	24.81	24.09	18.75	28.85	34.55	21.40	26.33	26.25	11.14	8.25	13.33	12.33	5.00
100s	1	0	0	0	3	0	3	0	0	0	1	0	0	0	0	0	0	0	0	0	0	0	0	0
50s	7	3	4	0	5	0	1	0	1	0	5	1	1	0	1	3	1	0	0	0	0	0	0	0
Catches/Stumpings	24/0	11/0	8/0	2/0	11/0	3/0	6/0	1/0	12/2	21/2	2/0	4/0	4/0	3/0	2/0	0/0	2/0	0/0	1/0	2/0	1/0	1/0	2/0	0/0

Home Ground: Headingley
Address: Headingley Cricket Ground, Leeds, LS6 3BU
Tel: 01132 787394
Fax: 01132 784099
Email: rachel@yorkshireccc.org.uk
Directions: From M1 South leave at junction 43 to M621 as far as junction 2. From M62 West leave at junction 27 to take M621 as far as junction 2. From M62 East leave at junction 29 to join M1 northbound to junction 2 of M621. At junction 2 of the M621 follow the signs for Headingley stadium along A643. Follow Leeds Inner Ring Road (A58(M)) to A660 which is signposted to Headingley stadium. Signs along this route will indicate when you have reached the Headingley area and on Test match days additional temporary signing will direct you to the free Park & Ride car park to the north of Headingley at Beckett Park.
Other grounds used: Scarborough
Year formed: 1863

Chief Executive: Colin Graves
Director of Operations: Geoff Cope
First XI Coach: David Byas
Captain: Craig White
County colours: Blue and gold

Website:
www.yorkshireccc.org.uk

Honours
County Championship
1867, 1869, 1870, 1893, 1896, 1898, 1901
1902, 1905, 1908, 1912, 1919, 1922, 1923
1924, 1925, 1931, 1932, 1933, 1935, 1937
1938, 1939, 1946, 1949, 1959, 1960, 1962
1963, 1966, 1967, 1968, 2001
Sunday League/NCL
1983
Benson & Hedges Cup
1987
Gillette Cup/NatWest/C&G Trophy
1965, 1969, 2002

YORKSHIRE CCC

FIRST-CLASS MATCHES
BOWLING

Match	RKJ Dawson	SP Kirby	JAR Blain	CEW Silverwood	TT Bresnan	DS Lehmann	C White	MAK Lawson	MJ Hoggard	A McGrath	IJ Harvey	ND Thornicroft	VJ Craven	AKD Gray	MJ Wood	MJ Lumb	RM Pyrah	PA Jaques	DJ Wainwright	Overs	Total	Byes/Leg-byes	Wickets	Run outs
Essex (Headingley) 21–24 April		23-5-72-2	15.2-1-63-2	23-7-44-2		10-3-20-2				17-8-24-1		9-1-28-1								97.2	262	11	10	
		16-3-50-2	16.3-3-52-3	20-5-60-2	11-2-25-2		9-2-20-0			13-2-32-1		6-1-20-0								91.3	273	14	10	
Nottinghamshire (Trent Bridge) 28 April–1 May	30.4-7-102-3		14-1-87-0	17-2-66-1	12-1-55-1	8-2-21-1	5-0-12-0			3-2-4-1										89.4	353	6	8	1
Hampshire (Headingley) 12–14 May	6-1-26-1		19-5-63-3	17-6-61-3			8-1-25-1		22-5-64-1	8-2-30-0	14-4-32-1									94	322	21	10	
	5.4-1-27-1		14-1-76-3	15-3-47-3			11-1-46-2		15-1-60-0	1-1-0-0	11-3-37-0									72.4	313	20	10	1
Nottinghamshire (Headingley) 19–21 May	18-2-74-2		15-3-66-2		19-2-91-2		12-3-40-1				7-1-26-0	15-6-34-0	9.3-2-37-2							95.3	393	35	10	1
	13-3-48-1		0.1-0-5-0		14.3-3-57-3		12-3-50-3				6-1-23-0		17.5-3-80-1							64.3	269	6	8	
Essex (Chelmsford) 2–5 June	22-7-101-2	21-2-86-3		22.3-1-84-3	6-2-16-0	20-4-61-1	3-2-2-0													104.3	359	9	10	1
	19-6-32-2	6.1-0-20-1		7-1-18-3		17-2-35-4														49.1	116	11	10	
Durham (The Riverside) 8–10 June	16.5-2-40-5	10-2-25-1			5-2-11-0	1-0-1-0	13-4-36-2							8-2-27-2						53.5	150	10	10	
	20.2-4-75-4	13-5-26-2			4-1-17-0	9-2-23-1	10-1-39-2							9-3-24-1						65.2	214	10	10	
Leicestershire (Headingley) 18–21 June	5.1-1-12-2	26-5-85-2		23-3-78-3	23-3-88-3	3.4-2-2-0	4-2-12-0													85.1	289	12	10	
Hampshire (The Rose Bowl) 23–26 June	15-2-51-0	14-4-44-2			13-4-37-0				20.4-6-50-3					8-2-29-2	7-1-20-1					77.4	259	28	8	
Somerset (Scarborough) 21–23 July	19-4-79-3	17-1-92-1			17-1-75-2		10-0-36-2	16.3-1-69-2					17-3-90-0							96.3	451	10	10	
								0.4-0-6-0												0.4	6	0	0	
Derbyshire (Derby) 28–31 July	5-1-23-0	21-1-76-2	19-5-58-2							22-7-39-5	21-4-73-0		11-1-51-0	19-2-56-1						118	406	30	10	
	16-5-45-2	21-3-75-3	11-1-58-2							16-4-41-0	15-4-38-0		7-2-18-2	5-0-13-0	1-0-2-0					92	305	15	9	
Derbyshire (Headingley) 12–15 August	9-0-30-0	17-3-41-1		12-3-38-4	6-0-15-1			11.2-1-39-1	7-0-22-0	17-4-38-3										79.2	240	17	10	
	26-7-53-1	13-4-25-0		10-1-78-2	10-2-22-1			13-1-48-0	7-2-21-0	11-1-28-0			2-0-10-0							92	245	10	5	1
Leicestershire (Leicester) 19–22 August	23-1-84-0	25-5-87-3		13-1-65-1	22-7-42-2					22-1-65-3				8-1-30-1						113	382	9	10	
	5-1-18-0	16-5-60-2		6-0-19-2	15-2-41-2					6-2-13-0				0.4-0-5-0						48.4	166	10	6	
Glamorgan (Colwyn Bay) 24–27 August																				-	-	-	-	-
Durham (Scarborough) 1–3 September		25-3-92-1		14-0-80-0	11-1-32-3			19-2-62-5	13-1-53-1						1-0-1-0					82	325	6	10	
		29-6-115-3		20-1-64-3	13-4-52-0			15-1-84-1	16.4-1-47-2											94.4	375	12	9	
Somerset (Taunton) 10–13 September		8-1-29-0		10-2-38-0	4-0-25-0				8-1-44-0										3-1-5-0	33	141	0	0	
Glamorgan (Headingley) 16–19 September	31-4-97-2	18-2-65-1	19-1-110-4		12-3-40-1				23.3-6-67-2								6-4-2-0	2-0-18-0		111.3	410	11	10	
	2-0-2-1	6-0-21-0	4-0-16-0						3-1-8-0											15	55	8	1	

	RKJ Dawson	SP Kirby	JAR Blain	CEW Silverwood	TT Bresnan	DS Lehmann	C White	MAK Lawson	MJ Hoggard	A McGrath	IJ Harvey	ND Thornicroft	VJ Craven	AKD Gray	MJ Wood	MJ Lumb	RM Pyrah	PA Jaques	DJ Wainwright
Overs	379.4	327.1	188	174.3	160.3	105.4	88.2	75.3	121.5	102	154	44.2	51.4	31	1	1	6	2	3
Maidens	71	53	26	33	31	19	18	6	22	21	41	10	8	3	0	0	4	0	1
Runs	1255	1132	804	570	557	261	282	308	393	280	430	168	191	89	1	2	2	18	5
Wickets	36	31	30	22	17	15	11	9	9	8	7	6	6	2	0	0	0	0	0
Average	34.86	36.51	26.80	25.90	32.76	17.40	25.63	34.22	43.66	35.00	61.42	28.00	31.83	44.50	-	-	-	-	-

FIELDING

- MJ Wood
- SM Guy (21 ct, 2 st)
- I Dawood (12 ct, 2 st)
- RKJ Dawson
- PA Jaques
- MJ Lumb
- A McGrath
- C White
- IJ Harvey
- CEW Silverwood
- TT Bresnan
- DS Lehmann
- MJ Hoggard
- VJ Craven
- SP Kirby
- AKD Gray
- AW Gale
- JAR Blain
- CR Taylor
- ND Thornicroft
- MAK Lawson
- RM Pyrah
- JJ Sayers
- DJ Wainwright